world development report 2014

Risk and Opportunity

Managing Risk for Development

A World Bank Group Corporate Flagship

world development report 2014

Risk and Opportunity

Managing Risk for Development

THE WORLD BANK
Washington, DC

1818 H Street NW, Washington DC 20433
Telephone: 202-473-1000; Internet: www.worldbank.org

1 2 3 4 16 15 14 13

ISBN, eISBN, DOI, and ISSN:
Softcover
ISSN: 0163-5085
ISBN: 978-0-8213-9903-3
e-ISBN: 978-0-8213-9982-8
DOI: 10.1596/978-0-8213-9903-3

Hardcover
ISSN: 0163-5085
ISBN: 978-0-8213-9964-4
DOI: 10.1596/978-0-8213-9964-4

Cover design: Heads of State
Interior design: Debra Naylor

The maps in the *World Development Report 2014: Risk and Opportunity—Managing Risk for Development* were produced by the Map Design Unit of the World Bank. The boundaries, colors, nominations and any other information shown on this map do not imply, on the part of the World Bank Group, any judgment on the legal status of any territory, or any endorsement or acceptance of such boundaries.

Contents

Boxes

Diagrams

Figures

Glossaries

Maps

Profile

Tables

Foreword

In recent years, the world has suffered a multitude of crises. Financial and economic turmoil have disrupted the world economy through loss of income, jobs, and social stability. Intense natural disasters have devastated entire communities from Haiti to Japan, leaving a trail of fatalities and economic losses in their wake. Concerns about global warming have grown, as have fears about the spread of deadly contagious diseases.

As I travel around the world, I hear the same concern: how can we become more resilient to such risks? The *World Development Report 2014 (WDR 2014), Risk and Opportunity—Managing Risk for Development,* helps provide answers to this pressing question.

Another concern is the missed development opportunities that arise when necessary risks are not taken. Pursuing opportunities requires taking risks, but many people, especially the poor, are often reluctant to do so, because they fear the potential negative consequences. Failure to act can trap people in poverty, leaving them vulnerable to negative shocks and even less able to pursue opportunities that would otherwise improve their well-being.

The inability to manage risk properly leads to crises and missed opportunities. This poses significant obstacles to attaining the World Bank Group's two main goals: ending extreme poverty by the year 2030 and boosting shared prosperity of the bottom 40 percent of the population in developing countries. Managing risk effectively is, therefore, absolutely central to the World Bank's mission. The *WDR 2014* demonstrates that effective risk management can be a powerful instrument for development—it can save lives, avert economic shocks, and help people build better, more secure futures.

This report calls for individuals and institutions to move from being "crisis fighters" to becoming "proactive and systematic risk managers." There is substantial evidence that recognizing and preparing for risk can pay off abundantly. For instance, many developing countries displayed resilience in the face of the recent global financial crisis because they had previously reformed their macroeconomic, financial, and social policies.

Protecting hard-won development gains by building resilience to risk is essential to achieving prosperity. That is true whether one is grappling with natural disasters, pandemics, financial crises, a wave of crime at the community level, or the severe illness of a household's chief provider. Risk can never be completely eliminated. But people and institutions can build resilience to risk by applying a balanced approach that includes structural policy measures, community-based prevention, insurance, education, training, and effective regulation. Countries have learned how to manage risk in diverse settings, but, until now, research related to risk management in the developing world has not been synthesized into a single source that is easily accessible and well-referenced.

This *WDR* aims to fill that gap. It serves as a valuable guide both for mainstreaming risk management into the development agenda, and for helping countries and communities strengthen their own risk management systems. The Report also offers important insight for changing the approach to risk in the Bank's own operations. The World Bank Group is currently undergoing a transformation, which calls for shifting the institutional culture regarding risk from one of extreme risk aversion to one of informed risk taking. This year's *WDR* cautions that the greatest risk may be taking no risk at all. I could not agree more.

My hope is that the *WDR 2014* will lead to risk management policies that allow us to minimize the danger of future crises and to seize every opportunity for development. Success on this front will help us build the world we all want: one free of poverty, with shared prosperity for all.

Jim Yong Kim
President
The World Bank Group

Acknowledgments

This Report was prepared by a team led by Norman Loayza, together with İnci Ötker-Robe. The other members of the core team were César Calderón, Stéphane Hallegatte, Rasmus Heltberg, Xubei Luo, Martin Melecky, Ana María Oviedo, and Kyla Wethli. Research analysts Sebastien Boreux, Kanako Goulding-Hotta, Rui Han, Harry Edmund Moroz, Anca Maria Podpiera, Jun Rentschler, Faiyaz Talukdar, and Tomoko Wada completed the team. Gilles Cols, Olga Jonas, Federica Ranghieri, and Anna Reva contributed to the Report's spotlights.

The Report was sponsored by the Development Economics Vice Presidency. Overall guidance for the preparation of the Report was provided by Kaushik Basu, Senior Vice President and Chief Economist, and Asli Demirgüç-Kunt, Director of Research, Development Economics. The team benefited from continuous engagement with and advice from Martin Čihák, Quy-Toan Do, Mary Hallward-Driemeier, Aart Kraay, and Sergio Schmukler.

An advisory panel comprising Laura Alfaro, Robert Barro, Thorsten Beck, Stefan Dercon, Ibrahim Elbadawi, Rohini Pande, Klaus Schmidt-Hebbel, Hyun Song Shin, and Jan Švejnar provided feedback and advice. The team also benefited from the advice of World Bank Chief Economists Augusto de la Torre, Shantayanan Devarajan, Marianne Fay, Ariel Fiszbein, Caroline Freund, Indermit Gill, Bert Hofman, Jeffrey Lewis, and Martín Rama.

The team would like to acknowledge the generous support for the preparation of the Report by the Canadian International Development Agency, the Knowledge for Change Program, the Japan Policy and Human Resources Development Fund, and the World Bank Research Support Budget. The team also thanks the German Federal Ministry for Economic Cooperation and Development and the Deutsche Gesellschaft für Internationale Zusammenarbeit, which co-organized and hosted the WDR International Policy Workshop in Berlin, November 2012.

Interagency consultations were held with the European Commission, the International Monetary Fund, the Organisation for Economic Co-operation and Development, several United Nations organizations, the World Economic Forum, and agencies for development cooperation in Denmark, Finland, France, Japan, the Netherlands, Norway, Spain, Sweden, Switzerland, and the United Kingdom. Valuable inputs were received from the World Bank Institute and all regional and anchor networks, as well as other parts of the World Bank Group, including the International Finance Corporation and the Multilateral Investment Guarantee Agency.

Country consultations were held in Austria, Belgium, Brazil, Chile, Denmark, Finland, France, Germany, Indonesia, Japan, the Netherlands, Norway, Peru, Rwanda, Singapore, Spain, Sweden, Switzerland, the United Kingdom, and the United States. Most included academics, members of civil society, and public entities and governments. Consultations with researchers and academics were aided by ad hoc conferences organized by the Centre for the Study of African Economies, Oxford University, and the Center on Global Governance at the School of International and Public Affairs, Columbia University. The team also received valuable feedback at the African Economic Conference 2012, the Asia Development Forum 2013, and the Latin American and Caribbean Economic Association Conference 2012.

The Report was skillfully edited by Nancy Morrison and Martha Gottron. Bruce Ross-Larson and Gerry Quinn provided additional editorial advice. The World Bank's Publishing and Knowledge Division coordinated the design, typesetting, printing, and dissemination of the Report. Special thanks to Mary Fisk, Stephen McGroarty, Stephen Pazdan, Denise Bergeron, Andres Meneses, Shana Wagger, and Paschal Ssemaganda, as well as to the Translation and Interpretation Unit's Bouchra Belfqih, Cecile Jannotin, and Michael Lamm. The Development Data Group contributed to the preparation of the Report's statistical annex, coordinated by Timothy Herzog. The team also thanks Merrell Tuck-Primdahl, Vamsee Krishna Kanchi, and Swati P. Mishra for their guidance on communications strategy, and Vivian Hon for her coordinating role. Barbara Cunha, Birgit Hansl, and Manal Quota reviewed some of the foreign language translations of the Overview.

The production and logistics of the Report were assisted by Brónagh Murphy, Mihaela Stangu, and Jason Victor, with contributions from Laverne Cook, Gracia Sorensen, and Tourya Tourougui. Ivar Cederholm, Elena

Chi-Lin Lee, and Jimmy Olazo coordinated resource mobilization. Irina Sergeeva and Sonia Joseph were in charge of resource management. Gytis Kanchas, Nacer Megherbi, and Jean-Pierre Djomalieu provided IT support.

Background papers were provided by Joshua Aizenman, Phillip R. D. Anderson, Maximillian Ashwill, Emmanuelle Auriol, Ghassan Baliki, Thorsten Beck, Najy Benhassine, Nicholas Bloom, Julia K. Brown, Martin Brown, Daniel Buncic, Julio Cáceres-Delpiano, Sara Guerschanik Calvo, Olivier De Jonghe, Alejandro de la Fuente, Philippe de Vreyer, Mark A. Dutz, Maya Eden, Penelope D. Fidas, Roberto Foa, Rodrigo Fuentes, Garance Genicot, Gary Gereffi, Ejaz Ghani, Sudarshan Gooptu, Mikael Grinbaum, Federico H. Gutierrez, Ronald Inglehart, Susan T. Jackson, Olga B. Jonas, Jan Kellett, Ilan Kelman, Tariq Khokhar, Auguste T. Kouame, Aart Kraay, Sadaf Lakhani, Sylvie Lambert, Esperanza Lasagabaster, Ethan Ligon, Samuel Maimbo, William F. Maloney, Tom Mitchell, Ahmed Mushfiq Mobarak, Hernan J. Moscoso Boedo, Andrew Norton, Eduardo Ortiz-Juárez, Patti Petesch, Florence Pichon, Patrick Premand, Carlos Rodriguez Castelan, Natalia Salazar, Luis Servén, Francis J. Teal, Maarten van Aalst, Guillermo Vuletin, Koko Warner, Tetyana V. Zelenska, and Nong Zhu. Details of their contributions are listed at the end of the Report.

For valuable contributions and advice, the team thanks Pablo Ariel Acosta, Tony Addison, Montek Ahluwalia, Ahmad Ahsan, David Aikman, Harold Alderman, Franklin Allen, Aquiles Almansi, Philippe Ambrosi, Goli Ameri, Walter J. Ammann, Dan Andrews, Paolo Avner, Edmar Bacha, Javier Baez, Hemant Baijal, Christopher Barrett, Scott Barrett, Kathleen Beegle, Tim Besley, Gordon Betcherman, Deepak Bhattasali, Indu Bhushan, Jörn Birkmann, Christiane Bögemann-Hagedorn, Uta Böllhoff, Patrick Bolton, Laura Elizabeth Boudreau, François Bourguignon, Carter Brandon, Juan José Bravo, Tilman Brück, Robin Burgess, Guillermo Calvo, Jack Campbell, Jason Cardosi, Michael R. Carter, Miguel Castilla, Michael Chaitkin, Marcos Chamon, Guang Zhe Chen, Maria Teresa Chimienti, Fredrick Christopher, Craig Churchill, Luis Abdón Cifuentes, Massimo Cirasino, Stijn Claessens, Daniel Clarke, Tito Cordella, Sarah E. Cornell, Gerardo Corrochano, Robert Cull, Julie Dana, Anis Dani, Jishnu Das, Joachim De Weerdt, Ximena Del Carpio, Jean-Jacques Dethier, Jacqueline Devine, Pierre Dubois, Patrice Dumas, Peter Ellehoj, Brooks Evans, Jessica Evans, Marcel Fafchamps, Paolo Falco, Shahrokh Fardoust, Thomas Feidieker, Wolfgang Fengler, James Fenske, Ana Margarida Fernandes, Adrián Fernández, Francisco Ferreira, Deon Filmer, Greg Fischer, James Foster, Marcel Fratzscher, Linda Freiner, Roberta Gatti, Francis Ghesquiere, Swati Ghosh, Antonino Giuffrida, David Gleicher, Markus Goldstein, George Graham, Margaret Grosh, Patricia Grossi, Mario Guadamillas, Conor Healy, Frank Heemskerk, Joachim Heidebrecht, Jesko Hentschel, Rafael Hernández, Matt Hobson, John Hoddinott, Niels Holm-Nielsen, Naomi Hossain, Andrew Hughes Hallett, Oh-Seok Hyun, Elena Ianchovichina, Ridzuan Ismail, Takatoshi Ito, Abhas K. Jha, Emmanuel Jimenez, Steen Jørgensen, Nidhi Kalra, Sujit Kapadia, Masayuki Karasawa, Corneille Karekezi, Supreet Kaur, Lauren Kelly, Igor Kheyfets, Beth King, Naohiro Kitano, Leora Klapper, Alzbeta Klein, Kalpana Kochhar, Kiyoshi Kodera, Friederike Koehler-Geib, Diane Koester, Robert Kopech, Anirudh Krishna, Jolanta Kryspin-Watson, Howard Kunreuther, Kiyoshi Kurokawa, Christoph Kurowski, Miguel Laric, Alexia Latortue, Sara Lazzaroni, Nick Lea, Daniel Lederman, Margaret Leighton, Robert Lempert, Sebastian Levine, Yue Li, Irina Likhacheva Sokolowski, Justin Yifu Lin, Kathy Lindert, Gladys Lopez, Augusto López Claros, Leonardo Lucchetti, Maria Ana Lugo, Olivier Mahul, Thomas Markussen, Will Martin, María Soledad Martínez Pería, Eric Maskin, Laura Mazal, J. Allister McGregor, Claire McGuire, Robin Mearns, Carlo Menon, Rekha Menon, Erwann Michel-Kerjan, Tim Midgley, Gary Milante, Suguru Miyazaki, Nuno Mota Pinto, Marialisa Motta, Joy Muller, Akira Murata, Lydia Ndirangu, Ha Nguyen, Giuseppe Nicoletti, Yosuke Nishii, Michel Noel, Alistair Nolan, Sharyn O'Halloran, Philip O'Keefe, Ory Okolloh, Michelle Ooi, Miguel Angel Ostos, Marcus C. Oxley, Robert Palacios, Pepi Patrón, Douglas Pearce, Brian Pinto, Russell Pittman, Jean-Philippe Platteau, Sandra Poncet, David Popp, Antonin Pottier, Prashant, John Primrose, Hnin Hnin Pyne, Ricardo Raineri, Anthony Randle, Martin Ravallion, Robert Reid, Ricardo Reis, Ortwin Renn, Changyong Rhee, Helena Ribe, Michelle Riboud, Jamele Rigolini, Dena Ringold, David Robalino, Jorge Luis Rodriguez Meza, Rafael Rofman, Jonathan Rothschild, Davinder Sandhu, Apurva Sanghi, Hans-Otto Sano, Yasuyuki Sawada, Stefano Scarpetta, Anita Schwarz, Paul Seabright, Junko Sekine, Amartya Sen, Rodrigo Serrano-Berthet, Shigeo Shimizu, Paul B. Siegel, Joana Silva, Emmanuel Skoufias, Marc Smitz, Irina Solyanik, Joseph Stiglitz, Adrian Stone, Stéphane Straub, Henriette Strothmann, Pablo Suarez, Kalanidhi Subbarao, Mark Sundberg, Olumide Taiwo, Tamanna Talukder, Kazushige Taniguchi, Finn Tarp, Gaiv Tata, Maria Hermínia Tavares de Almeida, Stoyan Tenev, Mehrnaz Teymourian, Erik Thorbecke, Klaus Tilmes, Carlos Tortola, Izabela Toth, Carolina Trivelli Ávila, Yvonne Tsikata, María Cristina Uehara, Tunc Tahsin Uyanik, Renos Vakis, Dominique Van De Walle, Ashutosh Varshney, Adrien Vogt-Schilb, Eiji Wakamatsu, Sophie Walker, Simon Walley, Christine Wallich, David Waskow, Masato Watanabe, Asbjorn H. Wee, Jonathan B. Wiener, Alys Willman, Lixin Colin Xu, Mohamed Mahdi Youssouf, and Asta Zviniene. The team also thanks the many others inside and outside the World Bank who provided comments.

Risk and opportunity

Risk management can be a powerful instrument for development

Managing risk for a life full of opportunities: a mother protects her child against malaria with a bed net in Ghana.

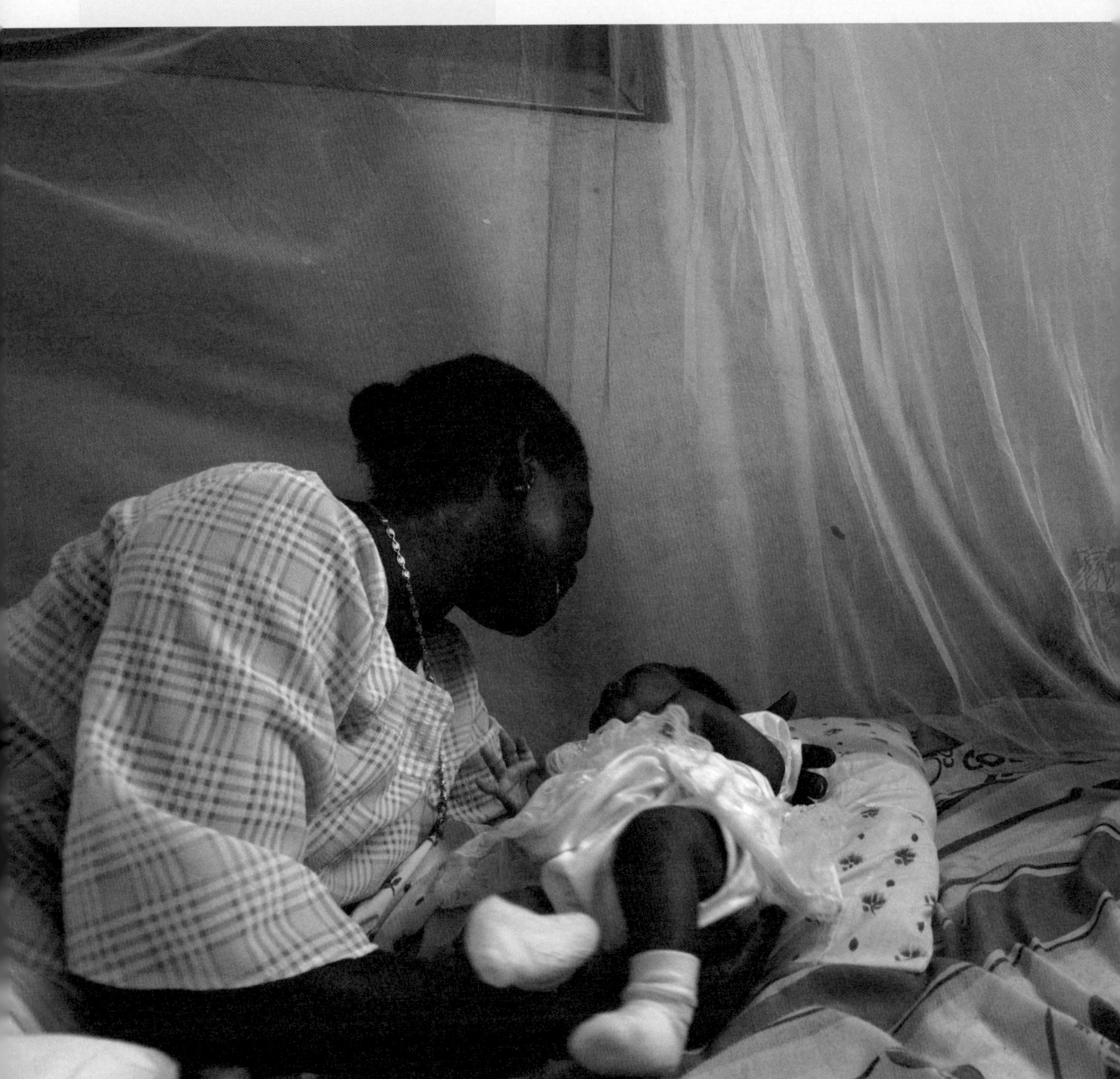

Risk and opportunity

Risk management can be a powerful instrument for development

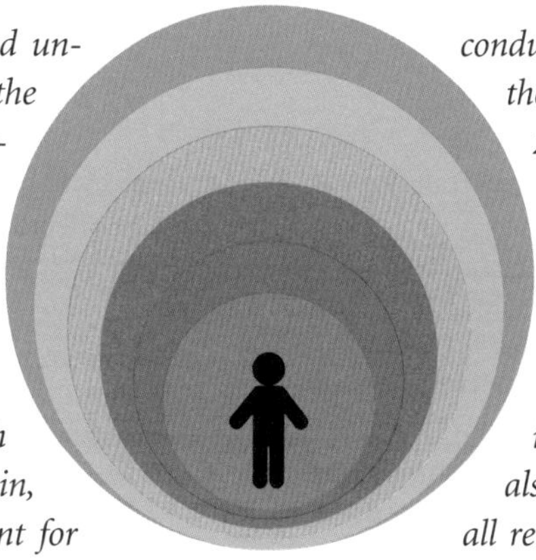

The past 25 years have witnessed unprecedented changes around the world—many of them for the better. Across the continents, many countries have embarked on a path of international integration, economic reform, technological modernization, and democratic participation. Although challenges and inequalities remain, economies that had been stagnant for decades are growing, people whose families had suffered deprivation for generations are escaping poverty, and hundreds of millions are enjoying the benefits of improved living standards and scientific and cultural sharing across nations. As the world changes, a host of opportunities arise constantly. With them, however, appear old and new risks, from the possibility of job loss and disease to the potential for social unrest and environmental damage. If ignored, these risks can turn into crises that reverse hard-won gains and endanger the social and economic reforms that produced these gains. The solution is not to reject change in order to avoid risk but to prepare for the opportunities and risks that change entails. Managing risks responsibly and effectively has the potential to bring about security and a means of progress for people in developing countries and beyond.

The World Development Report (WDR) 2014 *focuses on the process of risk management, addressing these questions: why is risk management important for development, how should it be conducted, what obstacles prevent people and societies from conducting it effectively, and how can these obstacles be overcome? The WDR 2014's value added resides in its emphasis on managing risks in a proactive, systematic, and integrated way. These characteristics underscore the importance of forward-looking planning and preparation in a context of uncertainty. They also highlight the necessity to address all relevant risks jointly, using all available tools and institutions. From a policy maker's perspective, a proactive, systematic, and integrated approach to managing risks involves striking a proper balance between the contribution from the state and the contribution from individuals, civil society, and the private sector, with the goal of ensuring that these contributions are coordinated and complementary.*

The WDR 2014 argues that risk management can be a powerful instrument for development—not only by building people's resilience and thus reducing the effects of adverse events but also by allowing them to take advantage of opportunities for improvement. The WDR 2014 is not devoted to a detailed analysis of specific risks. Its framework, however, can be implemented to address particular, relevant sets of risks in given regions and countries. Focusing on the process of risk management allows the WDR 2014 to consider the synergies, trade-offs, and priorities involved in addressing different risks in different contexts, with the single motivation of boosting development (box 1).

BOX 1 ***Five key insights on the process of risk management from the World Development Report 2014***

1. Taking on risks is necessary to pursue opportunities for development. The risk of inaction may well be the worst option of all.
2. To confront risk successfully, it is essential to shift from unplanned and ad hoc responses when crises occur to proactive, systematic, and integrated risk management.
3. Identifying risks is not enough: the trade-offs and obstacles to risk management must also be identified, prioritized, and addressed through private and public action.
4. For risks beyond the means of individuals to handle alone, risk management requires shared action and responsibility at different levels of society, from the household to the international community.
5. Governments have a critical role in managing systemic risks, providing an enabling environment for shared action and responsibility, and channeling direct support to vulnerable people.

Source: WDR 2014 team.

Risk is a burden but also an opportunity

Why worry about risk? In recent years, a multitude of crises have disrupted the world economy and have had substantial negative consequences on development. Because of the 2008–09 global financial crisis, most economies around the world experienced sharp declines in growth rates, with ensuing loss of income and employment and setbacks in efforts to reduce poverty. When food prices spiked in 2008, riots broke out in more than a dozen countries in Africa and Asia, reflecting people's discontent and insecurity and causing widespread political unrest. The 2004 Asian tsunami, the 2010 earthquake in Haiti, and the 2011 multiple hazard disaster in northeastern Japan—to name but a few—have left a trail of fatalities and economic losses that exemplify the increased frequency and intensity of natural disasters. Concerns about the impact of climate change worldwide are growing, and so are fears about the spreading of deadly contagious diseases across borders. Indeed, the major economic crises and disasters that have occurred in recent years and those that may occur in the future underscore how vulnerable people, communities, and countries are to systemic risks, especially in developing nations.

Idiosyncratic risks, which are specific to individuals or households, are no less important for people's welfare. Losing a job or not finding one because of inadequate skills, falling victim to disease or crime, or suffering a family breakup from financial strain or forced migration can be overwhelming, particularly for vulnerable families and individuals. Households in Ethiopia whose members experienced serious illness, for example, were forced to cut their consumption by almost 10 percent and continued to be negatively affected three to five years later.[1] Health costs from high levels of crime and violence amount to 0.3–5.0 percent of gross domestic product (GDP) a year for countries in Latin America, without even considering the impact of crime on lost output stemming from reduced investment and labor participation.[2] Loss of employment in countries as different as Argentina, Bulgaria, and Guyana not only has lowered income and consumption but has also reduced people's ability to find new work, worsened social cohesion, and in some cases increased domestic violence.[3]

Whether adverse consequences come from systemic or idiosyncratic risks, they may destroy lives, assets, trust, and social stability. And it is often the poor who are hit the hardest. Despite impressive progress in reducing poverty in the past three decades, a substantial proportion of people in developing countries remain poor and are vulnerable to falling into deeper poverty when they are struck by negative shocks (figure 1). The mortality rate from illness and injury for adults under age 60 is two and a half times higher for men and four times higher for women in low-income countries than in high-income countries, while the rate for children under age five is almost twenty times higher.[4] Mounting evidence shows that adverse shocks—above all, health and weather shocks and economic crises—play a major role in pushing households below the poverty line and keeping them there.[5] Moreover, realizing that a negative shock can push them into destitution, bankruptcy, or crisis, poor people may stick with technologies and livelihoods that appear relatively safe but are also stagnant.

FIGURE 1 *Many people around the world are poor or live very close to poverty; they are vulnerable to falling deeper into poverty when they are hit by negative shocks*

More than 20 percent of the population in developing countries live on less than $1.25 a day, more than 50 percent on less than $2.50, and nearly 75 percent on less than $4.00.

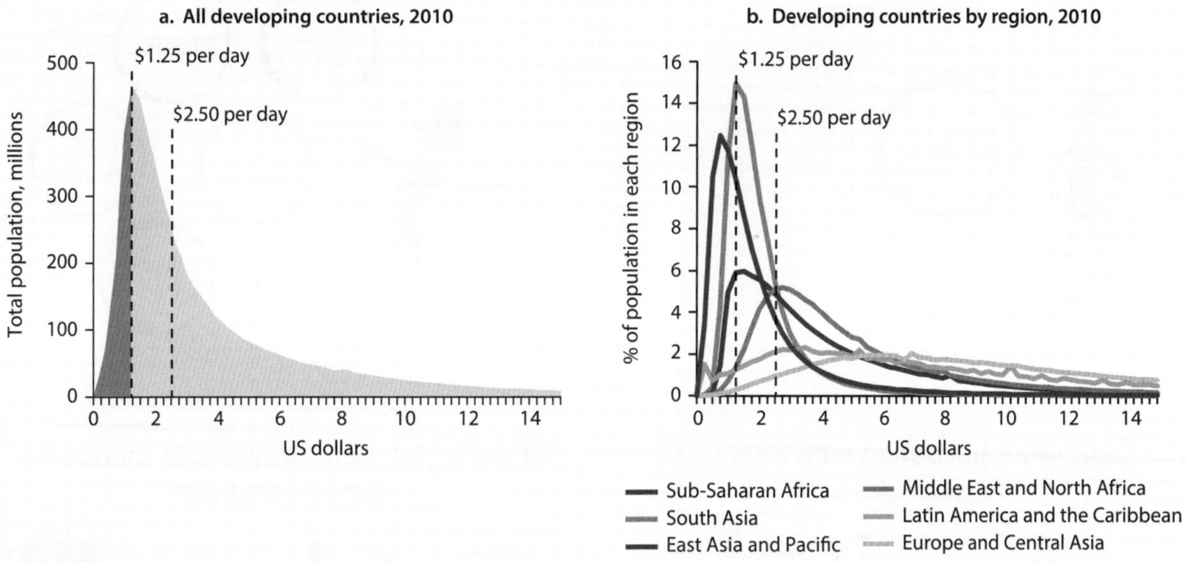

Source: WDR 2014 team based on data from World Bank PovcalNet (database).
Note: $1.25 per day is a widely used measure of extreme poverty. However, $2.50 per day is considered a more relevant measure of extreme poverty for some regions, such as Latin America and the Caribbean. See Ferreira and others 2013.

Yes, confronting risk, as the possibility of loss, is a burden—but it is also necessary to the pursuit of opportunity. Risk and opportunity go hand in hand in most decisions and actions taken by countries, enterprises, and families as they seek to improve their fate. Indeed, risk taking is intrinsic to the process of development. Consider a few examples. Since the 1990s, most developing countries have opened their borders to seek international integration and higher economic growth, but in the process they have also increased their exposure to international shocks. Firms around the world have made investments to upgrade their technologies and increase profitability, but the debt required to do so has made them more vulnerable to changes in demand and credit conditions. From Brazil to South Africa, millions of families have migrated to cities to seek better job opportunities and health and education services, where they have also become more exposed to higher crime and benefit less from communal support. The motivation behind these actions is the quest for improvement, but risk arises because favorable outcomes are seldom guaranteed.

Risk management can be a powerful instrument for development

Whether risks are systemic or idiosyncratic, imposed or taken on voluntarily, development can occur only by successfully confronting risk and pursuing opportunity. Many crises and development losses are the result of mismanaged risks. No less important, many opportunities are missed because preparation for risk is insufficient and necessary risks are not taken—the "risk of inaction." It is therefore essential to shift from unplanned and ad hoc responses when crises occur to proactive, systematic, and integrated risk management. As such, risk management can build the capacity to reduce the losses and improve the benefits that people may experience while conducting their lives and pursuing development opportunities (drawing 1 and profile 1).

Risk management can save lives. Consider the case of Bangladesh, where improved preparation for natural hazards has dramatically reduced loss of life from cyclones. In the past four decades, three major cyclones of similar magnitude have hit Bangladesh.

DRAWING 1 *Risk management for everyone: A visual representation of key concepts*

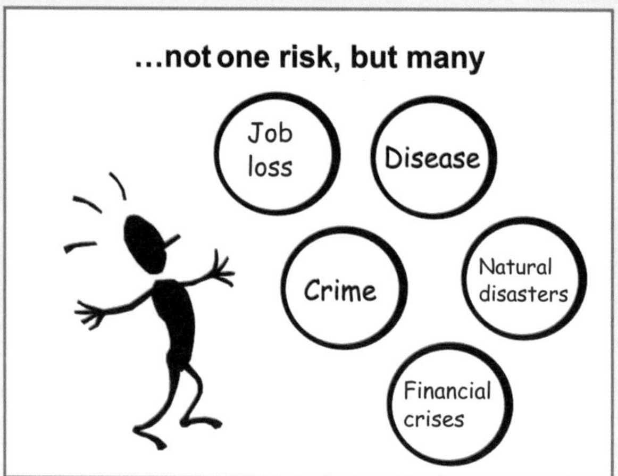

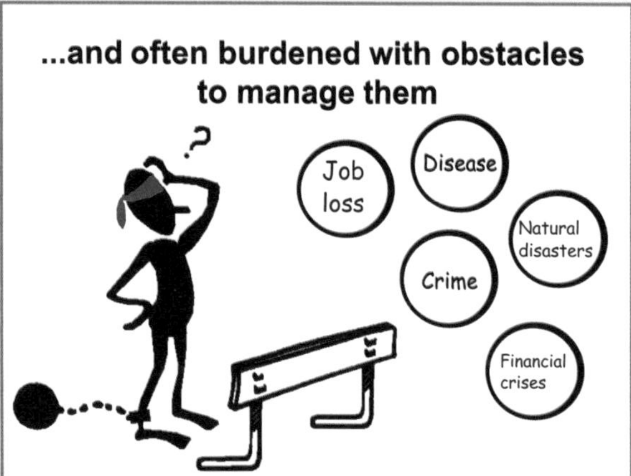

Drawing by Jason Victor for the WDR 2014.

PROFILE 1 *The Gomez family: A modern tale of risk and resilience*

The Gomez family lives in a shantytown on the outskirts of Lima. Only a few years ago, the family lived in a rural village in the Peruvian Andes, where they had a small farm. The region was prone to droughts, and they could never earn enough income to escape poverty. Many of their neighbors had migrated to the city in the 1980s, pushed by civil conflict in the countryside. The Gomez family refused to go for fear of losing their land and finding nothing better in the city. The risk was too large. Peru was a different place then: inflation and unemployment were rampant, and the threat of social unrest was ever present.

In the 1990s, the macroeconomy was stabilized and the civil war ended. New opportunities started to arise in urban and rural areas. At first, these opportunities eluded the Gomez family. A dam had been constructed near their village, but using its waters required the renovation of canals on their farm. They applied for a loan from a commercial bank but were denied, which came as no surprise since it was their first time applying. Mr. and Mrs. Gomez came to believe that their children had no future in the village and decided to migrate to the city. This time, however, they did not have to worry about losing their farm. They had been given a property title and were able to sell the farm to a neighbor, who had the capital to renew the canals. The money from the farm would give the Gomezes a cushion as they took the momentous challenge of migration.

Lima, with just under 10 million inhabitants, seemed like a huge and inhospitable place. That is why they decided to move to the shantytown where many members of their village had relocated. There, they would find companionship, cultural identity (all the festivals of their old village were properly celebrated here), and, of course, help finding a job. Mr. Gomez found work on a construction site, but it was irregular, with frequent layoffs. Mrs. Gomez had to pitch in, and she was fortunate to find work as a seamstress in a textile enterprise. The grandmother helped out, taking care of the children when they returned from school. Having two income earners (and a willing grandmother) made the Gomez household more resilient to whatever might happen.

And things did happen. Mario, the eldest son, was injured in a traffic accident. There was no car insurance, and the family had to bear the cost of Mario's medical treatment. They could not have done it alone, and they didn't have to. They relied on a public hospital, run and financed by the state. Medical treatment there was of uneven quality, but it provided basic services. The family had to spend some of their limited savings to supplement the hospital services and buy medication, but all that was worth it because Mario recovered.

The Gomezes had to dig into their assets once again, but this time for a very different purpose. Elena—the second daughter, whom everyone regarded as the brains in the family—came home one day and asked her parents if she could study English in the evenings. This was a good idea. Peru had recently signed several free trade agreements (one of them with the United States), and exporting companies had started to grow, offering jobs to young, qualified people. English would be a big plus.

Some months before, however, her parents would have declined her initiative on the grounds that it was not safe to be out at night. Police protection was scarce in the outskirts of the city, and criminals took advantage of that. When a crime wave eventually affected the Gomezes' shantytown, the community put together neighborhood patrols (effective, although at times unduly harsh). When Elena asked for English classes, the safety risk had been reduced, and she could go out to study in the evenings. As time passed, she and her family would be well prepared to benefit from the period of stability and sustained growth that Peru was experiencing.

Confronting risks and seizing opportunities may have put the Gomez family on the path out of poverty, possibly forever. It was their work, initiative, and responsibility that made it possible, but they could not have done it alone.

Source: WDR 2014 team.

Note: A video of this fictional story is available in nine languages on the *World Development Report 2014* website http://www.worldbank.org/wdr2014.

FIGURE 2 *The benefits of risk management often outweigh the costs*

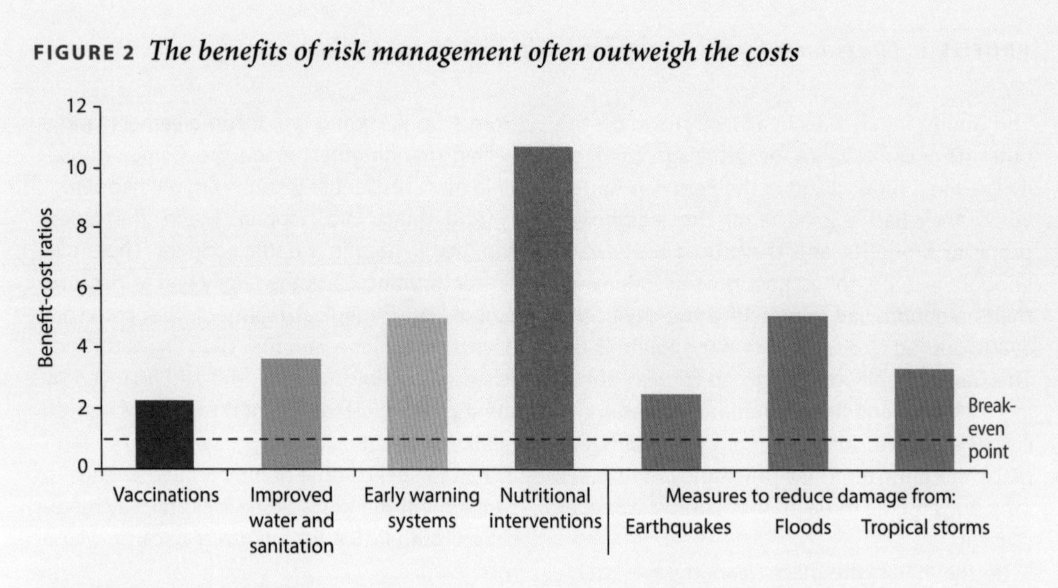

Source: Wethli 2013 for the WDR 2014.

Note: The figure shows the median of benefit-cost ratios across a range of studies in each category (with a minimum of at least four estimates in each category). Above the dotted line, expected benefits exceed expected costs. The range of estimates within each category can be substantial, reflecting a diversity of intervention types and locations, and the sensitivity of estimates to variations in underlying assumptions. However, in almost all cases, even the 25th percentile of the ranges are above the break-even point.

A cyclone in 1970 claimed over 300,000 lives, but one in 1991 claimed almost 140,000, and one in 2007 claimed about 4,000. Casualties have been greatly reduced by a nationwide program to build shelters—from only 12 shelters in 1970 to over 2,500 in 2007—along with improved forecasting capacity and a relatively simple but effective system for warning the population.[6]

Risk management can avert damages and prevent development setbacks. Countries as different as the Czech Republic, Kenya, and Peru offer recent compelling examples where macroeconomic preparation has shielded the economy from the negative effects of a global financial crisis. Having achieved lower fiscal deficits, disciplined monetary policy, and lower current account deficits, these countries experienced a smaller decline in growth rates in the aftermath of the 2008 international crisis than they did following the 1997 East Asian crisis. The same beneficial effect of macroeconomic preparation seems to have occurred in many other low- and middle-income countries.[7]

Risk management can unleash opportunity. Risk management tools—such as improved information, crop insurance, and employment diversification—can help people mitigate risk. The ability to mitigate risk, in turn, can allow people, especially the poor, to overcome their aversion to risk and be more willing to undertake new promising ventures. Some farmers in Ethiopia, for instance, choose not to use fertilizer because they fear drought and other potential shocks and thus prefer to retain savings as a cushion rather than investing in intermediate inputs.[8] In contrast, farmers in Ghana and India have been more willing to take on risk in search of higher yields—increasing their investments in fertilizer, seeds, pesticides, and other inputs—because they have rainfall insurance.[9] When aggregated, these gains can have much broader effects, contributing to improved productivity and growth for a country as a whole.

Crises and losses from mismanaged risks are costly, but so are the measures required to better prepare for risks. So, does preparation pay off? Benefit-cost analyses across a number of areas suggest that risk preparation is often beneficial in averting costs, sometimes overwhelmingly so (figure 2). There seems to be a lot of truth in the old adage that "an ounce of prevention is worth a pound of cure." For example, a regimen of mineral supplements designed to reduce malnutrition and its related health risks may yield benefits at least 15 times greater than the cost of the program.[10] Similarly, improving weather forecasting and public communication systems to provide earlier warning of natural disasters in developing countries could yield estimated benefits 4 to 36 times greater than the cost.[11]

BOX 2 *A risky world: Trends in risk across regions*

The risks that people face have changed considerably over time, although this evolution has sometimes varied across regions. Risks have eased in some areas—such as maternal health, where the mortality rate has declined in all regions. Conversely the incidence of crime has increased substantially in Latin America and Sub-Saharan Africa. Strikingly, the incidence of natural disasters has increased in every region of the world. While Latin America, the Middle East and North Africa, and Sub-Saharan Africa all have suffered significantly fewer years of recession in each decade since the 1980s, Organisation for Economic Co-operation and Development (OECD) countries have experienced more.

a. Maternal mortality

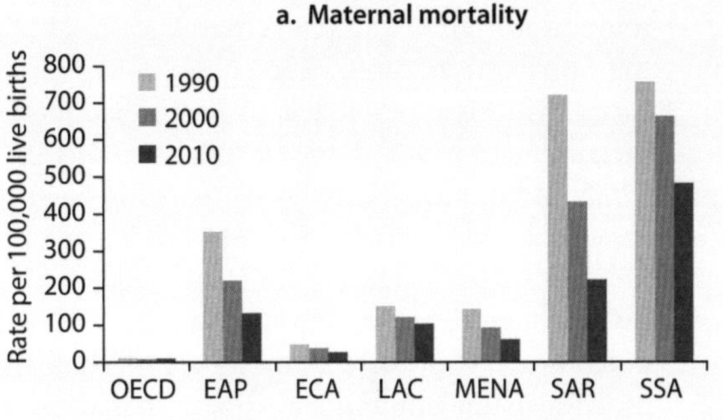

b. Homicides

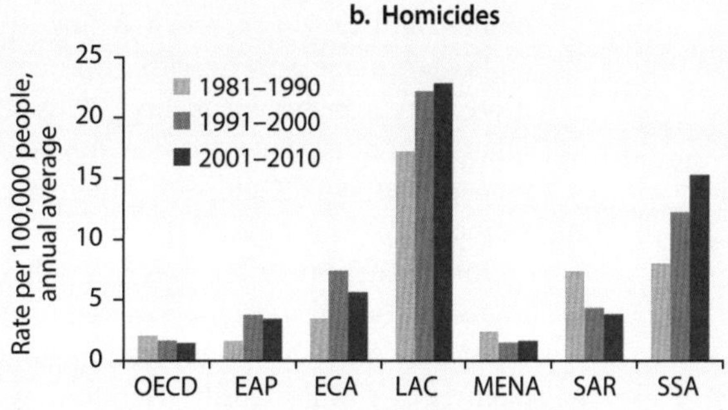

c. Incidence of natural disasters[a]

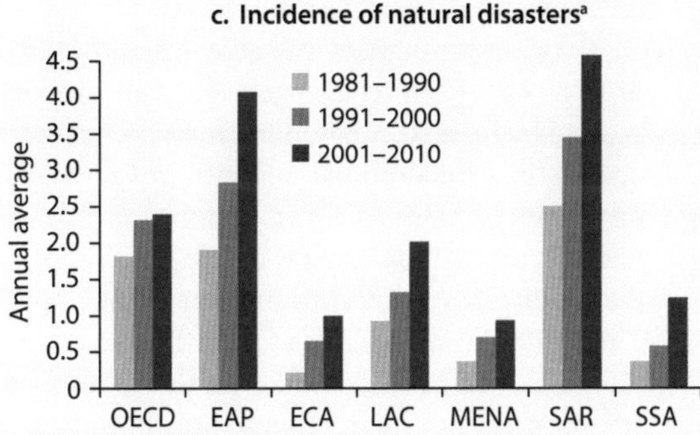

d. Large recessions[b]

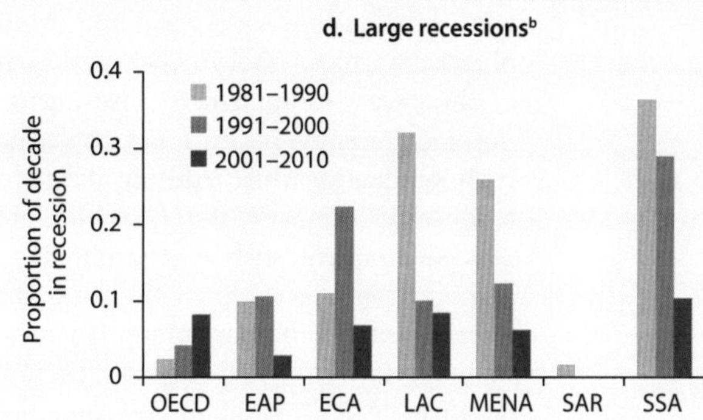

Source: WDR 2014 team based on data from World Bank World Development Indicators (database); EM-DAT OFDA/CRED International Disaster Database; United Nations Office on Drugs and Crime Homicide Statistics (database).

Note: Figures show the simple average across countries in each region. OECD countries in the figure are high-income countries that have been members of the OECD for at least 40 years. All other countries are grouped into geographic regions. EAP = East Asia and Pacific; ECA = Europe and Central Asia; LAC = Latin America and the Caribbean; MENA = Middle East and North Africa; SAR = South Asia; SSA = Sub-Saharan Africa.

a. Natural disasters include droughts, earthquakes, floods, and tropical storms.

b. Large recessions are identified by following Barro and Ursúa 2012 and using as a threshold a 5 percent decline in GDP per capita growth from peak to trough. There were no large recessions in South Asia from 1991 to 2010.

Comparing the cost-effectiveness of preparing for risk with that of coping with its consequences is one of the important trade-offs that must be assessed. The choice between these actions depends in part on how the (certain) costs of preparing for risk compare to the (often uncertain) benefits of doing so.[12] In addition, risk management requires considering different risks and the relative need of preparing for each of them (box 2). Given limited resources, setting priorities and making choices is both unavoidable and necessary. For instance, a family living in a violence-ridden community faces safety, health, and property risks and must choose how to allocate its limited budget to protect and insure against each of these risks. Likewise, a small country prone to torrential rains and also exposed to international financial shocks must decide how much to spend in flood prevention infrastructure and how much to save to counteract the effects of financial volatility.

When risks are taken on voluntarily in the pursuit of opportunity, another trade-off emerges: expected returns must be weighed against the potential losses of a course of action. This trade-off is intensified when a higher return is possible only if more risk is accepted. That is often the case with financial investments, where a lower yield is characteristic of a more secure position, and higher yields with riskier positions.[13] A risk-return trade-off may also be *perceived* for certain development actions: for instance, public opinion and certain experts may link the pursuit of higher economic growth with lower environmental protection or higher inequality.[14] Although this and other risk-return trade-offs may not be present, risk management entails addressing them as a legitimate possibility.

Risk management involves not only considering trade-offs but also taking synergies into account. These can make both preparation for and consequences of risk less costly. They can also diminish risks and increase expected benefits. These "win-win" situations are widespread and should be emphasized—which is not to say that they are costless or always easy to implement. Investments in nutrition and preventive health, for example, make people more productive while reducing their vulnerability to disease.[15] Similarly, improvements in the business environment, such as streamlining regulations and improving access to credit, can induce the enterprise sector to become more dynamic and grow more quickly, while also making it more resilient to negative shocks.[16] At the macroeconomic level, disciplined monetary and fiscal policies—reflected in moderate inflation and sustainable public deficits—accelerate economic growth while reducing high volatility in the face of external and domestic shocks.[17]

What does effective risk management entail?

As the ancient Greek philosopher Heraclitus wrote, the only thing constant is change. And with change comes uncertainty. Faced with choices for bettering their lives, people make virtually every decision in the presence of uncertainty. Young people decide what to study or train for without knowing exactly what jobs and wages will be available when they enter the labor market. Adults decide how much and how to save for retirement in the face of uncertain future income and investment returns, health conditions, and life spans. Farmers decide what to cultivate and what inputs to use not knowing with certainty whether there will be enough rain for their crops and what demand and prices their products will command in the market. And governments decide the level of policy interest rates and fiscal deficits in the presence of uncertain external conditions, domestic productivity growth, and changes in financial markets.

The analysis of choice under uncertainty in economics and public policy

It is only natural, therefore, that the analysis of choice under uncertainty and scarce resources has been at the heart of economics and public policy for centuries. The basic approach to decision under uncertainty—introduced by Daniel Bernoulli in the 1700s and modeled formally by John von Neumann and Oskar Morgenstern in 1944—is based on the notion that individuals optimize the expected "utility" (or subjective perception of welfare) of possible outcomes.[18] This expected utility approach relies on individuals making rational choices, based on their preferences for risk and their knowledge of potential outcomes and respective probabilities.

Notwithstanding its valuable insights, this approach has been challenged on two important grounds. The first is that individuals do not seem to operate in a fully rational manner, possibly because uncertainty makes the decision process so complicated that people prefer simple behavioral rules that evolve over time but are not always optimal. The work of Maurice Allais in the 1950s and Daniel Kahneman and Amos Tversky in the 1970s focused attention on the limitations and innate tendencies of human behavior when confronting decisions under uncertainty.[19]

The second challenge to the basic expected utility approach is that individuals do not make decisions in isolation but in groups, mainly because the potential outcomes can be greatly affected by how people act in coordination with others. The work of Duncan Black in the 1940s and James Buchanan and Mancur Olson in the 1960s emphasized the shortcomings of and obstacles to collective action.[20] Although originally concerned with the state's provision of public goods, the public choice approach extends to actions taken by any group, from households to communities of any size. The basic insight is how valuable and at the same time elusive it is to coordinate collective action, especially in the face of uncertainty.

A different strand of the economics literature is also concerned with the collective action problem and offers critical principles to overcome them. In their pioneering work in the 1960s and 1970s, Leonid Hurwicz, Roger Myerson, and Eric Maskin studied the problem of mechanism design to achieve efficiency in markets, organizations, and institutions. The critical insight here is that incentive constraints should be considered as important as resource constraints in understanding decision making in the presence of uncertainty.[21] This insight is vital when developing the best ways to coordinate the collective action of any group, especially under asymmetric information, diverging interests, and limited knowledge. It forces analysts and policy makers to see beyond aggregate resources and question what informs and motivates the actions of people and organizations, including actions related to managing risk.

An analytical framework for risk management

The insights derived from the economics of decision under uncertainty provide an analytical framework for risk management. The *World Development Report 2014* proposes that this framework consists of several interrelated steps:

- Assessing the fundamental goals of and motivations for risk management: that is, resilience in the face of adverse events and prosperity through the pursuit of opportunities (discussed in the first two sections above).
- Understanding the environment in which risks and opportunities take place (referred to below as the risk chain).
- Considering what risk management entails: that is, preparing for and coping with both adverse and positive events (presented below under "The components of risk management").
- Assessing the main obstacles that individuals and societies face in managing risk, including constraints on resources, information, and incentives (discussed below in the section entitled "Beyond the ideal").
- Introducing the potential role of groups and collective action at different levels of society to overcome the obstacles that people encounter in managing risk (presented below in the section "The way forward").

Understanding the environment in which risks and opportunities arise: The risk chain

The world is constantly changing and generating shocks that affect individuals and societies. *Shocks* may be positive (such as abundant rainfall or a windfall in terms of trade) or negative (illness or war). They may affect small groups (such as a family or a rural community) or large ones (a region or a country). And they may occur suddenly (such as natural hazards or financial shocks) or gradually (such as demographic transitions, technological trends, or environmental changes). Whether the *outcomes* from those shocks are positive or negative, large or small, individualized or widespread, depends on the interaction between shocks and the internal and external conditions that characterize a social and economic system (such as a household, a community, or a country). Importantly, the effect of shocks on people's outcomes is also mediated by their actions to prepare for and confront risk.

This interaction can be represented by a risk chain (diagram 1), which can be applied to different types of risks and contexts.[22] For example, whether someone becomes ill during a pandemic depends on how contagious the virus is (the initial shock); population density and living conditions in given areas (the external environment or exposure); people's individual susceptibility (internal conditions, such as their age or the strength of their immune system); and the steps they take to prevent becoming sick or contaminating others, such as frequently washing their hands or wearing a face mask (risk management). Similarly, whether an enterprise can successfully take advantage of new technology and innovation depends on the characteristics of the technology (the initial shock); the infrastructure in the country, which may affect the enterprise's access to the technology (the external environment); how innovative the enterprise is (internal conditions); and how much capital the enterprise has accumulated and how informed it is about the benefits and potential drawbacks of the new technology (risk management).

In this context, *risk* is defined as the possibility of loss. Risk is not all bad, however, because taking risks is necessary to pursue opportunity. *Opportunity* is defined as the possibility of gain, thus representing the upside of risk. People's *exposure* to risk is determined by their external environment. For example, whether a house is exposed to the risk of coastal flooding depends on its location. *Vulnerability* occurs when people are especially susceptible to losses from negative shocks because of a combination of large exposure, weak internal conditions, and deficient risk management. For example, a highly leveraged financial institution that has taken very risky positions without counterbalancing hedges is vulnerable

DIAGRAM 1 ***The risk chain: The nature and extent of outcomes depend on shocks, exposure, internal conditions, and risk management***

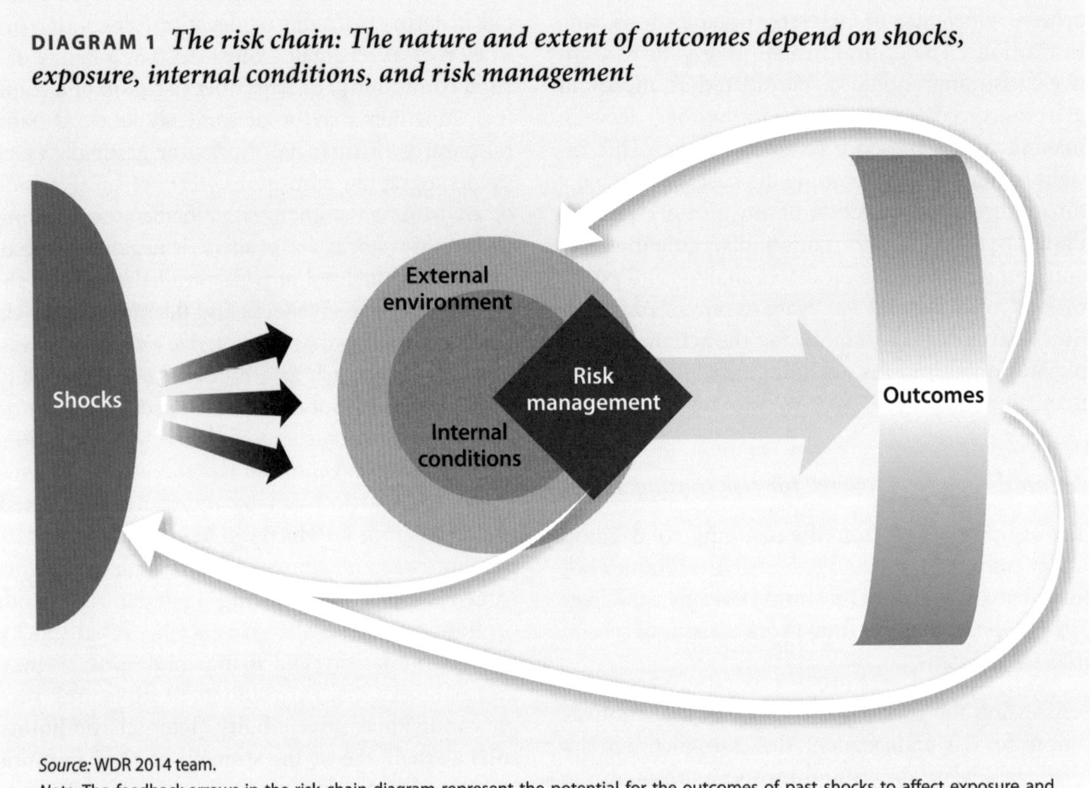

Source: WDR 2014 team.

Note: The feedback arrows in the risk chain diagram represent the potential for the outcomes of past shocks to affect exposure and internal conditions, as well as the propensity for future shocks. Similarly, the effectiveness of people's risk management can significantly affect the nature of and propensity for future shocks.

to an economic or financial shock. Likewise, a poor household with few assets and volatile income may be especially vulnerable to increased food prices.

Risk management is the process of confronting risks, preparing for them, and coping with their effects. *Resilience* is characterized by the ability of people, societies, and countries to recover from negative shocks, while retaining or improving their ability to function. Much of the emerging literature on risk in a development context emphasizes the important role that risk management can play in increasing resilience to negative shocks. However, to increase prosperity and well-being, risk management also has an essential role in helping people and countries successfully manage positive shocks. Indeed, successfully managing positive shocks is a critical part of increasing people's resilience to negative shocks over time. For example, a farmer's ability to withstand a drought may be substantially influenced by how the yields from years of good rainfall were managed. Thus the goal of risk management is to both decrease the losses and increase the benefits that people experience when they face and take on risk.

The components of risk management: Preparation and coping

To achieve that goal, risk management needs to combine the capacity to prepare for risk with the ability to cope afterward—taking into account how the up-front cost of preparation compares with its probable benefit. Building on the seminal contribution from Isaac Ehrlich and Gary Becker, *preparation* should include a combination of three actions that can be taken in advance: gaining knowledge, acquiring protection, and obtaining insurance.[23] Once a risk (or an opportunity) materializes, people take action to deal with what has occurred through *coping* (diagram 2). A strong risk management strategy would include all four of these components: knowledge, protection, insurance, and coping. They interact with each other, potentially improving each other's quality. For instance, better knowledge can lead to more efficient decisions regarding the allocation of resources between insurance and protection. Likewise, better insurance and protection can make coping less difficult and costly. Several obstacles, however, often make this risk management strat-

DIAGRAM 2 *The interlinked components of risk management*

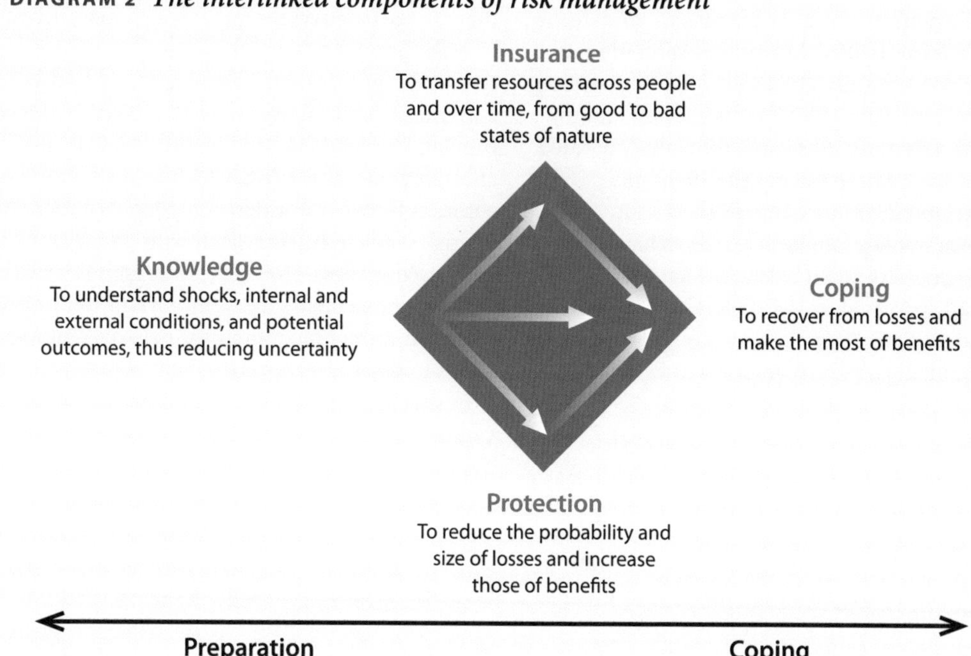

Source: WDR 2014 team.

egy difficult to achieve in practice, as is discussed in more detail below.

Knowledge

Obtaining knowledge and thus reducing the uncertainties that people face when they confront risk and pursue opportunities is the first component of risk management. Knowledge entails more than just amassing information: while obtaining information about possible events and their likelihoods is necessary, knowledge also involves using that information to assess exposure to those events and possible outcomes and then deciding how to act. Knowledge therefore contains elements of assessment and judgment. Furthermore, people's knowledge of risk depends not only on the information they can access but also on the quality of information that is provided by other social and economic systems. Indeed, public policy has an important role to play in improving the availability, transparency, and reliability of information that may be relevant for risk preparation, including national account and labor statistics, various market signals, and weather forecasts, among others. Moreover, the state can contribute by reducing the uncertainty that can be created by erratic policies, protracted implementation of reforms, and frequent regulatory changes.

While knowledge of risks often has been lacking in developing countries, it is increasing in several key areas, such as dealing with disease, economic cycles, and natural hazards. And new technologies are greatly helping to improve knowledge of potential shocks and inform responses to them. Farmers in Ghana and 15 other African countries, for example, receive specific market information through their mobile phones, which helps them improve their response to changes in agricultural prices and demand.[24] Globalization and scientific advances have also improved understanding of many pathogens, including how they can be detected and diagnosed rapidly to enable disease control. Improved technologies have also supported greater collaboration among scientists and policy makers, as well as enabling the media to inform people, even in remote parts of the world.

Protection

Protection includes any actions that lower the probability and size of negative outcomes or increase the probability and size of positive outcomes. Developing countries have made substantial improvements in some aspects of their risk protection in recent decades. The percentage of people in low- and middle-income countries with access to improved sanitation, for instance, increased from 36 percent in 1990 to 56 percent in 2010; meanwhile, the immunization rate for measles doubled from 41 percent to 83 percent between 1985 and 2010.[25] Improved sanitation and increased vaccinations, alongside other preventive health measures, have helped reduce infant and maternal mortality rates. Similarly, following repeated cycles of high inflation during the 1970s and 1980s, many developing countries established sound fiscal and monetary policy frameworks, which have helped reduce the intensity and incidence of large recessions (see box 2). Increased use of early warning systems has helped to protect populations exposed to natural hazards, reducing fatalities when major events occur.

Insurance

To the extent that protection cannot completely eliminate the possibility of negative outcomes, insurance can help cushion the blow from adverse shocks. Insurance includes any instruments that transfer resources across people or over time, from good to bad states of nature. In certain cases, insurance for particular risks is provided by specialized markets in the financial system. However, because formal insurance markets are often not widely available in developing countries, a larger burden is placed on self-insurance, which is often pursued through relatively costly and inefficient means, such as holding durable assets (like jewelry) that can be sold in the event of a shock. Large numbers of households also participate in informal, community-based risk sharing, and microfinance and microinsurance programs are increasingly providing new instruments that help people manage risk. Similarly, alongside traditional safety nets, conditional cash transfers and other social insurance programs are a means for the state to transfer resources to help the most vulnerable cope with adverse circumstances.[26]

There may be either synergies or trade-offs between insurance and protection as strategies to manage risk. To the extent that having insurance reduces people's incentives to prevent bad states from occurring, insurance and protection act as substitutes for each other. However, when the steps that people take to attain protection facilitate or make it cheaper to insure against adverse outcomes, protection and insurance can complement each other.[27] Being a nonsmoker, for instance, can make it easier and cheaper to obtain health insurance. Protection often must be observable for insurance and protection to be complements. While observability is already highly relevant for informal risk sharing in communities, technology may also make it increasingly relevant for formal insurance. For example, new devices for cars can allow insurers to vary the insurance premiums they charge based on the quality of people's driving.[28]

Together, knowledge, insurance, and protection constitute preparation. The assets of households, communities and governments, as well as services provided by markets and the public sector, all influence preparation for risk, which in turn affects outcomes. Overall, the extent of people's preparation for risk tends to be correlated with national income across countries. However, interesting variations within regions highlight the important role of policy in determining preparation for risk, over and above access to resources (box 3).

Coping

The final component of risk management is coping, which encompasses all actions that are taken once a risk (or, alternatively, an opportunity) has materialized. Coping, therefore, consists of deploying the knowledge, protection, and insurance resources that have been obtained during the preparation phase. The relationship between coping and preparation becomes very fluid when confronting an evolving risk. This includes updating relevant knowledge by monitoring and assessing emerging risks and then adapting and implementing any necessary and available responses.

The choice of how much to prepare for risk has implications for the kind of coping that is needed, which, in turn, can contribute to vicious or virtuous circles in risk management. When effective preparation limits the damages from adverse shocks, coping can be minimal—leaving more resources available for further investments in risk management, reducing vulnerability to future shocks, and so on. At the household level, for instance, having health insurance can facilitate medical treatment and recovery, while reducing out-of-pocket expenses, when a family member falls ill or suffers an accident. At the macroeconomic level, evidence suggests that by reducing losses from natural hazards, for example, preparation for risk may sustain and even accelerate economic growth.[29]

In contrast, when preparation is limited or a shock is unexpectedly large, coping can be haphazard and require costly measures—leaving few resources available for future risk management, worsening vulnerability to shocks, and weakening households' ability to undertake new opportunities. For example, the loss of assets that occurs from natural disasters in countries as different as Ethiopia and Honduras—caused by direct damage from a hurricane or

BOX 3 *How does preparation for risk vary across countries?*

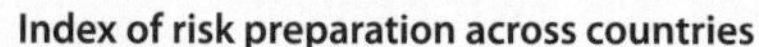

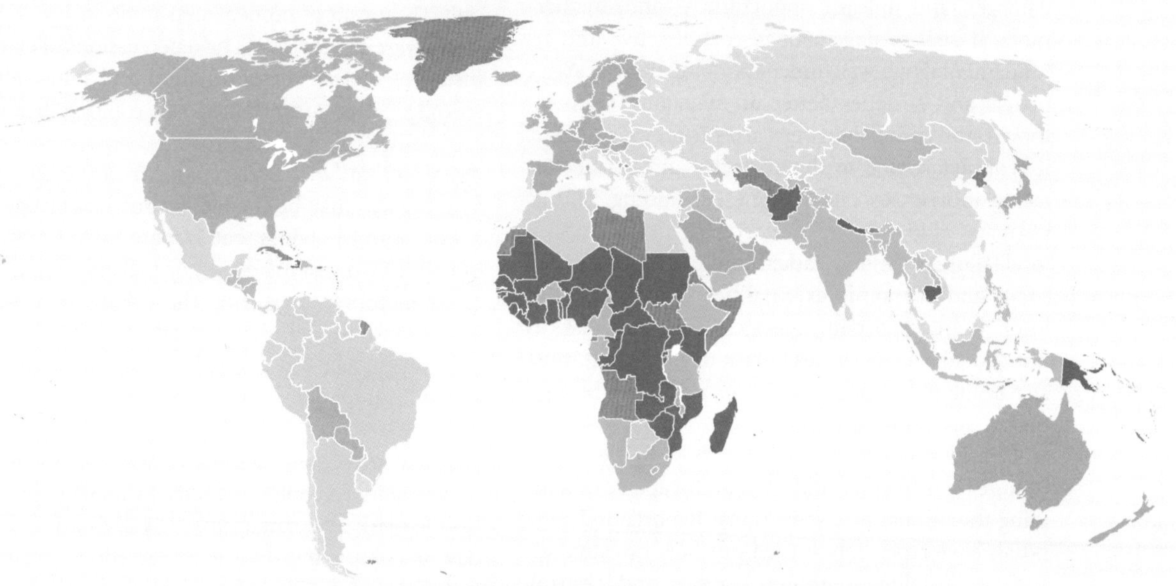

Least prepared quintile ■ ■ ■ ■ ■ Most prepared quintile ■ Missing data

People's preparation for risk at the country level includes actions by and contributions from all social and economic groups and institutions, including the state. An index of preparation for risk is charted on the map above. The index, developed for the *World Development Report 2014*, comprises measures of assets and services across four important categories—human capital, physical and financial assets, social support, and state support—that influence preparation for risk. The component indicators for the index include: average years of total schooling for the population aged 15 and over, and the immunization rate for measles (human capital); the proportion of households with less than $1,000 in net assets, and an index of access to finance (physical and financial assets); the percent of the workforce who contribute to a pension scheme, and the proportion of respondents stating that "in general, people can be trusted" (social support); and the percent of the population with access to improved sanitation facilities, and an indicator of fiscal space based on gross public debt as a percentage of revenues (state support).[a]

This index shows that the extent of people's preparation for risk tends to be correlated with national income across countries, but only to a certain extent. People tend to be the most prepared in high-income countries (particularly in North America and western Europe), and least prepared in low-income countries (especially in Africa), on average. However, substantial variation exists within regions. For example, Chile is reasonably well prepared for risk, while its neighbor to the east, Argentina, has only average risk preparation despite having a similar level of income per capita. Likewise, Ethiopia has better risk preparation than other countries in the region with similar or relatively higher income per capita. This underscores the importance of policies, over and above income level and access to resources, in determining preparation for risk.

Source: Foa 2013 for the WDR 2014. Map number: IBRD 40097.

a. Each indicator is rescaled to range between zero and one. The index, which is the average of the eight indicators, thus maintains the cardinal properties of the indicators, rather than simply being an average of rankings across the components. This approach follows in part the methodology used in the construction of the Worldwide Governance Indicators (see Kaufmann, Kraay, and Mastruzzi 2010). If necessary, each indicator is transformed so that an increase in its measure represents an improvement.

drought, lack of insurance, and distressed sale of assets—has substantial short-term as well as long-term effects: poor households can effectively become trapped in poverty, making them more vulnerable to future negative shocks and less able to undertake new ventures for improvement.[30] Similarly, while the coping responses by governments around the world in the midst of the 2008–09 crisis—including bailouts of large financial firms, fiscal stimulus, and extended periods of monetary easing—helped calm markets in the short-run, these responses may have negative longer-term effects, including substantially increased public debt and perverse incentives for financial institutions' risk taking.

Beyond the ideal: The obstacles to risk management

If risk management can save lives, avert economic damages, and unleash opportunity—and, furthermore, if risk management is cost-effective and its fundamentals are well understood—then, why aren't people and societies better at managing risk? Although the specific answer varies from case to case, it is always related to the obstacles and constraints facing individuals and societies, including lack of resources and information, cognitive and behavioral failures, missing markets and public goods, and social and economic externalities. This realization leads to an important message. Identifying risks is not enough: the obstacles to risk management must also be identified, prioritized, and addressed through private and public action (box 4).

Consider the case of Mumbai. Its drainage system is more than 100 years old and barely capable of handling the annual monsoon rains. Reports and proposals have repeatedly spelled out how investments, such as installing pumping stations and clearing out debris, are needed to expand the capacity of the storm drainage system. Yet with few exceptions, the proposals have not been acted upon. An exceptionally large monsoon hit the city in 2005, leading to more than 400 deaths, extensive damage to buildings and infrastructure, and interruption of economic and financial activity. Afterward, a fact-finding committee made recommendations for overhauling the drainage system that were distressingly similar to those made in the 1990s. As of 2013, however, implementation is again lagging. As a result, India's financial capital remains highly vulnerable to monsoon rains.

Why aren't people better at managing their own risk?

Lack of resources. Even when a risk management strategy is cost-effective, individuals and groups may find it difficult to undertake because of large upfront costs and limited access to credit. Shortages of assets and finance, which are especially acute in poor and developing countries, can make the trade-offs inherent in risk management harder to handle. Governments may decide that, given their limited budget, current consumption spending is more pressing than investments for disaster risk reduction.

Lack of information and cognitive failures. Relevant information may not exist or be available to decision makers, or they may lack the ability to understand this information. Cognitive shortcomings are relevant and pervasive obstacles to risk management in many circumstances, even in advanced countries. In the United States, for example, a survey revealed that only 31 percent of homeowners in flood-prone areas were aware of the risk.[31] The repercussions of extreme instances of lack of information and knowledge—so-called "deep" uncertainty—are explored below.

Behavioral failures. Even if information exists, decision makers may be unable to turn knowledge into actions and behaviors that prepare them for risk. In many cases, decision and policy makers seem to have short memories regarding the origins of crises of various sorts. Systemic financial crises, for instance, are almost always preceded by unusually high credit concentration and growth, and this process seems to be well understood.[32] Yet policy makers often do little to control credit booms. A false sense of security may underlie people's inability to manage preparation for risk in normal times (by saving for a rainy day or completing disaster preparedness plans, for instance). And a "paradox of protection" can arise: risk protection that suppresses losses for a long period creates a false sense of security, leading to decreased vigilance and risk awareness and potentially resulting in larger future losses.[33] In many cases what might be perceived as irrational behavior may in fact be the result of distorted incentives, incorrect or insufficient knowledge, or particular social norms and cultural beliefs.

Obstacles beyond the control of individuals hamper their risk management

Missing markets and public goods. Markets in areas critical for effective risk management—credit, insurance, jobs—are weak or even missing in many developing countries. So are public goods and services essential for risk management—economic and political stability, law and order, and basic infrastructure. In fact, well-developed markets may be missing because supportive public goods are flawed. If, for instance, the justice system does not enforce contracts, it makes little sense to buy health, vehicular, or house insurance, and no such market will exist.[34] There are many reasons why public goods are missing, but this discussion considers only the most pertinent ones for risk management. The first, already discussed, is lack of resources: the costly flood protections constructed in the Netherlands, for example, are simply not feasible for many similarly threatened developing countries, like Bangladesh or Vietnam. The second reason

BOX 4 *Bringing the essentials of and obstacles to risk management together in policy design*

Designing effective public policy must go beyond simply identifying potential risks to analyzing obstacles to risk management. Diagram a below presents a set of screens to assist in decision making—helping to identify critical gaps and revealing effective, low-cost interventions.

a. A set of screens to aid risk management

Risk assessment	Incentive assessment		Information assessment	Behavior assessment	Resource assessment	Policy design
How much risk are we facing?	Are bad incentives leading to too much or too little risk taking?		Are decision-makers ill informed?	Are cognitive and behavior biases impairing risk management?	Are resources and access to resources too limited?	What policies should be implemented?
	Because of market failures?	Because of government failures?				

This practical approach provides two important insights for the design of risk management policies:

Be realistic. Simple risk management instruments should be preferred when capacity is low. Policy makers should concentrate on low-hanging fruit and win-win solutions. Soft measures that change incentives (such as improving zoning regulations for coastal areas) are preferable as a starting point to engineered measures (such as dikes to prevent flooding). Furthermore, it is particularly cost-effective to strengthen the capabilities that are useful in managing risks of different natures, such as the ability to complete large-scale evacuations (which can be useful for either a hurricane or a nuclear accident, for example). Realistic policy options should ensure that risk management avoids unintended negative policy consequences; provides the right incentives to build on everybody's best capacities; and protects the most vulnerable, who are often least able to implement ideal but expensive solutions.

Build a strong foundation for improved risk management over time. It often makes sense to create institutional arrangements when the need for them is obvious, such as after a disaster event, and that cannot be easily reversed once the memory of the event has disappeared. This institutional irreversibility should be combined with flexible implementation and continuous learning. Policy makers should aim for robust policies that may not be optimal in the most likely future, but that lead to acceptable outcomes in a large range of scenarios and that are easy to revise as new information becomes available. Starting with a strong foundation for risk management requires a long-term perspective, creates the right incentives, and minimizes the risk of unintended negative effects. It also helps ensure that policies are flexible enough to be adjusted when new information becomes available. (For more on both these insights, see the discussion entitled "Five principles of public action for better risk management" at the end of this overview.)

Thinking about both the fundamental components of and obstacles to risk management with these lessons in mind can help identify which specific policies are most relevant in different contexts. For example, countries with limited resources or weak institutional capacity should focus on policies that are foundational, while countries that already have solid foundations for risk management in place can aim for more advanced policies. This framework is used throughout the *World Development Report 2014* to organize and prioritize risk management policies across the four main components of risk management (knowledge, protection, insurance, and coping) for different social and economic systems, from the household to the international community. These are summarized in corresponding tables for each of these systems (diagram b).

b. A framework for public policy priorities

	POLICIES TO SUPPORT RISK MANAGEMENT FOUNDATIONAL → ADVANCED		
Knowledge			
Protection			
Insurance			
Coping			

Source: WDR 2014 team.

is related to the political economy of risk management. Governments may be reluctant to spend on risk preparation because its costs are immediate and observable while its benefits, even if substantial, are longer term and less visible.

Government failures. Risk management can also be impaired by government failures stemming from capture by interest groups, corruption of government officials, and distortionary policies. On policy capture, enterprises and people who are negatively affected by certain risk management measures will naturally tend to oppose them and be vocal about it, while the people protected by these measures are often not aware of them (and therefore do not support them), or lack the commensurate influence of active lobbies. Powerful tobacco and asbestos lobbies, for instance, can block useful health regulations even in the presence of well-established scientific evidence. On distortionary policies, sometimes even well-intentioned measures can impair risk management by distorting people's incentives to manage their own risk. An example is poorly designed post-disaster support that creates moral hazard and discourages risk management by individuals and firms. Similarly, overly generous safety nets or financial sector bailouts can undermine incentives for risk preparation.

Social and economic externalities. Risk management actions undertaken by some people or countries may impose losses on others. For instance, overuse of antibiotics is creating ever more drug-resistant bacteria. Similarly, excessive exploitation of common natural resources such as oceans, forests, and the atmosphere—a phenomenon known in the literature as "the tragedy of the commons"—is leading to environmental degradation, climate change, and a future drop in economic growth.[35] In a different realm, an expansion in the money supply to stimulate the domestic economy in large advanced economies is creating destabilizing capital inflows to developing countries, as well as eroding the wealth of domestic savers and taxpayers. Similarly, instituting trade barriers to protect domestic producers during economic downturns imposes increased cost on trade partners and can lead to trade retaliation, possibly turning a downturn into a protracted world recession.[36] Other risk management actions can generate benefits for people other than those bearing their cost, therefore creating incentives to "free ride." That is the case, for instance, for countries that take costly measures to reduce greenhouse emissions, which can benefit the rest of the world. Both negative and positive externalities may complicate the process of risk management, making it less predictable and distorting its incentives. The solution is coordination and collective action, which can be difficult to obtain when there are wide differences in preferences, values, and exposures. For instance, externalities and collective action failures may be why reaching a binding international agreement on greenhouse gas emissions is proving so elusive.

Deep uncertainty and robust solutions

"Deep uncertainty" is an obstacle to risk management that deserves special attention. Also known as Knightian uncertainty in economic circles,[37] deep uncertainty refers to a situation for which even experts cannot agree on appropriate models to understand it, on the potential outcomes and probabilities of its occurrence, and on how much importance should be given to it. Taking a broad perspective, the difference between deep uncertainty and ordinary uncertainty is a matter of degree, fluid, and evolving. Building knowledge helps to reduce the degree of uncertainty. The history of science is full of cases where deep uncertainty gradually became ordinary uncertainty, amenable to management and control. But while this happens, what should be done in the presence of "unknown unknowns"?

Under conditions of deep uncertainty, it is preferable to implement adaptive and robust policies and actions that lead to acceptable outcomes in a large range of scenarios and that can be revised when new information is available and when the context changes.[38] For monetary and financial policy, a promising practice is the use of stress testing of banks and other financial institutions using a broad range of situations, including forward-looking crisis scenarios.[39] Above all, plans that are designed for the most likely outcomes but that increase the vulnerability to less likely events should be avoided. For instance, dike systems built only for standard rainstorms and tides can actually increase vulnerability by creating a false sense of security and dramatically increasing the damages when a flood does occur.

The way forward: A holistic approach to managing risk

Can individuals on their own overcome the obstacles to risk management they face? Although individuals' own efforts, initiative, and responsibility are essential for managing risk, their success will be limited without a supportive external environment. While individuals on their own may be capable of dealing with many risks, they are inherently ill-equipped to confront large shocks (such as the head of a household falling ill), systemic shocks (such as a natural hazard or an international financial crisis), or multiple shocks that occur either simultaneously or sequentially (for example, a drought followed by a food price shock and food insecurity).

People can successfully confront risks that are beyond their means by sharing their risk management with others. They can pool their risk collectively through various overlapping social and economic groupings (*systems*). Indeed, the need to manage risk and pursue opportunity collectively may often be a key reason why these groups or systems form in the first place.[40] These systems extend in size and complexity—from the household to the international community. They have the potential to support people's risk management in different yet complementary ways (diagram 3). Their different scope may allow them to handle shocks and exposures that match their scale (box 5).

- The *household* is the primary instance of support, pooling resources, protecting its members—especially the vulnerable—and allowing them to invest in their future.
- *Communities* provide informal networks of insurance and protection, helping people deal with idiosyncratic risks and pooling resources to confront common risks.
- *Enterprises* can help absorb shocks and exploit the opportunity side of risk, contributing to more stable employment, growing income, and greater innovation and productivity.
- *The financial system* can facilitate useful risk management tools such as savings, insurance, and credit, while managing its own risks responsibly.
- *The state* has the scale and tools to manage systemic risks at the national and regional levels, to provide an enabling environment for the other systems to function, and to provide direct support to vulnerable people. These roles can be achieved through the provision of social protection (social insurance and assistance), public goods (national defense, infrastructure, law and order), and public policy (sound regulation, economic management).

DIAGRAM 3 ***Key social and economic systems can contribute to risk management in complementary ways***

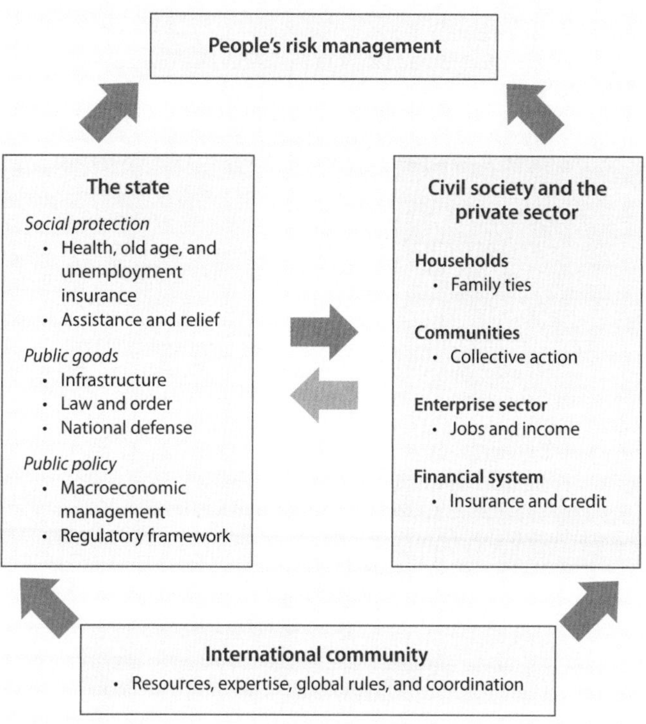

Source: WDR 2014 team.

- *The international community* can offer expertise, facilitate international policy coordination, and pool resources when risks exceed national capacity or cross national and generational boundaries.

These systems have mutual interactions, often complementing and sometimes substituting for each other's risk management functions. For instance, various mechanisms of protection and insurance provided by communities, enterprises, the financial system, and the state can complement and improve households' self-protection and self-insurance. Enterprises rely on macroeconomic stability, public services, and financial products to remain dynamic and continue to provide income and employment to people. The financial system can provide tools of insurance, saving, and credit only if enough households and enterprises are able to participate in the system, and if the economy features a certain degree of stability and predictability. Markets, in general, can provide risk management tools and resources at a growing scale if the necessary public services, such

BOX 5 *Which systems for which risks?*

Individuals face a multitude of risks, and various social and economic systems can help them manage risks that are beyond their means alone. But which systems are most appropriate for which risks? Two important principles provide a way to prioritize risk management across systems:

1. The *principle of subsidiarity* suggests that risks should be handled at the lowest level capable of handling them, to take advantage of the proximity to and greater knowledge of the agents most directly affected by a risk, as well as the ability to monitor both those agents and the risks that they face.
2. The *principle of comparative advantage* suggests that risks should be managed by the system that can handle them most effectively.

Individuals and households are well placed to handle idiosyncratic risks (such as minor injuries or income shortfalls) as long as the potential losses remain relatively small. They have an advantage in managing these types of risk because of their proximity to the level at which the main impact occurs and because of their ability to monitor conditions and efforts within the household.

As the size of potential losses increases, the tools that individuals have at their disposal can quickly be exhausted. The enterprise and financial systems can thus provide effective tools and mechanisms (discussed in more detail in the sections below) for individuals to manage potential losses from large idiosyncratic shocks (such as the job loss of the head of the household or a burned-down house). The state must sometimes provide substitutes for these functions when markets are missing or not available to some.

Because systemic risks affect large groups of people, they can hardly be managed by individuals alone. Communities have an advantage in managing small systemic risks (such as local violence or flooding) because of their proximity to the groups of people affected and their potential advantage in monitoring and resolving local tensions. The state also has an advantage in managing small systemic risks (such as moderate fluctuations in aggregate prices or regional food shortages) because of its capacity to control the national macroeconomy and transfer resources between different parts of a country.

Because many agents within a country are severely affected when large systemic shocks occur, such as economy-wide banking crises or natural disasters, the cross-support they can provide for one another is limited. In other words, it is difficult for the private sector alone to pool and insure for systemic risk. The state thus has a unique role in managing large systemic risks because it has the scale and tools to prepare at the national and regional levels. Support and coordination from the international community is needed when large systemic risks cross national borders or overwhelm national capacities. Spotlights in the WDR 2014 feature case studies of risk management by different support systems.

Types of risk that can be managed by different systems and examples featured in the WDR 2014 spotlights

	Small idiosyncratic risk	Large idiosyncratic risk	Small systemic risk	Large systemic risk
System best placed to manage risk	Individuals and households	The enterprise sector and financial system	The community and the state	The state and the international community
Spotlight examples	Health risks (Turkey and the Kyrgyz Republic) Loss of employment and income (India)		Food shortages (Ethiopia and El Salvador) Urban violence (Brazil and South Africa)	Natural hazards (the Philippines and Colombia) Financial crises (the Czech Republic, Peru, and Kenya) Pandemics (global)

Source: WDR 2014 team.

as the rule of law and a sound regulatory framework, are in place and effective. The international community relies in part on responsible governments that are willing to cooperate to address global risks; in turn, the international community can help governments and countries that lack resources and capacity for risk management.

The relative importance of these systems changes with the level of development. In less advanced countries, and especially in fragile and conflict-affected countries, informal mechanisms tend to be more prevalent and the relative roles of the household and the community are larger. For these countries, the international community may also play a larger role through financial assistance and capacity building. As countries advance—and informal mechanisms give way to formal ones—the relative importance of the contributions from the enterprise sector and the financial system grow. The *potential* role of the state is larger in less developed countries, but in these cases the state tends to suffer from more severe capacity and resource constraints. These limitations call for a mutual, symbiotic relationship between the state, civil society, the private sector, and the international community, as countries develop (see below).

The state, civil society, and the private sector: Helping one another manage risk

None of the social and economic systems presented above works perfectly. Indeed, in certain cases they hinder rather than help people's risk management. They have the potential, however, to become effective support systems when their weaknesses are resolved. The state thus has an important potential role to play by complementing and supporting the functions that households, communities, enterprises, and the financial system may serve. From this perspective, the state's role goes beyond the narrow purpose of correcting market failures and extends to addressing systemic risks, building institutions that enhance each component of risk management, and providing direct support to vulnerable populations.

It would be naïve, however, to ignore the fact that the state often falls short in fulfilling its potential role. Historically and throughout the world, examples of government failures are regrettably abundant.[41] This is all too vividly evident in the case of fragile and conflict-affected countries. What to do then? Civil society, the private sector, and the international community can provide badly needed public goods and services—albeit imperfectly. Especially, but not only, in democratic societies, they can also help improve governance and the delivery of public services by generating mechanisms to make the state responsive to the needs of the population and accountable for its actions.[42]

The discussion that follows assesses the potential contribution of each major system and suggests ways to improve their performance, individually and in combination with other systems. The state's potential contribution is presented in connection with each system, reflecting its overarching role and allowing for an elaboration of specific recommendations for public policy, as well as a discussion of their rationale and trade-offs.

The household

How can it foster resilience and prosperity?

For most people, the household—defined as a group of individuals related to one another by family ties—constitutes the main source of material and emotional support to confront risk and pursue opportunity. Extending Gary Becker's metaphor in *A Treatise on the Family,* households are "little factories" where goods and services of knowledge, protection, and insurance are produced, using both "intermediate inputs" obtained from the rest of society and the pooled efforts and skills provided by family members.[43] How can the household contribute?

Protection and risk pooling for its members. Protection and insurance at the household level are particularly important for idiosyncratic risks and even more relevant when market or social insurance is lacking. Protection against adverse shocks is especially important for the vulnerable within the household: the young, the old, and the ill. For this purpose, families can benefit from the resources that are available in society—all the more so if these resources are increasing and improving. Thus, for instance, higher incomes and better access to health services have increased immunization rates for measles to more than 70 percent in every region of the world, although Sub-Saharan Africa still has much room for improvement (figure 3a).

Moreover, sharing bad times (and good times) occurs naturally in the household. Indeed, pooling risk within and across family generations has been a basic form of insurance from time immemorial. The extended family plays an active role, especially in developing countries. For instance, evidence from Bangladesh, Ethiopia, India, Mali, and Mexico shows that extended family members step in to help out in a substantial way when their relatives fall ill.[44] Similarly, evidence from several countries around the world indicates that family members who migrate assist their families through remittances when negative shocks occur in their place of origin.[45]

Allowing its members, especially the young ones, to make investments for the future. The role of households extends well beyond protecting and insuring members against negative events. Households invest in the human capital and social skills of their members, especially the young, preparing future generations to manage the risks and opportunities they will face. Schooling is one important example where progress has occurred in recent decades. The average number of years of educational attainment has increased since 1960 in all regions—most substantially in regions that initially had the lowest attainment (figure 3b). However, the quality of education, as measured by international exams in science, math, and reading skills, is still lagging behind in many

FIGURE 3 *Education and health outcomes in developing countries are improving, but unevenly*

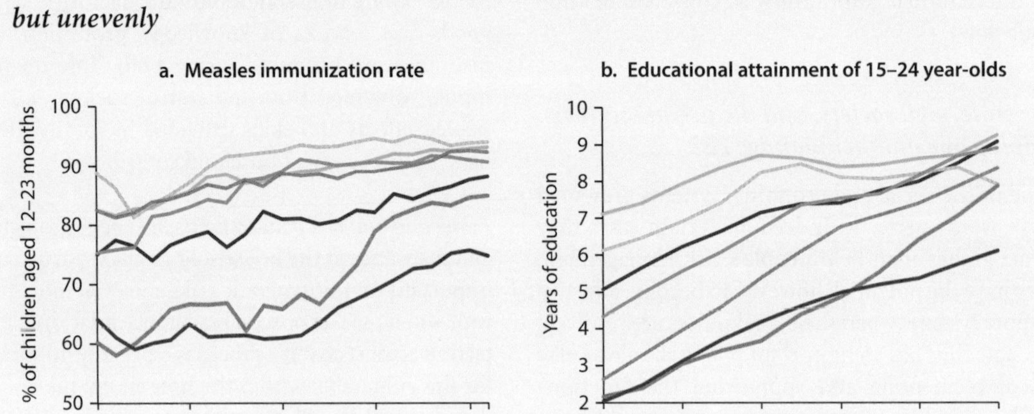

Source: WDR 2014 team based on data from World Bank World Development Indicators (database) (panel a) and Barro and Lee 2010 (panel b).

Note: Organisation for Economic Co-operation and Development (OECD) countries in the figure are high-income countries that have been members of the OECD for at least 40 years. All other countries are grouped into geographic regions.

low- and middle-income countries, without signs of converging yet.[46]

What characteristics improve the household's contribution to risk management?

Households are small but complex units. The motivations of their members can range from altruism to self-interest, the intrahousehold relationships can be based on common goals or relative bargaining power, and the household's connections to society can be fluid or remote. These characteristics can have great influence on how well the household functions as a first line of support to confront risk and opportunity.

Access and participation. Communities, labor and financial markets, and public institutions provide the "intermediate inputs" that families build upon to manage their risks. Continuous access to and participation in those markets and institutions is critical for families to be successful risk managers (so much so in the view of the *World Development Report 2014* that the following four sections are devoted to assessing how they can contribute). To give just one example: evidence from 59 countries suggests that access to programs that limit out-of-pocket health expenditures, such as social insurance and private health insurance, significantly reduces the incidence of catastrophic medical expenditures, especially for poor households.[47] Given the fundamental importance of health for everything else people do, there is indeed great need for health insurance and much room for improvement: only 17 percent of adults in developing countries report having contributed to health insurance, and this share is as low as 2 percent in some low-income countries.[48]

Fairness within the household. One would like to think of households as nurturing, cohesive units. All too often, however, abuse and discrimination occur within the family, making it a source of, rather than a solution to, risk. Compelling evidence shows that women's economic and social empowerment can strongly influence whether the allocation of resources within the household benefits children and promotes gender equality.[49] An evaluation of a cash transfer program in South Africa, for instance, found that pensions received by women improved the health and nutritional status of girls but that transfers received by men had no effect on either boys or girls.[50] One important ingredient for women's economic empowerment is access to the labor market, which in several contexts is limited by inadequate child care infrastructure and restrictive social norms.

Some countries and regions have much room for improvement: female labor participation rates are only 20–30 percent in the Middle East, North Africa, and South Asia, while in most of the rest of the world they are well above 50 percent.[51]

How can the state contribute?

The state has an important role to play in providing social services and countering harmful social norms. Policies that *empower households as a unit* and policies that *empower individuals within households* are necessary.

Providing essential social services. Access to good, even if basic, educational and medical services can prepare people to confront major health risks, handle life-cycle transitions, and take advantage of work opportunities. In this sense, the drive for "equality of opportunities" can also bring about resilience for households and individuals.[52] The efforts of Thailand and Turkey to offer universal access to quality health insurance deserve special mention. Universal access to health care is likely to require a partnership between the public and private sectors to ensure both fiscal sustainability and sufficient human resources.[53] For the most vulnerable, targeted safety nets can have a dramatic impact in preventing the coping responses that incur long-term costs—such as reducing basic consumption, withdrawing children from school, selling productive assets in distress sales, or resorting to crime. Ethiopia's Productive Safety Net Program is one successful example of protecting the most vulnerable from food insecurity while building community assets to better manage climatic risks and raise productivity.[54]

Increasing women's power in the household. This can be done first through economic empowerment: encouraging women's participation in the labor force and, for poor households, directly increasing their purchasing power. An example of the latter is conditional cash transfer programs that make payments to women directly; impact evaluations have shown that these programs improve family and, especially, children's outcomes, including health and cognitive development.[55] A second route is through social and legal empowerment: enforcing legal measures against abuse and domestic violence, eliminating regulations that discriminate against women in asset ownership or economic activity, and conducting educational campaigns to counter social norms that tolerate violence or discrimination against women and children. The campaigns should target both men and women: more than 20 percent of women in all regions, except Latin America and the Caribbean, believe a husband is justified in hitting or beating his wife for reasons like going out without telling him and arguing with him.[56]

The community

How can the community foster resilience and prosperity?

Communities are groups of people who interact frequently and share location or identity. Neighborhood groups, religious groups, and kinship groups are some examples. They work through informal networks based on trust, reciprocity, and social norms—what James Coleman and Robert Putnam call "social capital."[57] In this way, communities can help their members by sharing idiosyncratic risks and confronting common risks and opportunities.

Sharing idiosyncratic risks. Informal insurance is particularly important for low-income households and is sometimes their only real safety net. In the village of Nyakatoke in Tanzania, for instance, with a population of only 120 families, there are about 40 different insurance schemes (burial societies, rotating savings associations, and arrangements to share labor and livestock).[58] These practices are also relevant at the country level. Indonesian households, for instance, have informal insurance against 38 percent of the economic costs of serious health shocks and 71 percent of the costs of minor illness.[59] In Nigeria, informal credit and assistance make up 32 percent of all coping responses identified by households (figure 4).

Confronting common risks and opportunities. When communities channel their social capital for collective action, they can provide some publics goods (such as basic transport and irrigation infrastructure) to protect against common adverse events (such as epidemics, natural hazards, and crime and violence) and to facilitate taking advantage of common opportunities (such as new markets and technologies).[60] This collective action can be especially important when state capacity is low. The informal settlement of Orangi in Karachi, Pakistan, for example, financed and organized its own sanitation, vaccination, microfinance, family planning, and violence prevention, assisted by a local nongovernmental organization.

FIGURE 4 *People respond to shocks on their own and by pooling risk with others*

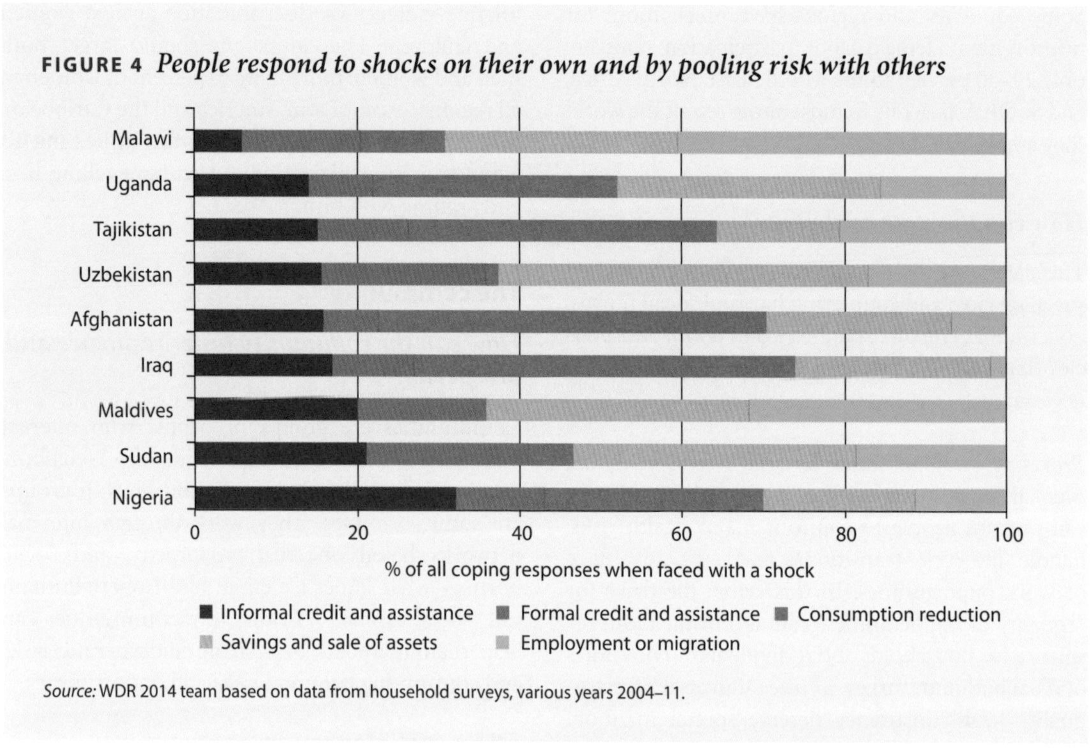

Source: WDR 2014 team based on data from household surveys, various years 2004–11.

What characteristics improve the community's contribution to risk management?

Cohesiveness. Communities with strong ties between their members—that is, those communities endowed with high "bonding" social capital—are better able to organize collective action on behalf of the group.[61] In fact, for local problems whose solution eludes markets and governments, a cohesive community can be the missing piece of the puzzle. Cohesiveness is not easy to achieve, however, when community members have different values and cultural identities, as is increasingly the case in urban communities. Moreover, community cohesiveness is seriously compromised when people are excluded or discriminated against.

Connectedness. Communities also need connections to other communities and to markets; without these connections they remain small and insular, lack political influence, and are unable to accomplish anything at scale. Communities with strong ties to one another—that is, those communities that have high "bridging" social capital—are more likely to collaborate with one another on mutually beneficial risk management projects and to coexist peacefully. Cities with high religious or ethnically motivated violence, for example, tend to lack routine interaction among members of different groups and to be characterized by divisive local leaders, media, and criminal gangs.

How can the state contribute?

Reliance on personal interactions and informal means of enforcement underlies the strength of communities, but it is also the source of their weakness. Communities struggle with systemic risk and falter when risk management requires complex and long-term preparation. Governments can help by providing essential public goods and promoting inclusion and respect for diversity.

Providing essential public goods, such as infrastructure and rule of law. Communities' autonomous coping and insurance mechanisms do not add up to adequate risk management; they also need national and local governments to complement their efforts. For example, neighborhoods are potentially able to maintain their own drains, but urban flood prevention requires citywide drainage and land use planning that only city governments can provide. Similarly, neighborhoods can patrol against petty criminals, but they are powerless against organized crime.

Promoting inclusion and respect for diversity. Communities are not necessarily fair or reliable and can be marked by strong inequalities in power and wealth.[62] They may exclude vulnerable people (chronically ill, widowed), new entrants (migrants, refugees), or those who happen to be different (ethnic minorities). The state can help by enacting antidiscrimination laws, conducting educational campaigns, and encouraging interactions that promote cohesiveness in the face of diversity.

Not only can governments support communities, but community participation can increase the quality of the governance process and improve the performance of government programs. People may not heed the call to evacuate when government sounds the disaster alarm, but they will run when warned by a trusted fellow community member. Mobilizing communities' voice, energy, and collective action can help overcome some of the obstacles to improving risk management in countries and regions with weak government capacity. For example, Afghanistan's National Solidarity Program is constructing rural infrastructure with community participation and also laying a foundation for improved local governance. In India and Uganda, disseminating information on health and education entitlements and outcomes through community-sponsored public meetings has improved both government services and community participation, leading to more vaccinations, more prenatal supplements, and fewer excess school fees.[63]

The enterprise sector

How can the enterprise sector foster resilience and prosperity?

The enterprise sector comprises workers and owners, the arrangements that organize their relationships, and the technologies that turn production factors into goods and services. Enterprises, the defining unit of the enterprise sector, range from informal to formal, from self-employment to partnerships to giant multinational corporations, and from agriculture to manufacturing and services. Whereas the owner of a single enterprise might seek to maximize its profits, the enterprise sector as a whole encompasses the interests of workers, owners, and consumers. Despite the possible important trade-offs among these interests, the enterprise sector can help people manage risk through several channels, as described below.

For workers and owners, being part of a multiperson enterprise—that is, a firm—offers the possibility of sharing the benefits and losses from specialization, collaboration, and innovation. Indeed, this is one of the main motives behind the formation of firms. As Frank Knight and Ronald Coase argued in their seminal studies, firms have an institutional advantage in providing cost-efficient ways of dealing with uncertainty and overcoming transaction costs.[64] Whereas most individuals on their own are naturally risk averse and thus reluctant to take on new ventures, in groups they become more willing to pursue projects that involve more risk but also promise higher returns. Firms, therefore, can serve as natural vehicles to exploit the upside of risk, with beneficial consequences for individuals' resilience and prosperity.[65]

Risk sharing. Enterprises allow risk sharing among workers through collaboration; among owners of firms through investment diversification; and between workers and owners through (formal or informal) contractual arrangements. For risk sharing within a given enterprise, achieving a certain size is an advantage. The enterprise sectors of many developing countries, however, are dominated by self-employment (figure 5). Rates of self-employment are around 70 percent in South Asia and exceed 80 percent in Sub-Saharan Africa and are also pervasive in developing countries in other regions. These high rates of self-employment suggest that the incomes of vast numbers of workers in developing countries are vulnerable to diverse shocks—a sick child, an equipment failure, or a change in the weather could mean the loss of a day's income and more. They also suggest that the enterprise sector is not benefiting from the specialization and increased productivity that multiperson enterprises make possible.

Innovation and resource reallocation. When fueled by competition, the enterprise sector can promote innovation by adopting new technologies and reallocating resources. In some instances, it may require exit and entry of enterprises in the economy. This process of "creative destruction," as first labeled by Joseph Schumpeter,[66] can generate substantial adjustment costs but may be the only way an economy remains resilient and prosperous in the face of constantly changing conditions. Improving this dynamic process can have significant effects both on reducing the risk of prolonged recessions and on increasing aggregate productivity. For instance, one estimate finds that making resource allocation as efficient in China and India as it is in the United States would increase total factor productivity by as much as 50 percent in China and 60 percent in India.[67] These large gains, however, would also require developing institutions and a business environment that can support a high degree of dynamism in the enterprise sector—not an easy task.

Worker, consumer, and environmental protection. Motivated by reputational considerations and properly

FIGURE 5 ***Self-employment is more prevalent in developing countries, especially in Sub-Saharan Africa and South Asia***

Self-employment, as percent of total employment, average 2004–06

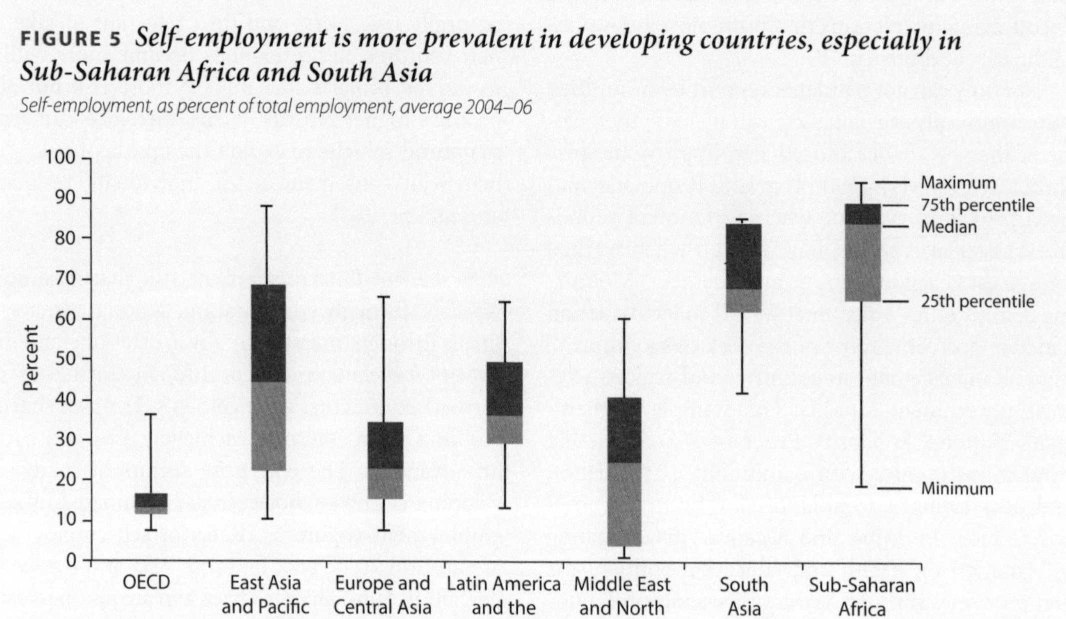

Source: WDR 2014 team based on data from World Bank World Development Indicators (database).
Note: Organisation for Economic Co-operation and Development (OECD) countries in the figure are high-income countries that have been members of the OECD for at least 40 years. All other countries are grouped into geographic regions.

regulated by the state, the enterprise sector can contribute to people's risk management by providing workplace safety, consumer protection, and environmental safeguards. These protections are not guaranteed, however; and in some cases enterprises do undermine them and generate losses for society. These harmful practices can be corrected with stewardship from the state, communities, and enterprises alike. Given the right incentives, firms that make these social protections a priority can have substantial benefits. A recent meta-analysis, for instance, found that workplace wellness programs reduce medical and absenteeism costs—gains that accrue to both workers and firms.[68]

What characteristics improve the enterprise sector's contribution to risk management?

Two characteristics enhance the ability of the enterprise sector to contribute to people's resilience and prosperity: *flexibility* and, over time, *formality.*

Flexibility. Flexibility is the capacity of the entire enterprise sector (owners, workers, technologies) to adjust to changing conditions. It should not be confused with the simple ease of firing workers. An enterprise sector that is flexible is more capable of responding to shocks by allocating resources within and across enterprises, promoting risk sharing, and innovating in an ever-changing world. In the recent global financial crisis, for instance, Denmark and Spain were hit hard, yet their labor outcomes were markedly different. In Denmark, job separations were high but unemployment spells were short. In contrast, in Spain the unemployment rate, which stood at 25 percent at the beginning of 2013, has shown few signs of abating since the start of the crisis. The difference is arguably explained by the rigidity within the enterprise sector in Spain, in contrast with Denmark's propitious business environment. This situation has prompted a serious debate and recent reform proposals in Spain to remedy the situation. More generally, the evidence indicates that countries with less flexibility in their enterprise sectors suffer deeper and more prolonged recessions when negative shocks occur.[69]

Formality. For enterprises, formality is defined as compliance with laws and regulations. Whether formality is beneficial (for enterprises and the economy) or not depends on the quality of the norms dictated by the state and the quality of the public services it offers. When these norms and services are sound, the enterprise sector is characterized by less self-employment and larger, more stable, and more formal firms. These characteristics are all related. Informal mechanisms may be effective for small firms and simple transactions, but they are insufficient for larger firms and complex relations with workers and markets. With adequate public regulations and services, formal firms can benefit from better legal protection (such as contract enforcement) and better use of public infrastructure (such as ports for international trade). That, in turn, can promote risk sharing and innovation among enterprises. Moreover, it can make enterprises more easily accountable for their impact on worker safety and on consumer and environmental well-being.[70]

There are both synergies and trade-offs between flexibility and formality. In countries with effective state institutions, formality enhances flexibility. In countries with weak state institutions and cumbersome regulatory regimes, however, the cost of formality can be too large for the majority of enterprises and workers. In this case, informality is a means for the economy to achieve a certain degree of flexibility and for workers to access a practical safety net.[71] Figure 6 provides a typology of countries based on the flexibility and formality of their product and labor markets.

How can the state contribute?

Public policy for the enterprise sector requires reforms that balance the economy's need for flexibility with society's need for legal and regulatory protections.

A better business environment. Several of the ways in which the state can contribute to productivity and innovation can also enhance the resilience derived from the enterprise sector. A better investment climate can improve risk management in the enterprise sector by encouraging adherence to sensible rules and regulations and by increasing the sector's capacity to adjust to new conditions. Most basically, secure property rights and regulatory certainty, along with low costs for firm entry and exit, are essential. In addition, although labor market reforms in isolation are unlikely to be successful, reducing the burden of labor taxes and streamlining regulations is a critical component of a comprehensive set of reforms—where the overall effect is larger than the sum of their parts.[72] Alongside such complementary reforms, recent cross-country evidence finds that moving a country from the quintile with the greatest labor rigidity to the one with the least rigidity improves the speed of adjustment to shocks by one-half and increases productivity growth by as much as 1.7 percentage points.[73] Furthermore, strong and inclusive social insurance is necessary so that flexibility in the enterprise sector does not come at the expense of the well-being of workers, their households, or their communities (box 6).

Stronger and enforceable regulations for worker, consumer, and environmental safety. While in many areas regulations can be excessive and disruptive of market forces, stronger and enforceable regulations are needed to ensure workplace safety, consumer protection, and environmental preservation. Market failures derived from externalities and asymmetric information are pervasive in these areas, requiring direct intervention by the state. The deadly garment factory collapse in Bangladesh in 2013—which claimed the lives of more than 1,100 workers—is a sad reminder of the importance of the state's monitoring and enforcement of regulations that cannot be overseen by people on their own. These regulations are important, particularly in states whose low institutional capacity requires them to prioritize their interventions carefully.

The financial system

How can the financial system foster resilience and prosperity?

Through the provision of useful financial tools and responsible management of its own risks, the financial system can shield people from the impact of negative shocks and better position them to pursue opportunities. Saving instruments (such as bank deposits and liquid securities) enable people to accumulate buffers for rainy days. Credit instruments (such as education or mortgage loans) alleviate financing constraints, helping people to smooth consumption following negative shocks but also to exploit opportunities with greater flexibility. Finally, market insurance (such as health and residential insurance) provides a means to cover the costs of damaging adverse events.

What characteristics improve the financial system's contribution to risk management?

Inclusion and depth. As Merton Miller and numerous followers have argued persuasively, when finan-

FIGURE 6 ***Countries vary widely in the flexibility and formality of their product and labor markets***

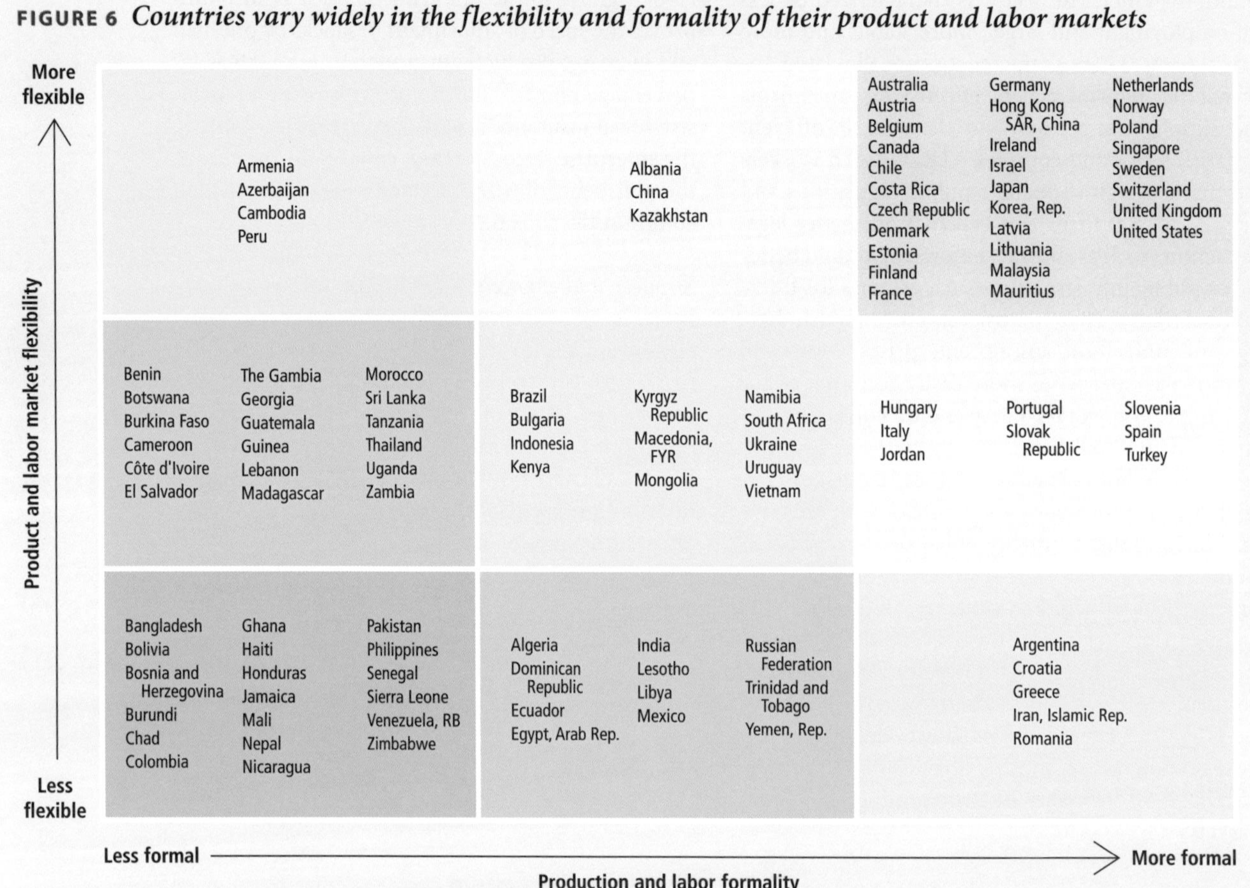

Source: WDR 2014 team based on data from World Bank Pensions (database); World Bank World Development Indicators (database); World Economic Forum 2012; and Schneider, Buehn, and Montenegro 2010.

Note: Economies in the top row are high (above the median value) in both product market flexibility and labor market flexibility; in the middle row they are high in one or the other of the two; and in the bottom row they are low (below the median value) in both flexibility indicators. Similarly, economies in the first column on the left are low in both formal production and formal labor; in the middle column they are high in one of the two formality indicators; and in the last column on the right they are high in both formality indicators. Only economies with data for all four indicators are considered, and median values are calculated within this sample.

cial markets are competitive and function without distortions, they can efficiently provide more and better tools and services to more people.[74] Indeed, financial markets can provide instruments and services that help people face risks of varying frequency, intensity, and nature, either idiosyncratic or systemic. However, about 70 percent of people in low- and middle-income countries do not use essential financial tools at all, compared with about 40 percent in high-income countries. Data on individuals' financial portfolios show that financial savings and insurance are each used by only about 17 percent of people in low- and middle-income countries (compared with 45 percent of people using financial savings tools in high-income countries), and credit is used by about 8 percent (compared with 14 percent in high-income countries)—although great heterogeneity exists across countries (figure 7).

Stability. The Achilles' heel of the financial system is its propensity for crisis. As observed in the seminal work of Douglas Diamond and Phillip Dybvig, the mismatch between the duration of banks' assets (long-term) and liabilities (short-term) makes the financial system inherently unstable.[75] If the financial system fails to manage the risk it retains, it can hurt people—directly by hindering their access to

BOX 6 *Should access to social insurance be tied to work status?*

The provision of *basic* insurance against the risks associated with illness and old age—especially for the vulnerable—is arguably a fundamental goal for public policy. But how is social insurance funded and whom does it benefit? Traditionally, it has been funded through mandatory payroll taxes levied on employers and employees, and it has benefited contributing workers. The problem with this approach is its limited coverage: in most developing countries, formal workers (who contribute and benefit from social insurance) make up less than half the labor force (and much less in Sub-Saharan Africa and South Asia). The traditional approach thus ends up excluding many workers—mostly those who are low-income, self-employed, or work in agriculture.[a]

To close the coverage gap, several countries have set up noncontributory systems for health and old-age pension insurance. Is it a good idea to combine noncontributory and mandated contributory systems? If the benefits from contributing to social insurance are uncertain and the enforcement of mandated payments is weak, having these parallel systems may undermine the incentives for employers to hire formally and for employees to seek formal employment. A vicious circle could then ensue: informality breeds low coverage, and the response to low coverage breeds further informality.[b]

One possibility that merits discussion is delinking social insurance from work status. This uncoupling would involve the following public action:

- Allowing people to participate in health and old-age insurance regardless of work status (employed or unemployed, and formal or informal), requiring reasonably short vesting periods and portable benefits.
- Making additional contributions to health and pension schemes voluntary and clearly linked to predictable benefits that are beyond the basic provisions granted by the state. Involving the private sector in the management and provision of the voluntary portion of social insurance contributions and benefits.
- Providing basic health care and old-age pensions funded by the state and directed to vulnerable populations but potentially open to everyone (at least for health care).[c]
- Funding this basic provision through general government revenues and user fees (for health care), to a level consistent with fiscal sustainability.
- Clearly communicating with the public the characteristics and limitations of basic provisions and the additional costs and benefits of voluntary contributions.
- Promoting financial literacy and fostering trust in the financial system regarding its insurance function by macroprudential actions and policy certainty.

Too ambitious or far-reaching? Maybe so—but worth discussing.

Source: WDR 2014 team.

a. Ribe, Robalino, and Walker 2012.

b. Evidence from Chile, Colombia, and Mexico shows that the interplay of contributory and noncontributory systems has led to declines in formal employment, and there is widespread evidence that smaller, informal firms tend to be less productive and pay lower wages. See Levy and Schady 2013; Pagés-Serra 2010; ILO 2009; La Porta and Shleifer 2008.

c. Developing countries such as Mauritius and South Africa already rely primarily on noncontributory systems for pensions, while several other countries—including China, India, Thailand, Turkey, and Vietnam—have also begun to offer universal access to health insurance. See Holzmann, Robalino, and Takayama 2009.

finance, or indirectly by hampering available credit for enterprises and straining public finances, thereby contributing to loss of jobs, income, and wealth. The experience from 147 banking crises that struck 116 countries from 1970 to 2011 (map 1) is telling: the average cumulative loss of output during the first three years of crises was 33 percent of GDP in advanced economies and 26 percent in emerging markets.[76]

Both synergies and trade-offs may exist between financial inclusion, depth, and stability. By making greater and more diversified domestic savings available to banks (and thereby reducing reliance on reversible foreign capital), greater financial inclusion and depth can enhance the stability of the financial system.[77] But excessive financial inclusion and rapid deepening can endanger stability. This applies especially to credit markets. For instance, the banking crises in Thailand (1997), Colombia (1982), and Ukraine (2008) were preceded by excessive annual credit growth of 25 percent, 40 percent, and 70 percent, respectively. Providing the right amount of credit—not too much and not too little—is a major concern for all countries.

How can the state contribute?

Providing sound financial infrastructure. Financial infrastructure consists of institutions that facilitate financial intermediation, including payment systems, credit information bureaus, and collateral registries. Financial infrastructure also includes a regulatory framework that fosters both consumer protection and competition among financial institutions. Mexico and South Africa, for instance, have enacted efficient consumer protection frameworks, which include ombudsmen to resolve disputes in consumer finance.[78] Competition can lead to innovation in financial inclusion, as in the Philippines, which has

FIGURE 7 ***Financial inclusion in savings, credit, and insurance across developing countries at different income levels***

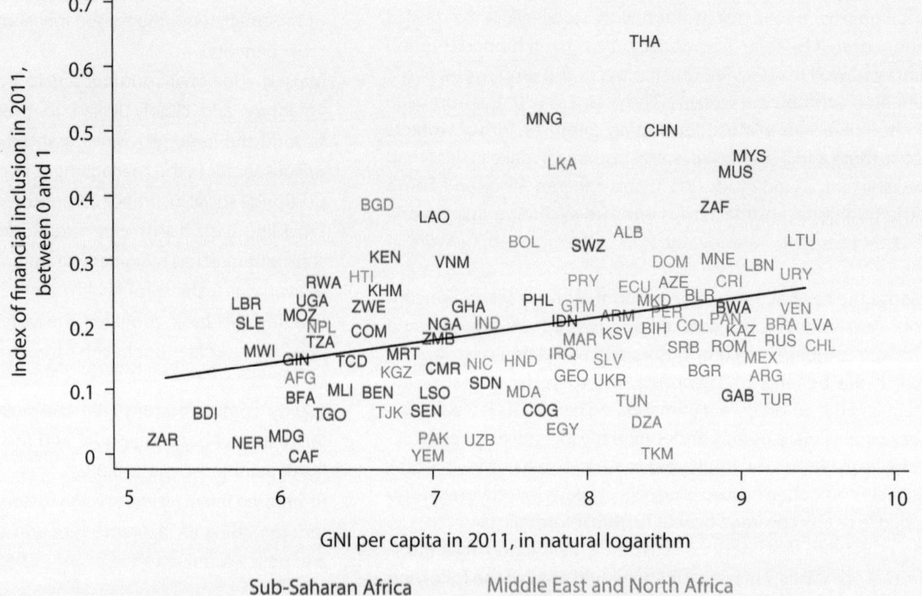

Source: WDR 2014 team based on data from World Bank Global Findex (database) and World Bank World Development Indicators (database).

Note: The index of financial inclusion is calculated based on Global Findex data on the use of savings (percentage of adults who saved money at a financial institution in the past year); credit (percentage of adults who borrowed from a financial institution in the past year); and insurance (percentage of adults who personally paid for health insurance, and percentage of adults working in agriculture who purchased agriculture insurance). GNI = gross national income.

allowed mobile network operators to take on many banking operations.[79] Moreover, to promote financial inclusion, the government can lead by example through innovative practices. An interesting case is India's National Rural Employment Guarantee Act, which has improved outreach to poor people living in rural areas through the introduction of government-to-person payments using a bank account.[80]

Enacting macroprudential regulation for systemic risks. To better manage the potential for systemic financial crises, countries should establish strong macroprudential regulatory frameworks—frameworks that consider the interconnectedness of financial institutions and markets and that address the financial system as a whole.[81] Making macroprudential regulators independent, possibly by placing them under the central bank, is the first step in this direction—as in the Czech Republic, which in 2006 gave the central bank explicit responsibility for fostering financial stability. Governments can then pursue proactive macroprudential supervision and intervene with timely and robust policy tools, as the Republic of Korea did in 2011 in the wake of the international financial crisis by imposing a levy on bank noncore financial liabilities to manage speculative capital flows.

Ideally, macroprudential regulation would prevent financial crises. Some crises, however, are unavoidable, and a crisis resolution system is necessary. How should losses be handled? In resolving crises, countries should seek to pass bank losses to existing shareholders, managers, and in some cases uninsured creditors—minimizing costs to taxpayers, threats to fiscal stability, and future moral hazard. To facilitate recovery from crises, governments and the international community can contribute by reducing regulatory uncertainty through timely decisions and effective global coordination.

Taking the trade-offs and synergies between inclusion, depth, and stability explicitly into account. Evidence suggests that in 90 percent of cases, national financial

MAP 1 *Banking crises around the world, 1970–2011*

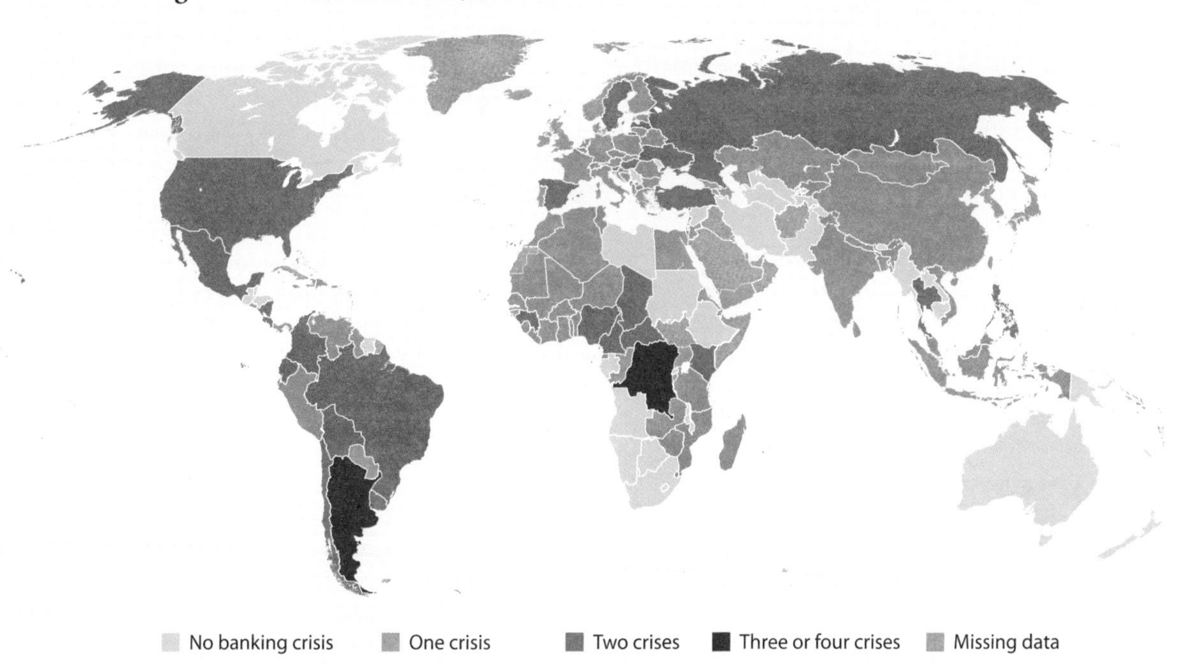

Source: WDR 2014 team based on data from Laeven and Valencia 2012. Map number: IBRD 40098.

sector strategies do not address specific trade-offs between financial development goals and the management of systemic risk, although more than two-thirds of countries commit to achieving both goals within their strategy.[82] A financial policy committee may provide a means for a country to better take trade-offs and synergies in the financial sector into account and improve policy coordination. An interesting example to consider is Malaysia, where the central bank takes the lead in engaging major stakeholders in financial sector policy, including the ministry of finance and private sector experts. The goal of this engagement is to prepare a national financial sector strategy for Malaysia that takes into account trade-offs between promoting financial inclusion and development and managing systemic risk in the financial sector.

The macroeconomy

How can the macroeconomy foster resilience and prosperity?

The macroeconomy is the platform where all economic activity takes place: from consumption to savings in households, from investment to production in enterprises, and from borrowing to lending in financial markets. Sound macroeconomic management can provide an environment where households, communities, and enterprises are able to plan for the long term and undertake their own risk management. Furthermore, macroeconomic policy can address large systemic risks, which households and other socioeconomic systems are unequipped to handle on their own. As Robert Barro, among others, has noted, macroeconomic crises with large welfare costs have marked the world economy for decades—palpably so since 2007.[83] Policy makers have an essential role to play in preventing these crises or at least in mitigating their effects.

Macroeconomic stability. Business cycles are intrinsic to modern economies, and some degree of volatility in aggregate prices, output, and employment is normal. Evidence indicates that the harmful effects of volatility do not derive from moderate fluctuations but from high inflation and abrupt moves in economic activity. These effects percolate throughout the economy—reducing employment, interrupting credit, and deferring investment—and produce losses that lead to a decline in long-term economic growth. Indeed, analysis across a set of developed and developing countries over four decades suggests that an increase in GDP volatility from normal to crisis-related levels can decrease long-run per capita GDP growth by around 2 percentage points a year.[84]

Continuous provision of public goods and services. Part of the reason why crises have an impact on long-run growth is that they can result in an interruption or deterioration in the provision of essential public goods and services. These interruptions occur especially when governments are forced to undertake drastic cuts in expenditures during downturns. This was the case, for instance, in several Latin American countries during the 1980s and 1990s, with more than half the fiscal adjustment consisting of spending cuts in infrastructure investment.[85] Similarly, social security spending dropped in nearly half the countries in the Middle East and North Africa following crises in the region.[86] During the latest global financial crisis, education budgets fell sharply in the majority of Eastern European countries: for instance, by 25 percent in Serbia and 10 percent in Hungary.[87]

What policies can best contribute to risk management?

Experts have argued that macroeconomic policies should be credible, predictable, transparent, and sustainable. This is sensible advice. It can also be presented more concretely in terms of risk management: macroeconomic policy makers should behave prudently during upswings to avoid costly coping during downturns.

Transparent and credible monetary policy. Endowed with independence and a drive for transparency and credibility, monetary policy authorities have successfully brought down inflation worldwide in the last 25 years: while 34 countries had annual inflation greater than 50 percent in 1990–94, only 1 country (Zimbabwe) registered that rate by the end of the 2000s. Adopting a monetary policy framework that creates incentives for long-term price stability, while accounting for the business cycle, has been crucial to defeating inflation.

The 2008–09 international financial crisis and the ensuing recession in developed countries have tested the improvements made in monetary policy in developing countries. All in all, they have proven to be resilient. One important issue to consider in the wake of the crisis is whether financial stability should be included as a direct objective of monetary policy. The jury is still out, but it can be argued that financial stability is best achieved through macroprudential instruments—aimed at curbing financial imbalances and volatile capital flows—rather than through monetary policy.[88]

Flexible exchange rate regimes. Although debated for a long time, flexible exchange rates have proven to be effective shock absorbers. That is true whether the shock originated inside or outside the domestic economy. Countries with flexible exchange rates tend to adjust better—recovering more quickly and more strongly—to deterioration in their terms of trade,[89] natural hazards such as earthquakes and storms,[90] and other shocks that may produce internal or external imbalances.[91]

Countercyclical and sustainable fiscal policy. Worldwide, fiscal policy has not made as much progress as monetary policy in terms of effective process and positive results. This is not surprising: fiscal policy is inherently more complex—having multiple objectives and instruments and being immersed in the political process. With respect to risk management, fiscal policy in developing countries has suffered from a procyclical bias that has tended to amplify upswings and worsen recessions.[92] In the past two decades, however, several developing countries around the world have put a premium on fiscal transparency and discipline, building buffers during good times with an eye toward future downturns. These institutional improvements explain the recent ability of a large fraction of developing countries to conduct countercyclical fiscal policy, mainly by turning investment and consumption spending in a direction opposite to that of the cycle in general economic activity (map 2 focuses on countercyclical consumption spending). Independent fiscal councils can provide an important means to further institutionalize such discipline (box 7).

Why is countercyclical fiscal policy useful? First, it allows governments to continue to provide goods and services and to maintain their public investment programs in a stable fashion, even if public revenues drop (as is normal in the downside of the business cycle). Second, it provides resources to increase social assistance and insurance to larger numbers of people in need who are suffering from adverse cyclical macroeconomic conditions. These two mechanisms make a significant contribution not only during the recessionary part of the cycle but also for the long-run welfare of people and the economy.[93] A third possible reason is to stimulate the economy. There is little evidence, however, that discretionary fiscal stimulus based on fueling consumption works. To the con-

MAP 2 *Government consumption became countercyclical in more than one-third of developing countries over the past decade*

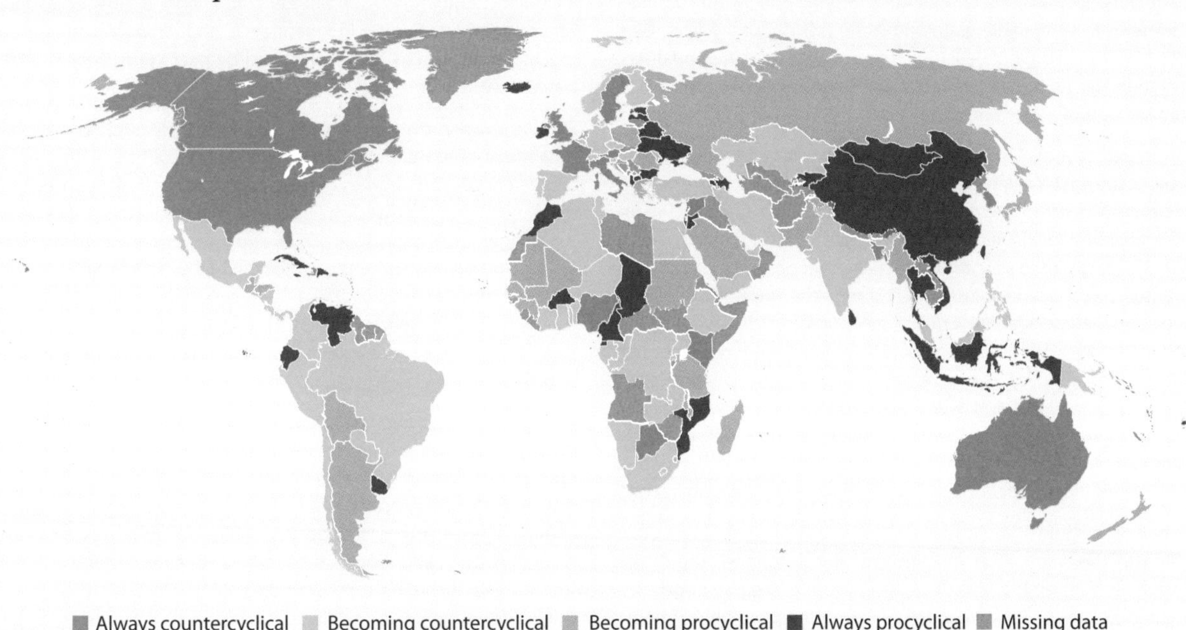

■ Always countercyclical ■ Becoming countercyclical ■ Becoming procyclical ■ Always procyclical ■ Missing data

Source: WDR 2014 team estimations based on Frankel, Végh, and Vuletin 2013 methodology. Map number: IBRD 40099.

Note: The map shows the evolution of the cyclical stance of fiscal policy from 1960–99 to 2000–12. The cyclical stance is measured in a regression of the (Hodrick-Prescott) cyclical component of general government consumption expenditure on its own lagged value, and the cyclical component of real GDP. The sign of the coefficient on the cyclical component of real GDP indicates whether government consumption expenditure is procyclical (positive sign) or countercyclical (negative sign). The coefficient on the cyclical component of real GDP was estimated separately for the periods 1960–99 and 2000–12. Then, countries are classified as always countercyclical (in both periods); becoming countercyclical (only countercyclical in 2000–12); becoming procyclical (only procyclical in 2000–12); and always procyclical (in both periods). The likely endogeneity of the cyclical component of real GDP was controlled for by using as instruments the (current and lagged value of the) cyclical component of real GDP of the country's main trading partners and international oil prices, as well as the lagged value of the country's own cyclical component of real GDP.

trary, estimates of the Keynesian fiscal multiplier—the increase in GDP for every dollar of additional government spending—range only between 0.4 and 0.6 for most developing countries and between 0.6 and 1.2 for most developed countries.[94] Once the cost of raising the necessary additional revenue (in terms of taxes, debt, and red tape) is factored in, the net multiplier is likely to be near zero or negative.

Finally, from a risk management perspective, fiscal sustainability requires being aware of contingent liabilities. Some of them are legitimate, such as reconstruction and assistance in the aftermath of natural disasters and the larger outlays required to cover social insurance and medical treatment for an aging population. Other contingent liabilities are more controversial; financial bailouts, for example, can represent a large burden for the state: around 50 percent of GDP in Indonesia and Thailand after the 1997 East Asia crisis, and over 40 percent of GDP in Iceland and Ireland during the 2008–09 crisis.[95]

Dealing with contingent liabilities requires a combination of measures: first, governments must provide the right incentives for self-reliance—for example, by replacing pay-as-you-go systems with fully capitalized old-age pension systems, and by letting risk-takers in financial markets suffer full losses from failed ventures. Second, market solutions should be encouraged by, for example, allowing the issuance of catastrophe bonds in international markets to insure against natural hazards. And, third, resources should be provisioned for residual liabilities that the state may have to bear.

The international community

When can the international community foster resilience and prosperity?

Unmanaged risks do not respect boundaries, and no one country or agent acting alone can deal effectively

BOX 7 ***An independent fiscal council can help overcome procyclical fiscal bias***

What is the problem? Fiscal authorities around the world routinely deviate from sustainable plans and suffer from a "procyclical" bias: they tend to run budget deficits and accumulate debt in good times, and then lack adequate resources and flexibility ("policy space") to stabilize output in bad times.

A proposed solution. The creation of an independent fiscal council can provide the right incentives for the government to build up resources to cope with cyclical downturns and long-run contingencies. The fiscal council would administer a set of flexible fiscal rules mandated by law: deciding on the allocation of deficits over time, signaling when countercyclical action is justified, and monitoring public debt sustainability. Full delegation of policy making to an independent fiscal council is unrealistic because of the political and redistributive nature of fiscal policy. The government, following its political mandate, would retain control over the distribution of expenditures and the structure of taxation. However, isolating some aspects of fiscal policy implementation from the political process and delegating them to an independent council can enhance fiscal credibility and accountability.[a]

How can this solution be implemented? Fiscal councils should be designed in a way that avoids political capture, the rise of government incentives to ignore council advice, or the possibility of being dismantled when conflicts within government occur. An effective fiscal council requires independence from the political process—including competitive appointment and long tenure of council board members, budget independence, and strong accountability mechanisms (such as being evaluated by peer councils or international organizations).[b]

Has this solution been implemented anywhere? By 2012, 22 national governments (and counting) had created fiscal councils, with varying characteristics and degrees of relevance.[c] The Netherlands' Centraal Planbureau and the Swedish Fiscal Policy Council are the closest to full-fledged fiscal councils. In Chile, two independent advisory bodies provide key inputs for the projection of the "structural" revenue, which in turn determines government expenditure through a fiscal rule. Acting as advisory bodies, fiscal councils in Morocco, Kenya, and Uganda provide ex ante and ex post assessment of fiscal policies for parliament.

If a council is not feasible, is there an alternative? Establishing an independent fiscal council requires the political appetite for autonomous institutions and strong governance underpinnings and thus may not be possible in all countries. Where an independent council is not feasible, a good foundation for fiscal sustainability would involve adopting transparent and comprehensive fiscal frameworks, including top-down approaches to budgeting. Since the 2000s, Armenia, for instance, has formulated a three-year rolling budgetary framework with expenditure ceilings and integrated it into budgetary law.[d]

Source: WDR 2014 team.

a. Debrun, Hauner, and Kumar 2009.
b. Calmfors and Wren-Lewis 2011.
c. IMF 2013.
d. World Bank 2013.

with a risk that crosses a national border. Once triggered, pandemics and financial or economic crises can circle rapidly around an increasingly interconnected world. Armed conflicts can devastate people and spill over into neighboring countries. Natural disasters can ruin a country or an entire region. Climate change is likely to intensify all these risks. Clearly, risks that spread across and affect multiple countries or generations call for international attention.

The international community is a fusion of rather diverse agents, including sovereign governments, international organizations, the global scientific community and media, and civil society. It can offer expertise and knowledge; provide protection through global rules and regulations, capacity building, and international coordination; and pool national resources to better prepare for risk and alleviate crisis situations.

Risks that exceed national capacity. The international community's engagement may be needed when countries face severe capacity constraints and have weak or dysfunctional governments.[96] That is especially the case in fragile and conflict-affected countries, where people face the most extreme risks and obstacles to risk management, with limited access to functioning markets, communities, and public institutions. People living in fragile and conflict-affected countries made up 15 percent of the world population in 2010, but about one-third of people living in extreme poverty.[97] Conflicts can transcend national borders, resulting in increased refugee populations, spread of communicable diseases, and growing pressure on public goods in neighboring countries absorbing affected populations. Sharing a border with a fragile state can reduce a country's economic growth by 0.4 percent annually.[98] By improving economic prospects and the environment for health, security, and education, engagement by the international community can reduce social and economic tensions that inflame and spread conflict, while nurturing opportunities.

International support is also needed when very large shocks, such as natural disasters and financial crises, result in losses that dwarf a country's resources. That can happen even in large and more developed countries, as the Euro Area crisis clearly demonstrates—although low-income countries are disproportionately affected by economic risks and disasters. For example, the Aceh province in Indonesia bore the brunt of a powerful earthquake and tsunami in 2004, leaving more than 500,000 people homeless and an estimated economic loss of 97 percent of Aceh's GDP. The international community set up a special multidonor fund to support reconstruction and establish early warning systems, efforts that almost 10 years after the tragedy have largely proven to be a success.[99] Success does not always follow, however, as illustrated by the disappointing results of the international community's intervention in Haiti after a powerful earthquake in 2010.[100]

Risks that cross national borders. Openness and modernization have made economic, social, and ecological systems increasingly interconnected (figure 8). Along with opportunities for growth and poverty alleviation, this interconnectedness has also created a set of risks that cross national borders and require critical risk management from the international community, including regional organizations.[101] Increased air travel and trade in goods and services, for instance, can provide free passage to pathogens that cause infectious diseases, some of which can travel around the world in less than 36 hours.[102] Similarly, financial crises can spread through an increasingly complex network of links across financial systems around the world. Rapid economic growth that has relied heavily on carbon-based energy is also related to slowly evolving risks such as climate change and environmental degradation, with potentially irreversible consequences for future generations.

What characteristics improve the international community's capacity to manage risk?

The effectiveness of the international community depends on how well it can fill in knowledge and capacity gaps, establish rules and standards that guide nations in managing their risks, and facilitate and coordinate collective action to manage risks that go beyond national borders. In turn, collective action is facilitated when agents within the international community are united by shared preferences and objectives, or when certain actors have the ability to mobilize resources and enforce agreements—even in the absence of cohesion or unity across nations.

FIGURE 8 *Economic, financial, and social interconnectedness are on the rise*

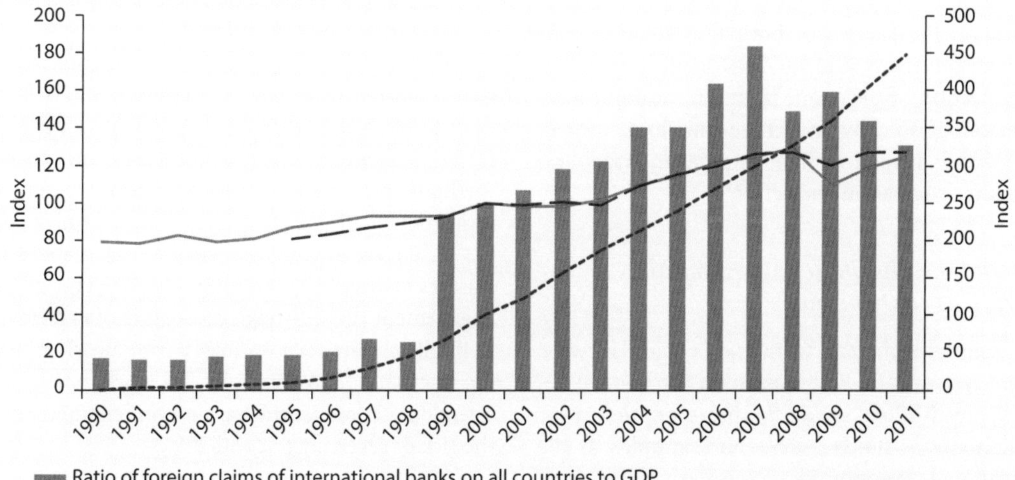

Source: WDR 2014 team based on data from World Bank World Development Indicators (database), Bank for International Settlements Consolidated Banking Statistics (database), and World Tourism Organization Yearbook of Tourism Statistics (database).

Note: All series are indexed to 100, with 2000 as the base year.

Cohesiveness through shared preferences and objectives. Mutual recognition of the need to address risks enables the international community to better prepare for risks that exceed national capacity—such as the arrangements to provide emergency lending to countries facing acute financing shortfalls, and support for regional insurance pools like the Caribbean Catastrophe Risk Insurance Facility.[103] Similarly, multilateral cooperation for risks that cross boundaries works best when the interests of various nations are well aligned and are not overruled by competing domestic policy priorities. By helping to align national interests, the almost universal agreement for the need to eliminate smallpox facilitated its eradication. In contrast, in cases where national interests diverge, such as resolving climate change risks and alleviating the plight of people living in fragile and conflict-affected countries, progress can be slow.

Power to mobilize resources and enforce agreements. The international community can have a substantial impact on the management of risks when there is a clear goal around which to mobilize resources. For example, with support from the international community, early warning systems have helped reduce deaths from many types of disasters.[104] Similarly, even if complete international consensus is lacking, the international community can make progress on risks that cross boundaries if it can devise mechanisms for enforcing agreements. That capacity depends crucially on the international community's ability to realign incentives around shared goals and to attract participation of major players. A key element in the success of both the Nuclear Non-Proliferation Treaty and the Montreal Protocol on the protection of the ozone layer, for example, were the threat of security and trade sanctions, respectively, which helped realign national interests and facilitate participation and action.

How can the international community improve its contribution?

The insights from the work by Leonid Hurwicz, Roger Myerson, and Eric Maskin on mechanism design for institutions are all the more important for a collectivity as fluid, diverse, and complex as the international community. Considering incentive constraints (and not only budget and informational constraints) is critical to devising effective mechanisms for the international community to contribute to risk management despite its multiple players, complicated power structures, and diverging goals.

If incentives are aligned: Pursue proactive and well-coordinated interventions. When incentives are aligned and a course of action is clear, scaling up risk management requires proactive and well-coordinated interventions by the international community. In dealing with risks such as pandemics or financial crises in an interconnected world, the effectiveness of these actions rests critically on supporting the capacity of individual countries to monitor and contain risks in their territory. For example, while 36 donors provided support to more than 100 developing countries to prepare for a possible pandemic of avian flu (H5N1) from 2005 to 2010, local monitoring was essential to contain the virus. More resources should be devoted to supporting capacity building for early warning, monitoring, and communication systems, and to designing risk-pooling solutions that reward preparation.

If incentives are not aligned: Use incremental approaches to global solutions. When incentives are not aligned, major sovereigns are not fully engaged, and the consequences of inaction are potentially catastrophic—as with climate change and other environmental risks such as loss of biodiversity—the international community should embrace incremental approaches that can increase traction toward global solutions (box 8). To preserve full participation as the ultimate goal, however, special attention should be given to steps that can help align incentives toward a common objective, even if alignment seems very difficult to achieve. For environmental risks, this effort may consist of dissemination of knowledge and advocacy that can help bring diverging views closer, financial and technology incentives to countries for steps such as preventing deforestation and inducing the use of cleaner technologies, and investments in research and development—for example to construct methods for counteracting greenhouse gas concentration in the atmosphere.[105] In a similar spirit, the New Deal for Engagement in Fragile States (the Busan Partnership) recognizes that the risk of nonengagement can outweigh most risks of engagement in fragile countries; it outlines a framework in which the international community can work to help them strengthen core institutions and policies and reduce the risk of reverting to conflict.[106]

An institutional reform to mainstream risk management

The *World Development Report 2014* offers dozens of specific policy recommendations to improve risk

BOX 8 ***For certain global risks such as climate change, the international community should embrace incremental approaches that can lead to global solutions***

What is the problem? Management of global risks requires proactive concerted action by sovereign nations. But limited progress in some areas has cast doubt on the possibility of fostering collective action among countries with diverging interests, capacity constraints, and incentives to free ride. Global negotiations to secure agreements with full participation have stalled—most spectacularly for climate change, where persistent inaction could have catastrophic and irreversible consequences. Some potentially useful international actions—including cooperation to develop and share technologies and existing financial instruments—have been postponed in the expectation that they will be part of a "soon-to-be-signed" global agreement.

The proposed solution. For certain global risks such as climate change, the international community should embrace incremental approaches that can increase traction toward global solutions. When incentives are misaligned, major sovereigns are not fully engaged, and the consequences of inaction are disastrous, progress can still be made outside a multilateral treaty. Incremental deals and actions by an initially small group of participants can serve as building blocks to global agreements. By demonstrating benefits from action, the expectation is that the group would include progressively more participant countries over time.

Are there successful examples? Some remarkable examples exist. The Montreal Protocol to protect the ozone layer was originally signed by 24 countries but won universal ratification during the 1990s with the combined efforts of governments, international organizations, nongovernmental organizations, and scientists.[a] Likewise, the Limited Test Ban Treaty, whose signatories expanded from 3 to 119 between 1963 and 1992, paved the way for the more comprehensive Nuclear Non-Proliferation Treaty.

How can it be implemented? Country governments, international organizations, and specialized entities can form a "coalition of the willing" to coordinate, advocate, and take action on climate change.[b] The coalition can create incentives for others to join over time by promoting technological change and funding that lowers participation costs (cheaper ways to reduce emissions, subsidies, or technology transfers). It can also partner with scientists, civil society, and the media to induce participants to comply and nonparticipants to join in. International institutions, including an international risk board, can provide platforms for policy debate and monitor, report, and aggregate actions to ensure incremental efforts are on the right path. Strategically, the coalition could anchor its actions to existing global frameworks to demonstrate that incremental and global deals can be connected.

Source: WDR 2014 team.

a. UNEP 2007.

b. Falkner, Stephan, and Vogler 2010; Goldin 2013; Hale 2011.

management at different and complementary levels of society (box 9 provides a summary of these policies). Its overarching advice, however, is that these recommendations should be implemented in a proactive, systematic, and integrated way to optimize their effectiveness. For this purpose, the *World Development Report 2014* advocates establishing a national risk board, which can contribute to mainstreaming risk management into the development agenda. This could be a new agency or come from reform of existing bodies: what is most important is a change in approach—one that moves toward a coordinated and systematic assessment of risks at an aggregate level. Implementing this recommendation may require a substantial change in the way national governments develop and implement their general plans, moving from planning under certainty to considering change and uncertainty as fundamental characteristics of modern economies. A national risk board can help governments overcome the political economy obstacles they face when managing risks at the country or even international levels.

Establish a national risk board to manage risks in a proactive, systematic, and integrated way

What is the problem? All too often, risk management strategies and implementation prove ineffective (or introduce other risks) because they are not coordinated among all relevant policy stakeholders. Managing risk in a proactive and integrated way has definite advantages: it can help define priorities, ensure that all contingencies have been considered, and avoid overspending to manage one risk in isolation while neglecting others. Some countries conduct national risk assessments that involve multistakeholder teams from various ministries and often include the private sector and civil society. The Netherlands, the United Kingdom, and the United States have completed this exercise, and other countries, such as Morocco, have begun a process toward it. However, this exercise is usually carried out by a temporary, ad hoc group that exists only while the assessment is taking place. Other countries have created multiministry bodies in charge of information exchange and

BOX 9 *Selected policy recommendations from the WDR 2014*

The state has an important role in supporting the contributions of all social and economic systems to people's risk management. The following summarizes selected policy recommendations from the WDR 2014, organized by system, as they are discussed in the Report:

For the household:

- Public health insurance, run in partnership with the private sector, with emphasis on preventive care and treatment of contagious diseases and accidents
- Public education, run in partnership with the private sector, with a focus on flexible skills, adaptable to changing labor markets
- Targeted safety nets for the poor, for instance conditional cash transfers with payments directly to women
- Enforceable laws against domestic abuse and gender discrimination, accompanied by educational campaigns

For the community:

- Public infrastructure for the mitigation of disaster risks, built in consultation with surrounding communities
- Transportation and communication infrastructure, especially to integrate and consolidate isolated communities
- Police protection against common and organized crime, especially targeted to communities under threat
- Enforceable laws against racial or ethnic discrimination, accompanied by educational campaigns

For the enterprise sector:

- Secure and respected private property rights
- Streamlined and predictable regulations for taxation, labor markets, and entry and exit of firms
- Enforceable regulations for workplace safety, consumer protection, and environmental preservation
- Consider the possibility of delinking social insurance (that is, health and old-age pension) from work status

For the financial system:

- Sound financial infrastructure (payment systems, credit information) to facilitate financial inclusion and depth
- Enforceable regulations that foster both consumer protection and competition among financial institutions
- Macroprudential regulation, for the financial system as a whole, to lessen financial crises and avoid bailouts
- A national financial strategy that addresses trade-offs between financial inclusion, depth, and stability

For the macroeconomy:

- Transparent and credible monetary policy, oriented to price stability and conducted by an autonomous central bank
- For the majority of countries, a flexible exchange rate regime, in a context of transparent and credible monetary policy
- Countercyclical and sustainable fiscal policy, aided by an independent fiscal council
- Provision for contingent liabilities, such as natural disasters, financial crises, and pensions of an aging population

For the international community:

- Engagement in bilateral, regional, and global agreements to share risks across countries, enhance national capacity, and confront common risks, favoring proactive and coordinated interventions
- For elusive global risks such as climate change, formation of a "coalition of the willing" with like-minded country governments, creating incentives for other countries to join in.

The WDR 2014 advocates that these recommendations be implemented in a proactive, systematic, and integrated way. For this purpose, it proposes establishing a national risk board to help mainstream risk management into the country's development programs and suggests the possibility of an international risk board to support the "coalition of the willing."

Source: WDR 2014 team.

coordination for risk management, but these bodies usually deal with a single risk—most often with natural disasters, as in Peru, or national security, as in Israel. Few countries actually have an integrated, permanent risk management agency that deals with multiple risks.

What is the solution? To facilitate proactive and integrated risk management at the country level, a national risk board can be set up as a standing (permanent) committee. It can analyze risks, including trade-offs across risks and across risk management policies; consider and publish assessments of risk management practices in the country; define priorities in risk management; and make recommendations about appropriate policies to be implemented. Institutionalizing the national risk board should add value by enabling risk management to be integrated across all sectors, by challenging inaction stemming from political interests, and by introducing clear accountability mechanisms for implementing agreed risk management measures.[107]

How can it be implemented? The national risk board should bring together a wide range of stakeholders. It could be either part of government or an autonomous agency. The board composition would include both policy makers (to reflect political priorities) and independent experts (to incorporate technical knowledge and private sector perspectives). It would have the power to issue "act-or-explain" recommendations to relevant authorities responsible for implementing policy—that is, relevant authorities would have to act upon the board's recommendations or explain why they had decided to reject them. Although the appropriate institutional design of the board will depend on the country's political and institutional context, the board's composition and powers should strive to achieve an adequate balance of expertise, credibility, relevance, and legitimacy—that is, to fall within the "balanced" region in diagram 4.

DIAGRAM 4 ***Balancing the trade-offs in the institutional design of a national risk board***

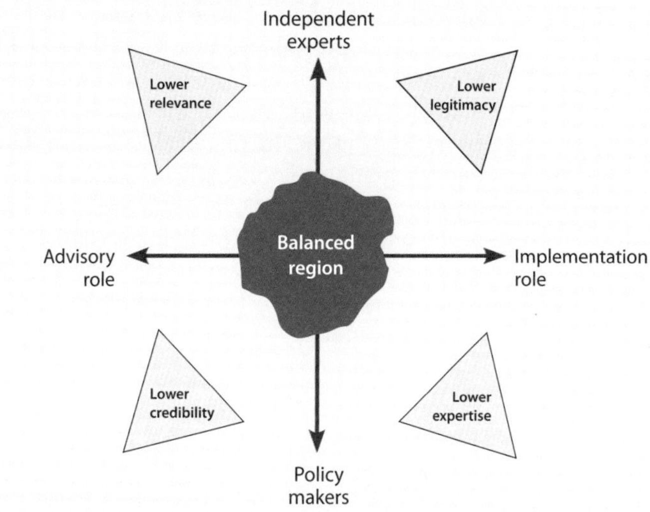

Source: WDR 2014 team.

The board's policy makers could be nominated by the executive branch of government, and the independent experts could come from academia, the business community, and civil society organizations. The board's expertise would cover the areas of military, security and terrorism risk; economic risk; environmental, health, and technological risk; and social risk. To avoid becoming a powerless body, the board should have sufficient prominence in the public eye. And it should be held accountable by regularly publishing its recommendations accompanied by analysis and statements of policy priorities and by being subjected to annual hearings in front of a legislative committee.

While an autonomous national risk board may have certain advantages, the board could also function as part of government. Indeed, countries as different as Jamaica, Mali, Mexico, Morocco, and Rwanda are considering establishing an integrated risk management function within the government structure—in part following a proposal by the World Economic Forum to establish a country risk officer, similar to the position of chief risk officer that has been created in many multinational companies.[108] This institutional design could be practical in countries with a strong framework for an effective and independent civil service, with the national risk board members appointed as expert technocrats with guaranteed positions for periods that extend beyond the political cycle.

Singapore's Whole-of-Government Integrated Risk Management framework is an example of an approach that has overcome "silos" within the government.[109] The institutional umbrella of the framework is the Strategy Committee, composed of permanent secretaries from various ministries across government and chaired by the Head of Civil Service. In addition, the Homefront Crisis Management system includes a ministerial committee chaired by the Minister of Domestic Affairs and supported by the Homefront Crisis Executive Group, comprising senior representatives from ministries and government agencies. This multirisk framework is complemented by agencies focused on specific risks, such as the National Security Coordination Secretariat. Singapore's institutional arrangement for integrated risk management involves a great deal of specialization and a complex coordination process that has evolved over time. For developing countries, a simpler arrangement that involves less specificity and specialization in its institutional design (and requires less demanding coordination mechanisms) may be a good starting point.

Finally, two important questions should be addressed. First, what can motivate a government to institute a national risk board? An initial impulse is necessary for leaders to overcome opposing incentives and establish a long-term institution. This impulse can come from within the country, through reform-minded political leaders and technocrats, and from outside, through incitement and support from the international community. Once created, the national risk board can challenge inaction or poor practices by introducing clear accountability mechanisms for risk management. A reformist government interested in the continuation of its beneficial legacy may want future governments to be accountable for their actions or their lack of action.

The second question is whether a similar body can be created at the global level—an international risk board—to help address risks that cross national boundaries. An international risk board could involve the scientific and expert community around the world to pool all available knowledge to identify, assess, and manage major global risks. Its major drawback would be that, in the absence of a governing body at the international level, it could lack implementation relevance. That could be remedied, however, if the international risk board were to work in conjunction with the "coalition of willing" countries (see box 8), setting priorities on issues to be tackled urgently and offering credibility and legitimacy to its efforts.

In conclusion: Five principles of public action for better risk management

Analysis throughout the *World Development Report 2014* suggests that, to improve the quality and delivery of social protection, public goods, and public policy that are essential to supporting people's risk management, public action can usefully be guided by some key principles. The five principles that follow reflect the lessons from best practice around the world and are relevant for different types of risks and countries. Their application should be tailored to specific contexts, however. Although at first glance these principles may appear uncontroversial, in application they involve tensions and trade-offs that make their implementation a challenge.

1. Do not generate uncertainty or unnecessary risks

The state's policies and actions should strive to reduce risks and lessen uncertainty. At a minimum, the state should not worsen them. How or why would a government do that? First, through its policies, it may perpetuate social norms that discriminate against certain groups and make them more vulnerable. For example, state policies that promote gender inequality or ethnic favoritism harm, rather than help, household and community resilience.

Second, the government may favor the group that supports it politically, whether a small elite or large constituency, against the legitimate interests of others. For instance, states that expropriate financial assets (like savings and pension funds) or private infrastructure (like residential buildings or factories) from some households may obtain short-run gains but end up hampering the ability of the financial system and the enterprise sector to grow, develop, and provide risk management resources to the entire population.

Third, an internally fragmented government that lacks organization and coordination may end up with ambivalent policies or ineffective implementation. This may occur, for instance, as result of a defective decentralization process, where local and regional governments do not have the necessary resources and capacities to fulfill their responsibilities, do not share the priorities and preferences of the national government, or attempt to free ride on other local and regional governments.

Finally, the government may be guided by ideology, wishful thinking, or simple desperation when confronting difficult and genuine problems, instead of relying on measures based on good evidence and analysis. A common example is labor market regulations that purport to defend workers' interests but wind up protecting only a few and contributing to the roots of a large informal sector. Inflationary financing of budget deficits or variable and inconsistent macroeconomic policies in the face of crisis are other examples: sooner rather than later, both paths lead to increased uncertainty, macroeconomic instability, and possibly even protracted recessions.

2. Provide the right incentives for people and institutions to do their own planning and preparation, while taking care not to impose risks or losses on others

The challenge for public policy is to create incentives for people to do their own risk planning and preparation, avoiding circumstances in which benefits are privately appropriated but losses are imposed on others.

Consider financial bailouts. They are detrimental not only because they can produce a large fiscal burden but also because they provide incentives for excessive risk taking. Yet bailouts are sometimes necessary to prevent a systemic collapse of financial intermediation. Bailouts should be avoided—mostly by using well-established, clear, and transparent macroprudential policies—but if bailouts occur, they should be designed to avoid providing the wrong incentives for the future. Good examples of orderly financial bailouts are hard to find, but the Turkish experience in the wake of the 2000–01 banking crisis (and especially the unwavering stance of the country's bank regulatory and resolution agencies) offers a case to analyze and follow.[110]

In a very different realm, social protection can be criticized for not encouraging personal self-reliance and being an unsustainable burden to the state. The evidence, however, demonstrates that these problems can be avoided by a design that takes people's incentives directly into account. Well-designed safety nets—such as conditional cash transfers or workfare programs, as implemented in Bangladesh, Brazil, India, and Mexico, to name a few—have promoted better household practices in the areas of education, health, and even entrepreneurship, while remaining fiscally sustainable.[111]

In all cases, to manage risks effectively, two changes in people's mindset related to individual and social responsibility are critical: moving from dependency to self-reliance, and from isolation to cooperation. Providing the right incentives can contribute in both regards.

3. Keep a long-run perspective for risk management by building institutional mechanisms that transcend political cycles

A major challenge for public action is to establish institutional mechanisms that induce the state to keep a long-run perspective that outlasts volatile shifts in public opinion or political alliances. For instance, the state's provision of education and health services is a large investment in risk preparation for families and communities that must be funded on a continuous and sustainable basis to succeed: that entails long-run planning. In the case of health services, Thailand and Turkey offer successful examples with their recent shift to universal health insurance programs.

Consider also the following two examples from financial and macroeconomic policy. For the financial system to support risk management, it is essential to strike the right balance between inclusion and stability. This balance can be assessed only through comprehensive long-run planning, like that being done in Malaysia, where the strategy for the financial sector is prepared by the central bank, in collaboration with the ministry of finance and the private sector. Countercyclical monetary and fiscal policies also require a long-run perspective, which allows them to manage the business cycle by using resources built over a prolonged time and in different scenarios. Best practice suggests targeting a long-run budget balance, as Chile, Colombia, and Norway, among others, are doing. Institutional mechanisms that transcend the political cycle—such as a national risk board and an independent fiscal council—can help maintain a long-run focus on risk management.

4. Promote flexibility within a clear and predictable institutional framework

Flexibility in adjusting to new circumstances is essential to promoting resilience and making the most of opportunities. Prime examples include household migration in response to shifting economic trends, rural communities' adaptation to climate change, and enterprise renewal in the face of technological and demand shocks. Flexibility should not imply arbitrary discretion or haphazard responses, however. A challenge for the state is to promote flexibility while preserving a sensible, transparent, and predictable institutional structure.

For enterprises, the Danish model of "flexicurity" offers such balance, combining ease of hiring and firing of workers alongside a strong social safety net and reemployment policies. The result is a dynamic economy with high turnover in employment but short spells of unemployment. For the macroeconomy, inflation targeting regimes with floating exchange rates offer a good model of flexible yet institutionally sound monetary policy. By 2012, 27 countries around the world had adopted an inflation targeting regime. With the onset of the European Monetary Union in 1999, many countries that had practiced inflation targeting in the 1990s abandoned the regime. Given the prolonged recession and uncertainty in the Euro Area, monetary flexibility could have been a useful tool these countries no longer have.

5. Protect the vulnerable, while encouraging self-reliance and preserving fiscal sustainability

The harsh reality is that throughout the world, many people do not have the material resources and information necessary to confront the risks they face. The everyday struggle to eke out a living can make planning ahead hard for the poor. The challenge for the state is to protect the vulnerable while preserving fiscal sustainability—and encouraging self-reliance.

For households that remain highly vulnerable to shocks, the state can provide safety nets to replace the costly coping mechanisms that undermine consumption, human capital, and productive assets. Safety nets are possible even in low-income countries, provided the support is targeted to vulnerable populations and is designed to incentivize work effort. Ethiopia's Productive Safety Net System, for example, demonstrates how a well-designed safety net can protect millions of households from food insecurity while investing in community assets.

The international community can also provide support to vulnerable populations with resources and expertise. Although much criticized, foreign aid has been successful when provided in coordination with accountable local institutions. Such was the case when foreign aid helped rebuild infrastructure and establish early warning systems in Indonesia after the 2004 tsunami.

At the end of the day, protection of the vulnerable entails taking the measures necessary for sustainable development—development that eliminates extreme poverty and allows people to escape vulnerability through the sustained growth that risk management can offer.

Some closing thoughts

The fate of individuals and families can change for the better if they plan and prepare to face the risks and opportunities that lie at the heart and core of modern life. So too can the fate of communities and countries improve, if they share the continuous responsibility required to manage risk successfully.

"I grew up in a war environment. And what I learned is that you can plan your fate, at least to some degree, if you assess your risk and do something about it."

—Klaus Jacob, disaster risk management expert at Columbia University and World War II survivor[112]

"There was a time I used to walk to work every day. The route I had to take was dangerous, and many people were victims [of] robbery and physical abuse. So, yes, I have overcome risk to pursue opportunity."

—Kariuki Kevin Maina, student, Kenya Contribution to the WDR 2014 website

Notes

1. Dercon, Hoddinott, and Woldehanna 2005.
2. Buvinić and Morrison 2000.
3. World Bank 2012d.
4. WHO 2013.
5. Baulch 2011 offers a useful survey.
6. Paul 2009.
7. Didier, Hevia, and Schmukler 2012.
8. Dercon and Christiaensen 2011.
9. See Karlan and others 2012 for Ghana; and Cole, Giné, and Vickery 2013 for India.
10. Hoddinott, Rosegrant, and Torero 2012.
11. Hallegatte 2012a.
12. While the costs of preparing for risk must be incurred predominantly up front, the benefits tend to accrue over time and are therefore more uncertain. The probability of a risk materializing is thus central to any assessment of a potential intervention. In formal benefit-cost analyses, this probability is usually taken into account either implicitly (by basing calculations of averted costs on average historical data) or explicitly (by weighting the potential benefit of a risk management intervention in the event of a shock by the probability of that shock occurring). See Wethli 2013 for the WDR 2014.
13. See, for example, Bodie, Kane, and Marcus 2011.
14. See Kuznets 1955 and Dasgupta and others 2002. The tradeoffs mentioned in the text are *perceived* to exist by some experts and a large share of the public, as reflected in opinion polls, but may not be present in reality. Recent analyses find, for instance, that economic growth and environmental protection as well as social inclusion are often complementary. See World Bank 2012b.
15. Hoddinott, Rosegrant, and Torero 2012.
16. Dethier, Hirn, and Straub 2011; Kehoe and Prescott 2007.
17. Bruno and Easterly 1998.
18. Bernoulli 1738; von Neumann and Morgenstern 1944.
19. Allais 1953; Kahneman and Tversky 1979.
20. Black 1948; Buchanan and Tullock 1962; Olson 1965.
21. Hurwicz 1960; Myerson 1979; Maskin 1999.
22. The concept of a risk chain is discussed and illustrated in Alwang, Siegel, and Jørgensen 2001. See also Barrett 2002; Heltberg, Siegel, and Jørgensen 2009.
23. Ehrlich and Becker 1972. See also the extension in Muermann and Kunreuther 2008 and the applications in Gill and Ilahi 2000; Holzmann and Jørgensen 2001; and Packard 2002.
24. Khokhar 2013 for the WDR 2014.
25. World Bank World Development Indicators (database).
26. World Bank 2012c.
27. For a rich discussion of the potential complementarity between insurance and protection, see Erlich and Becker 1972.
28. *Economist* 2013.
29. Hallegatte 2012b.
30. Carter and others 2007.
31. FEMA 2010.
32. Gourinchas and Obstfeld 2012; Schularick and Taylor 2012.
33. Hallegatte 2012b.
34. La Porta and others 1998.
35. See, for example, Tornell and Velasco 1992.
36. This kind of trade retaliation was avoided during the 2008–09 global financial crisis, in part because of successful coordination by the international community—in contrast to the well-known "beggar-thy-neighbor" trade policies that exacerbated the Great Depression (Eichengreen and Irwin 2010). However, the international community has been less successful in avoiding export restrictions during the food price crises in recent years (Martin and Anderson 2012).
37. Knight 1921.
38. Hallegatte and others 2012.
39. Čihák and others 2012.
40. For a review of the literature on risk sharing and family and network formation, see Fafchamps 2011.
41. Acemoglu and Robinson 2012 compile many examples of such failures.
42. Reinikka and Svensson 2005; Speer 2012; Devarajan, Khemani, and Walton 2011.
43. Becker 1993.
44. Oviedo and Moroz 2013 for the WDR 2014.
45. De Weerdt and Hirvonen 2013 for Tanzania; Yang and Choi 2007 for the Philippines; Paulson 2000 for Thailand.
46. WDR 2014 team based on OECD Programme for International Assessment (PISA).
47. Xu and others 2003.
48. Demirgüç-Kunt and Klapper 2012.
49. Duflo 2003; Thomas 1990.
50. Duflo 2003; see also Thomas 1990 and Lundberg, Pollak, and Wales 1997.
51. WDR 2014 team based on World Bank World Development Indicators (database).
52. World Bank 2005.
53. Thoresen and Fielding 2011 show how expanding health care coverage can put considerable pressure on the sustainability not only of fiscal resources, but also human resources.
54. Premand 2013 for the WDR 2014.
55. Paxson and Schady 2007 and references therein; Macours, Schady, and Vakis 2008; see also references in Fiszbein and Schady 2009.
56. WDR 2014 team based on Demographic and Health Surveys.
57. Coleman 1988; Putnam 1993.
58. De Weerdt 2001.
59. Gertler and Gruber 2002.
60. For example, Aldrich 2011 shows that social capital plays a key role in communities' ability to recover from natural disasters.
61. Alesina, Baqir, and Easterly 1999.
62. Narayan, Pritchett, and Kapoor 2009; Bowles and Gintis 2002.
63. Bjorkman and Svensson 2009; Pandey and others 2007.
64. Knight 1921; Coase 1937.
65. For seminal papers on the topic, see Baily 1974 and Azariadis 1975.
66. Schumpeter 1942.
67. Hsieh and Klenow 2009.
68. Baicker, Cutler, and Song 2010.
69. Bergoeing, Loayza, and Repetto 2004.
70. An interesting example of formalization leading to both enhanced environmental protection and higher incomes has recently occurred in Peru. In recent years, informal mines in Peru have sprung up in response to rising gold prices. Ignoring existing regulations, these informal mines have caused significant deforestation. The mercury used in the extraction process has contaminated rivers and the atmosphere and threatened human health. In the La Libertad region, the Poderosa Mining Company took an innovative approach to the problem after informal miners invaded one of its mining concessions. The company began to formalize the invading

miners, signing agreements that allowed them to continue mining under its direction. The agreements, which meet international environmental management quality standards, have increased the small miners' income and decreased the harm from deforestation and mercury contamination. UNEP 2012.
71. World Bank 2012d; Loayza and Rigolini 2011.
72. Calderón and Fuentes 2012.
73. Caballero and others 2013.
74. Miller 1986.
75. Diamond and Dybvig 1983.
76. Laeven and Valencia 2012.
77. Han and Melecky 2013 for the WDR 2014; Cull, Demirgüç-Kunt, and Lyman 2012.
78. Brix and McKee 2010.
79. Gupta 2013.
80. World Bank 2012a.
81. Borio 2003 provides a discussion of the differences between a traditional, microprudential regulatory framework and a macroprudential regulatory approach.
82. Maimbo and Melecky 2013 for the WDR 2014.
83. Barro 2009.
84. Hnatkovska and Loayza 2005.
85. Easterly and Servén 2003.
86. Prasad and Gerecke 2010.
87. Education International 2009.
88. Svensson 2012; Bruno and Shin 2013.
89. Edwards and Levy Yeyati 2005.
90. Ramcharan 2007.
91. Edwards 2004; Lane and Milesi-Ferretti 2012; Ghosh, Qureshi, and Tsangarides 2013.
92. Kaminsky, Reinhart and Végh 2005.
93. Parker 2011.
94. See Kraay 2012 and Ilzetzki and Végh 2008 for surveys of the literature on developing countries; and Barro and de Rugy 2013 and Ramey 2011 for surveys of the literature on developed countries.
95. Laeven and Valencia 2012.
96. DFID 2005; OECD 2011a, 2012; World Bank 2011.
97. OECD 2012.
98. DFID 2005.
99. See "Resilience Stories" at the Sendai Dialogue website at https://www.gfdrr.org/node/1308.
100. Larrimore and Sharkey 2013.
101. Not all risks that exceed national borders are truly global. Some risks, such as armed conflict between neighboring countries or disputes over natural resources, may affect only a few countries. Such risks may be more appropriately or effectively managed by regional institutions.
102. Jonas 2013 for the WDR 2014.
103. Mahul and Cummins 2009.
104. World Bank and United Nations 2010.
105. Royal Society 2009.
106. OECD 2011b.
107. Graham and Wiener 1995; World Economic Forum 2007.
108. World Economic Forum 2007.
109. OECD 2009.
110. Damar 2007; Ersel and Ozatay 2008.
111. Fiszbein and Schady 2009; Alderman and Yemtsov 2012.
112. Quoted in Eric Klinenberg, "Adaptation: How Can Cities be 'Climate-proofed'?" *The New Yorker*, January 7, 2013, 33.

References

Acemoglu, Daron, and James A. Robinson. 2012. *Why Nations Fail: The Origins of Power, Prosperity, and Poverty*. New York: Random House.

Alderman, Harold, and Ruslan Yemtsov. 2012. "Productive Role of Safety Nets." Social Protection and Labor Discussion Paper 1203, World Bank, Washington, DC.

Aldrich, Daniel P. 2011. "The Power of People: Social Capital's Role in Recovery from the 1995 Kobe Earthquake." *Natural Hazards* 56: 595–611.

Alesina, Alberto, Reza Baqir, and William Easterly. 1999. "Public Goods and Ethnic Divisions." *Quarterly Journal of Economics* 114 (4): 1243–84.

Allais, Maurice. 1953. "Le Comportement de l'Homme Rationnel devant le Risque: Critique des Postulats et Axiomes de l'Ecole Americaine." *Econometrica* 21 (4): 503–46.

Alwang, Jeffrey, Paul B. Siegel, and Steen L. Jørgensen. 2001. "Vulnerability: A View from Different Disciplines." Social Protection Discussion Paper 0115, World Bank, Washington, DC.

Azariadis, Costas. 1975. "Implicit Contracts and Underemployment Equilibria." *Journal of Political Economy* 83 (6): 1183–202.

Baicker, Katherine, David Cutler, and Zirui Song. 2010. "Workplace Wellness Programs Can Generate Savings." *Health Affairs* 29 (2): 304–11.

Baily, Martin N. 1974. "Wages and Employment under Uncertain Demand." *Review of Economic Studies* 41 (1): 37–50.

Barrett, Christopher B. 2002. "Food Security and Food Assistance Programs." In *Handbook of Agricultural Economics*, vol. 2B, edited by Bruce L. Gardner and Gordon C. Rausser, 2103–90. Amsterdam: Elsevier Science.

Barro, Robert J. 2009. "Rare Disasters, Asset Prices, and Welfare Costs." *American Economic Review* 99 (1): 243–64.

Barro, Robert J., and Veronique de Rugy. 2013. "Defense Spending and the Economy." Mercatus Center at George Mason University, Arlington, VA.

Barro, Robert J., and Jong-Wha Lee. 2010. "A New Data Set of Educational Attainment in the World, 1950–2010." Working Paper 15902, National Bureau of Economic Research, Cambridge, MA.

Barro, Robert J., and Jose F. Ursúa. 2012. "Rare Macroeconomic Disasters." *Annual Review of Economics* 4 (1): 83–109.

Baulch, Bob. 2011. *Why Poverty Persists: Poverty Dynamics in Asia and Africa*. Cheltenham, U.K.: Edward Elgar.

Becker, Gary S. 1993. *A Treatise on the Family*. Cambridge, MA: Harvard University Press.

Bergoeing, Raphael, Norman Loayza, and Andrea Repetto. 2004. "Slow Recoveries." *Journal of Development Economics* 75 (2): 473–506.

Bernoulli, Daniel. 1738. "Specimen Theoriae Novae de Mensura Sortis." *Commentarii Academiae Scientiarum Imperialis Petropolitanae* 5: 175–92. Translated in 1954 in "Exposition of a New Theory of the Measurement of Risk." *Econometrica* 22 (1): 23–36.

BIS (Bank for International Settlements). Consolidated Banking Statistics (database). BIS, Basel, http://www.bis.org/statistics/consstats.htm.

Bjorkman, Martina, and Jakob Svensson. 2009. "Power to the People: Evidence from a Randomized Field Experiment on Community-Based Monitoring in Uganda." *Quarterly Journal of Economics* 124 (2): 735–69.

Black, Duncan. 1948. "On the Rationale of Group Decision-Making." *Journal of Political Economy* 56 (1): 23–34.

Bodie, Zvi, Alex Kane, and Alan J. Marcus. 2011. *Investments*. 9th ed. New York: McGraw-Hill.

Borio, Claudio. 2003. "Towards a Macroprudential Framework for Financial Supervision and Regulation." *CESifo Economics Studies* 49 (2): 181–215.

Bowles, Samuel, and Herbert Gintis. 2002. "The Inheritance of Inequality." *Journal of Economic Perspectives* 16 (3): 3–30.

Brix, Laura, and Katharine McKee. 2010. "Consumer Protection Regulation in Low-Access Environments: Opportunities to Promote Responsible Finance." Focus Note 60, Consultative Group to Assist the Poor, Washington, DC.

Bruno, Michael, and William Easterly. 1998. "Inflation Crises and Long-Run Growth." *Journal of Monetary Economics* 41 (1): 3–26.

Bruno, Valentina, and Hyun Song Shin. 2013. "Assessing Macroprudential Policies: Case of Korea." Working Paper 19084, National Bureau of Economic Research, Cambridge, MA.

Buchanan, James M., and Gordon Tullock. 1962. *The Calculus of Consent: Logical Foundations of Constitutional Democracy*. Ann Arbor: University of Michigan Press.

Buvinić, Mayra, and Andrew R. Morrison. 2000. "Living in a More Violent World." *Foreign Policy* (118): 58–72.

Caballero, Ricardo J., Kevin N. Cowan, Eduardo M. R. A. Engel, and Alejandro Micco. 2013. "Effective Labor Regulation and Microeconomic Flexibility." *Journal of Development Economics* 101: 92–104.

Calderón, César, and J. Rodrigo Fuentes. 2012. "Removing the Constraints for Growth: Some Guidelines." *Journal of Policy Modeling* 34 (6): 948–70.

Calmfors, Lars, and Simon Wren-Lewis. 2011. "What Should Fiscal Councils Do?" *Economic Policy* 26 (68): 649–95.

Carter, Michael R., Peter D. Little, Tewodaj Mogues, and Workneh Negatu. 2007. "Poverty Traps and Natural Disasters in Ethiopia and Honduras." *World Development* 35 (5): 835–56.

Čihák, Martin, Sònia Muñoz, Shakira Teh Sharifuddin, and Kalin Tintchev. 2012. "Financial Stability Reports: What Are They Good For?" Working Paper 12/1, International Monetary Fund, Washington, DC.

Coase, Ronald H. 1937. "The Nature of the Firm." *Economica* 4 (16): 386–405.

Cole, Shawn, Xavier Giné, and James Vickery. 2013. "How Does Risk Management Influence Production Decisions? Evidence from a Field Experiment." Working Paper 13-080, Harvard Business School, Boston, MA.

Coleman, James S. 1988. "Social Capital in the Creation of Human Capital." *American Journal of Sociology* 94: S95–S120.

Cull, Robert, Asli Demirgüç-Kunt, and Timothy Lyman. 2012. "Financial Inclusion and Stability: What Does Research Show?" Brief 71305, Consultative Group to Assist the Poor, Washington, DC.

Damar, H. Evren. 2007. "Does Post-Crisis Restructuring Decrease the Availability of Banking Services? The Case of Turkey." *Journal of Banking & Finance* 31 (9): 2886–905.

Dasgupta, Susmita, Benoit Laplante, Hua Wang, and David Wheeler. 2002. "Confronting the Environmental Kuznets Curve." *Journal of Economic Perspectives* 16 (1): 147–68.

Debrun, Xavier, David Hauner, and Manmohan S. Kumar. 2009. "Independent Fiscal Agencies." *Journal of Economic Surveys* 23 (1): 44–81.

Demirgüç-Kunt, Asli, and Leora F. Klapper. 2012. "Measuring Financial Inclusion: The Global Findex Database." Policy Research Working Paper 6025, World Bank, Washington, DC.

Dercon, Stefan, and Luc J. Christiaensen. 2011. "Consumption Risk, Technology Adoption and Poverty Traps: Evidence from Ethiopia." *Journal of Development Economics* 96 (2): 159–73.

Dercon, Stefan, John Hoddinott, and Tassew Woldehanna. 2005. "Shocks and Consumption in 15 Ethiopian Villages, 1999–2004." *Journal of African Economies* 14 (4): 559–85.

Dethier, Jean-Jacques, Maximilian Hirn, and Stéphane Straub. 2011. "Explaining Enterprise Performance in Developing Countries with Business Climate Survey Data." *World Bank Research Observer* 26 (2): 258–309.

Devarajan, Shantayann, Stuti Khemani, and Michael Walton. 2011. "Civil Society, Public Action and Accountability in Africa." Policy Research Working Paper 5733. World Bank, Washington, DC.

De Weerdt, Joachim. 2001. "Community Organizations in Rural Tanzania: A Case Study of the Community of Nyakatoke, Bukoba Rural District." Economic Development Initiatives, Bukoba.

De Weerdt, Joachim, and Kalle Hirvonen. 2013. "Risk Sharing and Internal Migration." Policy Research Working Paper 6429, World Bank, Washington, DC.

DFID (Department for International Development, United Kingdom). 2005. "Why We Need to Work More Effectively in Fragile States." DFID, London.

Diamond, Douglas W., and Philip H. Dybvig. 1983. "Bank Runs, Deposit Insurance, and Liquidity." *Journal of Political Economy* 91 (3): 401–19.

Didier, Tatiana, Constantino Hevia, and Sergio L. Schmukler. 2012. "How Resilient and Countercyclical Were Emerging Economies during the Global Financial Crisis?" *Journal of International Money and Finance* 31 (8): 2052–77.

Duflo, Esther. 2003. "Grandmothers and Granddaughters: Old-Age Pensions and Intrahousehold Allocation in South Africa." *World Bank Economic Review* 17 (1): 1–25.

Easterly, William R., and Luis Servén 2003. *The Limits of Stabilization: Infrastructure, Public Deficits, and Growth in Latin America.* Palo Alto, CA: Stanford University Press.

Economist. 2013. "Gizmos That Track Driving Habits Are Changing the Face of Car Insurance." February 23.

Education International. 2009. "Education and the Global Economic Crisis: Summary of Results of the Follow-up Survey." Education International, Brussels.

Edwards, Sebastian. 2004. "Thirty Years of Current Account Imbalances, Current Account Reversals, and Sudden Stops." *IMF Staff Papers* 51 (Special Issue): 1–49.

Edwards, Sebastian, and Eduardo Levy Yeyati. 2005. "Flexible Exchange Rates as Shock Absorbers." *European Economic Review* 49 (8): 2079–105.

Ehrlich, Isaac, and Gary S. Becker. 1972. "Market Insurance, Self-Insurance, and Self-Protection." *Journal of Political Economy* 80 (4): 623–48.

Eichengreen, Barry, and Douglas A. Irwin. 2010. "The Slide to Protectionism in the Great Depression: Who Succumbed and Why?" *Journal of Economic History* 70 (4): 871–97.

Ersel, Hasan, and Fatih Ozatay. 2008. "Fiscal Dominance and Inflation Targeting: Lessons from Turkey." *Emerging Markets Finance and Trade* 44 (6): 38–51.

Fafchamps, Marcel. 2011. "Risk Sharing between Households." In *Handbook of Social Economics*, vol. 1B, edited by Jess Behabib, Alberto Bisin, and Matthew O. Jackson, 1255–79. San Diego: Elsevier.

Falkner, Robert, Hannes Stephan, and John Vogler. 2010. "International Climate Policy after Copenhagen: Towards a 'Building Blocks' Approach." *Global Policy* 1 (3): 252–62.

FEMA (Federal Emergency Management Agency, United States). 2010. "Local Official Survey Findings on Flood Risk." FEMA, Washington, DC.

Ferreira, Francisco H. G., Julian Messina, Jamele Rigolini, Luis-Felipe López-Calva, Maria Ana Lugo, and Renos Vakis. 2013. *Economic Mobility and the Rise of the Latin American Middle Class.* Washington, DC: World Bank.

Fiszbein, Ariel, and Norbert Schady. 2009. *Conditional Cash Transfers: Reducing Present and Future Poverty.* Washington, DC: World Bank.

Foa, Roberto. 2013. "Household Risk Preparation Indices–Construction and Diagnostics." Background paper for the *World Development Report 2014.*

Frankel, Jeffrey A., Carlos A. Végh, and Guillermo Vuletin. 2013. "On Graduation from Fiscal Procyclicality." *Journal of Development Economics* 100 (1): 32–47.

Gertler, Paul, and Jonathan Gruber. 2002. "Insuring Consumption against Illness." *American Economic Review* 92 (1): 51–70.

Ghosh, Atish R., Mahvash S. Qureshi, and Charalambos G. Tsangarides. 2013. "Is the Exchange Rate Regime Really Irrelevant for External Adjustment?" *Economics Letters* 118 (1): 104–109.

Gill, Indermit S., and Nadeem Ilahi. 2000. "Economic Insecurity, Individual Behavior and Social Policy." Working Paper 31522, World Bank, Washington, DC.

Goldin, Ian. 2013. *Divided Nations: Why Global Governance Is Failing and What We Can Do about It.* Oxford, U.K.: Oxford University Press.

Gourinchas, Pierre-Olivier, and Maurice Obstfeld. 2012. "Stories of the Twentieth Century for the Twenty-First." *American Economic Journal: Macroeconomics* 4 (1): 226–65.

Graham, John D., and Jonathan B. Wiener. 1995. *Risk versus Risk: Tradeoffs in Protecting Health and the Environment.* Cambridge, MA: Harvard University Press.

Gupta, Sunil. 2013. "The Mobile Banking and Payment Revolution." *European Financial Review* (February–March): 3–6.

Hale, Thomas. 2011. "A Climate Coalition of the Willing." *Washington Quarterly* 34 (1): 89–101.

Hallegatte, Stéphane. 2012a. "A Cost Effective Solution to Reduce Disaster Losses in Developing Countries: Hydro-Meteorological Services, Early Warning, and Evacuation." Policy Research Working Paper 6058, World Bank, Washington, DC.

———. 2012b. "An Exploration of the Link between Development, Economic Growth, and Natural Risk." Policy Research Working Paper 6216, World Bank, Washington, DC.

Hallegatte, Stéphane, Ankur Shah, Robert Lempert, Casey Brown, and Stuart Gill. 2012. "Investment Decision Making under Deep Uncertainty: Application to Climate Change." Policy Research Working Paper 6193, World Bank, Washington, DC.

Han, Rui, and Martin Melecky. 2013. "Financial Inclusion for Stability: Access to Deposits and Deposit Growth in the 2008 Crisis." Background paper for the *World Development Report 2014.*

Heltberg, Rasmus, Paul B. Siegel, and Steen L. Jørgensen. 2009. "Addressing Human Vulnerability to Climate Change: Toward a 'No-Regrets' Approach." *Global Environmental Change* 19 (1): 89–99.

Hnatkovska, Viktoria, and Norman Loayza. 2005. "Volatility and Growth." In *Managing Economic Volatility and Crises: A Prac-*

titioner's Guide, edited by Joshua Aizenman and Brian Pinto, 65–100. New York: Cambridge University Press.

Hoddinott, John, Mark Rosegrant, and Maximo Torero. 2012. "Investments to Reduce Hunger and Undernutrition." Paper prepared for the 2012 Global Copenhagen Consensus.

Holzmann, Robert, and Steen Jørgensen. 2001. "Social Risk Management: A New Conceptual Framework for Social Protection, and Beyond." *International Tax and Public Finance* 8 (4): 529–56.

Holzmann, Robert, David A. Robalino, and Noriyuki Takayama. 2009. *Closing the Coverage Gap: The Role of Social Pensions and Other Retirement Income Transfers*. Washington, DC: World Bank.

Hsieh, Chang-Tai, and Peter J. Klenow. 2009. "Misallocation and Manufacturing TFP in China and India." *Quarterly Journal of Economics* 124 (4): 1403–48.

Hurwicz, Leonid. 1960. "Optimality and Informational Efficiency in Resource Allocation Processes." In *Mathematical Methods in the Social Sciences*, edited by Kenneth J. Arrow, Samuel Karlin and Patrick Suppes, 27–46. Stanford, CA: Stanford University Press.

ILO (International Labour Organization). 2009. *The Informal Economy in Africa: Promoting Transition to Formality: Challenges and Strategies*. Geneva: ILO.

Ilzetzki, Ethan, and Carlos A. Végh. 2008. "Procyclical Fiscal Policy in Developing Countries: Truth or Fiction?" Working Paper 14191, National Bureau of Economic Research, Cambridge, MA.

IMF (International Monetary Fund). 2013. "Fiscal Adjustment in an Uncertain World." *Fiscal Monitor*, October, IMF, Washington, DC.

Jonas, Olga. 2013. "Pandemic Risk." Background paper for the *World Development Report 2014*.

Kahneman, Daniel, and Amos Tversky. 1979. "Prospect Theory: An Analysis of Decision under Risk." *Econometrica* 47 (2): 263–91.

Kaminsky, Graciela L., Carmen M. Reinhart, and Carlos A. Végh. 2005. "When It Rains, It Pours: Procyclical Capital Flows and Macroeconomic Policies." In *NBER Macroeconomics Annual 2004*, edited by Mark Gertler and Kenneth Rogoff, 11–82. Cambridge, MA: MIT Press.

Karlan, Dean, Robert Darko Osei, Isaac Osei-Akoto, and Christopher Udry. 2012. "Agricultural Decisions after Relaxing Credit and Risk Constraints." Working Paper 18463, National Bureau of Economic Research, Cambridge, MA.

Kaufmann, Daniel, Aart Kraay, and Massimo Mastruzzi. 2010. "The Worldwide Governance Indicators: Methodology and Analytical Issues." Policy Research Working Paper 5430, World Bank, Washington, DC.

Kehoe, Timothy J., and Edward C. Prescott. 2007. *Great Depressions of the Twentieth Century*. Minneapolis: Research Department, Federal Reserve Bank of Minneapolis.

Khokhar, Tariq. 2013. "Leveraging New Technology for Data-Driven Risk Mitigation and Management: Selected Examples and Summaries." Background paper for the *World Development Report 2014*.

Knight, Frank, 1921. *Risk, Uncertainty, and Profit*. Boston: Houghton Mifflin Company.

Kraay, Aart. 2012. "How Large Is the Government Spending Multiplier? Evidence from Lending by Official Creditors." *Quarterly Journal of Economics* 127 (2): 829–87.

Kuznets, Simon. 1955. "Economic Growth and Income Inequality." *American Economic Review* 45 (1): 1–28.

La Porta, Rafael, Florencio Lopez de Silanes, Andrei Shleifer, and Robert W. Vishny. 1998. "Law and Finance." *Journal of Political Economy* 106 (6): 1113–55.

La Porta, Rafael, and Andrei Shleifer. 2008. "The Unofficial Economy and Economic Development." *Brookings Papers on Economic Activity* 39 (2): 275–363.

Laeven, Luc, and Fabian Valencia. 2012. "Systemic Banking Crises Database, an Update." Working Paper WP/12/163, International Monetary Fund, Washington, DC.

Lane, Philip R., and Gian-Maria Milesi-Ferretti. 2012. "External Adjustment and the Global Crisis." *Journal of International Economics* 88 (2): 252–65.

Larrimore, J. T., and Brielle Sharkey. 2013. "Haiti Continues to Struggle Three Years after the Earthquake." Council on Hemispheric Affairs, January 18, http://www.coha.org/haiti-continues-to-struggle-three-years-after-the-earthquake/.

Levy, Santiago, and Norbert Schady. 2013. "Latin America's Social Policy Challenge: Education, Social Insurance, Redistribution." *Journal of Economic Perspectives* 27 (2): 193–218.

Loayza, Norman, and Jamele Rigolini. 2011. "Informal Employment: Safety Net or Growth Engine?" *World Development* 39 (9): 1503–15.

Lundberg, Shelly J., Robert A. Pollak, and Terence J. Wales. 1997. "Do Husbands and Wives Pool Their Resources? Evidence from the United Kingdom Child Benefit." *Journal of Human Resources* 32 (3): 463–80.

Macours, Karen, Norbert Schady, and Renos Vakis. 2008. "Cash Transfers, Behavioral Changes, and Cognitive Development in Early Childhood Evidence from a Randomized Experiment." Policy Research Working Paper 4759, World Bank, Washington, DC.

Mahul, Olivier, and J. David Cummins. 2009. *Catastrophe Risk Financing in Developing Countries: Principles for Public Intervention*. Washington, DC: World Bank.

Maimbo, Samuel, and Martin Melecky. 2013. "Financial Policy Formulation: Addressing the Tradeoff between Development and Stability." Background paper for the *World Development Report 2014*.

Martin, Will, and Kym Anderson. 2012. "Export Restrictions and Price Insulation during Commodity Price Booms." *American Journal of Agricultural Economics* 94 (2): 422–27.

Maskin, Eric S. 1999. "Nash Equilibrium and Welfare Optimality." *Review of Economic Studies* 66 (1): 23–38.

Miller, Merton H. 1986. "Financial Innovation: The Last Twenty Years and the Next." *Journal of Financial and Quantitative Analysis* 21 (4): 459–71.

Muermann, Alexander, and Howard Kunreuther. 2008. "Self-Protection and Insurance with Interdependencies." *Journal of Risk and Uncertainty* 36 (2): 103–23.

Myerson, Roger B. 1979. "Incentive Compatibility and the Bargaining Problem." *Econometrica* 47 (1): 61–73.

Narayan, Deepa, Lant Pritchett, and Soumya Kapoor. 2009. *Moving Out of Poverty: Success from the Bottom Up*, vol. 2. Washington, DC: World Bank.

OECD (Organisation for Economic Co-operation and Development). 2009. "Innovation in Country Risk Mangement." Studies in Risk Management, OECD, Paris.

———. 2011a. *Managing Risks in Fragile and Transitional Contexts. The Price of Success?* Paris: OECD.

———. 2011b. "A New Deal for Engagement in Fragile States." Paper prepared for the International Dialogue on Peacebuilding and Statebuilding organized by OECD, November 29–December 1.

———. 2012. *Fragile States 2013. Resource Flows and Trends in a Shifting World.* Paris: OECD.

Olson, Mancur, Jr. 1965. *The Logic of Collective Action: Public Goods and the Theory of Groups.* Cambridge, MA: Harvard University Press.

Oviedo, Ana María, and Harry Moroz. 2013. "The Impacts of Risk." Background paper for the *World Development Report 2014.*

Packard, Truman G. 2002. "Pooling, Savings, and Prevention: Mitigating the Risk of Old Age Poverty in Chile." Policy Research Working Paper 2849, World Bank, Washington, DC.

Pagés-Serra, Carmen, ed. 2010. *The Age of Productivity: Transforming Economies from the Bottom Up.* Washington, DC: Inter-American Development Bank.

Pandey, Priyanki, Ashwini R. Sehgal, Michelle Riboud, David Levine, and Madhav Goyal. 2007. "Informing Resource-Poor Populations and the Delivery of Entitled Health and Social Services in Rural India." *Journal of the American Medical Association* 298 (16): 1867–75.

Parker, Jonathan A. 2011. "On Measuring the Effects of Fiscal Policy in Recessions." *Journal of Economic Literature* 49 (3): 703–18.

Paul, Bimal Kanti. 2009. "Why Relatively Fewer People Died? The Case of Bangladesh's Cyclone Sidr." *Natural Hazards* 50 (2): 289–304.

Paulson, Anna L. 2000. "Insurance Motives for Migration: Evidence from Thailand." Unpublished manuscript, Kellogg Graduate School of Management, Northwestern University, Evanston, IL.

Paxson, Christina, and Norbert Schady. 2007. "Does Money Matter? The Effects of Cash Transfers on Child Health and Development in Rural Ecuador." Policy Research Working Paper 4226, World Bank, Washington, DC.

Prasad, Naren, and Megan Gerecke. 2010. "Social Policy in Times of Crisis." *Global Social Policy* 10 (2): 218–47.

Premand, Patrick. 2013. "From Risk Coping to Risk Management: Productive Safety Nets in Africa." Background paper for the *World Development Report 2014.*

Putnam, Robert D. 1993. "The Prosperous Community: Social Capital and Public Life." *American Prospect* 4 (13): 35–42.

Ramcharan, Rodney. 2007. "Does the Exchange Rate Regime Matter for Real Shocks? Evidence from Windstorms and Earthquakes." *Journal of International Economics* 73 (1): 31–47.

Ramey, Valerie A. 2011. "Can Government Purchase Stimulate the Economy?" *Journal of Economic Literature* 49 (3): 673–85.

Reinikka, Ritva, and Jakob Svensson. 2005. "Fighting Corruption to Improve Schooling: Evidence from a Newspaper Campaign in Uganda." *Journal of the European Economic Association* 3 (2–3): 259–67.

Ribe, Helena, David A. Robalino, and Ian Walker. 2012. *From Right to Reality: Incentives, Labor Markets, and the Challenge of Universal Social Protection in Latin America and the Caribbean.* Washington, DC: World Bank.

Royal Society 2009. "Geoengineering the Climate: Science, Governance and Uncertainty." Royal Society, London.

Schneider, Friedrich, Andreas Buehn, and Claudio E. Montenegro. 2010. "Shadow Economies All over the World: New Estimates for 162 Countries from 1999 to 2007." Policy Research Working Paper 5356, World Bank, Washington, DC.

Schularick, Moritz, and Alan M. Taylor. 2012. "Credit Booms Gone Bust: Monetary Policy, Leverage Cycles, and Financial Crises, 1870–2008." *American Economic Review* 102 (2): 1029–61.

Schumpeter, Joseph A. 1942. *Capitalism, Socialism and Democracy.* New York: Harper and Brothers.

Speer, Johanna. 2012. "Participatory Governance Reform: A Good Strategy for Increasing Government Responsiveness and Improving Public Services?" *World Development* 40 (12): 2379–98.

Svensson, Lars E. O. 2012. "Comment on Michael Woodford, Inflation Targeting and Financial Stability." *Sveriges Riksbank Economic Review* 2012 (1): 33–38.

Thomas, Duncan. 1990. "Intra-Household Resource Allocation: An Inferential Approach." *Journal of Human Resources* 25 (4): 635–64.

Thoresen, Stian H., and Angela Fielding. 2011. "Universal Health Care in Thailand: Concerns among the Health Care Workforce." *Health Policy* 99 (1): 17–22.

Tornell, Aarón, and Andrés Velasco. 1992. "The Tragedy of the Commons and Economic Growth: Why Does Capital Flow from Poor to Rich Countries?" *Journal of Political Economy,* 100 (6): 1208–31.

UNEP (United Nations Environment Programme). 2007. "A Success in the Making: The Montreal Protocol on Substances that Deplete the Ozone Layer." UNEP, Nairobi.

———. 2012. "Analysis of Formalization Approaches in the Artisanal and Small-Scale Gold Mining Sector Based on Experiences in Ecuador, Mongolia, Peru, Tanzania and Uganda: Peru Case Study." UNEP, Nairobi.

Université Catholique de Louvain. EM-DAT: The OFDA/CRED International Disaster Database. Université Catholique de Louvain, Brussels, http://www.emdat.be.

UNODC (United Nations Office on Drugs and Crime). Homicide Statistics (database). UNODC, Vienna, http://www.unodc.org/unodc/en/data-and-analysis/homicide.html.

von Neumann, John, and Oscar Morgenstern. 1944. *Theory of Games and Economic Behavior.* Princeton, NJ: Princeton University Press.

Wethli, Kyla. 2013. "Benefit-Cost Analysis for Risk Management: Summary of Selected Examples." Background paper for the *World Development Report 2014.*

WHO (World Health Organization). 2013. *World Health Statistics 2013.* Geneva: WHO.

World Bank. 2005. *World Development Report 2006: Equity and Development.* Washington, DC: World Bank.

———. 2011. *World Development Report 2011: Conflict, Security, and Development.* Washington, DC: World Bank.

———. 2012a. "Financial Inclusion Strategies Reference Framework." Prepared for the G20 Mexico Presidency. World Bank, Washington, DC.

———. 2012b. *Inclusive Green Growth: The Pathway to Sustainable Development.* Washington, DC: World Bank.

———. 2012c. "Resilience, Equity, and Opportunity." The World Bank 2012–2022 Social Protection and Labor Strategy, World Bank, Washington, DC.

———. 2012d. *World Development Report 2013: Jobs.* Washington, DC: World Bank.

———. 2013. *Beyond the Annual Budget: Global Experience with Medium-Term Expenditure Frameworks.* Washington, DC: World Bank.

———. Global Findex (database). World Bank, Washington, DC, http://data.worldbank.org/data-catalog/financial_inclusion.

———. PovcalNet (database). World Bank, Washington, DC, http://iresearch.worldbank.org/PovcalNet/index.htm.

———. Pensions (database). World Bank, Washington, DC, http://www.worldbank.org/pensions.

———. World Development Indicators (database). World Bank, Washington, DC, http://data.worldbank.org/data-catalog/world-development-indicators.

World Bank and United Nations. 2010. *Natural Hazards, UnNatural Disasters: The Economics of Effective Prevention.* Washington, DC: World Bank.

World Economic Forum. 2007. *Global Risks 2007: A Global Risk Network Report.* Geneva: World Economic Forum.

———. 2012. *The Global Competitiveness Report 2012–2013.* Geneva: World Economic Forum.

World Tourism Organization. Yearbook of Tourism Statistics (database). World Tourism Organization, Madrid, http://statistics.unwto.org/en/content/yearbook-tourism-statistics.

Xu, Ke, David B. Evans, Kei Kawabata, Riadh Zeramdini, Jan Klavus, and Christopher J. L. Murray. 2003. "Household Catastrophic Health Expenditure: A Multicountry Analysis." *Lancet* 362 (9378): 111–17.

Yang, Dean, and HwaJung Choi. 2007. "Are Remittances Insurance? Evidence from Rainfall Shocks in the Philippines." *World Bank Economic Review* 21 (2): 219–48.

PART I

Fundamentals of risk management

Cyclone warning in Bangladesh. With good preparation, simple but effective interventions can save lives and avert damages.

CHAPTER 1

Risk management can be a powerful instrument for development

Risk and opportunity

When food prices spiked in 2008, riots broke out in more than a dozen countries in Africa and Asia. As food prices, particularly bread prices, continued to rise in the Arab Republic of Egypt, Rashad Fahti, a factory worker, struggled to feed his wife and four children on his monthly salary of $34.[1] A continent away, in Indonesia, the village of Montei Baru-Baru lost more than one in five residents—67 people—when it was hit by a large tsunami that followed an earthquake in 2010.[2] Globally, in the aftermath of the 2008–09 global financial crisis, an estimated 53 million additional people will remain stuck in extreme poverty by 2015 who otherwise would not have been so poor.[3] The major economic crises and natural disasters that have occurred in recent years underscore how vulnerable people are to systemic risks, which cut across large groups of people—especially in developing countries.

Idiosyncratic risks, which are specific to individuals or households, are no less important to people's welfare. Losing a job or not finding one because of lack of skills, falling victim to disease or crime, or suffering a family breakup from divorce or forced migration can all be overwhelming, particularly for vulnerable households. Households in Ethiopia whose members experienced serious illness, for example, had to reduce their consumption by almost 10 percent and continued to be negatively affected three to five years later.[4] Health costs from high levels of crime and violence amount to 0.3 to 5.0 percent of annual gross domestic product (GDP) for countries in Latin America, without even considering the impact of crime on lost output because of reduced investment and labor participation.[5] Loss of employment in countries as different as Argentina, Bulgaria, and Guyana has not only lowered income and consumption but has also reduced people's ability to find new work, worsened social cohesion, and in some cases increased domestic violence.[6] Whether adverse events come from systemic or idiosyncratic risks, they may destroy lives, assets, trust, and social stability.

Risk is everywhere. While risks in some areas and some regions have diminished in recent years—in part because of improved macroeconomic and financial management and better preventive health care in developing countries—people in developing and developed countries alike continue to face a multitude of risks. Some types of risk—including those related to natural hazards, crime, environmental challenges, and food prices—have become more pronounced in recent decades (box 1.1).

It is often when risks are mismanaged that the consequences become severe, turning into crises with dire results. Poor outcomes do not always reflect bad risk management, however: extremely large and unexpected shocks can overwhelm even the best preparation. Such crises have damaging effects because they not only affect people's current living conditions but also weaken their ability and willingness to pursue new opportunities. Recognizing that a negative shock can push them into destitution, bank-

BOX 1.1 *A risky world: Risks vary over time and across regions*

In the past few decades, the patterns of risk that people have faced have diverged. The incidence of natural disasters, food price shocks, and risks from climate change have increased substantially. By contrast, fewer risks have materialized in other areas—including maternal health, where the mortality rate has declined in all regions.

For some risks, progress has varied across regions. Developed countries have experienced more large recessions and health epidemics over the past three decades, although the incidence of shocks is generally lower than in developing countries. By contrast, developing countries experienced fewer economic recessions in the 2000s than in the 1980s and 1990s, but they faced an increasing incidence of shocks in other areas, notably in epidemics in Sub-Saharan Africa, and homicide in Latin America.

a. Large recessions[a]

b. Incidence of natural disasters[b]

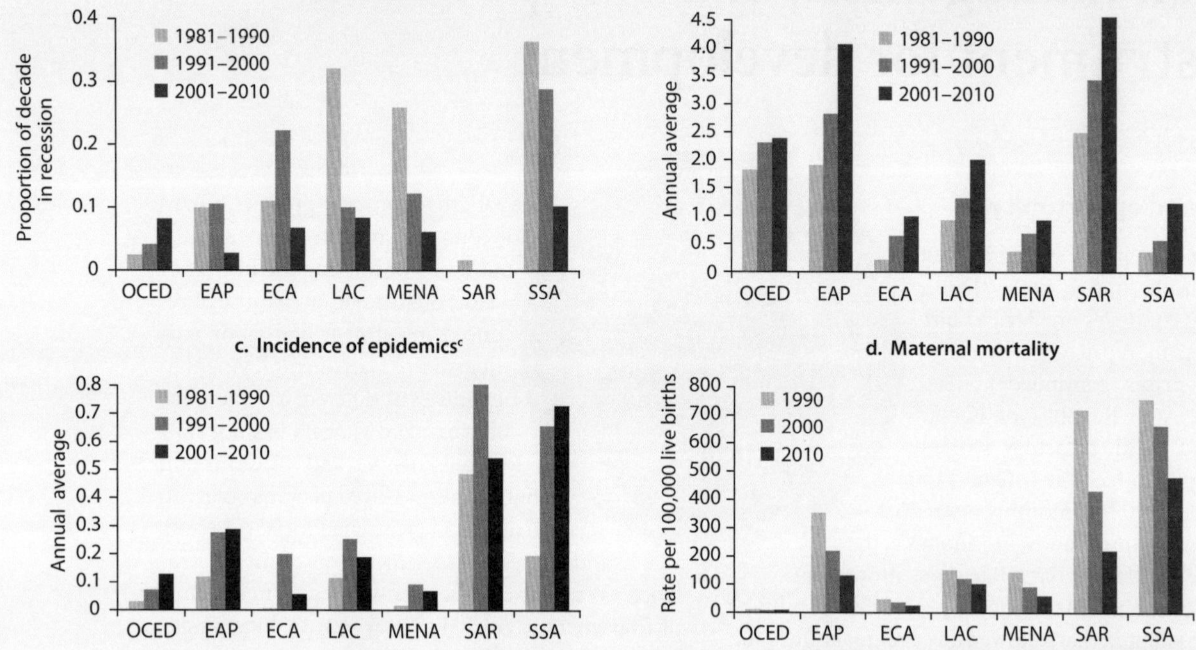

e. Homicides

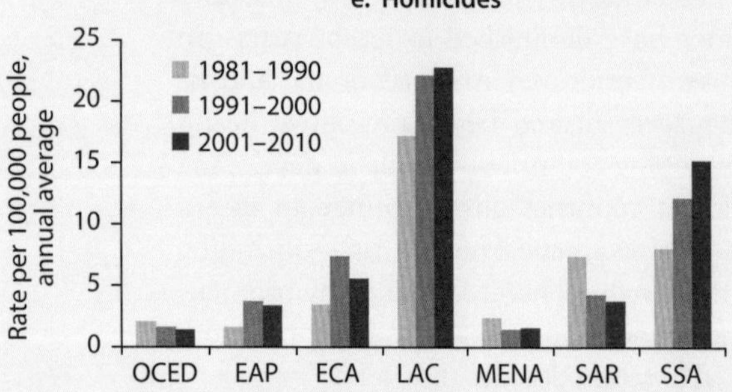

f. Food prices and global sea level rise

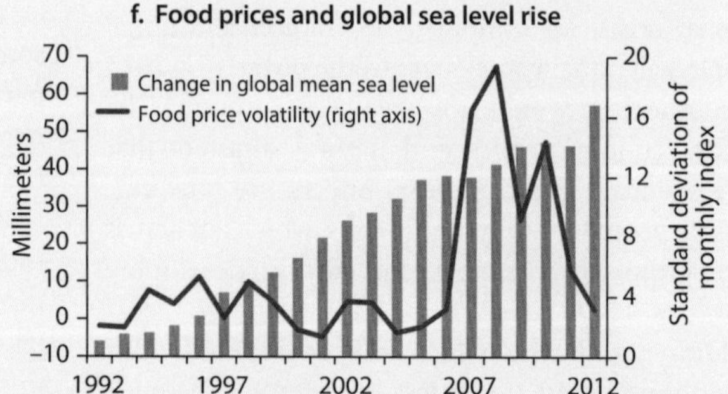

Source: WDR 2014 team based on data from World Bank World Development Indicators (database); EM-DAT OFDA/CRED International Disaster Database; Nerem and others 2010; United Nations Office on Drugs and Crime Homicide Statistics (database); Food and Agricultural Organization Food Price Index (database).

Note: Figures show the simple average across countries in each region. Organisation for Economic Co-operation and Development (OECD) countries in the figures are high-income countries that have been members of the OECD for at least 40 years. All other countries are grouped into geographic regions. EAP = East Asia and Pacific; ECA = Europe and Central Asia; LAC = Latin America and the Caribbean; MENA = Middle East and North Africa; SAR = South Asia; SSA = Sub-Saharan Africa.

a. Large recessions are identified by following Barro and Ursúa 2012 and using a 5 percent decline in GDP per capita growth from peak to trough as a threshold. There were no large recessions in South Asia from 1991 to 2010.

b. Natural disasters include droughts, earthquakes, floods, and storms.

c. Epidemics refer to either an unusual increase in the number of cases of an infectious disease, which already exists in the region or population concerned, or the appearance of an infection previously absent from a region.

ruptcy, or crisis, people may stick to technologies and livelihoods that appear safe but are also stagnant.

Risk need not be harmful, however, and is not always a burden. In many cases, people hoping to improve their standards of living may voluntarily take on risk. Indeed, risk taking is essential to the pursuit of opportunity. But those opportunities may bring their own risks. A country that opens its borders to foster international integration and higher economic growth may also increase its exposure to international shocks. An enterprise that upgrades to more advanced technologies to enhance its profitability may also become more indebted and financially vulnerable. Farmers who adopt new crops and use more inputs in expectation of higher yields may face larger losses if rainfall is low. A rural household that migrates to the city seeking better health care and education may expose its members to higher crime and less communal support. These actions are motivated by the quest for improvement, but the results are seldom guaranteed.

As the world changes, new opportunities and possibilities, as well as risks and complications, continually arise. Rejecting or ignoring change can lead to stagnation and impoverishment. In contrast, embracing change and proactively dealing with risks can open the way to sustained progress. Risk management should therefore be a central concern at all levels of society. By improving resilience, risk management has the potential to bring about a sense of security and the means for people in developing countries and beyond to achieve progress.

Why is risk management relevant for development?

Risk management is an essential tool for development because people in developing countries are exposed to many risks, and an inability to manage those risks can jeopardize development goals, including economic growth and poverty reduction. The prevalence of risk in everyday life in the developing world is apparent in table 1.1, which presents data from household surveys that count the number of respondents who have been affected by various shocks.[7] A majority of households across a sample of developing countries report having been exposed to a shock in the preceding year, and a substantial proportion were exposed to more than one. The shocks most frequently reported are natural hazards (such as droughts and floods) and health risks. Rural areas tend to be more severely affected by shocks, especially by droughts and floods. One exception is employment shocks, which tend to be concentrated in urban areas (possibly reflecting a greater share of informal employment in rural areas). Middle-income countries (such as Peru) report a smaller share of people affected by shocks than do low-income countries.

Surveys also show that people in developing countries feel susceptible to risk and are concerned by it. Figure 1.1 presents data from the latest World Values Survey, which asks respondents to provide a relative judgment about risks that have materialized or that concern them.[8] Once again, regions with more low-

TABLE 1.1 ***Households in developing countries face many shocks***

Percentage of respondents reporting type of shock

Shocks	Afghanistan[a]		India[b]	Lao PDR		Malawi		Peru		Uganda	
	Urban	Rural	Rural	Urban	Rural	Urban	Rural	Urban	Rural	Urban	Rural
One or more	16.4	48.9	61.6	34.4	72.1	40.0	66.8	20.7	34.4	29.7	56.2
Two or more	8.7	39.2	23.4	11.9	36.1	12.7	40.4	1.4	1.9	5.6	15.6
Natural disasters (drought, flood)	10.6	42.2	57.3	5.6	36.0	10.4	47.2	2.6	21.5	19.9	52.1
Price shocks[c]	0.2	3.0	—	4.4	4.9	21.1	42.0	—	—	1.7	3.2
Employment shocks	6.4	4.3	—	9.3	3.1	7.7	3.4	6.4	1.5	1.9	0.7
Health shocks (death, illness)	6.9	14.0	30.2	23.2	33.8	10.1	18.0	9.1	8.9	11.8	14.9
Personal and property crime	1.8	6.6	0.9	5.8	1.9	8.5	8.4	3.2	3.1	6.6	8.7
Family and legal disputes	—	—	1.9	0.0	0.9	1.7	4.3	0.7	0.3	—	—

Source: WDR 2014 team based on data from household surveys, various years 2005–11.
Note: — = not available.
a. The 2005 Afghanistan National Risk and Vulnerability Survey aims to be statistically representative at the national level. However, to the extent that it is difficult to access households most acutely affected by insecurity, the data may underestimate shocks for those households. Conversely, it shows that the risks faced by the households that were surveyed are not unlike those in other developing countries.
b. Data for India are based on representative surveys from rural Karnataka, Madhya Pradesh, and Orissa.
c. Price shocks refer to strong or unexpected changes in the price of agricultural outputs or inputs, or the price of staple food items.

FIGURE 1.1 *Households in developing countries feel susceptible to risk and are concerned by it*

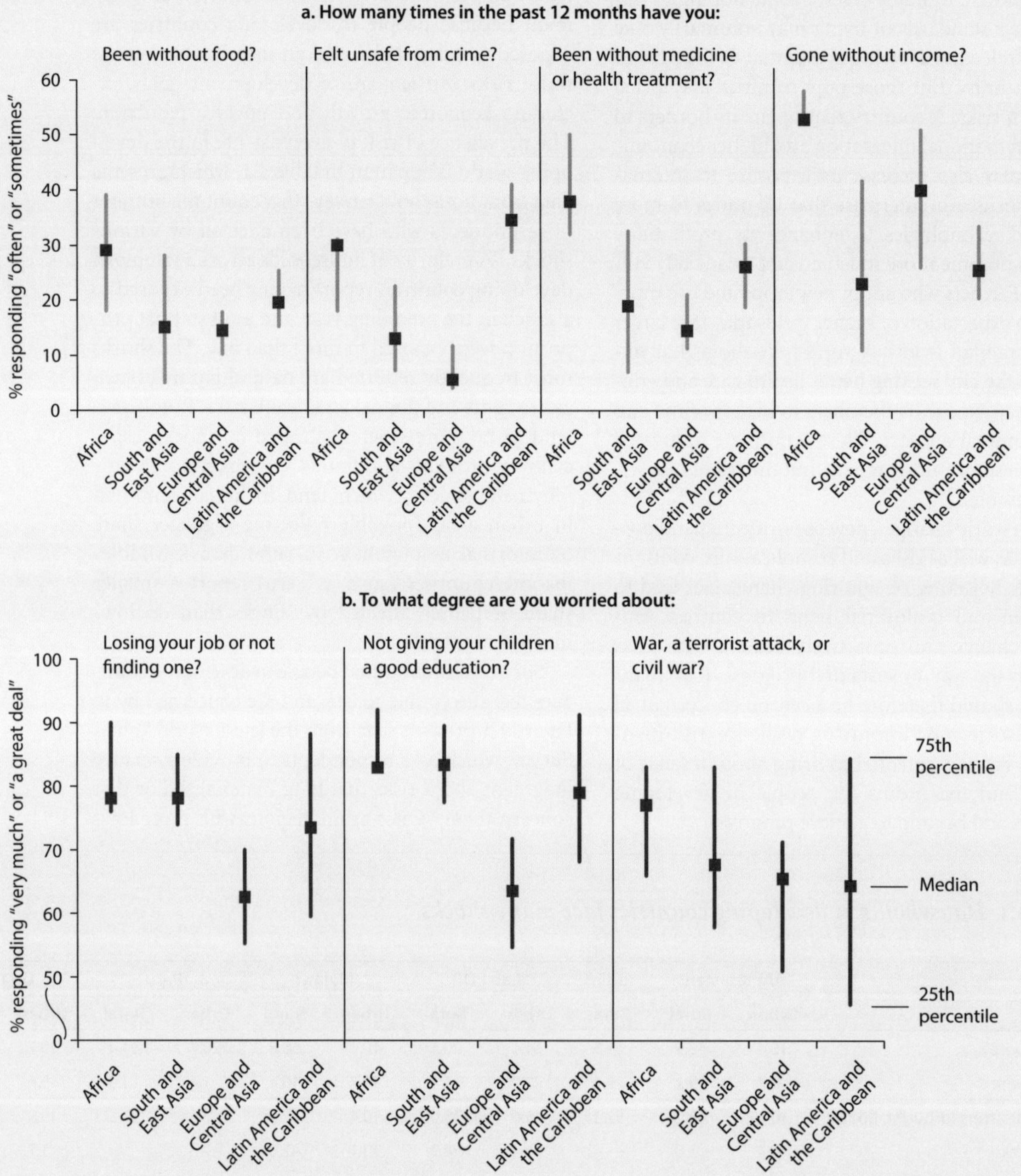

a. How many times in the past 12 months have you:

Been without food? / Felt unsafe from crime? / Been without medicine or health treatment? / Gone without income?

% responding "often" or "sometimes"

Africa / South and East Asia / Europe and Central Asia / Latin America and the Caribbean

b. To what degree are you worried about:

Losing your job or not finding one? / Not giving your children a good education? / War, a terrorist attack, or civil war?

% responding "very much" or "a great deal"

75th percentile / Median / 25th percentile

Source: WDR 2014 team based on data from the World Values Survey, 2010–12.

income countries are the most severely affected (panel a). A large number of people in Sub-Saharan Africa report having gone without cash income, food, or health treatment in the preceding year. Latin America, although a region with relatively more middle-income countries, faces a particular problem with crime. Forward-looking survey questions show that a majority of people are concerned by risks that might emerge in the future (panel b). Indeed, in some cases, the number of people who worry about future risks exceeds the number who have been affected by that risk in the past: more than 50 percent of people in all regions express concern about losing their jobs, for instance, while far fewer report having gone without income in the previous year. This differential underscores the very real psychological and emotional toll that risk can have on people.

Risk management saves lives

Failure to prevent and prepare for risk can have tragic consequences—often leading to widespread loss of life. Mortality is frequently higher in developing countries and disproportionately affects the poor. Developing countries tend to be more exposed to natural hazards, have less robust building structures, and have low capacity to prevent disasters. One stark statistic sums this up: more people die from drought in Africa than from any other natural hazard, whereas virtually no one has died from drought in developed countries in the past four decades.[9] Similarly, the mortality rate from illness and injuries is far higher in developing countries than developed countries. The mortality rate for adults under age 60 is two and a half times higher for men and four times higher for women in low-income countries than in high-income countries, while the rate for children under age 5 is almost twenty times higher.[10] Diseases that affect the poor take the biggest toll: the mortality rate from preventable infectious diseases including lung infections, diarrheal diseases, HIV/AIDS, and malaria is more than twenty times higher in low-income countries than in high-income countries.[11]

The loss of life that results from crises can often be avoided or reduced at moderate cost. For example, in January 2010, an earthquake measuring 7.0 on the Richter scale occurred close to Port-au-Prince, Haiti; 230,000 people died. By contrast, a month later, a much larger earthquake, measuring 8.8 on the Richter scale, struck off the coast of central Chile. While destruction was considerable, the total estimated death toll was far lower: 525 fatalities. One significant reason for the different outcomes is Chile's enforcement of building codes: buildings were more robust to ground tremors. When rebuilding following such events, the decision of how much to invest in better preparation depends in part on the probability of a similar event occurring in the future. What is essential, however, is thinking in advance about the possibility of such an event and deciding how to prepare. Bangladesh provides a good example, where improved preparation for natural hazards has dramatically reduced loss of life from cyclones. In the past four decades, three major cyclones of similar magnitude have hit Bangladesh. A cyclone in 1970 claimed over 300,000 lives, one in 1991 claimed just under 140,000, and one in 2007 claimed around 4,000.[12] This great reduction in casualties is a result of a nationwide program to build shelters, along with improved forecasting capacity and a relatively simple but effective system for warning the population.[13]

Risk management averts damages and prevents development setbacks

Crises can have substantial economic costs and lead to large-scale loss of property, infrastructure, and belongings. In the past 15 years, a number of developing countries—including the Dominican Republic, Ecuador, Indonesia, Jamaica, Thailand, and Turkey—have faced banking crises with fiscal costs equal to 20 percent of GDP or more.[14] The value of damages from natural disasters is often higher in developed countries, where property and infrastructure are more costly to rebuild and repair. However, relative to the size of their economies, the economic impact is often much larger for developing countries.[15] Households and firms may also be more acutely affected in developing countries because a smaller proportion of their damages are insured.[16] The costs of idiosyncratic risks can also be high. Households in developing countries may spend up to 20 percent of their annual income on the direct costs of treating a disease such as tuberculosis, for example.[17]

Large shocks can also cause serious long-term damage to human, social, and physical capital—especially for the poor. When shocks are large relative to a country's economy, they may have crippling long-term effects. For example, the hurricane that hit Honduras in 1998 is estimated to have caused total direct and indirect damages equal to 80 percent of GDP, leaving a legacy of substantially weaker public finances and current account deficits.[18] At times the effects from crises are permanent. A growing body of research documents the role that shocks—above all, health and weather shocks and economic crises—play in pushing households into poverty and keeping them there.[19] Following the 1999–2000 drought in Ethiopia, households in the two lowest income quintiles lost an estimated 60 to 80 percent of their assets; the wealthiest quartile lost just 6 percent.[20] Despite poverty reduction, a substantial proportion of people in developing countries are vulnerable to falling into poverty when they are hit by negative shocks (box 1.2).

Proactive risk management can help prevent or lessen damages. For example, early warning systems can curb the potential damage from natural hazards

BOX 1.2 ***While poverty has declined, many people around the world remain vulnerable to poverty***

In a significant achievement, poverty in developing countries has steadily declined over the past two decades. The share of people living below $2.50 a day has dropped from 72 percent in 1990 to 50 percent by 2010. Nonetheless, a substantial proportion of people remain vulnerable to poverty, with 89 percent of people in developing countries living on less than $10 a day in 2010, compared with 94 percent in 1990.[a] While chronic poverty has declined significantly, the large share of people in developing countries that live very close to poverty highlights the potential for substantial increases in transient poverty—which can have long-run consequences for people's health and livelihoods—when people are hit by negative shocks.

While all regions have reduced the shares of the population that live in or are vulnerable to poverty, progress has varied across regions. In Europe and Central Asia, where poverty was already relatively low, substantial progress has been made in reducing vulnerability to poverty. In East Asia and the Pacific, the rate of poverty was cut in half from 1990 to 2010, from 88 percent 40 percent, but 92 percent of the population continues to live in poverty or be vulnerable to it. Similarly, in the South Asia and Sub-Saharan Africa regions, 98 percent of the population lived on less that $10 a day as of 2010.

Share of population in developing countries living in or vulnerable to poverty

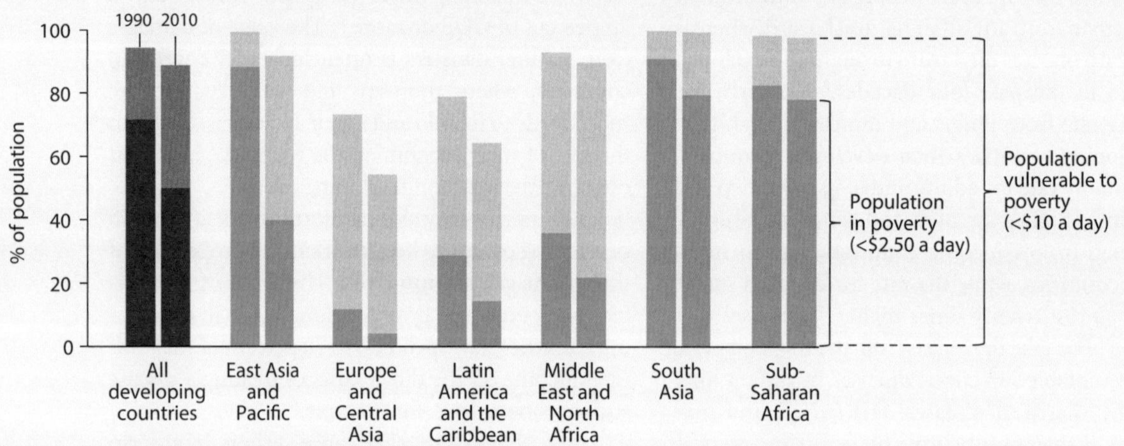

Source: WDR 2014 team based on data from World Bank PovcalNet (database).

a. $1.25 a day is a widely used measure of extreme poverty. However, $2.50 a day is considered a more relevant measure of extreme poverty for some regions, such as Latin America and the Caribbean. The $10-a-day measure is an approximate threshold for measuring vulnerability to poverty across regions, which correlates with asset holdings. The measure is based on studies suggesting that, for some regions, income of at least $10 a day is necessary to achieve the degree of economic stability and resilience to shocks that characterizes middle-class households. By contrast, those living below $10 a day are vulnerable to poverty, in the sense that they face the possibility of remaining in poverty or easily entering into poverty. See, for example, López-Calva and Ortiz-Juarez 2011; Ferreira and others 2013.

by moving people away from the areas likely to be most affected and by preparing buildings and infrastructure in advance. Forecasting capacity can also be helpful in minimizing the damage from other natural hazards. The introduction of seasonal forecasting models in the Philippines, for instance, helped farmers adjust their agricultural production plans ahead of the El Niño drought in 2002–03.[21] Similarly, improved macroeconomic management can reduce the severity of economic shocks by creating fiscal and monetary buffers to help lessen the impact of shocks. In the 2008–09 financial crisis, middle-income countries experienced a sharp decline in their GDP growth, similar to that in high-income countries—although not greater than that in high-income countries, as had been the case in previous global crises. Low-income countries, which were less exposed to financial markets, witnessed a more moderate decline in their GDP growth, both relative to other countries and to their own past experience. In both cases, sound macroeconomic management before the crisis—including better-controlled inflation, smaller fiscal and current account deficits, and increased international reserves—created a buffer that allowed countries to use countercyclical policies in response to their growth downturns, contributing to a much quicker recovery compared with previous global financial crises (see chapter 7).[22]

Risk management unleashes opportunity

No less important than people's concern about negative shocks is their desire to improve their circumstances. Some 68 percent of people in developing countries said that a high level of economic growth should be the first priority for their country; 70 percent said work was "very important" in their life.[23] A quarter of people in developing countries said they would like to permanently emigrate from their country: an aspiration to improve their standards of living was cited as the most important motivator by a substantial majority.[24]

While the desire for improvement is strong, the changes needed to bring improvement about can entail substantial risk. Sometimes fear of risk—which is often particularly acute for the poor—means that productive opportunities are not pursued. For example, low-income households in developing countries disproportionately choose to grow low-risk crops, which are also low return, thereby perpetuating poverty.[25] Farmers may choose not to use fertilizer because they fear negative shocks such as low rainfall or diminished demand, thus preferring to retain savings as a cushion rather than investing in intermediate inputs.[26] Similarly, fear of failure may inhibit rural households from taking opportunities to migrate temporarily during the lean season, despite potentially large gains from doing so.[27]

Beyond their own forgone opportunity, individuals' choices to avoid risk because they fear loss can also have national repercussions when aggregated. For example, evidence suggests that aversion to risk—which is especially strong in developing countries, where people often live close to subsistence levels—can explain two-thirds of the difference in the use of intermediate inputs (such as fertilizer) between developing and developed countries, amplifying differences in agricultural and overall productivity by as much as 50 and 80 percent, respectively, compared to a model without the risk of agricultural shocks.[28] Similarly, reluctance to undertake innovation in the absence of risk management tools can have implications for national economic growth, especially because innovation often brings positive spillover effects, with the benefits accruing to society and not just the individual.

Risk management can provide a means for people to better manage the potential downside from taking on risk—thereby fostering opportunity and ultimately reducing poverty. For example, by mitigating the potential for loss, insurance enabled farmers in Ghana to both invest more in production and pursue riskier, higher-yield types of production.[29] Similarly, farmers in India who were offered rainfall insurance shifted their production from drought-resistant to higher-yield crops and also made greater investments in fertilizer, hired labor, and other inputs (figure 1.2a).[30] Each year in rural Bangladesh, households face the prospect of famine and increased poverty in the lean season, when there is little agricultural work and grain prices are high, yet relatively few people migrate to urban areas to find employment for those few months. The offer of support, in the form of a modest loan or grant, led to substantially higher rates of temporary migration, with corresponding increases in consumption for remaining members of the family. Significantly, seasonal migration also remained higher in subsequent years, when an incentive to migrate was not provided, suggesting an important self-learning element that can help reduce fear of risky activities (figure 1.2b).

In many instances, risk management may provide a means both to increase economic returns and reduce the propensity for crises, especially in developing countries. For example, improvements in education not only increase productivity and income but also enhance risk management, because highly skilled workers are less likely to be unemployed or underemployed.[31] Investments in nutrition and preventive health allow people to be more productive, while also reducing communities' susceptibility to illness and disease.[32] A more flexible enterprise sector is both more productive and better able to respond to economic shocks (chapter 5). Policies to substantially reduce high inflation in developing countries can help reduce volatility as well as enhance long-run economic growth.[33] These win-win examples illustrate the potential to simultaneously manage risk and enhance development: there need not necessarily be a trade-off between resilience and growth.

What does risk management entail?

This section discusses in detail two important components of the analytical framework introduced in the overview. First, it explores the process by which decisions about risk are made, and the environment in which risks and opportunities arise. Then it describes what a strong risk management strategy looks like—encompassing actions to both prepare for and cope with risk. The obstacles that often make such a strategy difficult to achieve in practice are explored in chapter 2. The discussion that follows attempts to provide a unifying structure and set of terms to discuss risk and risk management across different areas

FIGURE 1.2 ***Risk management tools can help people pursue opportunity***

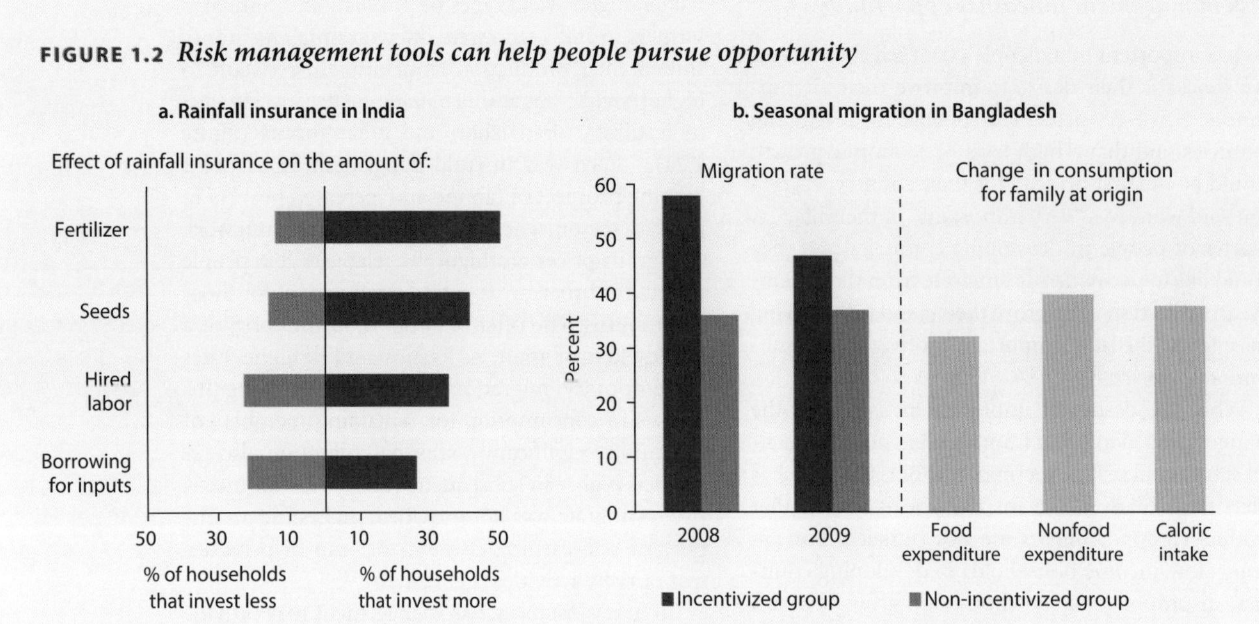

Source: WDR 2014 team based on data from Cole, Giné, and Vickery 2013 (panel a) and Bryan, Chowdhury, and Mobarak 2012 (panel b).
Note: The bars in panel a represent the self-reported investment decisions of 749 farmers who were provided rainfall insurance in a semi-arid area of India.

of expertise in development—although the terminology and use of concepts may differ from applications in some disciplines (glossary 1.1).

Managing risk under uncertainty

The world is constantly changing, and with change comes uncertainty. Amid this uncertainty, people must consider different options for how to prepare for risks they may face. They must decide the proper balance between taking on risk and preparing for it, or acting only after a shock has occurred. In some instances, the choice of how much risk to take on will be affected by a trade-off between risk and return—by reducing the riskiness of an undertaking, people may also diminish the potential return they can get. That is often the case for financial investments, for example. In many cases, however, risk management can be growth enhancing, allowing people both to decrease the risk they face and to improve their return. The choice of which actions to take then turns on how the up-front cost of preparation compares to the likely benefit,[34] as well as any potential obstacles to people's risk management—including lack of information and economic constraints.

Risk management can both increase economic returns and reduce the propensity for crises: there need not be a trade-off between resilience and growth.

Whether a risk management option is ultimately judged to be excessively costly depends in part on the relative prices of different actions and the availability of alternatives—particularly on whether people are able to rely on family, the state, or other networks for support, and on whether they can reasonably expect to borrow money if necessary. The perceived benefit of risk management depends, in turn, on assessments of the likely size of a future shock, the probability of it occurring, and how much people care about the future (when the benefits of risk management would accrue) compared with the present (when the costs are undertaken). Their personal preferences (including their tolerance and appetite for risk) will also affect their decision. These preferences can be influenced by several factors, including income and cultural norms. At very low levels of income, for example, risk aversion might be synonymous with loss aversion (box 1.3).

Understanding the environment in which risks and opportunities arise

Change can generate both negative shocks (such as natural hazards or financial crises) and positive shocks (such as resource booms or improvements in

GLOSSARY 1.1 *Terms related to risk management*

Term	Definition
Risk	The possibility of loss. It can be imposed from outside or taken on voluntarily in the pursuit of opportunities.
Opportunity	The possibility of gain. It can be regarded as the upside of risk.
Systemic risk	Risk that is common to most members of an entire system.
Idiosyncratic risk	Risk that is specific to some members of a system.
Risk management	The process that involves confronting risks, preparing for them (ex ante risk management), and coping with their effects (ex post risk management).
Shock	A change in the world that may be positive or negative and that may occur gradually or suddenly.
Exposure	The external environment that determines the shocks to which a system is subject.
Vulnerability	A high susceptibility to loss from negative shocks resulting from a system's exposure, internal conditions, and risk management.
Resilience	The ability of a person or system to recover from negative shocks while retaining or improving their functioning.
Crisis	A situation in which the adverse outcomes from risk become so severe and generalized that the functioning of the system is threatened.
Uncertainty	The situation of not knowing what the outcome will be.

Source: WDR 2014 team.

technology). Whether risk is imposed or taken on voluntarily, the impact of shocks can be amplified or reduced depending on people's external environment, their internal conditions, and their risk management.

Consider the tragic case of Sichuan province in China where 69,000 people, including thousands of children, died following a large earthquake in May 2008. What factors contribute to a death toll in an event like this? Clearly, the intensity of the initial shock can have a major influence (in this case, the earthquake measured 7.8 on the Richter scale). In addition, people's external environment may expose them to earthquakes to a greater or lesser extent (they may live in a densely populated region prone to earthquakes, for example). Their internal conditions (age, health, education, and so on) may also play a role. Their own preparation matters. For example, do children in schools practice emergency responses to earthquakes? Once a shock occurs, the outcome also depends on people's ability to cope—on how quickly emergency responders are able to

BOX 1.3 *When risk aversion becomes loss aversion: A view from utility theory*

In economic models, agents' risk aversion is represented by the curvature of their utility function. Agents who are risk averse, for example, have concave utility functions: they get greater utility from outcomes that occur with certainty than from outcomes that have the same average value but are uncertain. When constructing models, economists must make a choice about what type of utility function to use. Constant (relative) risk aversion utility functions are commonly used and relatively easy to work with. One drawback of this class of utility functions, however, is the characteristic that agents' risk aversion to (proportional) variations in consumption does not change with their income. It may be reasonable to think, however, that agents with different levels of income but otherwise similar characteristics have different preferences for risk. For example, people with higher levels of income may feel they have less to lose and be willing to take on more risk.

By contrast, people who are very poor and credit constrained may be particularly fearful of risk. For these people, risk aversion essentially becomes loss aversion: the possibility of loss weighs much more heavily in their minds than the possibility of gain. In these circumstances, it may be better to consider utility functions where (relative) risk aversion is not constant with income. In Stone-Geary utility functions, for example, utility depends not only on consumption but on the difference between current consumption and a minimum level of subsistence. Loss aversion has a strongly discouraging effect on people's willingness to pursue new ventures and opportunities. It can be mitigated, however, by access to financial markets (in the form of insurance and credit) and the availability of safety nets, especially in times of distress.

Source: WDR 2014 team.

get to the scene, and what equipment they have, for example. In Sichuan, questions have been raised about whether poor enforcement of building codes in rural schools made the disaster worse than it might have been. Coping was also made more difficult by damage to major highways in the region, and by landslides and mudflows, which made it hard to access the affected areas after the earthquake occurred.

By contrast, the discovery of valuable natural resources provides an example of a positive shock. Paradoxically, this windfall is sometimes seen as a kind of curse, although it need not be—as Chile has shown. Chile has been a major producer of copper for the past century, and copper continues to account for more than half of all exports. Chile's ability to benefit from this resource has depended in part on external conditions, including the level and volatility of the world copper price. Internal conditions have also mattered. In the postwar period, relatively weak technological capacity and a shortage of high-skilled workers arguably hampered the performance of domestic copper producers.[35] Over time, improvements in risk management have also played an important role. While imprudent spending by elites may partly explain why strong copper production did not feed through to stronger economic development for much of the twentieth century,[36] the government began to take an active and positive role in managing copper revenues follow-ing a renewed increase in Chilean copper production in the 1980s and 1990s. It now uses a fiscal rule linked to the price of copper, contributing to the government's Economic and Social Stabilization Fund and Pension Reserve Fund (see chapter 7). Today, Chile is seen as a leading example of managing a natural resource responsibly for the benefit of its citizens.

The goal of risk management is to mitigate the losses and improve the benefits that people experience when they face risk and opportunity.

More generally, the interactions between shocks, the external environment and internal conditions, approaches to risk management, and outcomes can be represented by a risk chain (diagram 1.1).[37] The source of any risk is the initial shock. Shocks, either positive or negative, may occur suddenly (such as natural hazards), or gradually (such as demographic transitions or technological changes). Some shocks are systemic, while others are idiosyncratic, affecting only certain individuals or households. As highlighted in the examples above, the outcomes of shocks depend on the external environment and people's internal conditions—and, to a considerable extent, on their preparation for risk and how they cope once a risk has materialized.

While this discussion has suggested that risks are propagated in a linear fashion, in reality the relationships represented in the risk chain involve several feedback effects (see diagram 1.1). The outcome of past shocks may affect people's exposure to shocks. For example, a family that moves to an urban area following a severe drought will be exposed to a whole new set of potential shocks. The outcome of past shocks may also affect the propensity for future shocks to occur. Contracting HIV/AIDS makes the risk of tuberculosis much more likely, for instance. While outcomes in a small system, such as a household, are unlikely to have large effects on their own, they may have a considerable effect when they are sufficiently correlated across systems. While one household with substantial debt may not seem too problematic, for instance, household indebtedness can be a source of instability at an aggregate level when many people are overleveraged. People's risk management can also greatly affect the propensity for future shocks. The use of insecticide-treated bed nets can substantially reduce the number of mosquitoes in an area, for example, decreasing the risk of malaria; managing soil erosion reduces the risk of landslides; and effective macroprudential regulation can reduce the likelihood of future financial crises (see chapter 6).

The goal of risk management

In this context, *risk* is defined as the possibility of loss. Even when risk is taken on in the pursuit of opportunity, the results are not guaranteed: risk thus implies a possibility of loss. By contrast, *opportunity* is defined as the possibility of gain (it can be regarded as the upside of risk). People's *exposure* to risk is determined by their external environment. For example, whether a house is exposed to the risk of coastal flooding depends on its location. Some people may be *vulnerable*—that is, especially susceptible to losses from negative shocks—as a result of their exposure, internal conditions, and risk management.[38] For example, a highly leveraged financial institution that has taken high-risk positions without counterbalancing hedges may be vulnerable to an economic or

DIAGRAM 1.1 ***The risk chain: The nature and extent of outcomes depend on shocks, exposure, internal conditions, and risk management***

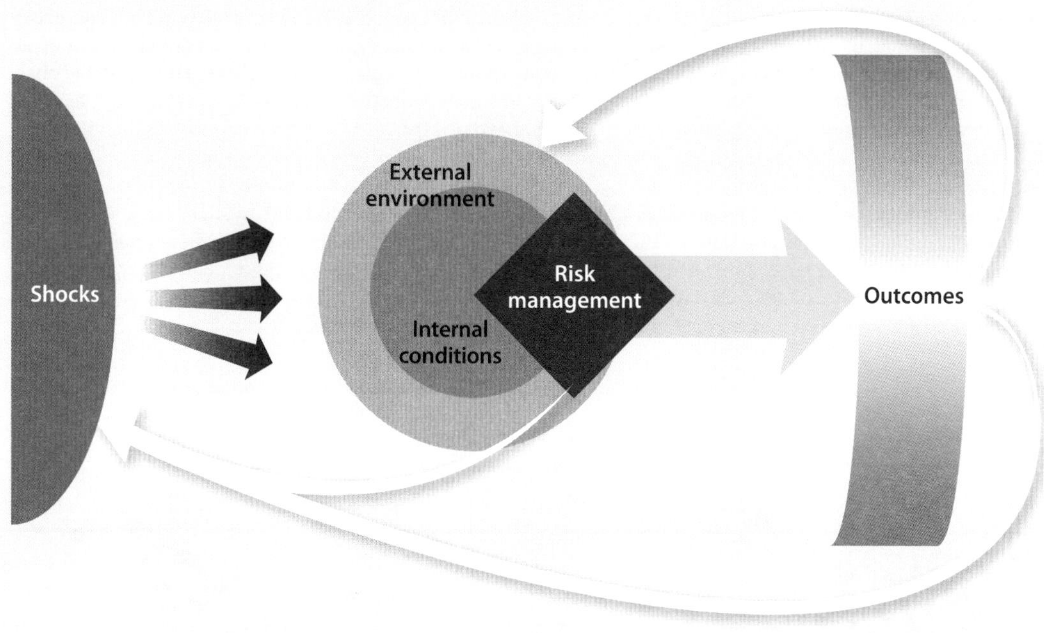

Source: WDR 2014 team.

Note: The feedback arrows in the risk chain diagram represent the potential for the outcomes of past shocks to affect exposure and internal conditions, as well as the propensity for future shocks. Similarly, the effectiveness of people's risk management can significantly affect the nature of and propensity for future shocks.

financial shock. Likewise, a poor household with few assets may be especially vulnerable to a food price shock.

Resilience is characterized by people's ability to recover from negative shocks while retaining or improving their functioning. One outcome of increased resilience is likely to be reduced volatility of household consumption and income growth (box 1.4). A considerable body of the emerging literature on risk in a development context emphasizes how resilience to negative shocks can be increased through better risk management. However, risk management also has an essential role in increasing prosperity by helping people and countries successfully manage positive shocks. Indeed, successfully managing positive shocks is a critical part of increasing people's resilience to negative shocks over time. Ignoring this aspect is particularly unsatisfactory in the context of chronic poverty, because it suggests that the best that a poor household can achieve through risk management is to not become any poorer over time.[39] Instead, the goal of risk management should be to increase the benefits as well as decrease the losses that people experience when they face risk.

Risk management requires preparation and coping

To achieve that goal, risk management needs to combine the capacity to prepare for risk with the ability to cope once a risk has materialized. Preparation (or ex ante risk management) includes a combination of three actions that can be taken in advance: acquiring knowledge (gathering information and making judgments about risk); obtaining protection (to influence the likelihood and magnitude of risk); and obtaining insurance (to transfer resources between good and bad periods). Risk cannot—and should not—be eliminated altogether, however, and exceptional shocks can always occur. Thus, once a risk (or an opportunity) materializes, people need to take action to cope with what has occurred (that is, engage in ex post risk management) (diagram 1.2).[40] Coping actions include updating knowledge and then deploying any insurance and protection.

Knowledge

Because people face uncertainty when they confront risk, increased knowledge is an essential component

BOX 1.4 *Developing countries have increased their resilience over time*

One feature that is likely to be characteristic of resilient households is the smoothness of their consumption and income growth over time. A household with good preparation and diversified assets will have less income volatility and will be able to smooth consumption when faced with shocks. By contrast, a household that is not resilient is more likely to have large drops (or increases) in consumption and income.

Panel a illustrates the volatility of consumption and income growth per capita from 2000–11 around the world.[a] Countries closer to the axis origin had more stable income and consumption growth. Moreover, in countries that are located to the right of the 45° line, per capita consumption growth was more stable than income growth—an important characteristic, given that consumption is most relevant for household welfare. Developed countries were the most resilient in this period, with lower volatility in both household consumption and income growth than in developing countries. In addition, consumption growth was relatively more stable than income growth in developed countries. By contrast, most developing countries have struggled with both unstable consumption and income.[b]

The stability of consumption growth has changed over time (panel b). Countries that are located to the right of the 45° line had more stable per capita consumption growth during the 2000s than in the 1990s. Although volatility of consumption remains high overall, several developing countries across all regions have become more resilient in the past decade.

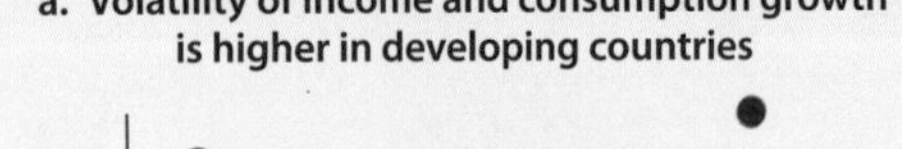

a. Volatility of income and consumption growth is higher in developing countries

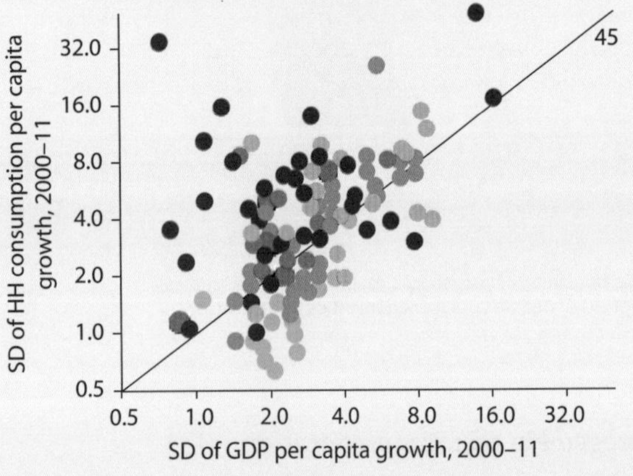

b. Volatility of consumption growth has stabilized over time

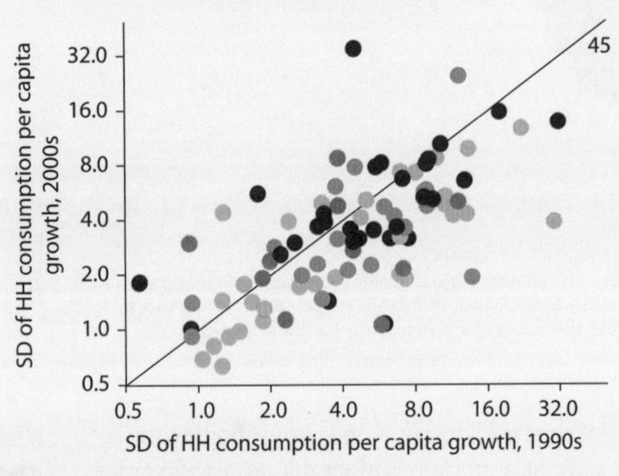

OECD ● East Asia and Pacific ● Europe and Central Asia ● Latin America and the Caribbean ● Middle East and North Africa ● South Asia ● Sub-Saharan Africa

Source: WDR 2014 team based on data from World Bank World Development Indicators (database).

Note: The data are presented on a logarithmic scale. Organisation for Economic Co-operation and Development (OECD) countries in the figure are high-income countries that have been members of the OECD for at least 40 years. All other countries are grouped into geographic regions. SD = standard deviation; HH = household; GDP = gross domestic product.

a. Since accurate household consumption and income data are not widely available across countries, household final consumption expenditure per capita and GDP per capita provide imperfect proxies. Volatility is measured by the standard deviation of the respective growth rates over the period.

b. This finding is consistent with the business cycle literature, which finds that output volatility is significantly higher in developing countries than in developed countries. See Agénor, McDermott, and Prasad 2000.

of risk management. Increased information about risk can help people better understand the nature and likelihood of risks they may face, thus reducing uncertainty. Knowledge of risk goes beyond simply obtaining information: knowledge also involves using that information to assess potential risks and then deciding how to act. Furthermore, not only can better knowledge of risk help people prepare for negative shocks, it is also relevant to the management of positive shocks. For example, better knowledge can inform decisions about investments in skills and education, which are often crucial to attaining better standards of living. Consider a family that is contemplating moving to a new location where the parents may be able to get better jobs, but which is also prone to malaria. The parents may want to learn about training that could improve their chances of getting work in the new area and, if they decide to undertake the opportunity, they could learn about the risk of malaria and then decide what actions to take to protect themselves. In this way, confronting risk can improve knowledge by creating a richer understanding

DIAGRAM 1.2 *The interlinked components of risk management*

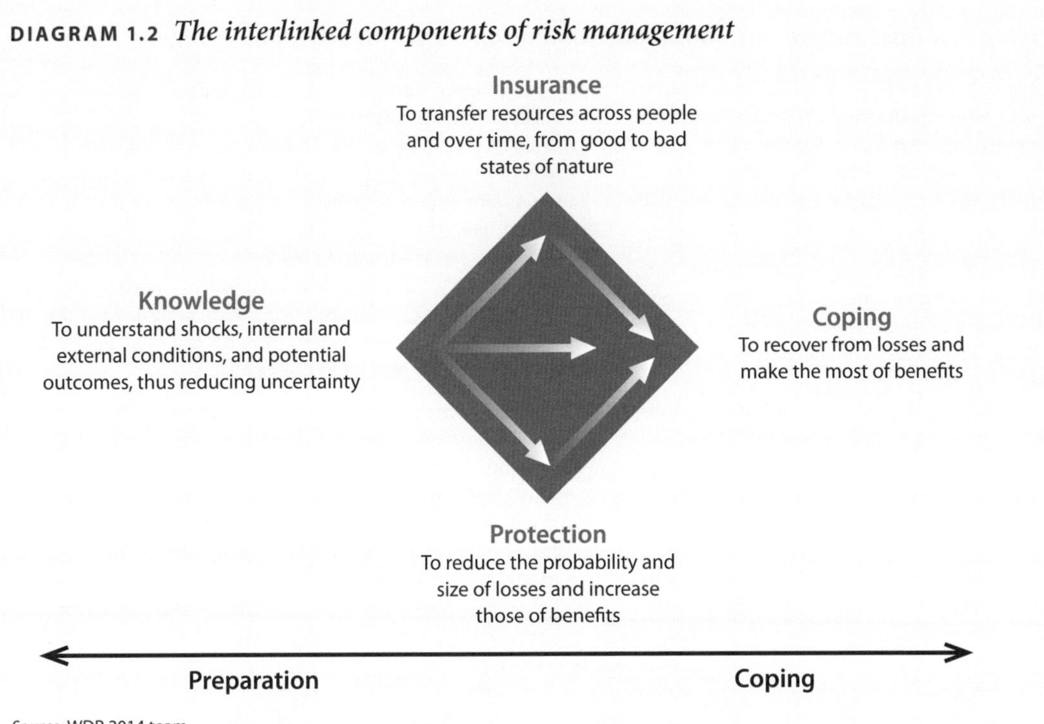

Source: WDR 2014 team.

of the potential consequences and informing future action.

Even with increased knowledge, many decisions must be made with imperfect information. In most cases, therefore, although people know what the possible outcomes are and can assess their probabilities, there is still uncertainty about what will actually happen. Beyond this, however, some areas (such as nuclear energy safety or climate change) are affected by "deep uncertainty," where either very little is known or even the experts cannot agree on underlying trends and possible outcomes, let alone the probabilities surrounding them. The presence of uncertainty requires devising strategies that can successfully manage risks in a wide variety of scenarios (see chapter 2).

Acquiring knowledge (and thereby reducing uncertainty) depends not only on the information that people can access themselves but also on the quality of information that is provided by other social and economic systems. Indeed, because uncertainty can be a substantial obstacle to people's risk management, public policy has an important role in improving access to, and presentation of, information on risk, particularly through the provision of timely and reliable data on risk. Governments can also reduce the uncertainty associated with their policies and regulations by providing regulatory stability and policy predictability. Health care is one area that has greatly benefited from increased provision and quality of information on potential health risks, as well as improved knowledge of how to manage those risks. More broadly, new technologies can further help improve knowledge of potential shocks and inform responses to them (box 1.5). Increased information is not a sufficient condition for better risk management, however, especially when people have difficulty interpreting information or acting on it (see chapter 2).

Protection

Protection, in turn, includes any actions that lower the probability and size of negative outcomes or increase the probability and size of positive outcomes. Thus protection includes action to prevent negative shocks from occurring or to mitigate their impact (especially for negative shocks that cannot be prevented)—or, in some cases, both. Similarly, it includes actions to increase the propensity for positive shocks and gains from them. Protection can be self-provided, purchased from the market, or provided publicly by the community or the state. Continuing with the example of malaria, family members could

BOX 1.5 *Leveraging new information and communication technologies for risk management*

New technologies that help to capture, assess, and communicate data more quickly and with greater reach have become more widely accessible over the past five years. Mobile phones, aerial and satellite imagery, social networks, and online platforms for collective and distributed work can improve risk management by enabling people to:

- *Be better informed of risks.* To help pinpoint people in need of assistance following the 2010 earthquake in Haiti, the Ushahidi crowdsourcing platform enabled citizens to report incidents via text messages to volunteers who tracked and mapped areas affected by the disaster (map).
- *Better evaluate evolving risks.* To identify areas hardest hit by Hurricane Sandy in the United States in 2012, more than 3,000 online volunteers helped inform official responders by conducting rapid damage assessments using fresh aerial imagery of houses in affected areas.
- *Better manage risks in pursuit of opportunity.* To improve their response to changes in agricultural prices and demand, farmers in Ghana can receive specific market information through their mobile phones. Farmers receiving information saw increases in their income of 10 to 30 percent.
- *Respond to risk more quickly.* To assist recovery following a 2008 earthquake in Rwanda, citizens in unaffected parts of the country used mobile phones to transfer "mobile money" to people in the affected area.
- *Evaluate the effectiveness of risk management and adjust their strategies accordingly.* To assess whether residents heeded warnings from the Mexican government to remain at home during the H1N1 flu outbreak in 2009, researchers have tracked population movements using data from mobile phone towers.

New technologies can make new types of information available, improve its timeliness, provide more flexible ways of handling information, and cut costs significantly. New technologies may also bring new challenges, however, including concerns about privacy, difficulties in judging the validity of information on the Internet, and a risk of information being used for violent or oppressive ends. The challenge for policy makers is to leverage the benefits of new technologies while respecting privacy and protecting sensitive information.

Disaster mapping in Haiti[a]

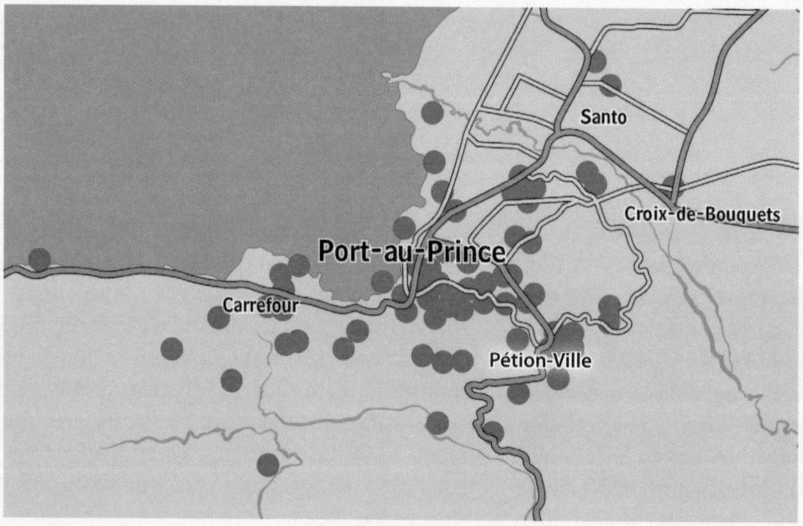

Source: Khokhar 2013 for the WDR 2014.

a. WDR 2014 team based on data from Ushahidi, http://community.ushahidi.com/index.php/deployments/. The red circles in the map depict localities in need of support from emergency responders.

use bed nets or wear long-sleeved clothing to avoid being bitten by mosquitoes (self-protection). They could purchase protection from the market, such as paying to treat the family's house with insect-repelling paint (market protection). They could join with local community members in draining standing water sources (community-based protection). Finally, the family could benefit from activities by local government authorities, such as spraying insecticide (state protection).

Different forms of protection may be relatively more effective for different types of risk. Self-protection is mostly effective for frequent risks that have a relatively low impact, although it can also be relevant for some risks with potentially large losses (such as driving safely, or using a condom to protect against sexually transmitted diseases). Investments in human capital, especially health and education, are an important means of helping people improve their self-protection. However, individuals may not be able to do much to protect themselves against some risks with very large impacts (which also tend to be less frequent), especially systemic risks. Such risks often require assistance from communities or the state. State protection for systemic risks such as natural hazards or economic crises includes physical investments (dikes, sea walls, better roads, sanitation, and so on), as well as investments in early warning indicators and contingency planning to improve emergency response.

Insurance

To the extent that protection cannot completely eliminate the risk of negative outcomes, insurance can help to cushion the blow from adverse shocks. Insurance includes any instruments that transfer resources between good and bad times (savings, formal insurance contracts, loans, credit lines, hedging instruments), as well as means of transferring resources to those especially in need in bad times (social safety nets, community support, or other risk-pooling mechanisms). It can be self-provided; achieved by pooling risk with others (formally through a market, or informally); or provided by the state. Continuing with the malaria example, the family could save to provide a financial buffer in case of illness (self-insurance) or buy health insurance to cover potential treatment costs (market insurance). Public insurance (by the community or the state) might include building social networks that could provide support to the family in case of illness, offering medical treatment in subsidized state hospitals, and providing unemployment insurance if workers in the family contract malaria.

With good preparation, only minimal coping may be needed to recover quickly—leaving more resources available for investment in risk management and reducing vulnerability to future shocks.

Self-insurance in the form of savings is an effective way to insure against frequent shocks that have a relatively small impact, but savings can quickly be exhausted as the size of potential losses grows. Market insurance can thus provide a useful means to insure against larger shocks. However, market insurance does not offer complete coverage for all types of risk for several reasons. Insurers may fear that having insurance will make people reckless (a problem described as moral hazard) or that insurance will be purchased by people who are the most prone to risk (adverse selection). In addition, the cost of recovery from some (infrequent) shocks may be so large that the likely payouts in the event of a shock would greatly exceed the amount that can reasonably be collected from insurance premiums. These factors may make the price of market insurance prohibitively expensive or eliminate market insurance for specific risks altogether.

In developing countries, new technology and distribution networks have contributed to substantial growth in formal insurance in recent years, but access still remains fairly limited overall. That places a larger burden on self-insurance, which is often pursued through relatively costly and inefficient means, such as holding durable assets (like jewelry) that can be sold in the event of a shock. Many households in developing countries also participate in informal risk-sharing schemes, but coverage is often incomplete.[41] Given the lack of market insurance in many developing countries, the state can help further improve access to, and use of, financial risk management tools, and in some cases directly intervene, by, for example, providing credit subsidies and guarantees (see chapter 6). While being careful not to crowd out private initiatives, the state may provide some forms of insurance directly, notably by using public resources to provide safety nets for the most vulnerable (see chapter 3). Communities and the state can also provide support for extreme shocks (such as large natural hazards or financial crises) that are not covered by market insurance.

As strategies to manage risk, insurance and protection may create synergies or require trade-offs. A considerable body of economic literature is premised on the view that insurance reduces people's incentive to try to prevent bad states of nature from occurring (in other words, insurance leads to moral hazard). To the extent that moral hazard occurs, insurance and protection act as substitutes for each other. An alternative view, however, is that protection and insurance may sometimes be complements. That happens when the steps that people take to attain protection are observable to insurers, who can then vary the premiums they charge different individuals (for example, lower prices for people who do not smoke than for people who do). In such cases, protection can make it cheaper to insure against adverse out-

BOX 1.6 ***Protection and insurance can provide complementary means of managing risk***

The relationship between the probability and severity of risk can be characterized as downward sloping: small losses tend to be frequent, while large losses are rare. Such a monotonically decreasing probability density function is represented in the figures below.

Protection can decrease the likelihood of very severe losses, thereby increasing the probability of routine losses relative to extraordinary losses (pivot from the solid to the dashed line in panel a). While self-protection is important for some risks with potentially large losses, public protection (either by the community or state) may be particularly important for reducing the probability of systemic risks with severe consequences (additional pivot to dotted line in panel b).

Self-insurance (savings) helps primarily to cover small losses. Market insurance is better for risks that are less frequent but have larger losses, while community and state support may be needed for risks that are so large that market insurance is not provided. Increased protection can complement insurance by increasing the availability of market insurance—both by reducing the cost of insuring for bad outcomes and increasing the supply of insurance for some risks that were not previously covered (pivot to dotted line and expansion of market insurance in panel b), in turn reducing the burden on self-insurance and the need for community and state support.

a. Protection increases the likelihood of normal times

Private protection
Public protection
Probability of loss
Routine
Severity of loss
Extraordinary

b. Protection can increase the availability of insurance

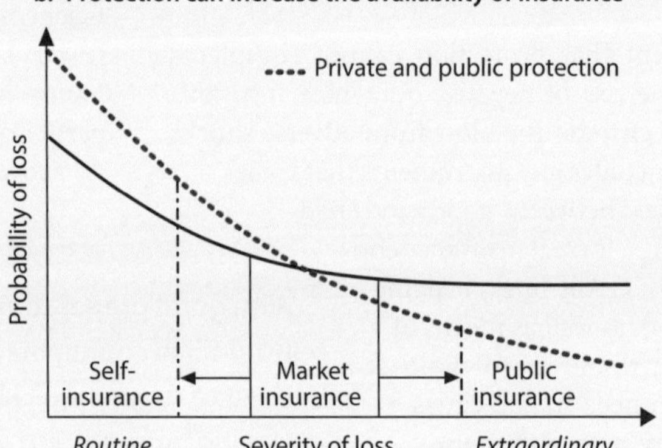

Source: WDR 2014 team based on Ehrlich and Becker 1972; Gill and Ilahi 2000.

comes by reducing the likelihood of their occurrence and may also induce insurers to insure some large shocks that were previously not covered because the risk was too great. Thus protection and insurance together may provide complementary means of managing risk (box 1.6).[42] While this aspect of observability of action is already highly relevant for informal risk sharing in communities, technology may also make it increasingly relevant for formal insurance. New devices for cars, for instance, can allow insurers to vary the insurance premiums they charge based on the quality of people's driving.[43]

Preparation

Together, knowledge, insurance, and protection constitute preparation (or ex ante risk management). Important progress to increase preparation has been made in some areas, which has helped prevent some risks from developing and has averted some serious losses. The institutions and instruments that were established to support conditional cash transfers in Brazil and Mexico—and social reforms in several other developing countries—have improved preparation for and resilience to shocks.[44] Growing numbers of children are immunized against infectious diseases; and households in developing countries increasingly buy old-age, health, and agricultural insurance. Furthermore, although international donors continue to spend predominantly on disaster response, their spending on disaster preparation has increased in recent years (see chapter 8).[45] The extent of people's preparation for risk tends to be correlated with national income across countries. However, interesting variations within regions highlight the important role of policy in determining preparation for risk, over and above access to resources (box 1.7).

Coping

Coping (ex post risk management) encompasses all actions that are taken once a risk (or alternatively an opportunity) has materialized. These actions include updating relevant knowledge by assessing the new

BOX 1.7 *Preparation for risk varies within and across regions and continents*

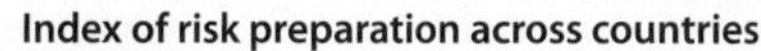

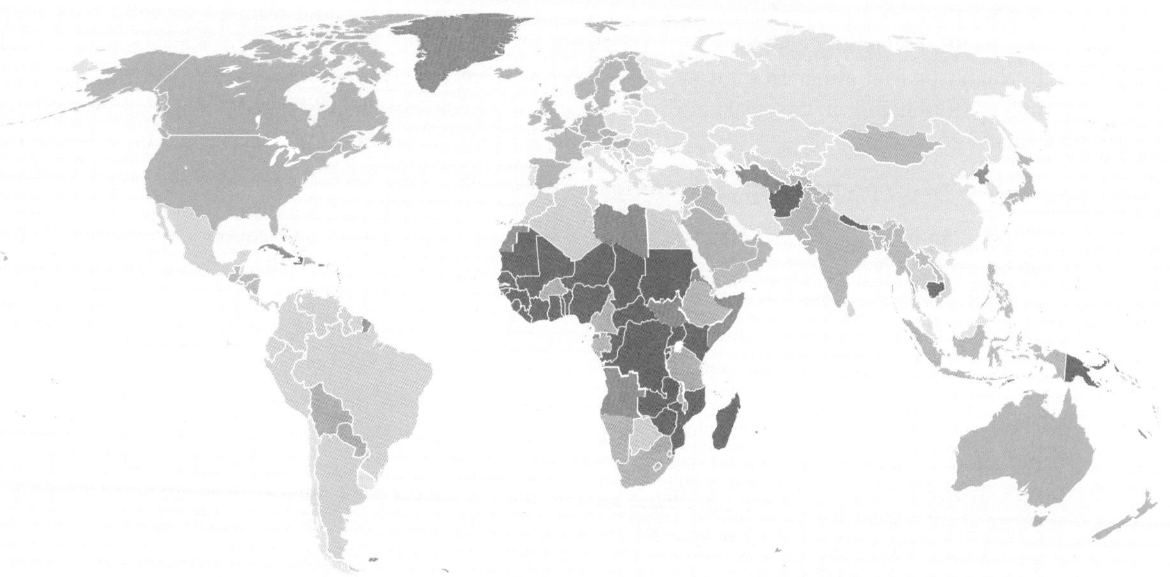

People's preparation for risk at the country level includes actions by and contributions from all social and economic groups and institutions, including the state. An index of preparation across countries is charted on the map above. The index, developed for this Report, comprises measures of assets and services that influence preparation for risk, which in turn affects outcomes.

The index shows that people's preparation for risk tends to be correlated with national income, but only to a certain extent. On average, people tend to be the most prepared in high-income countries (particularly in North America and western Europe). By contrast, people are the least prepared in low-income countries (especially in Africa). Substantial variation exists within regions, however, even for countries with similar levels of income per capita. For example, Chile is reasonably well prepared for risk, while its neighbor to the east, Argentina, has only average risk preparation despite having a similar level of income per capita. Likewise, Ethiopia has better risk preparation than other countries in the region with similar or relatively higher income per capita (Central African Republic, Sudan, Uganda). This variation underscores the importance of policies, over and above income and access to resources, in determining preparation for risk.

The index comprises measures from four important categories: human capital, physical and financial assets, social support, and state support.[a] A household's human capital, in the form of knowledge, skills, and health, plays a role in providing flexibility to prepare for risk. Physical and financial assets—whether in the form of accumulated savings or access to credit—provide a buffer in the face of shocks. Social support also plays a role in allowing households to respond to specific shocks. This support may include formal programs, such as pension schemes, health insurance, and unemployment compensation, or informal institutions, such as the presence of family and friends willing to provide care and support. Finally, state support has a critical bearing on risk preparation, through both the provision of public goods that help manage risk (such as public health and environmental protection) and the fiscal capacity of the state to intervene to counteract systemic shocks. The specific indicators selected are highly correlated with and representative of a wide selection of indicators in these categories.[b]

Source: Foa 2013 for the WDR 2014. Map number: IBRD 40097.

a. Each indicator is rescaled to range between zero and one. The index, which is the average of the eight indicators, thus maintains the cardinal properties of the indicators, rather than simply being an average of rankings across the components. This approach follows in part the methodology used in the construction of the Worldwide Governance Indicators (see Kaufmann, Kraay, and Mastruzzi 2010). If necessary, each indicator is transformed so that an increase in its measure represents an improvement.

b. Component indicators for the risk preparation index: Human capital: average years of schooling; immunization rate (measles). Physical and financial assets: proportion of households with less than $1,000 in net assets; access to finance index. Social support: contributors to a pension scheme (as percent of workforce); proportion of respondents stating that "in general, people can be trusted." State support: access to improved sanitation facilities (percent of population with access); gross public debt (as a percentage of revenues).

situation and then implementing necessary and available responses. Continuing with the malaria example, if members of the household contract the disease, coping could include making use of the family's health insurance and drawing on savings to pay for treatment. The family could also get treatment at public hospitals if available, or, if necessary, borrow money from friends in its social network.

Links between preparation and coping

Coping can be minimal, and lead to quick recovery, when good preparation for risk is in place, or more extensive, when preparation is limited or a shock is unexpectedly large. For example, a home with a reinforced roof and protected windows may suffer relatively little damage in a hurricane. Similarly, good macroeconomic management allowed a number of developing countries to recover relatively quickly from the 2008–09 global financial crisis. In some cases, some preparations that could help to minimize a shock might not be taken because of the costs involved, but other preparations can help make coping more efficient if a shock does occur. For example, while it may not always be cost-effective for cities to build high flood defenses, deciding in advance how to deploy disaster relief can help avoid conflicts over resource allocation following major floods and make coping more efficient. When preparation is weak, however, ex post risk management must deal with unexpected, new, and uncertain situations. Under those circumstances, coping can become ad hoc and often requires very costly measures. For example, households unprepared for income shocks may have to resort to measures such as cutting back food consumption or taking up hazardous work.[46]

The contrast between minimal and costly coping highlights the potential for vicious or virtuous circles in risk management. When effective preparation limits the damages from shocks, the need for coping is minimal and fewer resources are used for disaster response—leaving more resources available for investment in risk management, reducing vulnerability to future shocks, and so on. Evidence suggests that preparation for risk may accelerate economic growth by reducing losses from disasters and decreasing economic volatility during crises.[47] For example, analysis across a set of developed and developing countries over four decades suggests that "crisis volatility" can decrease per capita GDP growth by as much as 2.2 percentage points a year.[48] Conversely, very costly coping may leave few resources available for future risk management, worsening vulnerability to shocks, and weakening households' ability to undertake new opportunities. That may have a particularly harmful effect on the poor, who can become trapped in poverty as they face multiple shocks with little protection.[49] Similarly, at the national level, declines in public infrastructure (especially in health, sanitation, and education), employment, and social cohesion following disasters can weaken countries already in precarious positions.

Preparation and coping can also be affected by deep uncertainty. When knowledge is severely limited by uncertainty, it is difficult to predict how shocks will unfold and what the consequences might be and thus how best to prepare for them; that, in turn, affects coping because it is difficult to anticipate what actions will be needed after a shock. For example, uncertainty about how climate change is likely to affect different geographical areas can make it very difficult to prepare effectively for floods or drought, which may lead to ad hoc and chaotic coping. To avoid crisis and effectively manage risk in these areas, preparation needs to include contingency planning—and, more broadly, processes, expertise, and institutions that can facilitate a flexible response to unexpected events (see chapter 2). For example, regulators may not always be able to predict where and when risks in the financial system will arise, but by putting in place response procedures and coordination mechanisms, they can respond quickly to emerging risks (see chapter 6). In some cases, even when investment in risk prevention has been extensive, disaster response can be suboptimal if it is uncoordinated and inflexible (box 1.8).

Risk management is cost-effective—yet not always feasible

Not only can risk management save lives, avert damages, and unleash opportunities, but preparation for risk often has high returns. A regimen of mineral supplements designed to reduce malnutrition and its related health risks, for example, may yield benefits 15 or more times greater than the cost of the program.[50] Similarly, improving early warning systems in developing countries could yield estimated benefits 4 to 36 times greater than the cost.[51] More generally, benefit-cost analyses suggest that risk preparation is often beneficial in averting costs, sometimes overwhelmingly so, as illustrated by high median benefit-cost estimates across a number of areas (figure 1.3). Such analyses typically compare the likely cost of an intervention with the expected benefit in

BOX 1.8 *A "man-made" disaster: The Fukushima nuclear accident in Japan*

In 2011 Japan was hit by joint disasters that were unprecedented in scale and complexity. One of the largest earthquakes ever recorded, measuring 9.0 on the Richter scale, struck on March 11, 2011, generating an enormous tsunami that swept over part of Japan's eastern coastline. The earthquake's tremors, together with the flooding caused by the tsunami, resulted in a total loss of power at the Fukushima Daiichi Nuclear Power Plant. As workers struggled to cool the nuclear reactors, a massive nuclear leak occurred on March 15.

To provide an impartial assessment of the events that led to the radioactive leak, the Japanese government created the Fukushima Nuclear Accident Independent Investigation Commission. Although the earthquake and tsunami were the proximate causes of the leak, the commission concluded that the nuclear disaster was in fact "man-made." Both the regulators and plant operator were aware of the potential risk of a power outage in the event of a tsunami reaching the plant, and of the need for structural reinforcement of the plant, but failed to act.

Lack of flexibility and poor coordination proved especially problematic in managing the response to the disaster. Local authorities were unprepared for a nuclear disaster alongside a natural hazard, and plant technicians were initially isolated because of transport and communication failures. Both situations highlight the need to build capacity to respond flexibly to unexpected events. Responders and decision makers must be in a position to respond rapidly and flexibly—albeit within a well-established institutional framework—to events that may unfold in ways never previously imagined. Moreover, problems of coordination among the national government, regulators, local authorities, and the plant's operator underscore the importance of establishing coordination mechanisms in advance. These mechanisms should include establishing the chains of authority and means of coordination that will be deployed in the event of a crisis, and putting in place disaster coordination teams

Source: WDR 2014 team based on Fukushima Nuclear Accident Independent Investigation Commission 2012.

FIGURE 1.3 *The benefits of risk management often outweigh the costs*

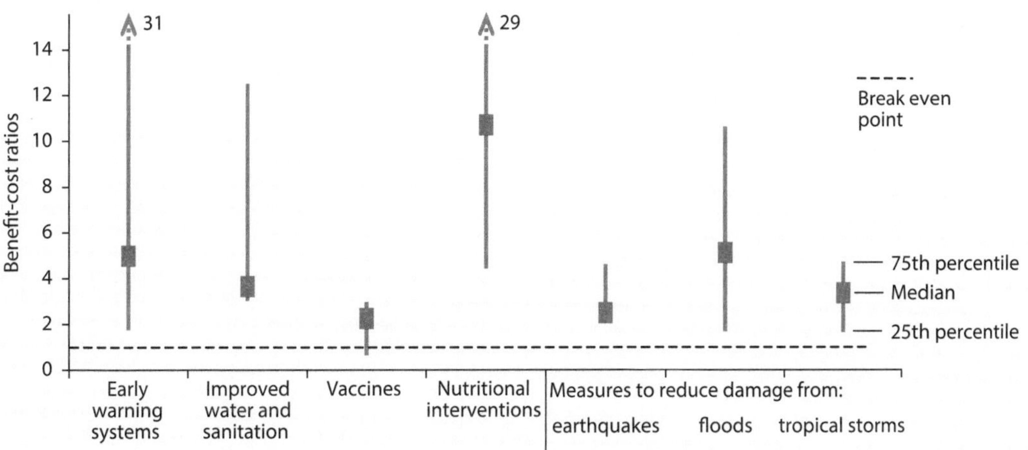

Source: Wethli 2013 for the WDR 2014.

Note: The figure shows the 25th percentile, median, and 75th percentile of benefit-cost ratios across a range of studies in each category (with a minimum of at least four estimates in each category). Above the dotted line, expected benefits exceed expected costs. The 75th percentiles for early warning systems and nutritional interventions are 31 and 29, respectively.

terms of averted loss of life or damages should a shock occur. Estimates vary considerably, reflecting the different local contexts and assumptions of the underlying studies.[52] Despite this caveat, such analyses provide a useful sense of the orders of magnitude involved and support the assertion that preparation is often cost-effective.

Spending on preparation is costly, however, while the benefits are not always immediately evident, and people in developing countries often have limited resources with which to manage their risks. That may help explain why, despite the potential to save lives and avert damages, more is not spent on preparation, and why spending on disaster response is often much higher than spending on preparation. Although spending on preparation is likely to be underestimated (and has increased more recently), international aid data shows that in the past three decades more than 96 percent of the total annual spending by international donors on disaster management has been directed to emergency response and reconstruction relief, on average, with only 3.6 percent of funds spent on disaster prevention and preparation (see chapter 8).[53] More generally, a number of internal and external obstacles may prevent people from successfully managing the risks they face. These and many other obstacles that confound risk management are discussed in detail in chapter 2, along with the potential role and limitations of the state in helping to alleviate them.

Notes

1. "Egypt Grants Bonuses after Deadly Food Riots," Associated Press, April 4, 2008.
2. "Death Toll from Indonesian Disasters Nears 430," *Jakarta Globe*, October 29, 2010.
3. World Bank and IMF 2010.
4. Dercon, Hoddinott, and Woldehanna 2005.
5. Buvinić and Morrison 2000.
6. World Bank 2012c.
7. Self-reported data on shocks entail a subjective assessment by households. In addition, household surveys do not provide information on the magnitude of shocks. In some cases, the shocks reported may be relatively small.
8. These perceptions appear comparable with the actual incidence of risk (see box 1.1) for risks that are similarly defined and that occur frequently. For some risks, however, especially those that evolve slowly, perceptions of risk can sometimes diverge from reality (see chapter 2).
9. EM-DAT OFDA/CRED International Disaster Database.
10. WHO 2013.
11. WHO 2013.
12. EM-DAT OFDA/CRED International Disaster Database.
13. Paul 2009.
14. Laeven and Valencia 2012.
15. World Bank and United Nations 2010.
16. For example, the ratio of total losses to insured losses from natural disasters in the United States is typically between 2 and 4, whereas in China it has often been close to 50. See Kunreuther and Michel-Kerjan 2012.
17. Russell 2004.
18. Mechler 2004.
19. Baulch 2011 provides a useful survey.
20. Little and others 2004.
21. Subbiah, Bildan, and Narasimhan 2008.
22. Didier, Hevia, and Schmukler 2012; IMF 2010.
23. 2010–2012 World Values Survey; median across 24 developing countries in survey.
24. Gallup 2006–08, 2010–12. Twenty-seven percent of people surveyed said they would like to permanently move to another country (median across 72 developing countries in survey). In the former Soviet Union, the main reasons for wanting to move were to improve their standard of living (52 percent), for their children's future (13 percent), or to get a good job (10 percent); in Latin America, the main reasons were to escape from poverty (38 percent), make money and help loved ones back home (29 percent), or to achieve higher personal and professional growth (17 percent).
25. See Rosenzweig and Binswanger 1993 for evidence from India, and Dercon 1996 for Tanzania.
26. Dercon and Christiaensen 2011.
27. Brown, Mobarak, and Zelenska 2013 for the WDR 2014.
28. Donovan 2012.
29. Karlan and others 2012.
30. Cole, Giné, and Vickery 2013; Mobarak and Rosenzweig 2012.
31. World Bank 2012c.
32. Hoddinott, Rosegrant, and Torero 2012.
33. Bruno and Easterly 1998.
34. While the costs of preparing for risk must be incurred predominantly up-front, the benefits tend to accrue over time and are therefore more uncertain. The probability of a risk materializing is thus central to any assessment of a potential intervention. In formal benefit-cost analyses, this probability is usually taken into account either implicitly (by basing calculations of averted costs on average historical data) or explicitly (by weighting the potential benefit of a risk management intervention in the event of a shock by the probability of that shock occurring). See Wethli 2013 for the WDR 2014.
35. Maloney 2007.
36. Maloney 2007.
37. The concept of a risk chain is discussed and illustrated in Alwang, Siegel, and Jørgensen 2001. See also Barrett 2002; Heltberg, Siegel, and Jørgensen 2009.
38. This definition is related to, but distinct from, how the term *vulnerability* is used in various disciplines. For example, microeconomic studies, which typically focus on income shocks, define vulnerability in terms of the probability that a person will enter into poverty following a shock. For a full discussion of the many ways in which vulnerability is defined in different disciplines, see Alwang, Siegel, and Jørgensen 2001.
39. See, for example, Christopher Barrett and Mark Constas, "Resilience to avoid and escape chronic poverty: Theoretical foundations and measurement principles," http://www.dyson.cornell.edu/faculty_sites/cbb2/presentations.htm.
40. The seminal paper in this field is Ehrlich and Becker 1972. See also the extension in Muermann and Kunreuther 2008, and the applications in Gill and Ilahi 2000; Holzmann and Jørgensen 2001; and Packard 2002.
41. Townsend 1994.
42. For a rich discussion of the potential complementarity between insurance and protection, see Erlich and Becker 1972.
43. *Economist* 2013.
44. World Bank 2012a.
45. World Bank 2012b.
46. Heltberg, Hossain, and Reva 2012.
47. Hallegatte 2012b; Hnatkovska and Loayza 2005.
48. Crisis volatility (as opposed to the small but frequent cycles that are typical of business cycles) is defined in terms of downward deviations below a common threshold. Careful instrumental variable analysis is needed to control for simultaneity between volatility and growth. See Hnatkovska and Loayza 2005.
49. For evidence on how loss of assets from natural disasters can create poverty traps, see Carter and others 2007.
50. Hoddinott, Rosegrant, and Torero 2012.
51. Hallegatte 2012a.
52. The set of assumptions used for benefit-cost analysis varies by study. Many studies provide a range of estimates, based on differing assumptions about the value of lost life and discount rates. Most studies do not make specific assumptions about governments' risk aversion, or the extent to which governments are credit constrained. Benefit-cost ratios typically increase with the time horizon considered, reflecting the increased likelihood of shocks over a longer time period. See Wethli 2013 for the WDR 2014 for further discussion.
53. WDR 2014 team based on data from AidData. Disaster prevention and preparation includes donor funding for early warning systems and protection of critical infrastructure, among other items. However, other spending that may improve preparation for disasters—for example, changing the location of roads—may often be classified as more general development spending. To that extent, these figures underestimate donor spending on preparation.

References

Agénor, Pierre-Richard, C. John McDermott, and Eswar S. Prasad. 2000. "Macroeconomic Fluctuations in Developing Countries: Some Stylized Facts." *World Bank Economic Review* 14 (2): 251–85.

Alwang, Jeffrey, Paul B. Siegel, and Steen L. Jørgensen. 2001. "Vulnerability: A View from Different Disciplines." Social Protection Discussion Paper 0115, World Bank, Washington, DC.

Barrett, Christopher B. 2002. "Food Security and Food Assistance Programs." In *Handbook of Agricultural Economics*, vol. 2B, edited by Bruce L. Gardner and Gordon C. Rausser, 2103–90. Amsterdam: Elsevier Science.

Barro, Robert J., and José F. Ursúa. 2012. "Rare Macroeconomic Disasters." *Annual Review of Economics* 4 (1): 83–109.

Baulch, Bob. 2011. *Why Poverty Persists: Poverty Dynamics in Asia and Africa.* Cheltenham, U.K.: Edward Elgar.

Brown, Julia K., Ahmed Mushfiq Mobarak, and Tetyana V. Zelenska. 2013. "Barriers to Adoption of Products and Technologies that Aid Risk Management in Developing Countries." Background paper for the *World Development Report 2014.*

Bruno, Michael, and William Easterly. 1998. "Inflation Crises and Long-Run Growth." *Journal of Monetary Economics* 41 (1): 3–26.

Bryan, Gharad, Shyamal Chowdhury, and Ahmed Mushfiq Mobarak. 2012. "Seasonal Migration and Risk Aversion." Discussion Paper 8739, Centre for Economic Policy Research, London.

Buvinić, Mayra, and Andrew R. Morrison. 2000. "Living in a More Violent World." *Foreign Policy* (118): 58–72.

Carter, Michael R., Peter D. Little, Tewodaj Mogues, and Workneh Negatu. 2007. "Poverty Traps and Natural Disasters in Ethiopia and Honduras." *World Development* 35 (5): 835–56.

Cole, Shawn, Xavier Giné, and James Vickery. 2013. "How Does Risk Management Influence Production Decisions? Evidence from a Field Experiment." Working Paper 13-080, Harvard Business School, Boston, MA.

Dercon, Stefan. 1996. "Risk, Crop Choice, and Savings: Evidence from Tanzania." *Economic Development and Cultural Change* 44 (3): 485–513.

Dercon, Stefan, and Luc J. Christiaensen. 2011. "Consumption Risk, Technology Adoption and Poverty Traps: Evidence from Ethiopia." *Journal of Development Economics* 96 (2): 159–73.

Dercon, Stefan, John Hoddinott, and Tassew Woldehanna. 2005. "Shocks and Consumption in 15 Ethiopian Villages, 1999–2004." *Journal of African Economies* 14 (4): 559–85.

Didier, Tatiana, Constantino Hevia, and Sergio L. Schmukler. 2012. "How Resilient and Countercyclical Were Emerging Economies during the Global Financial Crisis?" *Journal of International Money and Finance* 31 (8): 2052–77.

Donovan, Kevin. 2012. "Agricultural Risk, Intermediate Inputs, and Cross-Country Productivity Differences." Job Market Paper, Arizona State University.

Economist. 2013. "Gizmos That Track Driving Habits Are Changing the Face of Car Insurance." February 23.

Ehrlich, Isaac, and Gary S. Becker. 1972. "Market Insurance, Self-Insurance, and Self-Protection." *Journal of Political Economy* 80 (4): 623–48.

FAO (Food and Agricultural Organization). FAO Food Price Index (database), FAO, Rome, http://www.fao.org/worldfoodsituation/FoodPricesIndex/en/.

Ferreira, Francisco H. G., Julian Messina, Jamele Rigolini, Luis-Felipe López-Calva, Maria Ana Lugo, and Renos Vakis. 2013. *Economic Mobility and the Rise of the Latin American Middle Class.* Washington, DC: World Bank.

Foa, Roberto. 2013. "Household Risk Preparation Indices—Construction and Diagnostics." Background paper for the *World Development Report 2014.*

Fukushima Nuclear Accident Independent Investigation Commission. 2012. "The Official Report of the Fukushima Nuclear Accident Independent Investigation Commission." National Diet of Japan, Tokyo.

Gill, Indermit S., and Nadeem Ilahi. 2000. "Economic Insecurity, Individual Behavior and Social Policy." Working Paper 31522, World Bank, Washington, DC.

Hallegatte, Stéphane. 2012a. "A Cost Effective Solution to Reduce Disaster Losses in Developing Countries: Hydro-Meteorological Services, Early Warning, and Evacuation." Policy Research Working Paper 6058, World Bank, Washington, DC.

———. 2012b. "An Exploration of the Link between Development, Economic Growth, and Natural Risk." Policy Research Working Paper 6216, World Bank, Washington, DC.

Heltberg, Rasmus, Naomi Hossain, and Anna Reva. 2012. *Living through Crises: How the Food, Fuel, and Financial Shocks Affect the Poor.* Washington, DC: World Bank.

Heltberg, Rasmus, Paul B. Siegel, and Steen L. Jørgensen. 2009. "Addressing Human Vulnerability to Climate Change: Toward a 'No-Regrets' Approach." *Global Environmental Change* 19 (1): 89–99.

Hnatkovska, Viktoria, and Norman Loayza. 2005. "Volatility and Growth." In *Managing Economic Volatility and Crises: A Practitioner's Guide*, edited by Joshua Aizenman and Brian Pinto, 65–100. New York: Cambridge University Press.

Hoddinott, John, Mark Rosegrant, and Maximo Torero. 2012. "Investments to Reduce Hunger and Undernutrition." Paper prepared for the 2012 Global Copenhagen Consensus.

Holzmann, Robert, and Steen Jørgensen. 2001. "Social Risk Management: A New Conceptual Framework for Social Protection, and Beyond." *International Tax and Public Finance* 8 (4): 529–56.

IMF (International Monetary Fund). 2010. *Emerging from the Global Crisis: Macroeconomic Challenges Facing Low-Income Countries.* Washington, DC: IMF.

Karlan, Dean, Robert Darko Osei, Isaac Osei-Akoto, and Christopher Udry. 2012. "Agricultural Decisions after Relaxing Credit and Risk Constraints." Working Paper 18463, National Bureau of Economic Research, Cambridge, MA.

Kaufmann, Daniel, Aart Kraay, and Massimo Mastruzzi. 2010. "The Worldwide Governance Indicators: Methodology and Analytical Issues." Policy Research Working Paper 5430, World Bank, Washington, DC.

Khokhar, Tariq. 2013. "Leveraging New Technology for Data-Driven Risk Mitigation and Management: Selected Examples and Summaries." Background paper for the *World Development Report 2014.*

Kunreuther, Howard, and Erwann Michel-Kerjan. 2012. "Policy Options for Reducing Losses from Natural Disasters: Allocating $75 Billion." Paper prepared for the Copenhagen Consensus.

Laeven, Luc, and Fabian Valencia. 2012. "Systemic Banking Crises Database, an Update." Working Paper WP/12/163, International Monetary Fund, Washington, DC.

Little, Peter D., M. Priscilla Stone, Tewodaj Mogues, A. Peter Castro, and Workneh Negatu. 2004. "'Churning' on the Margins: How the Poor Respond to Drought in South Wollo, Ethiopia." BASIS Brief 21, Collaborative Research Support Program, Madison, WI.

López-Calva, Luis F., and Eduardo Ortiz-Juarez. 2011. "A Vulnerability Approach to the Definition of the Middle Class." Policy Research Working Paper 5902, World Bank, Washington, DC.

Maloney, William F. 2007. "Missed Opportunities: Innovation and Resource-Based Growth in Latin America." In *Natural Resources: Neither Curse nor Destiny*, edited by Daniel Lederman and William F. Maloney, 141–82. Washington, DC: World Bank.

Mechler, Reinhard. 2004. *Natural Disaster Risk Management and Financing Disaster Losses in Developing Countries.* Karlsruhe: Verlag Versicherungswirtschaft GmbH.

Mobarak, Ahmed Mushfiq, and Mark Rosenzweig. 2013. "Informal Risk Sharing, Index Insurance and Risk-Taking in Developing Countries." *American Economic Review: Papers and Proceedings* 2013 103 (3): 375–80.

Muermann, Alexander, and Howard Kunreuther. 2008. "Self-Protection and Insurance with Interdependencies." *Journal of Risk and Uncertainty* 36 (2): 103–23.

Nerem, R. Steven, Don P. Chambers, Chong-Deok Choe, and Gary T. Mitchum. 2010. "Estimating Mean Sea Level Change from the Topex and Jason Altimeter Missions." *Marine Geodesy* 33 (S1): 435–46.

Packard, Truman G. 2002. "Pooling, Savings, and Prevention: Mitigating the Risk of Old Age Poverty in Chile." Policy Research Working Paper 2849, World Bank, Washington, DC.

Paul, Bimal Kanti. 2009. "Why Relatively Fewer People Died? The Case of Bangladesh's Cyclone Sidr." *Natural Hazards* 50 (2): 289–304.

Rosenzweig, Mark, and Hans Binswanger. 1993. "Informal Risk Sharing, Index Insurance and Risk-Taking in Developing Countries." *Economic Journal* 103 (416): 56–78.

Russell, Steven. 2004. "The Economic Burden of Illness for Households in Developing Countries: A Review of Studies Focusing on Malaria, Tuberculosis, and Human Immunodeficiency Virus/Acquired Immunodeficiency Syndrome." *American Journal of Tropical Medicine and Hygiene* 71 (2): 147–55.

Subbiah, A. R., Lolita Bildan, and Ramraj Narasimhan. 2008. "Assessment of the Economics of Early Warning Systems for Disaster Risk Reduction." Background paper submitted to the World Bank Group Global Facility for Disaster Reduction and Recovery.

Townsend, Robert M. 1994. "Risk and Insurance in Village India." *Econometrica* 62 (3): 539–91.

UNODC (United Nations Office on Drugs and Crime). Homicide Statistics (database). UNODC, Vienna, http://www.unodc.org/unodc/en/data-and-analysis/homicide.html.

Université Catholique de Louvain. EM-DAT: The OFDA/CRED International Disaster Database. Université Catholique de Louvain, Brussels, http://www.emdat.be.

Wethli, Kyla. 2013. "Benefit-Cost Analysis for Risk Management: Summary of Selected Examples." Background paper for the *World Development Report 2014.*

WHO (World Health Organization). 2013. *World Health Statistics 2013.* Geneva: WHO.

World Bank. 2012a. "Resilience, Equity, and Opportunity." 2012–2022 Social Protection and Labor Strategy, World Bank, Washington, DC.

———. 2012b. "The Sendai Report: Managing Disaster Risks for a Resilient Future." World Bank, Washington, DC.

———. 2012c. *World Development Report 2013: Jobs.* Washington, DC: World Bank.

———. PovcalNet (database). World Bank, Washington, DC, http://iresearch.worldbank.org/PovcalNet/index.htm.

———. World Development Indicators (database). World Bank, Washington, DC, http://data.worldbank.org/data-catalog/world-development-indicators.

World Bank and IMF (International Monetary Fund). 2010. *Global Monitoring Report 2010: The MDGs after the Crisis.* Washington, DC: World Bank.

World Bank and United Nations. 2010. *Natural Hazards, UnNatural Disasters: The Economics of Effective Prevention.* Washington, DC: World Bank.

Preparing for the unexpected: An integrated approach to disaster risk management in the Philippines and Colombia

The frequency and severity of disasters resulting from natural hazards have been increasing. Losses from disasters amounted to $3.5 trillion between 1980 and 2011, with one-third occurring in low- and middle-income countries. The complexity of problems posed by natural hazards cannot be addressed by single-sector development planning. Thus many countries are responding with multisectoral approaches and are moving quickly toward mainstreaming the management of risks from natural hazards into all aspects of development planning and in all sectors of the economy. Recognizing that the risks from natural hazards can never be completely eliminated, a balanced approach incorporates structural measures, as well as community-based prevention, emergency preparation, insurance, and other nonstructural measures, such as education and training or land use regulation. Two of the most effective systemic approaches to disaster risk management (DRM) have been developed in Colombia and in the Philippines.

An inclusive, innovative, and coordinated approach in the Philippines

Located along the western rim of the Pacific Ring of Fire and the Pacific typhoon belt, the Philippines is vulnerable to earthquakes, tsunamis, volcanic eruptions, landslides, floods, tropical cyclones, and drought. With 268 recorded disaster events over the past three decades and more than 40 million people affected between 2000 and 2010, the Philippines ranks eighth among countries most exposed to multiple hazards, according to the World Bank's Natural Disaster Hotspot list.

As early as 1941, the Philippines established the Civilian Emergency Administration to formulate and execute policies and plans to protect the population in emergencies. Since then, the institutional and disaster management systems have focused on emergency response, with important measures defined and implemented for short-term forecasting, early warning and evacuation, and postdisaster relief. More recently, the DRM system has been enhanced through a shift in the policy framework that focuses on prevention and mitigation, above and beyond emergency relief and response. The Disaster Risk Reduction and Management Act of 2010 adopted a comprehensive and integrated approach that promotes the involvement of all sectors and all stakeholders at all levels, especially the local community. A national risk financing strategy is being undertaken to establish appropriate risk transfer instruments to complement resources at the national and local levels, including a contingency credit line (the Catastrophe Deferred Drawdown Option, or CAT DDO).[1]

The approach to DRM in the Philippines is distinguished by inclusiveness, innovation, and coordination. Overall policy and coordination comes through the National Disaster Risk Reduction and Management Council, which consists of 39 members from national government agencies, local governments, nongovernmental organizations, and the private sector, and is complemented by Regional and Local Councils. This multistakeholder composition is preserved even at the provincial and municipal levels, where Disaster Risk Reduction Councils operate in coordination with the national council. Local government units are in charge of disaster preparedness, prevention, mitigation, and response, and since the 1970s have been committed to working with communities to effectively promote resilience.

Innovation and inclusiveness also guide the approaches taken in risk assessment and communication. In 2006, five technical agencies, which traditionally had not worked together, started collaborating on multihazard mapping of the 27 provinces most vulnerable to disasters. The READY project marked the first attempt to approach disasters in a multihazard fashion. It included capacity-building activities in the provinces and established community-based early warning systems for tsunamis, floods, and landslides, which have been used extensively. Launched by the Department of Science and Technology in 2012, the Nationwide Operational Assessment of Hazards (NOAH) project aims to improve the disaster management capacity of local governments by spreading out risk assessment and hazard mapping that can trigger protective actions and early evacuation. By 2014 NOAH will provide high-resolution flood hazard maps and install automated rain gauges and water-level measuring stations for 18 major river basins of the Philippines. It provides not only information about weather conditions, the amount of rainfall, and potential flooding in a specific area but also timely warnings about severe weather, earthquakes, and floods, reaching out to a wide segment of the population.

Every year, a National Disaster Risk Reduction and Management Fund, formerly called the Calamity Fund, is appropriated in the national budget for disaster aid, relief, and rehabilitation services. A similar fund has been set up at the local level. Before 2010, most of the fund was used for postdisaster activities. With the enactment of the Disaster Risk Reduction and Management Act, 70 percent of the fund can be allocated for predisaster preparedness activities. This shift indicates that the government is moving toward an agenda more geared to risk reduction.

Integrating disaster management into the development process in Colombia

Colombia has established itself as a leader in Latin America in developing a comprehensive vision for risk and disaster management. Colombia's advanced DRM system is anchored on investments in structural measures, risk assessments, early warning and emergency response, institutional support, and financial and fiscal measures at the national and municipal levels, as well as the organization of national and local entities for emergency response. As a result of these measures, mortality rates per natural phenomenon have dropped by almost half from the 1970s to the 2000s, from 4,025 to 2,180. Housing damages increased almost fivefold during that period, however, mainly because of unplanned urbanization, which brought almost 80 percent of the population into cities, and lack of enforcement of building codes in some areas of the country.

Colombia's long history in organizing and designing risk management measures started with instruments such as the National System for Disaster Prevention and Response (1985) and the National Plan for Disaster Prevention and Response (1998). Recently, Colombia approved a new national policy and a National System for Disaster Risk Management. Law 1523 (2012) reflects a paradigm shift in which disaster risk management is explicitly recognized as a part of the development process, and stronger incentives for local governments to invest in risk reduction and strengthen technical assistance are provided. It also recognizes that natural disasters are an implicit contingent liability of the state (see chapter 7), and it establishes a fiscal risk management strategy, which includes sophisticated risk transfer mechanisms, such as the CAT DDO.

Decentralization and a growing focus on prevention are guiding the approach to DRM in the country. Since 1997, Colombia has required that land use plans be developed at the municipal level; these plans must consider the location of critical hazards and risk areas for purposes of disaster prevention. One of Colombia's risk prevention strategies is to resettle the at-risk population in safe areas, when risk cannot be mitigated by other means or only by methods that are more costly than resettlement. Enforcement of building codes is weak, and retrofitting of existing buildings is costly and inefficient—to the point that resettlement policies have been preferred.

Some cities are well advanced in their ability to carry out effective disaster risk management plans and implement them well. Since the 1990s, Bogotá has conducted various studies to identify hazards and assess risks. Detailed maps of hazards related to floods, landslides, and forest fires, as well as a seismic microzoning, have been produced. As a consequence, unstable zones have been identified and buffer zones have been established. The district planning department designed an integrated rehabilitation, reconstruction, and sustainable development plan in 2005. A three-stage methodology was developed to support the resettlement process, which includes community engagement and awareness, support with preparation for the move (including a special housing subsidy), and monitoring and follow-up after resettlement. Once families turned over their original properties, the process of rehabilitation and restoration of those high-risk lots started. This successful methodology has been replicated in other cities in Colombia and elsewhere in Latin America.

The actions in Colombia and the Philippines represent significant steps toward a holistic and multistakeholder approach to DRM, but more is needed. An even greater focus on risk reduction is required, especially at the local level, along with a better definition of roles, responsibilities, and coordination among players, and additional investments in specific sectors that are not fully integrated into the DRM system, such as housing, finance, and agriculture.

Notes

1. The CAT DDO is a World Bank financial instrument that offers eligible middle-income countries immediate liquidity of up to $500 million, or 0.25 percent of gross domestic product (whichever is less), in case of a natural disaster. The instrument was designed by the World Bank to provide affected countries with bridge financing while other sources of funding are mobilized.

Sources

Campos Garcia, Ana, Niels Holm-Nielsen, Carolina Díaz Geraldo, Diana M. Rubiano Vargas, Carlos R. Costa Posada, Fernando Ramírez Cortés, and Eric Dickson, eds. 2012. *Analysis of Disaster Risk Management in Colombia: A Contribution to the Creation of Public Policies.* Bogotá: World Bank and the Global Facility for Disaster Reduction and Recovery (GFDRR).

Correa, Elena, ed. 2011. *Preventive Resettlement of Populations at Risk of Disaster: Experiences from Latin America.* Washington, DC: World Bank and GFDRR.

Fernandez, Glenn, Noralene Uy, and Rajib Shaw. 2012. "Community-Based Disaster Risk Management Experience of the Philippines." In *Community-Based Disaster Risk Reduction,* edited by Rajib Shaw, 205–31. Bingley, U.K.: Emerald Group Publishing Ltd.

World Bank and the National Disaster Coordinating Council of the Philippines. 2004. "Natural Disaster Risk Management in the Philippines: Enhancing Poverty Alleviation through Disaster Reduction." World Bank, Washington, DC.

Whether on the road or confronting economic, natural, or health risks, local conditions can pose obstacles to proactive risk management.

CHAPTER 2

Beyond the ideal: Obstacles to risk management and ways to overcome them

Missed opportunities for good risk management

Nearly every year, Mumbai is hit by heavy rains, and for years, reports have spelled out precisely what to do to reduce the risk of flooding. Twenty years ago, a master plan (the Brimstowad Report) provided a list of recommendations to make the city more resilient to floods, and nearly $200 million was approved to implement the plan. But 12 years after the report was published, in 2005, only a fraction of this sum had been spent. Then an exceptional monsoon event hit the city. Almost half the average yearly rainfall fell in a single day, leaving in its wake more than 400 deaths and extensive damages to buildings and infrastructure. After the 2005 devastation, the government established a fact-finding committee (the Chitale Committee) to investigate the causes of the disaster and propose solutions. Perhaps not surprisingly, their recommendations were very similar to those of the Brimstowad Report. These measures were supposed to be implemented by 2015. But as of 2012, only about one-fourth of the 58 projects in the 1993 Brimstowad Report had been completed, while the tendering process for four major projects had not even begun.[1] The city remains highly vulnerable to the heavy rains that occur almost every year, despite well-identified solutions to reduce the risk (photo 2.1).

As in Mumbai, many crises—in many countries, in many sectors, and at many scales—are repeated that could have been prevented or at least mitigated (map 2.1). Significant progress in risk analysis has been made in recent decades, thanks to new tools such as remote sensing and satellite imagery, better weather forecasting systems allowing for more reliable warning, new epidemiological knowledge to better target public health interventions, and more experience about how to deal with violence or macroeconomic crises. Why isn't more being done with this knowledge? As the Mumbai story illustrates, even the first "no brainer" actions such as cleaning up the drainage system are sometimes challenging to implement. To cite some other distressingly common examples: Hand washing is unquestionably a good investment in good health; nevertheless, individuals often fail to do it. Early warning systems provide a cost-effective means of mitigating the damage from natural hazards, with benefits exceeding costs by a margin of four to one at the global level, but investment in and implementation of early warning systems remain limited.[2] There is widespread and vigorous consensus on the damage caused by excessive risk taking in the financial sector, but implementing strong regulations has proven difficult. On the other hand, sometimes too few risks are taken, as when firms are reluctant to take on the risk of innovation for new products or technologies, when farmers do not shift to planting more productive seeds, or when banks refuse to finance viable but risky economic activities. In all these cases, desirable steps to manage risk are not taken, leading to an excess of risk taking or an excess of prudence.

PHOTO 2.1 Difficulties implementing known and even low-cost solutions. Cleaning clogged drainage systems would mitigate the risk of flooding. However, such well-identified and cost-effective solutions often fail to be implemented. The Mumbai case illustrates a common problem (as seen in this picture from Jakarta).

This lack of action suggests that the risk management framework introduced in chapter 1 is an ideal and that its implementation, in practice, is impaired by a number of obstacles. The main ones include lack of resources and information, biases in behavior, and constraints that can be traced to social norms, market failures, and governance shortcomings. Fortunately, public action can help alleviate these constraints, especially by focusing on cost-effective interventions and general capabilities, improving coordination across levels of government and between the public and private sectors, and aiming for robust and adaptive policies in areas of deep uncertainty (glossary 2.1).

A public risk management strategy involves more than simply identifying and assessing risks. Indeed, the mere existence of a risk—even a large one—does not mean that public action is necessary. If individuals and firms are taking this risk based on an informed assessment of its potential costs and benefits and are able to cope with the consequences, there is no reason to prevent them from doing so. On the other hand,

MAP 2.1 ***Crises repeat themselves in the absence of effective prevention***

Flooding has resulted in widespread damage in New Orleans for more than 90 years.

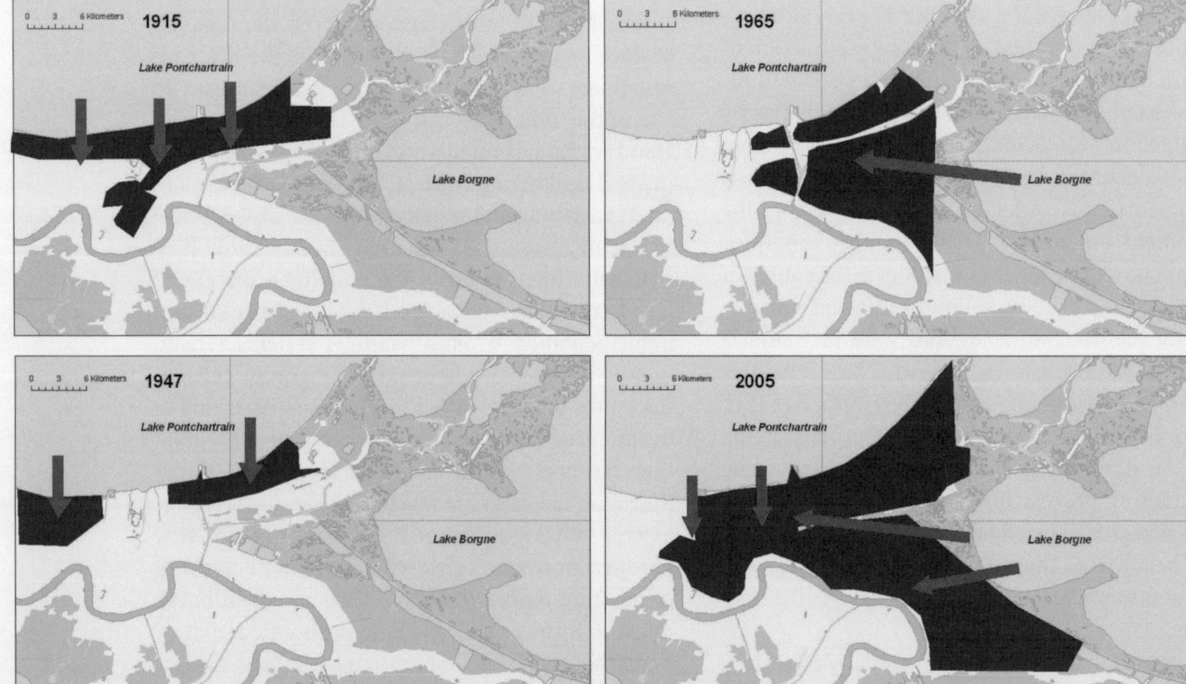

Source: Grossi and Muir-Wood 2006.
Note: Red arrows indicate the breaches in the levees. Blue areas indicate areas flooded by hurricanes.

GLOSSARY 2.1 *Economics terms used throughout the Report*

Asymmetric information	A situation in which one party in a transaction has more or better information than another party.
Adverse selection	A situation in which asymmetric information leads agents with privileged information to try to select products and services on advantageous terms, possibly skewing the transaction in their favor.
Common-pool problem	The problem that arises when individuals overuse common resources to which they have unrestricted access.
Coordination failure	A situation in which decision makers reach an outcome that is inferior because they are unable to jointly choose strategies that would result in a preferable outcome.
Deep uncertainty	A situation in which parties to a decision do not know or cannot agree on the key forces that shape the future, the probability distributions of the main variables and parameters in their models, or the value of alternative outcomes.
Moral hazard	A tendency for people to act less responsibly when they are protected from the harmful consequences of their behavior.
Myopia	A lack of long-range perspective in thinking or planning.
Principal-agent problem	The problem that arises when agents pursue their own goals, even when doing so entails poorer outcomes for the principals on whose behalf the agents are supposed to act.
Time inconsistency in policy	A situation in which policy makers announce policies in advance to influence the expectations of private decision makers, but then have an incentive to follow different policies after those expectations have been formed and acted upon.

Source: WDR 2014 team.

public action is needed if individuals and firms cannot manage a risk or its consequences properly. That is the case, for instance, if they take a risk without the proper information, if they cannot manage the consequences if the risk materializes into losses, or if the people or groups taking on the risk are not the same ones who would be affected by the loss.

Accordingly, the development of a public risk management plan should be based on the identification, prioritization, and correction of practical obstacles to risk management. This chapter therefore presents a typology of these obstacles, as shown in diagram 2.1. It suggests a methodology to prioritize the obstacles that require public action, starting with "soft" options based on institutional arrangements, communication and information campaigns, and behavioral approaches, and then looking at costlier approaches such as providing public goods (like dikes and drainage systems).

Many crises that occur repeatedly could be prevented with existing means—but even simple "no brainer" actions can be challenging to implement.

Why aren't people better at managing their own risk?

Ideally, people, firms, and organizations would manage the risks that are within their own capacity. They are best placed to estimate which risks are worth taking (such as moving to the city to find better-paying jobs and better public services) and which ones are too costly if things go wrong. Yet they face many obstacles in their assessment of and preparation for risk.

People may lack information and resources

Financial constraints. Lack of income, assets, and resources often hinders risk management, especially for the most vulnerable in developing countries. Even though some options for risk management are cheap or even almost cost-free (driving safely), others can be expensive. People would prefer to live in earthquake-proof houses, but the construction costs may be too high. Even when a risk mitigation investment is cost-effective from an economic perspective, people or firms may find it difficult to finance because of large up-front costs and limited access to credit. Households that have limited resources and are therefore more vulnerable to risks and more severely affected by losses may face poverty traps. Because of this higher vulnerability, they cannot accumulate the necessary resources for protecting themselves from further losses in the future (see chapter 3). These

DIAGRAM 2.1 *Individuals, firms, and countries face many obstacles in managing risks*

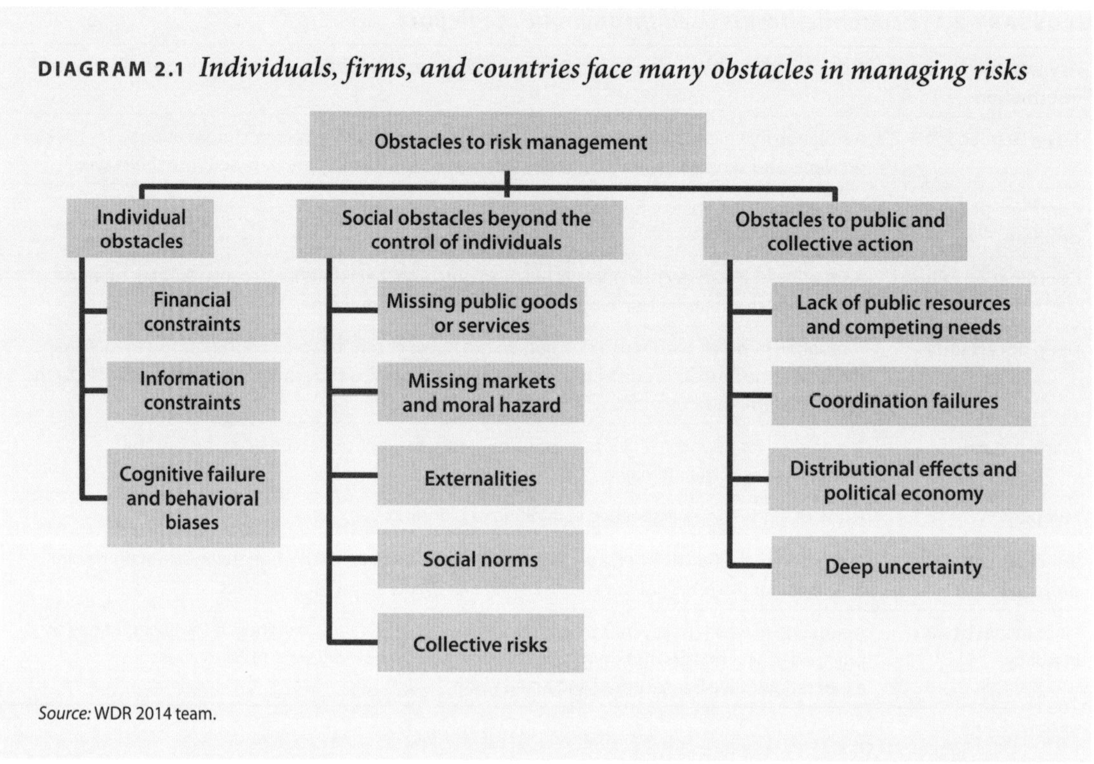

Source: WDR 2014 team.

effects may even occur at the macro level, when, for instance, immediate reconstruction needs after natural disasters crowd out longer-term development investment at the community or regional level.

Information constraints. Information may exist but may not be available to or known by the people who have to make risk-related decisions. For instance, only 31 percent of people living in areas prone to flooding in the United States were aware of this risk, and only 33 percent knew that federally backed flood insurance was available, a 2010 survey by the Federal Emergency Management Agency revealed.[3] Investors and banks may not have the knowledge to evaluate a loan application regarding innovative projects, leading them to reject profitable projects and thus constraining creative risk taking and innovation.[4]

Progress has been made in making information more widely available in many areas. New information and communication technologies help people access complex information from nearly anywhere on the planet. Data collection and access remain insufficient, however. Because information has aspects of a public good, it is underprovided by private actors; thus states have a large role in producing and disseminating it. Some countries have not made sufficient efforts in this direction, notably where data are not available for free—or not available at all. Hydrometeorological services, for example, often have to rely on revenues from the sale of data to strengthen and maintain their observation networks. As a result, the cost of one meteorological observation in Europe varies from zero (in Slovenia) to 0.40 euros (in Romania).[5] Costly data restrict access to valuable information and reduce the social benefits that are derived from them.[6]

People struggle to translate knowledge into action

Individual decision making in practice can veer quite a long way from the basic, idealized assumptions of economic theory, such as the "maximization of expected utility." To the extent this gap is linked to individual preferences and values, it is not a reason for public action. But part of the gap stems from the limited time and capacity people have to process information on risks and to decide which risk prevention measures they will implement. As a result, they sometimes make decisions that go against their own interests and preferences; this latter issue may justify public action.

A variety of studies shed light on just how inconsistent and incomplete people can be in their evaluation of risk (box 2.1). People are biased toward the status quo and tend to choose the default option. For

BOX 2.1 *The irrational, the uncertain, and the short-sighted: Some classic experiments reveal surprises about people's behavior*

A well-established economics concept known as expected utility theory holds that people try to maximize their expected gains. Yet in practice, when faced with risk and uncertainty, people behave differently, some classic experiments show. The first experiment reveals that people are very averse to uncertainty. They value a gain that is a "sure thing" more than one that is uncertain, beyond what would be predicted by the theory. In this experiment, individuals must choose between different lotteries, shown in table a. In the first choice, most people (65 percent) chose the first option. In the expected utility framework, this means that the benefit (or "utility," in economic terms) of winning $4,000 is larger than four-fifths (20 percent versus 25 percent) of the benefit of winning $3,000. But in the second choice, most people (80 percent) chose the "sure thing," even though in the expected utility framework this would mean that the benefit of winning $4,000 is *lower* than four-fifths of the benefit of winning $3,000 (80 percent versus 100 percent)—a direct contradiction of their first choice. This aversion to uncertainty—beyond what risk aversion in the expected utility theory would suggest—may be one reason behind the underinvestment in innovative projects and entrepreneurship, relative to other forms of more secure income.

The second experiment reveals that people are not able to process differences between small probabilities and so consider all low-probability events to be equally likely (table b). In the first choice, participants can select from two lotteries, each of which provides the same expected payoff. An overwhelming majority (86 percent) selected Lottery 2. This shows that, in general, people's decisions account not only for the expected outcomes but also for the associated probabilities. However, the second choice shows that they do not do so when probabilities are very small. As in the first choice, expected payoffs are the same for both lotteries, and the probability associated with the lower payoff is twice as high as for the higher payoff. In the second choice, however, the majority of participants opt for the choice with the higher payoff, rather than the choice with the higher winning probability. These results show that people treat high and low probabilities differently, which may explain why people are less likely to make investments to reduce the risk of low-probability events at the margin (such as investing to reduce the risk of a building collapse in an earthquake) or to make desirable trade-offs between different low-probability risks.

A third experiment shows how people's decisions depend on what they consider "the default situation." Again, people are asked to choose from two lotteries. This time, the chances of winning or losing are equivalent, but the amounts that can be won or lost differ. First, they are given $1,000 and must choose between definitely winning another $500 or having a 50 percent chance of winning another $1,000; 84 percent of the respondents select the sure outcome. Second, they are given $2,000 and they must choose between definitely losing $500 and having a 50 percent chance of losing $1,000; 68 percent of respondents select the latter lottery. Respondents react differently to the two choices, even though they are perfectly equivalent.

This experiment illustrates the role of the reference points. It also shows that individuals are often risk averse with gains and risk seekers for losses. Depending on whether the reference point is the best possible outcome (and the only possibility is a loss) or the worst possible outcome (and the only possibility is a gain), individuals will make different choices. Insurers have known for a long time that people are more likely to buy insurance if their reference point is the occurrence of a disaster.

a. People are averse to uncertainty in a way that contradicts expected utility theory

	First choice		Second choice	
Lottery properties	**Lottery 1**	**Lottery 2**	**Lottery 1**	**Lottery 2**
Lottery option	20% chance of winning $4,000, 80% chance of winning nothing	25% chance of winning $3,000, 75% chance of winning nothing	80% chance of winning $4,000, 20% chance of winning nothing	100% chance of winning $3,000
% of participants who choose the lottery	65	35	20	80

b. People treat high and low probabilities very differently

	First choice		Second choice	
Lottery properties	**Lottery 1**	**Lottery 2**	**Lottery 1**	**Lottery 2**
Lottery option	45% chance of winning $6,000, 55% chance of winning nothing	90% chance of winning $3,000, 10% chance of winning nothing	0.1% chance of winning $6,000, 99.9% chance of winning nothing	0.2% chance of winning $3,000, 99.8% chance of winning nothing
% of participants who choose the lottery	14	86	73	27

Source: WDR 2014 team based on Kahneman and Tversky 1979.

PHOTO 2.2 A preference for large voluntarily chosen risks compared with small externally imposed ones. People may take on large risks for their hobby (such as high-altitude mountaineering); however, they may find a much smaller risk to be unacceptable if it is imposed on them by others (such as the construction of a chemical plant in their neighborhood). © Gordon Wiltsie/National Geographic

example, the proportion of organ donors in countries where being a donor is the default choice (and people must opt out if they do not want to be donors) is nearly 60 percent higher than it is in countries where people must opt in to become donors.[7] People usually attribute a higher weight to rare events, but they also simply neglect the possibility that very rare ones will occur.[8] Individuals disregard the possibility of very bad futures, possibly because of the stress created in thinking about them.[9] There is also a difference in how people weight the individual risk they chose for themselves (when they drive, hike, or skydive) and the collective risks that are imposed upon them (when a chemical plant is built in their neighborhood): even if the benefits are similar, the level of risk is usually perceived to be higher when risks are imposed or when individuals feel they have little control over these risks (photo 2.2).[10] To account for this difference, the French government recommends that the cost-benefit analyses for investment in transport safety value one death avoided in public transport 50 percent higher than one death avoided in individual car accidents (1.5 million euros versus 1 million euros).[11]

People, including policy makers, make many decisions in the face of risk by using heuristics (rules of thumb) or by following social norms, instead of making deliberate calculations to identify the best option.[12] People use risks they consider similar to guide their decisions. That is why the "availability" of similar risks can explain why people care more about some risks and less about others. For example, because of their experience with the mad cow disease crisis, Europeans may be more concerned than Americans about nontraditional food production techniques, including genetically modified crops.[13] Education and communication campaigns and the provision of information in a form that individuals can easily process are thus key elements of a risk management strategy. That is why driving rules are learned not only in a theoretical setting but also through mandatory driving instruction, to the point where they become at least partially automatic.[14]

People are often overconfident about avoiding loss: they think they are able to drive safely under the influence of alcohol, and they think they can manage a flood and do not need to evacuate. They also have short memories about catastrophes, they discount the future too much and in inconsistent ways, and they fail to account for avoided losses that are not observable. After Hurricane Katrina hit New Orleans in 2005, the number of U.S. households with flood risk insurance increased more than three times more rapidly than observed in previous years. However, the average cancellation rate remained unchanged, at approximately 33 percent a year, suggesting a short effect of the disaster on household behavior.[15] A simulation-based study shows that the primary motivator of decisions to invest in protection is the size of losses already experienced, not losses that were avoided.[16] This tendency leads to a "paradox of protection": when protection against frequent events suppresses losses for an extended period of time, vigilance and risk awareness decrease. That leads to insufficient maintenance of protective measures and high investments in risky areas, resulting in future losses (and losses of increasing scale) if protections collapse or are overwhelmed by an exceptional event.[17] This lack of consistency in decision making is not unique to risk management; it also explains why individuals have so much trouble meeting their own objectives (such as a New Year's resolution to exercise more). It is why people often try to create irreversibility in their choices, by raising the cost of failing to reach their objectives (such as paying a high annual fee at a gym).[18] In many developing countries, this search for irreversibility also helps explain why people save "in kind." For instance, people protect their savings from capture not only by their extended family but also by themselves by slowly advancing the construction of a house each time resources become available, even though this practice is a very inefficient and risky way of saving.

These biases in behavior have consequences for the design of effective risk management policies. Excessive discounting of the future, short-sightedness (myopia), and the tendency to stick to the default option can, for example, explain insufficient saving where individuals are allowed to opt into a retirement saving scheme. The biases can also explain why flood insurance reaches large penetration only in countries where it is compulsory or during short periods of time following disasters. These biases can justify specific interventions, from tax incentives to compulsory enrollment in insurance or pension schemes. In this context, conditional cash transfer programs (for instance in Mexico and Brazil) have proven to be highly successful in helping individuals managing their health risks. By requiring compliance with certain behavior—such as adhering to a prescribed vaccination schedule for children—in order to receive a monthly cash transfer, such programs create a direct monetary incentive for taking socially and individually beneficial actions to reduce risk, such as medical treatments and checkups. Thus such programs can overcome the constraints discussed above (from resource and information constraints to behavioral biases and a tendency to postpone nonurgent medical checkups indefinitely); they thereby help reduce health risks for vulnerable individuals, their households, and their wider communities.

Obstacles beyond the control of individuals hamper their risk management

Missing public goods and markets, and even social norms, may prevent people from managing their own risk taking. Above and beyond individual risks, some risks are systemic and therefore cannot be managed without collective action.

Individuals must cope with market and government failures

Missing public goods and services. Public goods and services that provide an essential foundation for people's risk management are often missing. From the point of view of investors, for instance, risk can be managed only if contracts can be enforced, which requires the rule of law and an effective judiciary. Health insurance is of little use if poorly regulated health care providers are not competent or if the right medicine is not available. The low quality of road infrastructure is responsible for a fraction of the higher rates of traffic deaths observed in developing countries. In Poland, the number of crashes at "black spots," where accidents are frequent, decreased by 35 percent when danger signs were posted.[19]

Many risk-related decisions rely at least partially on basic infrastructure. The landfall of Hurricane Katrina in New Orleans in 2005 illustrates both the success of a road-traffic evacuation plan—the evacuation was quicker and smoother than previous ones for inhabitants who owned a car—and the failure to evacuate the population that relied on public transportation.[20] The lack of sanitation infrastructure is a major obstacle for individuals to manage their own health risks. For instance, in India open defecation and the absence of sanitary facilities in poor households have been shown to be a key reason for child stunting.[21] Stunting can have a significant impact on adult health, productivity, and economic prospects, and thus on development opportunities. Accordingly, as long as sanitation infrastructure is not provided, individual behavior changes and development programs such as child nutrition interventions are likely to have limited positive impacts. This example illustrates a general point: the importance of providing basic infrastructure as a basis for the success of further individual and collective risk management policies (photo 2.3)

Complicating matters, some people may be excluded from public services for risk management

PHOTO 2.3 Good infrastructure is needed for people to manage their risks. Thanks to a national project, people in Woukpokpoe, Benin, have gained access to safe, clean water, which enables them to manage health risks more effectively.

because of their gender, ethnicity, political affiliation, or lack of education or literacy. In Peru, for instance, legal proceedings are held only in Spanish, while many farmers speak only Quechua and Aymara, making it difficult for them to rely on the judiciary system to protect their rights and manage their risks.

Missing markets and the problem of moral hazard. Missing markets and instruments, such as insurance and hedging markets, are key obstacles to people's ability to manage risk. Even where instruments exist, they may be plagued by market failures. Insurers offer low-deductible (and higher-premium) policies to satisfy clients with high risk aversion. In Israel, however, it has been shown that "bad" drivers who have more accidents chose these policies more than average drivers. This is a classic case of adverse selection. The fact that people who are more vulnerable are likely to buy more insurance than individuals who are less vulnerable—and that insurers lack information about who is and is not more vulnerable, and thus cannot charge more to riskier customers—increases the cost of insurance for everyone, creates affordability issues, and limits the benefits from risk sharing.[22] The state may need to intervene to promote the creation of markets and instruments and to regulate them in a way that supports individuals in their management of risk.

Identifying risks is not enough: the obstacles to risk management must also be identified, prioritized, and addressed through private and public action.

Not all risks can be covered, however. Nonmonetary losses, such as health and psychological impacts or personal objects and photographs lost during floods or fires, can rarely be fully compensated. After the Bihar floods in India in 2008, for instance, the elderly suffered from depression more often than they did before the floods.[23] Even if all impacts could be compensated, doing so would remove all incentives for individuals and firms to mitigate risks themselves and would increase both adverse selection and moral hazard (the fact that insurance reduces the incentive for people to protect themselves against risks) and would therefore magnify losses.[24] It is thus rarely optimal to cover losses completely, which is why private insurers and public schemes (or mixes through public-private partnerships) always include a deductible that limits the amount of coverage.

Externalities. The actions of some actors may increase risks for others or reduce their incentives to manage their own risk. Overuse of antibiotics by some may make some harmful bacteria more resistant to treatment, threatening the health of all.[25] A firm that introduces a new chemical may create health risks to others, while reaping most of the financial benefit. Disasters cause indirect losses that create externalities.[26] In November 2012, for instance, Japanese automaker Honda cut the factory hours of its U.S. auto assembly workers in Ohio because it could not get parts from Thailand, affected at the time by large floods. Socially optimal risk management in one production unit (as in Thailand) should take into account these supply chain effects and the impact of interruptions in production on the ability of client factories to create value added. Such far-ranging consideration is not normally the case, however, leading to insufficient risk management. Cases like these highlight the need to design and implement public actions (like regulation) or collective action (like supply chain management) to ensure that individual incentives are aligned with collective objectives. The response to the 2011 earthquake and tsunami in Japan offers examples of such collective actions, with clients providing their suppliers free assistance to help them restore their production as quickly as possible.[27]

Social norms. Individual behavior regarding risk management is embedded in social norms, which can present obstacles to risk management—or facilitate it. For example, use of a face mask while sick prevents transmission of disease; in Asia, but not elsewhere, wearing a mask is a commonly followed social norm. By contrast, the "stigma of failure" is a social norm that works against innovation and entrepreneurship. To counter it, some governments and private institutions are rewarding innovation and risk taking, even when it fails: for instance, through the creation of prizes (such as India's Tata Group award of an annual prize for the best failed idea), or tax write-offs for research and development. Specific policy approaches may be necessary when lawmakers challenge a well-established social norm. In the United States, police at first opposed enforcing rape and domestic violence laws, until complementary measures changed social norms (such as "shaming penalties" for rape and portrayals of male violence against women as "cowardly" or "unmanly").[28] Changes in social norms can have many origins and channels. Lobbies and interest groups use communication campaigns to change perceptions about prevailing social norms. Marketing companies, seeking to maximize sales and revenues, use advertising campaigns to shape perceptions about products and services. Sometimes these campaigns come at the expense of risk management: for example, by encouraging eating and drinking habits that are detrimental to good health. In contrast, public health policies have had great successes in changing norms to improve hygiene and prevent diseases with sanitation or hand washing. Sometimes, changes in norms have unexpected drivers. *Telenovelas* (televised soap operas) in Brazil have had a large influence on fertility choices. The different life styles and ideals presented in the shows have influenced social norms, with a measurable impact on people's behaviors (photo 2.4).[29]

PHOTO 2.4 Changing social norms. *Telenovelas* in Latin America have changed social norms by exposing people to different lifestyles. © Globo Marcus

Some risks are collective by nature

Some risks are systemic—and therefore collective—by nature. Financial crises or economic slowdowns can be managed only at the country or even international level. When industrial policies are implemented to support a technology or a sector, a country takes a macroeconomic and fiscal risk that is socialized at the national level. If the technology or the sector fails, the loss is shared by all taxpayers. Furthermore, in an increasingly interconnected world, many risks, such as pandemics or financial crises, are now global. In all these cases, risk must be managed collectively, using public goods and services such as protective infrastructure, health care systems, financial regulations, and macroeconomic management. Many natural risks, especially in areas of geographically concentrated infrastructure and high density, also call for collective management. Because of various synergy effects, economic production and infrastructure tend to agglomerate geographically, often in at-risk zones such as coastal areas or river flood plains.[30] Moreover, protection infrastructure is "lumpy," meaning that it cannot be increased continuously and progressively—it often consists of a complex system (such as multiple rings of dikes and pumping stations) and it requires planning, is expensive with large up-front costs, and usually covers large areas. As a consequence, individuals or firms cannot provide hard protection to their houses or production facilities independently of what is put in place at the collective level. Thus managing natural risk is at least partly a collective issue.

In cases requiring collective action, the definition of the acceptable level of risk needs to be made at the social level, through a political process. Even though policy makers often claim that "disasters are unacceptable"—especially after a catastrophe—canceling all risks would be prohibitively costly. Thus a certain amount of risk must be accepted.[31] Defining an acceptable level of risk is difficult because of the complexity of some issues (box 2.2) and because preferences, values, and beliefs may differ widely. Some individuals are more risk averse than others and may prefer a more precautionary approach. Individuals use their "world views" as cognitive and emotional filters that influence how they perceive and act with respect to risky situations, and as a way of simplifying decision making. Working in a cultural theory setting, a study classified U.S. individuals according to three fundamental world views—"fatalist/hierarchical," "individualist," or "egalitarian"—and showed that these views largely explain people's preferences concerning many technological and environmental risks, such as nuclear energy, genetically modified crops, and climate change.[32]

Because factors that influence how people process information about risks are embedded in fundamental beliefs, judgments about these risks can differ markedly within a country and even more across countries. At the international level, strong disagree-

BOX 2.2 *Strengthening the interaction between experts and policy makers to improve risk management*

Many risk assessments are based on a classic risk matrix that represents the potential impact of an event on the horizontal axis and its likelihood (probability of occurrence) on the vertical axis. The risk can be considered "intolerable" if its likelihood and potential impact are too high; "acceptable" if both factors are low enough; or "tolerable," in the sense that it is not desirable to suppress it, but it nevertheless needs be managed or reduced (figure).

Scientists and other experts alone cannot define what risks are acceptable; they lack legitimacy to do so. Nor can policy makers by themselves define what risks are acceptable; they usually lack technical expertise. Thus closer and better interactions between science and policy are needed to codefine what is acceptable, tolerable, and intolerable.

Different countries have introduced different institutional systems to reach these definitions, in line with their political culture. Some countries (the United States) use what is referred to as an "adversarial" system, in which there is an open, procedure-based, and transparent confrontation of viewpoints, and the outcome is determined through a legal process. Other areas (parts of southern Europe) rely on a "patronage" system, in which a public entity is in charge of assessing risks, relying on in-house experts and processes, with little public scrutiny and participation. Finally, a "consensual" or "corporatist" approach is more common in northern Europe, based on closed-door negotiations between regulators and stakeholders, with little public control and the aim of creating compromise.

The adversarial system is better able to manage uncertainty and ensure accountability; however, this system is also very costly, may exclude some stakeholders, and is not able to benefit from collaboration and information exchanges between the regulator and the regulated private actors. In the U.S. system, for instance, regulation tends to occur only after the damage is done. Lawsuits for damages cost U.S. industry 1.9 percent of GDP ($180 billion) annually, in contrast to the United Kingdom, which has a more consensual system, and where liability costs industry less than 0.5 percent of GDP.[a]

Recent work suggests the existence of considerable flexibility in the type of risk regulations that can be implemented, regardless of the political and legal culture.[b] Regulatory instruments are disseminated and hybridized to make them appropriate for different country contexts, helping improve risk regulation globally.[c] In practice, most countries have tried to adapt risk regulation instruments to their cultural and institutional settings, in an effort to balance the cost and the transparency of their risk management institutions.

A risk matrix can be used to map hazards according to their probability and impact

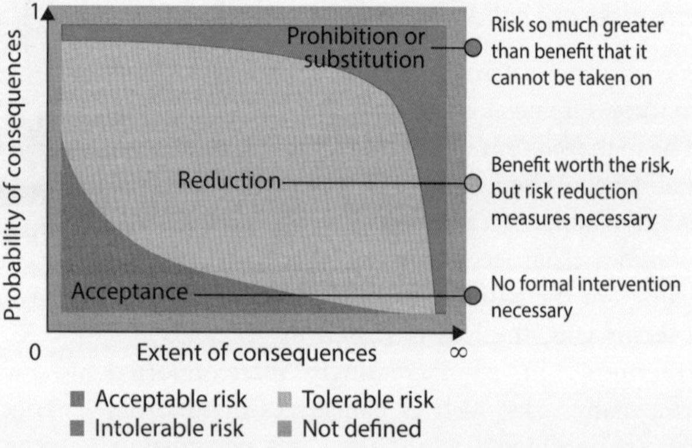

Source: WDR 2014 team adapted from Renn and Graham 2005.

Source: WDR 2014 team based on Renn and Graham 2005.

a. Loewenberg 2006.
b. De Francesco 2012.
c. Wiener 2013.

ments over acceptable levels of risk have led to trade disputes involving high-uncertainty risks such as beef hormones, mad cow disease, and genetically modified crops. An in-depth comparison of risk regulations in the United States and Europe highlights the role of cultures and world views on risk management practice, as well as the complexity of the matter, with European governments showing more risk aversion than the United States for some risks (beef hormones), but less for other risks (mad cow disease).[33] The difficulty in defining an acceptable level of risk in a given context means that prescriptive recommendations concerning risk management are very sensitive issues and need to be issued with caution.

Defining a social level of acceptable risk is also difficult because of differences in individual or collective sensitivity. Such differences are particularly important for health issues; some individuals are far more sensitive to pollutants than others, for instance. Investigating health effects of one type of air pollution (particulate matter), a study concluded that the most susceptible people (those in the 99.9th percentile) would feel negative effects at exposures only 0.2 to 0.7 percent of the level that would induce the same effects in people of median susceptibility.[34] In the presence of such heterogeneity, designing homogenous regulations is challenging and highly dependent on considerations of equity (especially when sensitivity is correlated with other social factors). The selected regulation is also unlikely to satisfy all individuals. The same problem exists at the international level. For instance, the international community committed to avoid "dangerous climate change" as long ago as 1992, through the United Nations Framework Convention on Climate Change. Countries have very different exposures and vulnerabilities to climate change, however, and thus have different views of what a "dangerous" change is, making it more difficult to reach an agreement on greenhouse gas emission reductions (see chapter 8).[35]

Why aren't states better at filling in the gaps?

Countries—or the international community—could do much to help people overcome obstacles to their management of risk, and these actions can be very cost-effective and supportive of development and poverty alleviation, as discussed in chapter 1. Correcting market failures and other social obstacles to realign the incentives of individuals with the goals of society is one of the main roles of governments and local authorities. Yet this help often does not happen, or it happens in a very imperfect way that can make risk management counterproductive or excessively costly. States face large obstacles themselves and have competing priorities that do not focus on managing risks and fostering resilience. First, decision makers and policy makers, as individuals, are susceptible to the biases that have been described earlier. For instance, they tend to have short memories and have a short-term bias, they tend to misestimate low probabilities, and they use rules of thumb and social norms instead of rigorous risk assessments to make many decisions. But obstacles to public action go beyond the obstacles to individual decision making, and include many other government failures.

Defining a government failure is difficult, however.[36] A government failure can be defined as a situation where the government does not operate in the public interest—that is, the interests of the taxpayers and the users of public services—but in the interests of "narrow interest groups who are able to exploit a privileged position for their own benefit."[37] This definition links government failure with capture by interest groups. Here, four broad categories of government failures are discussed. The first is linked to *insufficient resources and capacity* and to the involuntary implementation of government actions that are less desirable than what could be achieved. The second is related to *coordination failure* (within government or between public and private actors), including policy capture, such as a government that is manipulated by an interest group to introduce regulation that is detrimental at the social level. A third category is linked to *political economy issues* and voluntary decisions by the government to favor a subset of the population at the expense of the rest and for its own benefit (for example, a government provides protection to an industry in exchange for political support, or a regulation is captured by the regulator). A last category is linked to *uncertainty and the impossibility of identifying clear-cut solutions to a problem*—regardless of the capacity, resources, and goodwill of the government—because of lack of knowledge concerning the appropriate course of action; this situation is referred to as deep uncertainty and is discussed further later in this chapter.

Lack of resources and technical capacity hampers public policy

Resource and capacity constraints to pursue risk management can be a serious barrier to public action. The expensive disaster risk preventions that have been implemented in developed countries (such as flood protections in the Netherlands) are out of reach for many similarly threatened developing countries (such as the Arab Republic of Egypt, Bangladesh, or Vietnam). This gap is largely the result of financial constraints, including the lack of financial instruments appropriate for long-term investments with large social returns but limited cost recovery.[38] But it is also connected to the existence of many competing needs in developing countries, from health and education to infrastructure development. In addition, technical capacity is often lacking in developing countries, particularly so in countries where the public sector has well-identified difficulties in retaining its talented and skilled workers. The competencies needed to analyze risks and identify relevant management actions may thus be inaccessible even for governments willing to act.

Lack of resources may weaken institutions and impede enforcement of rules, which in turn may lead to poorly designed or implemented risk management policies. For example, the inability of government to enforce property rights and land titles has a negative impact on risk management: households with precarious tenure risk eviction and are unlikely to invest in risk-mitigating investments such as flood-proofing and earthquake-proofing their houses. They are also unable to use their home as collateral to obtain credit to finance such investments. Corruption often thrives amid weak institutions and is an obstacle to public risk management: for instance, when contractors do not respect building norms for public buildings in earthquake-prone cities. As illustrated in chapter 4, community-based solutions can help in instances when governments and local authorities are unable or unwilling to manage risks. Where school construction does not respect building norms because local authorities are unable to enforce them, the involvement of the community—and the parents who will send their children to the school—may be a solution. In situations where enforcement and compliance are weak, more effective enforcement of existing building norms can potentially have significant benefits. For instance, insurance experts estimate that insured losses in the United States from Hurricane Andrew in 1992 could have been reduced by 25 percent if building norms had been fully enforced.[39]

Lack of resources not only influences what can be achieved but also the type of solutions and measures that are desirable. For risk management, as for other productive investments, the "best" technology depends on the relative scarcity of production factors. In developing countries where capital and skilled labor are scarce and unskilled labor is underused, risk management solutions will necessarily be different from those selected by more developed countries where capital is cheap and labor is expensive. In particular, risk management strategies are likely to be based more on hard infrastructure (large dike systems) in higher-income countries. The appropriate risk management actions also depend on institutional and enforcement capacity. Where enforcement capacity is limited, strengthening building norms may worsen the situation. Increasing compliance costs can increase the number of noncompliant, high-vulnerability buildings, with an impact on aggregate risk larger than the risk reduction from more-resistant, compliant buildings.

Coordination failures impair risk management

Coordination failures between different state agencies may also hinder risk management. Horizontal coordination is needed to ensure that actions from different ministries are consistent and synergetic. For instance, the ministry of finance may create and regulate a health care insurance system, but the usefulness of the insurance will depend on the availability of competent health care providers, a responsibility of the health ministry. Vertical coordination is also crucial because risk management must be shared across different levels (from the neighborhood to the country and the global communities). A public-private insurance scheme (regulated by the ministry of finance at the national level) cannot be designed independently of the implementation of risk reduction measures such as land use plans and building norms at the local level (a task often led by local authorities). In the absence of cross-scale regulations, a "public moral hazard" may emerge, if local authorities rely on national support in case of disasters, reducing the incentive to implement preventive actions.[40]

Coordination is also required between public and private actors. The impact of a flood is highly dependent on the ability of private actors to reallocate resources and the ability of utilities and transport companies to restore basic services. The impact of epidemics is dependent on the ability of companies and organizations to maintain operations with a reduced workforce. In sectors where states often rely on private sector expertise (cyberattacks, finance), public-private cooperation is a critical ingredient in the design of a strategy. Such cooperation is often difficult to establish because of differences in culture and work habits, issues related to privacy and commercial secrecy, risks of capture and rent-seeking behaviors from private actors, and lack of incentives on both sides. The recent financial crisis illustrates the difficulty regulators face in determining the best course of action when their main advisers—professionals from the financial sector—have a large stake in the decision (see chapter 6).

To promote and improve coordination, multiple stakeholders need to be involved in decision-making processes for risk assessment and implementation (box 2.3). Stakeholder involvement is useful not only to disseminate information and increase the acceptability of risk management policies; it is also a means of enhancing the technical quality of the analysis and ensuring that risk management strategies are reasonable and well developed.[41] A collective approach allows the transfer of risks to the actors that are best able to manage them—for instance, because of their access to knowledge and resources. In the management of natural disaster risks, for example, a set of promising initiatives has been implemented to improve coordination, based on the creation of multiministry bodies in charge of information exchange and coordination. The responsibility for risk management is located in the highest office (the prime minister's or president's office) in about 25 percent of the countries and in a central planning or coordination unit in 10 percent of them.[42] In Peru, the responsibility for disaster risk management resides in a new agency within the president's office and is therefore able to coordinate across ministries. The time and resources consumed by coordination actions should not be underestimated, however, and the cost of doing so may be important in countries where

BOX 2.3 *Institutions to improve risk management: National risk assessments*

National risk assessments (NRAs) to improve policy related to preventing and planning for crises and emergencies have been conducted in the United Kingdom and in the Netherlands since 2005 and 2007, respectively.[a] In both countries, NRAs are used to assess the main risks faced by the country, regardless of the type and origin of risk (natural, technological, terrorist, other). They are based on similar approaches: identifying risks, generating scenarios, assessing the probability or plausibility and impacts of the risks, and constructing a national risk matrix. The matrix in the figure summarizes the main risks and organizes them according to their likelihood (x-axis) and severity of impact (y-axis).

Several major benefits emerge from conducting such an assessment. First, it helps with coordination and cooperation across ministries and organizations, thus avoiding "silo" effects. Ministries in charge of one risk (for instance, the ministry of health, for epidemics) have found that the NRA helped them mobilize other ministries to provide information and design their own response plan (for example, the ministry of education needs to set up a response plan to cover the event of many teachers becoming sick). Second, it anticipates trade-offs, helping to avoid conflicts between stakeholders during a crisis. In the Netherlands, that is the case during floods, when several regions compete for access to limited resources needed for emergency management. Third, it helps involve new actors. The private sector has a key role in risk and crisis management, and NRAs have been used to involve them in the development of risk management strategies. Finally, an NRA influences the distribution of resources dedicated to managing different risks.

Following a similar approach, the government of Morocco is considering a multirisk approach. With the support of the World Bank and the Global Facility for Disaster Reduction and Recovery, Morocco has conducted risk assessments in three key areas: natural disaster risk, volatility in commodity prices, and risks in the agricultural sector. The country is seeking to adopt an explicitly integrated approach to assessing its key risks and is now beginning to develop options on how best to mitigate the identified risks, including through developing a national risk management strategy and supporting institutions.

The United Kingdom has adopted a comprehensive risk management framework

Overall relative impact score	Between 1 in 20,000 and 1 in 2,000	Between 1 in 2,000 and 1 in 200	Between 1 in 200 and 1 in 20	Between 1 in 20 and 1 in 2	Greater than 1 in 2
5				Pandemic influenza	
4			Coastal flooding Effusive volcanic eruption		
3	Major industrial accidents	Major transport accidents	Other infectious diseases Inland flooding	Severe space weather Low temperatures and heavy snow Heatwaves	
2			Zoonotic animal diseases Drought	Explosive volcanic eruption Storms and gales Public disorder	
1			Non-zoonotic animal diseases	Disruptive industrial action	

Relative likelihood of occurring in the next five years

Source: Cabinet Office 2012.

Source: WDR team based on Vastveit 2011.

a. Ministry of the Interior and Kingdom Relations 2009; Cabinet Office 2012.

public resources are scarce. That is particularly the case where the public sector struggles to attract skilled and motivated workers.

Political economy problems hinder risk management

Political economy obstacles. Even when resources are available, politicians may be reluctant to devote them to risk management because the costs of risk management are immediate, concentrated, and observable, while the benefits are longer term, distributed more broadly, and often less visible. When regulating the use of new chemicals or the development of a new area, for instance, public decision makers have a strong and immediate influence on the revenues of one or a few firms (when regulating chemicals) or on the value of people's assets (landowners).[43] Affected firms and people will naturally tend to oppose any constraint and be very vocal about it. On the other hand, the people protected by the regulation—people negatively affected by pollution or future buyers of apartments in the newly developed areas—are often not aware that the regulation may eventually protect them and therefore rarely support it. Even more complicated are cases such as climate change, where beneficiaries are not born yet, because the benefit from risk management extends over the very long term (see chapter 8).

The existence of dispersed interests is a classic issue in institution building and is responsible for many government failures, especially when public goods are concerned.[44] Policy trade-offs are often determined by the ability of various interests to organize themselves: for instance, through lobbying organizations. Evidence shows that increasing transparency and providing a voice to dispersed interests help avoid capture by interest groups and improve policy decisions.[45] These political issues have beset many well-known efforts to control risks, such as those relating to asbestos, lead paint, and tobacco. These cases show that powerful lobbies can block health regulation even in the presence of well-established scientific evidence of negative health impacts. They also demonstrate that nongovernmental organizations, scientific organizations, and citizen associations play a key role in bringing these issues to the public and creating broad support for regulating these risks.[46] Risk management is thus more likely to be efficient where strong civil society organizations are able to conduct independent risk audits and assessments and to communicate their results to the wider public. To make these possible, however, the government should ensure free access to data; free dissemination of results through media, the Internet, and social networks; and some legal protection for whistleblowers. Many countries provide protection for individuals who report alleged dishonest or illegal activities that have been occurring in a government department or private company or organization (in the United States, the first whistleblower law was passed in 1863). Recent progress in this direction has been achieved by many countries, including Jamaica and India.

Lack of well-accepted indicators for risk. The lack of well-accepted indicators for risk makes it difficult to measure the performance of decision makers and to hold them accountable for their risk management choices. Controlling and coordinating the delivery of public services is difficult when the potential for competition in quasi-markets—that is, markets created and organized by the government to create competition among public service providers—is limited and when the quality of the service is not easily observable.[47] Health care is a common illustration of this problem: service quality is not directly observable, and results can evolve over the long term and are always very uncertain. Risk management is no different: while forgone profits and lost jobs from a chemical firm can be measured and published, the reduction in risk from banning some potentially carcinogenic product cannot be easily measured. In general, the fact that disaster relief is immediate and pertinent while prevention is less visible and more difficult to measure makes it impossible to enforce the accountability of decision makers, leading to biased spending decisions toward less cost-effective ex post action.

The long horizon of risk management actions and the lack of indicators mean that it is also difficult to use competition to control public risk management. In theory, competition across localities should be an incentive to risk management: localities often rely on local taxes on economic activity, and the risk level can be a determining factor for a private actor who wants to invest in one locality or another. But the risk level is often not directly observable, and decades can pass before a good risk management action translates into a lower risk level. Competition can thus hardly be used to discriminate between good and bad risk management. In such a context, regulatory approaches have high potential.[48] One promising option is the creation of national risk boards in charge of conducting risk assessments and assessing the quality of risk management of various agencies and organizations (including local authorities and their land use plans) through risk audits and benchmarking (see box 2.3; see also the "Focus on policy reform" at the end of this Report). Risk assessments could be used to create indicators that would help populations reward risk-sensitive policy making; they would also trigger risk-based competition across agencies and localities to encourage good risk management. National risk boards could also help with vertical coordination issues, by mitigating the public moral hazard created by the national support to affected subnational entities.

Preference for one policy in advance but another when the time comes to implement it (time inconsistency). Sometimes after a shock or crisis, a government will have an interest in acting in a way that contradicts its commitments before the event. To cite a recent and major example: to avoid excessive risk taking in the financial sector, the government may promise not to bail out bankrupt financial institutions; but if a large financial institution does go bankrupt, the government will have an interest in bailing it out, regardless of its previous commitments. These incentives reduce the credibility of the entire strategy and create a strong moral hazard issue. These problems are amplified by the lag between the short period of many political mandates and the longer period needed for risk management results to be observable. Disaster relief can even be used opportunistically, by being distributed close to an election or targeted to areas that vote for the ruling party.[49]

Under deep uncertainty, policies need to be robust in a large range of possible scenarios, and able to be revised as future circumstances warrant.

Distributional problems. All risk management policies redistribute wealth and power; at their worst, they can harm the poorest and the most vulnerable, raising important equity concerns. For instance, increasing building construction costs to improve earthquake and flood resilience may make it even more difficult for inhabitants of informal settlements to obtain decent housing. In Jakarta, flood- and earthquake-proofing a typical home costs $3,100, on average, only slightly less than the annual per capita GDP in Indonesia.[50] Even excise taxes on cigarettes, an efficient tool to prevent young people from starting smoking and protect them from addiction, have been criticized for their cost to the poor.[51] Complementary policies may be needed to mitigate these negative effects, and the risk management policy mix may need to include redistributive measures to be accepted by a majority and not harm the poorest.[52]

In this context, conditional cash transfers have proven to be able to deliver both distributional benefits to the poor, as well as positive impacts in terms of risk management. The Bolsa Família Program in Brazil, for instance, has not only been a main driver for significantly reducing inequality and extreme poverty in recent years but has also improved individual risk management. The underlying idea of the program is to provide poor households with monthly cash transfers that are conditioned on compliance with certain risk management behaviors, such as completing health check-ups, monitoring growth of children, or pursuing adequate care for pregnant women. The program has been able to achieve compliance rates for these health conditionalities of close to 100 percent, thereby significantly improving the management of health risks of 11 million poor households.

Uncertainty is sometimes severe

Sometimes, information about how to manage risks does not exist, and decisions involve a condition known as deep uncertainty. These cases occur when experts cannot agree on which models to use (disagreement on how to transfer the results of analyses of the health impact on animals to human beings, for example); on the probability distributions of key uncertain parameters (the probability of a long period without economic growth); or on the values of alternative outcomes (the acceptability of a total loss of the Amazon forest in the event of significant climate change).[53] In such cases, it may be impossible to define a probability for alternative outcomes, or even to identify the set of possible futures (including highly improbable events—like the famous "black swan").[54] Or it can be impossible to reconcile different views through a common estimation of probabilities of different outcomes. A situation of deep uncertainty is different from a situation of "large uncertainty," in which different actors can agree on the probabilities and values of different outcomes, even if the range of possible outcomes is very broad because knowledge is limited. In situations of deep uncertainty, different stakeholders or experts can have divergent opinions and may not even agree on the existence of large uncertainty. These situations lead to gridlock and lack of consensus, strong political opposition to any action, and therefore to paralysis. They are particularly difficult to manage when large and irreversible damages are possible, when decisions cannot be postponed until more information is available, and when policy or technical options are "brittle": that is, very sensitive to small errors in design.

To further complicate matters, uncertainty surrounds not only the risk itself, but also the risk management measures that are implemented and their efficiency and side effects. In practice, anticipating all consequences of risk management policies is impossible, and some policies may have unacceptable side effects or create other risks. The Koka reservoir in Ethiopia illustrates this problem: it was built to store water for agriculture and improve food security, but its impact on the mosquito population and thus on health was not anticipated: as a result, malaria case rates within three kilometers of the reservoirs are 2.3 times as great as for those living six to nine kilometers from the reservoir.[55] Around micro-dams, malaria prevalence is as much as 7 times greater than in the rest of Ethiopia.[56] Such side effects cannot always be avoided and need to be monitored and managed.[57]

Uncertainty is especially deep in "emerging risks" or in areas where scientific uncertainty is the greatest (genetically modified crops, hydropower dams, nuclear energy, climate change). A common example is the uncertainty about future changes in local climates. Different scientific teams develop simulations of climate systems that differ in their technical implementations, but these climate models are based on the same widely accepted laws of physics. And while these models agree on the large patterns of climate change, they can point in opposite directions at the local scale and for some parameters. For example, depending on the model, rainfall in West Africa could increase or decrease by 25 percent by the end of this century (map 2.2). Such uncertainty is clearly an obstacle to the design of water infrastructure able to deal with floods and droughts in the region. The experts' ability to forecast future energy demand has also been disappointing,[58] and few anticipated the rapid technological developments that have occurred in medicine, energy, or information and communications technology.

There are many other examples of cases where experts cannot agree on the assumptions that lie at the heart of their analysis, and thus reach results that cannot be reconciled (a situation labeled "dueling certitudes" by economist Charles Manski). These examples include the evaluation of the fiscal consequences of health care reforms—with large uncertainties concerning how medical practice will evolve—and the impact of various policies to reduce cocaine consumption.[59] In these cases, different stakeholders can rarely come to agreement on the "most likely" future on which planning should be based, or on the "most likely" consequences of a given action. Moreover, doing so would be dangerous if future risks and events deviate from this most likely case.

A special case of deep uncertainty that can paralyze action is regulatory and policy uncertainty (see chapter 5). Firms working on renewable energy tech-

MAP 2.2 ***Deeply uncertain futures: Different climate models project very different changes for precipitation in Africa***

CCSM3

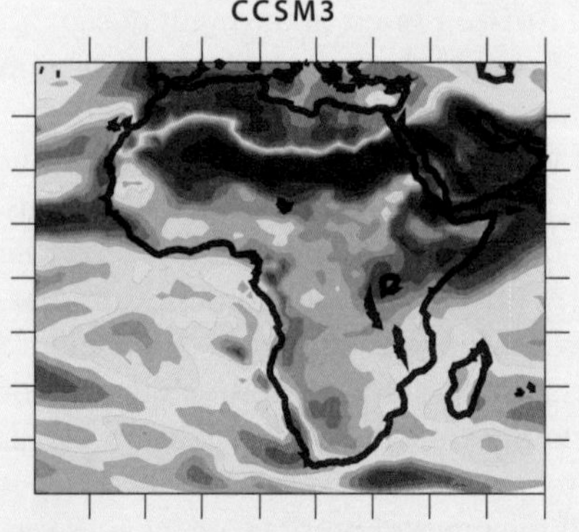

GFDL-CM2.0

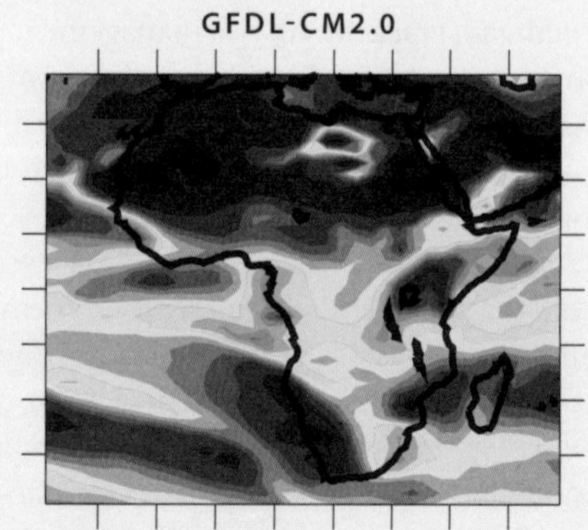

Source: IPCC (Intergovernmental Panel on Climate Change) 2007.

Note: The maps show simulations from two different climate models. The brown areas indicate decreases in annual precipitation. The green areas indicate increases in annual precipitation.

nologies, for instance, are dependent on environmental regulations and policy-determined carbon prices. They are highly vulnerable to policy reversals, and this uncertainty is a major obstacle to taking risk and innovating.[60]

In situations of deep or large uncertainty, many traditional methods for decision making under uncertainty are difficult to apply. And many well-identified biases toward overconfidence and against the provision of estimates of uncertainty become particularly dangerous.[61] Alternative tools are useful for communicating the presence and degree of uncertainty and for finding compromises, more consensual solutions, and options that are less brittle and more acceptable for stakeholders with different beliefs and values. In these cases, it is preferable to implement adaptive and robust policies that lead to acceptable outcomes in a large range of scenarios and that can be revised when new information is available or when the context changes.[62]

Many methodologies have been proposed for designing such policies, and the best approach depends on the context.[63] "Robust decision making" is one of these methodologies. The iterative process, by which multiple stakeholders can identify vulnerabilities and options to reduce them, and then implement them with appropriate monitoring and revision using new knowledge, is shown in diagram 2.2. Its advantage is that all actors do not have to agree on what is the most likely future and on the value of different possible outcomes before a decision is discussed. Moreover, it helps identify the uncertainties that do *not* matter for a given decision, thus focusing the process on what is most important (box 2.4). This approach also explicitly recognizes that different actors have different values and beliefs, and it makes the influence of these values on the decision much more apparent than with other methods (such as the cost-benefit analysis, in which values and preferences are captured in complex valuation techniques). As a result, it helps create a dialogue among stakeholders and facilitates reaching an agreement on solutions that are more widely acceptable.

Above all, decision makers should avoid plans that are designed for the most likely outcomes but that increase the vulnerability to less likely events. Huge dikes built to guard against tsunamis and typhoon storm surges may encourage investment in coastal areas and increase vulnerability to exceptional events that exceed the design level of the dikes.[64] Taking into account extreme cases requires defining a set of scenarios—including low-probability, high-impact ones—and evaluating the robustness of plans

DIAGRAM 2.2 ***An iterative process of decision making to prompt robust action in the face of uncertainty***

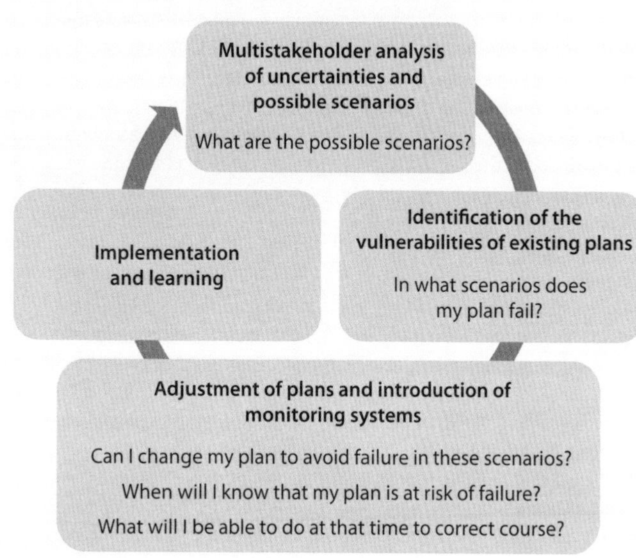

Source: WDR 2014 team.

and projects in these cases. Often low- or zero-cost options that reduce vulnerability in these extreme scenarios can be identified and implemented. For example, an early warning system is useful even when all floods are supposed to be prevented by hard protections.

A balance needs to be struck between the plausibility of scenarios and the need to explore the range of possible, if uncertain, events. This balance is difficult to define (as illustrated by applications of the precautionary principle, discussed in box 2.5). Decision makers have a tendency to be too conservative in their assessment of what is possible and plausible. The U.K. national risk assessment deals with this issue through the use of "reasonable worst-case scenarios," but there is no objective way of designing such scenarios, and subjective judgment will always be necessary. This subjectivity implies that the development and selection of scenarios must be done by policy makers working closely with experts (see box 2.2).

Putting it all together: A policy sequence

Diagram 2.3 presents a set of screens that aid in analyzing a risk in a given context, starting from the assessment of risk itself. But designing effective public policy must go beyond risk assessment, to analyze

BOX 2.4 *Applying a robust decision-making methodology to deal with the risk of flooding in Ho Chi Minh City*

Ho Chi Minh City, a low-lying and fast-growing metropolis of 7.4 million people, faces significant and growing flood risk. The city's planners are seeking to implement an integrated flood risk management strategy. However, many factors that would affect their choice of strategy are deeply uncertain, such as future population, economic growth, and the effects of climate change on rainfall and the sea level. In partnership with Ho Chi Minh City's Steering Center for Flood Control, researchers undertook a demonstration project to analyze how robust decision making (RDM) could improve flood management, using the Nhieu Loc-Thi Nghe canal catchment area as a case study. The analysis explored 12 different risk management portfolios, each consisting of combinations of options such as raising homes and retreating from low-lying areas. Each portfolio was simulated in 1,000 scenarios, where each scenario consisted of up to six different assumptions about socioeconomic development and climate change in the future.

The RDM analysis found that the current infrastructure plan reduces risk in best-estimate future conditions. Moreover, this plan is robust to a wide range of possible future population and economic trends; the uncertainty surrounding these aspects is therefore not a problem for designing a flood protection system. However, the current plan may not be sufficiently robust to plausible impacts from climate change. Relying exclusively on the currently planned infrastructure ("baseline") would keep risk below recent levels only if rainfall intensities increase by no more than approximately 5 percent and if the Saigon River rises less than 45 centimeters (figure). Various scientific estimates suggest that both these thresholds may be exceeded by mid-century. The RDM analysis considered additional measures to ensure risk reduction for increases in rainfall intensity of up to 35 percent and increases in the level of the Saigon River of up to 100 centimeters. The cost of these measures could be reduced if the city implements an adaptive plan, which adds some measures now and more in the future if needed. The results of the RDM analysis allow policy makers to evaluate robustness gains of certain strategies, and consider the associated trade-offs against their risk preferences and available budgets. Overall, the findings suggest that these additional actions would significantly improve the robustness of Ho Chi Minh City's risk management plans.

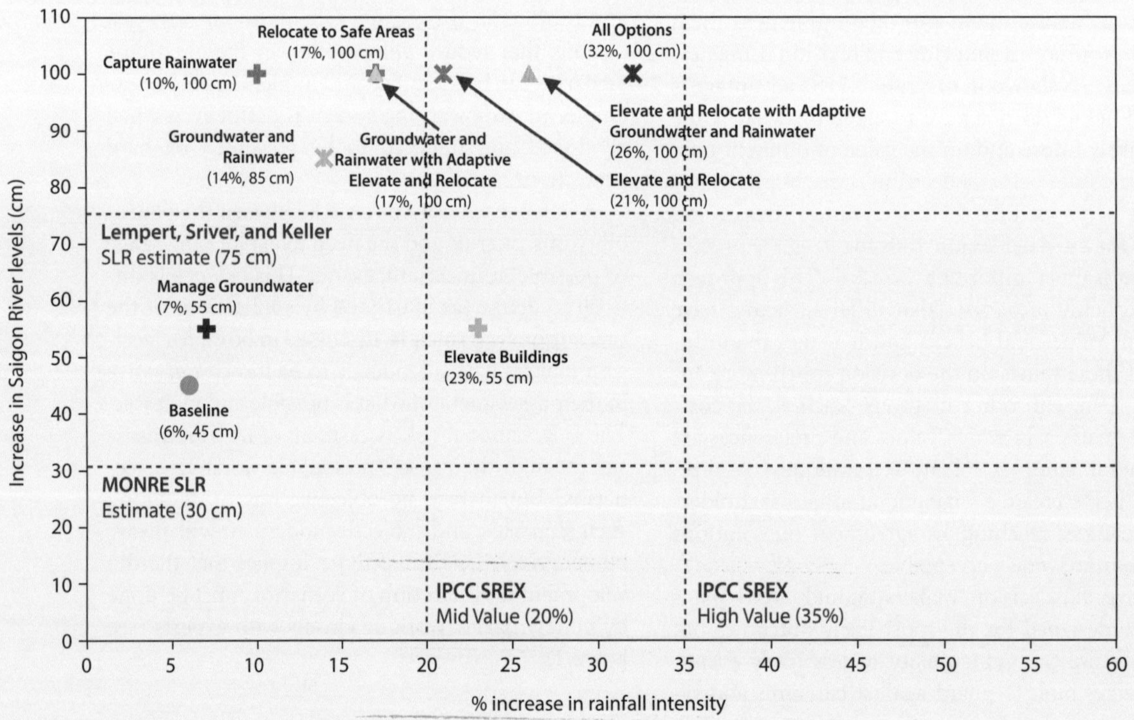

Source: WDR 2014 team based on Lempert and others 2013.

Note: Different estimates of potential rainfall and river levels in the figure are indicated by the blue dashed lines. MONRE = Ministry of Natural Resources and the Environment (Vietnam). SLR = sea level rise. SREX = IPCC special report (IPPC 2012).

BOX 2.5 *Precaution in the face of risk: Striking a balance between costs and benefits with the precautionary principle*

Precaution in the face of risk has been formalized in many countries in the form of a "precautionary principle." Three versions of the principle, in increasing level of stringency, have been identified by Wiener and Rogers:

- "Uncertainty does not justify inaction" (it is possible to regulate without full scientific certainty).
- "Uncertainty does justify action" (regulations are required when there is a possibility of danger).
- "Uncertainty requires shifting the burden and standard of proof" (potentially risky activities are prohibited until the proponent of the activity can prove it poses no risks or acceptable risks).

Implementation of the precautionary principle may be either explicit or implicit. German laws have mentioned the *Vorsorgeprinzip* since the 1970s, and France introduced the precautionary principle in its national constitution in 2005. In the United States, the concept of "precautionary actions" is regularly mentioned in court decisions and in laws and regulations. For instance, the Environmental Protection Agency banned leaded gasoline in the 1970s, when the benefits of doing so were still unclear; this measure is now known to be cost-effective and responsible for decreasing the number of children with lead-related learning deficits in the United States. But the United States has not adopted an overarching precautionary principle for all regulation; since the late 1970s, every U.S. president has instead required impact assessments of the benefits and costs of regulation. The precautionary principle is recognized at the international level: for instance, by the 1992 declaration of the United Nations Conference on Environment and Development.

The European Union (EU) seems to be following the first version of the principle in some areas. The Maastricht treaty (1992) states that EU policy on the environment "shall be based on the precautionary principle" (Art 130R). A communication from the European Commission published in 2000 states the following: "Where there are threats of serious or irreversible damage, lack of full scientific certainty shall not be used as a reason for postponing cost-effective measures to prevent environmental degradation." The communication provides implementation guidance, designed to ensure that the precautionary principle does not lead to paralysis or self-contradiction: the measures it recommends are supposed to be *temporary* (and to include a plan to collect the information needed to conduct a more classical risk analysis); *proportional* (the threat must be "serious" and the measures "cost-effective"); based on *significant evidence* of the existence of a risk ("full certainty" is not necessary, but the threat needs to be credible); and based on an *assessment* of benefits and costs.

Putting the precautionary principle into practice has been difficult in some cases. Precaution can prevent some risks but can also pose new risks as well as economic costs. Debates over the precautionary principle have been heated at times (such as when critics perceive high costs, low risks, or disguised trade protectionism). But the reality of actual application in policy making has been quite diverse, within the United States and the European Union and elsewhere, suggesting that concerns about costs and risks are shaping real policy choices. These issues also suggest that more learning, and an iterative process, are needed about how to apply and put into operation a precautionary approach, especially in lower-income environments.

Source: WDR 2014 team based on Charnley and Rogers 2011; European Commission 2000; Wiener and Rogers 2002; Wiener and others 2011.

the obstacles to risk management that are described in diagram 2.1 and discussed earlier. A sequence that policy makers might consider in conducting a risk management analysis follows:

1. Individuals and firms may fail to manage risks because decision makers (private or public) face incentives that are distorted toward too much or too little risk taking. These situations need to be identified and corrected as a priority, since other measures are unlikely to be effective in the presence of bad incentives.
2. If incentives are correct, then providing good information is critical to improving the quality of decisions.
3. Sometimes, correct incentives and good information are unable to trigger a change in behavior. Specific measures are required to correct cognitive failures and behavioral biases.
4. Stakeholders may be willing to improve their risk management, but may be unable to do so because they lack resources. In this case, the provision of additional resources—directly or indirectly—would help.

This sequence is only an example: in practice, the second, third, or fourth of these considerations could happen first or at the same time as the others. However, applying these screens in that order can help identify critical gaps that need to be addressed first and reveal early in the process relatively low-cost interventions that are highly effective (such as correcting incentives through market instruments or better coordination).

In theory, these measures to correct incentives should pay for themselves over time, since they correct externalities and market and government failures. But in the short run, costs may be high, and over time, there may be tough trade-offs, large dis-

DIAGRAM 2.3 *A set of screens for assessing obstacles to risk management, and formulating policy responses*

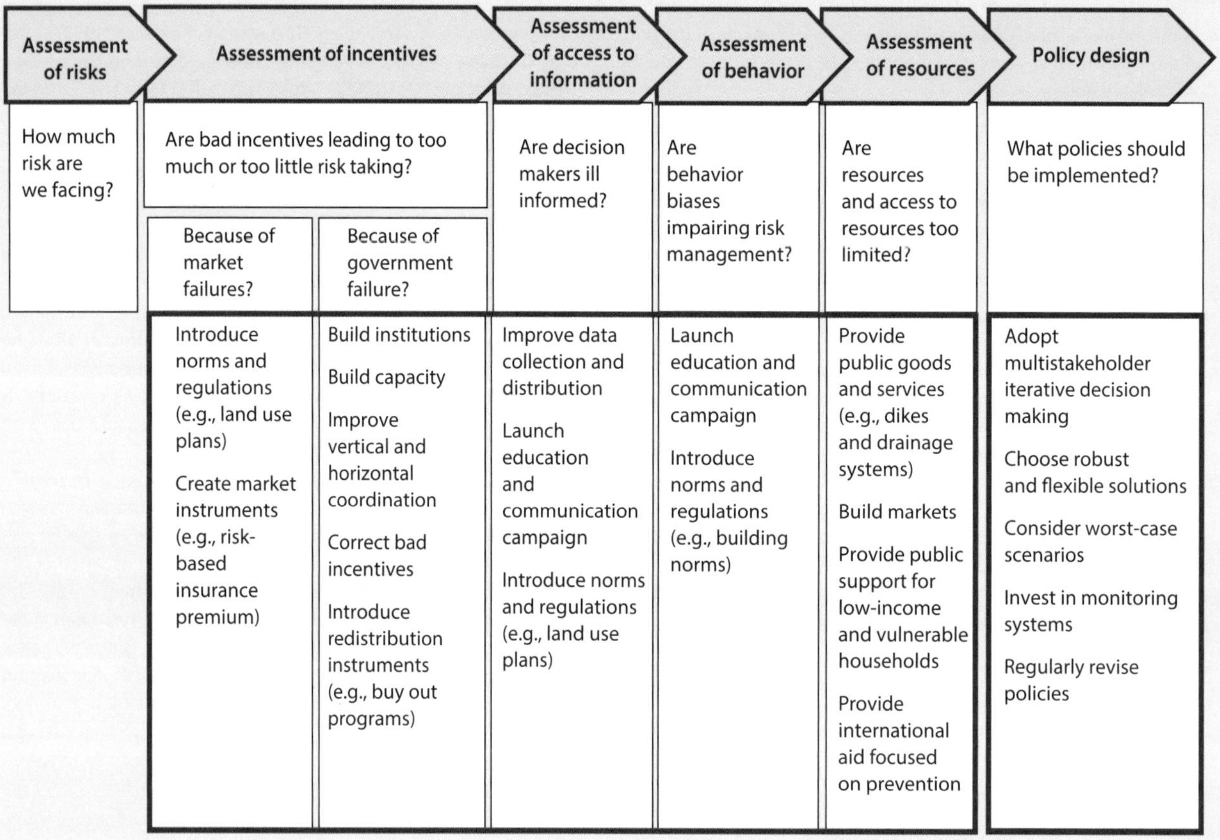

Assessment of risks	Assessment of incentives		Assessment of access to information	Assessment of behavior	Assessment of resources	Policy design
How much risk are we facing?	Are bad incentives leading to too much or too little risk taking?		Are decision makers ill informed?	Are behavior biases impairing risk management?	Are resources and access to resources too limited?	What policies should be implemented?
	Because of market failures?	Because of government failure?				
	Introduce norms and regulations (e.g., land use plans) Create market instruments (e.g., risk-based insurance premium)	Build institutions Build capacity Improve vertical and horizontal coordination Correct bad incentives Introduce redistribution instruments (e.g., buy out programs)	Improve data collection and distribution Launch education and communication campaign Introduce norms and regulations (e.g., land use plans)	Launch education and communication campaign Introduce norms and regulations (e.g., building norms)	Provide public goods and services (e.g., dikes and drainage systems) Build markets Provide public support for low-income and vulnerable households Provide international aid focused on prevention	Adopt multistakeholder iterative decision making Choose robust and flexible solutions Consider worst-case scenarios Invest in monitoring systems Regularly revise policies

Source: WDR 2014 team.

tributive impacts, or high political costs (when some actors oppose the measure). A low or negative aggregate cost does not mean that a policy is easy to implement. Complementary measures may be needed to cope with political obstacles or with negative side effects over the short term.[65] Other measures will be more costly (such as direct investment in building dikes), and they can be considered at a later stage.

A way past the obstacles: Choosing policy priorities

How can policy makers build a strong foundation for improved risk management over time? Given the obstacles they face, they must make hard choices. They must be practical in these choices. Their choices sometimes must be second-best: less than ideal, and more limited than desired.

In making those choices, policy makers should choose steps that can be taken now but allow for improvements later. This practical approach leads to specific priorities, building on the five policy principles discussed at the end of chapter 1.

Be realistic

Keep it simple. Simple risk management instruments should be preferred when capacity is low, even though they may be less efficient in theory. Simple regulations, for instance, may be easier to enforce than sophisticated (and theoretically more efficient) approaches based on market instruments. An example is car insurance in South Africa, where a fuel tax helps pay for third-party insurance for motor vehicles. Such an approach provides a simple and efficient way of compensating accident victims in a weak institutional environment where enforcing compulsory car insurance is difficult.[66] Selecting solutions that are appropriate for local capacity and resources is particularly critical to ensure that risk management does not cause unnecessary harm and excessive costs or create new risks through unintended negative policy consequences or political economy backlash.

Tailor technology to local circumstances. Adoption of the most recent vintage of technologies can help developing countries manage their risks. Technology transfers can help: for instance, by making available globally the most recent drugs and vaccines. What is required, however, is not a simple technology transfer but the adaptation of technology to fit local needs and social norms and constraints and to thus maximize adoption (see spotlight 1). Successful innovations in risk management in developing countries have often relied on modern technologies, but always through a complex process of adaptation. The Bangladesh hurricane early warning system, for instance, combines modern hurricane track forecast technologies with low-tech, locally designed communication tools, including handheld bullhorns, bicycle-mounted loudspeakers, and house-to-house contacts.[67]

Concentrate on low-hanging fruit and win-win solutions. Relatively low-cost interventions that are highly effective should be favored. Cleaning the storm drains in Mumbai helps flood control. But beyond that, it improves health and hygiene and even the quality of life in neighborhoods, leading to a virtuous cycle. Removing bad incentives can be extremely efficient and relatively inexpensive, even though it may not be easy to do. For instance, reforms can target fossil fuel subsidies that promote energy-inefficient transport and heating and thus increase health risks from local air pollution. Strengthening the *capabilities* that are generally useful to manage risks of different natures is particularly cost-effective.[68] For example, the ability to manage large-scale evacuation is the same whether the reason is a flood or a technological accident, as is the capacity to scale up cash transfers rapidly after a shock, whether the shock is a natural hazard or an economic crisis.

Build a strong foundation for improved risk management over time

Create institutional arrangements when the need for them is obvious in everybody's mind—such as after a disaster—and that cannot be easily reversed when the memory of the event has disappeared. Doing so helps prevent some of the negative consequences of people's short memory about risk and disaster and compensates for the implementation issues related to political economy challenges. While policy makers should not wait to initiate such institutional changes until a contingency occurs, the increased public awareness in such a situation will increase the momentum and support for institutionalizing best-practice risk management. For instance, the Netherlands reacted to the 1953 floods by implementing local maximum acceptable flood risk levels; these limitations are fixed by law, making it harder for people to disregard flood management as time goes by.[69] The creation of a national risk board is an option to create an irreversible institutional change that incentivizes long-term risk management and helps coordinate risk reduction actions.

Start with soft measures that change incentives or make them more effective. Hard measures (such as dikes) or complex risk-sharing mechanisms are very unlikely to be efficient and sustainable if incentives are distorted toward too much or too little risk taking. Obstacles to risk management related to incentives need to be identified and corrected as priorities, through institutional reforms and economic instruments (from regulation to market instruments), to communication and information campaigns, and behavioral approaches. Starting with soft measures can correct for a bias in risk management toward hard and capital-intensive solutions—even when cheaper and more flexible institutional solutions are available.

Choose flexible solutions and build in learning. To cope with uncertainty and differences in beliefs, values, and sensitivity, policy makers should aim for robust policies that may not be optimal in the most likely future but that lead to acceptable outcomes in a large range of scenarios and that are adaptive and flexible: that is, policies that are easy to revise as new information becomes available. More learning, and an iterative process of monitoring and learning, is needed about how to apply risk management approaches, especially in lower-income environments.[70] One way to maximize learning is to learn from other domains where experience is systematized and internationalized. An example is the International Civil Aviation Organization, a specialized agency of the United Nations that defines the protocols for investigations of aviation accidents and shares the results, ensuring that everybody can benefit from the mistakes of the others. "Learning from Megadisasters," a knowledge-sharing project sponsored by the government of Japan and the World Bank, collects and analyzes information, data, and evaluations on the Great East Japanese Earthquake of March 11, 2011, with the aim of sharing Japan's knowledge on disaster risk management and postdisaster reconstruction with other countries vulnerable to disasters. Improving the ability of the international community to share information on risks—from health and road-accident risks to large-scale disasters—would be a useful input into the design of more robust strategies (see chapter 8).

Notes

1. "Brimstowad May Miss Its 2015 Deadline," *Hindustan Times*, July 26, 2012.
2. World Bank and GFDRR 2013.
3. FEMA 2010.
4. Guiso 1998.
5. See the Ecomet's website at www.ecomet.eu.
6. World Bank and GFDRR 2013.
7. Johnson and Goldstein 2003.
8. Kahneman and Tversky 1979.
9. Banerjee and Duflo 2011.
10. Sjöberg 2000.
11. Commissariat Général du Plan 2001.
12. Weber and Johnson 2012.
13. Sunstein 2011.
14. Engel and Weber 2007.
15. Michel-Kerjan, de Forges, and Kunreuther 2012.
16. Meyer 2010.
17. Hallegatte 2012.
18. Banerjee and Duflo 2011.
19. Hyder and Aggarwal 2009.
20. Kiefer and Montjoy 2006.
21. Spears 2013.
22. Cohen 2005.
23. Telles, Singh, and Joshi 2009.
24. Laffont 1995.
25. Austin, Kristinsson, and Anderson 1999.
26. Lall and Deichmann 2012.
27. Todo, Nakajima, and Matous 2013.
28. Kahan 2000.
29. La Ferrara, Chong, and Duryea 2008.
30. UNISDR 2011.
31. Hallegatte 2012.
32. Peters and Slovic 1996.
33. Wiener and others 2011.
34. Hattis and others 2001.
35. World Bank 2009.
36. Krueger 1990.
37. James 2000, 330.
38. World Bank 2012.
39. Kunreuther 2006.
40. Michel-Kerjan 2008.
41. Stern and Fineberg 1996.
42. UNISDR 2007.
43. Viguie and Hallegatte 2012.
44. Olson 1965.
45. World Bank 2000, chapter 3.
46. Blanke 2011.
47. Ferlie 1992; James 2000.
48. James 2000.
49. Healy and Malhotra 2008.
50. Kunreuther and Michel-Kerjan 2012.
51. Jha and Chaloupka 2000.
52. Viguie and Hallegatte 2012.
53. Hallegatte and others 2012.
54. Taleb 2010.
55. Lautze and others 2007.
56. Ghebreyesus and others 1999.
57. Graham and Wiener 1995.
58. Craig, Gadgil, and Koomey 2002.
59. Manski 2011.
60. See the Climate Policy Initiative's website at http://climatepolicyinitiative.org/publication/risk-gaps.
61. Manski 2011.
62. Pate-Cornell 2012.
63. Hallegatte and others 2012.
64. Hallegatte 2012.
65. World Bank 2012.
66. Smith 2006.
67. Paul 2010.
68. Ministry of the Interior and Kingdom Relations 2007.
69. Slomp 2012.
70. Dewey 1927.

References

Austin, Daren J., Karl G. Kristinsson, and Roy M. Anderson. 1999. "The Relationship between the Volume of Antimicrobial Consumption in Human Communities and the Frequency of Resistance." *Proceedings of the National Academy of Sciences of the United States of America* 96 (3): 1152–56.

Banerjee, Abhijit V., and Esther Duflo. 2011. *Poor Economics: A Radical Rethinking of the Way to Fight Global Poverty.* New York: PublicAffairs.

Blanke, D. Douglas. 2011. "Tobacco." In Wiener and others, *The Reality of Precaution,* 91–120.

Cabinet Office (United Kingdom). 2012. "National Risk Register of Civil Emergencies." Cabinet Office, London.

Charnley, Gail, and Michael D. Rogers. 2011. "Frameworks for Risk Assessment, Uncertainty, and Precaution." In Wiener and others, *The Reality of Precaution,* 361–75.

Cohen, Alma. 2005. "Asymmetric Information and Learning: Evidence from the Automobile Insurance Market." *Review of Economics and Statistics* 87 (2): 197–207.

Commissariat Général du Plan. 2001. "Transports: Choix Des Investissements Et Coût Des Nuisances." Commissariat Général du Plan, Paris.

Craig, Paul P., Ashok Gadgil, and Jonathan G. Koomey. 2002. "What Can History Teach Us? A Retrospective Examination of Long-Term Energy Forecasts for the United States." *Annual Review of Energy and the Environment* 27 (1): 83–118.

De Francesco, Fabrizio. 2012. "Diffusion of Regulatory Impact Analysis among OECD and EU Member States." *Comparative Political Studies* 45 (10): 1277–305.

Dewey, John. 1927. *The Public and Its Problems.* New York: Henry Holt and Company.

Engel, Christoph, and Elke U. Weber. 2007. "The Impact of Institutions on the Decision How to Decide." *Journal of Institutional Economics* 3 (3): 323–49.

European Commission. 2000. "Communication from the Commission on the Precautionary Principle." Communication COM(2000) 1 final, European Commission, Brussels.

FEMA (Federal Emergency Management Agency). 2010. "Local Official Survey Findings on Flood Risk." FEMA, Washington, DC.

Ferlie, Ewan. 1992. "The Creation and Evolution of Quasi Markets in the Public Sector: A Problem for Strategic Management." *Strategic Management Journal* 13 (S2): 79–97.

Ghebreyesus, Tedros A., Mitiku Haile, Karen H. Witten, Asefaw Getachew, Ambachew M. Yohannes, Mekonnen Yohannes, Hailay D. Teklehaimanot, Steven W. Lindsay, and Peter Byass. 1999. "Incidence of Malaria among Children Living near Dams in Northern Ethiopia: Community Based Incidence Survey." *British Medical Journal* 319 (7211): 663–66.

Graham, John D., and Jonathan B. Wiener. 1995. *Risk Versus Risk: Tradeoffs in Protecting Health and the Environment.* Cambridge, MA: Harvard University Press.

Grossi, Patricia, and Robert Muir-Wood. 2006. "Flood Risk in New Orleans: Implications for Future Management and Insurability." Risk Management Solutions, Newark, CA.

Guiso, Luigi. 1998. "High-Tech Firms and Credit Rationing." *Journal of Economic Behavior & Organization* 35 (1): 39–59.

Hallegatte, Stéphane. 2012. "An Exploration of the Link between Development, Economic Growth, and Natural Risk." Policy Research Working Paper 6216, World Bank, Washington, DC.

Hallegatte, Stéphane, Ankur Shah, Robert Lempert, Casey Brown, and Stuart Gill. 2012. "Investment Decision Making under Deep Uncertainty: Application to Climate Change." Policy Research Working Paper 6193, World Bank, Washington, DC.

Hattis, Dale, Abel Russ, Robert Goble, Prerna Banati, and Margaret Chu. 2001. "Human Interindividual Variability in Susceptibility to Airborne Particles." *Risk Analysis* 21 (4): 585–99.

Healy, Andrew J., and Neil Malhotra. 2008. "Mass and Elite Preferences for Disaster Relief and Prevention Spending: Retrospective Voting and Failures in Electoral Accountability." Economics Department Working Paper, Loyola Marymount University, Los Angeles.

Hyder, Adnan A., and Anju Aggarwal. 2009. "The Increasing Burden of Injuries in Eastern Europe and Eurasia: Making the Case for Safety Investments." *Health Policy* 89 (1): 1–13.

IPCC (Intergovernmental Panel on Climate Change). 2007. *Climate Change 2007: The Physical Science Basis.* Contribution of Working Group I to the Fourth Assessment Report of the IPCC. Cambridge, UK: Cambridge University Press.

———. 2012. *Managing the Risks of Extreme Events and Disasters to Advance Climate Change Adaptation.* A Special Report of the Intergovernmental Panel on Climate Change. New York, NY: Cambridge University Press.

James, Oliver. 2000. "Regulation inside Government: Public Interest Justifications and Regulatory Failures." *Public Administration* 78 (2): 327–34.

Jha, Prabhat, and Frank J. Chaloupka. 2000. *Tobacco Control Policies in Developing Countries.* New York: Oxford University Press.

Johnson, Eric J., and Daniel Goldstein. 2003. "Do Defaults Save Lives?" *Science* 302 (5649): 1338–39.

Kahan, Dan M. 2000. "Gentle Nudges vs. Hard Shoves: Solving the Sticky Norms Problem." *University of Chicago Law Review* 67 (3): 607–45.

Kahneman, Daniel, and Amos Tversky. 1979. "Prospect Theory: An Analysis of Decision under Risk." *Econometrica* 47 (2): 263–91.

Kiefer, John J., and Robert S. Montjoy. 2006. "Incrementalism before the Storm: Network Performance for the Evacuation of New Orleans." *Public Administration Review* 66 (s1): 122–30.

Krueger, Anne O. 1990. "Government Failures in Development." *Journal of Economic Perspectives* 4 (3): 9–23.

Kunreuther, Howard. 2006. "Disaster Mitigation and Insurance: Learning from Katrina." *ANNALS of the American Academy of Political and Social Science* 604 (1): 208–27.

Kunreuther, Howard, and Erwann Michel-Kerjan. 2012. "Policy Options for Reducing Losses from Natural Disasters: Allocating $75 Billion." Copenhagen Consensus 2012 Challenge Paper, Copenhagen Consensus Center, Washington, DC.

La Ferrara, Eliana, Alberto Chong, and Suzanne Duryea. 2008. "Soap Operas and Fertility: Evidence from Brazil." Working Paper 172, Bureau for Research and Economic Analysis of Development, Durham, NC.

Laffont, Jean-Jacques. 1995. "Regulation, Moral Hazard and Insurance of Environmental Risks." *Journal of Public Economics* 58 (3): 319–36.

Lall, Somik V., and Uwe Deichmann. 2012. "Density and Disasters: Economics of Urban Hazard Risk." *World Bank Research Observer* 27 (1): 74–105.

Lautze, Jonathan, Matthew McCartney, Paul Kirshen, Dereje Olana, Gayathree Jayasinghe, and Andrew Spielman. 2007. "Effect of a Large Dam on Malaria Risk: The Koka Reservoir in Ethiopia." *Tropical Medicine & International Health* 12 (8): 982–89.

Lempert, Robert, Nidhi Kalra, Suzanne Peyraud, Zhimin Mao, Sinh Bach Tan, Dean Cira, and Alexander Lotsch. 2013. "Ensuring Robust Flood Risk Management in Ho Chi Minh City." Policy Research Working Paper 6465, World Bank, Washington, DC.

Loewenberg, Samuel. 2006. "US Chemical Companies Leave Their Mark on EU Law." *Lancet* 367 (9510): 556–57.

Manski, Charles F. 2011. "Policy Analysis with Incredible Certitude." *Economic Journal* 121 (554): F261–F89.

Meyer, Robert. 2010. "Why We Still Fail to Learn from Disasters." In *The Irrational Economist: Making Decisions in a Dangerous World*, edited by Erwann Michel-Kerjan and Paul Slovic, 124–31. New York: Public Affairs.

Michel-Kerjan, Erwann. 2008. "Disasters and Public Policy: Can Market Lessons Help Address Government Failures?" Proceedings of the 99th National Tax Association Annual Conference, Boston, MA.

Michel-Kerjan, Erwann, Sabine Lemoyne de Forges, and Howard Kunreuther. 2012. "Policy Tenure under the U.S. National Flood Insurance Program (NFIP)." *Risk Analysis* 32 (4): 644–58.

Ministry of the Interior and Kingdom Relations (the Netherlands). 2007. *National Security: Strategy and Work Programme 2007–2008*. The Hague: Ministry of the Interior and Kingdom Relations.

———. 2009. *Working with Scenarios, Risk Assessment and Capabilities in the National Safety and Security Strategy of the Netherlands*. The Hague: Ministry of Interior and Kingdom Relations.

Olson, Mancur. 1965. *The Logic of Collective Action: Public Goods and the Theory of Groups*. Cambridge, MA: Harvard University Press.

Pate-Cornell, Elisabeth. 2012. "On 'Black Swans' and 'Perfect Storms': Risk Analysis and Management When Statistics Are Not Enough." *Risk Analysis* 32 (11): 1823–33.

Paul, Bimal K. 2010. "Why Relatively Fewer People Died? The Case of Bangladesh's Cyclone Sidr." *Natural Hazards* 50 (2): 289–304.

Peters, Ellen, and Paul Slovic. 1996. "The Role of Affect and Worldviews as Orienting Dispositions in the Perception and Acceptance of Nuclear Power." *Journal of Applied Social Psychology* 26 (16): 1427–53.

Renn, Ortwin, and Peter Graham. 2005. "Risk Governance: Towards an Integrative Approach." White Paper 1, International Risk Governance Council, Geneva.

Sjöberg, Lennart. 2000. "Factors in Risk Perception." *Risk Analysis* 20 (1): 1–12.

Slomp, Robert. 2012. "Flood Risk and Water Management in the Netherlands: A 2012 Update." Rijkswaterstaat, Ministry of Infrastructure and the Environment, The Hague.

Smith, Stephen. 2006. "Taxes on Road Transport." In *Excise Tax Policy and Administration in Southern African Countries*, edited by Sijbren Cnossen, 117–50. Pretoria: University of South Africa Press.

Spears, Dean. 2013. "How Much International Variation in Child Height Can Sanitation Explain?" Policy Research Working Paper 6351, World Bank, Washington, DC.

Stern, Paul C., and Harvey V. Fineberg. 1996. *Understanding Risk: Informing Decisions in a Democratic Society*. Washington, DC: National Academy Press.

Sunstein, Cass R. 2011. "Precautions against What? Perceptions, Heuristics, and Culture." In *The Reality of Precaution*, 492–517.

Taleb, Nassim N. 2010. *The Black Swan: The Impact of the Highly Improbable*. New York: Random House.

Telles, Shirley, Nilkamal Singh, and Meesha Joshi. 2009. "Risk of Posttraumatic Stress Disorder and Depression in Survivors of the Floods in Bihar, India." *Indian Journal of Medical Sciences* 63 (8): 330–34.

Todo, Yasuyuki, Kentaro Nakajima, and Petr Matous. 2013. "How Do Supply Chain Networks Affect the Resilience of Firms to Natural Disasters? Evidence from the Great East Japan Earthquake." Discussion Paper Series 13-E-028, Research Institute of Economy, Trade and Industry, Tokyo.

UNISDR (United Nations International Strategy for Disaster Reduction). 2007. "Hyogo Framework for Action 2005–2015: Building the Resilience of Nations and Communities to Disasters." United Nations, Geneva.

———. 2011. "Global Assessment Report on Disaster Risk Reduction: Revealing Risk, Redefining Development." United Nations, Geneva.

Vastveit, Kirsti R. 2011. "The Use of National Risk Assessments in the Netherlands and the UK." Master's dissertation, University of Stavanger, Stavanger, Norway.

Viguie, Vincent, and Stéphane Hallegatte. 2012. "Trade-Offs and Synergies in Urban Climate Policies." *Nature Climate Change* 2 (5): 334–37

Weber, Elke U., and Eric J. Johnson. 2012. "Psychology and Behavioral Economics Lessons from the Design of a Green Growth Strategy." Policy Research Working Paper 6240, World Bank, Washington, DC.

Wiener, Jonathan B. 2013. "The Diffusion of Regulatory Oversight." In *The Globalization of Cost-Benefit Analysis in Environmental Policy*, edited by Michael A. Livermore and Richard L. Revesz, 123–41. New York: Oxford University Press.

Wiener, Jonathan B., and Michael D. Rogers. 2002. "Comparing Precaution in the United States and Europe." *Journal of Risk Research* 5 (4): 317–49.

Wiener, Jonathan B., Michael D. Rogers, James K. Hammitt, and Peter H. Sand. 2011. *The Reality of Precaution: Comparing Risk Regulation in the United States and Europe*. Washington, DC: RFF Press.

World Bank. 2000. *World Development Report 2000/2001: Attacking Poverty*. Washington, DC: World Bank.

———. 2009. *World Development Report 2010: Development and Climate Change*. Washington, DC: World Bank.

———. 2012. *Inclusive Green Growth: The Pathway to Sustainable Development*. Washington, DC: World Bank.

World Bank and GFDRR (Global Facility for Disaster Reduction and Recovery). 2013. "Weather, Climate and Water Hazards and Climate Resilience: Effective Preparedness through National Meteorological and Hydrological Services." World Bank, Washington, DC.

SPOTLIGHT 2

Protecting the food consumption of the poor: The role of safety nets in Ethiopia and El Salvador

Around the world, 870 million people are chronically undernourished. Environmental degradation, climate change, and food price spikes put additional pressures on the ability of poor people to meet their basic food consumption needs. The experiences of Ethiopia and El Salvador show that investments in safety nets can be an effective mechanism to reduce chronic food insecurity and respond to spikes in food prices.

Building resilience to droughts in Ethiopia

For more than 30 years, emergency food aid was the primary response to food insecurity in Ethiopia. The aid saved lives, but it did not prevent asset depletion, nor did it help households rebuild their livelihoods after droughts. To move from crisis response to prevention, the government of Ethiopia launched the Productive Safety Net Program (PSNP) in 2005. Its main objective is to protect food consumption and prevent asset depletion of rural households that lack food security. The program includes a public works component and provides direct grants for those who cannot work. By 2009 the PSNP had become the largest program of its kind in Sub-Saharan Africa, supporting 7.6 million chronically food insecure people. In 2011, when the Horn of Africa suffered its worst drought in 60 years, the PSNP was expanded to cover 9.6 million people. It relies on donor contributions but is managed by the government; its budget is about 1.2 percent of gross domestic product.

The program provides predictable cash and food transfers for six months of the year corresponding to the so-called "lean season," when households tend to run out of food. The transfers cover about 40 percent of a recipient's annual food needs. A complimentary initiative, the Household Asset Building Program (HABP), provides microcredit, agricultural extension, and business advice to help PSNP recipients improve their asset base, so that eventually they can manage without aid. About three of every four PSNP beneficiaries also had access to some HABP services from 2006 to 2010.

Program participants are chosen through a combination of geographic and community targeting. At the start of the program, the government identified the most food insecure districts based on a long history of emergency food aid. Within these districts, household eligibility is determined through a community-based selection process according to predefined criteria. The wage rate for the public works program was set low, to discourage better-off households from applying.

Steps were also taken to respond to the needs of the transitory poor. These included annual retargeting to respond to changes in the relative positions of households; a contingency budget to cover households that might become chronically food insecure; a risk-financing facility to provide funding during a crisis should the contingency budget be exhausted; and an emergency response system to cover districts that are not participating in the PSNP.

Evaluations have shown that the program has reduced household food insecurity. Receiving PSNP transfers for five years is associated with an increase of food security for 1.05 months a year compared with having received no transfers, and 1.53 months when households receive both PSNP and HABP services. The PSNP also reduced distress sales of assets, from 51 percent of beneficiary households at the start of the program to 34 percent by 2010. In addition, the public works projects helped create valuable community assets such as roads, schools, and clinics, and improved agricultural productivity through water and soil conservation.

The program has outperformed traditional humanitarian responses in timeliness of disbursements during major droughts. During the 2011 drought, the government provided aid within two months after a drought warning, using the risk financing facility—the typical humanitarian response is eight months.

The PSNP has demonstrated that receipt of timely and predictable assistance enables households to manage risks more effectively and reduce the use of costly coping mechanisms. The program also has positive community-wide impacts through creation of public assets and environmental restoration, which should facilitate long-term improvements in livelihoods. It also demonstrates the benefits of shifting the donor community's approach from meeting short-term food needs through emergency relief to addressing the underlying causes of household food insecurity and investing in permanent systems with the ability to manage risk proactively.

Ensuring food security in the face of natural disasters and economic shocks in El Salvador

El Salvador is exposed to multiple shocks that threaten food security, including natural disasters—floods, earthquakes, and hurricanes—as well as shocks to the economy, which is small, dollarized, and dependent on remittances. To mitigate the impact of these shocks, the government has introduced several safety nets: conditional cash transfers (CCTs) and pensions in rural areas, school feeding in all public schools, and an income support program in cities.

While the programs were designed with donor support, they are fully owned and managed by the government. These safety nets were effective in protecting the consumption of recipients during food price spikes in 2007–08, job losses and reduction of remittances due to the global economic crisis in 2009, and severe storms in 2010.

The Comunidades Solidarias Rurales, or CSR (formerly Red Solidaria), launched in 2005, provides short-term assistance to the extreme poor in rural areas and increases incentives for investments in human capital. Pregnant women and mothers of children up to age 5 receive monthly cash transfers of $15. Families with children aged 6 to 18 also receive the transfers if they comply with regular health checkups and preschool and school attendance requirements. In addition, the program supports improvement of basic services—water, sanitation, electricity, health and nutrition, and income-generating activities—in target localities. In 2012, CSR had about 85,000 beneficiaries in 100 of the poorest rural communities.

CSR was effective in smoothing food consumption and preventing increases in stunting among children in beneficiary households when food price inflation doubled in 2008. Beneficiaries of the CCTs reported improvements in nutrition and health as a result of program participation. In 2009, as part of the crisis response program, the government also introduced monthly pensions of $50 for people older than 70 in CSR-supported communities. An evaluation by the International Food Policy Research Institute has shown that CSR is well targeted, ranking third in its targeting effectiveness in Latin America after programs in Brazil and Chile.

The government has also taken steps to address rising food insecurity and poverty in cities following job losses and the increase of food prices associated with the global economic crisis. A Temporary Income Support (PATI) Program, launched in 2009, provides six months of income support to the urban poor who participate in community projects ranging from rehabilitating infrastructure to providing social services. An innovative feature of the program is that it conditions income support on attendance of training activities, and thus aims to address income vulnerability and longer-term employability with one integrated instrument. Experienced social workers teach participants not only technical skills such as sewing, cooking, or car repair, but also entrepreneurship skills and soft skills such as how to prepare for job interviews or write resumes.

PATI targets municipalities with the highest urban poverty rates, giving preference to two groups with above-average unemployment rates: young people and female household heads. The program started as a pilot in two municipalities in 2009, was rapidly expanded to 11 municipalities affected by severe storms in 2010, and reached 40,000 beneficiaries in 36 municipalities by 2012. It has proven helpful in rehabilitating urban infrastructure and smoothing beneficiaries' food consumption. Preliminary World Bank evaluations show that PATI had a positive impact on improving job readiness and willingness to start a business. Once considered a short-term crisis response program, PATI is now a core element of El Salvador's new Comunidades Solidarias Urbanas Strategy, modeled after the CSR but adapted to an urban context. The urban CCT program is currently being piloted in 25 municipalities, with plans for expansion.

El Salvador is an example of a small, relatively poor country that has been able to design and implement several complex safety net programs. The government learned from international practice but adapted the programs to the local context and added some innovations. These include combining CCTs with activities to improve infrastructure and generate income, and conditioning short-term income support on training to facilitate longer-term improvements in livelihoods of beneficiaries. Political commitment to reducing food insecurity and poverty was an important element of El Salvador's success; the programs were developed continuously under several different administrations. A sequenced approach was another characteristic. Beginning with a small rural safety net in 17 poor rural communities, the government gradually added more rural areas as administrative capacity improved, then a pension component, and is now expanding to urban areas. The government is currently working with donor agencies on building a more integrated social protection system that could provide protection against risks across the entire life cycle.

Sources

Ethiopia

Hobson, Matt, and Laura Campbell. 2012. "How Ethiopia's Productive Safety Net Programme Is Responding to the Humanitarian Crisis in the Horn." *Humanitarian Exchange Magazine* 53 (March).

Subbarao, Kalanidhi, Carlo del Ninno, Colin Andrews, and Claudia Rodriguez-Alas. 2012. *Public Works as a Safety Net: Design, Evidence and Implementation*. Washington, DC: World Bank.

World Bank. 2010. "Designing and Implementing a Rural Safety Net in a Low-Income Setting: Lessons Learned from Ethiopia's Productive Safety Net Program 2005–2009." World Bank, Washington, DC.

———. 2012. "Before Crisis Hits: Can Public Works Programs Increase Food Security?" *From Evidence to Policy*. World Bank, Washington, DC (September).

El Salvador

De Brauw, Alan, and Edmundo Murrugarra. 2011. "How CCTs Help Sustain Human Capital during Crises. Evidence from Red Solidaria in El Salvador during the Food Price Crisis." Unpublished manuscript, World Bank, Washington, DC.

IFPRI (International Food Policy Research Institute), and FUSADES (Fundación Salvadoreña para el Desarrollo Económico y Social). 2008. "Evaluación de Impacto Externa de la Red Solidaria: Informe de la Eficacia de la Focalización." IFPRI and FUSADES, Washington, DC.

Soares, Fábio Veras. 2012. "What Is Happening with El Salvador's CCT Programmes?" One Pager 168, United Nations Development Programme, Brasilia.

World Bank. 2010. "Accessing Good Quality Jobs: Priorities for Education, Social Protection, Science and Technology." World Bank, Washington, DC.

———. 2012. "The Evolution of Poverty and Equity in El Salvador, 2000–2010." Unpublished manuscript, World Bank, Washington, DC.

PART II

The role of key social systems

Three generations living together in Indonesia. Household members can increase their resilience by pooling individual energy and resources to manage risks, but internal and external obstacles limit their ability to do so efficiently.

CHAPTER 3

Households are the first line of support to confront risk and pursue opportunity

Sharing good times and bad times

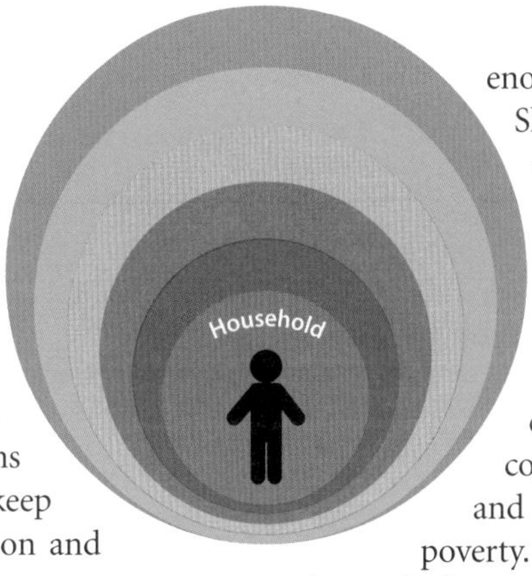

Shamsun Nahar and her family have helped one another in good times and bad as they struggle to leave poverty behind. Shamsun is 44 years old and lives in a village in central Bangladesh with her 16-year-old daughter. Two sons live with their wives nearby but keep separate households; her eldest son and his family live in Dhaka.

Fifteen years ago, when Shamsun's husband, Mobarak Molla, was 35, he felt the first symptoms of tuberculosis. Unable to afford proper treatment, he died at age 40. The couple had owned about an acre of land and an ox. When Mobarak died, Shamsun had to sell their ox to cover funeral expenses and buy food. Her three sons continued to work in the field, but because they had no ox, they had to share the plot with another farmer, so they harvested a smaller crop. Slowly, Shamsun managed to improve her situation, thanks to a few loans she obtained from her village savings group and a local nongovernmental organization (NGO). This money enabled her to send her eldest son, Masud, to work for part of the year as a rickshaw driver in Dhaka—where he eventually stayed permanently—as well as to set up a very small shop, where she sells necessities such as soap and biscuits. Having two sons nearby and one in the city means Shamsun can get help in times of crisis. The steady income from her shop enables her to provide the basics for herself and her daughter. However, Shamsun worries about being able to save enough for her daughter's marriage. She also feels vulnerable to illness and other negative shocks because of her limited assets.[1]

This story illustrates some of the risks that vulnerable families face and how they attempt to build resilience together. Large shocks can force poor people to use costly coping measures that set them back and undermine their ability to escape poverty. In contrast, families that are able to invest in human capital, accumulate financial and physical assets, and share risks among their members can become resilient to shocks and are better positioned to pursue opportunity.

Jean-Jacques Rousseau wrote in *The Social Contract* that "the oldest of all societies, and the only natural one, is that of the family." Indeed, for most people, the members of their household constitute the main source of material and emotional support. A household is defined here as a group of individuals related to one another by family ties (kinship).[2] They might live under the same roof or not, and they might be a small nuclear family of parents and children, or a large extended family including grandparents and other relatives. In any event, households form a very strong and tightly knit community, where members often pool their resources to consume, invest, and care for the most vulnerable, among them children and elderly adults.

Many households, however, particularly poor ones, struggle to help individuals cope with shocks and are unable to support their search for opportunities. As units, they face the challenges both of protecting and insuring their members against common shocks, such as illness and income losses, and of accumulating sufficient assets and human capital to grow their income.[3] To meet these challenges, households need to have sufficient resources and to be closely connected to their community, to markets, and to good-quality public goods and services. In addition, family dynamics and social norms sometimes limit the extent to which members can collaborate effectively, increasing the vulnerability of certain individuals within the household—typically women, children, and elderly adults—in the face of shocks.

Government policies can strengthen households' ability to manage risk by facilitating their access to information, financial tools, and labor markets. Public policies should also ensure access to education and provide basic protection against health and income risk, especially for the poor. And they can address inequalities within the household through a mix of regulation and interventions to empower and protect the most vulnerable members.

This chapter focuses on the internal and external obstacles that prevent households from building adequate preparation and from sharing risk within the household; the implications of those obstacles for the vulnerability and resilience of households and individuals; and the actions households can take to improve their preparation in the face of risk and opportunity. It also focuses on public policies to help households prepare for and cope with risk. It starts by describing the main shocks that affect households in developing countries, the different strategies that households use to manage risk, and the obstacles they encounter. It then discusses how a systemic approach to policy for risk management should consider the multiple risks that households face, and all the different instruments that they need to manage these risks effectively. This systemic approach has the benefit of highlighting complementarities and synergies across policies, in particular for protecting households against risk while enhancing their access to opportunity.

What risks do households face and how do they cope?

Every day, millions of people all over the world fall sick, lose their jobs, fall victim to crime, or are hit by natural hazards. The wide variation in both the incidence and the nature of the shocks that affect household members is shown in figure 3.1, which reports survey data from six countries documenting shocks

FIGURE 3.1 ***Shocks to households vary considerably across countries***

Percentage of households reporting shocks in each category

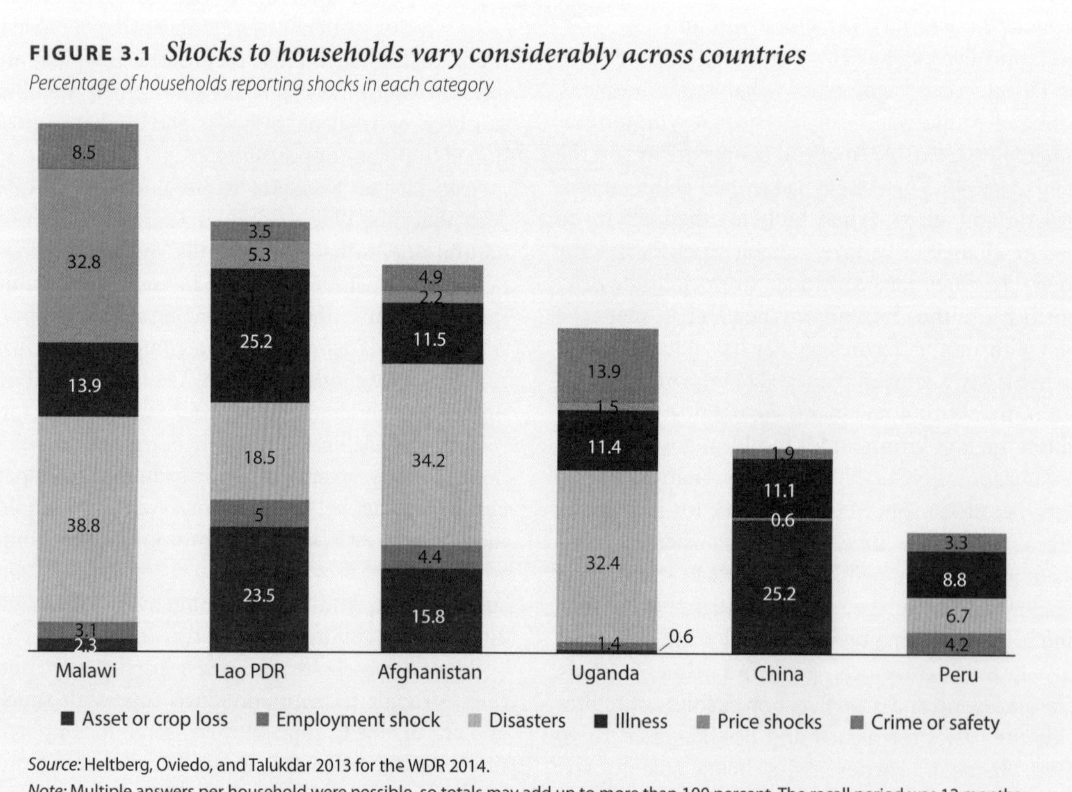

Source: Heltberg, Oviedo, and Talukdar 2013 for the WDR 2014.

Note: Multiple answers per household were possible, so totals may add up to more than 100 percent. The recall period was 12 months.

that household members suffered over the previous 12 months. Disasters, illness, and asset losses are the most common shocks across countries, followed by price shocks. Rural and urban households are exposed to different risks: weather shocks typically affect rural households disproportionately, whereas urban households are more exposed to price shocks, crime, and unemployment (see chapter 1).[4]

Household members can help one another manage risk and pursue opportunity

When household members share risks, they can increase their own resilience and that of the household. Economic theory suggests that individuals should be able to smooth consumption over their life cycle. As chapter 1 argues, they are better able to do so when protection and insurance mechanisms—either formal or informal—are available to help them absorb income shocks and maintain stable consumption. In particular, when perfect credit and insurance markets are not available, household members can increase their resilience by pooling individual energy and resources to invest in protection and insurance, and to cope with shocks—particularly with idiosyncratic shocks.

By and large, empirical research shows that households manage to protect their consumption from shocks, albeit not fully. Research in Bangladesh, Ethiopia, India, Mali, and rural Mexico has found that households protect their consumption—at least in part—after illness shocks by using several strategies, including increasing labor supply within the household.[5] A recent study for Indonesia reveals that while households face significant income risk from several kinds of shocks, they manage to achieve a level of insurance representing at least 60 percent of this risk. On average, however, expected consumption represents 65 percent of the expected income, suggesting that households are willing to incur a large cost to insure their consumption.[6] Looking more closely at how the composition of the household affects shock responses, a study of households in Senegal shows that in urban areas, larger households that include extended family members experience smaller declines in basic consumption after being hit by a negative shock, compared with smaller households. At the same time, heads of household supporting extended families experience the largest relative declines in (food) consumption, to preserve the consumption of the other household members.[7]

Concern and attention to the most vulnerable members distinguish the household from other groups. Several factors, including altruism, reciprocity, and social norms, explain why household members care for one another (box 3.1). Whatever the motivation, abundant evidence shows that in all socioeconomic and cultural contexts, the family is seen as a key pillar of support to the individual. To cite an

BOX 3.1 *Altruism, exchange, or social norms: What motivates family members to care for one another?*

Why do parents invest in their children's education? Why do adult children take care of their elderly parents? Why do spouses pool their resources, siblings lend money to one another, and extended family members check on their relatives? Economists and sociologists have long pondered these questions and have come up with three broad theories for why family members care for one another.

According to the theory of altruism, an individual's welfare depends on the welfare of others. Maximizing utility then involves transferring a portion of one's resources to others.[a] More recent research suggests that evolutionary forces such as genes or sociocultural influences may be behind this altruism.[b] The second theory suggests that social norms define how family members should help one another.[c] The third theory, one emphasizing exchange, hypothesizes that familial support is rooted in reciprocal arrangements, which can (but need not) be reinforced by social norms: people provide assistance now in the expectation that they might require assistance later.[d]

Empirical evidence suggests that each of these theories has merit.[e] For example, reciprocal arrangements such as time-for-money exchanges between parents and children are more common in countries where government support is weak and access to markets is limited, suggesting the presence of exchange motives. Kinship norms may explain why grandparents frequently care for their grandchildren in certain countries in Sub-Saharan Africa and in China. Altruism explains why parents have been found to transfer money to children on the basis of need, and children to devote greater amounts of time to parents with the worst health. Other evidence, however, reveals that motives are not always altruistic: the extent of parental investment in children has been shown to influence children's support for their parents.

Source: WDR 2014 team.

a. Becker 1974.
b. Alger and Weibull 2010.
c. Alesina and Giuliano 2013.
d. Bernheim, Shleifer, and Summers 1985.
e. Silverstein and Giarrusso 2010.

FIGURE 3.2 ***Elderly people frequently live with other family members***

Share of households with at least one member aged 60+ years, and share of population aged 60+ years

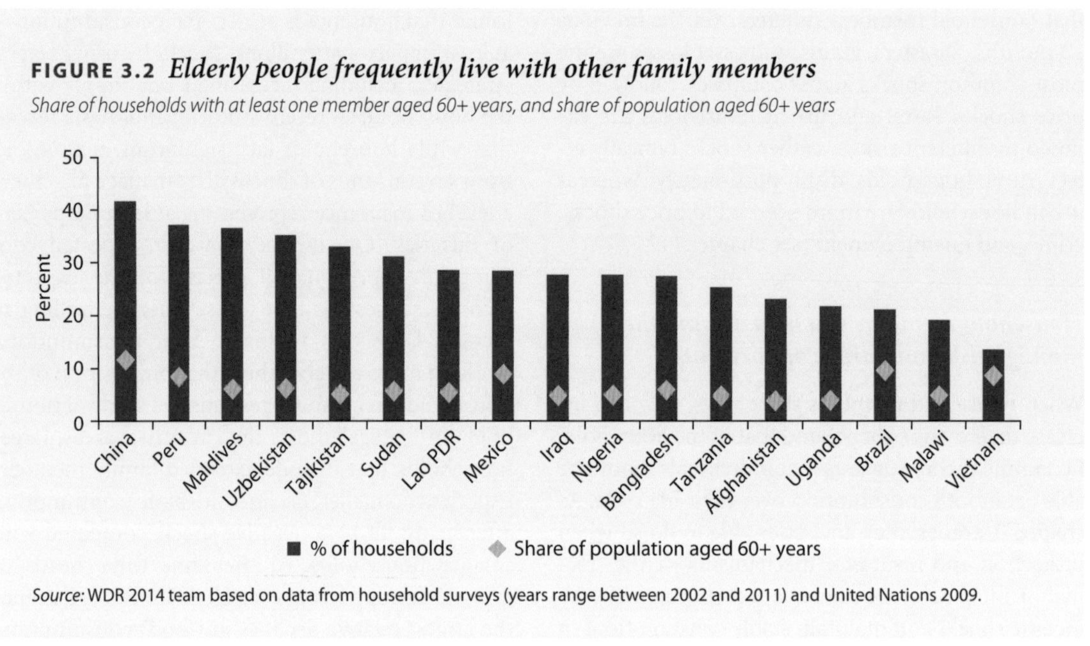

Source: WDR 2014 team based on data from household surveys (years range between 2002 and 2011) and United Nations 2009.

example, evidence on living arrangements in 17 developing countries shows that on average 28 percent of households have members over the age of 60, a significantly higher share than this age group represents in the total population (figure 3.2). In many circumstances, children and grandchildren take care of older relatives. For example, in China, 90 percent of elderly with disabilities living with their families have access to support, compared with 73 percent of elderly living alone.[8] In other cases, the elderly take care of younger relatives. In Sub-Saharan Africa and China, for instance, grandparents are often the main caregivers of their grandchildren.[9]

Pooling risk within the family has been a basic form of insurance from time immemorial.

Obstacles internal and external to the household limit the ability of its members to manage risks efficiently, however. As chapter 2 describes in detail, financial constraints, information constraints, and an inability to translate information into knowledge and knowledge into action all limit the ability of individuals to manage risks effectively. Social obstacles such as missing markets and public goods, moral hazard, externalities, and social norms limit the range of instruments that households have at their disposal to manage risk. In this context, poor households in particular try to reduce their exposure to shocks by opting for low-risk, low-return activities and are forced to take costly measures to cope with shocks once they hit—a strategy that increases their vulnerability to future shocks even more.

Moreover, complex dynamics within the household may increase the vulnerability of some members. Empirical evidence shows that household members—who often have different preferences—allocate resources (labor, capital, and output) following a bargaining process that in many instances appears to be inefficient.[10] For example, in Burkina Faso, husbands and wives cultivate separate plots, following the traditional division of labor among rural couples. Plots run by wives are significantly less productive, which implies that household income could be increased with a different allocation of labor across plots. In Côte d'Ivoire, husbands and wives cultivate "gender-specific" crops in separate plots, and they strictly allocate the income of each crop to specific consumption categories, such as personal consumption, food, and education. Thus, as the income from one crop fluctuates, so do the consumption expenditures tied to that income. Consumption decisions based on pooled incomes would increase the stability of consumption for both spouses as well as for their children.[11] Experimental evidence from games comparing the behavior of husbands and wives also shows that in many cases their choices fail to maximize joint income.[12]

To respond to shocks, poor households use costly strategies, with unequal effects on household members

When shocks damage substantial proportions of households' assets and slash their income, households with limited savings or insurance mechanisms must take difficult steps to maintain a minimum level of consumption, mainly of food. The shock survey data mentioned earlier reveal that more than half of households affected by health and income shocks in Afghanistan, China, and Tajikistan, and almost half of households in Lao People's Democratic Republic and Uganda, reported having cut consumption.[13] Regression analysis of the data shows that in several countries, poor households tend to use costly coping mechanisms, including selling a productive asset such as livestock, cutting food consumption, or consuming lower-quality food (table 3.1). Selling productive assets is particularly harmful because it curtails the household's ability to generate adequate income for a long time after the shock. Strategies such as working longer hours, taking on more work, or migrating seem to be less clearly associated with poverty. However, households with higher wealth and better access to infrastructure and services more frequently report using their savings or borrowing money, either formally or informally.

The impacts of the more costly coping strategies can be long term and even permanent, particularly for children. Empirical evidence from studies of the impact of large shocks (usually natural hazards) on economic and human development outcomes typically finds that while all household members experience hardship, adult outcomes tend to revert to their long-term trends eventually, whereas children can suffer permanent effects, especially during the critical development period of the first two years of life.[14] These effects, which tend to be more prevalent in poor households, translate into lower earnings and worse health in adult years. In some cases, larger negative impacts have been documented for girls than for boys.

Shocks can cause long-term damages to human capital when the nutrition of very young children is compromised. Children who are heavier and longer at birth tend to develop better cognitive skills that enable them to attain more education and get better

TABLE 3.1 *Poorer households are more likely to report using costly mechanisms to cope with shocks*

	Type of household most likely to report coping strategy				
Country	**Use savings/ credit/assets**	**Work more/ migrate**	**Assistance (government/family/ community/NGOs)**	**Sell productive assets**	**Reduce consumption quantity/quality**
Afghanistan	Richer	Richer	Richer	Poorer	Poorer
China	—	Richer	—	Richer	Richer
Iraq	Richer	Richer	—	—	Poorer
Malawi	Richer	—	—	—	—
Mexico	Poorer (credit/asset sales)	—	—	—	Poorer
Nigeria	Richer	—	—	—	—
Peru	Richer	—	—		—
Sudan	Richer	Poorer	Poorer	Poorer	Poorer
Tajikistan	—	—	—	Richer	Poorer
Uganda	Richer (savings/sell assets), poorer (credit)	—	Richer	—	Poorer
Uzbekistan	Poorer (credit)	Poorer	—	Poorer	—

Source: Heltberg, Oviedo, and Talukdar 2013 for the WDR 2014.
Note: The table presents the results of regression estimations where socioeconomic indicators (either consumption quintile or asset-based measure of wealth) significantly affected the probability of reporting the corresponding coping strategy (significance at least 5 percent). Regressions include region and urban fixed effects, household size, gender, education and occupation of head (where available), dependency ratio, consumption quintile, and the principal factor of access to piped water, quality of roof/floor, having a cell phone, and distance to public services and main roads.
— = Socioeconomic indicators not significant. No data were available for the sale of productive assets in Peru.

jobs. Birth weight is closely related to the quality of the mother's nutrition during pregnancy. Therefore, reducing food intake during pregnancy can cause large and irreversible damage to the development of children in utero. Extreme shocks, such as the 1919 influenza pandemic and the great Chinese famine of 1959–61, caused losses in height, cognitive development (measured in years of schooling), and overall health outcomes for the generation born during those years. Shocks can also compromise the quality of nutrition available to children in their first two years, which is also essential to physical and cognitive development. The 1994–95 drought in rural Zimbabwe cut growth by 1.5 to 2.0 centimeters among children aged 12 to 24 months. Children who were 3 years old or younger during the 1998–2000 economic crisis in Ecuador had a significantly lower height-for-age score and a lower vocabulary test score than children of same age in noncrisis times.[15] Moreover, in a few countries, shocks have been found to hurt early nutritional and developmental outcomes for girls disproportionately.[16]

In the face of disaster, some households also sacrifice investments in education in exchange for having an additional member—usually a school-age child—enter the workforce. School attendance dropped by almost 7 percent among those households more heavily hit by two strong earthquakes in El Salvador in 2001, while children in these households were two and a half times more likely to be working after the earthquake than before (the share rose from 6.5 percent to 16.5 percent). Sometimes, the temporary use of child labor has permanent consequences for their human capital. In northern Tanzania, children who had to work an additional 5.7 hours a week after a rainfall shock attained one year less of school, compared with those who did not work more.[17]

Stress, fueled by shocks, can increase domestic abuse. Adult stress levels increase significantly with shocks. The Asian financial crisis of 1997 increased depression and anxiety in Indonesia and Thailand, particularly among the less educated, urban, and landless populations. In Kenya, farmers experience increased levels of cortisol (a hormone produced in times of stress) when rainfall is too low.[18] Focus group participants in Cambodia, Jamaica, and Mongolia reported that the hardship generated by the 2008 crisis had increased men's violence toward wives and children.[19] Shocks can also lead to increased abuse of elderly people. A study in rural Tanzania found that during years of low rainfall, the number of murders of elderly women—accused of witchcraft and killed by their family members—nearly doubles.[20]

Physical and psychological abuse experienced during childhood can have long-lasting effects on identity and behavior, not only undermining the self-esteem that is crucial for decisions regarding risk taking and pursuing opportunities but also increasing the likelihood of violent behavior in adulthood.[21] A survey of men in six countries found that those who had been victims of abuse during childhood were twice as likely to have been violent toward their partners (figure 3.3).

FIGURE 3.3 ***Men who experienced violence in the household when young are more likely to act violently as adults***

Percentage of men who have perpetrated violence on an intimate partner as adults

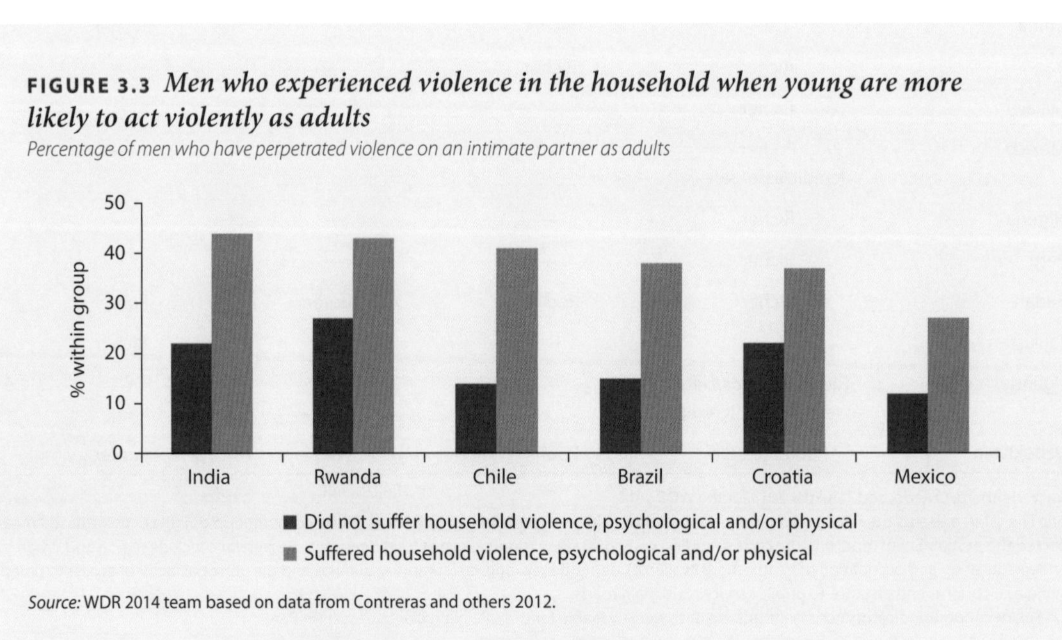

Source: WDR 2014 team based on data from Contreras and others 2012.

How do households prepare to manage risks, and what obstacles do they face?

To confront risk and pursue opportunity, household members acquire knowledge and invest in protection and insurance. The quality of their risk management depends on their access to information, markets, public services, and infrastructure, as well as on the level of risk sharing within the household.

Acquiring and sharing knowledge about risk and opportunity

Obtaining information is crucial for managing risk. News about such matters as prices, weather risks, better agricultural technologies, and job openings can immediately improve the ability of a household to prepare for and respond to risk. Mobile phones have increasingly become indispensable tools to obtain and exchange information for many households in the developing world, which account for nearly two-thirds of the world's 4.77 billion users. First, by drastically reducing communication costs, mobile phones improve cohesiveness of disperse social groups and networks, enabling people to respond more quickly to the income shocks of other family members.[22] Second, readily available information on risks, such as weather updates and early warnings, can assist households in preparing for disasters. Third, mobile phones can reduce information asymmetries and price uncertainties, enabling farmers to increase their surplus. Finally, mobile banking offers opportunities for household members to transfer money to one another and undertake other financial transactions in a safe and cost-efficient way.[23]

Investing in human capital to increase protection and access to opportunity

Better nutrition, sanitation, and access to preventive health care increase productivity and reduce the risks of morbidity and mortality. Historically, one of the leading causes of premature death in the developing world has been the high risk of maternal mortality and the exposure of young children to malnutrition and disease. In recent years, however, more investment in prevention, better health services, and higher income have led to a significant decline in infant, child, and maternal mortality. Immunization rates for measles, for example, which were as low as 60 percent in South Asia and 64 percent in Sub-Saharan Africa in 1990, are now above 75 percent in every region of the world (figure 3.4a). Since 2002, infant mortality rates have declined significantly as well (figure 3.4b). On the other hand, dietary risks (leading to obesity) and smoking continue to increase, which has made noncommunicable disease a leading cause of death (figure 3.5).

FIGURE 3.4 *Immunization rates have increased and infant mortality has declined everywhere*

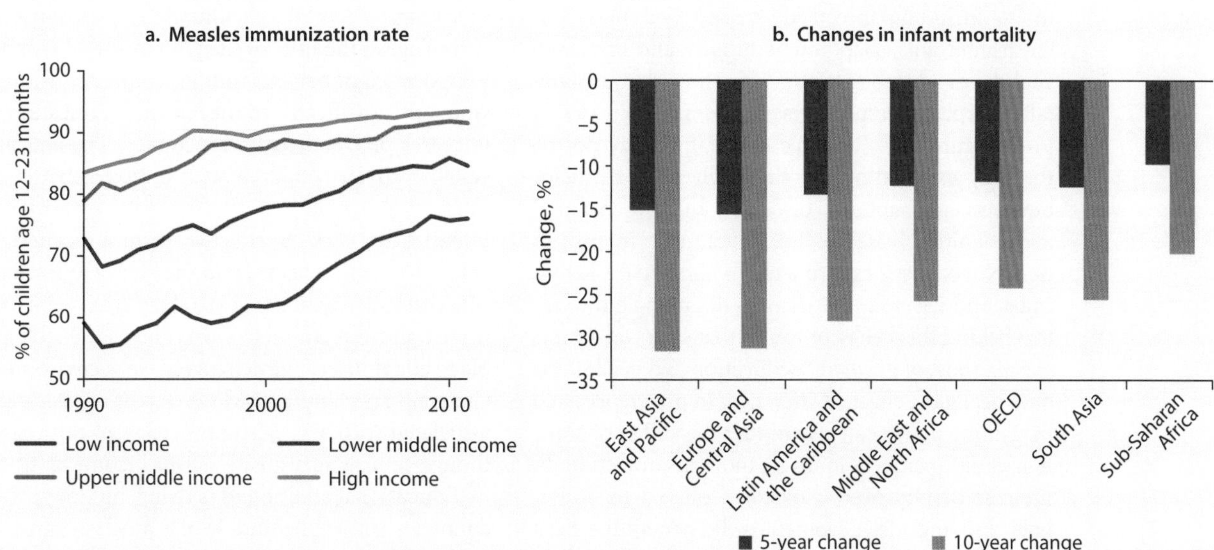

Source: WDR 2014 team based on data from World Bank World Development Indicators (database).

Note: The 5-year change indicates the change in the infant mortality rate between 2007 and 2011. The 10-year change indicates the change between 2002 and 2011. Organisation for Economic Co-operation and Development (OECD) countries in the panel b are high-income countries that have been members of the OECD for at least 40 years. All other countries are grouped into geographic regions.

FIGURE 3.5 *The risk of death from noncommunicable disease is growing in all developing regions*

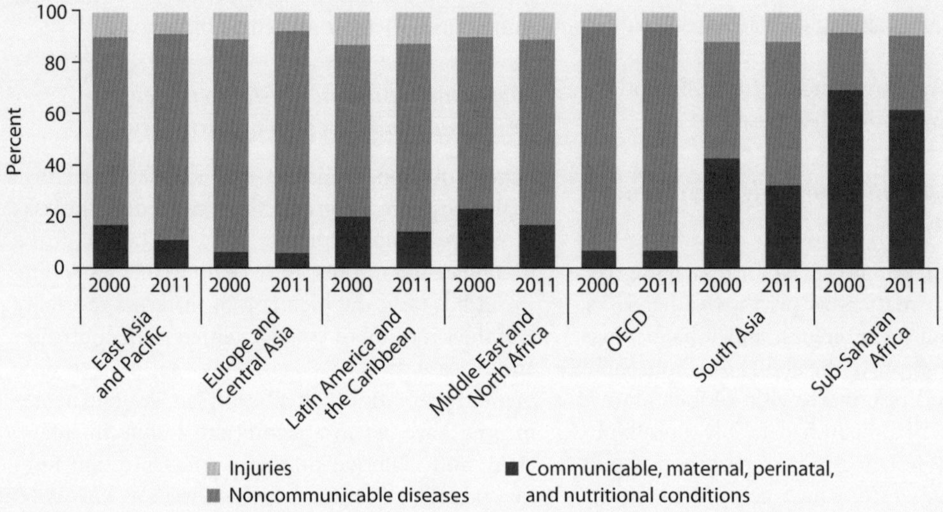

Source: World Health Organization Global Health Estimates Summary Tables: Deaths by Cause, Age and Sex, available at http://www.who.int/healthinfo/global_burden_disease/en/ (regional tabulation prepared specifically for the *World Development Report 2014*).

Note: Organisation for Economic Co-operation and Development (OECD) countries in the figure are high-income countries that have been members of the OECD for at least 40 years. All other countries are grouped into geographic regions.

Despite the clear benefits of disease prevention in reducing risk and improving welfare, demand for tools to reduce the risk of disease can be surprisingly low among poor households.[24] For example, experimental trials that have provided several such tools—including insecticide-treated bed nets, water disinfectants, soap, multivitamins, and improved cookstoves—to poor households show that demand falls sharply in response even to small increases in price (figure 3.6). Resource constraints may not be the only explanation for this high price elasticity, however; as chapter 2 discusses, many behavioral and cognitive biases reduce investment in protection. Nonetheless, experiments in Guatemala, Kenya, India, and Uganda that tried to disentangle the factors behind this behavior found that cash constraints explain most of it, whereas education and peer effects have negligible effects. Differences in preferences and bargaining power can also hinder the ability of some household members to invest more in protection. In the case of improved cookstoves offered to households in Bangladesh, women—who benefit the most from this technology—were unable to purchase them because they have little say over financial decisions.

Households also invest in education to manage risks better and to take advantage of opportunity. Education helps people achieve better health outcomes. For example, young people with more education are less likely to engage in substance abuse, violence, and unprotected sex.[25] In Taiwan, China, the 1968 expansion of compulsory education from six to nine years reduced the likelihood that girls of primary school age at the time of the reform would give birth to underweight babies as adults, compared with girls who were not affected by the reform.[26] Education also increases productivity and income.[27] The education system provides children with critical generic skills (literacy and math), as well as "soft" or socioemotional skills, such as effective communication, the ability to work in teams, and the ability to learn new concepts and methods. These skills are crucial in the transition from school to work, and they enable people to adapt to a rapidly changing work environment. Generally speaking, an additional year of education is associated with a 12 percent increase in earnings, although returns vary greatly across income levels.[28]

Educational attainment is rising, but low-income countries still lag behind. While much progress has been made toward the Millennium Development Goal of ensuring that all children complete primary school, less progress has been made for higher grades of attainment (figure 3.7a). The low attainment,

FIGURE 3.6 *Demand for preventive health care products falls steeply as the price increases*

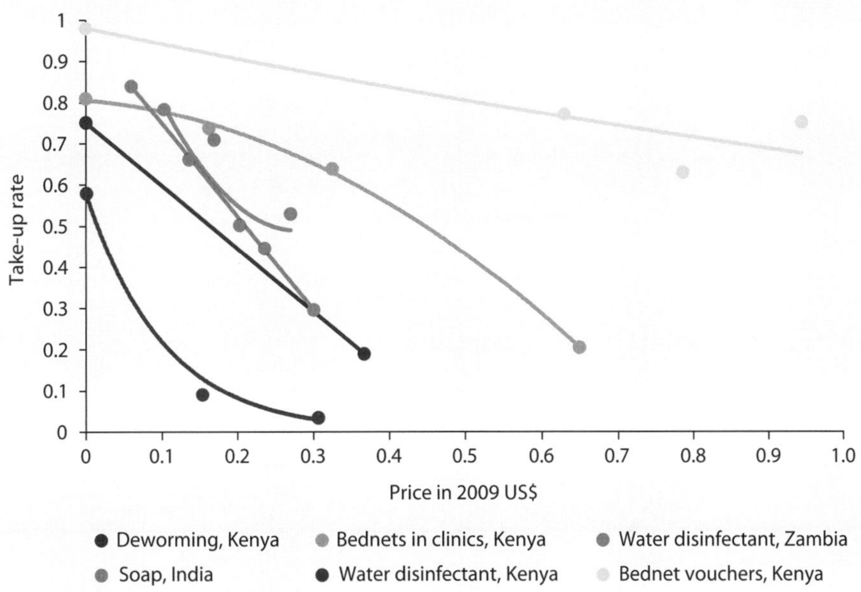

Source: Abdul Latif Jameel Poverty Action Lab (J-PAL) 2011.

FIGURE 3.7 *Low-income countries still lag in educational attainment, and some middle-income countries suffer from gaps in quality*

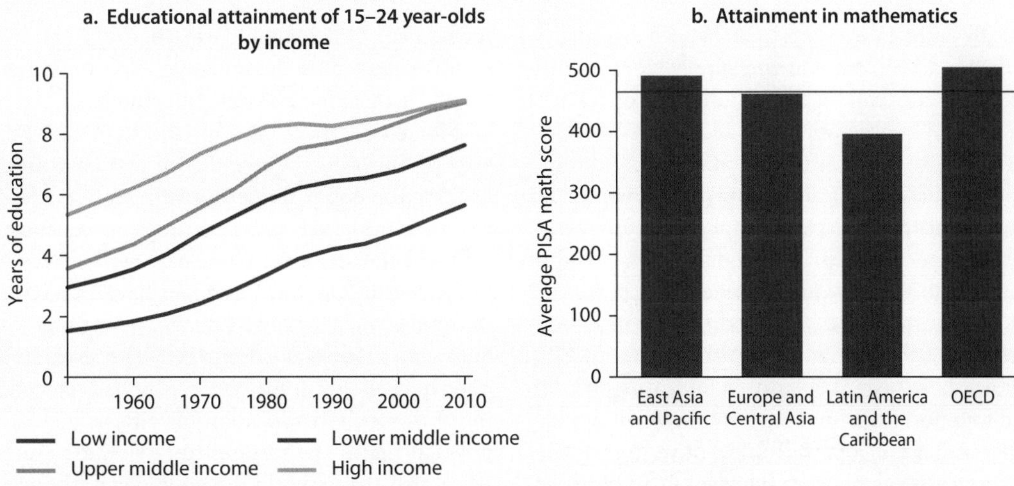

Source: WDR 2014 team based on data from Barro and Lee 2010 (panel a) and OECD Programme for International Student Assessment (database) (panel b).

Note: In panel b, the red line indicates overall average score. Organisation for Economic Co-operation and Development (OECD) countries in the figure are high-income countries that have been members of the OECD for at least 40 years. All other countries are grouped into geographic regions. PISA = Programme for International Student Assessment.

FIGURE 3.8 ***Educational attainment is still uneven for boys and girls from poor households, especially in lower-income countries***

Gender gap in primary education by level of income

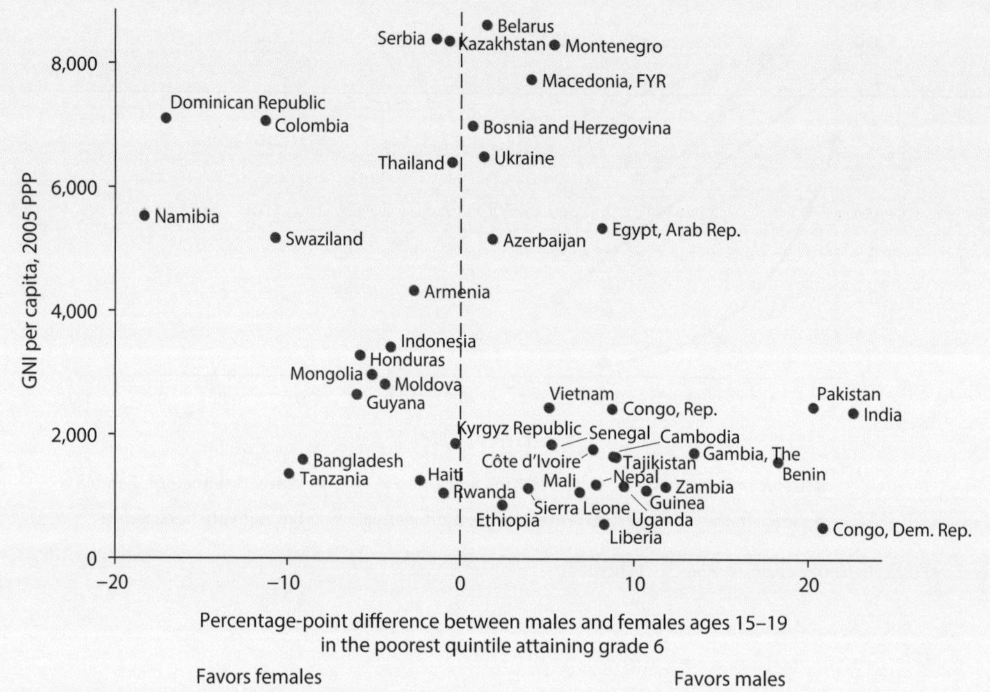

Source: WDR 2014 team based on data from World Bank EdAttain (database).

Note: Positive differences denote a lower percentage of females attaining grade 6 relative to males. Household poverty is based on an index of assets and housing characteristics. Years are between 2005 and 2008. GNI = gross national income. PPP = purchasing power parity.

especially among the poorest, can be seen as a supply and demand problem. On the supply side, insufficient and inadequate infrastructure, lack of teacher training, and weak monitoring and enforcement of basic standards (such as teacher attendance) diminish the quality of education. On the demand side, resource constraints, lack of employment opportunities, or limited information about returns to education add to the low quality, reduce the perceived value of education, and increase dropout rates.[29] Research shows that conditional cash transfer (CCT) programs have been successful in increasing the demand for education. But better employment opportunities also act as a powerful incentive to invest in education, as research from Bangladesh and Mexico shows.[30]

While middle-income countries are catching up to high-income countries on attainment, there are still large differences in quality between countries, as shown by the average scores of 15-year-olds in the standardized Programme for International Student Assessment (PISA) math test (figure 3.7b). These quality gaps reduce the potential effect of education on skill acquisition and job opportunities.

Moreover, gender gaps in education continue to exist within poor households in certain countries, limiting the opportunities for women to participate in the labor market years later. Gaps in education enrollment and attainment have narrowed impressively in the developing world, and they have even reversed in some groups, with women surpassing men in attainment in several countries.[31] However, among poor households, some parents are still reluctant to invest as much in education for girls as they do for boys. In many low-income countries, for example, fewer girls than boys in the poorest quintile achieve six years of education (figure 3.8). Low educational attainment also affects women's participation in the labor force; in Nicaragua, for example, women with complete tertiary education were almost twice as likely to participate in the labor force as women with only primary education.[32]

Accumulating financial and physical assets to build insurance and investment opportunities

The ability to maintain liquid savings and tap credit in safe and flexible ways is important for managing risks and investments. Even among the poor, saving rates and the number of financial instruments used (mostly informal) are high.[33] But many obstacles impede poor households from keeping significant amounts of liquid savings to manage risks more effectively or to undertake investment opportunities. First, for very poor households, satisfying immediate needs takes most of their income, making the opportunity costs of saving very high. Second, informal risk-sharing mechanisms and the associated pressure to share income might affect decisions about how much to save and what instruments to use.[34] Despite these obstacles, having access to saving and credit options is highly valued, which is evident from the substantial fees that some people are willing to pay to be able to save safely; these include rotating savings and credit associations, which do not pay interest and bear significant risk for loss, and deposit collectors, who *charge* fees, rather than pay interest, to keep the customers' savings. The growing number of clients—137.5 million in 2010—of microfinance providers is also a sign of the substantial demand and the potential benefits of expanding financial products among the poor.[35] As chapter 6 discusses, however, wider access to financial products for households, if not well-managed, can increase demand for credit beyond amounts these households can reasonably handle and lead to overindebtedness. That, in turn, can affect aggregate financial stability.

Physical assets—while less efficient than liquid savings—are another important resource for managing risk. Most poor households save in part by accumulating physical and productive assets such as livestock, jewelry, or appliances, all of which have low liquidity and uncertain returns. Physical and productive assets may be exposed to risk from disasters, crime, or expropriation, and some forms of assets, such as land, may not be transferable. Asset price fluctuations can also hurt the ability of households to use assets effectively as insurance mechanisms.[36]

Moreover, the ability to own and accumulate assets is unequal within many households. Laws in most of the world allow women to own assets, but several countries—particularly in South Asia and Sub-Saharan Africa—still have gender-specific ownership rights that limit women's ability to acquire, sell, transfer, or inherit property. Such laws weaken the bargaining position of the woman in the household, leaving her and her children more vulnerable to shocks and less able to pursue opportunities.[37] For instance, in southern Ethiopia, where divorces are rare and divorced wives get no share of joint assets, women from poor households—but not their husbands—reduce their food consumption when they get sick and are unable to work.[38]

Few households in developing countries rely on market insurance products. As noted in chapter 1, the risks that concern people the most relate to insurable events: illness, loss of income, and loss of assets. Although these events can be difficult to insure against when they affect large numbers of people, as in the case of an epidemic or a natural disaster, insurance products are widely available in high-income countries. Health, property, and unemployment insurance are common, and in some cases even mandatory. Yet in developing countries, only about 1 percent of total asset losses from natural hazards were formally insured between 1980 and 2004, compared with 30 percent in high-income countries.[39] The low penetration of market insurance products in developing countries results from high transaction costs (for assessing claims), which translate into high premiums. Instead, most people rely on informal risk-sharing arrangements with their extended family and community members (see chapter 4).

A low supply of formal insurance only partly explains low coverage. Demand for insurance tends to be low among many households even when people repeatedly suffer from or are exposed to shocks such as illness or disasters. Several explanations have been advanced for this low observed demand. First, resource constraints often restrict people's ability to purchase insurance. Second, people with limited education and low numeracy skills might find the concept of insurance complex and therefore prefer informal reciprocity arrangements. Third, subscribers must trust that the provider will deliver the payment if the shock occurs. Building trust becomes more challenging if the institutional environment offers few avenues to enforce the contract. Finally, the high noncovered risk (or "basis" risk) of many insurance schemes reduces the expected payment and undermines the value of the insurance policy and the trust associated with it.[40]

Building insurance informally through family formation, fertility, and marriage

In places where social protection and access to financial markets are limited, the process of family formation can be highly related to risk.[41] Agreements for mutual support among family members can be one of the limited options available in contexts where access to other forms of support are missing, either from the market or the state (see box 3.1). In Andhra Pradesh and Maharashtra in southern India, for example, many parents marry their daughters into households in distant villages to diversify income risks among households exposed to different climatic shocks. In these cases, a daughter's marriage becomes an informal insurance mechanism to protect consumption. In countries where parents must provide a dowry to their daughters, the financial pressure can lead them to marry their daughters at younger ages or to other members of the extended family (family ties act as a form of credit because parents can commit to later payments). These practices limit the potential for investing in daughters' human capital and expose them to risk of abuse by their spouses, as well as increasing health risks for future children when girls marry biological relatives.

Parents may also have to rely on their children to confront the risk of income loss.[42] For example, rural households in Bangladesh with higher risk exposure, fewer credit sources, and weaker ties to their community have higher rates of fertility than similar households in India. One of the driving factors behind this difference is that women in rural Bangladesh, unlike women in rural India, lack job opportunities outside the home. Women who cannot participate in the labor market face more difficulties in responding effectively to large shocks—such as widowhood—and hence must rely more heavily on support from their children. High fertility has negative consequences for human capital accumulation in developing countries, where children from larger families receive fewer vaccinations and have lower school attainment. This quantity-quality trade-off suggests that these families have less leeway to make adjustments in their resource allocation as the number of children increases.

Diversifying income sources and increasing labor supply

In developing countries, where exposure to income shocks is large and formal insurance is unavailable, households often diversify their sources of income. Throughout the developing world, household income often comes from more than one sector (for example, farming and services), location (urban and rural, domestic or foreign), or product. For example, 10 to 20 percent of households in Mexico, Nicaragua, Panama, and Timor Leste; 50 percent in Indonesia; 72 percent in Côte d'Ivoire; 84 percent in Guatemala; and 94 percent in Udaipur, India, report earning income from more than one type of activity.[43] Having a diversified income portfolio including farm and nonfarm activities might reduce income fluctuations, but it does not always do so—in part because incomes from different activities tend to be more correlated during crises.[44] In addition, because household effort is divided into many different activities, diversification often leads to lower average incomes. Greater access to markets and safety nets reduces the need for people to diversify their income activities to lower their exposure, as a recent study in Bangladesh found, and it also opens possibilities for them to enter higher-income activities.[45]

Other households—typically those with no access to credit markets, formal or informal—opt for activities that have low risk exposure but also have low returns, such as drought-resistant crops, which tend to have low yields. Households with very few assets cannot self-insure against shocks, either by selling these assets or by using them as collateral for credit. At the same time, diversifying income sources often requires a minimum amount of starting capital (say, for purchasing an animal). As a result, many asset-poor households have no other option but to opt for activities where income risk is minimal. Studies in India, Tanzania, and other countries have found that poor rural households grow disproportionately more low-risk, low-return crops, such as sweet potatoes.[46]

Increasing their labor supply can help households cope with shocks, provided that household members can work and that sources of employment are available. In such cases, households with excess labor supply, which can be readily tapped as needed, can protect consumption more effectively. Regression analysis shows that, for example, members of larger households in China, Iraq, Peru, and Uzbekistan respond to shocks by increasing the hours they work, taking on more jobs, or working in a different location.[47]

The ability of a household to increase its labor supply either temporarily or permanently depends critically on the ability of women to participate in the labor force. Female participation has increased significantly in recent decades, but a large share of the female population still remains outside the labor force. Only one in five women in the Middle East and North Africa and less than one in three in South Asia were either working or looking for work in 2011 (figure 3.9). Economic factors including higher labor demand, better infrastructure, and higher educational attainment play a pivotal role in increasing female labor market participation. However, because women tend to be the main providers of child care, lack of good-quality child care alternatives can create a trade-off between

FIGURE 3.9 *Female labor force participation is still limited in some regions*

Percentage of females in the labor force

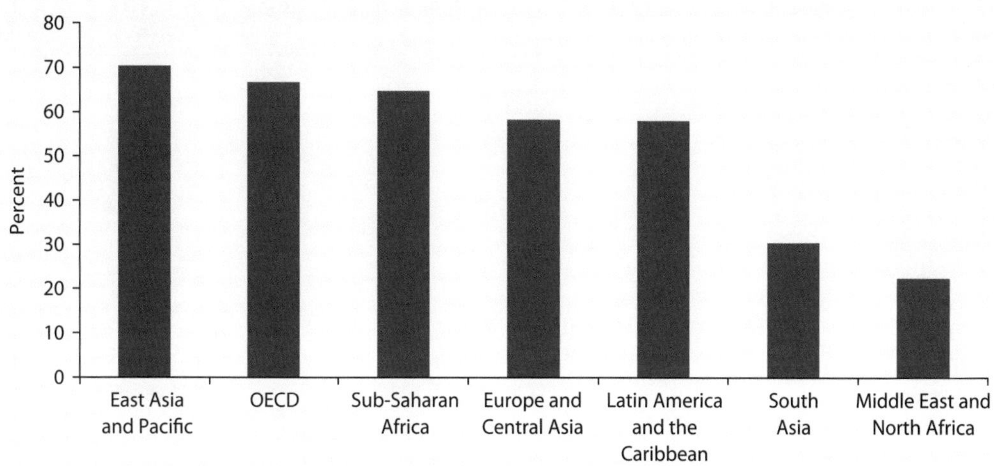

Source: WDR 2014 team based on data from World Bank World Development Indicators (database).

Note: Data are as of 2011. Organisation for Economic Co-operation and Development (OECD) countries in the figure are high-income countries that have been members of the OECD for at least 40 years. All other countries are grouped into geographic regions.

female participation in the labor force and child development. In addition, social norms that limit the participation of women in economic activity may slow down gains in female participation in the regions with historically low participation.[48]

Migration is also an effective way to diversify risk and can be a coping response to a shock. Although migration can weaken social ties within the family and with the rest of the community, its net economic effect is still likely to be positive for the entire household—a fact reflected in the growing movement of people within and across countries and in the volume of remittances worldwide. Temporary migration for work from rural to urban areas is the dominant form of migration; there are 740 million internal migrants worldwide, nearly four times the number of international migrants.[49] Most studies on migration, which focus on international migration, find positive and substantial contributions to migrant income, although the effects on family members who remain behind are less clear. Still, in the Philippines for example, an unexpected increase in a migrant's income leads to higher educational expenditures, enhanced entrepreneurship, and lower poverty rates at the origin. A growing body of literature finds that remittances are an informal insurance against consumption shocks at the origin. For instance, in the Philippines, Tanzania, and Thailand, migrant workers are more likely to send remittances to members of their family who are hit by a shock.[50]

Experimental evidence shows that poor households fail to take advantage of migration opportunities that would improve their response to shocks. A study in a famine-prone rural area of Bangladesh found that people are not willing to migrate temporarily to the city during the lean season, despite the harsh conditions. For them, the cost of migrating and the possibility of not finding a job opportunity in the city make it too risky an enterprise, even if expected returns are positive. As part of the study, a small cash incentive was offered to farmers to migrate. Those who took the incentive and migrated increased the consumption of their family members by 30 percent, increased the calorie intake by 550–700 calories a person a day, and were also more likely to migrate again in following years, when the incentive was no longer offered.[51]

How can government strengthen protection and foster better opportunities for households?

Households face multiple risks every day, and they use as many tools as they have available to manage them. Poor households, however, tend to have only limited access to protection and insurance mechanisms provided by markets and public services. These limitations increase vulnerability, particularly for risks that are not equally shared within the household. Government policies can substantially improve

TABLE 3.2 *A systemic approach for policies to address multiple risks using multiple instruments*

	Types of policy instruments						
Goal	Facilitate savings	Social insurance	Cash transfers	Information/ training	Wage subsidies	Access to services	Access to credit/ grants
Preparing and coping with:							
Illness	X	X	X	X		X	
Disability	X	X	X	X	X	X	X
Old age	X	X	X	X		X	X
Death	X	X	X				
Unemployment	X		X	X	X	X	X
Weather shocks/ disasters	X	X	X	X		X	X
Investment in human capital			X	X		X	
Poverty reduction			X	X	X	X	X

Source: WDR 2014 team based on Robalino, Rawlings, and Walker 2012.

household risk management and increase households' access to better opportunities by taking a systemic approach to risk management. Such an approach implies a sound understanding of the risks that households face, the interactions between them, the range of obstacles to better risk management, and the right combination of instruments that can strengthen risk management while increasing access to opportunities. Table 3.2 shows how various kinds of policy instruments address multiple sources of risk and suggests how they might be used from a systemic perspective; for example, providing health services in combination with other instruments, such as insurance and information on preventive practices, can deliver better outcomes in protecting people against the risk of disease and the financial burden it causes. Some tools, such as cash transfers, also contribute to investment in human capital and poverty alleviation.

Taking a systemic approach to policy making for risk management also implies that instruments need to be put in place before shocks take place and that coordination is essential. In practice, different programs and policies are the responsibility of different government agencies; institutional mechanisms are thus needed to coordinate these programs and policies to align goals, set monitoring and performance standards, and establish common infrastructure that enables risk management tools to function seamlessly. Moreover, just as households need to prepare in anticipation of shocks, governments need to have these systems in place before shocks hit, incorporating features that enable a quick response to changes in households' needs. The following recommendations describe different policy instruments that can help households address barriers to building better protection, insurance, and coping strategies, as well as instruments that can improve risk sharing within the household, keeping in mind that single-instrument solutions are rare and that the most successful policies involve a combination of them.

Designing policies with a risk management lens

Policies often have indirect effects on people's behavior, and understanding these effects can be useful for improving incentives to invest in protection at the household level. Property rights are a telling case. Secure property rights increase the value of the asset to the owner, because the asset can be safely transferred and also used as collateral, increasing access to credit. Beyond that, secure land tenure rights increase the value of investments in land conservation and infrastructure, which reduce risk exposure and increase productivity. Secure land tenure rights have also been found to increase labor market participation and reduce child labor.[52] Another example is cash transfers. They are a very direct way to help households overcome financial constraints to invest in human capital, but incentives to invest are even greater when the transfers are conditioned on making the investments. A recent experimental comparison of conditional and unconditional cash transfers for girls in Malawi shows that conditioning plays an important role in improving school attendance and even learning outcomes.[53]

Leveraging technology and partnering with the private sector

Systemic policies addressing multiple risks require not only close coordination among different government agencies but also partnering with other actors in the society. The ability to share data and to track beneficiaries across programs is one example—simple in theory—that many countries struggle with in practice. The availability of affordable technologies to collect biometric data is opening opportunities for governments to identify beneficiaries and deliver services to them, in particular for the poor, who are often "invisible" populations for lack of proper proof of identity. India's pioneering identification project aims to issue a unique identification number, or *Aadhaar,* to every resident of the country, linked to basic demographic information and biometrics, as a formal proof of identity. The scheme has assigned more than 300 million *Aadhaars* so far, at a cost of less than $3 per capita. The *Aadhaar* is a gateway to both public and private services: the government uses it to deliver public benefits directly to individuals with fewer leakages, and the private sector—particularly financial services providers—can use the *Aadhaar* to expand access to financial services.[54] More generally, public service delivery can benefit from public-private partnerships in many areas, from health to social assistance (box 3.2).

Addressing disparities within households

Public policies can also redress the balance of power and reduce inequities within the household. In many cases, a combination of regulatory reforms, targeting of public programs, and social norms that empower women to take greater control over decisions regarding family planning, work, and financial management can increase their bargaining power in the household, while reducing the vulnerability and improving opportunities for children.

Many women in poor households—particularly in poor and rural areas—have little control over fertility decisions, in part because good-quality family planning information and services are not available. Women in these areas should have reliable access to these services through health care providers, together with a range of contraceptive options. This task requires putting in place an efficient supply chain. In addition, providers need to communicate effectively and transparently with their patients about the benefits and potential side effects of different contraception methods, while respecting women's preferences and privacy.[55] To be truly effective, however, family planning services need to be accompanied by other interventions to increase women's bargaining power in the household, notably those that increase their economic clout and legal standing.

Access to labor markets for women is particularly important because it allows households to diversify their sources of income and improve the risk management of entire households.[56] But women's access to the labor market is extremely limited in some

BOX 3.2 *Improving service delivery by partnering with the private sector*

Public-private partnerships are an increasingly important component of efficient and effective service delivery. In India, government-sponsored health insurance schemes—which aim to expand access to health insurance to half the country's population by 2015—have engaged private sector firms as both administrators and health care providers. In São Paulo, Brazil, private nonprofit operators were permitted to run new hospitals based on a performance-based contract model. While implementation was not without challenges, impact evaluations have found that the nonprofit hospitals have been more efficient than for-profit ones, without sacrificing quality. Improvements in human resources and management practices seem to be responsible. In education, public-private partnerships can cut costs and improve student achievement. Colombia's Programa de Ampliación de Cobertura de la Educación Secundaria (PACES) provided 125,000 children with vouchers to attend private secondary academic and vocational schools. The program was cost-effective and increased student achievement.

The private sector can also play an important role in government transfer programs. In Brazil, banks now pay the government for the valuable right to distribute social security benefits; this is a reversal from the past, when the Brazilian government would pay banks. In making the transition, the government has saved money, beneficiaries have gained more places to obtain their benefits, and banks have acquired additional customers for their credit products. Conditional cash transfer (CCT) programs in Ecuador and South Africa also partner with private financial institutions to deliver payments. CCT programs in Bangladesh, Chile, and Colombia allow beneficiaries to use private providers to fulfill their education and health commitments. The private sector may be critical for meeting the increased service demands stimulated by CCTs in many countries.

Source: WDR 2014 team based on La Forgia and Nagpal 2012; Lewis and Patrinos 2012; Fiszbein and Schady 2009; La Forgia and Harding 2009; and Ortiz d'Avila Assumpção 2012.

places. Public policies can help, starting by ensuring that girls, in particular in poor households, complete their education. Providing child care alternatives and promoting family-friendly workplace policies can encourage women to stay in the labor force when they have children. Public action (through the media, for example) can also help counter social norms that keep women at home (see chapter 2).

Giving women more voice in household decision making has positive consequences for risk management and investment in human capital.[57] Women's empowerment can be achieved not only by enhancing access to the labor market but also by making women the beneficiaries of cash transfer and other social programs. Moreover, regulatory reforms that increase women's land tenure and inheritance rights, such as the reforms to the Hindu Succession Act, have been found to increase women's bargaining power as well as human development outcomes for girls.[58]

Abuse and discrimination within the family makes it a source of, rather than a solution to, risk.

Legal action against domestic violence is necessary to counter social norms that tolerate violence against women and children. In East Asia and the Pacific, the Middle East and North Africa, and Sub-Saharan Africa, more than 20 percent of women believe that a husband is justified in hitting or beating his wife for commonplace reasons such as going out without telling him and arguing with him (figure 3.10). As argued earlier, domestic violence can be both the outcome of an environment dominated by risk as well as a source of risky behavior. Better risk management tools can reduce the incidence of violence by reducing the stress factors associated with risk. Beyond that, legal sanctions against violent behavior provide a strong signal that, regardless of social norms, domestic violence has serious consequences.

Enhancing access to labor markets

To increase investment in skills, interventions should tackle demand and supply constraints. The first step is providing information about job opportunities and returns to education. Research from the Dominican Republic shows that receiving information on returns to education significantly reduces the likelihood that students will drop out of school before completion. In India, providing recruitment services

FIGURE 3.10 ***Social norms in many regions tolerate domestic violence***

Percentage of women who say that a husband is justified in hitting or beating his wife

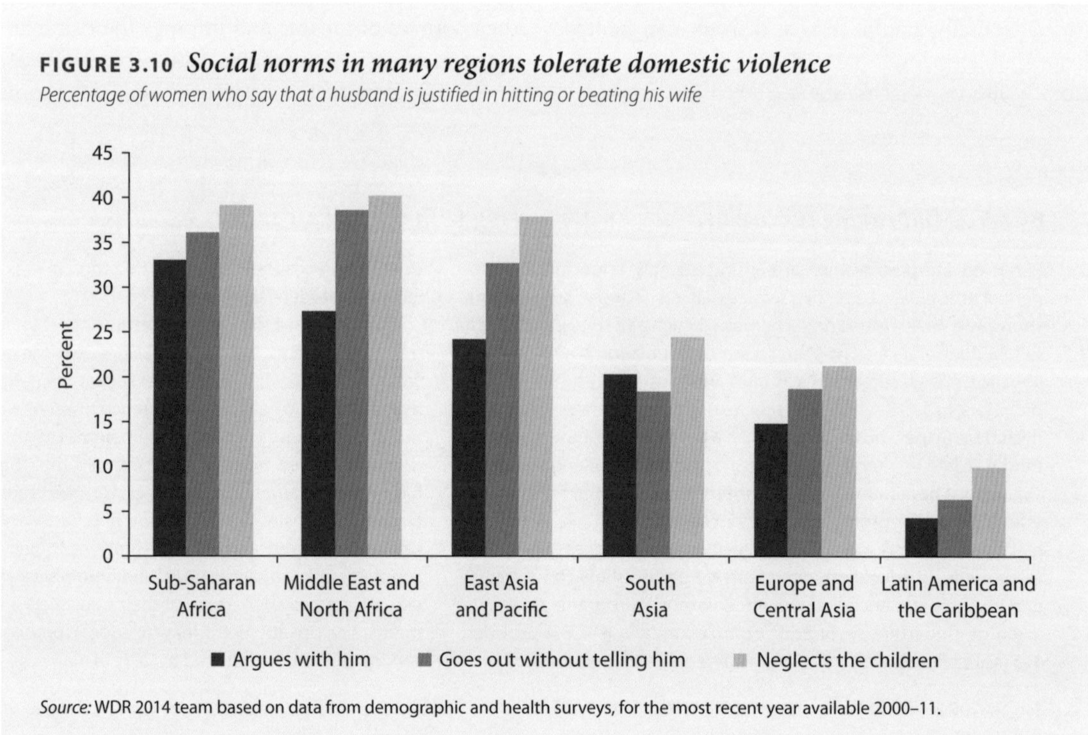

Source: WDR 2014 team based on data from demographic and health surveys, for the most recent year available 2000–11.

for jobs to women delayed their decision to marry and have children and increased their reported desire to obtain training and work more steadily.[59]

Second, education and training systems should help students develop the skills that employers want, which include soft skills, such as communications ability, in addition to reading and numeracy skills, according to employer surveys throughout the world. Evaluations of training programs for out-of-school youth that combine soft skills with technical training have shown positive results in increasing beneficiaries' chances of job placement and the quality of their jobs. Evidence also suggests that the delivery model that works best involves partnering with (accredited) private providers. Finally, many people need specific assistance to navigate the labor market and find the best opportunities available. Countries with sufficient implementation capacity can establish employment services to facilitate the matching process of employers and employees; these services have proven highly effective in high-income countries, particularly for unskilled workers.[60] These skill-enhancement strategies can deliver better job opportunities, however, only if there is an accompanying demand for these skills. For that, a dynamic enterprise sector is crucial (see chapter 5).

Facilitating migration and remittances

Lowering barriers to domestic and international migration also helps households diversify incomes and respond to shocks. As discussed, domestic migration provides millions of families with alternative income opportunities outside farming. But for poor households, even temporary migration is a risky venture that many are not willing to pursue. In many cases, indirect policies that, for instance, lower transportation costs, can encourage temporary migration. International migration also presents people with better income opportunities, but increasing movements of undocumented migrants across countries have increased social tensions and violence and even cost lives. To mitigate these risks, sending countries can play a more proactive role in facilitating legal migration, protecting the rights of migrants abroad, and respecting migration policies of receiving countries. A few countries have implemented programs of regulated migration. While these programs might not always be able to ensure proper treatment of migrants, they offer an avenue to migrate legally. Programs in Morocco, the Philippines, St. Lucia, and Tonga, for example, offer workers the opportunity to migrate temporarily to countries that demand labor in specific sectors, such as agriculture, construction, or health care. Receiving and sending countries establish agreements on quotas, wages, and duration of stay. If workers fulfill the requirements, they can migrate legally for a preestablished period, with a fixed contract and wage. Workers can reapply to the program upon their return, which lowers their incentive to stay illegally once their contract expires.[61]

Lower transaction costs for remittances can improve households' ability to mitigate income losses, while opening the door to better income opportunities. Worldwide in 2011, migrants sent approximately $372 billion in remittances to their families in developing countries (see chapter 6). Migrants often pay hefty transaction costs to send small amounts of money through large carriers. Lowering transaction costs by encouraging competition and promoting transparency can increase the benefits of remittances significantly for receiving countries. Simply providing information about fees for different carriers can help. The project Envía CentroAmérica, financed in part by the World Bank and the Inter-American Development Bank, provides detailed information about the fee variation across carriers for sending money to seven Central American countries. For example, fees for sending $200 from Washington, D.C. to Guatemala ranged from 1.29 percent to 17.42 percent, depending on the institution and the modality of payment. Mobile phones have also enabled many migrants, especially in countries like Kenya, to send remittances in a safe and affordable way.[62]

Increasing access to financial products

Financial products are a crucial component of a household's risk management strategy, and governments can facilitate access to formal financial products in several ways. As discussed earlier, poor households face significant barriers to access formal financial services. In addition to promoting the financial inclusion of the poor through an appropriate regulatory framework (such as consumer protection laws) and by expanding financial literacy (see chapter 6), governments can leverage social programs to connect beneficiaries with the financial sector through payment systems. This link has been made successfully in Brazil, Ecuador, and South Africa, where beneficiaries of pensions and cash transfer programs receive their payments electronically through the financial system (see box 3.2). In addition, carefully designed public subsidies can help expand the supply of certain commercial financial products, such as index insurance, that significantly

BOX 3.3 ***Index-based insurance: The potential and the challenges***

Index-based insurance can be a viable instrument to manage agricultural risk. Index-based, or parametric, insurance provides payments based on physical triggers (such as variation in rainfall) rather than loss claims. This type of insurance is less subject to moral hazard and has significantly lower transaction costs. Although some farmers bear significant "basis risk" because their risk is imperfectly correlated with the risk insured by the index contract, several studies show that index-based insurance increases investment and improves yields. In Tamil Nadu in India, for example, offering farmers index-based insurance made them more likely to plant higher-yield (but riskier) rice varieties and less likely to plant lower-yield but drought-tolerant ones. And when basis risk is large, having an informal network can help by providing insurance against basis risk. Thus the presence of informal risk sharing actually increases demand for index-based insurance in the presence of basis risk.

Still, the coverage of index-based insurance remains low. In particular, providers need to find better ways to market it by taking into account the context in which farmers operate, the variety of risks that they face, and their lack of experience with formal financial products. For instance, the studies for India show that selling insurance to landless laborers, not just land owners, provided significant protection to their income and their ability to invest, because they bear a disproportionate share of agricultural risk. In Kenya and Rwanda, Kilimo Salama, an index-based insurance program for small farmers, has managed to increase its client base by insuring inputs instead of harvests, using "aggregators" such as cooperatives to insure groups rather than single farmers, creating premium-sharing arrangements between farmers and agribusinesses, selling through local businesses that are frequented by the farmers, and paying claims immediately using mobile phones.

Governments also have a role to play. The Mexican Catastrophe Climate Contingency Insurance Program provides state governments with funding for the purchase of insurance, most of which is index-based and targeted at subsistence producers below the threshold for commercial agricultural insurance. India's Weather Based Crop Insurance Scheme has significantly expanded the use of index-based insurance by subsidizing premiums. However, government premium subsidies create tensions in the market that are difficult to resolve. For example, selling subsidized index-based insurance to landless agricultural laborers (who technically do not possess an insurable interest) opens the market to others (such as urban residents) to gamble with the product because the subsidized premiums make the insurance product, in effect, look like an attractive lottery ticket. Government resources might be better targeted to covering the up-front cost of installing weather stations needed to monitor rainfall at high density (to reduce basis risk), and to scaling up these investments, rather than subsidizing the price of the premiums.

Source: WDR 2014 team based on Brown, Mobarak, and Zelenska 2013 for the WDR 2014; Alejandro de la Fuente for the WDR 2014; "Fact sheet: Kilimo Salama ("Safe Agriculture")," available at http://kilimosalama.files.wordpress.com/2010/02/kilimo-salama-fact-sheet-final11.pdf.

improve risk management for the poor but that face scaling-up challenges (box 3.3).

Building health and social protection systems that protect the most vulnerable

Because health and income shocks can be particularly destructive for the poor, protecting them against these risks is a priority. This section discusses how countries can expand the coverage of health and social protection, starting with the most vulnerable populations, while striving to improve service delivery and results and still maintain fiscal sustainability.

Health insurance reforms are increasingly improving protection for the most vulnerable. In many developing countries, public health systems are fragmented, inefficient, and inequitable. Typically, health insurance systems are available to a minority of people, usually workers in the formal sector, while everyone else has access to lower-quality national health care systems financed by general revenues. Such duplication puts financial pressure on health systems, creates tiered-quality services, and may be regressive.[63] As a result, poor people receive substandard treatment while bearing large out-of-pocket costs. Many countries have undertaken efforts to reform their health care systems to deliver better services to the poor—while maintaining sustainability—by moving toward a model of universal health insurance (see the cases of Turkey and the Kyrgyz Republic in spotlight 3). A growing consensus is focusing on three basic goals for reform: enhancing risk pooling to ensure that health expenditures do not overwhelm the household's saving capacity; ensuring financial sustainability and equitable access by defining specific benefit packages and providing insurance at a low cost (or free) for the poor; and improving efficiency by delinking financing from service provision.

Table 3.3 summarizes some recent efforts in different countries to expand access to health insurance. While many features respond to the unique context of each country, a few patterns are apparent. First, these efforts provide subsidies so that poor and vulnerable populations can obtain access to insurance. For example, China's rural health insurance program subsi-

TABLE 3.3 *Common features of programs to expand coverage of health insurance*

What	Who	How
Use of general revenue financing to include the poor	Colombia	The Régimen Subsidiado health insurance program offers free and heavily subsidized health care to the poorest.
	India	The Rashtriya Swasthya Bima Yojna (RSBY) insurance program requires payment of a small nominal fee (5 percent of the combined registration fee and premium).
	Indonesia	The Jamkesmas program covers the poor and near-poor population at no cost.
	Mexico	The Seguro Popular program offers a full subsidy to informal sector households.
	Thailand	Any person outside the formal/civil service sector is covered for a nominal fee.
	Turkey	Premiums of the poor are covered by the state.
	Vietnam	Those below the poverty line and other selected groups are fully subsidized; the near-poor receive partial subsidization.
Higher quality and efficiency	India	Authorizations and case management in RSBY and Rajiv Aarogyasri are fully electronic.
Defined service package	Brazil	The Sistema Único de Saúde (SUS) offers a comprehensive package that includes essential drugs and dental care.
	Mexico	Package includes coverage of catastrophic illness.
	South Africa	The Antiretroviral Program provides testing, monitoring, and treatment for HIV/AIDS, based on a financial sustainability study.
	Turkey	Comprehensive basic benefits package includes diagnostic services, inpatient treatment, and hospitalization for emergency care.
Incentives on the supply side	Brazil	SUS transfers to municipal governments depend on meeting performance and coverage targets.
	Colombia	Capitation (per capita fees) and fee-for-service are commonly used in the Régimen Subsidiado.
	India	Private insurers are selected through competitive bidding and paid on the basis of enrollment.
	Indonesia	Providers are paid capitation at the primary level, and negotiated fees at the secondary level.
Services tailored to vulnerable populations	Brazil	The Family Health Strategy uses outreach activities to expand use of primary care and to identify and treat common diseases.
	Ethiopia	The Health Extension Workers program trains households to adopt best practices and to become role models in their community.
Data-driven	India	Biometric data collected at enrollment are used for monitoring use and outcomes.
	Kyrgyz Republic	Payment and utilization are analyzed to identify outliers and barriers to access and to forecast needs and costs.
	South Africa	Expenditures on personnel, drugs and supplements, lab services, and information systems are actively monitored.

Source: WDR 2014 team based on Cotlear, forthcoming, for Brazil, Colombia, Ethiopia, India, the Kyrgyz Republic, Mexico, South Africa, Turkey, and Vietnam. For India, Indonesia, and Thailand, see Adam Wagstaff 2011, "Health reform: A Consensus Emerging in Asia?" *Let's Talk Development* (blog), April 12. http://blogs.worldbank.org/developmenttalk/.

dizes at least 80 percent of the premium cost, and it aims to cover the entire rural population. In India, the Rashtriya Swasthya Bima Yojna scheme requires beneficiaries to pay only a nominal registration fee to join; the premium is paid by taxpayers. Indonesia's Jamkesmas scheme also covers the poor and near-poor at taxpayers' expense. In Thailand, the Universal Coverage scheme provides insurance for a nominal fee to everyone who is not in the civil service or the formal sector. Second, most insurance programs cover only a defined range of services, which can vary widely from country to country. Some countries have focused on covering primary care, while others cover only catastrophic illness, and still others offer a mix. Finally, several countries include the private sector in service delivery and make innovative uses of technol-

FIGURE 3.11 ***Noncontributory pension programs have expanded coverage in developing countries, especially for the poorest***

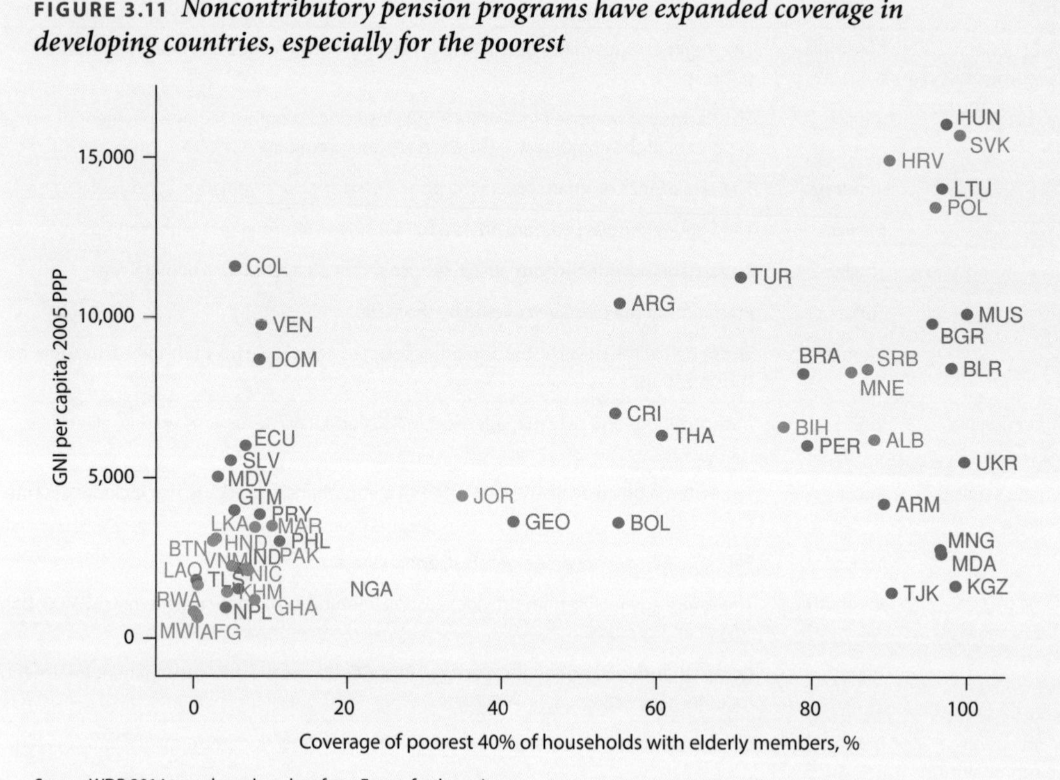

Source: WDR 2014 team based on data from Evans, forthcoming.

Note: Years vary between 2003 and 2010. Countries marked in blue have noncontributory pensions. GNI = gross national income; PPP = purchasing power parity.

ogy to improve efficiency. It is still too early to pass definitive judgment on the impact of these trends on health outcomes and household health expenditures, as well as their fiscal sustainability. But learning from these cases will be crucial as more countries move toward universal health insurance.

Providing income support for old age

Life-cycle transitions such as old age reduce the ability of individuals to earn sufficient income to remain out of poverty. In addition, time-inconsistent behaviors discussed in chapter 2 justify policies to encourage people in their earning years to save for the future. In many countries, however, social insurance systems (mostly for pensions and health) cover a minority of the population, usually the nonpoor. This exclusion occurs because so-called contributory insurance systems are financed by payroll taxes and contributions levied on employers and employees, typically only in the formal sector—which effectively denies access to the large proportion of self-employed and agricultural workers who work in the informal sector. In other countries, where contributory pension systems are supporting a rapidly growing elderly population, declining ratios of workers to retirees and a higher life expectancy make the current model unsustainable.

As a result, more and more countries are expanding coverage of basic pensions by introducing noncontributory pensions financed by general revenues. For example, 13 countries in Latin America and the Caribbean now have noncontributory pensions for those not covered by the contributory system.[64] Others, like Mauritius, South Africa, and several high-income countries, have historically relied on noncontributory pensions. As figure 3.11 shows, aside from the former socialist countries in Eastern Europe and Central Asia, all developing countries that cover more than half of the poorest 40 percent of households with elderly members have noncontributory systems.[65] Several studies show that noncontributory pensions have increased coverage and reduced poverty among the elderly.[66]

When contributory and noncontributory systems coexist, however, incentives to participate in mandatory contributory systems may diminish. That occurs because contributory systems may be ill-designed or because contributory and noncontributory systems may not be well integrated. Workers who move between formal and informal jobs or in and out of the labor force might not contribute sufficiently to be eligible to receive benefits or might achieve very low income-replacement rates.[67] Workers in rapidly aging countries might contribute toward increasingly uncertain benefits, creating a perception of contributions as a pure tax on labor and encouraging them to underreport wages or opt for informal employment.

To ensure that social insurance systems are equitable, fiscally sustainable, and minimize distortions in the labor market, countries should reconcile the need to expand coverage with the need to encourage private savings. Specifically, noncontributory systems that provide a basic level of benefits should be financed through general revenues just like any other basic government function. But not all countries are in a position to provide adequate benefits universally in a fiscally sustainable manner. In practice, many developing countries may be able to provide only a minimum level of benefits and possibly to only a targeted population. That is true in particular for countries where the old-age dependency ratio is growing fast. Thus countries need to consider their long-term fiscal capacity in relation to their future commitments to decide what the appropriate levels of coverage and benefits are. Importantly, they need to consider the different options to collect the necessary tax revenues (see the "Focus on policy reform" at the end of this Report).

Contributory systems can help to increase the adequacy of insurance benefits, but they need to be designed in a way that does not create distortions in the labor market. In some contexts, distortions will be avoided only if contributions are made voluntary and open to all, regardless of work status or if the mandatory contribution rates are reduced. In all cases, contributory systems should provide benefits that are clearly linked to contributions. Further, incentives to save—automatic enrollment, matching contributions, simplifying processes, and lowering information barriers through financial literacy—can have a significant impact. New Zealand's KiwiSaver scheme is an interesting example of an automatic enrollment program (with an "opt-out" option) that increased retirement savings for about half the population.[68]

Offering safety nets for bad times

Safety nets are also crucial to help the most vulnerable households manage risk and protect consumption in the face of shocks. Studies show that safety net programs such as public works and cash transfers help people build assets, take more risk in their productive activities, and accumulate human capital. Beneficiaries of programs in Bangladesh, Brazil, India, Mexico, Nicaragua, and other countries have invested more resources in high-risk, high-return ventures (such as fertilizer), have diversified their income away from agriculture, and have gained access to credit.[69]

For example, public works programs provide labor income while contributing to local economic development. These programs are particularly beneficial in countries with large rural populations, like those in Sub-Saharan Africa. Indeed, the region has more than 150 public works programs and more than 120 cash transfer programs.[70] Public works programs protect households' consumption in the face of income losses, while enabling them to build crucial growth-enhancing assets; examples include building water infrastructure and improving land management at the local level. Moreover, public works programs have positive local economic spillovers, similar to other safety nets. For instance, the Extended Public Works program in South Africa boosted local economies, because 67 percent of the beneficiaries purchased food from local shops.[71] Most of these programs are targeted geographically, and beneficiary selection is done through self-targeting (by offering low wages, the programs attract those who most need the income, while encouraging them to continue to seek other work). These programs also have the flexibility to respond to specific adverse conditions in certain households; for instance, the Ethiopian Productive Safety Net Program uses family targeting, which allows the program to adjust the quota of days that a family can benefit from the program to the size of the family.

A systemic approach to social protection is helping governments exploit synergies across instruments and deliver better service to all those who need it.[72] For instance, several programs have recently implemented strategies that combine protection with access to opportunity.[73] These programs seek to "graduate" beneficiaries sustainably by building pathways to better income through self-employment or wage employment opportunities. In most cases, these strategies require combining a range of instruments beyond simply providing cash transfers, such as providing links to financial services or training. Safety net beneficiaries in Côte d'Ivoire, Rwanda, and Tanzania are encouraged to save part of their earnings by obtaining access to bank accounts and community saving groups. Public works programs in El Salvador, Sierra Leone, and South Africa also provide some basic and technical skills training.[74] In Cameroon, beneficiaries of the new cash transfer program attend financial literacy and business training activities. Evaluation from pilot programs that provide cash and training to beneficiaries in Ethiopia, Ghana, and Nicaragua show that the combination of instruments leads to entry into higher-income activities in the short to medium term.

Both policies that empower households as a unit and policies that empower individuals within households are necessary.

Putting it all together: Guidelines for policy implementation

The policy recommendations to improve households' risk management can be roughly categorized into two complementary groupings: policies to *empower households*, and policies to *empower individuals within households* to better manage their risks.

The first set of policies addresses obstacles that households face as units, such as lack of information, lack of resources, and limited access to labor and financial markets. The second group addresses challenges to risk sharing within the household and impediments that increase the vulnerability of certain members, including underinvestment in human capital, using children to manage risk, excluding women from financial decision making, and exposure to domestic violence. Table 3.4 presents a summary of the policy recommendations discussed in this chapter, highlighting how combining different instruments may contribute to strengthening risk management, and the possible complementarities between them. This systemic approach requires strong coordination across government institutions

TABLE 3.4 *Policy priorities to improve risk management at the household level*

	POLICIES TO SUPPORT RISK MANAGEMENT FOUNDATIONAL →		→ ADVANCED
Knowledge	Basic literacy and training	Secondary education and training	Higher education and training
	Media and community campaigns	Teaching preventive health in schools	
	Facilitating informed fertility decisions	Access to mobile technology	
Protection	Sanitation infrastructure and preventive health care (including women's health)		
	Migration assistance/access to labor and other markets (especially for women)		
	Regulation to guarantee equal property rights for women	Policies to promote gender parity in leadership positions	
	Promulgation and enforcement of domestic violence and abuse laws		
Insurance	Index insurance	Financial inclusion of the poor	
	Lower remittance costs		
	Health insurance	Pensions (old age, disability, death)	Unemployment insurance
Coping	Self- and community-targeted income support	Means-tested income support	
	Transfers targeted to women		

Source: WDR 2014 team.

Note: The table presents a sequencing of policies based on the guidance of chapter 2 for establishing policy priorities: *be realistic* in designing policies tailored to the institutional capacity of the country, and *build a strong foundation* that addresses the most critical obstacles sustainably and that can be improved over time.

as well as between the government and the other economic and social actors, and depends on the country's institutional capacity.

A country's initial conditions also affect the use and effectiveness of each policy instrument. Hence, policies in table 3.4 are grouped according to a country's initial conditions and follow the guidelines presented in chapter 2: first, to be realistic, with policies adapted to the country's capacity; and second, to build a strong foundation, with policies that address the most important obstacles first and upon which more advanced policies can be designed and implemented over time. Thus countries with limited resources and low institutional capacity can begin by focusing on the most foundational policies: ensuring access to basic services, while also improving the efficacy of informal mechanisms, for example, by facilitating migration and remittances. Countries that have laid the foundations for risk management can go beyond the basics and focus on expanding access to services and raising productivity to foster the ability of households to take advantage of opportunity—by improving access to formal risk management products, and expanding coverage of social insurance.

In most countries, and in particular in those with limited capacity, implementing coordinated policies using multiple instruments can be very difficult. As discussed in chapter 2, obstacles inherent in public policy undermine the effectiveness of many government actions in helping people manage risk. These obstacles include limited capacity and resources, coordination failures within the government and with other actors, political economy constraints, and deep uncertainty. A few basic principles—following the guidelines to be realistic and build a strong foundation—can help policy makers overcome these obstacles as they design and implement policies.

Keep a long-run perspective

To ensure their long-run sustainability, governments should make sure that policies are fiscally sustainable and that institutional arrangements transcend the political cycle. Often, governments come into office eager to establish ambitious "flagship" programs, which turn out to be unaffordable, especially during economic downturns. Moreover, many of these programs are operated in isolation, rather than in coordination with similar and complementary programs run by other agencies. Instead of taking this short-term approach, governments should focus on building a legacy through stable institutional arrangements that improve coordination and efficiency across agencies, such as unified registries and data-sharing protocols, and by building strong technical capacity among civil servants. In addition, key programs that help people manage risk, such as social assistance programs, need to be properly funded when they are needed the most: that is, during downturns. To do that, governments should exploit good times to set up safety nets that can be scaled up to cover more people and offer more benefits in bad times, when more households face illness, unemployment, and other losses.

Promote flexibility

Within the institutional framework proposed above, government policies and programs should also be sufficiently flexible to adapt to changing circumstances. One example is the labor market. Demographic and economic changes can cause deep changes in the labor market; thus labor market policies, including education and training policies, should be flexible enough to adapt to such changes. Similarly, safety net programs require both effective instruments to identify the most vulnerable households and individuals when crises hit and the necessary infrastructure to deliver services in a timely manner. They should also be able to scale back their coverage when the crisis passes.

Provide the right incentives

Increasing incentives for members of the household to take personal responsibility is an important part of empowering households to manage risk. Many social assistance programs are now taking incentives into account: for instance, by establishing benefits and setting time limits on receipt to avoid discouraging beneficiaries from working. Public policy should also aim to change incentives within the household so that members decide to pool their resources for the benefit of all. This goal might require a mix of regulation reforms and specific design features in public programs (such as targeting of beneficiaries, combined with legal reforms). For instance, targeting women in cash transfer programs can empower them economically, but can also have negative repercussions (such as an increased risk of domestic violence) if their legal protection is not guaranteed.[75]

Protect the vulnerable

The first priority for policies to improve risk management should be those households that face the largest barriers to preparation. Too often, however, the definition of vulnerability is determined by interest groups. In the United States, the government spends 2.2 times as much on the elderly as on children, yet 22 percent of children under 18 live in poverty, compared with 9 percent of adults aged 65 and older.[76] Similarly, Brazil has practically eradicated poverty among the elderly, but not among children. Transparent policies with clearly defined priorities and goals, but with the flexibility to reallocate public funds when these goals are not met or when they change, can help.

Do not generate uncertainty or unnecessary risks

Policies should not create new obstacles to risk management. Most of the policies discussed in this chapter seek to overcome obstacles to risk management for households. In some cases, however, design flaws may create new barriers. For example, private saving incentives can be undermined if governments use the funds in public saving programs to finance current expenditures. Price caps imposed on food staples to keep them affordable to the poor often result in massive shortages and speculation, making people worse off. In more extreme cases, governments enact regulations that legitimize social norms that may weaken household risk management, such as those that limit the economic and social participation of women. Anticipating the additional risks and other unintended consequences for risk management that policies might generate should help governments avoid implementing policies where "the medicine is worse than the disease."

Notes

1. This story is adapted from Davis 2011.
2. See Hoff and Sen 2005.
3. Dercon 2002.
4. Heltberg, Oviedo, and Talukdar 2013 for the WDR 2014.
5. See references in Oviedo and Moroz 2013 for the WDR 2014.
6. Genicot and Ligon 2013 for the WDR 2014.
7. De Vreyer and Lambert 2013 for the WDR 2014.
8. Giles, Guo and Zhao 2013.
9. Silverstein and Giarrusso 2010.
10. See literature discussion in Alderman and others 1995.
11. Udry 1996 for Burkina Faso; Duflo and Udry 2004 for Côte d'Ivoire.
12. See, for example, Iversen and others 2011.
13. Heltberg, Oviedo, and Talukdar 2013 for the WDR 2014.
14. Oviedo and Moroz 2013 for the WDR 2014.
15. See references in Friedman and Sturdy 2011; Oviedo and Moroz 2013 for the WDR 2014.
16. Dercon 2002; Friedman and Sturdy 2011.
17. See references in Oviedo and Moroz 2013 for the WDR 2014.
18. Haushofer, de Laat, and Chemin 2012; Friedman and Sturdy 2011.
19. Heltberg, Hossain, and Reva 2012.
20. Miguel 2005.
21. World Bank 2011.
22. See Kusimba and others 2013, for example.
23. See discussion and references in Brown, Mobarak, and Zelenska 2013 for the WDR 2014.
24. See references in Brown, Mobarak, and Zelenska 2013 for the WDR 2014.
25. Heckman, Stixrud, and Urzua 2006; Grossman 2006.
26. Chou and others 2010.
27. For instance, see Card 1999.
28. Barro and Lee 2010. Returns to an additional year range from 6 percent in Sub-Saharan Africa to close to 14 percent in high-income economies.
29. See the discussion on this topic in Banerjee and Duflo 2011.
30. See references in Brown, Mobarak, and Zelenska 2013 for the WDR 2014.
31. World Bank 2011.
32. World Bank 2012.
33. Collins and others 2009.
34. See Di Falco and Bulte 2011 and Baland, Guirkinger, and Mali 2011 for examples.
35. Ledgerwood 2013.
36. Dercon 2002.
37. World Bank 2011.
38. Dercon and Krishnan 2000.
39. Linnerooth-Bayer, Mechler, and Hochrainer-Stigler 2011.
40. See references in Brown, Mobarak, and Zelenska 2013 for the WDR 2014.
41. See references in Cáceres-Delpiano 2013 for the WDR 2014.
42. See references in Cáceres-Delpiano 2013 for the WDR 2014.
43. See references in Brown, Mobarak, and Zelenska 2013 for the WDR 2014.
44. Dercon 2002.
45. Bandyopadhyay and Skoufias, forthcoming.
46. Dercon 2002.
47. Heltberg, Oviedo, and Talukdar 2013 for the WDR 2014.
48. See in-depth discussion in World Bank 2011.
49. See references in Brown, Mobarak, and Zelenska 2013 for the WDR 2014.
50. Paulson 2000; De Weerdt and Hirvonen 2013.
51. See references in Brown, Mobarak, and Zelenska 2013 for the WDR 2014.
52. Field 2007; World Bank 2003.
53. Baird, McIntosh, and Özler 2011.
54. Nilekani 2013.
55. World Bank 2011.
56. See, for example, Basu 2006.
57. World Bank 2011.
58. Deininger, Goyal, and Nagarajan 2013.
59. Jensen 2010; Jensen 2012.
60. Brown, Mobarak, and Zelenska 2013 for the WDR 2014; Almeida, Behrman, and Robalino 2012; Almeida and others 2012.
61. Ruiz 2008.
62. Kusimba and others 2013.
63. Ribe, Robalino, and Walker 2012.
64. See Holzmann, Robalino, and Takayama 2009.
65. Evans, forthcoming; Levy and Schady 2013.
66. See, for instance, Holzmann, Robalino, and Takayama 2009; Levy and Schady 2013; Frölich and others, forthcoming.
67. Ribe, Robalino, and Walker 2012.
68. Hinz and others 2013.
69. Alderman and Yemtsov 2012.
70. Premand 2013 for the WDR 2014.
71. Alderman and Yemtsov 2012.
72. Robalino, Rawlings, and Walker 2012.
73. See references in Premand 2013 for the WDR 2014.
74. See spotlight 2 on promoting food security in El Salvador.
75. World Bank 2011.
76. Isaacs and others 2012.

References

Abdul Latif Jameel Poverty Action Lab (J-PAL). 2011. "The Price Is Wrong: Charging Small Fees Dramatically Reduces Access to Important Products for the Poor." *J-PAL Bulletin* April 2011.

Alderman, Harold, Pierre-André Chiappori, Lawrence Haddad, John Hoddinott, and Ravi Kanbur. 1995. "Unitary Versus Collective Models of the Household: Is It Time to Shift the Burden of Proof?" *World Bank Research Observer* 10 (1): 1–19.

Alderman, Harold, and Ruslan Yemtsov. 2012. "Productive Role of Safety Nets." Social Protection and Labor Discussion Paper 1203, World Bank, Washington, DC.

Alesina, Alberto, and Paola Giuliano. 2013. "Family Ties." Working Paper 18966, National Bureau of Economic Research, Cambridge, MA.

Alger, Ingela, and Jörgen W. Weibull. 2010. "Kinship, Incentives, and Evolution." *American Economic Review* 100 (4): 1725–58.

Almeida, Rita, Juliana Arbelaez, Maddalena Honorati, Arvo Kuddo, Tanja Lohmann, Mirey Ovadiya, Lucian Pop, Maria Laura Sanchez Puerta, and Michael Weber. 2012. "Improving Access to Jobs and Earnings Opportunities: The Role of Activation and Graduation Policies in Developing Countries." Social Protection and Labor Discussion Paper 1204, World Bank, Washington, DC.

Almeida, Rita, Jere R. Behrman, and David A. Robalino. 2012. *The Right Skills for the Job? Rethinking Training Policies for Workers.* Human Development Perspectives. Washington, DC: World Bank.

Baird, Sarah, Craig McIntosh, and Berk Özler. 2011. "Cash or Condition? Evidence from a Cash Transfer Experiment." *Quarterly Journal of Economics* 126 (4): 1709–53.

Baland, Jean-Marie, Catherine Guirkinger, and Charlotte Mali. 2011. "Pretending to Be Poor: Borrowing to Escape Solidarity in Cameroon." *Economic Development and Cultural Change* 60 (1): 1–16.

Bandyopadhyay, Sushenjit, and Emmanuel Skoufias. Forthcoming. "Rainfall Variability, Occupation Choice, and Welfare in Rural Bangladesh." *Review of Economics of the Household.*

Banerjee, Abhijit V., and Esther Duflo. 2011. *Poor Economics: A Radical Rethinking of the Way to Fight Global Poverty.* New York: PublicAffairs.

Barro, Robert J., and Jong-Wha Lee. 2010. "A New Data Set of Educational Attainment in the World, 1950–2010." Working Paper 15902, National Bureau of Economic Research, Cambridge, MA.

Basu, Kaushik. 2006. "Gender and Say: A Model of Household Behaviour with Endogenously Determined Balance of Power." *Economic Journal* 116 (511): 558–80.

Becker, Gary S. 1974. "A Theory of Social Interactions." *Journal of Political Economy* 82 (6): 1063–93.

Bernheim, B. Douglas, Andrei Shleifer, and Lawrence H. Summers. 1985. "The Strategic Bequest Motive." *Journal of Political Economy* 93 (6): 1045–76.

Brown, Julia K., Mushfiq A. Mobarak, and Tetyana V. Zelenska. 2013. "Barriers to Adoption of Products and Technologies That Aid Risk Management in Developing Countries." Background paper for the *World Development Report 2014.*

Cáceres-Delpiano, Julio. 2013. "Literature Review: Family Formation and Fertility as Risk Coping Mechanisms." Background paper for the *World Development Report 2014.*

Card, David. 1999. "The Causal Effect of Education on Earnings." In *Handbook of Labor Economics*, vol. 3A, 1801–63. Amsterdam: Elsevier.

Chou, Shin-Yi, Jin-Tan Liu, Michael Grossman, and Ted Joyce. 2010. "Parental Education and Child Health: Evidence from a Natural Experiment in Taiwan [China]." *American Economic Journal: Applied Economics* 2 (1): 33–61.

Collins, Daryl, Jonathan Morduch, Stuart Rutherford, and Orlanda Ruthven. 2009. *Portfolios of the Poor.* Princeton, NJ: Princeton University Press.

Contreras, Manuel, Brian Heilman, Gary Barker, Ajay Singh, Ravi Verma, and Joanna Bloomfield. 2012. "Bridges to Adulthood: Understanding the Lifelong Influence of Men's Childhood Experiences of Violence." International Center for Research on Women, Washington, DC.

Cotlear, Daniel. Forthcoming. "The Challenges of Implementing Universal Health Coverage in Developing Countries: Lessons from 25 Countries from around the World." Unpublished manuscript. World Bank, Washington, DC.

Davis, Peter. 2011. "Patterns of Socio-Economic Mobility in Rural Bangladesh: Lessons from Life-History Interviews." Working Paper 197, Chronic Poverty Research Center, Bath, U.K.

Deininger, Klaus, Aparajita Goyal, and Hari Nagarajan. 2013. "Women's Inheritance Rights and Intergenerational Transmission of Resources in India." *Journal of Human Resources* 48 (1): 114–41.

Dercon, Stefan. 2002. "Income Risk, Coping Strategies, and Safety Nets." *World Bank Research Observer* 17 (2): 141–66.

Dercon, Stefan, and Pramila Krishnan. 2000. "In Sickness and in Health: Risk Sharing within Households in Rural Ethiopia." *Journal of Political Economy* 108 (4): 688–727.

De Vreyer, Philippe, and Sylvie Lambert. 2013. "Household Risk Management in Senegal." Background paper for the *World Development Report 2014.*

De Weerdt, Joachim, and Kalle Hirvonen. 2013. "Risk Sharing and Internal Migration." Policy Research Working Paper 6429, World Bank, Washington, DC.

Di Falco, Salvatore, and Erwin Bulte. 2011. "A Dark Side of Social Capital? Kinship, Consumption, and Savings." *Journal of Development Studies* 47 (8): 1128–51.

Duflo, Esther, and Christopher Udry. 2004. "Intrahousehold Resource Allocation in Côte d'Ivoire: Social Norms, Separate Accounts and Consumption Choices." Working Paper 10498, National Bureau of Economic Research, Cambridge, MA.

Evans, Brooks. Forthcoming. "An Examination of Pension Coverage of Elderly in the Developing World." Social Protection and Labor Policy Note, World Bank, Washington, DC.

Field, Erica. 2007. "Entitled to Work: Urban Property Rights and Labor Supply in Peru." *Quarterly Journal of Economics* 122 (4): 1561–602.

Fiszbein, Ariel, and Norbert Schady. 2009. *Conditional Cash Transfers: Reducing Present and Future Poverty.* Washington, DC: World Bank.

Friedman, Jed, and Jennifer Sturdy. 2011. "The Influence of Economic Crisis on Early Childhood Development: A Review of Pathways and Measured Impact." In *No Small Matter: The Impact of Poverty, Shocks, and Human Capital Investments in Early Childhood Development*, edited by Harold Alderman, 51–83. Washington, DC: World Bank.

Frölich, Markus, David Kaplan, Carmen Pagés-Serra, Jamele Rigolini, and David Robalino. Forthcoming. *Social Insurance and Labor Markets: How to Protect Workers While Creating Good Jobs.* Washington, DC: World Bank, Inter-American Development Bank, and Institute for the Study of Labor.

Genicot, Garance, and Ethan Ligon. 2013. "Risk and the Extent of Insurance." Background Paper for the *World Development Report 2014.*

Giles, John, Junjie Guo, and Yaohui Zhao. 2013. "Community, Family and Household Support for the Elderly in the Wake of Rapid Urbanization: Evidence from Rural China." Research in progress supported by the Knowledge for Change Program, World Bank, Washington, DC.

Grossman, Michael. 2006. "Education and Nonmarket Outcomes." In *Handbook of the Economics of Education*, vol. 1, edited by Eric Hanushek and Finis Welch, 578–633. Amsterdam: Elsevier.

Haushofer, Johannes, Joost de Laat, and Matthieu Chemin. 2012. "Poverty Raises Levels of the Stress Hormone Cortisol: Evidence from Weather Shocks in Kenya." Unpublished manuscript. J-PAL, Cambridge, MA.

Heckman, James J., Jora Stixrud, and Sergio Urzua. 2006. "The Effects of Cognitive and Noncognitive Abilities on Labor Market Outcomes and Social Behavior." *Journal of Labor Economics* 24 (3): 411–82.

Heltberg, Rasmus, Naomi Hossain, and Anna Reva, eds. 2012. *Living through Crises: How the Food, Fuel, and Financial Shocks Affect the Poor.* Washington, DC: World Bank.

Heltberg, Rasmus, Ana Maria Oviedo, and Faiyaz Talukdar. 2013. "What Are the Sources of Risk and How Do People Cope? Insights from Household Surveys in 15 Countries." Background paper for the *World Development Report 2014.*

Hinz, Richard, Robert Holzmann, David Tuesta, and Noriyuki Takayama. 2013. *Matching Contributions for Pensions: A Review of International Experience.* Washington, DC: World Bank.

Hoff, Karla, and Arijit Sen. 2005. "The Kin System as a Poverty Trap?" Policy Research Working Paper 3575, World Bank, Washington, DC.

Holzmann, Robert, David A. Robalino, and Noriyuki Takayama. 2009. *Closing the Coverage Gap: The Role of Social Pensions and Other Retirement Income Transfers.* Washington, DC: World Bank.

Isaacs, Julia, Katherine Toran, Heather Hahn, Karina Fortuny, and C. Eugene Steurle. 2012. "Kids' Share 2012: Report on Federal Expenditures on Children through 2011." Urban Institute, Washington, DC.

Iversen, Vegard, Cecile Jackson, Bereket Kebede, Alistair Munro, and Arjan Verschoor. 2011. "Do Spouses Realise Cooperative Gains? Experimental Evidence from Rural Uganda." *World Development* 39 (4): 569–78.

Jensen, Robert. 2010. "The (Perceived) Returns to Education and the Demand for Schooling." *Quarterly Journal of Economics* 125 (2): 515–48.

———. 2012. "Do Labor Market Opportunities Affect Young Women's Work and Family Decisions? Experimental Evidence from India." *Quarterly Journal of Economics* 127 (2): 753–92.

Kusimba, Sibel, Harpieth Chaggar, Elizabeth Gross, and Gabriel Kunyu. 2013. "Social Networks of Mobile Money in Kenya." Working Paper 2013-1, Institute for Money, Technology, and Financial Inclusion, Irvine, CA.

La Forgia, Gerard M., and April Harding. 2009. "Public-Private Partnerships and Public Hospital Performance in São Paulo, Brazil." *Health Affairs* 28 (4): 1114–26.

La Forgia, Gerard, and Somil Nagpal. 2012. *Government-Sponsored Health Insurance in India: Are You Covered?* Washington, DC: World Bank.

Ledgerwood, Joanna. 2013. *The New Microfinance Handbook: A Financial Market System Perspective.* Washington, DC: World Bank.

Levy, Santiago, and Norbert Schady. 2013. "Latin America's Social Policy Challenge: Education, Social Insurance, Redistribution." *Journal of Economic Perspectives* 27 (2): 193–218.

Lewis, Laura, and Harry Anthony Patrinos. 2012. "Impact Evaluation of Private Sector Participation in Education." Research Report, CfBT Education Trust, Reading, U.K.

Linnerooth-Bayer, Joanne, Rainhard Mechler, and Stefan Hochrainer-Stigler. 2011. "Insurance against Losses from Natural Disasters in Developing Countries: Evidence, Gaps and the Way Forward." *Journal of Integrated Disaster Risk Management* 1 (1): 1–23.

Miguel, Edward. 2005. "Poverty and Witch Killing." *Review of Economic Studies* 72 (4): 1153–72.

Nilekani, Nandan. 2013. "The Aadhaar Project." Presentation at Development Economics Lecture Series, World Bank, Washington, DC, April 24.

OECD (Organisation for Economic Co-operation and Development). Programme for International Student Assessment (PISA) (database). OECD, Paris, http://www.oecd.org/pisa.

Ortiz d'Avila Assumpção, Rodrigo. 2012. "How Brazil Stopped Paying the Banks: A Brazilian Perspective on Social Security Payments." Presentation at Social Protection and Labor Sector Seminar Series, World Bank, Washington, DC, October 26.

Oviedo, Ana María, and Harry Moroz. 2013. "The Impacts of Risk." Background paper for the *World Development Report 2014.*

Paulson, Anna L. 2000. "Insurance Motives for Migration: Evidence from Thailand." Kellogg Graduate School of Management, Northwestern University, Evanston, IL.

Premand, Patrick. 2013. "From Risk Coping to Risk Management: Productive Safety Nets in Africa." Background paper for the *World Development Report 2014.*

Ribe, Helena, David A. Robalino, and Ian Walker. 2012. *From Right to Reality: Incentives, Labor Markets, and the Challenge of Universal Social Protection in Latin America and the Caribbean.* Washington, DC: World Bank.

Robalino, David A., Laura Rawlings, and Ian Walker. 2012. "Building Social Protection and Labor Systems: Concepts and Operational Implications." Social Protection and Labor Discussion Paper 1202, World Bank, Washington, DC.

Ruiz, Neil G. 2008. "Managing Migration: Lessons from the Philippines." Migration and Development Brief 6, World Bank, Washington, DC.

Silverstein, Merril, and Roseann Giarrusso. 2010. "Aging and Family Life: A Decade Review." *Journal of Marriage and Family* 72 (5): 1039–58.

Udry, Christopher. 1996. "Gender, Agricultural Production, and the Theory of the Household." *Journal of Political Economy* 104 (5): 1010–46.

United Nations. 2009. "World Population Prospects: The 2008 Revision." Department of Economic and Social Affairs Population Division, United Nations, New York.

World Bank. 2003. *Land Policies for Growth and Poverty Reduction.* Washington, DC: World Bank.

———. 2011. *World Development Report 2012: Gender Equality and Development.* Washington, DC: World Bank.

———. 2012. "Better Jobs in Nicaragua: The Role of Human Capital." Policy Note, World Bank, Washington, DC.

———. Educational Attainment and Enrollment around the World (EdAttain) (database). World Bank, Washington, DC, http://iresearch.worldbank.org/edattain/.

———. World Development Indicators (database). World Bank, Washington, DC, http://data.worldbank.org/data-catalog/world-development-indicators.

Moving toward universal health insurance coverage in Turkey and the Kyrgyz Republic

The economic consequences of an illness are often devastating in developing countries. About 100 million people fall into poverty annually struggling to cover health care costs. The experiences of Turkey and the Kyrgyz Republic show that countries at all levels of development can improve access to and affordability of medical services by increasing the efficiency of government health spending and protecting the poor through publicly financed health insurance.

Increasing equity in access to health care in Turkey

Turkey has achieved impressive results in access, affordability, and quality of health care. Health insurance covers 95 percent of the population, and 76 percent of Turkish citizens are satisfied with health care services. Before 2003, however, use of health services was very uneven among regions, and health care in rural areas was both hard to obtain and more costly than in cities. Health financing was fragmented among four different insurance schemes. A separate Green Card Program for the poor covered only inpatient services and therefore was not widely used. Most public health resources were allocated to costly hospital-based services, rather than primary care.

To address these problems, the government launched a comprehensive Health Transformation Program in 2003. All health insurance schemes were merged into a universal health insurance program managed by the newly created Social Security Institution. Every insured person, including the poor, has the same benefits package, which covers inpatient and outpatient services, dental care, diagnostic tests, emergency care, and pharmaceuticals. The poor are exempt from co-payments if they use public facilities. The expanded benefits led to greater demand for the Green Card; participation more than tripled from 2003 to 2011, from 2.5 million to 9.1 million. Targeting of the program has also improved substantially: Green Card benefits to those in the lowest income quintile increased from 55 percent in 2003 to 71 percent in 2012.

Premiums are based on household income and increase with wealth. The government pays the premiums for the poor—defined as households with per capita income less than one-third the minimum wage, or about $163 a month. The poor are identified through the national Integrated Social Aid Services System, which is also used to determine eligibility for other social assistance programs. The integrated system helps avoid duplication of information and improves benefits administration. The near-poor (those with per capita income between one-third and the full minimum wage) are also well protected, with premiums set at about $20 a month. The rest of the population pays higher premiums, depending on income.

The government sought to strengthen primary care by promoting family medicine. This decision was in keeping with global evidence that systems oriented to primary care produce better health for the population at lower cost. The government introduced several incentives, including raising salaries of family doctors, introducing performance guidelines, and regularly monitoring the quality of service delivery through facility visits and patient surveys. Providers risk paying up to 20 percent of their base salary in penalties for failure to meet certain performance targets, such as immunizations and antenatal care. The government also introduced monthly bonus payments of up to 40 percent of base salary for doctors who relocate to underserved locations, a step that has reduced the gap in access to health care between rural and urban locations.

These reforms have significantly improved access to services and financial protection against medical costs throughout the country. Use of health services has more than doubled since 2003, satisfaction with the quality of health care has also risen, and key health indicators—life expectancy, and child and maternal mortality—have improved. A World Bank evaluation of the Green Card Program showed that it provided an effective safety net for the poor during the economic crisis of 2008, with beneficiaries less likely than those with no insurance to reduce their use of curative and preventive care. Improvements in access to health care were achieved without excessive public health spending: at 5.1 percent of gross domestic product (GDP), Turkey's public health spending is comparable to that of other countries at similar levels of development. Going forward, it will be important to strengthen mechanisms to contain costs and further increase efficiency of health spending.

Improving affordability of health care in the Kyrgyz Republic

At independence in 1991, the Kyrgyz Republic had a standard Soviet health care system, characterized by a large network of providers, a focus on curative hospital care rather than preventive services, and a centrally planned, input-based financing system. Although inefficiencies plagued this system, every Kyrgyz citizen enjoyed access to free medical services. During the early 1990s, the young state experienced a deep economic crisis, GDP declined by more than half, and the government was unable to maintain the oversized health care system. Informal out-of-pocket payments to health care providers became common to compensate for low salaries. Hospitalized patients often had to help pay for medicine, bed linens, and even light bulbs. For many of the poor, health care was unaffordable and thus unused.

Starting in 2001, the government introduced a series of reforms to improve the efficiency of health sector spending and decrease out-of-pocket costs. The sequencing of reforms was important to the success of the approach. First, the Mandatory Health Insurance Fund (MHIF) was introduced, funded by a 2 percent payroll tax paid by employers. The government makes contributions for the retired and the unemployed, and the self-employed can purchase health insurance for about $10 a year. Significant efficiency gains were obtained by consolidating separate pools of public health care funding at the district and regional levels into a single pool managed by the MHIF. This arrangement has reduced overhead costs and resulted in more equitable allocation of resources across administrative units. Second, purchase of health services was centralized under the MHIF, which contracts with providers across the country under output-based payment mechanisms. This approach has enhanced efficiency, giving facility managers some flexibility in how to use the funds. Third, primary care was made a priority. The oversized hospital sector was reduced by about 40 percent, and savings were allocated to medical supplies and salaries of health providers.

A major outcome of the reforms was the explicit definition of benefits and regulation of entitlements. The State Guaranteed Benefit Package establishes free primary and emergency care for all citizens and subsidized secondary care with exemptions from co-payments for vulnerable groups: children under age 5, retirees older than 70, the disabled, pregnant women, and those with medical conditions with high expected use of health care (diabetes, cancer, tuberculosis, and asthma). These groups also benefit from access to subsidized medications.

The impact of the reforms has been very positive. Use of health care is now roughly the same at all income levels (figure S3.1). Households are less likely to fall into poverty as a result of illness. Out-of-pocket health expenditures have declined among all income groups since the start of reforms and constituted only 4.4 percent of total household spending among the poorest quintile in 2009 (see figure S3.1). The incidence of catastrophic health spending (more than 20 percent of total household expenditures) declined from 8 percent in 2000 to 5 percent in 2009. Several health indicators, such as infant and under-five mortality rates, have improved, and the country has much better health outcomes than the average low-income nation. Public health spending constitutes about 3.5 percent of GDP, which is somewhat higher than the average for low-income countries and reflects the government's prioritization of health spending.

The experience in the Kyrgyz Republic shows that more efficient use of public resources can reduce the patient financial burden in a low-income country. This experience can be particularly valuable for other transition economies with limited fiscal space and overcapacity in the health sector. The positive outcomes were achieved thanks to a comprehensive approach rather than reliance on a single instrument. Introduction of strategic purchasing through the MHIF, giving providers greater autonomy and allowing them to manage some of the savings, downsizing the hospital sector, and increasing investments in primary care have resulted in significant efficiency gains that were directed toward greater financial protection of the population. The

FIGURE S3.1 *Use of health care and out-of-pocket health expenditure by income status, the Kyrgyz Republic, 2009*

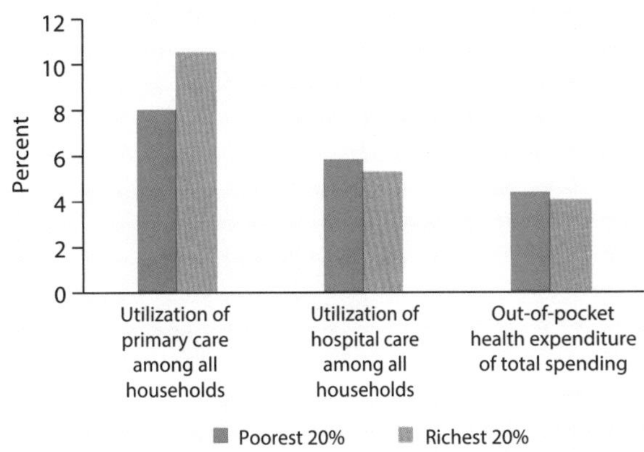

Source: WDR 2014 team based on data from Giuffrida, Jakab, and Dale 2013.

Kyrgyz Republic also has a rather developed health information system for a low-income country, which allows the government to forecast income from co-payments, plan annual expenditures, and monitor the impact of new policies.

Future reforms should focus on improving sustainability of health care financing. Further rationalization of health care financing will entail introducing targeting of co-payment exemptions by poverty status, as is done in Turkey and many other countries. Additional efficiency gains could be realized by reducing hospitalization rates and overuse of medication, cutting utility costs of health facilities, and streamlining funding on drug procurement.

Sources

Turkey

Aran, Meltem A., and Jesko S. Hentschel. 2012. "Protection in Good and Bad Times? The Turkish Green Card Health Program." Policy Research Working Paper 6178, World Bank, Washington, DC.

Menon, Rekha, Salih Mollahaliloglu, and Iryna Postolovska. 2013. "Toward Universal Coverage: Turkey's Green Card Program for the Poor." UNICO Studies Series 18. World Bank, Washington, DC.

OECD (Organisation for Economic Co-operation and Development) and World Bank. 2008. *OECD Reviews of Health Systems: Turkey.* Paris: OECD.

Ministry of Health of Turkey. 2012. *Health Statistics Yearbook 2011.* Ankara: Ministry of Health of Turkey.

Kyrgyz Republic

Giuffrida, Antonio, Melitta Jakab, and Elina M. Dale. 2013. "Toward Universal Coverage in Health: The Case of the State Guaranteed Benefit Package of the Kyrgyz Republic." UNICO Studies Series 17. World Bank, Washington, DC.

Ibraimova, Ainura, Baktygul Akkazieva, Aibek Ibraimov, Elina Manzhieva, and Bernd Rechel. 2011. "Kyrgyzstan: Health System Review." *Health Systems in Transition* 13 (3): 1–152.

WHO (World Health Organization). 2010. *Health Systems Financing: The Path to Universal Coverage.* Geneva: WHO.

Yazbeck, Abdo S. 2009. *Attacking Inequality in the Health Sector: A Synthesis of Evidence and Tools.* Washington, DC: World Bank.

Strength in numbers: members of a women's self-help group in rural Madhya Pradesh, India, attend a skills training program.

CHAPTER 4

Cohesive and connected communities create resilience

Community

Communities confront many risks

More than 750 people died when a heat wave struck Chicago in 1995, many of them elderly poor who avoided opening their windows at night for fear of crime. These deaths were not uniformly distributed across the city, even controlling for income. In some Chicago neighborhoods, the elderly poor perished, while in others they weathered the heat wave. Cohesive neighborhoods with strong social networks had lower mortality.[1]

In the rural community of Nyakatoke in Tanzania, a population of 120 households has formed at least 40 different community groups, such as burial insurance societies, rotating savings and credit associations, and labor and livestock sharing groups. These groups offer helpful (if partial) insurance to villagers, and most residents belong to several groups. Groups have verbal or written rules governing contributions and payouts for specific events, as well as sanctions against noncontributors. Some groups complement their rules with ceremonies that emphasize unity and the importance of mutual help. Most groups offer some form of insurance, and there is also a group that patrols the village at night.[2]

While local communities are at the epicenter of many crises, conflicts, and disasters, they are also part of the solution. Unmanaged risk causes loss of life, health, and property and deters investment.[3] Unlocking the potential of cities as centers of productivity and opportunity requires managing risks such as crime, pollution, and epidemics. Citizens are not defenseless: they may take steps to stop crime and disorder by mobilizing against gangs, mentoring at-risk youth, or stopping provocations from flaring into ethnic riots; they may petition authorities for sanitation, health services, and law and order; and they may provide mutual insurance and assistance.

Communities are groups of people who interact frequently and share identity or location. Neighborhood groups, religious groups, and kinship groups are some examples. Community relationships are not as close and long term as family relationships, in part because community groups are larger than families. People usually share gains and losses to a larger degree within their family than within their communities. At the same time, communities involve more personal interaction than market relationships; as a result, members of the community have better knowledge about one another's successes and failings, luck and misfortune. This knowledge helps them enforce norms about contributing to the common good and sharing with those in need.

Relying on norms, shame, guilt, and personal interaction allows well-functioning communities to solve many problems that markets and governments struggle with: preventing crime, managing natural resources, affecting behavior change, getting credit to the poor, and insuring risks that are hard for outsiders to monitor. Communities can mobilize for social change and responsive governance, as in the Arab

Spring. Community-driven projects can deliver public goods and services in fragile settings where government capacity is lacking, as in Afghanistan's National Solidarity Project. But communities can also exclude people and foment violent conflict with neighboring communities. And they struggle to create insurance pools and public goods of sufficiently large scale to address systemic risk and exploit more complex opportunities.[4]

This chapter focuses on how communities help their members confront risk and pursue opportunities and how development actors—including governments, donors, and nongovernmental organizations (NGOs)—can support them in this role. The chapter describes how many communities have evolved mechanisms of insurance, protection, and coping that help them address local risks; how some communities prosper while others expose their members to terrible risks; how free rider problems, unresponsive authorities, resource constraints, and other obstacles obstruct better community risk management; and how social cohesion and connections with other communities, markets, and government shape communities' chances at succeeding. The chapter also argues that communities can become much better risk managers with outside support.

> **For problems whose solution eludes markets and governments, a cohesive community could be the missing piece of the puzzle.**

Addressing risk is increasingly recognized as complementary to combating poverty in its many dimensions. When agencies listen to communities, they often discover that communities are keenly aware of risk and request support preparing for it. But what does risk management entail in a community context? This chapter explores various approaches governments, donors, and civil society organizations can use to foster communities' resilience, building on what is already there. The chapter advocates the types of policies that empower communities as risk managers by creating favorable legal regimes, fostering their own capacity to manage local risks, promoting their "voice" and ability to hold government accountable and providing complementary public goods and services. It also cautions against policies that ignore communities and create risk and instability.

Communities as risk managers

People and their communities face risk from many sources, both idiosyncratic and systemic. Surveys in many countries have asked people which shocks they have recently experienced: natural disasters, health shocks, price shocks, and asset loss tend to be the most frequent and severe (see also chapters 1 and 3). Evidence from many locations indicates that idiosyncratic shocks such as death, illness, and accidents are common and create high costs.[5] Systemic risk is important as well. In Tanzania, for example, six of the seven most frequently self-reported shocks—including spikes in food prices, floods, and water shortages—are systemic, in that they affect many members of the local community (figure 4.1a). In rural China, individual health and more widespread agricultural shocks are both major concerns. Agricultural shocks are more frequent, while health shocks tend to be more severe (figure 4.1b). In Nigeria, health shocks are the most common (35 percent of all severe shocks reported by urban households, and 27 percent by rural ones), followed by price and employment shocks in urban areas and disasters, price shocks, and asset loss in rural areas. Some systemic shocks are rather localized (drought, crop loss), while others are nationwide or global (swings in food and input prices).

What "community" means in the context of risk management can be defined in two complementary (and sometimes overlapping) ways, one centered on location, the other on cultural identity.[6] *Communities of location* are exactly what they sound like: people sharing a location, such as the long-term residents of a village or urban neighborhood. Communities of location can provide credit, insurance, and assistance against idiosyncratic risk and organize protection against local risks such as crime, disaster, and infection—for example, through policing, drainage, sanitation, or solid waste collection—provided they can overcome people's tendency to free ride and shirk on their responsibility to contribute or pay for their fair share of local public goods. Communities of location can either organize their own protection or petition government to provide the necessary services and infrastructure. Shared spaces such as parks and sports facilities strengthen people's ties to a local community.

The informal urban settlement of Indio Guays in Guayaquil, Ecuador, exemplifies a location-based community. The settlement sprang up in 1975, when poor people began acquiring land and building simple bamboo-walled houses. At that time, the new settlement sat in a swamp connected by dangerous

FIGURE 4.1 ***People and their communities are affected by both idiosyncratic and systemic shocks***

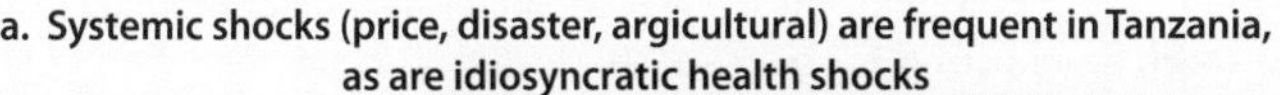

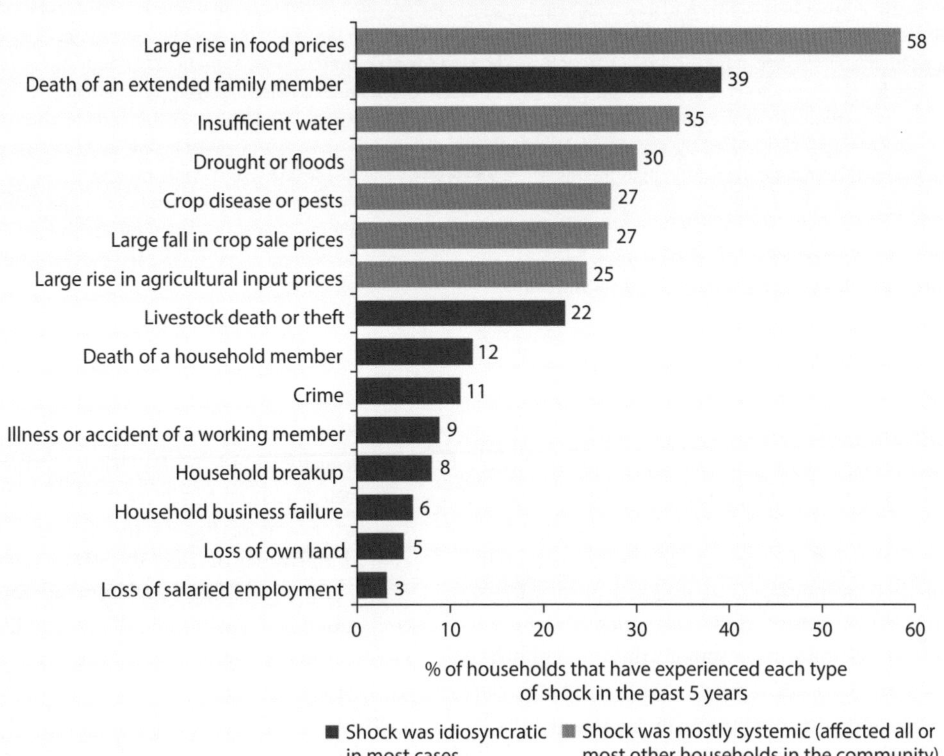

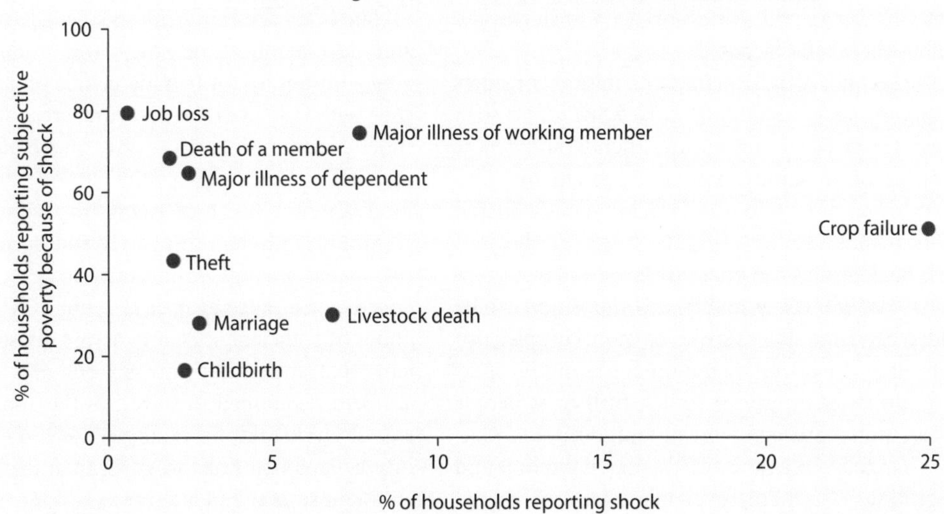

Source: WDR 2014 team based on data from the Tanzania National Panel Survey 2010/11 (panel a), and the China Rural Social Protection Survey 2004 (panel b) covering rural areas in three provinces (Fujian, Gansu, and Zhejiang) and one autonomous region (Guangxi) of China.

BOX 4.1 *When sharing wealth is a religious mandate: The use of* zakat *in Islamic communities*

Many religious traditions encourage or even mandate charitable giving to the poor and needy. *Zakat*—one of the Five Pillars of Islam—is a system ingrained in Islamic society in which every person has a duty to give a certain share of his or her income and assets to help specific categories of people defined by the Qur'an, including widows, orphans, people with disabilities, and others living in dire poverty. Interpretation varies from country to country. In some countries, *zakat* is collected and distributed by the government, while in others it remains a private matter distributed by donors directly to the chosen beneficiary or through a community affair in which donors deliver funds to the mosque for distribution. It is normally given once or twice a year, during Ramadan and Eid.

In the Republic of Yemen, *zakat* is not an obligatory tax but a transfer; the amount is calculated by the donor and distributed directly to the chosen beneficiary or delivered to the mosque or neighborhood leader for distribution. Survey data from the capital, Sana'a, show that around one-third of the poor receive *zakat* and that it is fairly well targeted, in that about 60 percent of it reaches households in the bottom 40 percent. However, poor households lacking social connections are sometimes excluded. As a lump-sum donation given once or twice a year, *zakat* is not an effective instrument for consumption smoothing in the face of shocks. Similar shortcomings are observed in Pakistan, where the *zakat* system is overseen by the government and implemented locally by community committees. Implementation is fraught with problems, such as mistargeting, infrequent and unpredictable delivery of benefits, and widespread perception of patronage and petty corruption.

Source: WDR 2014 team based on Levin, Morgandi, and Silva 2012 and World Bank 2007.

walkways with no physical or social infrastructure of any kind. The new neighbors formed a cohesive self-help committee and elected dynamic women to run it. Over the next decades, the committee successfully petitioned authorities and political parties for services, infrastructure, and land titles. By the early 2000s, it had become a stable urban neighborhood with cement houses, paved roads, running water, lighting, sanitation, schools, clinics, and people taking advantage of overseas migration opportunities.[7] Collective accomplishments, often involving risk management achieved through cohesion and links to authorities, combined with private accumulation of assets, housing, and education to transform the neighborhood and its people.

The second, complementary definition considers *community as a cultural, identity-based group* such as a kinship or ethnic group. Friends and fellow members of the same kin or ethnic group are a frequent source of help to people facing shocks. Shared identity—not location—grants access to the network. Such groups can offer assistance and insurance against loss of income, and their composition can be fluid: when large shocks strike, or more complex opportunities (involving migration, for example) arise, the boundaries of groups stretch further as people seek assistance through more distant social ties.[8] Culture—language, religious rituals, shared symbols and celebrations—strengthens people's sense of shared identity.

Religion and faith-based institutions play an important role in tying together cultural communities. Around the world, people often rely on religious institutions to provide both spiritual comfort and material relief in times of adversity (box 4.1). In Indonesia, for example, the financial crisis in 1997–98 caused the price of rice, the main staple food, to nearly triple, resulting in widespread economic distress, political transition, and social upheaval. Many Indonesians responded by more active participation in organized religion such as Qur'an study groups, which seemed to offer both spiritual relief and access to informal insurance. Religious participation was associated with a reduced need for alms or credit and was most pronounced in locales where formal credit was unavailable.[9]

The examples from Chicago, Ecuador, Indonesia, and Tanzania illustrate how communities often are vitally important for helping people prepare for and cope with risk, in urban and rural areas alike. Sometimes communities are the only source of assistance, the lifeline that helps people survive disaster and food scarcity. But these examples also suggest that community mechanisms rarely add up to adequate risk management. Communities struggle to provide effective insurance against systemic risk and public goods at sufficient scale and across divisions (problems that enterprises and governments sometimes are better equipped to solve). In the Tanzanian village of Nyakatoke, for example, none of 40 community groups had links to government or to NGOs, although several had attempted to forge them, realizing that such links often are necessary to solve larger problems and help people escape from poverty. Communities also tend to be better at coping with than preparing for risk and exploring opportunity. No communities are utopian ideals of equality and peace: hierarchies, inequalities, violence, and exclusion are always factors to reckon with, to different degrees.

Many of the obstacles facing communities as they confront risk can be traced to the informal organizational mechanisms communities tend to use. The community sphere is where norms of morality, fairness, reciprocity, a sense of duty to the common good, and occasionally altruism play out; markets are ruled by contracts and monetary reward. In the markets, agreements are ultimately enforced through the credible threat of legal sanctions; communities are just as likely to rely on shame, guilt, ostracism, or violence to settle disputes and to solve problems of adverse selection, moral hazard, and free riders (see glossary 2.1, chapter 2). These informal mechanisms work better in small cohesive groups than in larger and less dense groups. Accordingly, the need for in-group bonding and cohesion limits the size of the insurance pools and public goods that communities are able to create; it can also lead to exclusion of certain people. Communities' risk management mechanisms, geared for small groups, therefore perform best to ease idiosyncratic and small systemic risks; adapting them to larger and more complex problems requires research and careful organization.

Communities as providers of insurance

Families are usually the first port of call when someone is faced with a shock such as illness, disability, or job loss, but when family support proves inadequate, people turn to their communities for assistance. Loans and assistance from family, friends, and neighbors are among the most frequent responses to shocks (of any kind) in many developing countries (figure 4.2). In Nigeria, for example, informal credit and assistance was the most prevalent coping response, accounting for 32 percent of all responses. Informal credit and assistance is particularly important for low-income households, and sometimes is their only real safety net. Cutting back on food is also common; it makes up 20 to 22 percent of all coping responses reported by households in Afghanistan, Iraq, and Uganda. Across Eastern Europe and Central Asia, people with strong social capital in the form of trust and networks are significantly less likely to rely on costly coping such as reducing consumption of stable foods and forgoing medical care, probably because of better informal support (figure 4.3). People confronted with shocks also rely on savings and asset sales and seek more work. In contrast, credit from formal lenders and assistance from government and NGOs usually play lesser roles.

FIGURE 4.2 ***People respond to shocks on their own and by pooling risk with others, relying on informal credit and assistance to cope with shocks***

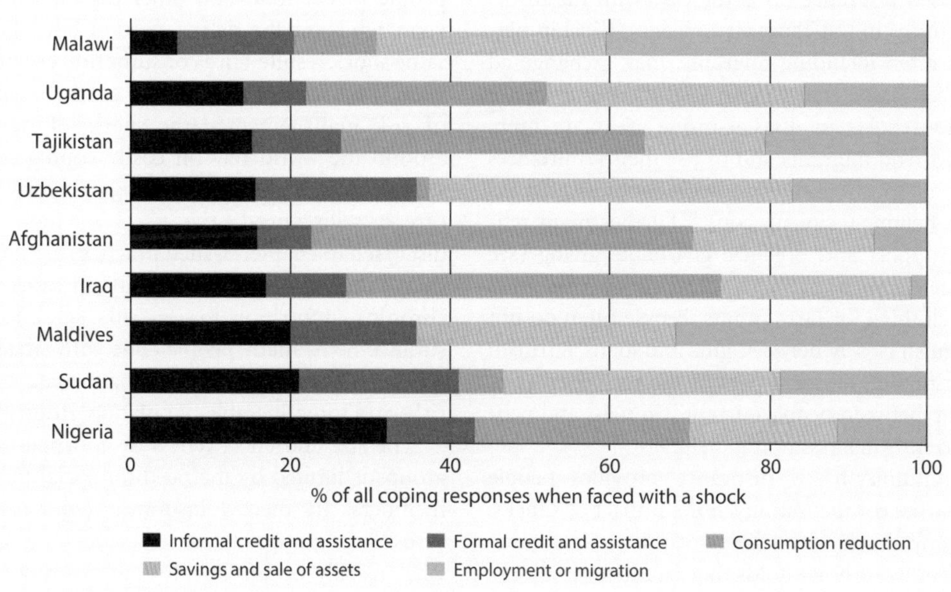

Source: WDR 2014 team based on data from household surveys, various years 2004–11.

FIGURE 4.3 ***Social capital helps reduce costly coping in Eastern Europe and Central Asia***

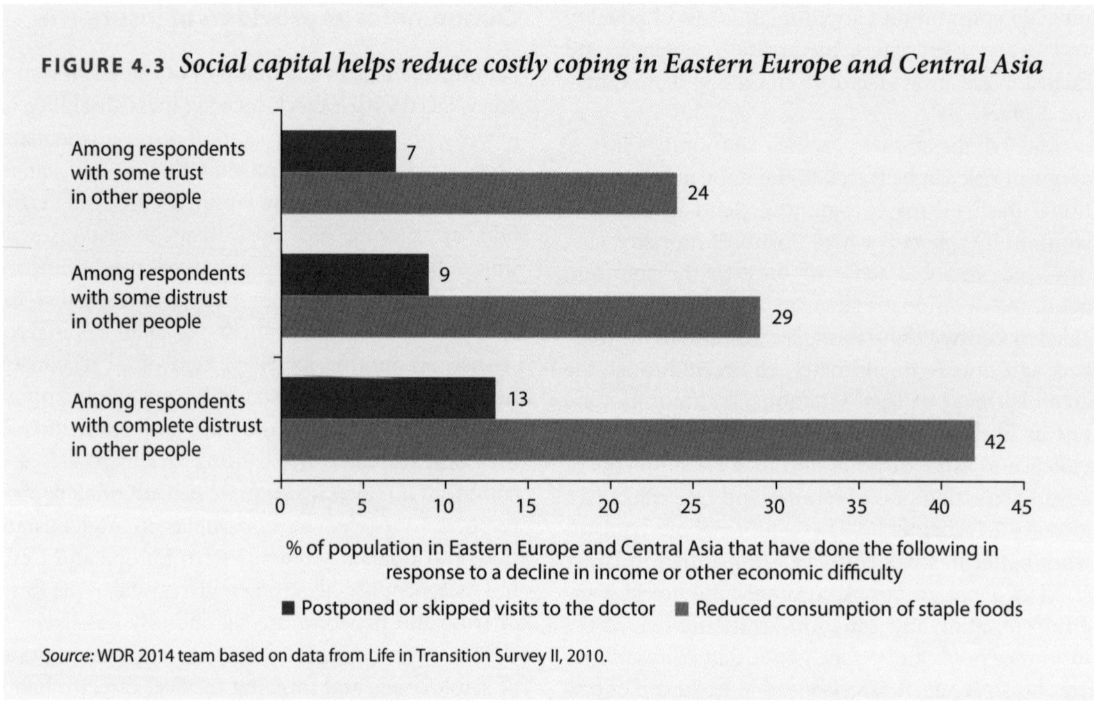

Source: WDR 2014 team based on data from Life in Transition Survey II, 2010.

The organization of informal insurance and coping support varies widely around the world. Community insurance—sometimes also called informal safety nets, risk pooling, and mutual insurance—tends to be based more on kin and reciprocal relationships than on formal contracts. Within those parameters, it can assume many different organizational forms. Membership-based groups operate rule-based insurance (as is the case with the insurance groups in the Tanzanian village). Kinship networks, often including migrants, may exchange ad hoc, need-based transfers. In fact, there is evidence that households in disaster-prone areas are more likely to send migrants and to use their remittances to prepare for shocks. Remittances shoot up after disasters, helping recipients cope.[10] Further, many religions support and organize charitable giving (see box 4.1). Transfers can be in the form of cash, food, labor, clothing, or farm inputs. People often do not distinguish closely between gifts and loans, altruism and insurance; all form part of the reciprocal relationship between people currently in need and people currently in a position to help.

Community-based insurance provides people with partial compensation for the impact of shocks, but many shocks nevertheless cause serious hardship. Studies of households that face income shocks show that their consumption falls less than income: in other words, some risk is insured away and some is retained.[11] Indonesian households insured themselves against 38 percent of the economic costs of more serious health shocks and 71 percent of the costs of more minor illness.[12] In the Philippines, remittances compensate for 65 percent of the cost of rainfall shocks.[13] The poorest are the least insured. For example, in rural China, for the poorest tenth of the population, a loss of income of 100 yuan led people to cut food and other expenditures by 40 yuan, while for the richest third of households, the same shock resulted in a consumption cut of only 10 yuan.[14] Because of these limits on the effectiveness of risk management, large shares of households around the world rely on costly coping responses such as skipping meals, forgoing necessary medical care, or selling productive assets (see figure 4.2). As discussed in chapter 3, such practices are hardest on the youngest and can lead to infant mortality and chronic malnutrition. In sum, although informal insurance helps many people cope with smaller idiosyncratic shocks, it is often inadequate for other risks and for vulnerable population groups.[15]

The size and effectiveness of informal insurance groups is limited by the need for social ties among members. In theory, insurance requires pooling across large groups of diverse people—but that is not what usually occurs in informal insurance groups, which tend to be small and homogeneous and therefore susceptible to aggregate risk.[16] Communities use direct observation of one another and frequent personal communication to control the scope for adverse selection and moral hazard and keep insurance pools financially viable. Kinship and intermarriage help foster strong ties. Some kinship groups have evolved strong norms about sharing with kin members in need, helping to extend the size of the insurance pool beyond the ancestral village. In-group social ties reduce problems of information asymmetry and enforcement of shared norms. But there are also drawbacks. Insurance arrangements that rely on social ties are easily challenged by in-migration (new settlers may lack the shared norms) and often exclude minorities.[17] Community arrangements are more difficult to sustain in larger groups where people lack direct interpersonal connections and communication. Such arrangements therefore work best for small or one-off idiosyncratic shocks that are easy to verify, such as funerals, and are least effective when communitywide shocks affect many members simultaneously.[18] Linking communities to market-based credit and insurance can help them overcome limitations of small size and in turn can benefit these programs. For example, community insurance groups in Ethiopia are helping to market crop insurance to their members and, by also sharing risk within the group, to overcome the problem of basis risk.

Communities' own support mechanisms are vital—in fact, they are often people's only source of help in hard times—but they are not enough and need to be augmented with outside assistance. Viewed as a form of risk management, informal insurance suffers certain deficiencies:

- *Informal insurance is insufficient in the face of systemic shocks.* Small informal groups cannot effectively smooth large shocks. Qualitative research during the global food, fuel, and financial crises that started in 2008 found that many people relied on costly coping responses as waves of systemic shocks strained informal mechanisms; reductions in the quality and quantity of food and in nonfood consumption were reported in study sites in all 13 countries studied; crime increased in 10 of them. The most important sources of assistance were relatives (sites in 13 countries), friends and neighbors (11 countries), and mutual solidarity groups (7 countries), but such informal support became less available and more rationed along ethnic or religious lines as the ability of better-off community members to contribute declined. Credit dried up as banks and moneylenders lent smaller amounts at higher interest rates. People also sought additional employment (12 countries), usually in informal occupations such as retail and services, where competition intensified and demand fell. Social cohesion sometimes declined, with upticks in petty theft reported in 10 countries and in sex work in 2 countries.[19]
- *The most vulnerable are excluded or are included on very adverse terms.* Exclusion keeps people with high needs and limited ability to contribute out of the insurance pool, partly in defense against adverse selection. One study among pastoralists in Ethiopia, for example, found that poorer people lacking cattle are excluded from informal credit, in part because of repayment risk and in part because they are socially invisible.[20] Chronically ill people may experience the same exclusion. A Somali proverb puts it succinctly: "Prolonged sickness and persistent poverty cause people to hate you."[21] Bonded labor, child labor, and early marriage are often the adverse consequences of informal arrangements. Bonded labor results from informal credit arrangements in which labor is used to guarantee repayment.

Communities as providers of protection

Exposure to risk is closely tied to location. Population growth and land scarcity are pushing more and more people into neighborhoods that lack basic infrastructure, are scarred by crime and violence, are marred by pollution, and face disaster risk. Latin America's 20 largest cities, for example, are all located in areas prone to flooding or earthquakes or have steep slopes; they are also plagued by crime.[22]

Confronting disasters and climate change

Safety, like so much else, has its price. In slums of Santo Domingo in the Dominican Republic, rents are almost twice as high in the safer areas than for residences near rivers and gullies.[23] Almost one-third of Nicaragua's population lives in areas that residents say are exposed to disaster, flooding, or contamination. Among these, half a million people live on or at the bottom of hills where they are exposed to landslides. This risk is 10 times higher for the poorest 20 percent than for the richest quintile.[24] In Djibouti City, a poor neighborhood is known as Bach à l'eau (underneath the water) because of its frequent flooding.

Evidence suggests that countries and communities are ill-prepared for the impacts of climate change, such as the higher frequency of extreme weather events. Disaster losses have grown significantly in recent decades as a consequence of climate change, population pressures, environmental degradation, and other factors. Countries with historically heavy exposure to tropical cyclones are better adjusted to this risk than countries with weaker exposure, but more recent increases in cyclone risk have not been matched by increases in preparation. One estimate finds that countries are unprotected against virtually all of the additional damage caused by intensified cyclone risk.[25]

Proactive and cost-effective measures to manage disaster risk are often available but not adopted because of inertia, short-sightedness, or reasons of political economy. For example, early warning systems, preparedness drills, sustainable land use planning, and ecosystem restoration are often good risk management but bad politics. In many countries, environmental changes and unsustainable agricultural practices have reduced the productivity of farm lands. Farmers respond by cutting down forests to plant on the rich soils beneath—a practice that may yield income in the short term but reduces soil fertility and increases sensitivity to climate change in the medium term. Changing such behaviors is hard because the benefits are immediate while the costs are diffuse and long term.[26] Smallholder communities in dry areas often rely far too much on a few drought-sensitive crops, such as corn (maize). Better options exist—drought-tolerant varieties, forestry, tree crops, migration, small businesses—but lack of credit and resources, a preference for traditional staple foods, and similar obstacles often block change. Poorer households usually respond to drought and impacts of climate change by selling assets, eating fewer and cheaper meals, borrowing at high cost, and migrating on a seasonal basis. Some of these practices can be counterproductive, resulting in a loss of human, physical, and environmental assets and undermining long-term prosperity.

Containing crime, violence, and conflict

More than one in ten people in many African and Latin American countries are victims of crime every year (figure 4.4). Some 1.5 billion people live in fragile or conflict-affected states or in countries with high levels of violent crime. Young men are the chief perpetrators. Men are more likely to be the victims of robbery and assault, while women are more likely to face sexual assaults and personal theft. More than half of all women in places such as rural Bangladesh, Peru, and Tanzania experience domestic violence on a regular basis (see chapter 3), although it is hugely underreported in official statistics. Rates of crime and violence are usually higher in cities than in rural areas, and within cities, crime and violence are frequently clustered in poorer communities. In Cape Town, South Africa, 44 percent of all homicides occur in

FIGURE 4.4 *Insecurity affects more than the victims*

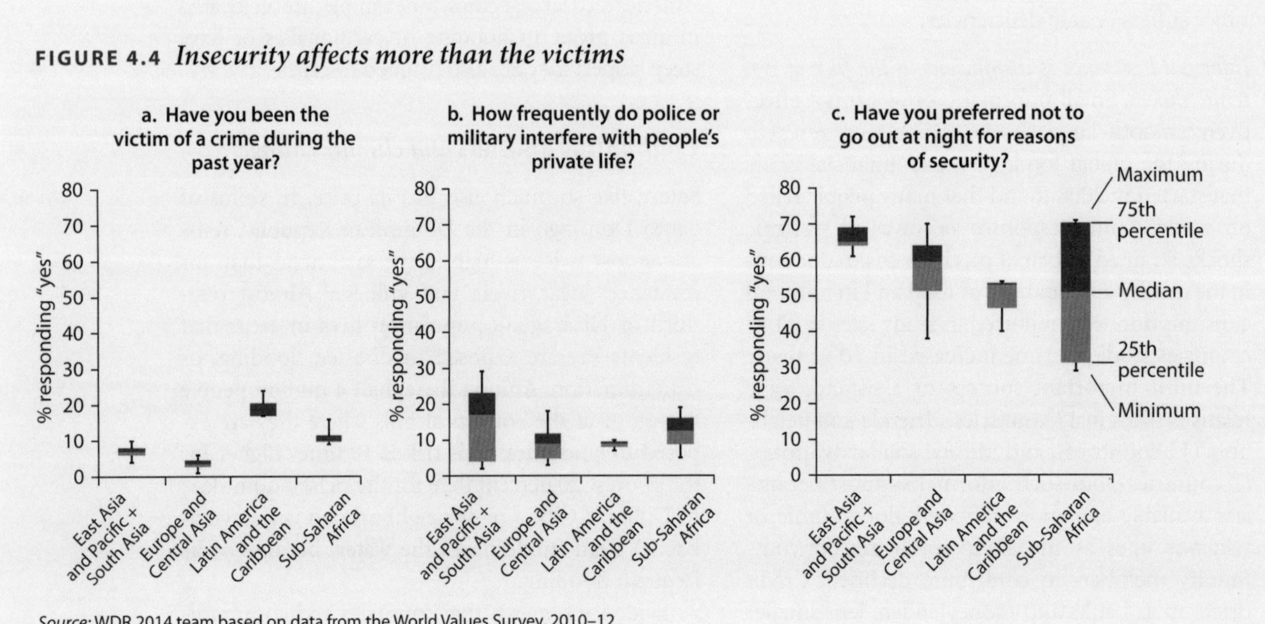

Source: WDR 2014 team based on data from the World Values Survey, 2010–12.

DIAGRAM 4.1 *Three major types of violence and their spillovers*

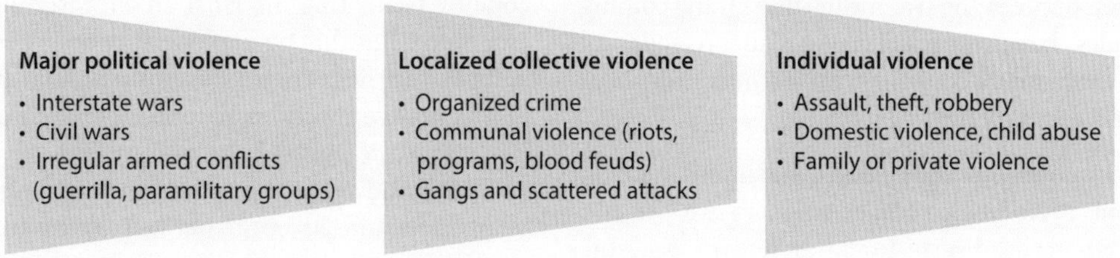

Major political violence	Localized collective violence	Individual violence
• Interstate wars • Civil wars • Irregular armed conflicts (guerrilla, paramilitary groups)	• Organized crime • Communal violence (riots, programs, blood feuds) • Gangs and scattered attacks	• Assault, theft, robbery • Domestic violence, child abuse • Family or private violence

Source: Petesch 2013 for the WDR 2014.

three neighborhoods that are among the city's poorest. Rural areas often endure less violence but not necessarily less conflict, and disputes over land, livestock, or infidelity can erupt into blood feuds and revenge killings. The weak presence of the state in many rural areas leaves it up to local informal institutions to address such feuds.[27] Not that the security forces are all that helpful: in many regions, more than one in ten people say that police or the military interfere "frequently or quite frequently" in people's private life.

Collective forms of violence have far more severe societal consequences than individual violence and petty crime because they also destroy social institutions, displace people, deter investment, trigger fear, and cause short-term thinking (diagram 4.1). Farmers grow food crops instead of perennials. According to one estimate, half the losses stemming from the conflict in northern Uganda result from cautious responses to risk (forgone opportunities) rather than from direct exposure to attacks—with significant risk-related losses also occurring in households that did not suffer a direct attack. Risk of violence may have reduced per capita expenditure in the affected region by some 70 percent.[28]

Most conflicts today have strong ethnic or religious components, but that does not mean that ethnic differences necessarily cause antagonism. Ethnicity is often exploited for political or economic gain, leading to a sharpening of ethnic divisions and tensions.[29] The literature is divided on the causes of conflict and the role of ethnicity, but it appears that conflict is more likely when social groups lack institutions to bridge their divides, states are weak, and there are strong external stressors. Four broad types of stressors stand out and result in spillovers between types of violence:

- *Weak states and links between politicians and criminals.* The supply of local violence is often linked to contests for power among elite actors with ties to armed groups and criminal networks. Weak state institutions permit such contests to play out violently. States with stronger institutions and rule of law constrain these conflicts and settle them in a more peaceful manner. Sometimes, there are localized pockets of fragility with dysfunctional state institutions within otherwise well-functioning states.
- *Grievances.* Patterns of inequality and marginalization across groups holding grievances—sometimes historical ones—play a major role in fueling many conflicts. Tensions often have historic causes or stem from disputes over land and natural resources, which can be worsened by environmental changes. High inequality, perceptions of injustices committed by the state, and politicians playing up ethnic divisions for their own purposes can spur ethnic violence and conflict.[30]
- *Conflict legacies.* Major political violence is often followed by long periods of heightened crime and violence facilitated by ex-combatants, widespread availability of arms, and breakdown of social norms. Trauma caused by past violence, colonization, or a history of state oppression (perhaps under the dominance of a particular ethnic group) makes it difficult to trust the state.[31] Although time heals, its healing effects can be measured in decades.[32] Collective violence such as organized crime and political violence spill over to individual violence.
- *Climate change.* Extreme climatic events (high temperatures, unusually low rainfall) are associated with violence, instability, and state collapse. A recent meta-analysis finds a strong association between climatic deviations and a wide range of measures of individual violence, intergroup violence, and state

collapse, both in recent time and historically. The mechanisms through which climate changes make conflict more likely are not yet clear. But the association between the two means that, in the coming decades, large projected changes in precipitation and temperature could help drive a major uptick in violence and conflict.[33]

Cross-cutting social ties help communities remain peaceful, even when conflict stressors are present. Most ethnically diverse localities remain peaceful, whereas others with the same diversity experience frequent outbursts of violence. The most violent cities tend to lack routine interaction among members of different groups and to be characterized by divisive local leaders, media, and criminal gangs. In contrast, cities with strong civic networks to bridge ethnic groups tend to remain peaceful, because those networks constrain political leaders from using violent means and quell rumors and tensions before they erupt into riots. These networks are not designed with violence prevention in mind: they can be film clubs, sports clubs, community associations, and so on. Crucially, they span ethnic groups.[34] Cross-cutting social ties also aid in recovery following conflicts and disasters.[35] However, community mechanisms are almost always completely overwhelmed when violence is linked to organized criminal networks.

Communities need connections to other communities and to markets; without them communities remain insular, lack political influence, and are unable to accomplish anything at scale.

Cohesive and connected communities are more effective

Risk need not imply vulnerability if communities can put risk protection in place, either by organizing it themselves or by mobilizing to demand risk protection from local authorities. In higher-income countries, local governments routinely clear drains and provide policing, sanitation, and clean water. In poor countries—and particularly in poor neighborhoods—local governments often do not provide these basic public goods of common protection. The alternative facing communities is therefore to mobilize collective action to create, demand, or maintain mutual protection, or else suffer exposure to risk. Communities vary enormously in how effectively they manage collective risks.

Social cohesion and connections to markets, governments, and other communities are the ingredients of effective community risk management. Where communities operate in relative isolation, social cohesion (or *bonding social capital*) helps them cope by facilitating informal credit, insurance, and assistance. But this type of social cohesion is rarely sufficient to help communities thrive and prosper. Horizontal connections to other communities (or *bridging social capital*) help communities solve larger problems and prevent conflict. Vertical connections to markets and governments help them access resources and opportunities.

The tight-knit rural village of Santa Ana, Paraguay is an example of a community that has mastered collective action. Everybody contributes toward the common good by helping, for example, to maintain roads, bridges, water supply, and electricity lines whenever repairs are needed. They confront cattle thieves and provide housing to a bus driver to ensure that his route covers their village. A sense of civic duty rather than written rules ensures that all contribute. Homogeneity and trusted local leaders contribute to their exceptionally high cohesion. The community did not do it all on its own. Roads, electricity, and water supply were constructed by government agencies (often with donor support); the community handles only the maintenance. Although comparative statistics are lacking, the majority of the worlds' location-based communities are far less cohesive than Santa Ana and achieve at best a fraction of its accomplishments.

What makes people mobilize? Common interests and trusted leaders motivate people to mobilize in community groups and social movements. Risk—and the perceived injustice of mismanaged risk—can be a forceful motivating factor. Historically, many efforts to control risk, reduce pollution, and improve social policies have resulted from successful social mobilization; a campaign started by antislavery activists and parliamentarians in 1787 led Britain to ban its slave trade in 1807, perhaps the first-ever victory by a social movement. The neighborhood committee in the informal settlement of Indio Guays in Guayaquil, Ecuador, discussed earlier, was formed to help settle land and other disputes and to petition authorities to provide basic infrastructure, health, and other services. India's Self Employed Women's Association (SEWA) mobilizes 1.3 million members around work security, income security, food security, and social security.[36]

FIGURE 4.5 ***Membership in voluntary organizations varies widely around the world***

Percentage of survey respondents who belong to a voluntary organization

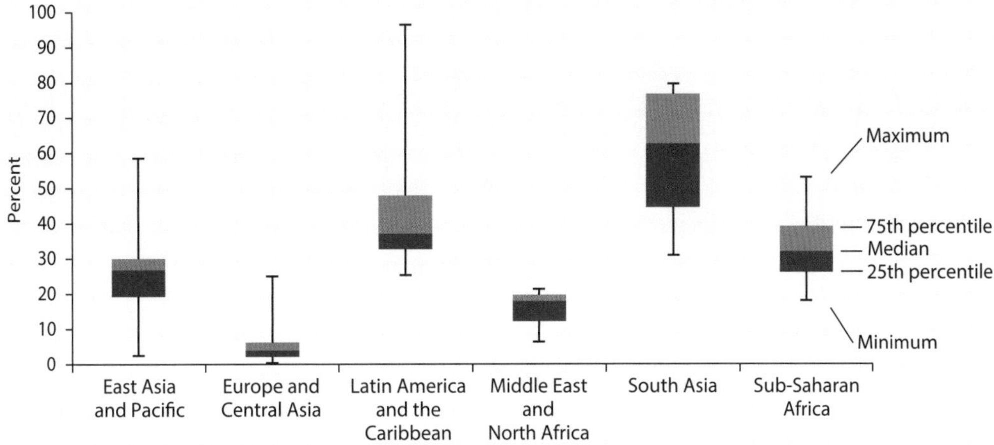

Source: WDR 2014 team based on data from African Barometer Round 5, 2010–11; East Asia Barometer, 2005–08; Latinobarómetro, 2005; South Asia Barometer, 2005–08; Arab Barometer, 2005–08; and Life in Transition Survey, II 2010. Figures are broadly comparable and, outside Africa, include religious organizations (but not attendance at worship).

Groups vary widely in their size and degree of formality. Burial societies and church groups are typically very small and informal. Community-based organizations are slightly larger and sometimes employ a few staff. NGOs are larger still and constituted legally. Jointly, these groups are often referred to as civil society. They pursue many causes such as providing credit, insurance, assistance, and services; managing common resources; and providing citizen "voice" demanding services, protection, and accountability from authorities and employers.[37] Although difficult to estimate, the size and importance of civil society varies significantly. Organizational membership tends to be highest in South Asia, Africa, and Latin America (figure 4.5). In Bangladesh and Sri Lanka, 80 and 77 percent of people, respectively, report they are members of at least one such organization.

Unless they receive outside support, communities need to overcome free rider problems to be effective. Groups of people find it hard to take collective action for joint benefits because some members of the group free ride on others' efforts: that is, they consume more or pay less than their fair share of a common resource. The problem is illustrated by the "public goods game." In this experimental game, each player is given a small amount of money that he or she can choose either to keep or to put in a pot that is shared by a group of players. A facilitator multiplies the content of the pot by a factor larger than one but smaller than the number of players and distributes the sum equally among all players, regardless of whether they contributed to the pot or kept the money. In this game, the common good is maximized when all players contribute their entire amount, although the individually rational choice is to contribute nothing. The game has been played in different cultures. Inevitably a significant number of players contribute—as long as they believe that others will reciprocate. The game has also been modified to allow for repeated interactions and punishment. Punishing of free riders (those who do not put funds in the common pot) leads to greater group cooperation, and some people are willing to punish even at a personal cost. Researchers believe that such punishment of free riders is crucial for sustaining collaboration in the real world.[38]

Without sustained cooperation, there would be no public goods, no collective management of natural resources, no social movements, and no society in any meaningful sense. Groups overcome the free rider problem by devising ways to enforce rules of contribution that reward cooperation and punish those who fail to contribute their fair share. Many social norms and institutions also serve to reinforce mutual collaboration based on reciprocity and punishment. The Tanzanian village of Nyakatoke, for example, operates a villagewide mutual insurance scheme for funerals and hospitalization that includes almost all the women in the village. To guard against free riding, nonmembers are categorically refused help, and there are punishments for members who are caught helping nonmembers.[39]

Researchers, including the Nobel Prize winner Elinor Ostrom, have documented considerable regularity in the factors that promote or hinder local governance and public goods provision. From the perspective of community risk management, some of the most important findings show that:[40]

- Communities whose rights to organize and govern local affairs are legally recognized are more likely to succeed. They must own the fruits of their labor.
- Rules need to be enforced. Access to local and timely dispute resolution mechanisms are critical because conflicts among community members or with local government are inevitable and need to be resolved.
- In larger systems, governance activities are often best organized in multiple, *nested* layers. For instance, when many communities share a common water supply, each may manage its own water distribution branch, while a higher body manages the entire system.
- Communities with low inequality, few ethnic divisions, equal treatment, and relatively low discrimination are more likely to create public goods, in part because of dense interpersonal interactions and shared norms about in-group reciprocity.

These findings imply that governments should create a favorable legal regime that enables communities to undertake their own risk management and dispute resolution—provided these function in a reasonably fair manner. The high costs and slow pace of the formal justice system make it unsuitable for many of the small, frequent disputes of community life. Responsibility for managing local risks and disputes can often be delegated to local actors. Decentralized management of disaster risk has been found to be cost-effective, for example, in part because local knowledge of risk can help keep people's lives, assets, and businesses out of harm's way. Moreover, many countries have enacted laws that undermine communities' customary arrangements for settling disputes and managing common property such as forests without providing adequate formal justice and resource management systems. The resulting governance vacuum has weakened forest management and caused forest degradation in many places. In recent years, many countries have devolved aspects of forest management to communities, with promising results for sustainability of forest resources.[41] However, when communities are rife with divisions, there is a crying need for neutral institutions with capacity to foster transparency, inclusion, and accountability.

In-group bonding and social cohesion sustains communities' risk management but often excludes outsiders and may lead to antagonism toward other ethnic and religious groups. Social exclusion stems from attitudes, policies, and laws that discriminate against certain groups on the basis of their ethnic, gender, or religious identity, for example. Attitude surveys suggest that tolerance of members of "out-groups" such as immigrants and ethnic minorities is *not* on the rise (figure 4.6). Excluded groups face discrimination that increases their risks and weakens their access to risk management. They often live in areas marked by high risk and have little access to services, markets, and institutions that could otherwise help them manage risks. They may face harassment, particularly when seeking to explore new opportunities or when demanding accountability and equal treatment. People displaced by violence often face debilitating exclusion in their new location (box 4.2). Exclusion can lead to risky behaviors such as excessive drug and alcohol consumption, crime, riots, and violence.

The Indian state of Kerala has often been hailed for its achievements in health, education, and social development, but it was once a bastion of exclusion. Kerala has high ethnic and religious heterogeneity. Until the middle of the nineteenth century, it was deeply divided by rigid caste barriers that denied opportunity to most castes. A movement of assorted ethnic groups started creating a common identity, based on shared language, culture, and values. Over time, demands for participation in governance grew, as did petitions for collective welfare in the form of schools and hospitals. By the 1940s, Kerala was a forerunner among Indian states in many areas of social development.[42]

Collaboration within groups is increasingly insufficient and in need of being complemented by cross-group collaboration. Cross-cutting social ties, or bridging social capital, mitigates social polarization, promotes trust in the system, inoculates society against identity politics and ethnic riots, and facilitates collective action. These ties need to include a sufficiently large number of groups.[43] How can they be encouraged and supported? Tanzania under President Julius Nyerere from 1964 to 1985 famously

FIGURE 4.6 ***Social exclusion based on ethnicity is not declining in many parts of the world***

Percentage of the population that would not welcome a neighbor of a different race or ethnic group

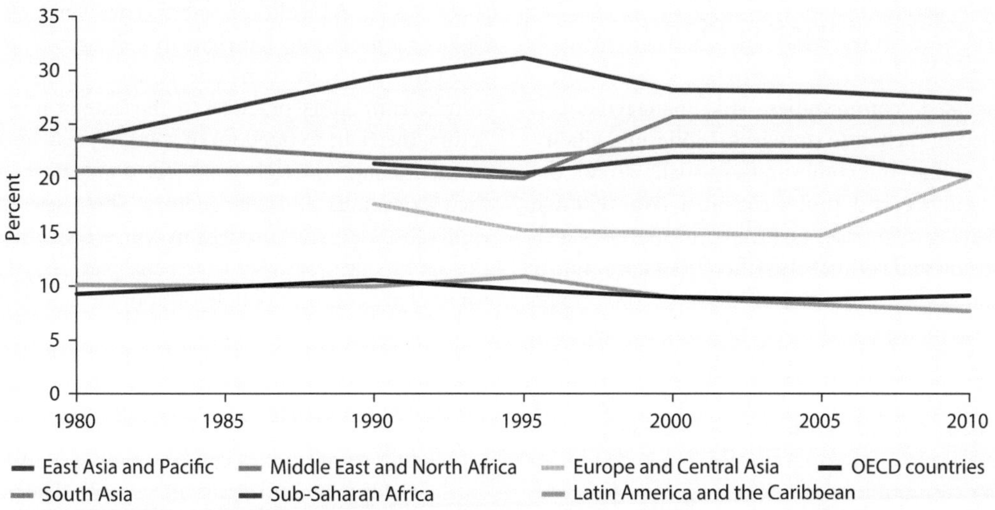

Source: Foa 2012 based on data from the World Values Surveys and European Values Study.

Note: Organisation for Economic Co-operation and Development (OECD) countries in the figure are all high-income countries that are members of the OECD. All other countries are grouped into geographic regions.

downplayed the role of ethnic identity and built a shared national Tanzanian identity, fostered through a national language, equitable public spending, and a common discourse of the nation's history. Thanks to this foresight, ethnic rivalry never rose to prominence in Tanzania and did not spill over into conflict as happened in so many neighboring countries. Other approaches used in various countries and cities include integrating schools, neighborhoods, and economic life; more-or-less mandatory participation in community self-help groups; "truth and reconciliation committees"; quotas for historically disadvantaged groups; and local peace committees.[44] The lessons are that ethnic differences need not result in

BOX 4.2 ***Refugees and internally displaced people: Moving from managing displacement to facilitating opportunities***

A staggering 43 million people are forcibly displaced. Some 15.2 million people are currently refugees because of violent conflict, and at least 27.5 million people are internally displaced in more than 40 countries. The displaced are often surprisingly resourceful. Leaving behind homes, assets, and familiar environments, they employ dynamic coping strategies to find new livelihoods and even prosper in their areas of displacement. But policies often constrain them.

Efforts to address displacement have not been successful. The average length of time that a refugee or internally displaced person lives in displacement is close to 20 years, yet displacement is most often managed as a short-term humanitarian crisis. Many problems arise as a result: prolonged residence in camps, dependency on assistance, restrictions on mobility, and failure to integrate in new locations. Tensions with host communities are common. International humanitarian assistance to the displaced totals around $8.4 billion annually, or 6 percent of all official development assistance.[a] There is little accountability for long-term results.

A better approach would recognize the long-term nature of displacement and help the displaced pursue economic opportunities. National legislation needs to recognize the displaced, remove discrimination, and lift mobility restrictions on refugees. Support could emphasize housing, education, infrastructure, livelihoods, and accessing any assets left behind by the displaced. To reduce tensions, support should also benefit host communities, as is being done in a World Bank–supported project for displaced people in Azerbaijan. Greater convergence of humanitarian and development funding could help promote long-term approaches.

Source: WDR 2014 team based on Lakhani 2013 for the WDR 2014.

a. OECD Development Assistance Committee estimates.

divided and antagonistic societies if there is trust and ties across groups and that both state and nonstate actors can promote such ties.

Public policies to improve local risk management

As discussed, communities' risk management is grounded in their core strengths—cohesion, vitality, survival skills—but communities usually do not deliver insurance and protection at a large enough scale, leaving many risks uncovered; weaknesses such as exclusion and conflict also often limit community risk management. Communities can become much better risk managers with the right form of support. NGOs, donors, and local and national governments can all help strengthen local risk management using four broad approaches. The first is to create a favorable legal regime for communities. The second is to mobilize communities as risk managers by fostering their own capacity to manage local risks. The third is to promote their "voice" and ability to influence government-provided risk management. The fourth is to provide public goods and services that complement communities' capacities, involving users as appropriate. These broad approaches all empower communities in different ways, as discussed next.

Create a favorable legal environment

Ideally, the state provides a neutral system of law and order where enforcement is impartial, property rights are enforced, crime and violence is kept in check, members of different social groups are equally respected, and communities' ability to organize and exercise voice for risk management is protected. However, that is not how many people see the state.

Instead, many people experience state institutions as unpredictable and unaccountable, one more source of risk one has to navigate. In parts of Africa and South Asia, chaotic land governance has led to corruption and land conflicts. Moreover, case studies and media reports abound of instances where street vendors have their goods confiscated; slum dwellers are violently evicted without notice; workers are prevented from forming unions that can voice their demands for workplace safety; undignified treatment by service providers make excluded groups reluctant to use basic services, leaving them less protected; governments provide arms to unaccountable local militias; and police and security forces demand bribes and commit abuses (see figure 4.4). In these instances, actions by agents of the state may result in social instability. How can this be countered?

Progress countering abuse and discrimination has often resulted from building greater respect for social, civil, and political rights. These include the right to association; the right to security of people and property from crime and violence; the right to nondiscriminatory practices by the state or nonstate actors; the right to freedom of speech, press, and information; and the right for affected groups to voice their grievances and seek redress. These and other rights foster an environment in which collective action and social mobilization can take place and flourish so that groups of people can pursue actions that reduce their collective risks.

Empower communities to manage risks

Mobilizing communities can be a powerful force of local development and risk management. The informal settlement of Orangi in Karachi, Pakistan, for example, financed its own low-cost sanitation as part of the "Orangi Pilot Project," started in 1980 by the social activist Akhtar Hameed Khan, assisted by a local NGO. The project also helped the community organize housing, vaccinations, microfinance, family planning, and steps to prevent violence, and elicited local government responses to problems too large for the community to handle. Its success rested on the insight that when the state does not supply essential services and public goods, communities can be mobilized to do so.[45] The project, which has been replicated in other cities of Pakistan and other countries, helped identify many of the essential ingredients of community-driven development: let communities themselves define priorities; maintain a long-term presence; and adjust project details over time as new problems, solutions, and opportunities emerge.

Such spontaneous social action has inspired donors and governments to promote community-driven development projects that induce communities to mobilize and build their capacity to plan their own development. Projects put self-help groups in charge of resources and decision making, supported by community mobilizers. NGOs, governments, and donors, including the World Bank, have promoted such projects in many sectors in both urban and rural areas in numerous countries. Indonesia, for example, has made the National Program for Community Empowerment (also known by its acronym, PNPM), a pillar of its antipoverty strategy. The program, which started in 1998 at a time of economic

BOX 4.3 *New communication technologies help communities manage violence and local conflict*

On the ground, patterns of violence are always varied and dynamic. Confusion, uncertainty, and misinformation can make it hard for people to know what is going on and how to stay out of trouble. To track, report, and warn of violence, people around the world are developing a host of information and communication technologies and platforms. Many of these information systems rely on a mix of "crowdsourcing" and maps to report the different forms of violence and crime and locate emerging hotspots, in real time and in ways that are both authoritative and widely accessible. The spread of cell phones helps community members both to report incidences of crime and violence and to access aggregated results.

A software platform called Ushahidi (Swahili for *testimonial*) was initially developed to map violence during Kenya's 2008 postelection riots. It aggregates reports sent by citizens using mobile phones or the web and, according to Ushahidi, had 45,000 users in Kenya at the time. It has since been expanded and adapted to various other uses in crisis situations, including in Haiti after the 2010 earthquake. An initiative based in Cairo, called Harassmap, is a mobile phone–based reporting system used by women who encounter harassment as they move about city streets. It is raising awareness of the problem and warning women of trouble spots. Across Latin America, people are setting up blogs, websites, and Internet applications, and using Twitter to report and share information on all forms of crime, violence, and police abuse. Helpful as these are, there are also downsides, such as deliberate misinformation.

View of Cairo showing incidents of sexual harassment reported by the public[a]

Source: Petesch 2013 for the WDR 2014.

a. WDR 2014 team based on data from Harassmap at http://harassmap.org. The red circles in the figure depict the number of reported incidents in that locality.

crisis, political transition, and a sharp spike in poverty, uses a community-driven development approach to build local infrastructure, improve health and education in the poorest regions, respond to climate change and environmental degradation, and target particularly marginalized groups. Evaluations of community-driven development interventions have shown mixed but overall good results on poverty; infrastructure costs and quality; and access to and utilization of health, education, and drinking water. Evaluations have also criticized projects for restricting themselves to short time frames and failing to create feedback loops to learn from experience and adjust accordingly.[46]

Regardless of their stated objectives, projects have repeatedly discovered that risk management is high on communities' list of priorities: for example, managing droughts and disasters in rural areas or violence and sanitation in urban ones. Modest but persistent technical and organizational assistance can reduce risk greatly. Microfinance can unlock communities' entrepreneurial potential. Civil society has helped Bangladesh advance its disaster risk management with low-cost, community-based disaster early warning systems. Maps and electronic applications that show where most crime and violence occurs help people avoid trouble spots and shame local police forces to take action (box 4.3). A project in the Lao

People's Democratic Republic helped communities integrate disaster risk management into village development plans. In Afghanistan, the National Solidarity Program has constructed rural infrastructure with community participation and laid the foundations for inclusive local governance in all parts of the country. Win-win projects can provide local employment in building protective physical assets or in managing or restoring ecosystems as part of disaster preparedness. Community-driven development projects have responded to disasters with speed and agility in many countries, including Indonesia, Pakistan, and the Philippines.[47]

Whereas some community-driven approaches have been on a modest scale, Andhra Pradesh and several other Indian states have assisted hundreds of thousands of self-help groups with microfinance and in diversification of local livelihoods. Groups are also helped to link up across villages and form associations covering larger areas, creating a movement made up of millions of poor people, largely women. The resulting strength in numbers permits these associations to buy food, obtain credit, access social programs, and organize insurance on favorable terms. Crucially, it also gives them collective voice and influence, which they use, for example, to gain access to social programs or to seek election to the village council.[48] This approach is now central policy under India's National Rural Livelihoods Mission. The NGO Bangladesh Rural Advancement Committee (BRAC) is another example of community-based development that has gone to scale. BRAC, which started as a relief organization in Bangladesh in 1972, is now active in 11 countries and assists an estimated 125 million people.

Empower communities with voice and accountability

Government institutions are essential for managing the many risks that exceed the capacity of communities, yet these institutions often disappoint. Public health workers are absent more than one-quarter of the time in Bangladesh, India, Indonesia, Peru, and Uganda.[49] The Orangi Pilot Project mentioned earlier could cost-effectively supply improved toilets and feeder sewers but had to rely on the municipality's outdated main sewer lines, making its overall sanitation effort less effective. Flooding, a growing problem in many African cities, is caused by deficient drainage and unregulated urban development—problems that only governments can solve. Communities bear the cost of flooding but have little idea about how to make authorities pay attention to the problem.[50]

The disconnect between communities and government came through loud and clear in a multi-country study, *Voices of the Poor,* which asked thousands of poor people around the world which institutions they found most and least effective.[51] Across locales, respondents considered kin, family, and community-based and religious organizations among the most effective support systems. Municipalities, police, and ministries were considered the least effective and were often regarded as unaccountable and unresponsive to the needs of the poor. Accounts of neglect, petty corruption, and extortion at the hand of officials abounded; the police were perceived the most negatively and were often described as a source of insecurity. Overall, state institutions constituted 33 percent of effective and 83 percent of ineffective institutions. By contrast, civil society organizations constituted 60 percent of the institutions considered effective and only 15 percent of those considered ineffective. These findings are echoed—although in a slightly muted manner—in the World Values Survey, where confidence in religious leaders is far higher than confidence in police and government (figure 4.7).

Local democracy, government capacity, and political economy influence how accountable decentralized government is to risks faced by low-income groups. Local governments in many countries lack the capacity, resources, and decision-making authority needed to be effective. Electing (rather than appointing) local governments can help by adding an element of accountability. Research, mostly from India, finds that decentralized electoral systems tend to deliver benefits to citizens—or at least to the "median voter"—but that they also can induce rent seeking by opportunistic local politicians.[52] Government capacity to deliver is often a critical bottleneck: In Peru, for example, many local governments underspend their allocated budget to a considerable degree, with average spending in 2009 ranging from 63 to 97 percent of the allocation depending on the type of funds. Many smaller municipalities lack a trained engineer to oversee construction projects.[53]

Stronger accountability mechanisms where citizens, service users, and communities demand better services directly from police, authorities, and utilities can help ensure that public spending is responsive to local risks and delivers results.[54] For example, experiments in India and Uganda involved public meetings where information on health and education entitlements and achievements were disseminated. After

FIGURE 4.7 *Who do you trust? Confidence in police, government, and religious leaders*

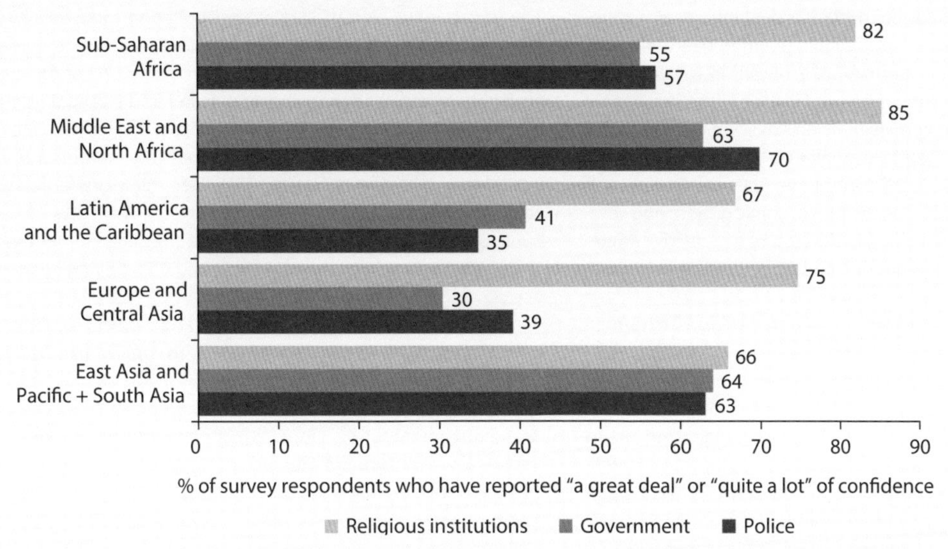

Source: WDR 2014 team based on data from the World Values Survey, 2005.

one year and four to six meetings, one intervention in India resulted in 27 percent more tetanus vaccinations, 24 percent more prenatal supplements, 25 percent more infant vaccinations, and fewer excess school fees compared with control villages where no meetings were held.[55] These results indicate that community participation can improve outcomes for health and education investments, reduce absenteeism, increase enrollment and health care use, and reduce maternal and infant mortality.

Citizen participation works best when higher-tier government is responsive.[56] Localized accountability mechanisms are useful but may not be transformative on their own. Local accountability is more powerful when the state creates complementary mechanisms to sanction corruption, inadequate services, and abuse of authority. These mechanisms can entail an independent judiciary or auditing institutions. Moreover, rights and social guarantees can galvanize social movements and foster collective action by offering critical entry points for citizens and NGOs demanding better risk management. Modern information and communication technologies make it simpler and faster for individuals and communities to mobilize. The right to assembly and political participation enables citizens to demand economic and personal protection and better services.

India's Mahatma Gandhi National Rural Employment Guarantee Act illustrates how good governance and social mobilization go hand-in-hand. This law, enacted after pressure from the Right to Food Campaign and others, creates an entitlement of 100 days of unskilled employment per year, at minimum wage, to all workers in rural areas who demand it. The law also provides for social audits and redress of grievances. Demand for work is massive, mostly from poor and disadvantaged groups, and at times of the year where no other work is available. Not only does the program offer a useful safety net, but it also helps spread awareness of rights and promotes dignity. Implementation varies across states: no state is able to offer all workers all the employment they demand and are entitled to. A state such as Rajasthan, which promotes transparency and accountability and has a long history of popular mobilization, performs relatively better: in Rajasthan, 84 percent of job seekers report being successful (against 56 percent nationwide), receiving 71 days of employment (against 37 nationwide), on average. The fact that the law is organized as a right motivates job seekers' collective action to hold authorities accountable for supplying employment instead of siphoning off the allocated funds.[57]

Provide infrastructure and services that complement communities' capacities

Basic infrastructure enables people to manage risk and seize opportunities. Mobile phone penetration

BOX 4.4 *Clean, green, and blue: Managing water and flooding in Singapore*

In the 1960s, Singapore imported most of its drinking water, was frequently flooded, and suffered from highly polluted rivers, air, land, and streets. Singapore's transformation, achieved in four decades, shows that the rapidly growing urban population in the developing world can aspire to a safe and clean living environment with sufficient water. Singapore moved forward with a long-term vision that the country could achieve more control over its water supply and become a livable city without sacrificing economic growth and competitiveness. It relied on research and development; effective implementation; and a combination of engineering, political commitment, and community-based measures.

In water resource management, Singapore's efforts focused on building up its local catchment water resources by capturing, storing, and using more of its heavy rainfall, as well as creating sources of water less dependent on the weather. The city built reservoirs to store rainwater collected from rivers, streams, canals, and drains that converted large parts of the city-state into a rainwater catchment area. Developing separate collection systems for used water and rainwater at the outset allowed Singapore to integrate its drainage system and channel rainwater to its reservoirs without affecting water quality. To maintain the cleanliness of the water supply, streams and culverts had to be kept free of garbage and pollution. The government closed or relocated polluting industries such as pig and duck farms, informal manufacturers, and street vendors; it built new food centers and markets to house food vendors; and it engaged the population to conserve water and stop pollution and littering. Today, Singapore has put in place a diversified water supply strategy known as the Four National Taps comprising water from local catchments, imported water, high-grade reclaimed water, and desalinated water. A large dam, the Marina Barrage, was built to create a freshwater reservoir that has a catchment area of 10,000 hectares, while regulating flooding of low-lying areas in the city center.

Singapore recognizes that climate change effects could result in more intense rainfall and rising sea levels. To cope with more intense rainfall, it is strengthening its drainage infrastructure and introducing measures to better control storm water. One measure includes a new requirement for developers to implement on-site measures to slow down surface runoff and reduce the peak flow of storm water into the public drainage system. In anticipation of rising sea levels, Singapore has added to its minimum reclamation. Since 2011, newly reclaimed land must be raised by a minimum of 1 meter in addition to the previous level of 1.25 meters above the highest recorded tide level observed before 1991.

Source: WDR 2014 team based on Soon, Jean, and Tan 2009 and contributions from PUB, Singapore's national water agency.

has skyrocketed, even in the most remote, low-income regions; meanwhile, 88 percent of the global population now has access to an improved water source. Singapore is an example of a city-state that took a proactive approach to bring health and environmental risks under control and in the process created one of Asia's most livable cities (box 4.4). But such an approach to managing risks to the public remains elusive in many low- and lower-middle-income countries, where 2.7 billion people lack access to sanitation (figure 4.8) and 1 billion defecate in the open. Open sewers and garbage still mar many slums. Such environmental conditions cause much disease. In Sub-Saharan Africa, one of every eight children, and in South Asia, one of every fifteen, die before their fifth birthday.

Understanding the strengths and limitations of communities' risk management can help governments design complementary policy actions.

Many health, sanitation, security, and other programs have concluded that involving and partnering with user communities improves outcomes (photo 4.1); such partnerships may even be necessary for success. Simply providing a toilet does not necessarily improve sanitation (box 4.5) in the same way that provision of more police does not necessarily reduce crime (spotlight 4). Communities can help create awareness, knowledge, and changes in norms and behavior—something India is exploiting with a campaign that discourages young women from marrying men who do not have a toilet. To reduce the spread of HIV, changes in sexual behavior are needed, in particular among high-risk groups such as sex workers and men who have sex with men. Community-based organizations can reach such groups far better than can governments. They can tailor interventions to key obstacles blocking the adoption of risk-reducing behaviors. In western Kenya, for example, community-based organizations provided awareness and knowledge that increased the use of condoms; in other localities, where knowledge was already high, community-based HIV interventions instead targeted the stigma that stops people from seeking testing and provided empowerment and motivation for behavior change.[58] Working closely with affected communities helps programs like these discover the obstacles for low uptake of risk management and redesign approaches accordingly.

FIGURE 4.8 *More people have cell phones than have toilets—illustrating a failure to provide the most basic protection*

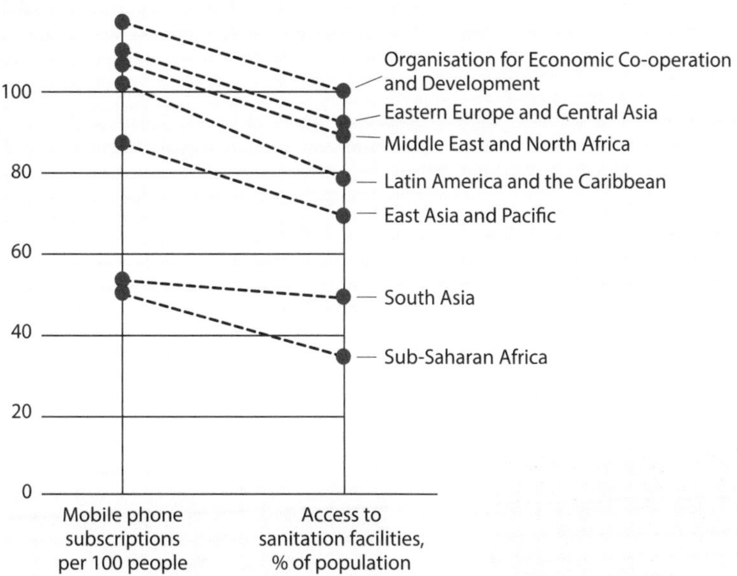

Source: WDR 2014 team based on data from World Bank World Development Indicators (database).

Note: Organisation for Economic Co-operation and Development (OECD) countries in the figure are high-income countries that have been members of the OECD for at least 40 years. All other countries are grouped into geographic regions. Data are as of 2010.

Income-support programs can often benefit from community participation, particularly in low- and lower-middle-income countries. Central authorities are better at identifying poor localities than at identifying the poor within them. Community participation in targeting can help by exploiting local knowledge and keeping elite capture of benefits in check—although the way the process is designed matters crucially.[59] An experiment in Indonesia compared community-based targeting conducted in villagewide meetings with a proxy means test. The community method resulted in slightly worse targeting at the $2 poverty line, equal targeting at $1 a day, and greater satisfaction and legitimacy overall (fewer complaints, fewer difficulties in distributing the funds, and greater acceptance of the beneficiary list).[60] Participation is equally important in providing relief after disasters: humanitarian assistance to people affected by disasters is often more effective when it takes local conditions into account and uses communities' own capacities. Likewise, an emphasis on rapid reconstruction, without adequate community involvement, can lead to recovering in ways that recreate vulnerabilities.[61]

PHOTO 4.1 Clean water and community-led sanitation improve hygiene and reduce diarrheal and other diseases. Children draw water from a water pump in North Sudan.
© Fred Noy/UN Photo

BOX 4.5 *Using social marketing to increase access to sanitation in rural Tanzania*

Around 1 billion people worldwide defecate in the open, creating vast risks for infants and children that often play amid excreta and waste water. Poor sanitation is responsible for an estimated 1.7 million deaths each year, is a cause of high medical bills, and is linked to disease and stunting among children. It can also impair dignity, gender equality, and quality of life. Agencies have learned that simply giving households toilets does not work. Instead, sanitation needs to be understood within the context of the obstacles households face.

Social marketing is being used in sanitation projects in rural Tanzania, where most toilets are basic pit latrines and diarrhea is common among children. The World Bank's Water and Sanitation Program conducted outreach activities with rural Tanzanians to understand their experience using toilets. People considered improving toilets and sanitary practices to be a low priority, costly, and complicated. Although people were very dissatisfied with their situation, affordable options were lacking, sanitation was not seen as a high priority, and a sense of powerlessness prevailed.

The program developed an inspirational promotion platform, called *Choo Bora Chawezekana!* (A Good Toilet Is Possible!) and delivered the message to an estimated 160,000 people in rural districts through radio spots, radio soap opera, and local events. District and ward authorities, masons, and village committees were employed as front-line promoters of the *Choo Bora* brand. Local masons produced an affordable cement slab for the toilet. The work of learning how Tanzanian households use sanitation continues. Findings from focus groups were incorporated into the National Sanitation Campaign, which aims to convince 6 million rural Tanzanians to invest in and use improved sanitation facilities by 2015.

Community-event in rural Tanzania promoting the *Choo Bora* message

Two women after purchasing a cement slab for a new toilet

Source: Jacqueline Devine and Jason Cardosi for the WDR 2014.
Photos: © Water and Sanitation Program staff.

Win-win investments should be favored. Not only can public works offer employment to unemployed workers; they can also boost preparation for crises and shocks by building local public goods or enhancing employment skills. Public works projects often build dams, shelters, drainage, and rural roads, and undertake soil, water, and forest conservation that protects communities against disasters. Djibouti, for example, started a workfare program when the economic crisis hit in 2008. The program offers short-term employment in community-based, labor-intensive works. It also supports improved nutrition practices, focusing on preschool children and pregnant or lactating women.[62] Many programs aim to impart skills that people can use to diversify their income sources. Latvia has used workfare to create temporary labor-intensive employment for people who had lost their jobs but were ineligible for unemployment benefits. The program has benefited communities by creating and maintaining infrastructure and providing social services.[63] (For more win-win examples, see spotlight 2.)

Earlier concerns that income-support programs might crowd out community mechanisms seem exaggerated, at least in developing countries. Some studies find that public safety nets displace informal transfers to a moderate or even significant extent.[64] As with credit, some substitution of formal sources for informal ones is to be expected. But displacement of private transfers does not translate to a net social loss when recipients share their benefits with other poor people or are able to increase their labor supply. This process has been studied extensively for South Africa's relatively generous old-age social pensions. Unemployment is high in South Africa and supporting unemployed family members drags many people into poverty, particularly families without any pensioner. When an elderly person starts receiving a pension, working-age family members are more likely to migrate for work—not less so—as the pension finances migration.[65] This way, access to risk management enables migration, employment, and escape from poverty.

Putting it all together: Policy principles and research priorities to foster resilient communities

Communities can become much better risk managers when supported by a favorable legal regime; when their organizational capacity is strengthened; when there is voice, transparency, and accountability; and when complementary public goods and services are provided, including those that link them to markets and other communities. Many different policies can be used to this end. These policies are summarized in table 4.1 by type of risk management instrument and by applying the lens of the five simple policy principles in the discussion that follows.

Do not generate uncertainty or unnecessary risk

Consult communities on important local decisions that involve them. When decisions on services, infrastructure, and land acquisition are taken without consulting the people they affect, opportunities to identify potential risks are missed.

Promote inclusion and accountability. State institutions need to strive for neutrality and reduce discrimination and practices that are unpredictable, abusive, or illegal. Ethnic favoritism, and perceptions thereof, should be avoided when targeting income support, services, and public sector employment, particularly in fragile environments. Local militias should not be armed, as they often become unaccountable or even criminal over time. Civil society and the press should not be constrained in their ability to serve as watchdogs. The press, on the other hand, needs to behave responsibly and refrain from playing up ethnic tensions and stereotypes.

Think long run

Prepare for disasters and emergencies in advance. Much disaster and humanitarian response is impeded by an absence of preparation: agencies raise funding for response on an ad hoc basis once emergencies have been declared; competition over funds limits coordination; a disaster's ability to grab head-

TABLE 4.1 *Policy priorities to improve risk management at the community level*

	POLICIES TO SUPPORT RISK MANAGEMENT FOUNDATIONAL →	→ ADVANCED
Knowledge	Transparency and freedom of the press	
	Simpler conflict filters for fragile settings	Violence and disaster hotspot maps
Protection	Law and order for all; anti-discrimination measures	
	Local institutions that bridge divided groups (particularly for fragile settings)	Community-based crime prevention
	Community infrastructure and capacity for disaster management	
Insurance	Credit and savings (group-based or microfinance)	Credit, savings, and insurance (bank-based)
Coping	Workfare for employment and basic infrastructure	Workfare for skill building
	Making humanitarian relief accountable for long-term results	Support delivered via permanent government systems
	Community-targeted income support	Means-tested income support

Source: WDR 2014 team.

Note: The table presents a sequencing of policies based on the guidance of chapter 2 for establishing policy priorities: *be realistic* in designing policies tailored to the institutional capacity of the country, and *build a strong foundation* that addresses the most critical obstacles sustainably and that can be improved over time.

lines determines funding; there are few incentives (and little funding) to invest ex ante in risk protection and preparedness; and permanent systems for delivering income and other support are missing. Moreover, since most humanitarian funding is spent on complex, protracted emergencies and not on intensive disasters, support that is inherently meant to be temporary and short-term in many cases ends up carrying on for the long haul (see box 4.2). Putting in place a coordinated funding mechanism for disaster and humanitarian preparation and response would help ensure timely responses, investment in preparation, and accountability for long-term outcomes (see also chapter 8).[66]

Build transparent, accountable, inclusive, and scalable institutions, and realize that fostering communities' cohesion and capacity to organize their own risk management takes time and patience. In fragile and conflict-affected countries, in particular, restoring confidence and institutional capacity may take a generation. Therefore, it is best to stay engaged for the long haul, and to use that time to experiment with ways to scale up.

Promote flexibility

Listen to communities, allow local actors discretion in devising local solutions, adopt learning-by-doing, and build feedback loops. All of these activities can help with adaptation of interventions over time and across space as local risks evolve as well as offer opportunities for managing them.

Provide the right incentives

Promote social accountability and transparency at local and national levels. Local accountability measures can contribute to better and more consistent delivery of local services and risk management by making service providers perform better, ensuring that spending meets local needs, and reducing corruption. To work well, local accountability measures often require complementary national action such as open flow of information, freedom of the press, and mechanisms for holding authorities accountable.

Include the vulnerable in protection

Focus public action on ways to protect people's basic consumption and access to health and education during systemic shocks. (This recommendation builds on chapter 3.) Income support is a useful complement to informal community coping and insurance—which are likely to be overwhelmed by systemic shocks—and can avoid costly and irreversible coping responses. Income-transfer programs need to be scalable and flexible in order to increase coverage in communities facing shocks and be scaled back once crisis abates. The beneficiary selection process should be able to identify those most affected by shocks, not just the chronic poor. Community-based targeting can help in this regard, often in conjunction with geographic targeting to affected regions, or self-targeting.

A final note: Refocus research priorities from diagnostics to solutions

Refocus research priorities to investigate the underlying causes of vulnerability, how to address them, and how to promote opportunity. Among all the topics covered in this chapter, by far the most researched has been informal insurance in rural areas. Urban areas have received less attention. Preparation for risk, which arguably can have the farthest reaching effects, seems underresearched. In general, research tends to be stronger on the diagnostics—the nature of shocks, their impacts, and the ways people cope—than on the particular policies to address vulnerability and ways they might promote opportunity. Financial and social protection instruments have attracted more research interest, particularly in economics, than broader policies pertaining to participation, fostering collective action, scaling up local initiatives, upgrading slums, improving governance, and fighting exclusion and discrimination; yet such "softer" approaches may well have more transformational impacts.

Make it easier to consider communities in development planning. Preventing local interventions from having unintended harmful consequences often requires detailed understanding of specific contexts, knowledge that can be time-consuming for planners to acquire. It would therefore be useful if social scientists could develop simpler and quicker tools (sometimes known as "conflict filters") to ensure that development planning takes local situations into account. More broadly, research on organizational models such as associations of the poor that can scale up community-based solutions and also deal better with large, complex problems would help fill a major void.

Notes

1. Klinenberg 2002.
2. De Weerdt 2001.
3. Dercon 2008; Jalan and Ravallion 2001.
4. Bowles and Gintis 2002.
5. Christiaensen and Subbarao 2005 for Kenya; Dercon and Krishnan 2000 for Ethiopia; Heltberg and Lund 2009 for Pakistan; Townsend 1994 for rural India; and Dercon and De Weerdt 2006 for community networks to help with illness. See also chapters 1 and 3.
6. The term *community* has its origins in the Latin term *communis*—shared by all or many. Communities are defined by relationships and connections, not affection (Bowles and Gintis 2002). *Community* denotes the group. *Social capital* refers to aspects of relationships within the group, such as norms and trust.
7. Moser 2009.
8. Fafchamps and De Weerdt 2011.
9. Chen 2010.
10. Mohapatra, Joseph, and Ratha 2012.
11. Fafchamps and De Weerdt 2011; Morduch 2002; Ravallion and Chaudhuri 1997; Townsend 1994.
12. Gertler and Gruber 2002.
13. Mohapatra, Joseph, and Ratha 2012.
14. Jalan and Ravallion 1999.
15. Dercon 2002.
16. Fafchamps and Gubert 2007.
17. Attanasio and others 2012; Coate and Ravallion 1993; De Janvry and others 2002.
18. De Janvry and others 2002; Genicot and Ray 2003.
19. Heltberg, Hossain, and Reva 2012.
20. Santos and Barrett 2011.
21. World Bank 2000, 16.
22. Fay 2005.
23. Fay 2005.
24. WDR 2014 team analysis based on Nicaragua Encuesta Nacional de Hogares sobre Medición de Nivel de Vida 2005.
25. Hsiang 2012.
26. Ashwill and Heltberg 2013 for the WDR 2014.
27. Petesch 2013 for the WDR 2014; World Bank 2010.
28. Rockmore 2011.
29. Esteban, Mayoral, and Ray 2012.
30. Varshney 2002; see also Lederman, Loayza, and Menendez 2002.
31. Marc and others 2013.
32. Collier 2009, 89; Petesch 2013 for the WDR 2014; World Bank 2010, ch. 2.
33. Hsiang, Burke, and Miguel 2013.
34. Varshney 2002.
35. Narayan, Nikitin, and Petesch 2010.
36. World Bank 2012.
37. Mansuri and Rao 2012.
38. Bowles and Gintis 2002; Ostrom 2000 offers an insightful survey of the literature.
39. This refusal has serious consequences, since funerals are elaborate affairs and there are bound to be logistical disasters without help. See De Weerdt 2001.
40. Ostrom 2000; Bowles and Gintis 2002; see also Habyarimana and others 2007 and the sources cited therein.
41. Ostrom 2000; Mansuri and Rao 2012.
42. Singh 2011.
43. Marc and others 2013; Singh 2011.
44. World Bank 2010.
45. Khan 1996.
46. Mansuri and Rao 2012.
47. World Bank 2006.
48. Narayan, Prennushi, and Kapoor 2009.
49. Chaudhury and others 2006.
50. Douglas and others 2008.
51. Narayan and others 2000, 198–202.
52. Besley, Pande, and Rao 2012; Mansuri and Rao 2012.
53. Loayza, Rigolini, and Calvo-Gonzalez 2011.
54. Mansuri and Rao 2012 and Speer 2012 provide recent surveys; see also World Bank 2003.
55. Pandey and others 2007. Bjorkman and Svensson 2009 found broadly similar results in Uganda, while Banerjee and others 2010 did not find significant impacts on services of giving information, perhaps because their experiment was of shorter duration.
56. Devarajan, Khemani, and Walton 2011; Mansuri and Rao 2012.
57. Dreze and Khera 2011; Liu and Barrett 2013.
58. Rodriguez-Garcia and others 2013.
59. Coady, Grosh, and Hoddinott 2004; Mansuri and Rao 2012.
60. Alatas and others 2012.
61. IPCC 2012.
62. Levin, Morgandi, and Silva 2012.
63. Azam, Ferre, and Ajwad 2012.
64. Cox, Hansen, and Jimenez 2004; Dercon and Krishnan 2003.
65. Ardington, Case, and Hosegood 2009.
66. van Aalst and others 2013 for the WDR 2014.

References

Alatas, Vivi, Abhijit Banerjee, Rema Hanna, Benjamin A. Olken, and Julia Tobias. 2012. "Targeting the Poor: Evidence from a Field Experiment in Indonesia." *American Economic Review* 102 (4): 1206–40.

Ardington, Cally, Anne Case, and Victoria Hosegood. 2009. "Labor Supply Responses to Large Social Transfers: Longitudinal Evidence from South Africa." *American Economic Journal: Applied Economics* 1 (1): 22–48.

Ashwill, Maximillian, and Rasmus Heltberg. 2013. "Is There a Community-Level Adaptation Deficit?" Background paper for the *World Development Report 2014.*

Attanasio, Orazio, Abigail Barr, Juan C. Cardenas, Garance Genicot, and Costas Meghir. 2012. "Risk Pooling, Risk Preferences, and Social Networks." *American Economic Journal: Applied Economics* 4 (2): 134–67.

Azam, Mehtabul, Celine Ferre, and Mohamed Ihsan Ajwad. 2012. "Did Latvia's Public Works Program Mitigate the Impact of the 2008–2010 Crisis?" Policy Research Working Paper 6144, World Bank, Washington, DC.

Banerjee, Abhijit V., Rukmini Banerji, Esther Duflo, Rachel Glennerster, and Stuti Khemani. 2010. "Pitfalls of Participatory Programs: Evidence from a Randomized Evaluation in Education in India." *American Economic Journal: Economic Policy* 2 (1): 1–30.

Besley, Timothy, Rohini Pande, and Vijayendra Rao. 2012. "Just Rewards? Local Politics and Public Resource Allocation in South India." *World Bank Economic Review* 26 (2): 191–216.

Bjorkman, Martina, and Jakob Svensson. 2009. "Power to the People: Evidence from a Randomized Field Experiment on Community-Based Monitoring in Uganda." *Quarterly Journal of Economics* 124 (2): 735–69.

Bowles, Samuel, and Herbert Gintis. 2002. "Social Capital and Community Governance." *Economic Journal* 112 (483): 419–36.

Chaudhury, Nazmul, Jeffrey S. Hammer, Michael Kremer, Karthik Muralidharan, and F. Halsey Rogers. 2006. "Missing in Action: Teacher and Health Worker Absence in Developing Countries." *Journal of Economic Perspectives* 20 (1): 91–116.

Chen, Daniel L. 2010. "Club Goods and Group Identity: Evidence from Islamic Resurgence during the Indonesian Financial Crisis." *Journal of Political Economy* 118 (2): 300–54.

Christiaensen, Luc J., and Kalinidhi Subbarao. 2005. "Towards an Understanding of Household Vulnerability in Rural Kenya." *Journal of African Economies* 14 (4): 520–58.

Coady, David, Margaret E. Grosh, and John Hoddinott. 2004. *Targeting of Transfers in Developing Countries: Review of Lessons and Experience.* World Bank Regional and Sectoral Studies. Washington, DC: World Bank.

Coate, Stephen, and Martin Ravallion. 1993. "Reciprocity without Commitment: Characterization and Performance of Informal Insurance Arrangements." *Journal of Development Economics* 40 (1): 1–24.

Collier, Paul. 2009. *Wars, Guns, and Votes: Democracy in Dangerous Places.* New York: Harper Collins.

Cox, Donald, Bruce E. Hansen, and Emmanuel Jimenez. 2004. "How Responsive Are Private Transfers to Income? Evidence from a Laissez-Faire Economy." *Journal of Public Economics* 88 (9–10): 2193–219.

De Janvry, Alain, Rinku Murgai, Elisabeth Sadoulet, and Paul Winters. 2002. "Localized and Incomplete Mutual Insurance." *Journal of Development Economics* 67 (2): 245–74.

Dercon, Stefan. 2002. "Income Risk, Coping Strategies, and Safety Nets." *World Bank Research Observer* 17 (2): 141–66.

———. 2008. "Fate and Fear: Risk and Its Consequences in Africa." *Journal of African Economies* 17 (2): 97–127.

Dercon, Stefan, and Joachim De Weerdt. 2006. "Risk Sharing Networks and Insurance against Illness." *Journal of Development Economics* 81 (2): 337–56.

Dercon, Stefan, and Pramila Krishnan. 2000. "In Sickness and in Health: Risk Sharing within Households in Rural Ethiopia." *Journal of Political Economy* 108 (4): 688–727.

———. 2003. "Risk Sharing and Public Transfers." *Economic Journal* 113 (486): 86–94.

Devarajan, Shantayanan, Stuti Khemani, and Michael Walton. 2011. "Civil Society, Public Action and Accountability in Africa." Policy Research Working Paper 5733, World Bank, Washington, DC.

De Weerdt, Joachim. 2001. "Community Organizations in Rural Tanzania: A Case Study of the Community of Nyakatoke, Bukoba Rural District." *The Nyakatoke Series* 3.

Douglas, Ian, Khurshid Alam, Maryanne Maghenda, Yasmin McDonnell, Louise McLean, and Jack Campbell. 2008. "Unjust Waters: Climate Change, Flooding and the Urban Poor in Africa." *Environment and Urbanization* 20 (1): 187–205.

Dreze, Jean, and Reetika Khera. 2011. *The Battle for Employment Guarantee.* New Delhi: Oxford University Press.

Esteban, Joan, Laura Mayoral, and Debraj Ray. 2012. "Ethnicity and Conflict: An Empirical Study." *American Economic Review* 102 (4): 1310–42.

Fafchamps, Marcel, and Joachim De Weerdt. 2011. "Social Identity and the Formation of Health Insurance Networks." *Journal of Development Studies* 47 (8): 1152–77.

Fafchamps, Marcel, and Flore Gubert. 2007. "The Formation of Risk Sharing Networks." *Journal of Development Economics* 83 (2): 326–50.

Fay, Marianne. 2005. *The Urban Poor in Latin America.* Directions in Development. Washington, DC: World Bank.

Foa, Roberto. 2012. "Trends in Tolerance of Social Minorities across the World." Unpublished manuscript, World Bank, Washington, DC.

Genicot, Garance, and Debraj Ray. 2003. "Group Formation in Risk-Sharing Arrangements." *Review of Economic Studies* 70 (1): 87–113.

Gertler, Paul, and Jonathan Gruber. 2002. "Insuring Consumption against Illness." *American Economic Review* 92 (1): 51–70.

Habyarimana, James, Macartan Humphreys, Daniel N. Posner, and Jeremy M. Weinstein. 2007. "Why Does Ethnic Diversity Undermine Public Goods Provision?" *American Political Science Review* 101 (4): 709–25.

Heltberg, Rasmus, Naomi Hossain, and Anna Reva. 2012. *Living through Crises: How the Food, Fuel, and Financial Shocks Affect the Poor.* Washington, DC: World Bank.

Heltberg, Rasmus, and Niels Lund. 2009. "Shocks, Coping, and Outcomes for Pakistan's Poor: Health Risks Predominate." *Journal of Development Studies* 45 (6): 831–946.

Hsiang, Solomon. 2012. "Are We Well Adapted to Our Climate? And What Might That Mean for Future Climate Changes?" *Earth Magazine* 57 (8): 8.

Hsiang, Solomon, Marshall B. Burke, and Ted Miguel. 2013. "Quantifying the Climatic Influence on Human Conflict, Violence and Political Instability." *Science* DOI: 10.1126/science.1235367.

IPCC (Intergovernmental Panel on Climate Change). 2012. "Managing the Risks of Extreme Events and Disasters to Advance Climate Change Adaptation." Special Report, IPCC, New York.

Jalan, Jyotsna, and Martin Ravallion. 1999. "Income Gains to the Poor from Workfare: Estimates for Argentina's Trabajar Program." Policy Research Working Paper 2149, World Bank, Washington, DC.

———. 2001. "Behavioral Responses to Risk in Rural China." *Journal of Development Economics* 66 (1): 23–49.

Khan, Akhter Hameed. 1996. *Orangi Pilot Project: Reminiscences and Reflections.* Karachi: Oxford University Press.

Klinenberg, Eric. 2002. *Heat Wave: A Social Autopsy of Disaster in Chicago.* Chicago: University of Chicago Press.

Lakhani, Sadaf S. 2013. "Forced Displacement: Moving from Managing Risk to Facilitating Opportunity." Background paper for the *World Development Report 2014.*

Lederman, Daniel, Norman Loayza, and Ana Maria Menendez. 2002. "Violent Crime: Does Social Capital Matter?" *Economic Development and Cultural Change* 50 (3): 509–39.

Levin, Victoria, Matteo Morgandi, and Joana Silva. 2012. *Inclusion and Resilience: The Way Forward for Social Safety Nets in the Middle East and North Africa.* Middle East and North Africa Development Report. Washington, DC: World Bank.

Liu, Yanyan, and Christopher B. Barrett. 2013. "Heterogeneous Pro-Poor Targeting in India's Mahatma Gandhi National Rural Employment Guarantee Scheme." *Economic and Political Weekly* 48 (10): 46–53.

Loayza, Norman, Jamele Rigolini, and Oscar Calvo-Gonzalez. 2011. "More Than You Can Handle: Decentralization and Municipal Spending Ability in Developing Countries." Policy Research Working Paper 5763, World Bank, Washington, DC.

Mansuri, Ghazala, and Vijayendra Rao. 2012. *Localizing Development: Does Participation Work?* Policy Research Report. Washington, DC: World Bank.

Marc, Alexandre, Alys Willman, Ghazia Aslam, Michelle Rebosio, and Kanishka Balasuriya. 2013. *Societal Dynamics and Fragility: Engaging Societies in Responding to Fragile Situations.* Washington, DC: World Bank.

Mohapatra, Sanket, George Joseph, and Dilip Ratha. 2012. "Remittances and Natural Disasters: Ex-Post Response and Contribution to Ex-Ante Preparedness." *Environment, Development and Sustainability* 14 (3): 365–87.

Morduch, Jonathan. 2002. "Consumption Smoothing across Space: Testing Theories of Risk-Sharing in the Icrisat Study Region of South India." United Nations University Wider Discussion Paper 55, United Nations University–World Institute for Development Economics Research, Tokyo.

Moser, Caroline O. N. 2009. *Ordinary Families, Extraordinary Lives: Assets and Poverty Reduction in Guayaquil, 1978–2004.* Washington, DC: Brookings Institution Press.

Narayan, Deepa, Robert Chambers, Meera K. Shah, and Patti Petesch. 2000. *Crying Out for Change.* Vol. 2 of *Voices of the Poor.* Washington, DC: World Bank and Oxford University Press.

Narayan, Deepa, Denis Nikitin, and Patti Petesch. 2010. "Building States from the Bottom Up in Conflict-Affected Countries." In *Rising from the Ashes of Conflict.* Vol. 4 of *Moving out of Poverty*, edited by Deepa Narayan and Patti Petesch, 1–190. Washington, DC: World Bank and Palgrave Macmillan.

Narayan, Deepa, Giovanna Prennushi, and Soumya Kapoor. 2009. "People's Organizations and Poverty Escapes in Rural Andhra Pradesh." In *The Promise of Empowerment and Democracy in India.* Vol. 3 of *Moving out of Poverty*, edited by Deepa Narayan, 234–85. Washington, DC: World Bank and Palgrave Macmillan.

Ostrom, Elinor. 2000. "Collective Action and the Evolution of Social Norms." *Journal of Economic Perspectives* 14 (3): 137–58.

Pandey, Priyanka, Ashwini R. Sehgal, Michelle Riboud, David Levine, and Madhav Goyal. 2007. "Informing Resource-Poor Populations and the Delivery of Entitled Health and Social Services in Rural India." *The Journal of the American Medical Association* 298 (16): 1867–75.

Petesch, Patti. 2013. "How Communities Manage Risks of Crime and Violence." Background paper for the *World Development Report 2014.*

Ravallion, Martin, and Shubham Chaudhuri. 1997. "Risk and Insurance in Village India: Comment." *Econometrica: Journal of the Econometric Society* 65 (1): 171–84.

Rockmore, Marc. 2011. "The Cost of Fear: The Welfare Effects of the Risk of Violence in Northern Uganda." Working Papers 109, Households in Conflict Network, Brighton, UK.

Rodriguez-Garcia, Rosalia, Rene Bonnel, David Wilson, and N'Della N'Jie. 2013. *Investing in Communities Achieves Results: Findings from an Evaluation of Community Responses to HIV and AIDS.* Directions in Development. Washington, DC: World Bank.

Santos, Paulo, and Christopher B. Barrett. 2011. "Persistent Poverty and Informal Credit." *Journal of Development Economics* 96 (2): 337–47.

Singh, Prerna. 2011. "We-Ness and Welfare: A Longitudinal Analysis of Social Development in Kerala, India." *World Development* 39 (2): 282–93.

Soon, Tan Yong, Lee Tung Jean, and Karean Tan. 2009. *Clean, Green and Blue: Singapore's Journey towards Environmental and Water Sustainability.* Singapore: Institute of Southeast Asian Studies.

Speer, Johanna. 2012. "Participatory Governance Reform: A Good Strategy for Increasing Government Responsiveness and Improving Public Services?" *World Development* 40 (12): 2379–98.

Townsend, Robert M. 1994. "Risk and Insurance in Village India." *Econometrica: Journal of the Econometric Society* 62 (3): 539–91.

van Aalst, Maarten, Jan Kellett, Florence Pichon, and Tom Mitchell. 2013. "Incentives in Disaster Risk Management and Humanitarian Response." Background paper for the *World Development Report 2014.*

Varshney, Ashutosh. 2002. *Ethnic Conflict and Civic Life: Hindus and Muslims in India.* New Haven, CT: Yale University Press.

World Bank. 2000. *World Development Report 2000/2001: Attacking Poverty.* New York: Oxford University Press.

———. 2003. *World Development Report 2004: Making Services Work for Poor People.* New York: Oxford University Press.

———. 2006. *Hazards of Nature, Risks to Development: An IEG Evaluation of World Bank Assistance for Natural Disasters.* Washington, DC: World Bank.

———. 2007. "Social Protection in Pakistan: Managing Household Risks and Vulnerability." World Bank, Washington, DC.

———. 2010. *World Development Report 2011: Conflict, Security, and Development.* Washington, DC: World Bank.

———. 2012. *World Development Report 2013: Jobs.* Washington, DC: World Bank.

———. World Development Indicators (database). World Bank, Washington, DC., http://data.worldbank.org/data-catalog/world-development-indicators.

SPOTLIGHT 4

Where criminal justice is not enough: Integrated urban crime and violence prevention in Brazil and South Africa

Levels of urban crime and violence differ within countries, within regions, and even within states and provinces, as do the drivers of crime, which are influenced by historical, political, cultural, and socioeconomic factors. Despite these differences, successful strategies to reduce and prevent crime and violence have common elements, often referred to as an integrated approach to urban crime and violence prevention. Three cities in Brazil and one in South Africa are emblematic of this integrated approach to urban crime and violence prevention, which includes communities and moves beyond mere policing.

Understanding risk factors, combining prevention and criminal justice reform, and pursuing inclusive approaches that engage actors at all levels of government, in civil society, and in the private sector are crucial in fighting and preventing urban crime and violence. A transition away from a criminal justice–first approach is frequently the first step. Preventive strategies—particularly those targeting young people through education, job training, psychological support, and early childhood development—usually follow. Because the benefits of prevention materialize in the longer run, strategies that aim to reduce crime and violence more quickly are also important. Among these strategies are inclusive citizen security, public health programs such as drug and alcohol rehabilitation, and the construction of youth-friendly spaces.

Although crime rates in some cities remain very high (figure S4.1), the improvements in crime and violence in Diadema, Belo Horizonte, and Rio de Janeiro in Brazil and in Johannesburg in South Africa highlight the benefits of complementing traditional criminal justice approaches with prevention strategies.

FIGURE S4.1 *Homicide rate in selected cities*

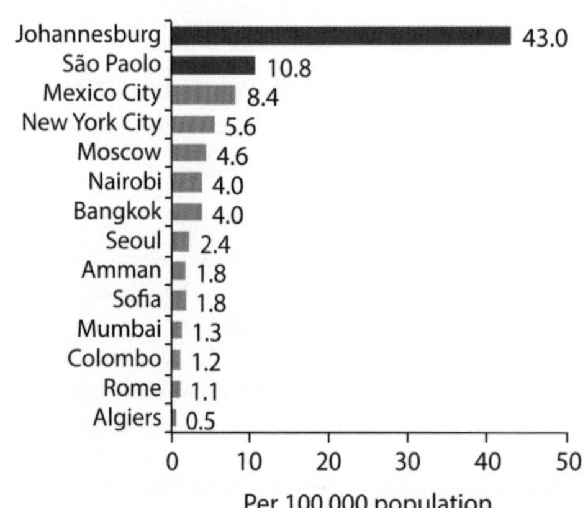

Source: WDR 2014 team based on data from the United Nations Office on Drugs and Crime Homicide Statistics database.

Note: All rates are for 2009, except for Algiers (2008), Amman (2006), Johannesburg (2007–08), Nairobi (2008), and Rome (2008).

Making cities safer in Brazil

Brazil is a heterogeneous country, which is reflected in the variation in crime rates across its different regions. While the homicide rate has increased significantly in areas such as the northeastern portion of the country, over the past 25 years some regions, particularly those in the south, have experienced large declines in their homicide rates. In São Paulo, for instance, the homicide rate fell 67 percent between 2000 and 2010.

Crime reduction approaches that have shown good results in the southeast include educational programs, programs for youth, and gun and alcohol control, all of which involved inclusive citizen security components at the municipal level. The strategies of three different Brazilian municipalities are particularly noteworthy.

Diadema, a city in the state of São Paulo where violence increased 49 percent between 1995 and 1998, enacted a new public security policy in 2000. Important components of the policy included a limit on alcohol sales after 11 p.m. and monitoring of the number and legality of alcohol licenses in the city. Diadema also improved public lighting and installed security cameras in areas with high crime rates. The public security policy contributed to a decline in the homicide rate from 389 per 100,000 inhabitants in 1999 to 167 in 2003. The alcohol policy seemed particularly effective: the homicide rate fell 44 percent and the rate of assaults against women fell 56 percent compared with levels expected in the absence of the alcohol policy.

Homicide rates also increased significantly in the late 1990s in Belo Horizonte, Brazil's third-largest city. Crime in the city often occurred in slums and was frequently perpetrated by young men. Following a public outcry, city officials in 2002 piloted the Fica Vivo (Stay Alive) program in the city's most violent slums. The program involved the city council; the municipal, federal, and military police; the public prosecutor's office; private businesses; nongovernmental organizations; and local communities. Preventive actions, including support for education, job training, and youth sports and arts programs, aimed to reduce violence through the combination of crime control and social development programs. Information sessions about violence, drugs, and sexually transmitted diseases were also offered. Thirty months after the implementation of Fica Vivo, homicides had fallen by 47 percent and attempted homicides by 65 percent.

The homicide rate jumped in the state of Rio de Janeiro, as well, more than doubling between 1980 and 1997 from 26 to 59 homicides per 100,000 inhabitants. Crime began to drop in the 2000s as a result of 2003 national gun control legislation and a small-arms buyback campaign. By 2008, homicide rates in the state and in the City of Rio had fallen to less than 34 per 100,000 habitants.

However, drug trafficking persisted in Rio's *favelas,* the informal settlements of Brazilian cities. In 2008, an initiative combining criminal justice and prevention was launched in response. The initiative relied on elite police units to clear *favelas* of drug traffickers. Once they were gone, UPPs (Police Pacification Units) entered the *favelas* and focused on building trust between the community and the police, while also providing a continued security presence. The UPPs helped accelerate the decline in the homicide and violent crime rates. A second phase, UPP Social (UPPS), links residents of those *favelas* that have been cleared of drug traffickers with social assistance. Dialogue is encouraged among residents, service providers, government agencies, and the private sector to help ensure that community needs are met. To ensure the sustainability of the approach, this phase also involves efforts to formalize services such as electricity, gas, cable, and Internet; rehabilitate youth formerly involved in criminal activity; and revitalize the urban area. By 2012, more than 25 UPPs had been established. The government plans to serve 165 communities through the establishment of 45 UPPs and UPPSs by 2014.

Combining prevention and criminal justice in South Africa

In the past, South Africa took a more reactive approach to crime, relying heavily on the criminal justice system. This reactive approach led to one of the highest rates of incarceration in the world but did little to stem crime. For instance, the country's homicide rate was 39 per 100,000 in 2007–08, higher than Brazil's rate of 26. A shift to a multisector preventive approach to crime reduction appears to be making some progress, however. In 1996, shortly after the end of apartheid, the South African government launched a National Crime Prevention Strategy, which advocated a greater focus on prevention. In recent years, the South Africa Police Services have used Community Police Forums to put this proposal into action. Consisting of schools, businesses, and civil and religious institutions, the forums facilitate partnerships and joint problem identification and problem solving between the police and the community. The partnerships are designed to lead to the development of multistakeholder community safety plans.

Johannesburg adopted a strategy in line with the rethinking of crime prevention taking place in the rest of the country. Indeed, the homicide rate in Johannesburg was even higher than in South Africa as a whole in 2007–08, reaching almost 43 homicides per 100,000 inhabitants. The Joburg City Safety Strategy, part of Johannesburg's development plan, is designed to cut the city's high crime rate. The strategy prioritizes actions that are critical to economic development and foresees a gradual broadening of the boundaries of crime reduction and prevention interventions. Key programs include targeted surveillance, patrols, closed circuit television, and other tools to deter criminals and increase people's perception of safety.

Reforms continue along these lines. In 2012, South Africa undertook a review of the criminal justice system in an effort to increase conviction rates, speed trials, improve the rehabilitation capacity of the prison system, and promote released prisoners' reentry into society. The country is also increasing the budget for and expanding locations of the police, courts, and prisons. Civil society organizations, such as the Open Society Foundation and the Center for Justice and Crime Prevention, have helped launch safety audits in poor communities and have assisted with the design of crime prevention programs tailored to the local context. The private sector is also heavily involved. For example, Business against Crime, a coalition of South African companies, collaborates with the government to develop public-private partnerships to reduce crime.

Sources

Greenwood, Peter W., Karyn Model, and C. Peter Rydell. 1998. "Diverting Children from a Life of Crime: Measuring Costs and Benefits." RAND Corporation, Santa Monica, CA.

Moser, Caroline. 2006. "Reducing Urban Violence in Developing Countries." Policy Brief 2006-01, Brookings Institution, Washington, DC.

Petesch, Patti. 2013. "How Communities Manage Risks of Crime and Violence." Background paper for the *World Development Report 2014.*

UNODC (United Nations Office on Drugs and Crime). Homicide Statistics. UNODC, Vienna, http://www.unodc.org/unodc/en/data-and-analysis/homicide.html.

World Bank. 2011. *Violence in the City: Understanding and Supporting Community Responses to Urban Violence.* Washington, DC: World Bank.

———. 2012a. "Bringing the State Back into the *Favelas* of Rio de Janeiro." World Bank, Washington, DC.

———. 2012b. "Making Brazilians Safer: Analyzing the Dynamics of Violent Crime." World Bank, Washington, DC.

Assembling computers in China. Jobs are drivers of development and pillars of resilience for people.

CHAPTER 5

Fostering resilience and prosperity through a vibrant enterprise sector

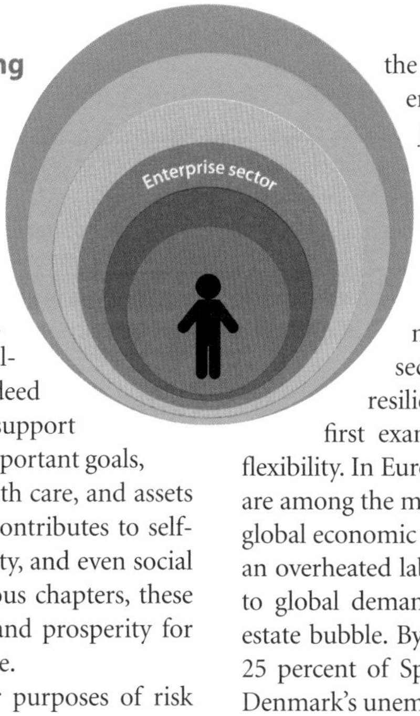

Creating jobs and supporting innovation

The fear of losing or not finding a job is a primary concern for most people. About three-quarters of respondents in developing countries worry a "great deal" about being unemployed, according to the latest World Values Survey. Having a job is indeed valuable: it produces income to support consumption and to help meet important goals, such as providing education, health care, and assets for family members. A job also contributes to self-esteem, a sense of personal security, and even social cohesion.[1] As discussed in previous chapters, these benefits are pillars of resilience and prosperity for households and communities alike.

Not all jobs are the same for purposes of risk management, however. From the perspective of workers, jobs that provide secure and increasing income and a safe working environment are preferable to jobs that do not carry those benefits. Moreover, jobs that produce goods and services that consumers want and can rely on and jobs that respect and conserve the environment are better from society's perspective. Where can these good jobs be found? This chapter argues that a vibrant enterprise sector is best situated to provide such jobs through its potential to mitigate the risk of unemployment, reallocate resources to create opportunities, and contribute to worker, consumer, and environmental protection. The chapter further argues that two characteristics—*flexibility* (the capacity to adapt to changes to the potential mutual benefits of workers and firm owners) and, gradually, *formality* (abiding by sensible laws and regulations)—can greatly help enterprises support people's risk management.

Two examples, continents apart, illustrate how flexibility and formality can improve the enterprise sector's capacity to foster people's resilience and promote prosperity. The first example illustrates the importance of flexibility. In Europe, Denmark, Germany, and Spain are among the many countries hit hard by the recent global economic and financial crises: Denmark from an overheated labor market, Germany from a shock to global demand, and Spain from a popped real estate bubble. By the beginning of 2013, more than 25 percent of Spain's labor force was unemployed. Denmark's unemployment rate also increased, but to a much lower 7.4 percent. In Germany, the rate was just 5.3 percent.[2] Many factors explain the different experiences of these three countries. For one thing, the shock that hit Spain was larger than those affecting Denmark and Germany. But explanations of the widely different unemployment outcomes should also consider the flexibility of the labor markets in those countries. Labor market reforms in Germany helped moderate wage increases before the international crisis and enabled employees and firms to adjust hours worked through work sharing without the need for layoffs. In Denmark, job separations were high, but unemployment spells were short and eased by a robust safety net and retraining programs for the unemployed. In Spain, in contrast, where a high percentage of the workforce was employed in the hard-hit construction sector, stringent employment regulations with significant severance costs, along with other structural factors such as the relatively high share of unskilled young labor, have added to the high and persistent unemployment.[3]

The second example shows the benefits for enterprises of becoming formal. In Peru in recent years, informal mines have sprung up in response to rising gold prices. Ignoring existing regulations, these informal mines have caused significant deforestation. The mercury used in the extraction process has contaminated rivers and the atmosphere and threatened human health.[4] In the La Libertad region, the Poderosa Mining Company took an innovative approach to the problem after informal miners invaded one of its mining concessions. The company began to formalize the invading miners, signing agreements that allowed them to continue mining under its direction. The agreements, which meet international environmental management quality standards, have increased the small miners' income and decreased the harm from deforestation and mercury contamination.[5]

These two stories convey the chapter's main message: flexibility and formality enhance the enterprise sector's ability to contribute to people's resilience and prosperity. An enterprise sector that is flexible is more capable of responding to shocks by reallocating resources within and across enterprises and of innovating in an ever-changing world. An enterprise sector that is formal is better situated to take advantage of legal protection and contract enforcement and to make better use of public infrastructure. In addition, formal enterprises can be more easily held accountable for their impact on worker safety and on consumer and environmental well-being.

There are both synergies and trade-offs between flexibility and formality. In countries with responsible and strong state institutions and streamlined regulations, formality enhances flexibility. In countries with weak state institutions and cumbersome regulatory regimes, however, the cost of formality can be too large for the majority of enterprises and workers. In this case, "informal is normal," and informality is a means for the economy to achieve a certain degree of flexibility and for workers to access a practical safety net.[6] A diverse array of workers and enterprises then remains informal because they are excluded from or choose not to join a formal sector that offers limited benefits.[7]

Informality is often a second-best response, however. The majority of the poor work in the informal sector out of necessity rather than choice. In Ghana, for example, more than 60 percent of informal salaried and self-employed workers without employees would rather have formal wage jobs.[8] Informal mechanisms may be effective for small firms and simple transactions, but are insufficient for larger firms and complex relations with workers and markets. That may be why wage employment as a share of total employment increases as a country develops. Notwithstanding significant variation across and within regions, self-employment—a large part of which is likely of a subsistence nature—is widespread in the developing world (figure 5.1).

If the enterprise sector is to fulfill its role in supporting people's risk management, public policy for the sector requires reforms that balance the economy's need for flexibility with society's need for legal and regulatory protections. The chapter argues for a combination of reforms to help the enterprise sector become flexible as it gradually becomes formal. These reforms include improving the basic foundations of the enterprise sector by strengthening property rights and reducing uncertainty about government policy; implementing and enforcing sound regulations; and providing inclusive social protection. In the longer run, when sound regulations for flexibility are in place, the government can pursue reforms that encourage both flexibility and formality by spurring innovation; increasing the skill level of the labor force; and enhancing worker, consumer, and environmental protections. These reforms are necessary not only to increase growth but to enhance people's resilience and to promote prosperity. Although the risks that enterprises themselves face and their risk-taking decisions are very important aspects of a vibrant enterprise sector, this chapter maintains the Report's focus on risks faced by people. It thus focuses on the enterprise sector as a sector and on its function of supporting people and society in managing risk in different ways.

The ways that the enterprise sector can help people confront risks

Let's step back for a moment and consider what the enterprise sector is. The enterprise sector comprises workers, owners, the arrangements that organize their relationships within an individual enterprise, and the technology that turns labor and capital into goods and services. Enterprises, the defining unit of the enterprise sector, range from informal to formal, from self-employment to partnerships to giant multinational corporations, and from agriculture

FIGURE 5.1 *Wage employment rises with the level of economic development*

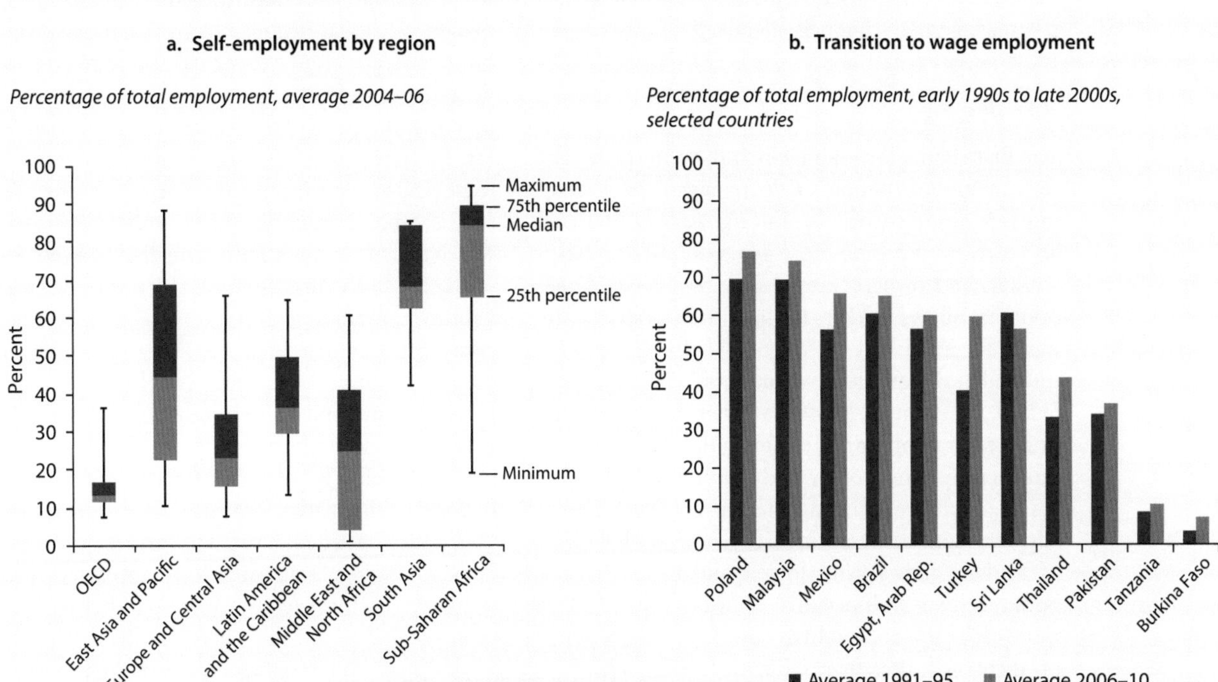

Source: WDR 2014 team based on data from World Bank World Development Indicators (database).
Note: Total employment consists of wage employment and self-employment. Organisation for Economic Co-operation and Development (OECD) countries in panel a are high-income countries that have been members of the OECD for at least 40 years. All other countries are grouped into geographic regions.

to manufacturing and services. Whereas a single enterprise might seek to maximize its profits, the enterprise sector as a whole is not confined to this objective. The sector encompasses the interests of workers, owners, and consumers, and—despite the possible important trade-offs between these interests—has the potential to help them manage risk through several channels discussed below. Flexibility and formality are important ways of ensuring that the enterprise sector can fulfill this function.

Enterprises include firms—enterprises in which two or more people work together. For workers and owners, being part of a firm widens the possibility of sharing the benefits and losses from specialization, collaboration, and innovation. Indeed, this is one of the main motives behind the formation of firms and, as such, has featured prominently in economic thinking at least since Adam Smith. Frank Knight and Ronald Coase, in their seminal studies, demonstrated the institutional advantage firms have in providing cost-efficient ways of dealing with uncertainty and overcoming the transaction costs inherent in direct exchanges.[9] Whereas most individuals on their own are naturally risk averse and thus reluctant to take on new ventures, in groups and subject to contractual arrangements, they become more willing to pursue projects involving more risk but also promising higher returns. Firms can thus serve as natural vehicles to exploit opportunities, with beneficial consequences for individuals' resilience and prosperity.[10]

More specifically, the enterprise sector has the potential to support people's risk management through three channels: sharing risk; allocating resources and promoting innovation; and protecting workers, consumers, and the environment. This potential is not always realized, however. In reality, each of the channels can entail significant costs that are often borne by the most vulnerable. Every day, newspapers are filled with stories about enterprises—especially those with short-term horizons—that behave in ways harmful to workers, consumers, the environment, and even the enterprise sector itself. Government has a role to play in helping the enterprise sector achieve its potential to support people's risk management. In practice, however, governments that lack the capacity, the appropriate incentives, and the correct strategy for public policy may undermine the flexibility and formality of the enterprise sector that can make these risk management channels effective.

Risk sharing

The first channel through which the enterprise sector can support people's risk management is sharing risk among workers, among owners of firms and owners of capital more generally, and between workers and owners. Firms serve as a kind of risk pool that allows workers to share the workload, filling in for an absent coworker or helping out with unfamiliar or complex assignments. When a worker falls ill, for example, another worker can assume his or her tasks temporarily, reducing the risk of unemployment for the worker and helping to guarantee his or her income during the illness. More generally, the complementarities between skills of workers allows firms to respond to both positive and negative shocks more easily than individuals could on their own, thereby stabilizing and enhancing aggregate productivity and income growth. For this type of risk sharing, size is often an advantage. Smaller firms tend to be more volatile. A recent study found that in the United States, which has a highly developed and diversified enterprise sector, aggregate sales growth of the median small firm is five times more volatile than that of the big publicly traded ones.[11]

For risk sharing, achieving a certain size of firm is an advantage. While self-employment—so common in many developing countries—is a safety net, it is also a symptom of vulnerability.

The enterprise sectors of many developing countries, however, are dominated by self-employment (see figure 5.1a); as a result, risk sharing among workers is limited. Rates of self-employment are around 70 percent in South Asia and exceed 80 percent in Sub-Saharan Africa, on average. This increases the vulnerability of the majority of workers in these regions to income shocks; a sick child, an equipment failure, or a change in the weather could mean the loss of a day's income. Such high rates of self-employment also suggest that the enterprise sectors in these regions are not benefiting from the specialization and increased productivity that multiperson firms make possible. As figure 5.1b indicates, a transition to wage employment is taking place in several developing countries, including Turkey, where the share of wage employment increased 50 percent between the early 1990s and the late 2000s.

The enterprise sector can also create opportunities for owners of firms—and owners of capital more generally—to share investment risk. When the owners of capital invest in firms that are exposed to different types and levels of risk, they are able to reduce the impact of a given negative shock on their investments through diversification, while still reaping the rewards of normal returns. An important legal risk-sharing mechanism for addressing capital risk is limited liability, which limits the losses for which a firm's owners are responsible and thus helps overcome individuals' natural risk aversion. Limited liability can encourage firms to take more creative risks, which in turn can increase productivity and facilitate the enterprise sector's provision of steady or increasing income and employment. The development of stock markets and the exploitation of economies of scale have arisen in large part as a result of limited liability. Risk sharing among firm owners can occur even without formal mechanisms. In places where the business climate is unfriendly, informal networks and business groups often spring up to facilitate cooperation among firm owners in the face of changing commercial, economic, and political circumstances.

Labor arrangements also permit risk sharing between workers and firm owners. Workers can offer a form of insurance to firms, in which they agree to reductions in wages or cutbacks in hours and benefits during temporary shocks in exchange for higher wages in normal times. This type of risk sharing has been found, for example, in manufacturing firms in Cameroon, Ghana, Kenya, and Zimbabwe.[12] Alternatively, firm owners willing to take chances on new ventures and to accept greater profit variability can still offer steady wages to their workers, who are generally more concerned about the stability and predictability of their income. A similar dynamic applies when the source of variability is specific to the workers. For example, firms provide insurance to workers, in the form of a steady wage, for idiosyncratic risks such as illness.[13] Labor contracts can facilitate these arrangements by clearly defining responsibilities and enhancing enforceability.

In sum, firms can serve as vehicles for risk sharing, providing insurance for shocks to individual workers and for shocks in the production process, allowing workers to specialize, and enabling owners of capital to make more profitable investments.

Resource reallocation and innovation

Resource reallocation and innovation is the second channel through which the enterprise sector can support risk management. Resource reallocation occurs when enterprises shift resources, expand and contract, and enter and exit markets. Reallocation can take place across enterprises and industries, as less productive enterprises collapse and other more productive ones are launched. This is the process of creative destruction described vividly by Austrian economist Joseph Schumpeter. The enterprise sector is often faced with large external shocks that can be positive or negative, and can include large and sudden changes in supply and demand, increases and decreases in input prices, advances in or obsolescence of technology, and natural disasters. The sector can absorb these shocks, and reduce the damage they cause or take advantage of opportunities, by reallocating resources efficiently within and across enterprises and industries to more productive areas, while still providing the income, employment, and products that facilitate people's risk management. Without this process of resource reallocation, the enterprise sector would stagnate, become more volatile, and experience more prolonged recessions, with dire economic and social implications.

Making resource allocation in China and India as efficient as in the United States—provided that other factors such as institutional capacity were in place—could potentially increase total factor productivity by as much as 50 percent in China and 60 percent in India, recent research suggests.[14] In the United States, one of the world's most dynamic economies, creative destruction accounts for more than 50 percent of productivity growth.[15] Higher productivity can also translate into greater job security. For instance, in Romania, when the financial crisis hit in 2008–09, more productive firms were less inclined to fire workers.[16] So while job turnover can carry high costs of adjustment (which need to be addressed through inclusive social protection and other measures, as discussed later in this chapter), rigid rules prohibiting layoffs can also carry high costs.

The enterprise sector can also support risk management by allocating resources to the most productive enterprises and innovating to adjust to the world's ever-changing conditions. Innovation includes adoption and adaptation of new technologies and processes, especially by firms in the developing world. Resource reallocation and innovation are the essence of a process of experimentation and learning that can enhance productivity while improving the capacity of the enterprise sector to respond to future shocks. Insufficient experimentation can sap the sector's ability to absorb such shocks. Innovation—investing in physical and knowledge-based assets—is at the heart of the ability of the enterprise sector to exploit the opportunities offered by new discoveries, particularly those opportunities that involve substantial risks.[17] Firms, which as entities can take on more risks than their owners and workers individually, are in a better position to promote the implementation of daring ideas that can lead to potentially productive ventures. Some ventures will fail—and should be allowed to do so. The success of the rest can provide both innovative processes for enterprises to absorb shocks better and innovative products for people to manage risk better. In the presence of risk sharing, risk taking and tolerance for failure on a broad scale can be the engine of growth and poverty alleviation for an entire country.

Worker, consumer, and environmental protection

The enterprise sector has the potential to support risk management by facilitating the development and implementation of employment standards and production processes that protect workers, consumers, and the environment. Sound regulation and strong enforcement are crucial to bolster such protections. Firms that voluntarily adopt quality and environmental standards, such as those codified by the International Organization for Standardization (ISO), internalize costs of protection to their advantage, by improving their reputation or enhancing their productivity; at the same time, they can also contribute to worker, consumer, and environmental protection.

Worker health and workplace safety are key components of productivity. In the best scenario, enterprises that recognize this connection will strive to improve their work environment as part of their strategy to maximize profits. For example, a recent meta-analysis found that workplace wellness programs reduce medical costs by $3.27 for every dollar spent on the program, and absenteeism costs by $2.73; these are benefits that accrue to both workers and enterprises.[18] Because they can affect the bottom line, reputational concerns have the potential to shape how enterprises treat workplace health and safety standards.

Such considerations with respect to productivity and reputation can encourage enterprises to develop quality standards for consumer products (box 5.1). Standards designed to minimize defects and

BOX 5.1 *Worker, consumer, and environmental protection can also be profitable business*

The interests of firms and those of workers, consumers, and the environment are not always aligned. But when they are, significant benefits can arise.

Nestlé's entrance into the milk business in India is an example of how the global supply chain can improve local conditions for workers. To establish a well-functioning milk business in the Moga district of India, Nestlé had to work closely with local farmers, providing financing for wells, veterinarians for sick animals, and instruction in milk quality. This collaboration benefited Nestlé's milk business, which established a reliable supply chain. But the farmers of Moga benefited, as well. According to Michael Porter and Mark Kramer in their analysis in the *Harvard Business Review*, "Nestlé has been able to pay higher prices to farmers than those set by the government, and its steady biweekly payments have enabled farmers to obtain credit." Nestlé has embarked on similar campaigns in Brazil, Thailand, and elsewhere.

While consumer and environmental protection often require public action, there are many examples of businesses launching initiatives to improve their production to benefit consumers and the environment. McDonald's Corp., for instance, has redesigned its packaging to allow consumers to access nutritional information using smartphones. Firms manufacturing bottled water, such as PepsiCo Inc. and Coca-Cola Co., have introduced bottle designs that use less plastic. Unilever, a consumer goods company, launched "Project Medusa" to increase the efficiency of the company's water usage by reusing water evaporated during cooking for equipment cleaning and for cooling.

Source: WDR 2014 team based on Porter and Kramer 2006.

increase product safety can raise consumer satisfaction and lead to higher profits. In recent years, many firms have begun to adopt a "quality philosophy" that extends from production to identification of consumer needs, to product design and assurance, to customer service.[19] Reputational effects can also discipline firms' treatment of the environment. At their best, social norms can discourage environmental mistreatment, civil society groups can watch for environmentally harmful production practices, and consumers can become informed about the environmental impact of the products they purchase.

At the same time, there are also many cases in which the enterprise sector undermines these protections or creates new risks for people, especially where institutions and regulations are weak. In some places, rapid economic growth has outpaced the development of workplace standards. Workers experience both hazardous workplaces and degraded environmental conditions created by those workplaces. For example, residents in the Madre de Dios department in Peru, a center of the informal mining highlighted in the beginning of the chapter, have significantly higher levels of mercury than other Peruvians, which is likely related both to the use of mercury in the mining process and to the consumption of fish from contaminated waters.[20] Child labor also remains a significant problem in many countries. More than half of all child laborers—some 115 million children—work in hazardous conditions, the International Labour Organization estimates. Even in more developed settings, there are cases where the safety and health of workers and consumers are compromised. The government has a crucial role to play in designing and enforcing sensible regulations.

Flexibility and formality in the enterprise sector improve people's resilience and prosperity

The shift to greater flexibility and formality can take time, and it requires complementary reforms to strengthen institutional capacity and improve regulations. When state institutions are weak and regulations are cumbersome, there are trade-offs between flexibility and formality. When state institutions are strong and regulations are sound, flexibility and formality can be symbiotic.

The role and importance of flexibility

Flexibility is the capacity to adapt to changing circumstances. The flexibility of the enterprise sector, and of individual enterprises, goes far beyond the narrow ability to hire and fire workers easily. Rather, it extends to the capacity to reallocate resources efficiently to more productive areas to respond to short-term shocks without seriously disrupting operations, and to increase capacity to respond to longer-term trends. Flexibility includes adjustments to risk-sharing arrangements among workers, among firm owners and owners of capital more generally, and between workers and firm owners. A flexible enterprise sector is one in which workers' skills are transferable, capital owners have abundant options for investment, and workers and firms

FIGURE 5.2 ***The flexibility of the enterprise sector varies around the world***

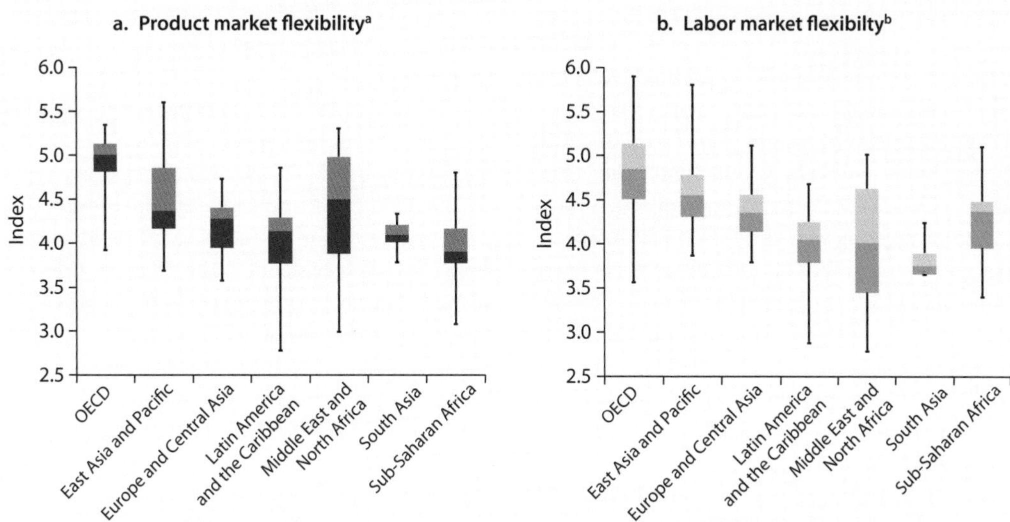

Source: WDR 2014 team based on data from World Economic Forum (WEF) 2012.

Note: The box plots show the minimum value, the range from the 25th percentile to the median (shaded dark), the range from the median to the 75th percentile (shaded light), and the maximum value for each region. The degree of flexibility rises with the numerical value, with 1 being the least and 7 being the most flexible. Organisation for Economic Co-operation and Development (OECD) countries in the figure are high-income countries that have been members of the OECD for at least 40 years. All other countries are grouped into geographic regions.

a. Product market flexibility corresponds to the WEF's measure of goods market efficiency and consists of intensity of local competition, extent of market dominance, effectiveness of antimonopoly policy, extent and effect of taxation, total tax rate, number of procedures and time required to start a business, agricultural policy costs, prevalence of trade barriers, trade tariffs, prevalence of foreign ownership, business impact of rules on foreign direct investment, burden of customs procedures, imports as a percentage of GDP, degree of customer orientation, and buyer sophistication.

b. Labor market flexibility corresponds to the WEF's measure of labor market efficiency and consists of cooperation in labor-employer relations, flexibility of wage determination, hiring and firing practices, redundancy costs, pay and productivity, reliance on professional management, brain drain, and female participation in the labor force.

are empowered to modify wages and employment levels potentially in their mutual interest. In a flexible enterprise sector, enterprises can expand and contract and enter and exit markets smoothly, and can innovate to capture new opportunities. Figure 5.2 shows two different measures of flexibility—one that corresponds to the efficiency of the market for goods (panel a) and the other to the efficiency of the market for labor (panel b). Both show that flexibility tends to be lower in the developing world.

Why is flexibility important? Flexibility enhances each of the three channels through which the enterprise sector supports people's risk management. Flexibility facilitates the risk sharing that allows workers and firm owners to respond to shocks, while providing opportunities for steady income and employment at the aggregate level. Complementary skills and specialization can help firms, especially larger ones, take advantage of increases in demand or the introduction of a new technology. In contrast, when labor arrangements between workers and owners are rigid, even small, idiosyncratic shocks can be very costly and threaten a firm's survival. Finally, the broader the opportunities in which firm owners can invest, the more diversified the risk they will bear. A shallow capital market or one with high transaction costs can cause investors to forgo good investment opportunities.

An enterprise sector that generates income opportunities even during times of economic difficulty is particularly vital in countries with weak social protection systems. In these countries, people without a job cannot rely on public help and must find some source of income. Where the costs of formality are high, this income very often comes from informal work—recent research shows that in the majority of countries, informality functions as a safety net for those who are not part of the formal economy.[21] The informal sector often provides the flexibility that people need for survival.

A flexible enterprise sector supports the reallocation of resources within enterprises and across enterprises and industries. Flexibility means that in response to shocks, the sector can efficiently redeploy labor and capital to more productive enterprises and more productive industries, potentially in the mutual interests of workers and firm owners. As the *World Development Report 2013: Jobs* indicated, jobs are drivers of development, and all types of employment, including informal jobs, can be transformational in improving living standards, productivity, and social cohesion.[22] The ease of dismantling collapsed businesses and of creating new ones is crucial to ensuring that new employment opportunities are created. Adjustment costs during this reallocation process can be significant, however, particularly for newly unemployed workers. Inclusive social protection systems need to be in place to protect the vulnerable.

Research on recovery from negative shocks demonstrates the harmful effects that rigidity can have. Using empirical evidence from 76 countries, a recent study found that economies with policy-induced rigidities such as excessive labor protections, barriers to firm entry, burdensome bankruptcy laws, and industry supports suffer deeper and more prolonged recessions (figure 5.3) than more flexible economies do. The study substantiated this evidence by modeling the recovery of an undistorted (flexible) economy and the recovery of an economy in which the government intervenes with subsidy after a shock. The results are striking. The flexible economy suffered a loss of 13 percent of preshock gross domestic product (GDP)—84 percent of which occurred in a single quarter—whereas the economy in which the government intervenes suffered a loss of 36 percent of preshock GDP spread out over five years. A smaller, faster loss implies a quicker recovery.

An examination of recent great depressions corroborates this evidence (box 5.2), as does cross-country research: impediments to resource reallocation to more productive firms reduce the pace of economic recovery. For example, by propping up banks and requiring them to maintain nonperforming loans to firms that otherwise would have failed in the late 1990s and early 2000s, Japan prevented their resources from flowing to more productive uses.[23] Better regulation, in contrast, can promote the reallocation of resources to more productive firms.[24]

Factors other than governmental regulation also can impede flexibility. One example is gender segregation in employment, which often hampers labor market flexibility; this issue is discussed extensively in

FIGURE 5.3 ***Countries with a higher regulatory burden experience more severe recessions***

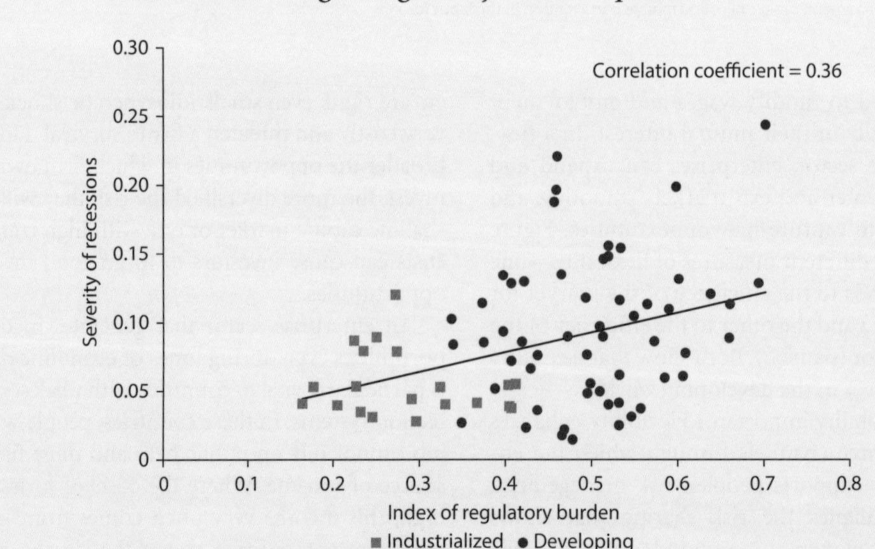

Source: WDR 2014 team based on data from Bergoeing, Loayza, and Repetto 2004.

Note: Index of regulatory burden varies from 0 to 1, where 1 indicates the heaviest burden. Data on regulatory burden cover financial restrictions, trade barriers, firm entry costs, inefficient bankruptcy procedures, bureaucratic red tape, tax burden, and labor regulations for the 1990s. The severity of recessions is measured by the sum of downward output deviations from trend for each country during 1990–2000. The solid (regression) line in the figure depicts the fitted linear relationship between the y- and x-axis variables, allowing for an intercept.

BOX 5.2 *Lessons from great depressions*

How should public policy respond to unusually large declines in output? While the benefits and limitations of expansionary monetary and fiscal policy in such cases have been examined and debated extensively, enterprise policy may play an especially important role, according to comprehensive analysis of the historical evidence by Timothy Kehoe and Edward Prescott in their exhaustive work, *Great Depressions of the Twentieth Century.*

In contrast to the relatively shallow and brief recessions that are typical of business cycles, "great depressions" are unusually deep, painful, and long.[a] The Great Depression of 1929–39 in the United States is perhaps the best-known example, but several European countries had similar experiences in the period between the first and second world wars, and some recent examples have occurred in Latin America, New Zealand, and Switzerland.

Such experiences have often been treated by economists as exceptions to which standard macroeconomic models may not apply. Instead, Kehoe and Prescott seek to use the modern tools of macroeconomics (specifically, growth accounting and the general equilibrium growth model) to scrutinize the underlying drivers of depressions in more than a dozen countries. Their findings suggest that the level of productivity growth is often the dominant driver of depression dynamics, while changes to labor input are also important in some cases.

What policies dampen productivity growth during depressions? First, not letting inefficient firms fail is crucial. For example, Chile and Mexico both experienced depressions in the early 1980s, but productivity growth recovered, and even exceeded trend, in Chile, while it remained 30 percent below trend in Mexico nearly 15 years later. Banking and bankruptcy procedures appear to have been central to the different outcomes. By the early 1980s, unproductive firms in Chile were allowed to go bankrupt, with new investments determined by market interest rates, whereas the state-controlled banking system in Mexico continued to channel loans to some unproductive firms through the early 1990s. Second, studies of the manufacturing, construction, and mining industries suggest competition policy may be important, insofar as more competitive industries tend to be more creative and productive in the aftermath of a large output decline.[b] Finally, tax increases and rigid wage policies have been shown to reduce labor input during great depressions. For example, rigid real wage policies appear to have been a key factor in prolonging the great depression of 1928–37 in Germany. In contrast, flexible labor regulations helped Germany escape the worst of the recent crisis (see box 5.5).

Recent microeconomic evidence finds that, besides the types and productivity of the technology used within individual firms, resource allocation across firms is a crucial determinant of cross-country differences in productivity.[c] The emerging literature in this field supports the view that facilitating resource reallocation can be an essential part of bringing depressions to an end.

Source: WDR 2014 team based on Kehoe and Prescott 2007.

a. Kehoe and Prescott 2007 define great depressions as declines in output per capita of at least 20 percent below trend, with at least 15 percent of the decline occurring within the first decade of the depression, and annual per capita output growth remaining below trend for each year of the depression.

b. Baily and Solow 2001.

c. See Restuccia and Rogerson 2013 for a useful review of the recent literature.

World Development Report 2012: Gender Equality and Development.[25] In most countries, women are more likely than men to participate in low-productivity activities, in the informal sector, and in family employment. Another factor involves exclusive business relationships. In Sub-Saharan Africa, for example, relationships formed through business activities can exclude unconnected communities from more profitable investment opportunities and perpetuate existing patterns of production.[26]

Innovation and flexibility are closely linked. The more easily resources flow to entrepreneurs and firms that offer new products, better technologies, and more efficient processes, the more quickly the enterprise sector can generate new opportunities at lower costs. Nonetheless, innovation can have adverse consequences for employment: for example, process improvements may allow an enterprise to produce the same output with less labor, leading to cutbacks or unemployment. Even innovation that results in positive (or zero) job creation might have a "skill bias" against unskilled labor.[27] That said, these negative effects can be counterbalanced when cost reductions associated with innovation spur price reductions, which in turn stimulate growth in aggregate terms, leading to greater demand and output over time. Product innovation, in contrast to process innovation, tends to stimulate domestic and foreign demand and so enhance an enterprise's demand for labor.

Flexibility is also closely related to worker, consumer, and environmental protection. In Bulgaria, for example, a firm's capacity to change—based on measures such as leadership, trust, innovation, and accountability—was found to be strongly positively associated with environmental performance.[28] Without flexibility, an enterprise will be unable to adjust its products or production techniques in response to the displeasure of consumers and civil society or to take appropriate action in the case of a defective, environmentally harmful, or dangerous product.

Although corporate responses to complaints about product and worker safety are often (rightly) criticized for being insufficient or ineffective, enterprises do seem to be able to adjust to and, at least at times, remedy such deficiencies. One famous case involved the Johnson & Johnson painkiller Tylenol, whose market share plummeted from 37 percent to 7 percent after several bottles were found to have been contaminated with cyanide. The firm removed all Tylenol from the market and adopted and advertised a "triple safety seal." In less than two years, the company had nearly regained its previous market share.[29] The incident led the U.S. Food and Drug Administration to issue regulations regarding drug packaging, and safety shields became the norm in the industry. Many enterprises operating in developing countries have also responded to concerns about product and worker safety, although these measures have had only limited success.[30]

The role and importance of formality

Enterprises are considered formal if their activities comply with laws and regulations governing taxes, registration, labor and workplace standards, product quality and safety requirements, and environmental guidelines—all of which can be costly to implement. In exchange, formal enterprises are entitled to enhanced access to legal protection and public infrastructure. Formality and informality, however, are a matter of degree. Some enterprises are in compliance in some but not all dimensions of formality. For example, some enterprises that comply with registration procedures may substantially underreport their sales and profits or only partially fulfill requirements to provide benefits and workplace protection to workers. Moreover, there is a wide gap between de jure formality and de facto formality, particularly in countries with weak institutional capacity.

Formality varies widely across countries (figure 5.4). The large differences in labor and production formality across countries and regions suggest the existence of a massive labor pool yet to be mobilized in formal—and likely more productive—activities. That is especially likely to be the case in countries with relatively high production formality but low labor formality. Informality is not a cause, but rather a symptom, of underdevelopment. In general, formal

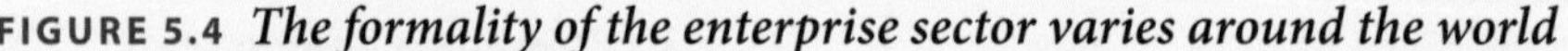

FIGURE 5.4 ***The formality of the enterprise sector varies around the world***

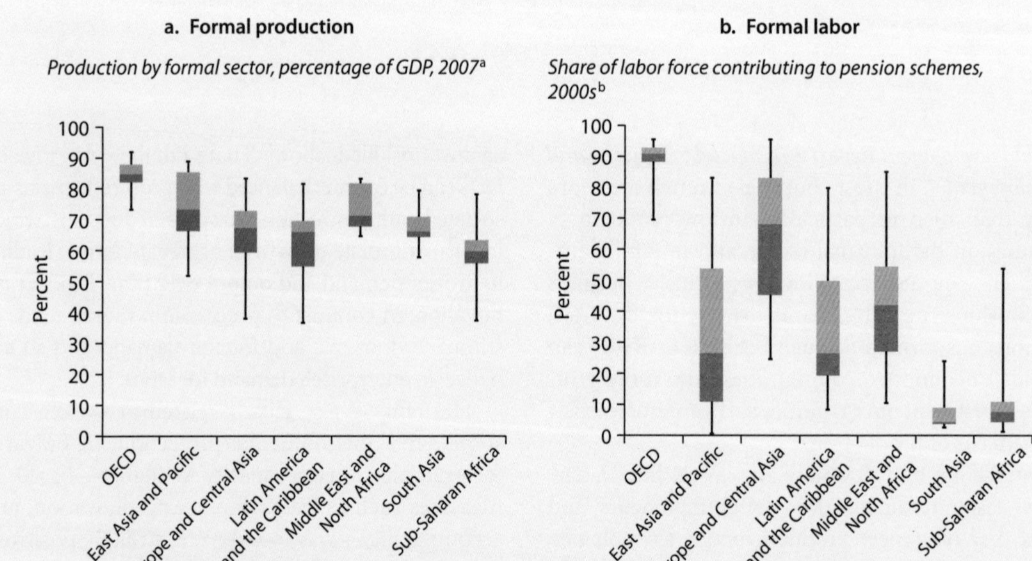

Source: WDR 2014 team based on data from Schneider, Buehn, and Montenegro 2010 (panel a); World Bank Pensions (database) and World Bank World Development Indicators (database) (panel b).

Note: The box plots show the minimum value, the range from the 25th percentile to the median (shaded dark), the range from the median to the 75th percentile (shaded light), and the maximum value for each region. Organisation for Economic Co-operation and Development (OECD) countries in the figure are high-income countries that have been members of the OECD for at least 40 years. All other countries are grouped into geographic regions.

a. Values computed as 100 minus estimates on the size of shadow economies by Schneider, Buehn, and Montenegro 2010.
b. Figure based on the latest data available in the 2000s.

employment tends to increase with the level of development. By helping to ensure that wages are paid and contracts honored, that property will not be seized, and that financial resources are available and affordable, formality helps both workers and enterprises to plan for the future. Compliance with labor, consumer, and environmental protections—while costly—can also lay the basis for growth, as discussed throughout this chapter.

Why is formality important? Like flexibility, formality enhances each of the three channels through which the enterprise sector supports people's risk management. Formal firms tend to be bigger, more stable, and better able to provide steady work for their employees. Because formal firms have a more predictable environment in which to grow and hire more employees, workers are better able to share the risk. Capital owners can invest in formal firms to diversify their own risk and jump-start growth for the business, thanks to the legality of contractual arrangements. Finally, formality means that contracts between workers and firms are more easily enforced and so less likely to be broken. Even in the absence of contracts, formality can provide both workers and employers with legal recourse if a labor arrangement is perceived to have been broken, reducing the risk to both parties of noncompliance. Small firms may be able to rely on informal institutions to enforce contracts. Such informal mechanisms become less effective, however, as firms grow and the relationships between owners and workers become more complex.

The stronger risk-sharing arrangements promoted by formality improve people's level and stability of income, one of the most significant factors in improving risk management. For example, average monthly earnings in Zambia generally increase with formality. In Tanzania, income volatility generally decreases with formality. Only 9 percent of informal employees in francophone West Africa had a written contract with their employers.[31]

Lack of formality can inhibit risk sharing across firms, as well. In Zimbabwe, for instance, the risk that suppliers will not comply with contracts has led manufacturing firms to increase inventories and liquidity reserves to protect against late delivery, nonpayment, or late payment.[32] This imbalanced type of risk sharing is unlikely to be efficient in a world in which just-in-time delivery is becoming the norm.

The laws and regulations that accompany formality can expedite the process of reallocating resources. Well-designed and consistently applied procedures are essential for resources to flow efficiently out of collapsed enterprises and toward new ones. Bankruptcy law and the depth of resale markets are particularly important to liberate productive resources from an unproductive enterprise and to ensure that creditors, and potential investors in other enterprises, are protected if a business fails. Laws that protect the intellectual property of established enterprises and entrepreneurs alike are often an important incentive for innovation. Finally, formality provides the legal documents that are frequently necessary to access credit and other financial resources. Such access supports business expansion, promotes new enterprises, and can provide a lifeline to enterprises in the face of shocks. Overall, cross-country analysis suggests that an increase of one standard deviation in informality leads to a decline of 0.7 to 1.0 percentage point in the rate of per capita GDP growth.[33] Further, countries with high informality cannot fully capture the benefits of globalization (box 5.3).

Formality may strengthen an enterprise's incentives to provide worker, consumer, and environmental protection. Good regulation can induce enterprises to internalize the social costs of their activities. That is particularly clear in the case of environmental rules that force firms to absorb some or all of the costs of polluting. It is also true of workplace protections that prohibit firms from paying very low wages when the supply of labor is abundant. Governmental regulation can thus create a level playing field for firms to compete by increasing worker productivity and consumer satisfaction through provision of a healthy workplace and environmental stewardship, rather than by paying poor wages, providing poor working conditions, or cutting costs at the expense of the environment. The legal identity provided by formality strengthens a firm's incentive to cultivate a reputation consistent with a healthy workplace, product quality, and environmental protection.

Employee access to benefits and safe workplaces tends to improve with formality. In Mozambique, the share of paid employees with a range of employment benefits, such as remunerated sick leave and severance payments, generally increases with the formality of employment, as does the share of workers in Zambia who use protective clothing when working.[34]

At the same time, formality is not a sufficient condition for worker, consumer, and environmental protections. These protections can be weak or absent even when firms are large multinationals or linked in a global value chain. In fact, the growth of global value chains has a dual effect, putting pressure on enterprises to comply with more stringent labor and production standards while increasing pressure to reduce labor costs, even by resorting to informal work. This situation results in improved employment for some workers, but informality and instabil-

BOX 5.3 *The complex relationship between globalization and formality*

Globalization brings new opportunities and risks. As many as 20 million people are directly employed in the manufacturing sector for global value chains. A large proportion of these are women and rural migrants in poor countries.[a]

In Costa Rica, investment from Intel has translated into accelerated formation of technical and English skills for workers. Standards of practice from the U.S. market, especially regarding worker and environmental protection, were actively transferred to the local economy, with Intel requiring its suppliers and subcontractors to meet strict worker safety qualifications and sending its employees to promote recycling programs and environmental awareness. Following Intel's socioeconomic contributions, the National Insurance Institute, Costa Rica's autonomous insurance institution, has created the nation's first job safety and health standard.[b]

In Mexico, the influx of export manufacturing jobs from 1985 to 2000 increased female formal employment nearly fivefold. These jobs offered higher wages than agriculture and other alternatives. The higher earnings increased the bargaining power of these women within their households and led to observable improvement in child health: the children of women who worked in formal export manufacturing were more than one standard deviation taller than the children whose mothers did not have their first job in manufacturing, and this effect was stronger for girls.[c] In Indonesia, during the East Asian crisis in the late 1990s, the aggregate adverse effect on employment was smaller for female workers because they were concentrated in larger firms and firms that exported, which were less hard hit.[d] On the other hand, the influx of relatively low-skill jobs also induced high school students to drop out of school; for every 20 new jobs created, one student left school in Mexico.[e] More recently, the trade collapse after the global crisis resulted in large layoffs in the *maquiladora* and in related industries.

Benefits from globalization accrue more to the formal economy because informal enterprises often do not have the appropriate standards and qualifications from the suppliers' standpoint to compete. Economies with high rates of informality are thus often positioned at the lower end of the global value chain, and their workers are more vulnerable to global shocks and less likely to benefit from opportunities. Recent research suggests that globalization has contributed to the prosperity of many countries, although sometimes at the cost of rising inequality.[f]

In the long run, economies that are more open tend to have a lower incidence of informal employment. In several countries in Asia, an increase in a country's openness has been associated with a reduction in the incidence of its informal employment. In Mexico, reductions in tariffs after joining the North American Free Trade Agreement significantly reduced the likelihood of informality in the tradable sectors.[g] In the short run, however, the impact of globalization on informality may be mixed, depending on the nature of the globalization process and the various economic fundamentals of the economy. For example, an overly rapid trade liberalization can wipe out the protected formal sectors and push their workers into self-employment or informal sectors. Given the high informality in many developing countries, particularly in agriculture, retail, and other services, the benefits of globalization may not reach many segments of the population, while shocks from the global arena can negatively impact their lives. Overall, globalization exposes enterprises to competition in the world market, providing incentives for productive enterprises to expand and pressures for unproductive ones to exit.

Source: WDR 2014 team.

a. UNCTAD 2013.
b. World Bank 2006.
c. Atkin 2009.
d. Hallward-Driemeier, Rijkers, and Waxman 2011.
e. Atkin 2012.
f. Kremer and Maskin 2006.
g. Aleman-Castilla 2006.

ity for others. A case study of garment factories in Morocco, for example, found that some high-skilled workers involved with the final product and with oversight of packaging, storage, and logistics for buyers had stable contracts and protections. However, factories also hired irregular workers to meet buyers' demands. These workers had casual contracts and were often subjected to discrimination.[35] In addition, because global value chains are not always linked to local value chains, the safety and quality benefits from industry standards that are enjoyed by global consumers may bypass domestic consumers.[36]

Furthermore, formality is not a guarantee against negligent or criminal acts. For instance, in 2012, more than 250 workers died in a fire at a garment factory in Pakistan that had been certified as meeting international health and safety standards.[37] Industrial disasters such as the Bhopal gas leak in 1984 and, more recently, the Deepwater Horizon oil spill in the Gulf of Mexico and the Fukushima Daiichi nuclear disaster in Japan continue to put people and the environment at risk.

The relationship between flexibility and formality

Burdensome laws and regulations can raise the costs of formality. Complicated and lengthy business application processes, onerous taxes, stringent hiring and firing rules, poor-quality public services such as police and courts, and a lack of educated workers can discourage informal enterprises from becoming formal. In these cases, there is a trade-off between flexibility and formality: to maintain flexibility, enterprises remain informal. While remaining informal may be optimal for individual enterprises, the enterprise sector as a whole suffers, because the advantages of formality are sacrificed. The seminal work of Hernando De Soto quantified the costs of formality and the extent to which excessive regulation can lead to abuses and foster informal activities.[38] As the cost of formality declines, the trade-off between flexibility and formality also declines.

When laws and regulations are focused, well-designed, and consistently applied, the costs of complying with them are low relative to their benefits. In this case, formality and flexibility reinforce each other. As the economy moves from high-cost formality to low-cost formality, trade-offs decline and flexibility and formality become symbiotic. Formality helps enterprises adapt to changing circumstances, with laws and regulations that make it easier to renegotiate labor arrangements, reallocate resources, and encourage innovation, and that level the competitive playing field. Flexibility, in turn, makes it easier for enterprises to comply with laws and regulations while remaining productive.

Flexibility is a reasonable short-term goal. Formality is a longer-term objective. In the short term, helping enterprises adjust to the world's ever-changing circumstances is critical, even without formality. In many low-income countries, especially in Sub-Saharan Africa and South Asia, even if economic growth rates are high, the formal sector cannot generate enough wage employment in the near future to absorb the majority of the labor force. The informal sector remains the main contributor to GDP and to employment. Self-employment and household enterprises serve as important means of survival for the most vulnerable. An empirical study covering eight countries in Africa, for example, found that household enterprises were responsible for the creation of most new nonagricultural jobs.[39] Increasing the flexibility of the enterprise sector to create more, and more-productive, jobs—both formal and informal—is crucial in helping people manage risk and reduce poverty.

In the longer run, however, formality strengthens the contribution of the enterprise sector to making people resilient to shocks. Increasingly, formality is becoming a necessary condition for joining the global supply chain. The quality and performance requirements (including standards and certifications) for global exports are too strict to be met by the informal economy on the supply side. When international competitive pressures intensify, the informal economy can actually be pushed out of the global value chain. As economists Rafael La Porta and Andrei Shleifer put it recently, "Informal firms keep millions of people alive but disappear as the economy develops."[40]

The transition to flexibility and formality is not easy. There is no single recipe for success; the transition depends on the specific country context, including factor endowment, history, and culture. In Malaysia, reforms in business and labor market regulations contributed to a more flexible economy.[41] In Costa Rica, relatively high education levels and fiscal incentives attracted large inflows of foreign direct investment that, together with advanced technology and product standards, helped create more formal jobs and reinforce skills building. With the right steps, pace, and sequence, countries can become flexible and formal in the longer run (figure 5.5).

How can the government help enhance the flexibility and formality of the enterprise sector?

In the transition to formality and flexibility, the quality and enforcement of policy and regulation are essential. The government can play a key role in lowering the costs and increasing the benefits of formality and flexibility. The government's focus should be on improving the attractiveness of formality; penalizing informality would damage the safety net that informal enterprises can provide when the state is weak or formality is prohibitively costly. The government should also focus on reforming complementary areas at the same time. If policy reforms are to have the desired effect, they must also be tailored to specific country conditions, such as institutional capacity, political environment, and the stage of development of the labor market.

The government can help in four main ways. It can lay the basic groundwork for enterprises to operate by strengthening property rights and reducing uncertainty about government policy. It can implement and enforce sound regulation. It can put in place inclusive social protection to protect workers, particularly the vulnerable. Finally, over time, it can strengthen policies that improve both flexibility and formality in the longer run.

FIGURE 5.5 *Typology of countries by the flexibility and formality of their product and labor markets*

Product and labor market flexibility ↑ / Production and labor formality →	Less formal		More formal
More flexible	Armenia Azerbaijan Cambodia Peru	Albania China Kazakhstan	Australia Austria Belgium Canada Chile Costa Rica Czech Republic Denmark Estonia Finland France Germany Hong Kong SAR, China Ireland Israel Japan Korea, Rep. Latvia Lithuania Malaysia Mauritius Netherlands Norway Poland Singapore Sweden Switzerland United Kingdom United States
	Benin Botswana Burkina Faso Cameroon Côte d'Ivoire El Salvador The Gambia Georgia Guatemala Guinea Lebanon Madagascar Morocco Sri Lanka Tanzania Thailand Uganda Zambia	Brazil Bulgaria Indonesia Kenya Kyrgyz Republic Macedonia, FYR Mongolia Namibia South Africa Ukraine Uruguay Vietnam	Hungary Italy Jordan Portugal Slovak Republic Slovenia Spain Turkey
Less flexible	Bangladesh Bolivia Bosnia and Herzegovina Burundi Chad Colombia Ghana Haiti Honduras Jamaica Mali Nepal Nicaragua Pakistan Philippines Senegal Sierra Leone Venezuela, RB Zimbabwe	Algeria Dominican Republic Ecuador Egypt, Arab Rep. India Lesotho Libya Mexico Russian Federation Trinidad and Tobago Yemen, Rep.	Argentina Croatia Greece Iran, Islamic Rep. Romania

Source: WDR 2014 team based on data from World Bank Pensions (database); World Bank World Development Indicators (database); World Economic Forum 2012; and Schneider, Buehn, and Montenegro 2010.

Note: Economies in the top row are high (above the median value) in both product market flexibility and labor market flexibility (figure 5.2); in the middle row they are high in one or the other of the two; and in the bottom row they are low (below the median value) in both flexibility indicators. Similarly, economies in the first column on the left are low in both formal production and formal labor (figure 5.4); in the middle column they are high in one of the two formality indicators; and in the last column on the right they are high in both formality indicators. Only economies with data for all four indicators are considered, and median values are calculated within this sample.

Several of the policies discussed in this section are frequently associated with productivity and growth policy. This is no accident. A better investment climate can improve risk management in the enterprise sector: improving respect for rules and regulations and increasing flexibility can help the sector respond to negative shocks and take advantage of opportunities. The more capable the enterprise sector is of managing risk, the more productive it can become. A government that supports the rule of law and transparent contracts and that does not act capriciously toward local and international investors can be the cornerstone for a vibrant enterprise sector (see box 5.4).

Lay the groundwork for a vibrant enterprise sector

Some policies, such as securing property rights and reducing uncertainty about government policy, are foundational in the sense that they lay the basic groundwork for the enterprise sector to operate. In fragile and conflict-afflicted states, strengthening national institutions and improving governance to provide citizen security, justice, and jobs are crucial first steps to break cycles of violence.[42]

Secure property rights. Secure property rights are essential to assure investors that their risk taking

BOX 5.4 *The resilience of the power sector during a period of civil unrest in Côte d'Ivoire was driven by protections for contracts*

Côte d'Ivoire is one of the countries in Sub-Saharan Africa that has pioneered private sector participation in the power sector. Since 1990, a private operator (Compagnie Ivoirienne de l'Electricité, or CIE) has managed the country's power sector. As of 2006, independent power producers (IPPs) accounted for nearly two-thirds of energy production. Severe droughts, a significant currency devaluation immediately before the IPPs were set up, civil war, and the suspension of a large part of revenue from power sales for an extended period of time have all affected the sector's performance. Rather than buckle under the combined pressures of these events, the sector has largely thrived, in part because of a combination of flexibility and formality among sector participants.

The two main IPPs, Compagnie Ivoirienne de Production de l'Electricité (CIPREL) and Azito Energie SA (Azito), continued to deliver electricity throughout the period of civil unrest; at times, employees guarded the plants around the clock—an act of resilience of which both owners and staff remain justifiably proud. Perhaps even more impressive has been the companies' decision to continue to supply power even when the government could not meet the terms of its contracts. The contracts require the companies to provide a certain amount of power each year, according to a fixed price or schedule of prices. Two major civil conflicts in the past decade significantly affected revenues and collection. Political fragility at the national level also made tariff adjustments next to impossible. From late 2010, at the peak of the most recent crisis, arrears to the IPPs built up, but rather than exercise penalty clauses under the contracts or shut down production, the two IPPs instead exercised forbearance, recognizing both the underlying robustness of the contracts and the central role played by their companies in the economy. The enterprises understood that the payment arrears had arisen from a temporary shortage of funds, rather than any intention on the part of the government to default. Indeed, the government signaled its good faith by paying all the parties in fixed proportions, according to its ability to pay. Ultimately, the IPPs understood that the sanctity of the contracts would be honored. With the consolidation in political power under a new government, this belief has been validated and the arrears have now been repaid.

Since the recent stabilization, both CIPREL and Azito have announced plans to expand their operations, which will increase investment and the energy supply and support economic growth and political stability in the postconflict state.

Source: Conor Healy for the WDR 2014.

will yield rewards. Government nationalization and expropriation of private sector assets undermine incentives to invest in a country. Countries with sound investor protections tend to grow faster than those with poor investor protections; countries with weak enforcement of contracts are characterized by greater macroeconomic volatility; and countries with reliable law and order have smaller informal enterprise sectors.[43]

Reduce uncertainty about government policy. A stable policy environment and certainty about regulation is a key determinant of domestic as well as foreign investment (see chapter 7). In Thailand in the mid-2000s, for instance, political instability was perceived as a major constraint on doing business, contributing to a decline in business sentiment and in private investment growth, despite improvement in several other aspects of the business environment.[44] When investors are uncertain about the future, they may demand higher rates of return to compensate them for the extra risk involved. They may also shorten their planning horizons, thus influencing their level and form of investment, choice of technology, and willingness to train workers. Policy uncertainty can have dire consequences for private investments, particularly those in infrastructure and other decisions that involve large sunk costs. Uncertainty increases the value to investors of waiting and can lead to significant declines in hiring, investment, and output.[45] Improving the predictability in the way the rule of law is applied and the credibility of reforms is crucial for private sector development. In Côte d'Ivoire, for example, the power sector thrived, even in a fragile environment, thanks in part to the private operator's trust in contract durability (box 5.4).

Implement sound regulations

Reform of burdensome and costly regulations that reduce enterprise sector flexibility and discourage the operation of formal enterprises should be a priority. Flexibility does not mean the absence of regulations; rather, sound regulations are needed to improve the business environment and mitigate risks for enterprises and their owners and workers.

Improve the regulations that affect the enterprise sector. Weak or obstructive regulations can needlessly hinder the development of the enterprise sector and impede competition. Worldwide, some 23 percent of registered firms consider tax administration to be a major or very severe obstacle, for example.[46] More broadly, research suggests that countries that move from the worst quartile of business regulations to the best could enjoy a 2.3 percentage point increase in annual growth.[47] Several important aspects of regulations identified in the *Doing Business* reports, such as starting a business, paying taxes, and resolving insolvencies, are generally more cumbersome in low-income countries than in middle- and high-income countries.[48]

Streamline business registration. An enterprise that demonstrates compliance with the appropriate rules and regulations should not have to wait for years to receive a permit to operate. Many countries have successfully increased the efficiency of registration by establishing online procedures and linking the relevant agencies with a single interface. Cross-country research suggests that reducing the cost of registration procedures to the level in the United States could increase the number of new firms by more than 20 percent.[49] In India after licensing reforms, innovation in the formal manufacturing sector increased by roughly 5 percentage points.[50] Reducing the cost and time of registration processes alone is not always enough to promote business formalization, however. In Brazil, where obtaining a business license has been eased but still remains complicated and where the tax burden associated with the registration is high, most informal firms choose to stay informal.[51]

A better business environment is good not only for productivity growth but also for resilience in the face of adverse shocks.

Reduce rigidities in labor market regulation. Reforming a single policy, such as labor market regulations, on its own will probably not have a large impact. Yet when labor market regulations are too rigid, they can undermine the resilience of the economy (see spotlight 5). An empirical study covering some 60 countries finds that moving from the 20th to the 80th percentile in regulatory labor rigidity reduces the speed of adjustment to shocks by one-third and lowers annual productivity growth by as much as 1.7 percent.[52] Evidence from 20 European countries shows that in countries with high firing costs, firms are more likely to hire temporary workers as their employment needs grow.[53] In Nicaragua, a 10 percent increase in the minimum wage from 1998 to 2006 raised wages by 5 percent for workers whose wages were within 20 percent of the minimum wage but also reduced regulated private sector employment by 5 percent. Those who lost their jobs generally did not find new ones and left the formal labor force.[54] Rigid labor market regulations that reduce incentives for firms to offer more stable jobs with enforceable contracts might disproportionately hurt the most vulnerable, such as women and young workers. In Indonesia, for example, the minimum wage is more binding for small firms and results in disproportionate job loss for female workers.[55]

Improve measures for resolving insolvency. Long and expensive bankruptcy procedures clutter the market with failed firms that block opportunities for new enterprises. Enhanced predictability and improved bankruptcy procedures can help facilitate responsible risk taking and reduce associated costs. Effective bankruptcy can help avoid many distortions—including, in some cases, taxpayer commitments in the form of bailouts.[56] The government can streamline corporate bankruptcy and encourage rapid reuse of assets to reduce the time and cost of bankruptcy and increase recovery of losses for creditors and investors. Reorganization may be an option for firms with proven viability that are in temporary financial distress. The challenges for the state are to balance the protection of failed entrepreneurs' rights with that of creditor rights and to limit the moral hazard for entrepreneurs to act imprudently.

Improve enforcement of regulations. Improving regulatory certainty also requires strengthening the implementation and enforcement of laws. For example, when countries such as Azerbaijan and the Kyrgyz Republic were initially moving up in the World Bank's *Doing Business* rankings, the local private sector reported that the business environment had not improved much because the reforms were not fully implemented. Investor Motivation Surveys show a correlation between the amount of discretion allowed in applying regulations and variance in delays in compliance. Overall, governments with less discretion in applying regulations present lower investment risk. That is particularly the case where institutional capacity is weak and effective safeguards against corruption are not in place. Governments can start to address the problem by drafting laws and regulations with as much clarity as possible to limit discretion in interpretation. To reduce the incidence of discriminatory implementation, the government can strengthen its accountability system, both by increasing the transparency of regulations and by improving feedback mechanisms to ensure fair and timely treatment of all entrepreneurs.[57]

Provide inclusive social protection and insurance

Policies to improve labor market flexibility and provide social protection need to be pursued in parallel. Increased flexibility improves efficiency by reallocating resources between and within firms, but can be costly for those who lose their jobs. To protect the vulnerable, including those in employment transitions, the government needs to put in place a system to provide voice and inclusive social protection. In turn, an inclusive system that covers basic health and education needs and targets the vulnerable may also promote a more dynamic enterprise sector (see chapter 3).

Build an inclusive social protection system. Flexible labor market policies can increase aggregate employment, as an empirical study with panel data from 97 countries reports.[58] Yet flexibility can lead to increased job turnover, which can increase the risk of unemployment and income loss for workers in transition. Promoting flexibility need not mean that workers who lose their jobs are completely at peril of prolonged unemployment, however. Germany and Denmark provide interesting but diverse examples of policies that combine labor market flexibility with social support. In their specific contexts, the German model highlights the potential to maintain stable employment through internal flexibility—in particular through adjustments to working hours and work-sharing—while the Danish "flexicurity" model is characterized by easy hiring and firing alongside a strong safety net and reemployment policies (box 5.5).

Provide support for training and retraining, especially for the vulnerable. Public support for training works best when enterprises and workers themselves have an incentive to invest in skills. To the extent that lack of resources is an obstacle to training, however, the

BOX 5.5 *Labor market flexibility alongside social support: Examples from Germany and Denmark*

As mentioned at the beginning of the chapter, during the most recent global recession, Germany has offered one model of how to combine labor market flexibility and stable employment. Labor market reforms enacted in the first half of the 2000s provided incentives for older workers to return to work, supported job search efforts, and implemented stricter monitoring of eligibility for unemployment benefits. In response, the share of permanent full-time jobs declined, while the share of flexible or nonstandard jobs increased.

In addition, two instruments that allowed flexible work hours played a key role in stabilizing employment. Working-time accounts enabled firms to adjust workers' hours in response to short-term fluctuations in demand. This tool lowers labor costs for firms in a downturn, helping them weather the storm without laying off workers. An estimated 320,000 jobs were saved through the use of this arrangement. A separate short-time work arrangement was backed by a government subsidy. Firms paid employees for the hours they worked, while the Federal Employment Agency partly compensated workers for the hours lost during the downturn. The number of short-time workers sharply increased, peaking at more than 1.5 million in May 2009. An estimated 400,000 jobs were saved through the use of short-time work.[a]

Denmark highlights another model of labor market flexibility. The Danish "flexicurity" model is characterized by easy hiring and firing, compensated by a generous social safety net and active labor market policies, which include job counseling and requalification, job training, and employment with wage subsidies. Light employment protections aim to promote firms' competitiveness by reducing their employment costs. However, a generous social safety net has high coverage and high replacement ratios: low-income groups receive up to 90 percent of the income they had been receiving before they were laid off. Active labor market policies help people reenter the labor market.

After the global crisis, Denmark's GDP growth fell to minus 5.2 percent in 2009. The unemployment rate jumped from 3.3 percent in 2008 to more than 6 percent in 2009 and hovered around 7.5 percent afterward. Most of the unemployed found jobs fairly quickly, however: 60 percent after 13 weeks, and 80 percent after 26 weeks. Nearly 70 percent of Danish workers surveyed say they are fairly or very confident that they can find a job if they are laid off—the highest rate for any European Union country.[b] Firms are also confident that they can find workers with the right skills with little cost or delay when the economy recovers.

While it is too early to say whether the German or Danish models coped well with the crisis and remain fiscally affordable in the longer run, they show that flexibility in the enterprise sector can both differ across countries and complement social safety nets. The choice of policy tools should be based on careful analyses of the institutional, historical, and socioeconomic contexts unique to each economy.

Source: WDR 2014 team based on Andersen and others 2011; Rinne and Zimmermann 2012.

a. Boeri and Bruecker 2011.

b. European Commission 2010.

government can channel public funding through public education institutions and build partnerships with the private sector to develop enterprise-based skills training. The government can also provide targeted support to help unskilled workers who are unemployed or employed in informal sectors with low-paying jobs, young people transitioning from school to work, and skilled workers transitioning between jobs to (re)integrate into the labor market. Specific policies may also be needed for certain groups of people. The provision of affordable and quality child and elderly care and the possibility of flexible working arrangements, for example, are particularly important for integrating female workers into the labor market.

Use general revenue to finance social insurance. In developing countries where the labor market is less formalized, however, social insurance that is based on mandatory contribution from employers and employees in the formal sector often protects only insiders, leaving the most vulnerable, such as informal workers and the unemployed, unprotected. In many cases, labor taxes can create market distortions and reduce firms' incentives to offer formal and stable contracts, particular for women, youth, and other vulnerable groups. In Mexico, for example, the close tie between employment and social insurance provision has made formal employment less attractive for firms.[59] It is a question for policy debate whether to use general revenue and user fees to fund basic social protection, such as basic health insurance and old age pensions (see the "Focus on policy reform" at the end of this Report).[60] Income taxes, property taxes, value-added taxes, and, in resource-rich countries, commodity taxes are potential sources of financing.

Such a shift in finance has the potential to help alleviate the undue burden on formal firms and move from protecting workers to protecting citizens. It can facilitate the government's efforts to meet its basic function of introducing a social protection system that provides basic services to all and supports the vulnerable, whether employed or not. Keeping benefits modest is often necessary for fiscal sustainability and for limiting moral hazard. In less developed countries, where the needs are larger and the capacity is more limited, fiscal sustainability and the efficiency of service delivery are likely to be more challenging. Tailoring the design of social protection schemes to country conditions given the stage of development of the labor market, institutional capacity, and the political environment is crucial to success. Building institutional capacity and strengthening accountability to enhance the efficiency of tax collection and the allocation of public expenditures are often among the key areas in which to begin.

Pursue policies that improve both flexibility and formality in the longer run

With sound regulations and incentives for flexibility in place, the government can pursue policies that improve both flexibility and formality. Policies aimed at increasing innovation and the share of highly skilled workers in the labor market require investments that typically come to fruition only in the long run.

Increase innovation by addressing constraints in access to finance. Access to finance for innovation can be a major constraint for enterprises. Because potential investors may not have the information an enterprise has about the likely success of a project, obtaining financing for innovative projects—which are especially uncertain—can be difficult, especially for new and small enterprises. The government can address this market failure by creating a business environment that includes appropriate resource support so that the private sector is able to provide financing at the three stages crucial for innovative enterprises: the early concept stage, when entrepreneurs need to develop ideas into viable concepts and products; the start-up stage, when entrepreneurs need seed funding to establish enterprises; and the growth stage, when entrepreneurs need venture capital to expand. The challenges for the state are to identify the best means for offering support depending on the prevailing business context and needs; to ensure that financing remains short term; to prevent the creation of dependent industries; and to contain the associated fiscal burden.

Facilitate the adoption of technology and global collaboration. Creating capacities and incentives to generate new-to-the-world knowledge will be relatively more important in developed economies, with industries at or closer to the technology frontier. In developing economies with less sophisticated technological capabilities and less abundant resources, the adoption of existing knowledge and its adaptation to local context might be relatively more important.[61] Indeed, external sources of technology account for 90 percent of the growth in total factor productivity in most developing countries.[62] The government can help to improve the links between research centers and universities and the private sector in research and product extension, support managerial skills training for entrepreneurs, and build the capacity to absorb new technology in the general workforce. Depending on the country's innovative capacities, the government can adopt appropriate intellectual property rights policies, which provide incentives for innovation that can be widely adopted or adapted, and facilitate technology sharing between countries. Finally, the government can facilitate access to international sources of knowledge through trade, technology licensing, foreign direct investment, joint ventures, links to the diaspora community, and other international networks, such as those for research and development collaboration.

In an ever-changing world, a vibrant enterprise sector that allocates resources efficiently, promotes innovation, and protects workers and consumers is crucial to resilience and prosperity.

Build the skills level of the labor force. A more skilled labor force, whose workers can take on more sophisticated tasks and are equipped with more fungible skills, is a necessary condition for a flexible and formal enterprise sector. Education and lifelong learning are crucial for mitigating the negative impact and taking on the opportunities of technology innovation. In India, for example, a higher level of education of a district's workforce is strongly linked to higher entry rates of formal enterprises.[63] Skills shortages and mismatches are among the top concerns of enterprises. Worldwide, some 27 percent of registered enterprises consider the lack of skilled workers to be one of the major constraints to doing business.[64] Informational barriers are a primary contributor to this constraint—people do not know either what skills are needed or what training is available. For example, modern management practices tend to diffuse slowly between firms. But field experiments on large Indian textile firms show that increasing awareness of the necessary management skills—gleaned through free consulting on modern management practices—raised average productivity by 11 percent by improving quality and efficiency and reducing inventory.[65] The government can help the product market and the labor market work better by disseminating information about training and labor market outcomes.

Build a regulatory framework that enhances worker, consumer, and environmental protection. Once a sound basic regulatory framework is in place, governments can gradually add targeted regulation to spur competition and protect workers, consumers, and the environment. Basic workplace safety standards can be crucial to prevent the exploitation of workers. The collapse of a factory building in Bangladesh in 2013, which killed more than 1,100 people, demonstrates the need for such regulation—the building was constructed illegally, with poor materials, and did not comply with existing building codes. Clear guidelines for testing and labeling consumer products, and for recalls in the case of product defects, can enhance consumers' confidence in the goods they buy. Environmental regulations are particularly important to prevent firms from socializing the costs of their activities. Consistent implementation of regulation is also a concern, because interest groups frequently use regulation as a tool to limit entry and handicap competitors. Without effective implementation, regulation can also become a governmental stamp of approval that does little to protect workers, consumers, or the environment. In these cases, regulation cannot fulfill its function of supporting people's risk management. To prevent regulatory capture, regulation must address specific problems and be implemented consistently.

Putting it all together

Helping the enterprise sector remain flexible as it gradually becomes formal

In an ever-changing world, a key to resilience and prosperity is a vibrant enterprise sector that promotes innovation; reallocates resources efficiently; and protects workers, consumers, and the environment. By promoting the rule of law and contract security, the state can provide an enabling environment that encourages both flexibility and formality in the enterprise sector. Not only will flexibility and—in the longer run—formality increase the resilience of workers, firm owners, and investors to negative shocks and improve their ability to take advantage of opportunities, but these characteristics will also help drive economic growth and alleviate poverty.

Creating such an enabling environment remains a challenge, however, because of the trade-off in developing countries between flexibility and formality. In the short run, the informal economy can be a way out of poverty for many of the poor and vulnerable. In the longer run, formality strengthens the benefits of flexibility and ensures that the entire population can enjoy these benefits. Formalization based on

TABLE 5.1 *Policy priorities to improve the enterprise sector's role in risk management*

	POLICIES TO SUPPORT RISK MANAGEMENT FOUNDATIONAL → ADVANCED	
Knowledge	Provide education and job-matching information	
	Basic skills and vocational training	Innovative skills training
Protection	Improve policy certainty and secure property rights	
	Streamline basic regulations, such as those on entry/exit	Spur innovation, including technology adoption/adaptation and innovation at the frontier
Insurance	Extend social insurance coverage, possibly delinking it from work status	
	Facilitate access to credit	Facilitate access to capital markets, for both debt and equity
Coping	Facilitate adaptability of wages and work hours	
	Develop insolvency mechanisms	Facilitate appropriate reorganization and avoid bailouts

Source: WDR 2014 team.

Note: The table presents a sequencing of policies based on the guidance of chapter 2 for establishing policy priorities: *be realistic* in designing policies tailored to the institutional capacity of the country, and *build a strong foundation* that addresses the most critical obstacles sustainably and that can be improved over time.

rigid enforcement of laws and regulations is not the solution, however: the entire enterprise sector would be worse off in a fully formal but sclerotic economy. What is needed is a business environment that is good for all enterprises, improvement of the regulatory framework, provision of public services, and enhanced worker skills to strengthen the advantages of becoming formal while retaining the advantages of being flexible. Done at the right pace and in the right sequence, the same policy elements that focus on increasing the flexibility of the enterprise sector can contribute to increasing both flexibility and formality in the long run.

Table 5.1 presents public policies that can improve the enterprise sector's socially beneficial role of risk management. Foundational policies include focusing on streamlining regulations and strengthening basic public services. For countries that already have those foundations in place, policy priorities should move on to facilitating innovation and the entry of efficient, productive enterprises, and easing the exit of inefficient, unproductive ones.

Following basic principles

Do not generate uncertainty or unnecessary risks. Securing property rights and providing a predictable political and policy environment are prerequisites for the enterprise sector to play any beneficial role. For this, improving legal institutions, reducing bureaucratic discretionary power, and strengthening transparency are fundamental.

Promote flexibility. Efficient labor and capital reallocation are crucial for the enterprise sector to adjust to ever-changing business conditions. Adaptable worker skills and clear mechanisms to resolve firm insolvency are needed.

Provide the right incentives. Competition, streamlined regulations, and fair enforcement can provide the incentives that the enterprise sector needs to remain flexible as it gradually becomes formal. Bailing out ailing firms is seldom an advisable policy action.

Protect the vulnerable. A social protection system that covers basic health and education needs can enhance the flexibility of the enterprise sector and protect the vulnerable, whether employed or not. The possibility of delinking social insurance from work status (employed/unemployed, formal/informal, urban/rural) deserves further consideration.

Keep a long-run perspective. While informality can act as a safety net to workers and provide flexibility to the enterprise sector in the short run, in the long run striving for formality should remain a goal for public policy.

Notes

1. World Bank 2012.
2. Eurostat, http://epp.eurostat.ec.europa.eu/portal/page/portal/statistics/themes.
3. Wölfl and Mora-Sanguinetti 2011.
4. Gardner 2012.
5. UNEP 2012.
6. Loayza and Rigolini 2011; World Bank 2012.
7. Maloney 2013 for the WDR 2014.
8. Falco and others 2012.
9. Knight 1921; Coase 1937.
10. For seminal papers on the topic, see Azariadis 1975 and Baily 1974.
11. D'Erasmo and Moscoso Boedo 2013.
12. Bigsten and others 2003.
13. Gutierrez 2013 for the WDR 2014.
14. Hsieh and Klenow 2009.
15. Caballero 2008.
16. Merotto, Kanematsu, and Huang, forthcoming.
17. Dutz 2013 for the WDR 2014.
18. Baicker, Cutler, and Song 2010.
19. Mitra 2008, 6.
20. Gardner 2012.
21. Loayza and Rigolini 2011.
22. World Bank 2012.
23. Hoshi and Kashyap 2010.
24. Andrews and Cingano 2012.
25. World Bank 2011.
26. Fafchamps 2001.
27. Pianta 2006.
28. Judge and Elenkov 2005.
29. Mitchell 1989.
30. Schrage 2004.
31. ILO 2009.
32. Fafchamps, Gunning, and Oostendorp 2000.
33. Loayza and Wada 2010.
34. ILO 2009.
35. Barrientos, Gereffi, and Rossi 2011.
36. Henson and Humphrey 2009.
37. "Inspectors Certified Pakistani Factory as Safe before Disaster," *New York Times*, September 19, 2012.
38. De Soto 1989.
39. Fox and Sohnesen 2012.
40. La Porta and Shleifer 2008.
41. See Ritchie 2004 and references therein for the history of reforms in Malaysia.
42. World Bank 2010.
43. Loayza and Wada 2010.
44. World Bank 2008.
45. Bloom 2009.
46. Enterprise Surveys 2006–11, http://www.enterprisesurveys.org.
47. Djankov, McLiesh, and Ramalho 2006.
48. World Bank 2013.
49. Bartelsman, Haltiwanger, and Scarpetta 2004.
50. Seker 2011.
51. Bruhn and McKenzie 2013.
52. Caballero and others 2013.
53. Dräger and Marx 2012.
54. Alaniza, Gindling, and Terrell 2011.
55. Del Carpio, Nguyen, and Wang 2012.
56. Ayotte and Skeel 2010.
57. Fidas and Benhassine 2013 for the WDR 2014.
58. Bernal-Verdugo, Furceri, and Guillaume 2012.
59. Levy 2008.
60. See Ribe, Robalino, and Walker 2012 for a full discussion.
61. Lasagabaster 2013 for the WDR 2014.
62. Coe, Helpman, and Hoffmaister 1997.
63. Ghani 2013 for the WDR 2014.
64. Enterprise Surveys 2006–11, http://www.enterprisesurveys.org.
65. Bloom and others 2013.

References

Alaniza, Enrique, Thomas H. Gindling, and Katherine Terrell. 2011. "The Impact of Minimum Wages on Wages, Work and Poverty in Nicaragua." *Labour Economics* 18 (Supplement 1): S45–S59.

Aleman-Castilla, Benjamin. 2006. "The Effect of Trade Liberalization on Informality and Wages: Evidence from Mexico." Discussion Paper 763, Center for Economic Performance, London School of Economics and Political Science, London.

Andersen, Torben M., Nicole Bosch, Anja Deelen, and Rob Euwals. 2011. "The Danish Flexicurity Model in the Great Recession." VoxEU.org, April 8. http://www.voxeu.org/article/flexicurity-danish-labour-market-model-great-recession.

Andrews, Dan, and Federico Cingano. 2012. "Public Policy and Resource Allocation: Evidence from Firms in OECD Countries." Economics Department Working Papers 996, Organisation for Economic Co-operation and Development, Paris.

Atkin, David G. 2009. "Working for the Future: Female Factory Work and Child Health in Mexico." Unpublished manuscript, Yale University, New Haven, CT.

———. 2012. "Endogenous Skill Acquisition and Export Manufacturing in Mexico." Working Paper 18266, National Bureau of Economic Research, Cambridge, MA.

Ayotte, Kenneth, and David A. Skeel, Jr. 2010. "Bankruptcy or Bailouts?" *Journal of Corporation Law* 35 (3): 469–98.

Azariadis, Costas. 1975. "Implicit Contracts and Underemployment Equilibria." *Journal of Political Economy* 83 (6): 1183–202.

Baicker, Katherine, David Cutler, and Zirui Song. 2010. "Workplace Wellness Programs Can Generate Savings." *Health Affairs* 29 (2): 304–11.

Baily, Martin N. 1974. "Wages and Employment under Uncertain Demand." *Review of Economic Studies* 41 (1): 37–50.

Baily, Martin N., and Robert M. Solow. 2001. "International Productivity Comparisons Built from the Firm Level." *Journal of Economic Perspectives* 15 (3): 151–72.

Barrientos, Stephanie, Gary Gereffi, and Arianna Rossi. 2011. "Economic and Social Upgrading in Global Production Networks: A New Paradigm for a Changing World." *International Labour Review* 150 (3–4): 319–40.

Bartelsman, Eric, John C. Haltiwanger, and Stefano Scarpetta. 2004. "Microeconomic Evidence of Creative Destruction in Industrial and Developing Countries." Policy Research Working Paper 3464, World Bank, Washington, DC.

Bergoeing, Raphael, Norman Loayza, and Andrea Repetto. 2004. "Slow Recoveries." *Journal of Development Economics* 75 (2): 473–506.

Bernal-Verdugo, Lorenzo E., Davide Furceri, and Dominique Guillaume. 2012. "Labor Market Flexibility and Unemployment: New Empirical Evidence of Static and Dynamic Effects." Working Paper 12/64, International Monetary Fund, Washington, DC.

Bigsten, Arne, Paul Collier, Stefan Dercon, Marcel Fafchamps, Bernard Gauthier, Jan Willem Gunning, Abena Oduro, Remco Oostendorp, Cathy Pattillo, Mans Söderbom, Francis Teal, and Albert Zeufack. 2003. "Risk Sharing in Labor Markets." *World Bank Economic Review* 17 (3): 349–66.

Bloom, Nicholas. 2009. "The Impact of Uncertainty Shocks." *Econometrica* 77 (3): 623–85.

Bloom, Nicholas, Benn Eifert, Aprajit Mahajan, David McKenzie, and John Roberts. 2013. "Does Management Matter? Evidence from India." *Quarterly Journal of Economics* 128 (1): 1–51.

Boeri, Tito, and Herbert Bruecker. 2011. "Short-Time Work Benefits Revisited: Some Lessons from the Great Recession." *Economic Policy* 26 (68): 699–765.

Bruhn, Miriam, and David McKenzie. 2013. "Using Administrative Data to Evaluate Municipal Reforms: An Evaluation of the Impact of Minas Facil Expresso." Policy Research Working Paper 6368, World Bank, Washington, DC.

Caballero, Ricardo J. 2008. "Creative Destruction." In *The New Palgrave Dictionary of Economics*, edited by Steven N. Durlauf and Lawrence E. Blume. Basingstoke, U.K.: Palgrave Macmillan.

Caballero, Ricardo J., Kevin N. Cowan, Eduardo M. R. A. Engel, and Alejandro Micco. 2013. "Effective Labor Regulation and Microeconomic Flexibility." *Journal of Development Economics* 101: 92–104.

Coase, Ronald H. 1937. "The Nature of the Firm." *Economica* New Series 4 (6): 386–405.

Coe, David T., Elhanan Helpman, and Alexander W. Hoffmaister. 1997. "North-South R&D Spillovers." *Economic Journal* 107 (440): 134–49.

D'Erasmo, Pablo N., and Hernan J. Moscoso Boedo. 2013. "Intangibles and Endogenous Firm Volatility over the Business Cycle." Unpublished manuscript, University of Maryland, College Park, MD, and University of Virginia, Charlottesville, VA.

Del Carpio, Ximena, Ha Nguyen, and Liang Choon Wang. 2012. "Does the Minimum Wage Affect Employment? Evidence from the Manufacturing Sector in Indonesia." Policy Research Working Paper 6147, World Bank, Washington, DC.

De Soto, Hernando. 1989. *The Other Path: The Economic Answer to Terrorism.* New York: Harper & Row Publishers.

Djankov, Simeon, Caralee McLiesh, and Rita Ramalho. 2006. "Regulation and Growth." *Economics Letters* 92 (3): 395–401.

Dräger, Vanessa, and Paul Marx. 2012. "Do Firms Demand Temporary Workers When They Face Workload Fluctuation? Cross-Country Firm-Level Evidence on the Conditioning Effect of Employment Protection." Discussion Paper 6894, Institute for the Study of Labor (IZA), Bonn.

Dutz, Mark A. 2013. "Resource Reallocation and Innovation: Converting Enterprise Risks into Opportunities." Policy Research Working Paper 6534, World Bank, Washington DC.

European Commission. 2010. *Monitoring the Social Impact of the Crisis: Public Perceptions in the European Union (Wave 4).* Flash Eurobarometer Series. Brussels: European Commission.

Fafchamps, Marcel. 2001. "Networks, Communities and Markets in Sub-Saharan Africa: Implications for Firm Growth and Investment." *Journal of African Economies* 10 (Supplement 2): 109–42.

Fafchamps, Marcel, Jan Willem Gunning, and Remco Oostendorp. 2000. "Inventories and Risk in African Manufacturing." *Economic Journal* 110 (466): 861–93.

Falco, Paolo, William F. Maloney, Bob Rijkers, and Mauricio Sarrias. 2012. "Heterogeneity in Subjective Wellbeing: An Application to Occupational Allocation in Africa." Policy Research Working Paper 6244, World Bank, Washington, DC.

Fidas, Penelope, and Najy Benhassine. 2013. "Transparency and Access to Information in Business Regulations." Background paper for the *World Development Report 2014.*

Fox, Louise, and Thomas Sohnesen. 2012. "Household Enterprises in Sub-Saharan Africa: Why They Matter for Growth, Jobs, and Livelihoods." Policy Research Working Paper 6184, Word Bank, Washington, DC.

Gardner, Elie. 2012. "Peru Battles the Golden Curse of Madre De Dios." *Nature* 486: 306–07.

Ghani, Ejaz. 2013. "Why Do Enterprises Get Attracted to Some Cities? Not to Others?" Background paper for the *World Development Report 2014.*

Gutierrez, Federico H. 2013. "Labor Contracts and Risk Sharing." Background paper for the *World Development Report 2014.*

Hallward-Driemeier, Mary, Bob Rijkers, and Andrew Waxman. 2011. "Ladies First? Firm-Level Evidence on the Labor Impacts of the East Asian Crisis." Policy Research Working Paper 5789, World Bank, Washington, DC.

Henson, Spencer, and John Humphrey. 2009. "The Impacts of Private Food Safety Standards on the Food Chain and on Public Standard-Setting Processes." Paper prepared for the Joint FAO/WHO Food Standards Programme, Codex Alimentarius Commission, Thirty-second Session, Food and Agriculture Organization, Rome, June 29–July 4.

Hoshi, Takeo, and Anil K. Kashyap. 2010. "Will the U.S. Bank Recapitalization Succeed? Eight Lessons from Japan." *Journal of Financial Economics* 97 (3): 398–417.

Hsieh, Chang-Tai, and Peter J. Klenow. 2009. "Misallocation and Manufacturing TFP in China and India." *Quarterly Journal of Economics* 124 (4): 1403–48.

ILO (International Labour Organization). 2009. *The Informal Economy in Africa: Promoting Transition to Formality: Challenges and Strategies.* Geneva: ILO.

Judge, William Q., and Detelin Elenkov. 2005. "Organizational Capacity for Change and Environmental Performance: An Empirical Assessment of Bulgarian Firms." *Journal of Business Research* 58 (7): 893–901.

Kehoe, Timothy Jerome, and Edward C. Prescott, eds. 2007. *Great Depressions of the Twentieth Century.* Minneapolis, MN: Federal Reserve Bank of Minneapolis.

Knight, Frank. 1921. *Risk, Uncertainty, and Profit.* Boston: Houghton Mifflin Company.

Kremer, Michael, and Eric Maskin. 2006. "Globalization and Inequality." Working Paper 2008-0087, Weatherhead Center for International Affairs, Harvard University, Cambridge, MA.

La Porta, Rafael, and Andrei Shleifer. 2008. "The Unofficial Economy and Economic Development." *Brookings Papers on Economic Activity* 39 (2): 275–363.

Lasagabaster, Esperanza. 2013. "Policy Priorities for Innovative Entrepreneurship." Background paper for the *World Development Report 2014.*

Levy, Santiago. 2008. *Good Intentions, Bad Outcomes: Social Policy, Informality, and Economic Growth in Mexico.* Washington, DC: Brookings Institution Press.

Loayza, Norman, and Jamele Rigolini. 2011. "Informal Employment: Safety Net or Growth Engine?" *World Development* 39 (9): 1503–15.

Loayza, Norman, and Tomoko Wada. 2010. "Informal Labor in the Middle East and North Africa: Basic Measures and Determinants." Unpublished manuscript, World Bank, Washington, DC.

Maloney, William. 2013. "Measuring Labor Market Risk." Background paper for the *World Development Report 2014.*

Merotto, Dino, Kosuke Kanematsu, and Tao Huang. Forthcoming. "Why Policy Makers Concerned about Jobs Need a BuDDy." PREM Premise Note, World Bank, Washington, DC.

Mitchell, Mark L. 1989. "The Impact of External Parties on Brand-Name Capital: The 1982 Tylenol Poisonings and Subsequent Cases." *Economic Inquiry* 27 (4): 601–18.

Mitra, Amitava. 2008. *Fundamentals of Quality Control and Improvement.* 3rd ed. Hoboken, NJ: John Wiley & Sons.

Pianta, Mario. 2006. "Innovation and Employment." In *The Oxford Handbook of Innovation,* edited by Jan Fagerberg, David C. Mowery, and Richard R. Nelson. New York: Oxford University Press.

Porter, Michael E., and Mark R. Kramer. 2006. "Strategy and Society: The Link between Competitive Advantage and Corporate Social Responsibility." *Harvard Business Review* 84 (12): 78–92.

Restuccia, Diego, and Richard Rogerson. 2013. "Misallocation and Productivity." *Review of Economic Dynamics* 16 (1): 1–10.

Ribe, Helena, David A. Robalino, and Ian Walker. 2012. *From Right to Reality: Incentives, Labor Markets, and the Challenge of Universal Social Protection in Latin America and the Caribbean.* Latin American Development Forum Series. Washington, DC: World Bank.

Rinne, Ulf, and Klaus F. Zimmermann. 2012. "Another Economic Miracle? The German Labor Market and the Great Recession." *IZA Journal of Labor Policy* 1: 3.

Ritchie, Bryan K. 2004. "Politics and Economic Reform in Malaysia." William Davidson Institute Working Paper 655, University of Michigan Business School, Ann Arbor.

Schneider, Friedrich, Andreas Buehn, and Claudio E. Montenegro. 2010. "Shadow Economies All over the World: New Estimates for 162 Countries from 1999 to 2007." Policy Research Working Paper 5356, World Bank, Washington, DC.

Schrage, Elliot J. 2004. "Promoting International Worker Rights through Private Voluntary Initiatives: Public Relations or Public Policy?" A Report to the U.S. Department of State on behalf of the University of Iowa Center for Human Rights, Iowa City.

Seker, Murat. 2011. "Effects of Licensing Reform on Firm Innovation." Policy Research Working Paper 5876, World Bank, Washington, DC.

UNCTAD (United Nations Conference on Trade and Development). 2013. *Global Value Chains and Development: Investment and Value Added Trade in the Global Economy: A Preliminary Analysis.* Geneva: United Nations.

UNEP (United Nations Environment Programme). 2012. "Analysis of Formalization Approaches in the Artisanal and Small-Scale Gold Mining Sector Based on Experiences in Ecuador, Mongolia, Peru, Tanzania and Uganda: Peru Case Study." UNEP, Nairobi.

Wölfl, Anita, and Juan S. Mora-Sanguinetti. 2011. "Reforming the Labour Market in Spain." Economics Department Working Papers 845, Organisation for Economic Co-operation and Development, Paris.

World Bank. 2006. *The Impact of Intel in Costa Rica: Nine Years after the Decision to Invest.* Washington, DC: World Bank and Multilateral Investment Guarantee Agency.

———. 2008. *Thailand: Investment Climate Assessment Update.* Washington, DC: World Bank.

———. 2010. *World Development Report 2011: Conflict, Security, and Development.* Washington, DC: World Bank.

———. 2011. *World Development Report 2012: Gender and Development.* Washington, DC: World Bank.

———. 2012. *World Development Report 2013: Jobs.* Washington, DC: World Bank.

———. 2013. *Doing Business 2013: Smarter Regulations for Small and Medium-Size Enterprises.* Washington, DC: World Bank.

———. Pensions (database). World Bank, Washington, DC, http://www.worldbank.org/pensions.

———. World Development Indicators (database). World Bank, Washington, DC, http://data.worldbank.org/data-catalog/world-development-indicators.

WEF (World Economic Forum). 2012. *The Global Competitiveness Report 2012–2013.* Geneva: WEF.

SPOTLIGHT 5

Moving toward greater labor market flexibility: India's uneven path

About 1.5 billion people in developing countries are employed in low-productivity informal sector jobs with no social security benefits and poor working conditions. What can governments do to create better jobs, and more of them? India's experience shows that states with more flexible labor regulations and lower costs of compliance tend to have greater labor mobility and higher productivity and employment in the formal manufacturing sector.

India has one of the most rigid labor markets in the world. Labor market issues are governed by 45 central government laws and more than 100 state statutes, many of which overlap. The most controversial laws regulate worker firings and closures of manufacturing firms. A statute dating back to 1947, the Industrial Disputes Act (IDA), requires factories with more than 100 workers to obtain government permission to lay off employees and close their operations. Such permissions are rarely granted, and employers face substantial fines and even a prison sentence if they fire workers illegally. Many other laws govern work conditions, minimum wages, and benefits. Firms with 10 or more workers that use electric power are required to register under the Factories Act and to keep records and file regular reports on such matters as overtime work, wages, attendance, sick leave, and worker fines. Compliance with these requirements, as well as multiple inspections, is costly, particularly for smaller firms.

Although the regulations are meant to enhance the welfare of workers, they often have the opposite effect by encouraging firms to stay small and thus circumvent labor laws. To avoid compliance costs, firms reportedly break down their operations into several small separate units. In many states, firms are increasingly relying on contract laborers, who do not receive the same benefits as regular employees. Excessive protections stipulated by labor laws also discourage hiring. Large Indian firms use less labor than is justifiable given the prevailing low wages. As a result of these distortions, nearly 9 in 10 Indian workers are employed in the informal sector and have little or no social insurance or fringe benefits. This informality is associated with markedly lower productivity. Value added per worker in India's informal manufacturing sector averages about one-eighth that in the formal sector.

A varied regulatory burden within India by state

Because Indian states have the authority to amend central labor laws, the regulatory burden on enterprises varies greatly by state. Some states have made their labor laws more flexible relative to the provisions of the central acts, while others have adopted additional restrictions. This variation has created the ideal conditions (a "natural experiment") to assess the economic effects of labor laws because, while individual states have changed their labor regulations, most other legislation has remained similar across states. This has prompted a number of studies, several of which are summarized in table S5.1.

Learning from the experience of labor reform in India and elsewhere

Most of the reforms in Indian states were aimed at improving procedures and reducing the costs of regulatory compliance, rather than at enacting comprehensive structural changes. Only two states (Uttar Pradesh and Uttaranchal) relaxed the threshold for applying IDA's restrictions on worker layoffs. The more common reforms eased the regime for use of contract labor; simplified reporting requirements; limited the number of registers that need to be kept; allowed shift work; and introduced self-certification of compliance with labor regulations to streamline or reduce the number of inspections. Two other states (Haryana and Punjab) introduced a single annual inspection for compliance with all labor laws, and several states now require government authorization for surprise inspections. The reforms have improved the business environment and reduced transaction costs. These efforts are mostly piecemeal, however; few states have addressed the vast body of administrative requirements systematically.

To create the sort of labor flexibility that promotes formalization and the benefits that accompany it, India needs to reduce the number of and simplify labor laws, modernize the IDA, and further improve administrative procedures. Although no single blueprint exists for how to design and implement effective labor market reforms, several developing countries offer examples of policy changes that increase labor market flexibility.

Malaysia does not limit the duration of fixed term contracts, prohibit night and weekend work, or require government permission to fire redundant workers. Labor regulations protect the interests of workers but are generally not too burdensome for employers and thus do not discourage them from hiring formal workers. The level of informality, estimated at about 35 percent of total employment, is low relative to other developing countries. Colombia has reduced severance payments for employees and introduced a wider definition of fair dismissals. To process mass dismissals more quickly, it has eased the requirement for advance notice of firings. The Czech Republic and Slovakia

TABLE S5.1 *Studies of labor regulations in India*

Study	Methodology	Findings
Besley and Burgess 2004	Constructed an index summarizing state-level amendments to the Industrial Disputes Act (IDA) between 1949 and 1992.	• States with less flexible labor regulations had lower output, productivity, investment, and employment in formal manufacturing than they would have had if their regulations were not so rigid. • Output in informal manufacturing increased in the same states.
Sharma 2009	Used the Besley-Burgess methodology to estimate the impact of reforms in 1991 that removed licensing requirements to set up and expand factories.	• After deregulation, the number of informal establishments declined by 25 percent in states with more flexible labor laws, compared with states with more rigid regulations.
Ahsan and Pagés 2009	Updated the Besley-Burgess index, and estimated the effects of difficulties in resolving labor disputes and restrictions on labor layoffs.	• States that increased labor law rigidity above the level stipulated in the IDA experienced declines in registered manufacturing and output relative to states that did not implement such changes. • Rigid regulations for settling disputes reduced output more than the IDA provisions on layoffs. • West Bengal has lost more than 620,000 manufacturing jobs because of its restrictive regulations in these two aspects of the law alone. Andhra Pradesh and Tamil Nadu have created more than 130,000 formal manufacturing jobs, thanks to improvements in their dispute resolution regulations.[a]
Dougherty 2008	Examined a broader range of labor regulations in 21 states. Analyzed 8 major labor legal areas. Constructed an Organisation for Economic Co-operation and Development (OECD) labor reform index based on 50 subjects of possible reform, many of which could be implemented by administrative procedure rather than through formal amendments to the law.	• The most common area of reform was contract labor; the least common were changes in rules governing inspections. • Overall, the degree of reform was modest: no state has introduced more than 28 reforms out of a possible 50 reform subjects measured. • States with higher labor reform indexes had greater job turnover rates—vital for technological change and economic growth.
Goldar 2011	Used the labor reform index developed by Dougherty	• States with higher labor reform indexes tended to have greater employment elasticity and a higher growth of organized employment in manufacturing compared with states that introduced few reforms.

a. World Bank 2010a.

increased the maximum duration of fixed term contracts and reduced redundancy costs.

India may well choose a different path, but the overall principle guiding reform efforts should be protecting workers—through such means as social assistance, skill building, and help finding jobs—rather than protecting jobs.

Sources

Ahsan, Ahmad, and Carmen Pagés. 2009. "Are All Labor Regulations Equal? Evidence from Indian Manufacturing." *Journal of Comparative Economics* 37 (1): 62–75.

Besley, Timothy, and Robin Burgess. 2004. "Can Labor Regulation Hinder Economic Performance? Evidence from India." *Quarterly Journal of Economics* 119 (1): 91–134.

Dougherty, Sean. 2008. "Labor Regulation and Employment Dynamics at the State Level in India." Economics Department Working Papers 624, Organisation for Economic Co-operation and Development, Paris.

Goldar, Bishwanath. 2011. "Growth in Organized Manufacturing Employment in Recent Years." *Economic and Political Weekly* 46 (7): 20–23.

Sharma, Siddharth. 2009. "Entry Regulation, Labor Laws and Informality." Enterprise Note 1, World Bank, Washington, DC.

World Bank. 2010a. *India's Employment Challenge: Creating Jobs, Helping Workers*. New York: Oxford University Press for the World Bank.

———. 2010b. *Malaysian Economic Monitor: Inclusive Growth*. Washington, DC: World Bank.

———. 2012. *World Development Report 2013: Jobs*. Washington, DC: World Bank.

———. 2013a. "Doing Business 2013. Smarter Regulations for Small and Medium Enterprises. Economy Profile: Malaysia." World Bank, Washington, DC.

———. 2013b. *Doing Business 2013: Smarter Regulations for Small and Medium-Size Enterprises*. Washington, DC: World Bank.

Finance doesn't need to be complex, and it can actually be helpful: an elderly man views stock prices at the Shanghai stock exchange.

CHAPTER 6

The role of the financial system in managing risk

More financial tools, fewer financial crises

The financial system can fulfill a socially beneficial function of risk management

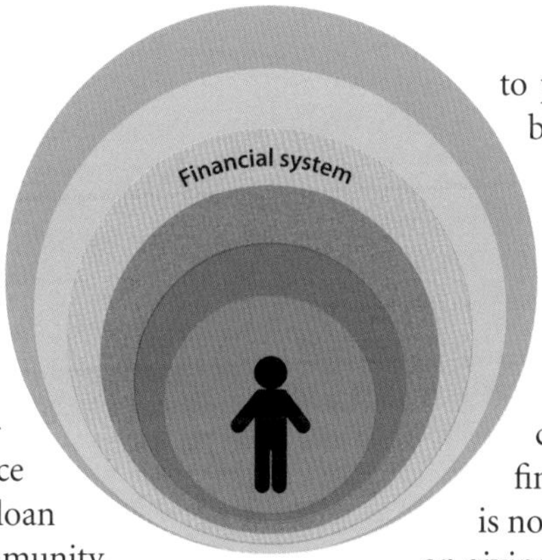

In 1990, after the Velvet Revolution ushered in an era of reform in the Czech Republic, Jan Sarkis, the son of a Greek immigrant, decided to start a business to produce bottled juices. He took out a bank loan and, on the advice of his local community, bought flood insurance and put his savings in a bank to protect against local theft. When banks plunged into a crisis in 1997, Jan's loan repayments spiked; then his savings were frozen for 14 months because his bank went bankrupt. A one-in-one-hundred-year-flood in 2002 swept away his business, but, fortunately, his insurance settlement covered a majority of the losses. The twin experiences left Jan with mixed feelings about the financial system.

In 2006, the Czech National Bank, a credible public institution, became the integrated supervisor of financial services, and confidence in the Czech financial system rose. An entrepreneurial risk taker, Jan took out another credit line and consolidated his savings in one bank account for greater efficiency. Two years later, the global financial crisis hit. Thanks to conservative supervision, the Czech banking system was well prepared. But the Czech koruna depreciated, pushing up the price of imported goods, including drinks.

Jan took a big risk, using his credit line to introduce a new sparkling drink. It was a success! Mindful of past shocks and possible future ones, Jan decided to protect his wealth by spreading his business risks and opportunities and taking his company public. The initial public offering on the regional Warsaw Stock Exchange was well subscribed, and he was able to diversify his wealth by buying stocks and bonds of other companies. Because of his wise decisions, and the financial system to support them, Jan is now a wealthy, respected man, focused on giving back to the community.[1]

As the ups and downs of Jan Sarkis's story illustrate, the financial system can help people manage risk by providing them with useful financial tools, protecting them from bad shocks, and better positioning them to take advantage of opportunities. Banks, insurance companies, brokerage houses, stock exchanges, other financial institutions, and the financial infrastructure (such as payment systems) that form the financial system can collectively fulfill this socially beneficial function of providing financial services and helping society manage risks. They can do so by offering people market insurance (such as disaster or life insurance), self-insurance (saving deposits), and self-protection (safe and efficient payments). People, including the poor, need not just credit but a range of financial tools to manage risk and pursue opportunity effectively and responsibly. However, the financial system can also hurt people if it fails to manage the risk it retains. It can generate bad shocks that affect people directly by hindering access to finance or indirectly by hampering refinancing of enterprises, straining public finances, and leading to loss of jobs, income, and wealth.

Public policy thus has two important roles, both of which help people manage risk. It can encourage the financial system to broaden the share of people with access to financial services (financial inclusion), giving more people more and better financial risk management tools. It can also encourage the financial system to better control systemic financial risk. Public policy should be selective, using direct interventions (such as subsidies and guarantees) sparingly to avoid distorting incentives in the financial market. It should focus on providing adequate financial infrastructure (payment systems, credit history information) and on implementing enabling regulation to promote greater competition and use of diverse financial tools by people. At the same time, the state needs to implement supervision of systemic risk in the financial sector that is prudent but promotes development in the sector. Specific recommendations to achieve these ends are discussed throughout the chapter.[2]

This chapter focuses on the risk-managing function of the formal financial system, whereas chapters 3 and 4, and, to some extent, chapter 5 address informal financial arrangements. The formal financial system can be defined in various ways. Here, the formal financial system is defined as consisting of firms whose primary business activity is financial activity. The system thus ranges from banks and insurance companies to microcredit and microinsurance firms. Financial systems perform several interconnected functions, including reallocating resources from savers to investors; monitoring managers and exerting corporate control; and facilitating trading, hedging, diversifying, and pooling of risk; this chapter concentrates on the risk management function.[3] Given the Report's focus on people, this chapter particularly examines the tension between financial inclusion and financial stability. Broader trade-offs between financial development and stability are discussed later in the context of institutional reforms to improve the formulation of financial sector policy.

For good risk management, people need a range of financial tools

Different financial tools serve different purposes

The financial system supports risk management by offering various financial tools to people and their support systems (households, the community, enterprises, the state, and even the international community).[4] With these tools, people can smooth consumption, finance their own or their children's education, deal with health and income shocks, improve nutrition, and plan for a better future, among other socially useful activities. In this way, the financial system can advance overall development and help create an environment of equal opportunity and a level playing field, including for the poor. Different types of financial risk-managing tools are designed to achieve different outcomes:

- *Payment and foreign exchange services* increase the security and ease of domestic transactions and international remittances, thus helping people self-protect.
- *Saving instruments* (bank deposits and liquid securities) help people smooth consumption and accumulate buffers for rainy days, thus providing self-insurance. Sometimes, savings can be a vehicle to finance unusually large expenses (investment) and to self-protect.
- *Credit* (such as education loans) helps people and their support systems alleviate financing constraints over time and exploit opportunities with greater flexibility and resilience, thus improving people's ability to self-protect. Access to credit in bad times, including credit they have lined up in advance to tap in event of shocks (contingent debt), can help people and support systems cope better.
- *Market insurance*, including hedging instruments, helps people and their support systems insure against the consequences of extreme adverse events such as death, impaired health or injury, or loss of income or wealth. The state can also benefit from market insurance against extreme losses.
- *Debt and equity investments* help people diversify wealth into a robust portfolio of instruments according to their risk preference, thus facilitating self-protection—and, if liquid, self-insurance, as well.
- *Risk-taking capital* (such as private equity or venture funds) enables firms, from small ones to international corporations, to take informed risks and innovate, including through innovation-driven start-ups and firm expansion.
- *Public trading of assets* (commodities, securities, financial derivatives) provides a mechanism for discovering and determining prices that match demand and supply. People then use this information to make decisions about their consumption and

saving, business opportunities, portfolio allocation, and strategic management of risks.

- *Risk pricing* information embedded in interest rates, insurance premiums, and other financial prices is provided by the financial system, thanks to its comparative advantage in this area. The financial sector "puts a price tag" on risk and thus helps the users of financial tools understand the cost and benefits of different strategies for managing their risks.

Because people face multiple risks, they must employ a range of tools for their financial strategies to be effective and reliable.

Each financial tool can manage only certain risks efficiently, based on their frequency, intensity, and impact. Self-insurance and market insurance help in coping with losses. Deposit accounts and electronic payment methods can make payment of current (expected) expenditures more efficient and secure. Remittances can also be securely and efficiently transferred to their receivers using electronic payments and foreign exchange services (box 6.1). When expenditures jump unexpectedly in the wake of a bad shock, the first wave of losses can be efficiently coped with by tapping saving deposits and liquid financial investments, which act as a self-insurance buffer (diagram 6.1a). Using savings to self-insure against larger, less probable losses can be inefficient, however. Ideally, those types of losses can be insured efficiently through credit, but only if people and their support systems have access to credit in bad times or can arrange for a loan that they can rely on when bad times come (contingent debt). Even credit can be too expensive a financial tool to prepare for one-in-one-hundred-year events, however. For these events and losses, market insurance is the most efficient financial tool. And even market insurers are unable to efficiently price, retain, and manage losses from extreme unexpected events, whose impact is hard to predict; in those cases, social safety nets and other solidarity schemes can offer support. In their risk management strategy, enterprises can use risk-taking capital for losses larger than those efficiently covered by contingent credit and smaller than those efficiently covered by market insurance. Another type of hybrid financial tool is provided by religion-based (Islamic) finance. Islamic banking products such as partnership loans (under *mudaraba* or *musharaka*

DIAGRAM 6.1 *Combining financial tools improves preparation for losses of different probability and severity*

a. Self-insurance and market insurance tools make it easier to cope with losses of different severity

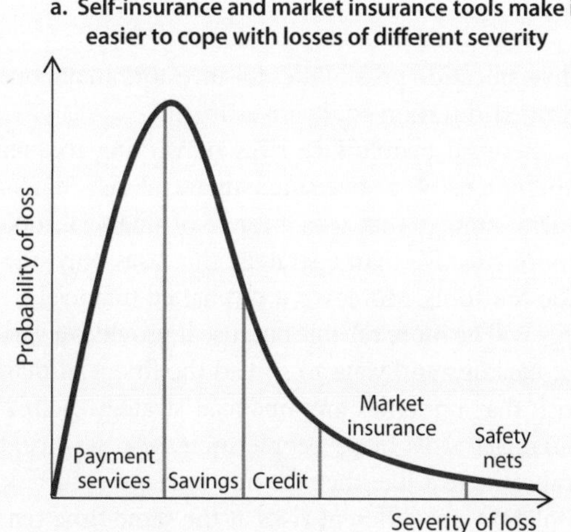

b. Self-protection tools help decrease the probability of a given loss

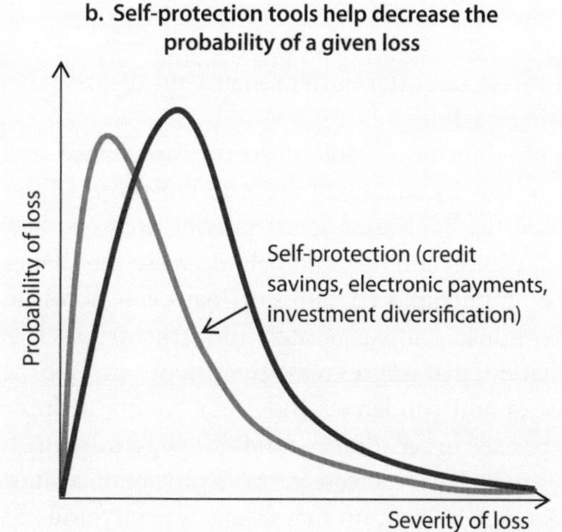

Source: WDR 2014 team.

Note: The diagrams depict a stylized loss distribution with fitted financial tools according to their efficiency to insure and protect against possible losses (risk) of varying frequency and intensity. The personal loss distribution function (dark red line in panels a and b) improves (shifts down and to the left) when people use financial self-protection (light red line in panel b).

BOX 6.1 *Better than cash: Electronic payments reduce risk and costs*

Cash may still be king at times, but compared with electronic payments, cash payments are inefficient, can carry significant handling and transportation costs, and run the risks of theft, loss, and counterfeiting. The use of cash also perpetuates the shadow economy by allowing business transactions and sales to stay off official books of accounts. Greater use of electronic payments, rather than cash, could save Brazil 0.7 percent of its gross domestic product (GDP) a year,[a] and India as much as 1.6 percent of GDP.[b]

Individuals and small firms using electronic payments benefit from convenient online authorizations, easier record keeping, and the availability of dispute resolution mechanisms. By promoting electronic payment, government policies have drastically reduced the risk of crime and have enabled beneficiaries to keep up with their financial obligations without delay. Importantly, electronic payment instruments must be linked to a deposit account either at a deposit-taking institution (bank) or in the form of e-money that can be used by banks, other financial firms, or mobile network operators. For the financially unserved and underserved, electronic payments are usually the first contact with formal financial services. In Pakistan, for example, more than 1.8 million branchless banking accounts process more than 10.4 million transactions monthly.[c]

Electronic transfers and payments of remittances offer significant benefits not only to migrants and their families but also to receiving countries. Remittances from 192 million international migrants (3 percent of the world's population) totaled $501 billion in 2011, of which $372 billion went to developing countries. Branchless banking and banking partnerships with mobile operators can extend remittance services to millions of people who were previously unbanked in remote, rural areas. For example, in the Philippines, "G-Cash" and "SMART Money" serve the Filipino diaspora by providing remittances over their mobile money platforms.[d]

Electronic payments, however, involve some risks that can dampen consumer confidence: the risk of fraud, the risk that the payment product issuer will go bankrupt, and the risk that records of the customer's account will be corrupted or destroyed because of problems with the issuer's operating system. For payment products linked to bank accounts, the second and third risks can be mitigated by prudential and operational requirements for the bank, as well as by deposit insurance. Such arrangements may not cover nonbank issuers, but other mechanisms to mitigate these risks can be enforced. The industry actively manages security risks, and targeted consumer protection measures are being implemented.

Electronic payments can help manage fraud and leakage risks in government payment programs and ultimately improve transparency and accountability. For example, in Saudi Arabia, the implementation in 2002 of the SADAD payment system, an electronic bill payments and settlement platform, saves the government 10–15 percent of annual revenues previously lost to human error, fraud, and delay. In Brazil, a corporate card payment program (Cartão de Pagamento do Governo Federal) has replaced the use of cash and checks for low-value procurement that is not subject to a bidding process; it has allowed agencies and cardholders to track expenses, while a government website openly discloses the value of transactions, date, and type of merchants.

Source: Maria Teresa Chimienti for the WDR 2014.

a. Central Bank of Brazil, "Efficiency and Costs on Retail Payment Instruments Usage," http://www.forodepagos.org/pdf/Custo_Eficiencia_English.pdf.

b. Ehrbeck and others 2010.

c. Consultative Group to Assist the Poor (CGAP), "An Overview of the G2P Payments Sector in Pakistan," http://www.cgap.org/publications/overview-g2p-payments-sector-pakistan.

d. See CGAP website, http://www.cgap.org/topics/paymentsremittances, for more information on payments and remittances.

contracts) can offer entrepreneurs profit-loss risk-sharing qualities.[5]

Other financial tools decrease the chance and size of loss by enabling people to self-protect (diagram 6.1b). Education loans provide access to better education and thus can help decrease the chance of being unemployed. Housing loans ease access to better housing and associated infrastructure, such as sanitation, that can decrease the risk of water-borne diseases and pandemics (box 6.2). Saving deposits can be used to accumulate funds for large, infrequent investments that increase people's protection against risks (such as a pump that cleans water). Similarly, a greater variety of investment securities (stocks, bonds), issued by various companies and funds with varying risk characteristics, can help people diversify their assets and protect against loss of income and wealth. Investment deposits of Islamic banks, which finance partnership loans to entrepreneurs, offer diversification possibilities for investors analogous to limited-duration equity investment.[6]

Because people face risks of varying frequency and intensity, a diversified financial risk management strategy that uses a range of financial tools is more effective than a strategy that uses only one or too few tools. Moreover, a diversified financial strategy will be more reliable because it provides a variety of backups and ways to spread the financial market risk that underlies any financial strategy. A mix of financial tools helps people increase resilience, because in real life, they do not manage each risk in isolation but different risks at the same time (chapter 1, table 1.1). Moreover, these risks are more or less either idiosyncratic or systemic in nature. To prepare for a large idiosyncratic risk (such as long-term illness), market insurance (such as health insurance) can be the most efficient financial risk management tool to use. Market insurance might be a bad tool for

BOX 6.2 *Housing finance can improve household resilience and opportunities*

A house can be a lifelong investment. Housing finance allows individuals to acquire property at an early age and spread repayments over time, as their income rises. Without proper financing, the alternative is to spend years saving while living in unsatisfactory conditions, or building housing little by little at a higher cost. In old age, home ownership provides security and resilience when income is lower and would not easily cover rent payments.

Housing finance can bring economic opportunity to households. By expanding access to secured credit collateralized by housing, housing finance can release family wealth for other diversified investments, unlocking the power of so-called "dead capital."[a] A properly functioning titling system and housing finance products can thus play a role in creating economic opportunity.

Housing finance improves people's resilience and helps them avoid poverty traps. To obtain a mortgage, households usually need to accumulate significant savings for the down payment. This "forced" saving alone can contribute substantially to a household's resilience.[b] Through housing finance products, people have access to better housing with better sanitary conditions, thus improving their resilience to disease. Having utility connections, sanitation, a waterproofed dwelling, and warmth or shade can all improve health conditions, especially among the more vulnerable young and elderly. Simple improvements like having a concrete floor can reduce mosquito breeding grounds and thus lead to lower levels of malaria. The availability of high-quality affordable homes enables families to spend a greater share of their household income on nutritious food, health care, and other essentials that promote good health. Greater residential stability also reduces the stress and disruption associated with frequent or unwanted moves and provides a stable base for individuals with chronic illnesses and other conditions to receive needed care.[c]

Improved housing contributes to safer and more resilient communities. In Honduras, for instance, criminal gangs are widespread, and lower-income communities are by far the most affected by the criminal activity. Improved housing through higher investment has helped reduce criminal activity and antisocial behavior. Effective housing projects have the power to change socioeconomic classification. Such projects have helped very low-income communities to achieve lower-middle income status and good educational levels, and otherwise marginal communities to enjoy higher security in Honduras.[d]

Source: Simon C. Walley for the WDR 2014.

a. De Soto 2000.
b. Collins and others 2009, 179.
c. Cohen 2007.
d. RTI International 2005.

protecting against a systemic risk (such as financial crisis) because it may fail if many insurance companies go bankrupt. At the individual level, people can prepare and cope better with systemic shocks by increasing their self-reliance (self-insurance and self-protection), including by using a range of suitable financial tools.

Some financial systems are better than others at offering access to variety

The range of financial tools supplied by the formal financial system varies considerably with the stage of development and personal income within a country. On average, people in high-income countries save through bank deposits much more than people in middle- and low-income countries (figure 6.1a). Even the poorest 40 percent of people in high-income countries (figure 6.1b) are much more likely to use formal saving deposits than people in middle-income and low-income countries. Formal credit is commonly used in high- and low-income countries; people in middle-income countries use credit much less. The use of private health insurance across middle- and low-income countries differs greatly, both on average and for the poorest 40 percent. Savings is the most frequently used financial tool around the world, followed by insurance and credit. This pattern, however, may reflect various obstacles to implementing better financial risk-managing strategies, on both the supply and demand side.

Supply-side factors that influence access

In theory, it should not matter whether the financial instruments are provided by banks, microfinance firms, insurance companies, or capital markets as long as people have access to the range of financial tools they need.[7] In practice, however, the institutional form does matter because each financial firm is licensed to provide only a specific range of financial tools, even though several institutions can be integrated under one financial group or holding company. At lower levels of financial development, financial systems tend to be concentrated in banking; at higher levels of development, there is greater diversification into capital markets, insurance companies, and mutual funds (figure 6.2). Thus having a financial system heavily concentrated in banks may constrain the provision of insurance. Similarly, the absence of capital markets, mutual funds, or brokerage houses can constrain people's options to diversify wealth.

FIGURE 6.1 ***The range of formal financial tools used by individuals varies by country and income***

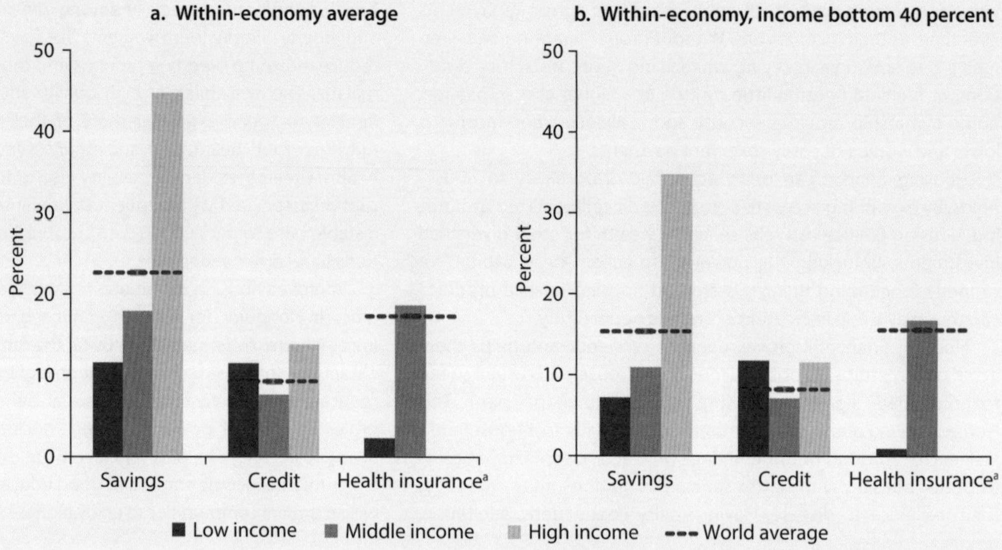

a. Within-economy average

b. Within-economy, income bottom 40 percent

Savings | Credit | Health insurance[a]

Low income | Middle income | High income | World average

Source: WDR 2014 team based on data from World Bank Global Findex (database); Demirgüç-Kunt and Klapper 2012.

Note: The figure measures the percentage of adults using formal financial risk-management tools.

a. Data on self-paid health insurance were not available for high-income countries.

FIGURE 6.2 ***As financial systems deepen, they diversify their institutional structure***

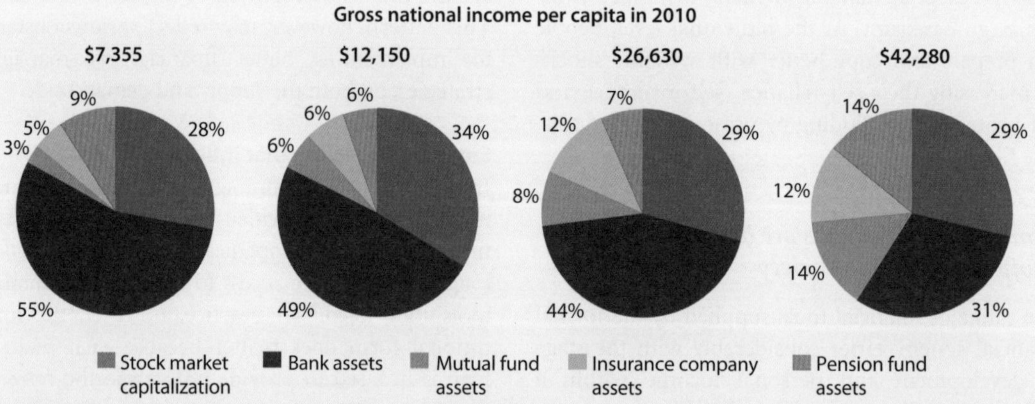

Gross national income per capita in 2010

$7,355 | $12,150 | $26,630 | $42,280

Stock market capitalization | Bank assets | Mutual fund assets | Insurance company assets | Pension fund assets

Source: WDR 2014 team based on data from World Bank Global Financial Development Database.

Note: Size of financial system calculated for 56 countries (6 lower-middle-income, 20 upper-middle-income, and 30 high-income countries) as the sum of bank assets, stock market capitalization, mutual fund assets, insurance company assets, and pension fund assets.

Financial firms themselves may be constrained in risk management by not having access to needed financial infrastructure (electronic payment systems, credit information) or hedging tools (such as cross-currency or interest rate swaps). That, in turn, could limit their ability to offer a wider range of better financial tools to people and their support systems, and to efficiently absorb more risk. Likewise, private firms may lack the capacity to assess and price certain risks (such as major natural catastrophes, terrorism, and epidemics) and thus focus on providing financial tools only for better-understood risks.

BOX 6.3 *Innovative insurance mechanisms in Mongolia and Mexico*

Insuring against livestock mortality in Mongolia

Forty percent of Mongolia's workforce is engaged in agriculture, mainly in herding. Harsh climatic conditions periodically lead to catastrophic losses of livestock, posing a systemic risk to herders' livelihoods and to Mongolia's economy. In 2006, the government of Mongolia introduced an index-based livestock insurance project (IBLIP) to provide livestock mortality insurance to herders and increase the financial resilience of Mongolia's herders and its economy. When, in 2010, for example, a devastating winter killed nearly 22 percent of Mongolia's livestock, the IBLIP provided $1.42 million in indemnity payments to 4,706 of the 5,628 covered herders.

The insurance program uses an index based on the average mortality of adult livestock in each of Mongolia's counties to determine payouts. The IBLIP has proven to be an effective tool for segmenting risk among herders, the domestic private insurance sector, the government, and the international reinsurance market. It ensures that each risk layer is effectively financed by the most appropriate stakeholder. Participating herders retain livestock mortality risk of up to 6 percent. From 6 to 30 percent, a commercial insurance product transfers this risk to a domestic pool of private insurers. Above 30 percent, the government finances a social safety net product. Herders who purchase the commercial insurance product are automatically registered for the social safety net product at no additional cost. The government also ring-fences its fiscal exposure to extreme livestock losses by ensuring that its liability is triggered only in the most extreme years, during which safety nets are required. Finally, by tapping international reinsurers, the IBLIP also facilitates the transfer of livestock mortality risk out of the country.

Financing postdisaster expenditures in Mexico

Mexico is exposed to earthquakes, hurricanes, floods, and a wide variety of other geological and hydrometeorological phenomena. Postdisaster recovery and reconstruction costs can jump because of delays in funding or the reallocation of budgets intended for development purposes. In 1996, the government of Mexico established the Fund for Natural Disasters (FONDEN) to provide adequate financial resources for federal and state postdisaster reconstruction efforts without compromising government spending already committed. It has evolved significantly to include broader disaster risk management activities, such as funding risk assessment and risk reduction and rebuilding infrastructure to higher standards.

FONDEN, which supports an integrated risk financing strategy for the government's contingent liabilities from disasters, has three key features. The first is a risk assessment profile. The government has a well-defined loss-reporting mechanism that provides accurate information about expenditures from past events. To support evidence-based public decision making about disaster risk management, the government has invested in exposure data and an in-house probabilistic risk model. The second key feature is clarification of contingent liability. FONDEN rules and guidelines clarify how total authorized resources will be determined for rapid reconstruction of public infrastructure, low-income housing, and eligible natural environment assets, as well as how the liability will be split among federal and state governments. The third feature is risk financing. FONDEN's integrated disaster risk financing strategy relies on a combination of risk retention instruments (self-funding, exceptional budget allocation) to finance recurrent expenditures, and risk transfer instruments to provide additional financing for immediate response (catastrophe bonds) and longer-term reconstruction (reinsurance of excessive losses) after major disasters.

The federal and state governments spent $1.46 billion a year on disaster response from 1999 to 2011, two-thirds of which was financed through FONDEN. The system is continuously evolving to integrate lessons learned from experience and to incorporate new budgetary tools and technology to make FONDEN more effective and efficient.

Source: Laura E. Boudreau, Daniel J. Clarke, and Olivier Mahul for the WDR 2014.

When firms offer a financial product to manage a risk they do not fully understand, they often misprice the product, jeopardizing their own stability and, if failing to pay out claims, damaging customer confidence as a result. For example, a private retirement insurance product in the Philippines was initially so underpriced that the offerer nearly went bankrupt.

In a competitive environment possibly enhanced by new entry of foreign firms, the financial industry can increase the share of people using financial services through responsible actions that account for risk.[8] Overall, the best way for financial firms to help advance financial inclusion is to offer simple, readily accessible, and reliable financial tools. For example, Kenya's M-PESA and M-KESHO projects have greatly broadened the use of electronic payments and mobile savings, and South Africa's Mzansi accounts are now used by one in six South Africans who use banks.[9] The delivery of other financial tools, such as insurance and capital market investments, needs to include clear and thorough communication between the seller and the client to ensure that the seller understands the expectations (risk management needs) of the client and that the client is aware of the properties of the financial tool. For instance, clearly explaining to a buyer of insurance the risk that the insurance may not cover the complete insured loss (basis risk) is crucial for increasing take-up and renewal.[10] To provide financial tools that offer more complete solutions for risk management, financial firms should also innovate through partnerships with the state, including in the area of insurance (boxes 6.3 and 6.4).

The large size of the financially underserved population worldwide indicates that microfinance institutions (microcredit, microsavings, microinsurance) can play an important role. There have been waves of

BOX 6.4 ***Private pension insurance to confront the risk of income loss in old age***

Some 700 million people worldwide are over 60 years of age—a number that is expected to increase to 1.6 billion within the next 40 years. A majority of these people live in developing countries, where there are few government income programs to support them in their old age. The governments of advanced economies have various types of public income support programs for people who have not provided adequately for their retirement. But a rising elderly population and a shrinking working population are threatening the fiscal viability of these programs at their existing levels. Issues of viability aside, developing countries have very few such arrangements because their governments lack the capacity to finance and administer them.

In the absence of government support, income for the aged traditionally comes through the family and social networks, but these are breaking down. Decreases in birth rates are resulting in smaller families, and rapid urbanization is building a distance between the aged and their families and social networks. Increasingly, developing countries are turning to private pension systems to fill the vacuum.

Providing formal income support to the aged poses many challenges for policy makers and private providers alike, including making people aware of the need and motivating them to save for old age, establishing trust in the institutions that can provide support, and developing cost-effective distribution systems. These challenges have been addressed effectively in some of the very few private sector programs that have been implemented over the past two decades:

- Early unsuccessful attempts by CARD, a nongovernmental organization in the Philippines, illustrate the importance of planning and pricing retirement income products. In 1996, CARD introduced a product that provided members with ₱300 ($5.45) a month from their 65th birthday until death, in return for premiums of ₱2.50 ($0.05) a week paid from the date of membership until retirement. This product was extremely popular. CARD, however, had not adequately assessed the impact of this product on the financial conditions of its institution. A later assessment showed that two years of premiums would cover just one month of benefits, a situation that threatened the capital of the entire institution, which also sold other insurance products. In 1999, the retirement income activities were separated from the institution and converted into a defined contribution scheme, with a significant loss to the original contributors.
- In 2001, Grameen Bank in Bangladesh introduced the Grameen Pension Scheme. The scheme attaches a mandatory retirement savings product to its loan products and requires borrowers to contribute a minimum of Tk 50 a month. Prospective borrowers are thus instructed in the need to save for old age. The bank generously subsidizes the earnings on the contributions—doubling the amounts contributed by individuals who make regular contributions. In turn, the bank benefits from the pension fund, which increases the pool of funds available to the bank to pursue its main business activity of providing microloans.
- The National Jua Kali Pension Scheme in Kenya is a voluntary pension savings program developed in 2011 by the National Federation of Kenya Jua Kali Associations and the Retirement Benefits Authority. In the first 12 months of operation, it attracted 25,000 members. By June 2012, the quarterly contribution flows exceeded K Sh 7 million ($82,000). The key features that have contributed to the early success of the scheme are strong endorsement by the supervisor and the well-respected trade organization, low distribution costs (access is only through mobile phone), and an investment manager that is prepared to subsidize fund management costs.

The success of any private pension initiative will require a sound legal and regulatory framework, strong and capable supervisors, good corporate governance, prudent investment practices, and cost-effective administration and distribution systems.

Source: Anthony Randle for the WDR 2014.

euphoria and criticism concerning microcredit and, more recently, microinsurance. Microfinance needs to assume a more realistic role in financial inclusion, taking into account business sustainability. Good examples exist in this respect, and it is time for others to follow. Procredit, established in 1996, is the first multinational microfinance bank; as of 2008, it was operating in 26 countries with 17,000 employees and $6 billion in assets. It enjoys an investment-grade rating that enables it to raise long-term finance in the German bond market, in addition to mobilizing and providing access to saving deposits locally. In developing countries, microinsurance firms, requiring an insurance premium as low as 50 cents, insure anything from television sets to burial costs. The world's largest comprehensive contributory social security scheme for workers in the informal economy is India's Integrated Social Security Programme, which insures more than 100,000 women workers and covers health insurance (including a maternity component), life insurance, and asset insurance. As many credit and insurance markets in advanced economies become saturated, multinational financial institutions (banks and insurance companies) are looking for sustainable growth opportunities; these include microfinance, which is increasingly becoming a mainstream activity in emerging markets.[11]

Demand-side factors that influence access

The large share of people who use only informal financial tools (savings, loans, insurance) or no financial tools at all reveals a great pool of potential clients

FIGURE 6.3 ***The shares of formal and informal saving and borrowing change as countries develop***

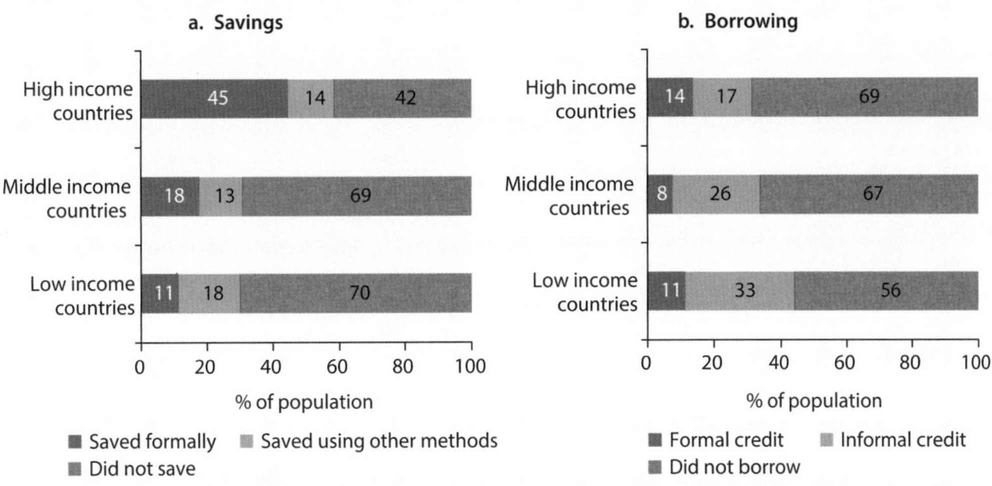

Source: WDR 2014 team based on data from World Bank Global Findex (database); Demirgüç-Kunt and Klapper 2012.
Note: The figure shows the percentage of adults saving or borrowing any money in the past year.

that could be commercially viable for the formal financial sector. For credit, it is probably not desirable to include everybody—not everyone is creditworthy or can handle credit responsibly—but a prudential limit may not exist for deposits and insurance.[12] More people use formal financial tools, such as savings and credit, as their countries develop and their average income rises (figure 6.3). However, even the poor use formal saving deposits that enable them to make investments and better plan how to break out of poverty. As countries develop, informal saving arrangements continue to coexist with formal ones. Informal saving and borrowing arrangements apparently have certain features that formal financial tools cannot provide. Completely replacing informal financial tools with formal ones may thus be neither feasible nor desirable.

People may not use formal financial tools for several reasons. The main reasons people give for not using a formal savings account are that "they do not have money to use it" (66 percent); "someone else in the family already has an account," which suggests there are indirect users (23 percent); "bank accounts are too expensive" (24 percent); and "banks are too far away" (20 percent).[13] Lack of necessary documentation (17 percent) and mistrust in banks (13 percent) also discourage people from using bank accounts and may keep some from using banks altogether. People also might prefer to stay in the informal sector (for example, refusing to use electronic payments), or they do not understand the benefit of using financial tools for risk management. In addition, low financial literacy often leads people to join Ponzi schemes, which frequently emerge and collapse in many developing countries (such as Albania, Nigeria, or the Philippines) and which may have damaged consumer confidence in any saving arrangements, including formal ones.

People are not the only ones to blame for the deficient use of financial tools. Bad corporate governance of financial firms contributes to low financial inclusion. Distorted incentives that focus on maximizing short-term profits are a particular problem: it takes time, effort, and up-front investment to broaden a client base and the range of financial tools. Many financial firms have not taken client needs sufficiently into account, including their risk profile and risk management goals, in designing and delivering financial tools. In Mexico, low-income consumers found greater price transparency at pawn shops than at microfinance institutions; they also trusted department stores to hold their savings more than they trusted banks. "They [department stores] don't give us anything, but at least they don't take anything away," some consumers noted, in reference to the various fees and hidden charges banks levied on their savings accounts. One consumer reported that "dormancy" and other charges had reduced the value of her bank savings account from 15,000 Mexican pesos to 9,000 over three years.[14]

Public policy can help broaden the use of financial tools

Experience teaches that direct policy interventions in the financial sector can have unintended consequences and distort proper incentives, especially with regard to shared responsibility for risk management. Prime examples of possibly distortive interventions include credit subsidies and guarantees.[15] Political capture and lobbying have often led to misallocation of credit within the economy, and poorly designed financial literacy programs have often failed to deliver desired results, become quickly obsolete, or built up false confidence of consumers in their financial skills.[16] Many small developing economies lack adequate financial infrastructure, which cannot be viably developed by the private sector because of the small scale of the market. Thus the infrastructure must be developed with the participation of the state, possibly through private-public partnerships, to enable greater financial inclusion and development.[17] Even where access to financial services exists, sound financial inclusion may be endangered by a lack of consumer protection regarding delivery of the services.[18]

What can public policy do to broaden the availability and use of financial tools to manage risk? Lessons from experience, as well as the conceptual framework of this Report, suggest the following:

Minimize unintended consequences of policy interventions.

- Direct public interventions should be implemented sparingly and be carefully designed to avoid distorting incentives and undermining risk management efforts of the financial firms and their clients. In some cases, subsidies and public guarantees could be useful to encourage take-up of private insurance, thereby shifting some of the government's contingent liabilities to private insurers: possibilities include agricultural, health, or pension insurance (see box 6.3).
- The state should implement well-designed and well-targeted financial education programs to ensure the cost-effectiveness of its intervention and avoid unintended results. To overcome these problems, the state should consider incorporating financial examples in regular public education curricula and partnering with the private sector to ensure proper design, implementation, and continuity of financial education programs.[19]

Help overcome obstacles to introducing useful, innovative financial instruments.

- Other direct interventions may be desirable. The state can help viable innovative financial products achieve scale and increase financial inclusion by, for example, introducing government-to-person (G2P) payments (as in India's NREGA G2P program),[20] making car or mortgage insurance mandatory, or requiring that large transactions or tax-deductible expenses be made with electronic payments. In seeking the best solutions to advance financial inclusion, the state should consider partnering with the private sector (see boxes 6.3 and 6.4).
- Improving infrastructure is particularly important for payment and security settlement systems, credit information infrastructure (public credit registries and credit bureaus), and collateral frameworks (registries of movable and immovable collateral, collateral appraisal, execution and sale). In providing financial infrastructure, the state should partner with the private sector as much as possible to improve governance of the infrastructure providers, ensure timely upgrades of technology, and encourage continuous innovation. The 2013 *Doing Business* indicators suggest that the quality of collateral frameworks and the depth of credit information in developing countries are about 30 percent and 60 percent lower, respectively, than the quality and depth in advanced economies. Further, the state postal network could be used to house properly regulated financial agents, who could offer financial tools in an easily accessible manner, including in hard-to-reach neighborhoods and rural areas.

Provide the right incentives, and heighten confidence in financial institutions.

- The state should provide an enabling environment for market development by including a legal framework for electronic payments; by requiring the introduction of simple, low-cost bank accounts for vulnerable populations such as the poor and the young; and by allowing banks, nonbank financial institutions, and electronic payment providers to compete against each other in similar market segments where appropriate. For example, the Philippines allowed Mobile Network Operators to take on many banking operations.[21]

- Regulatory reforms should focus on setting up an effective consumer protection framework that includes proper enforcement and dispute resolution mechanisms, such as a financial ombudsman (both Mexico and South Africa have established financial ombudsmen to resolve disputes in consumer finance).[22] A key goal is to instill trust in financial institutions, including through adequate insurance of retail deposits and improved quality of microprudential supervision. Microprudential and business conduct regulation should cover—using differentiated supervisory regimes—nonbank deposit-taking financial firms, such as saving houses, co-ops, and credit unions; nonfinancial firms that provide credit at the point of sale; microcredit and microinsurance companies; and payment and remittance services providers.[23]

Build in information gathering and learning from impact evaluations of reforms.

- The state should also develop data collection frameworks to continually assess gaps in financial inclusion and monitor and evaluate reforms. An example is Mexico's strategy of comprehensive data collection to better understand all challenges in access to finance; the data inform policy decisions, influence the business models of providers, and monitor progress. In 2011, the National Households Survey of Financial Services Usage was launched—and is to be repeated every three years—to understand household motivation for using financial services, as well as barriers to greater usage.[24]

Enable the poor to break out of poverty traps by offering financial tools fitted to their needs.

- When developing financial tools to help the poor, policy makers and microfinanciers should keep in mind the elements of reliability, convenience, flexibility, and structure. The great challenge of living on $2 a day is that even those $2 do not always come.[25] So second best to having reliable income is having reliable financial partners and portfolios. Convenience and flexibility are also important because the poor need to be able to deposit and withdraw savings and take out and repay loans frequently, close to home, and without obstacles. They need flexibility in building long-term savings so that short-term difficulties do not prevent them from benefiting from the advantages of a saving account (such as forgoing interest caused by delays in depositing money). Similarly, flexible loan schedules that can be readily renegotiated or forborne in "hungry months" and prepaid when extra liquidity arrives are very useful to the poor. Finally, providing some structure helps sustain self-discipline and commitment: for instance, through planned savings and loan repayments schedules, supported by visits from microfinance workers. Microfinance institutions and some mainstream financial institutions could learn many useful lessons for expanding their client base and searching for new and sustainable business opportunities by looking at the successful programs run by nongovernmental organizations to improve financial inclusion of the poor and the extreme poor.[26]

When financial inclusion works, it promotes development and helps alleviate poverty. But when financial inclusion is excessive or risks in the financial system are mismanaged, financial crises can erupt with large costs to entire societies (cartoon 6.1). The origins, impacts, and ways to avoid or manage financial crises are discussed next.

CARTOON 6.1 Finance can help but also hurt.
© Matt Cartoon, *The Daily Telegraph*, January 18, 2009

Financial crises hurt people: How can they be prevented?

Financial crises hurt people directly and indirectly

Banking crises can affect people's wealth, human capital, income, health, and even safety. By one measure, the average loss of output during banking crises in the past four decades has been substantial in both advanced countries (32.9 percent of GDP) and emerging economies (26 percent).[27] The average loss was much smaller in low-income countries (1.6 percent of real GDP), most likely because the penetration of financial services is low. Europe and Central Asia were especially affected by the 2008 wave of banking crises; about 62 percent of households in the region suffered a negative income shock mainly as a result of wage reduction (job loss, lower wage, or lower remittances). The costly coping strategies deployed by households to cope with this income shock included cuts in basic consumption, health care, and education.[28]

Financial shocks such as banking crises hurt people through four channels: the financial system, labor markets, product markets, and social services. Evidence from 147 banking crises in 116 countries from 1970 to 2011 suggests that the impact of banking crises is transmitted to households most strongly through the labor market channel.[29] The impact through the credit market seems to be less important. Only when banking crises coincide with currency crises (large local currency depreciations) are large changes in relative prices transmitted through the product market channel, where they affect urban households more than rural households. As for the social services channel, evidence from the Russian Federation suggests that the public sector cushioned rather than aggravated the impact of the 1998 banking, currency, and sovereign debt crisis.

Macroeconomic policy, the structure and infrastructure of the financial sector, and the design of formal safety nets play critical roles in amplifying or mitigating the propagation of financial crises to people. Household characteristics and microeconomic systems also play a crucial role. Evidence indicates that the most important mitigators of income shocks transmitted to households through the labor market channel are diversified household income, access to informal credit, and the buildup of a stock of durable consumption goods. Access to informal credit was an important microeconomic mitigator of the impact of the 2008 crisis in emerging and developing economies but not in advanced economies. In countries in which the banking crisis was accompanied by a sharp currency devaluation (Hungary, Ukraine), the accumulation of foreign currency debt (euros, Swiss francs) by some households before the crisis may have amplified the impact of income shocks.[30]

Access to and the use of formal financial tools can also help people cope better with the impact of financial crises. In the 2008 banking crises, among households in Europe and Central Asia suffering income shocks, those that did not have a bank account or access to bank credit used costly coping strategies much more often (by 14 to 16 percent) than households that had such tools.

In banking crises, income redistribution effects between the wealthy and the poor can be large. For example, wealthy investors tend to be better informed and are able to liquidate their position first and limit their losses. Further, wealthy individuals tend to receive favorable treatment or evade controls imposed during crises. Moreover, large financial transfers and opportunities for arbitrage emerge during crises, which allow investors with deep pockets to purchase assets at deep discounts and make large profits.

How does systemic risk turn into a financial crisis?

Systemic risk builds up over the financial cycle. The financial system is naturally procyclical. Procyclicality can originate from the behavior of financial intermediaries or from the procyclicality of the real economy.[31] Financial cycles are strongly related to business cycles. Notably, collapsing housing prices coincide with longer and deeper recessions, while rapid growth in credit and increases in housing prices coincide with stronger recoveries. Moreover, financial cycles are highly synchronized within a country (credit and housing price cycles) and across countries (credit and equity cycles). Not only do the financial and real cycles move together but banking crises can spill over to macroeconomic (sovereign debt or currency) crises, such as in Malaysia in 1997, or be triggered by a spillover from macroeconomic crises, such as in Russia in 1998.

Banking crises in Colombia (1982), Thailand (1997), and Ukraine (2008) were preceded by excessive credit growth of 40 percent, 25 percent, and 70 percent a year, respectively.[32] Accordingly, a major concern for all countries is provision of the right amount of "equilibrium" credit: not too much and not too little. International standard setters have proposed estimating equilibrium credit as the trend in the credit-to-GDP ratio, obtained through statistical filtering. Although such an approach can seem simple and transparent, its purely statistical nature disregards fundamental changes in equilibrium credit caused by economic and financial developments. To strike a better balance between financial development and stability, the academic literature has proposed structural frameworks to account for the impact of development on equilibrium credit.[33]

Banking systems in developing countries can incur additional exposures to systemic risk. Large investment needs alongside short-term and often small domestic savings add to systemic risk because banks can finance only short term (generally 6 to 12 months) compared with the investment financing needs of the real economy (typically, 7 to 8 years, with a 2-year grace period). Using foreign savings to obtain longer-term financing can expose the banking sector to aggregate refinancing risks, and the banks or the borrowers to foreign currency mismatches between their assets and liabilities (figure 6.4). Another, often neglected, systemic risk for small developing economies comes from lending that is concentrated in a small number of borrowers or sectors of the real economy. In early stages of development, countries initially specialize as they open to foreign trade, which naturally concentrates lending in fewer economic sectors. The economic structure diversifies only later when countries reach higher income levels. Lending concentration can also arise because of an underdeveloped financial infrastructure, related-party lending, pyramid ownership schemes, and overall lack of competition in the financial system.[34]

Interconnectedness can transform the risk from a single institution (idiosyncratic risk) into systemic risk. On the one hand, interconnectedness of financial institutions can have a positive impact on financial development because it promotes greater completeness of financial markets and better distribution of financial risks in normal times, including through innovative financial instruments, or derivatives. On the other hand, the interconnected balance sheets of financial firms, through their participation in joint financial infrastructure, can spread a shock throughout the national and even international financial system and sometimes amplify those shocks.[35] Adverse shocks can originate from problems in one systemic institution or from exposure of many financial firms to a single asset class, such as commercial real estate. The interconnectedness and common exposures of the U.S and European banks transmitted the 2007 U.S. subprime mortgage crisis first to Europe, and then, through the links between European parent banks and their subsidiaries and branches, to emerging Europe. Two aspects of interconnectedness are especially

FIGURE 6.4 ***Banks' aggregate refinancing risk and foreign currency mismatches can increase systemic risk in developing countries***

a. Europe and Central Asia's unusually heavy reliance on foreign savings

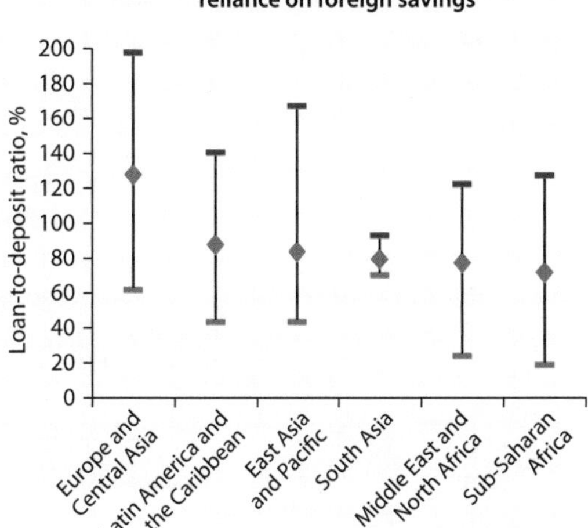

b. Foreign currency mismatches on bank balance sheets around the world

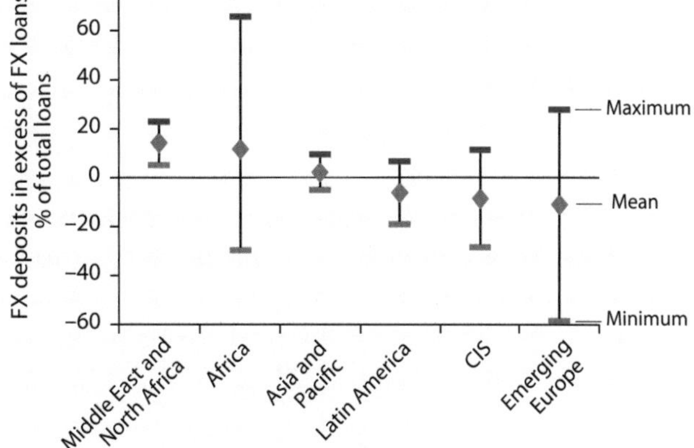

Source: WDR 2014 team based on data from World Bank FinStats (internal database) (panel a) and Chitu 2012 (panel b).

Note: Data for panel a are as of end-2008. Regions in panel b are grouped as in Chitu 2012, with data as of end-2006. CIS = Commonwealth of Independent States. FX = foreign currency.

important for developing countries: banks' ties to the shadow banking system, and cross-border banking.

In developing countries, the shadow banking sector comprises financial firms focused on providing alternative sources of financing to the economy.[36] These firms include leasing and factoring companies, credit unions, cooperatives, microfinance companies, and pawn shops. In Thailand, the sector covers nearly 40 percent of the financial system, while in Bulgaria, its share grew rapidly by 14 percentage points from 2003 to 2010. The concerns about shadow banking relate to regulatory arbitrage (lending through firms with the lowest capital requirements), mostly among banks and nonbank credit institutions. Developing countries need to ensure that shadow banks help provide alternative but safe financial services, without generating unacceptable systemic risks. In addition, other modes of finance such as Islamic banking (and insurance) have grown into systemic importance in some countries (such as Saudi Arabia, United Arab Emirates, and Malaysia), even though they account for only about 1.5 percent of global banking assets, or $0.9 trillion in 2011. While Islamic banks could be less cost-effective compared with conventional banks, they tend to be better capitalized, have higher asset quality, and be less likely to disintermediate during crises.[37]

Financial globalization, involving cross-border activities of banks, has been accompanied by many benefits, including protecting domestic economies from domestic shocks. From 2002 to 2012, the funds provided by banks from advanced economies to banks in developing countries increased from about $0.4 trillion to $1.7 trillion, translating into an average inflow of $130 billion a year.[38] By 2012, the global systemically important financial institutions (G-SIFIs) had 71 systemically important subsidiaries or branches (local SIFIs) in 43 developing countries. Brazil, Mexico, Peru, and Uruguay have the greatest systemic links to G-SIFIs, with six, four, four, and four local SIFIs linked to G-SIFIs, respectively.[39] This growing exposure to advanced economies can also pose potential dangers for financial stability, including exposing the domestic economy to foreign shocks. For instance, in response to a negative shock in the home country, foreign banks may decide to curtail lending or withdraw from the host country entirely. Many countries have managed such risk by requiring foreign banks to operate through an incorporated subsidiary with its own capital, rather than through a branch. Regional policy efforts to manage cross-border banking risk include the Vienna Initiative, which prevented regional banking groups from withdrawing liquid funds from Central and Eastern Europe in 2009.[40]

Possibility of contagion can further amplify systemic risk. Contagion typically relates to the breakdown in confidence as systemic risk materializes; contagion can cause runs on bank deposits, freezes of money and asset markets, or both. A recent example is the collapse of Lehman Brothers in 2008, which shattered confidence in money market mutual funds. Four days after Lehman's bankruptcy, the U.S. government was forced to announce guarantees for the entire sector. In developing countries, contagion risk relates mainly to depositor confidence. Because banks finance their long-term, illiquid assets with demandable debt in the form of first-come, first-serve deposits, depositors can consider them inherently unstable. Bank runs can occur when depositors fear others will withdraw before they do, leaving nothing for them. Important contagion effects for developing countries can also arise in the context of cross-border banking.[41]

Where did financial firms and past public policies fail the most?

Recently, bad corporate governance, distorted private incentives, short-term horizons for profit maximization, and coordination failures have resulted in excessive risk taking.[42] Financial firms have been largely unsuccessful in implementing good corporate governance, so the prevailing perverse incentives, including bad compensation policies, led bankers (from managers to loan officers) to maximize short-term profits and disregard prudent risk. Bank managers generally lack adequate personal responsibility for taking too much financial risk and are not held legally accountable for their bad practices. Further, financial firms, including SIFIs, ignored their own contributions (negative externalities) to systemic risk, and market discipline failed to enforce consideration of these externalities. Transparency and clear disclosure of information are important to achieve proper incentives, but for the most part the financial system has not implemented these mechanisms. In this environment, investors (bond holders and equity holders) failed to perform their basic monitoring and disciplining functions to correct the incentives of financial firms.

Some public policies have distorted private sector incentives for managing risk responsibly, have lacked a systematic approach, and have aided moral hazard behavior. Regulatory failures raise questions about the appropriate level of government involvement in the operation of the financial system. Supervisors have failed to measure banks' risks accurately or to set and enforce sufficient capital requirements for banks to be able to absorb unexpected losses reliably. Supervisors have also failed to design and enforce timely resolution of failing banks, which would limit the exposure of taxpayers to problem SIFIs.[43] The ineffective resolution frameworks for SIFIs have led to expectations of government bailouts. The SIFIs have thus tended to privatize their profits and socialize their losses. Moreover, various public guarantees and subsidies (implicit and explicit, including for lending to households) have distorted the incentives for risk management of both banks and their clients. Most recently, the regulatory uncertainty caused by the failure of governments in several developed countries to promptly decide on, coordinate, and implement financial sector reforms held back operations of the financial system and the recovery of the real economy. Too much has been expected of government regulation and supervisory capacity, in many cases. More selective policy interventions, minimizing unintended consequences, would be more appropriate, in some instances.

Making macroprudential regulators independent and giving them adequate policy tools are the basics for successful management of systemic risk.

Moreover, some public policies regulating systemic risk have been subject to capture by the financial industry.[44] The observations from the 2008 global financial crisis suggest significant influence of the industry lobby on the supervision of systemic risk, resolution of the crisis, and future regulatory reforms. The enduring challenge is to create mechanisms that can negate the "grabbing hand" of the financial industry and politicians, while creating strong incentives for official agencies to improve social welfare.[45] Making regulators politically and financially independent is the first step in this direction.

What are the best-practice policies for managing systemic risk and banking crises?

Pursue macroprudential policy. Macroprudential policy seeks to foster financial stability by managing systemic risk and keeping it at a socially acceptable level. Such policy is needed because policy measures focusing on the financial stability of financial institutions and their actions at the individual level are insufficient to foster financial stability at the aggregate level. The actions of individual financial firms can generate negative externalities that can allow systemic risk to build up. Moreover, monetary and fiscal policies can be ineffective in managing systemic risks in the financial system, especially in developing countries.

Central banks (as in the Czech Republic, South Africa, and Thailand) seem to be best equipped to assume the responsibility for macroprudential policy.[46] First, they have an advantage in monitoring macroeconomic developments. Second, centralizing macroprudential supervision in the central bank improves coordination of crisis management activities, especially if the central bank is also the banking sector regulator. Third, monetary policy decisions undertaken by the central bank have potential implications for financial leverage (debt load) and risk taking. As an emerging best practice, implementation of macroprudential policy is being conducted by macroprudential policy committees—an analog to monetary policy committees (for example, the macroprudential committee of the Bank of England).[47]

Choose the right indicators of systemic risk. To assess and monitor systemic risk, the macroprudential supervisor uses analytical tools, such as stress tests, early warning models, and assessments of systemic importance. Systemic risk assessment and monitoring need to be forward-looking, timely, and presented in a user-friendly way to ensure that policy makers act on the information received. Macroprudential stress tests are "what if" scenario exercises to assess the resilience of the system as a whole to extreme but plausible shocks.[48] Early warning models and assessments of systemic importance are less common in developing countries that are still working on building and using practical approaches to stress testing. From the points of view of practicality and accountability, monitoring a selected set of simple and robust financial indicators could be preferable to a more complex approach involving composite indicators or outputs from complex models.[49] Central banks often publish these systemic risk assessments as part of their financial stability reports to alert market participants, inform the public, and increase accountability of the macroprudential supervisors.[50]

Calibrate macroprudential tools to the specifics of the country. To manage systemic risk, macroprudential

TABLE 6.1 *A taxonomy of macroprudential tools*

Selected measures	Main characteristics	Country examples
Aimed at borrowers		
Loan-to-value caps	Reduces vulnerability arising from highly geared borrowing	Brazil; Bulgaria; Canada; Chile; China; Colombia; Croatia; France; Hong Kong SAR, China; Hungary; India; Italy; Korea, Rep.; Malaysia; Mexico; Norway; Philippines; Poland; Romania; Singapore; Spain; Sweden; Thailand; Turkey
Debt-to-income caps	Reduces vulnerability arising from highly geared borrowing	China; Colombia; Hong Kong SAR, China; Korea, Rep.; Poland; Romania; Serbia
Aimed at financial institutions (addressing the asset side)		
Credit growth caps	Reduces credit growth directly	China, Colombia, Malaysia, Nigeria, Serbia, Singapore
Foreign currency lending limits	Reduces vulnerability to foreign exchange risks; reduces credit growth directly	Argentina, Austria, Brazil, Hungary, Poland, Romania, Serbia, Turkey
Aimed at financial institutions (addressing the liabilities side)		
Reserve requirements	Reduces vulnerability to funding risks; reduces credit growth indirectly	Brazil, Bulgaria, China, Colombia, Russian Federation
Aimed at financial institutions (addressing bank buffers)		
Dynamic loan-loss provisioning	Increases resilience and reduces credit growth indirectly	Brazil, Bulgaria, Colombia, India, Mongolia, Peru, Russian Federation, Spain, Uruguay
Countercyclical capital requirements	Increases resilience and reduces credit growth indirectly	Brazil, India
Profit distribution restrictions	Limits dividend payments in good times to help build up capital buffers in bad times	Argentina, Colombia, Poland, Romania, Slovak Republic, Turkey

Source: WDR 2014 team based on Claessens, Ghosh, and Mihet, forthcoming.
Note: Countries listed in the table adopted corresponding macroprudential tools in various years from 2000 to 2010, some of them temporarily.

supervisors use policy tools such as variable capital buffers and dynamic provisioning, as well as caps on leverage, credit growth, and the debt-to-income ratio (table 6.1).[51] The use of macroprudential policy tools has been increasing, particularly in managing systemic risk in the financial sector. Macroprudential tools, such as capital controls, could also be used more broadly in the context of macroeconomic management (chapter 7). Interestingly, emerging markets have been three to four times more likely to use macroprudential tools than advanced economies.[52] For instance, in 2011, the Republic of Korea imposed a levy of up to 0.2 percent on bank noncore financial liabilities to manage speculative inflows of foreign capital.[53] Some macroprudential tools are intended to mitigate externalities that occur in the upturn of the financial cycle, while others are deployed to build buffers to mitigate any bust. For example, caps on debt-to-income and loan-to-value ratios could be effective in reducing risk exposures in booms, while countercyclical buffers, such as additional capital and reserve requirements, could help mitigate excessive deleveraging in severe downturns. In any case, the use of macroprudential tools needs to be calibrated to the specifics of a given country.[54]

Focus on crisis preparedness for effective management of future financial crises. In crises, policy makers face deep uncertainty about market conditions. They must be able to mobilize expertise to decide and act, transparently deploy legislated crisis management tools, communicate with the public to contain uncertainty, and ensure adequate loss sharing to avoid moral hazard going forward (box 6.5). The resolution of banking crises will always be country specific because of differences in legal framework, but resolution should not compromise the bottom line of minimizing the fiscal cost and avoiding moral hazard in the future. Concerns of widespread liquidity runs on banks usually mean that blanket guarantees are given to all bank creditors. While liquidity assistance to banks needs to be provided early on, open-ended liquidity support has proven to prolong crises and could result in future macroeconomic risks (chap-

BOX 6.5 *Preparing for a banking crisis with crisis simulation exercises*

To test crisis preparedness and practice using existing or proposed arrangements for crisis management, the World Bank, since 2009, has been encouraging financial policy makers to participate in financial crisis simulation exercises. During the exercise, participants receive a stream of (generally bad) news describing the "scenario" they must deal with and the tools provided by their (real or assumed) legal, regulatory, and operational frameworks. This news arrives in two forms: as "public information," understood to be simultaneously available to all participant teams (including financial sector supervisory authorities, the central bank, the finance ministry, and the deposit insurer) and the market; and as "private information" from several fictional characters (analysts, bank inspectors, advisers, bankers, journalists, foreign authorities, politicians). Participants must share their respective pieces of information and analyses to understand the scenario and coordinate their actions.

Areas for improvement are identified through exhaustive analysis of the exchanges that take place among the participants (typically running into the hundreds of written memos and e-mails), as well as between them and the fictitious characters.

While comparisons and generalizations are difficult, given the small sample size and highly localized conditions (reflected both in the institutional identity of the participating teams and the situations proposed by the fictional scenario), it is nonetheless possible to offer tentative impressions about the adequacy of participant responses to some common challenges and about the way participants tend to underestimate and underreact, or overestimate and overreact, to bad news:

- Most participants—often the nation's top decision makers—take these exercises quite seriously, typically spending one or more days fully concentrating on them. Their actions tend to be conditioned by whether they perceive the exercise as a (perhaps imposed) "test" or as a (freely requested) "drill." Ownership of the exercise by the participating public representatives is thus crucial for the success of the exercise.
- Public representatives frequently overestimate parent bank or shareholder capacity and willingness to provide support. This overestimation then typically leads to public agencies' inaction before and during the crisis, and protracted coping and recovery from the crisis.
- Formal arrangements to share information and coordinate action tend to spring up voluntarily and ignore possible conflicts of interest.
- Simple information sharing is much more common than joint analysis of all relevant information by all responsible parties.
- Governments tend to postpone decisions on resolution of problem banks—including restructuring, recapitalization, merger, closure, or liquidation—by implicitly or explicitly nationalizing them.
- Coordination of public communications is limited, if not entirely absent.

Some of the judgment and behavior observed in the exercises reveals cognitive and behavioral failures in policy-making decisions and actions in the face of risk, as discussed in chapter 2.

Source: Aquiles A. Almansi for the WDR 2014.

ter 7).[55] Emergency liquidity assistance from the central bank should be provided only to solvent banks.[56] Insolvent banks should be closed transparently to avoid moral hazard in the future. Prompt interventions can reduce costs and improve efficiency.[57]

Seek private sector solutions to pass bank losses to existing shareholders, managers, and in some cases uninsured creditors first. For systemwide crises, finding domestic private sector solutions could be difficult, and reliance on foreign takeovers or government-assisted mergers may be needed. The fiscal cost of banking crises averaged almost 7 percent of GDP during 1970–2011 (4 and 10 percent of GDP in advanced and developing countries, respectively). The two costliest banking crises occurred in Indonesia (1997) and Argentina (1980), with fiscal costs reaching 57 and 55 percent of GDP, respectively.[58] Overall, government interventions and assistance in managing banking crises need to be based on a sound legal framework to avoid ad hoc interventions outside the existing legal framework, which can have large redistribution effects. Countries must devote time and resources to preparing such frameworks in normal times because crises are not likely to go away.

Resolve failures of systematically important financial institutions fairly and effectively. Failing SIFIs must be resolved promptly in the view of the trade-off between minimizing negative spillovers to the rest of the financial system and minimizing future moral hazard, while protecting taxpayers' money (box 6.6). To improve the resilience of global and national SIFIs, recent proposals recommend that SIFIs hold more capital and other instruments that can promptly increase their capacity to absorb losses and mitigate the possibility of negative spillovers to the rest of the financial system in advance.[59] To further enhance crisis preparation, SIFIs should be required to prepare so-called "living wills" to assist the management and the authorities in prompt resolution of failing SIFIs, including through partitioning and sales. Resolution could also involve the injection of public capital or other government support, provided that sufficient fiscal space exists for such contingent liabilities, that costs to taxpayers are minimized, and that large re-

BOX 6.6 *Financial bailouts: "Too big to fail" versus moral hazard*

Domestic systemic banks are banks whose failure or severe problems might generate significant negative externalities for the rest of the domestic financial system and the economy. While in many cases banks of systemic importance can be identified ex ante using appropriate assessment methodology, it is hard to assess ex ante which banks will not be systemically important in stressed market conditions. Thus if a bank is in trouble, policy makers first need to determine whether the bank is systemically important in current market conditions, with a view to available legal resolution options and fiscal space, political economy factors, and uncertainty about possible spillovers to the financial system and the real economy.[a] This box focuses on systemic banks with insolvency problems after those banks have exhausted all possible insurance and protection measures arranged ex ante, such as capital buffers, bail-in or contingent debt, or sale of assets.

Available resolution options are an important factor shaping the possibility frontier of resolving systemic banks (panel a). Market solutions are preferable at all times and may include indirect support (mergers forced by the supervisor) or direct support from the government (purchase and assumption, with credit enhancement from the deposit insurance fund). However, if the market is small or in distress, private sector solutions may not be available. In contrast, injecting public capital into failing systemic banks may be fiscally unsustainable, counterproductive by increasing moral hazard, and potentially inequitable by introducing large redistribution effects, benefiting shareholders or creditors of the failing bank at the expense of taxpayers. Other resolution options, which are preferable in certain market conditions, include establishing a bridge bank so that the systemic part of failing bank is transferred to a new entity owned by the ministry of finance and operated by the bank supervisor or resolution agency, with little or no permanent support of public capital.[b]

If public funds are used in systemic bank resolution, political economy constraints become an even more important factor shaping the possibility frontier (panel a) because the legislature or the ministry of finance that provides public capital get involved in the decision making. The decision about the resolution method, timing of the intervention, and its particular execution (placing government deposits in the bank, nationalizing it, or using the bridge bank) will be influenced by politicians and the political lobby.[c] For systemic banks, the least-cost solution must consider the cost to society rather than the deposit insurance fund (bank resolution agency), given the likely spillover of the problem to the real economy.

The possibility frontier of systemic bank resolution

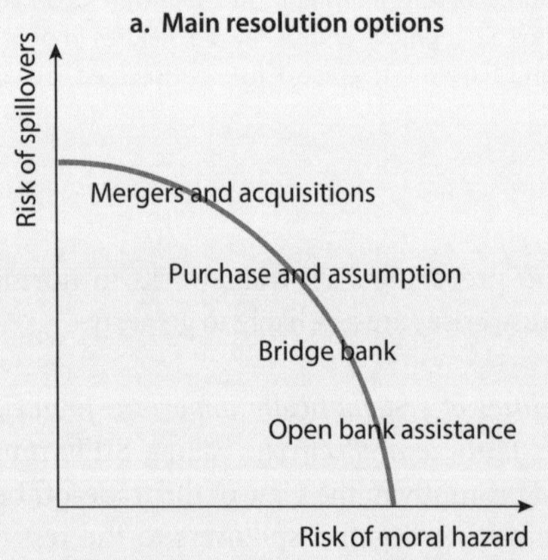

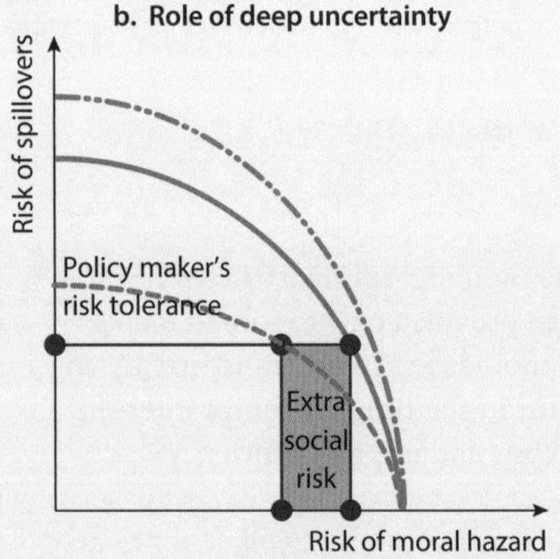

Source: WDR 2014 team based on Beck 2011.

In times of financial stress, policy makers face the additional challenge of deep uncertainty about negative spillovers that can be triggered by the closure of a systemic bank. They typically have some idea about the trade-offs, thanks to prior systemic risk and resolvability assessments (solid line, panel b). However, if such assessments are not being performed, policy makers can underestimate the real spillover potential, represented by the upper dashed line. To complicate matters, financial firms do not fully share all private information. In times of stress, they can use this information asymmetry to their advantage to lobby for higher public support than would be appropriate. This private information, if revealed, could show that the spillover potential is much smaller in reality, as depicted by the lower dashed line. Unnecessarily large bailouts using public money then reinforce moral hazard and result in larger redistribution effects, to the detriment of market discipline and taxpayers (shaded area depicting extra social risk, panel b).

Resolution of Turkey's 2001 systemic banking crisis through a public recapitalization program provides some elements of good practice in the presence of a too-important-to-fail and too-many-to-fail problem. The Turkish crisis started from mounting weaknesses in the banking system and collapse in investor confidence after the fall of a medium-sized bank. A successful design of the 2002 public recapitalization program prevented misuse of public funds through strict eligibility criteria, an in-depth audit to transparently disclose capital shortfalls, and the mandatory participation of bank owners in recapitalization. Between 1997 and 2004, 21 banks

(continued)

BOX 6.6 *Financial bailouts: "Too big to fail" versus moral hazard* **(continued)**

representing about 20 percent of banking sector assets were transferred to the bank resolution agency, and all but one bank were resolved through mergers, sales, and liquidation by 2004. The efforts of Turkish authorities to minimize the fiscal costs of the restructuring program and future moral hazard have contributed to greater self-reliance and self-discipline on the part of the Turkish banking sector, including improvements in bank risk management. This in turn underpinned the resilience of the Turkish banking sector to the spillovers from the 2008 global financial crisis.[d]

Systemic banks are likely to experience troubles in the future, especially if system-wide financial stresses emerge. Governments should therefore be well prepared to resolve troubled systemic banks while minimizing moral hazard and redistribution effects. Developing a legal framework for resolving systemic banks, preparing recovery and resolution plans (living wills) for banks of systemic importance in any market conditions, and preparing systemic risk assessment approaches to determine systemic importance of banks in specific market conditions should be essential parts of any crisis preparedness efforts. In particular, recovery plans can help increase the resilience of systemic banks and their ability to recover from stresses, thus indirectly enhancing overall financial stability.[e] To address political economy issues, decisions about troubled systemic banks should be broad-based, and involve the banking supervisor, resolution agency, central bank (the financial stability supervisor), and ministry of finance. The right platform for such decisions can be the financial stability committee (table 6.3), in which all these agencies typically participate. In addition, if the impact of resolving a domestic systemic bank crosses national borders, such as the case of the Icelandic bank Kaupthing, the resolution will require cross-country or regional coordination.[f]

Source: WDR 2014 team.

a. BIS 2012.
b. Beck 2011.
c. Brown and Dinc 2005.
d. Josefsson 2006.
e. BIS 2012.
f. BIS 2010b.

distribution effects are avoided. Another option is to close the SIFI and transfer its systemically important part to a temporary bridge bank, owned, managed, and then sold in a timely manner by public authorities.[60]

Reduce regulatory uncertainty. Regulatory uncertainty can paralyze recovery from a crisis. Government interventions to manage banking crises could have large repercussions for the government fiscal position and redistribution effects from taxpayers to creditors and shareholders (consider the Euro Area crisis resolution, for instance).[61] For this reason, the government could be forced to reset its tax policy and reform financial regulation as it learns about the causes of the crisis. This process could involve many stakeholders and might need to be coordinated at the regional or international level. As a result, regulatory reforms could be protracted and their outcomes very uncertain. Banks uncertain about how much capital and liquidity they will need to hold will curtail their lending. Investors will hold back their projects because once they take into account the uncertainty about future taxes and the cost of finance, most projects will become financially unviable. Thus tax and regulatory reforms in response to crises need to be timely and decisive to ease recovery. For that to happen, improved coordination at the national, regional, and international level needs to be established and put into practice.

Resolving the tension between financial development and financial stability

Important complementarities and trade-offs exist between boosting financial inclusion and fostering financial stability (cartoon 6.2). This section focuses on these complementarities and trade-offs, as well as on financial sector development and stability more generally.

Financial inclusion can aid stability

Greater financial inclusion can improve the efficiency and stability of financial intermediation by making greater and more diversified domestic savings available to banks. As a result, a country's banking system can ease its reliance on reversible foreign capital and thereby enhance its stability. Indeed, preliminary evidence suggests that a broader use of bank saving deposits made the banking systems of middle-income countries more resilient to deposit withdrawals and the slowdown in deposit growth during the 2008 crisis (figure 6.5a). Similarly, the performance of loan portfolios of Chilean banks suggests that aggregated losses on small loans present less systemic risk than large, infrequent, but also less predictable losses on large loans.[62] Thus greater financial inclusion and diversified credit allocation may coincide with greater stability of individual financial firms and of the entire

CARTOON 6.2 Trade-offs in financial sector policy pose a challenge.

© John Cole/*The (Scranton) Times-Tribune*

system. Greater financial inclusion can also enhance financial stability indirectly by providing households (and firms) with access to savings, credit, and insurance tools that can bolster resilience and stability of the real economy and thus the financial system that serves it.

If financial inclusion can enhance financial stability, can exclusion from formal financial services lead to greater instability? Households (and small firms) in countries with high levels of financial exclusion must rely on informal financial services that can be poor substitutes for formal services.[63] In extreme cases, informal services can increase people's risk exposure to shocks and be a source of instability themselves. For example, pyramid schemes organized as informal savings and investment opportunities have been known to trigger both political and social unrest and lack of confidence in the banking system.[64]

Stability is endangered when financial inclusion is excessive

Inclusion of everybody in each and every financial service cannot be the social objective. The U.S. subprime crisis showed that subsidized, excessive access to credit, combined with tolerated predatory lending, is bad policy. Similarly, in Russia, where consumer loans grew from about $10 billion in 2003 to more than $170 billion in 2008, people with low financial literacy underestimated the increased burden of debt-servicing costs in bad times, which significantly impaired their spending capacity.[65] Preliminary evidence suggests that excessive credit growth can impose heavy financial burdens on people when market conditions deteriorate (figure 6.5b). Households that purchase the "wrong" financial tools that add to their risk, whether a result of their own irresponsible risk taking or irresponsible delivery of financial services by financial firms, jeopardize their own financial stability—and collectively, possibly the stability of the financial system. Such risk exposures at the micro level can be mitigated by an adequate level of financial education and consumer protection. Financial tools with a risk profile matching that of the clients can improve outcomes in financial markets.

Stability is also impaired if the system tries to do more than its development permits

There appears to be a limit on how much and what services the financial system can provide to whom at a given stage of its development. This limit (a financial-possibility frontier) is affected by many development factors driving the provision of financial services on the supply side (financial system) and constraining participation on the demand side

FIGURE 6.5 ***Prudent financial inclusion can enhance financial stability but, if excessive, can weaken it***

a. Greater access to bank deposits can aid financial stability

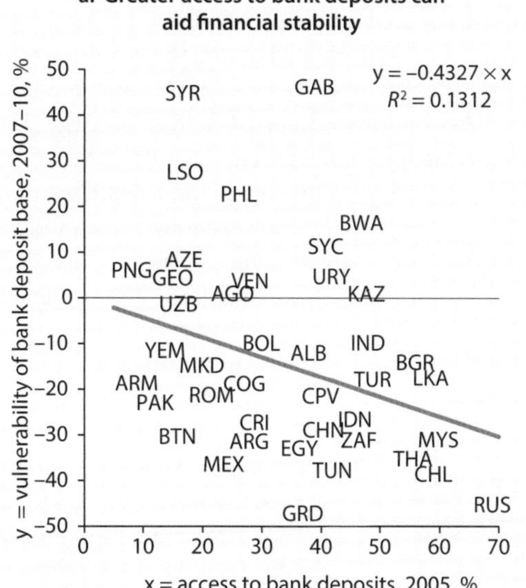

b. Excessive consumer credit can result in excessive indebtedness

y = 0.2649 × x
R^2 = 0.3544
GRC
BGR
ROM
ISL
LVA
HUN
ITA
ESP
SVK
AUT
POL
EST
LTU
NOR
SVN
CZE
PRT
BEL
DNK
y = household arrears on loan, 2010, %
x = annual growth in consumer credit, 2004–07, %

Source: WDR 2014 team based on data from Han and Melecky 2013 for the WDR 2014 (panel a); European Credit Research Institute Lending to Households in Europe (database), and European Union Statistics on Income and Living Conditions (EU-SILC) Survey (panel b).

Note: The solid (regression) lines in the figures depict the fitted linear relationships between the y- and x-axis variables. For panel a, the vulnerability of the bank deposit base is conditional on per capita income, bank z-score, occurrence of a banking crisis, and implemented explicit deposit insurance. For measurement of access to bank deposits, the composite index of access to financial services by Honohan 2008 was used. Regression results are available upon request. All middle-income countries for which data are available are included. For panel b, the countries are the EU-27 (excluding Ireland and Cyprus) plus Norway and Iceland. The arrears are on consumer loan repayments. The results hold if arrears are replaced by self-reported financial burden, or if the annual growth in consumer credit in 2004–07 is controlled for the size of subsequent bust in consumer credit in 2008–10.

(individuals and firms).[66] Following the concept of financial-possibility frontiers, countries can face three broad challenges. First, the frontier of a given country may be low relative to its level of economic development because of deficient structural factors (such as low population density or a high degree of economic informality) or nonstructural factors (such as inadequate contract enforcement or protection of property rights, or macroeconomic stability). Second, a country's financial system can be below its frontier because of demand constraints (such as self-exclusion stemming from low financial literacy and trust in banks) or supply-side constraints (such as lack of competition due to poor financial infrastructure or regulatory restrictions on new products). Third, a country's financial system can move beyond the frontier, expanding unsustainably through excessive investment and risk taking by market participants in environments of weak supervision, corporate governance, and market discipline. In such environments, financial innovation—which can promote financial deepening and inclusion in other contexts—could pose a challenge for financial stability, especially if it becomes self-interested and unnecessarily complex.

Bank competition can be beneficial if it improves financial inclusion, deepens financial markets, and generates useful innovative services at the acceptable level of systemic risk. More intense competition among banks can have positive effects on financial depth, income distribution, growth, and efficiency. At the same time, it can also negatively affect the stability of the banking system; with more pressure on profits, bankers have incentives to take excessive risks.[67] However, competitive lending rates reduce entrepreneurs' cost of borrowing and increase the success rate of entrepreneurs' investments. Banks, in turn, experience lower default rates on their loan portfolio, and the banking system as a whole enjoys greater stability. The role of regulatory frameworks could be critical in shaping the tension between bank competition and financial stability. Recent evidence, more attentive to systemic risk measurement, confirms that greater bank competition can be associated with greater financial stability.[68]

Policy, to succeed, must consider trade-offs and synergies in finance

At the level of the national government, the national financial sector strategy formulates the policy for the financial sector. A well formulated strategy should set development targets that take into account the systemic risk involved in achieving them and that communicate the systemic risk appetite (tolerance) of the country in the financial area. Preliminary evidence from a survey of national financial sector strategies indicates that most strategy documents have a clear statement of intent, but less than half have a quantifiable indicator included in their objective statements (table 6.2). Although most documents refer to systemic risk in general terms, very few refer to specific measures of systemic risk. With a few exceptions, the strategy implementation plans do not discuss specific trade-offs between financial development goals and the management of systemic risk, even though many countries commit to achieving both goals within the same strategy document. While the strategies include a rich numerical analysis of recent developments in the sector, the use of quantifiable data to specify their forward-looking objectives is weak. Instead of choices (which would lead to a discussion of trade-offs), conventional strategies tend to focus on issues.[69] Governments should instead adopt an approach that explicitly addresses policy trade-offs and begins by recognizing that the government must make choices and that each choice has consequences.

Financial policy must consider the synergies and trade-offs between promoting access to more and better financial tools and controlling systemic risk in the financial sector.

The national financial sector strategy should clearly assign implementation of the targeted financial development at the (identified) acceptable level of systemic risk to individual government agencies in accord with their mandate. For instance, the ministry of finance (or economy) could be responsible for financial development, while the central bank could be responsible for the supervision of systemic risk (as in Moldova). In their financial sector strategies, most countries broadly identify the implementing government agencies based on their overall mandates (table 6.2). Countries less often clearly assign specific agency responsibility for implementing measures to achieve development goals or to manage systemic risk at acceptable levels. Financial sector strategies should not only include such assignments in the implementation plan but should also present a mechanism through which the implementation will be coordinated, such as a standing committee.

A financial policy committee with an effective governance structure that includes major stakeholders in

TABLE 6.2 *National financial sector strategy documents rarely consider the trade-off between financial development and stability*

Development objectives	Clear development goals set	94
	Development goals quantified	42
	Tools to achieve goals identified	58
Systemic risk	Risk associated with achieving goals identified	94
	Systemic risk quantified	6
	Tools to manage systemic risk identified	53
Trade-off	Trade-off in development and systemic risk is communicated	11
Implementation plan	Agencies to execute the strategy identified	92
	Agencies to implement development goals assigned	64
	Agencies to manage systemic risk assigned	33

Source: WDR 2014 team based on Maimbo and Melecky 2013 for the WDR 2014.

Note: The table summarizes the percentage of countries meeting each requirement in a sample of 36 countries, consisting of six countries in each of the six regions: Latin America and the Caribbean, Sub-Saharan Africa, East Asia and Pacific, Europe and Central Asia, Middle East and North Africa, and South Asia.

TABLE 6.3 *Composition of financial stability committees in selected developing countries*

Country	Coordination body	Chair	Members
India	Financial Stability and Development Council	Minister of finance	CB, MOF, regulators for securities, insurance, and pension
Indonesia	Financial System Stability Coordination Forum	Minister of finance	CB, MOF, regulators for deposit insurance and financial services
Mexico	Financial Systemic Stability Council	Minister of finance	CB, MOF, regulators for securities and banking, insurance, pension and deposit insurance
Poland	Financial Stability Committee	Minister of finance	CB, MOF, and the regulator for financial services
South Africa	Financial Stability Oversight Committee (interim)	CB governor and minister of finance	CB, Treasury, and the regulator for financial services
Turkey	Financial Stability Committee	Deputy prime minister	CB, Treasury, regulators for banking, capital markets and deposit insurance

Source: WDR 2014 team based on information from the International Monetary Fund, national central banks, and ministries of finance.
Note: CB = central bank. MOF = ministry of finance.

financial sector policy, can improve policy coordination and produce balanced policies. To set compatible and sustainable policies, a group of policy makers and experts that understands the trade-offs between risk and development in the financial sector should be established. Many countries have established financial stability committees to manage systemic risk and crises, notably in the aftermath of the 2008 crisis (table 6.3). These committees are chaired by a high-level public official and include major policy makers in the financial area. It would be practical to extend a mandate to these high-level committees to prepare a holistic, national financial sector strategy, including with the participation of relevant experts from academia and the financial industry. Intermediate solutions also exist. For instance in Malaysia, the central bank engages with major stakeholders in financial sector policy, including the ministry of finance and private sector experts, to prepare a national financial sector strategy that takes into account tradeoffs between financial (inclusion) development and systemic risk in the financial system.

In implementing the financial sector strategy, some direct policy interventions (such as provision of financial infrastructure) could be beneficial, while others (support of state-owned banks, for example) could be controversial. Most public policies should be indirect and focused on proper regulation, because direct policy interventions can lead to unintended consequences, including large redistribution effects and distorted incentives in the private sector.[70] Coordination of policy implementation should also be the task of the proposed financial policy committee, which can revise the strategy periodically in light of new circumstances and newly identified gaps or policy tools concerning financial development and stability. In improving regulatory frameworks and adopting best practices in regulation, national policy makers are supported by international standard setters such as the Financial Stability Board, Basel Committee on Bank Supervision, International Association of Insurance Supervisors, and International Organization of Securities Commissions. The standard setters, apart from developing guidelines for best-practice regulation, provide assistance in building capacity, so that national regulators advance their knowledge and skills to further develop their national financial markets. At the regional level—closer to implementing regulatory frameworks—global best-practice guidelines could be elaborated on or turned into rules by regional standard setters. At the level of the European Union, these standard setters would include the European Systemic Risk Board, the European Banking Authority, European Securities and Markets Authority, and European Insurance and Occupational Pensions Authority.

Implementation should focus on enforcing good corporate governance to correct the incentives of financial firms and the financial system to take on excessive risk or pursue too much or too little financial inclusion, and to ensure that private decision making is governed by a long-term view and attention to business sustainability. Enforcing good standards of corporate governance pertains to both the development and offering of *useful*, *accessible*, and *reliable* financial services and to responsible risk taking that accounts for systemic externalities. The key areas to improve bank corporate governance include the following:[71]

- Boards should incorporate a balance of expertise to approve and monitor the overall business strategy of the bank, considering its long-term financial interests, exposure to risk, and ability to manage risk effectively.
- Senior management should ensure that bank activities are consistent with the bank's business strategy, risk appetite (tolerance), and policies approved by the board.
- Risk management, compliance, and internal audit functions should be established, each with sufficient authority, independence, resources, and access to the board.
- Compensation schemes should encourage an orientation to client needs, responsible provision of financial services and risk taking by the bank employees, and a long-term view in business conduct.[72]
- The board and senior management should understand and guide the bank's overall structure and its evolution, ensure that the structure is justified, and avoid undue complexity.
- Disclosure requirements should enhance accountability of banks to depositors, creditors, and other clients and stakeholders; for instance, key points on its governance structure and risk appetite should be clearly disclosed.

In addition, external auditors should monitor compliance with any mandatory or voluntary corporate governance codes adopted by the financial industry, and identify in their reports any gaps between the existing practice and the adopted code.

The jury is still out on the effects of bank (financial institutions) specialization versus diversification—for instance in lending—on financial development and stability. On the one hand, lending expertise gained through specialization in certain sectors can benefit banks by enhancing their screening and monitoring efficiency. On the other hand, diversification of lending risk across many sectors can enhance the stability of an individual bank by protecting it from correlated losses. At the system level, the impact of lending specialization as opposed to diversification could be critical. Diversified banks that look alike or purposely herd can actually reduce systemic stability.[73] Hence, from the system's perspective, promoting diversity among banks could be an important area of policy reforms. In this regard, promoting diverse business models, including that of Islamic banking, can increase the system's diversity along with greater financial inclusion. Furthermore, promoting diversity beyond the banking sector could be equally important and can involve insurance companies and nonbanking credit institutions.

Overall, public policy should encourage diversification of financial intermediation away from banks into capital markets to enhance the stability of the financial system. Recent evidence suggests that although bank lending to firms declined during the global crisis, bond financing actually increased to make up much of the gap in some countries.[74] Although banks may have practical advantage in developing countries, building local currency capital markets is desirable. Certain preconditions must be established, involving both the government and the private sector, such as adequate property rights, a legal framework, infrastructure (payment and security settlement systems), corporate governance, financial accounting standards, and a credible auditing industry. Some economies may still be far from establishing these preconditions, and some small economies may never generate the necessary scale. Still, firms in those countries could list on regional or global stock exchanges, and individual investors could access foreign capital markets through brokers or investment funds. Small economies with necessary preconditions in place and problems of small scale could consider developing local trading platforms integrated with regional or global stock exchanges—the way that Estonia, Latvia, and Lithuania integrated under the Baltic Stock Exchange. Regional and international initiatives have emerged to aid diversification of financial intermediation into capital markets. They include the 2003 Asian Bond Markets and Asian Bond Fund Initiatives; the 2008 Global Emerging Markets Local Currency Bond program of the World Bank; and the Vienna Initiative, a regional public-private coordination framework for development of local currency capital markets.

A summary of policy recommendations

This chapter has explored the tension between financial inclusion and stability and stressed that this tension must be addressed when financial sector policy is formulated and implemented. On the one hand, excessive and reckless financial inclusion can endanger financial stability. On the other hand, responsible financial inclusion can enhance the financial system's stability directly or indirectly through greater resil-

TABLE 6.4 ***Policy priorities to improve the financial system's role in risk management***

	POLICIES TO SUPPORT RISK MANAGEMENT FOUNDATIONAL → ADVANCED			
Knowledge	Collection and analysis of data on gaps in financial inclusion	Targeted financial education	IT solutions for better access to financial prices	
	System-wide collection of macroprudential data	Financial stability reports	Early warning models	
	Public communication of concerns about systemic risk and steps to resolve the crisis			
Protection	Legal frameworks and financial infrastructure	Consumer protection	G2P payments	Access to capital market instruments
	Independent financial regulators	Macroprudential regulation	Crisis preparedness frameworks	Crisis simulation exercises
	Corporate governance standards (for example, disclosure of ultimate controllers, risk management and internal controls, compensation policies)			
Insurance	Legal frameworks and financial infrastructure	Consumer protection	Compulsory insurance (for example, car, mortgage)	Fiscal insurance including PPPs
	Macroprudential capital buffers	Systemic risk surcharges	Foreign exchange reserves	Fiscal contingent liabilities
Coping	Contract enforcement	Efficient insolvency regimes and bad debt workouts	Preserved access to credit	Consumer protection
	Failing bank resolution	Emergency liquidity assistance	Blanket deposit guarantees	Lending guarantees

Source: WDR 2014 team.

Note: The table presents a sequencing of policies based on the guidance of chapter 2 for establishing policy priorities: *be realistic* in designing policies tailored to the institutional capacity of the country, and *build a strong foundation* that addresses the most critical obstacles sustainably, and that can be improved over time. G2P = government to person. IT = information technology. PPPs = public-private partnerships.

ience of the financial system's clients (individuals, firms, the state). In practice, middle-income countries face the greatest tension between allowing rapid financial inclusion and fostering financial stability. Low-income countries cannot mobilize as much savings from households that are often constrained in their consumption. Nor are low-income countries well-enough integrated into global finance to import large amounts of foreign savings. In contrast, financial inclusion in high-income countries approaches 90 to 100 percent, and high-income countries focus mainly on fostering financial stability.

Table 6.4 summarizes policy recommendations to promote financial inclusion and enhance financial stability in view of this tension. The recommendations are grouped according to the main components of effective risk management (knowledge, protection, insurance, and coping) and follow a foundational approach from the most needed to advanced measures in support of risk management. To broaden the availability and use of financial tools for managing risk, public policy should focus on overcoming obstacles related to financial infrastructure, the small scale of the market, and adoption of innovative financial instruments. The state should promote competition among different types of financial institutions and support delivery of financial tools within efficient consumer protection frameworks. To enhance management of systemic risk in the financial system, public policy should focus on establishing strong macroprudential frameworks, including crisis preparedness and resolution measures, that are equipped with adequate macroprudential tools, while fostering the safety and efficiency of financial market infrastructure. Most important, the process of public policy formulation must account for the trade-offs and synergies in finance to produce balanced policies that respect both a country's development goals and risk appetite in the financial area.

Notes

1. This story is a composite of events and recent business practices in the Czech Republic.
2. This chapter focuses on the financial system, not on individual financial institutions. Thus it does not discuss issues related to microprudential supervision and deposit insurance, for instance.
3. Levine 1997.
4. For a more extensive discussion of financial inclusion, see World Bank 2013.
5. Beck, Demirgüç-Kunt, and Merrouche 2013.
6. Beck, Demirgüç-Kunt, and Merrouche 2013.
7. Levine 1997.
8. The picture of competition in the financial system, based on available studies and data, is incomplete. Studies have focused mostly on banking; much less research has been done on competition in the insurance sector, capital markets (pension funds, mutual funds, brokerage houses), and the sector of nonbank credit institutions and payment services providers. For an extensive discussion of bank competition and enabling public policies, see World Bank 2012b, chapter 3. See BIS 2004 on the benefits of foreign direct investment in financial systems.
9. Demombynes and Thegeya 2012; Bankable Frontier Associates 2009.
10. Clarke and others 2012; Mobarak and Rosenzweig 2013.
11. Green 2008.
12. This section is focused on development. It thus does not deal with issues such as unmet demand for credit that results from tight credit standards in recessions or crisis periods.
13. Allen and others 2012.
14. Collins, Jentzsch, and Mazer 2011.
15. Dowd 2009; Honohan 2010. Similarly, public deposit insurance should strike a balance between protecting the vulnerable and discouraging moral hazard; it should not, for example, distort market discipline by letting depositors ignore bank risk and simply deposit funds for the highest interest rates.
16. Braun and Raddatz 2010; Willis 2009.
17. Beck 2013 for the WDR 2014.
18. OECD 2011.
19. See OECD, http://www.financial-education.org; World Bank, http://responsiblefinance.worldbank.org; and Russia Trust Fund on Financial Literacy and Education and Trust, http://www.finlitedu.org, managed by the World Bank, for information on designing financial education programs.
20. In 2008, India's National Rural Employment Guarantee Act (NREGA) made more than 45 million payments to poor people living in rural areas. People can receive their G2P payment from post office saving accounts, bank accounts, and village officials.
21. Gupta 2013.
22. Brix and McKee 2010.
23. World Bank 2012a.
24. World Bank 2012a, box 3.
25. Collins and others 2009.
26. Faz and Breloff 2012; Hashemi and de Montesquiou 2011.
27. Output losses are computed as the cumulative sum of the differences between actual and trend real GDP over the period (T, $T + 3$), expressed as a percentage of trend real GDP, with T the starting year of the crisis. See Laeven and Valencia 2012 for more details.
28. Mongolia, Nigeria, and the United States are the only countries outside that region that experienced a banking crisis from 2007 to 2011 (Laeven and Valencia 2012; Brown 2013 for the WDR 2014).
29. Brown 2013 for the WDR 2014.
30. See Brown 2013 for the WDR 2014 for further details and references.
31. Claessens, Ghosh, and Mihet, forthcoming; Claessens, Kose, and Terrones 2012.
32. World Bank FinStats (internal database), calculated as the three-year average growth of nominal credit before the crisis.
33. Reinhart and Rogoff 2009; BIS 2011a; Buncic and Melecky 2013a for the WDR 2014.
34. Beck and De Jonghe 2013 for the WDR 2014.
35. Allen and Gale 2000; Claessens, Ghosh, and Mihet, forthcoming.
36. Ghosh, Gonzalez del Mazo, and Ötker-Robe 2012.
37. Beck, Demirgüç-Kunt, and Merrouche 2013.
38. WDR 2014 team calculations based on data from the Bank for International Settlements on locational banking statistics by residence (claims of Bank for International Settlements reporting banks on banks in developing countries).
39. WDR 2014 team calculations based on Bankscope data and the initial list of 29 G-SIFIs issued by the Financial Stability Board. Local SIFIs are defined as the top 10 banks of the domestic financial system ranked by assets.
40. Empirical studies confirm that lending by subsidiaries is more stable than direct cross-border lending (Allen and others 2011); Vienna Initiative, http://vienna-initiative.com/vienna-initiative-part-1/.
41. Laeven and Valencia 2012. Contagion can occur through depressed asset prices (as a result of fire sales) and information (where one institution's failure can cause investors to withdraw their investments in other banks in the country). Similarly, as retail runs on banks occur, cross-border wholesale and interbank runs on solvent domestic banks can also happen because of coordination problems (Allen and others 2011).
42. BIS 2010a; Cole, Kanz, and Klapper 2012; Aebi, Sabato, and Schmid 2012.
43. Calomiris 2011; FSB 2010.
44. Braun and Raddatz 2010; Hardy 2006.
45. Senior Supervisors Group 2009; Beck, Demirgüç-Kunt, and Levine 2003.
46. BIS 2011b.
47. BIS 2011b; Bank of England 2013. Some proposals suggest that macroprudential policy committees consist of five members, all from outside government and international organizations: a macroeconomist, a microeconomist, a research accountant, a financial engineer, and a practitioner. The board should not include supervisors and regulators. Its composition should provide for objective and independent judgment.
48. IMF 2012b; Melecky and Podpiera 2012. See Buncic and Melecky 2013b for applications of practical stress-testing approaches for macroprudential policy.
49. Arnold and others 2012; Bank of England 2013.
50. Cihak and others 2012.
51. See also Lim and others 2011 for detailed country examples of the use of macroprudential tools.
52. Claessens, Ghosh, and Mihet, forthcoming.
53. Shin 2010; IMF 2012a.
54. For an example of a policy statement outlining a detailed approach to implementing macroprudential buffers in the United Kingdom, see Bank of England 2013. Lim and others 2011, figure 1, offers a useful conceptual framework on how to use macroprudential instruments.

55. Hoggarth, Reidhill, and Sinclair 2004.
56. In principle, the framework for emergency liquidity assistance should allow central bank lending against a broader pool of collateral (including highly rated corporate bonds or foreign governments bonds) that is properly discounted to avoid situations in which the central bank takes on excessive counterparty (credit) risk and needs to be recapitalized by the ministry of finance.
57. Dziobek and Pazarbasioglu 1997.
58. Laeven and Valencia 2012.
59. See FSB 2010; BIS 2011a. The instruments comprise systemic capital surcharges, obligatory issuance of contingent capital obligations (CoCOs), and bail-in debt instruments.
60. See, for instance, BIS 2012.
61. De Grauwe 2010.
62. Adasme, Majnoni, and Uribe 2006.
63. Collins and others 2009; Cull, Demirgüç-Kunt, and Lyman 2012.
64. CGAP 2011.
65. Klapper, Lusardi, and Panos 2012.
66. Beck 2013 for the WDR 2014.
67. Beck and De Jonghe 2013 for the WDR 2014.
68. Anginer, Demirgüç-Kunt, and Zhu 2012.
69. Lafley and others 2012.
70. World Bank 2012b.
71. BIS 2010a; FSB 2013.
72. European Commission 2009.
73. Beck and De Jonghe 2013 for the WDR 2014.
74. Adrian, Colla, and Shin 2012.

References

Adasme, Osvaldo, Giovanni Majnoni, and Myriam Uribe. 2006. "Access and Risk: Friends or Foes? Lessons from Chile." Policy Research Working Paper 4003, World Bank, Washington, DC.

Adrian, Tobias, Paolo Colla, and Hyun Song Shin. 2012. "Which Financial Frictions? Parsing the Evidence from the Financial Crisis of 2007–2009." Paper prepared for the National Bureau of Economic Research Macro Annual Conference, April 20–21.

Aebi, Vincent, Gabriele Sabato, and Markus Schmid. 2012. "Risk Management, Corporate Governance, and Bank Performance in the Financial Crisis." *Journal of Banking & Finance* 36 (12): 3213–26.

Allen, Franklin, Thorsten Beck, Elena Carletti, Philip Lane, Dirk Schoenmaker, and Wolf Wagner. 2011. *Cross-Border Banking in Europe: Implications for Financial Stability and Macroeconomic Policies.* London: Centre for Economic Policy Research.

Allen, Franklin, Asli Demirgüç-Kunt, Leora Klapper, and María Soledad Martínez Pería. 2012. "The Foundations of Financial Inclusion: Understanding Ownership and Use of Formal Accounts." Policy Research Working Paper 6290, World Bank, Washington, DC.

Allen, Franklin, and Douglas Gale. 2000. "Financial Contagion." *Journal of Political Economy* 108 (1): 1–33.

Anginer, Deniz, Asli Demirgüç-Kunt, and Min Zhu. 2012. "How Does Bank Competition Affect Systemic Stability?" Policy Research Working Paper 5981, World Bank, Washington, DC.

Arnold, Bruce, Claudio Borio, Luci Ellis, and Fariborz Moshirian. 2012. "Systemic Risk, Macroprudential Policy Frameworks, Monitoring Financial Systems and the Evolution of Capital Adequacy." *Journal of Banking & Finance* 36 (12): 3125–32.

Bank of England. 2013. "The Financial Policy Committee's Powers to Supplement Capital Requirements: A Draft Policy Statement." Bank of England, London.

Bankable Frontier Associates. 2009. "The Mzansi Bank Account Initiative in South Africa." Report commissioned by FinMark Trust, Bankable Frontier Associates, Somerville, MA.

Beck, Thorsten. 2011. "Bank Failure Resolution: A Conceptual Framework." In *Financial Regulation at the Crossroads: Implications for Supervision, Institutional Design and Trade,* edited by Panagiotis Delimatsis and Nils Herger, 53–71. Alphen aan den Rijn, NL: Kluwer Law International.

———. 2013. "The Supply-Demand Mismatch in Provision of Financial Services." Background paper for the *World Development Report 2014.*

Beck, Thorsten, and Olivier De Jonghe. 2013. "Lending Concentration, and Its Implications for Systemic Risk and Public Policy." Background paper for the *World Development Report 2014.*

Beck, Thorsten, Asli Demirgüç-Kunt, and Ross Levine. 2003. "Bank Supervision and Corporate Finance." Working Paper 9620, National Bureau of Economic Research, Cambridge, MA.

Beck, Thorsten, Asli Demirgüç-Kunt, and Ouarda Merrouche. 2013. "Islamic vs. Conventional Banking: Business Model, Efficiency and Stability." *Journal of Banking & Finance* 37 (2): 433–47.

BIS (Bank for International Settlements). 2004. "Foreign Direct Investment in the Financial Sector of Emerging Market Economies." CGFS Publications 22, BIS, Basel.

———. 2010a. "Principles for Enhancing Corporate Governance." BCBS Publications 176, BIS, Basel.

———. 2010b. "Report and Recommendations of the Cross-Border Bank Resolution Group." BCBS Publications 169, BIS, Basel.

———. 2011a. "Basel III: A Global Regulatory Framework for More Resilient Banks and Banking Systems—Revised Version June 2011." BCBS Publications 189, BIS, Basel.

———. 2011b. "Central Bank Governance and Financial Stability: A Report by Study Group." Other Publications 14, BIS, Basel.

———. 2012. "A Framework for Dealing with Domestic Systemically Important Banks." BCBS Publications 233, BIS, Basel.

Braun, Matias, and Claudio Raddatz. 2010. "Banking on Politics: When Former High-Ranking Politicians Become Bank Directors." *World Bank Economic Review* 24 (2): 234–79.

Brix, Laura, and Katharine McKee. 2010. "Consumer Protection Regulation in Low-Access Environments: Opportunities to Promote Responsible Finance." Focus Note 60, Consultative Group to Assist the Poor, Washington, DC.

Brown, Craig O., and I. Serdar Dinc. 2005. "The Politics of Bank Failures: Evidence from Emerging Markets." *Quarterly Journal of Economics* 120 (4): 1413–44.

Brown, Martin. 2013. "The Transmission of Banking Crises to Households: Lessons from the ECA Region 2008–2012." Background paper for the *World Development Report 2014.*

Buncic, Daniel, and Martin Melecky. 2013a. "Equilibrium Credit: The Reference Point for Macroprudential Supervisors." Background paper for the *World Development Report 2014.*

———. 2013b. "Macroprudential Stress Testing of Credit Risk: A Practical Approach for Policy Makers." *Journal of Financial Stability* 9 (3): 347–70.

Calomiris, Charles W. 2011. "An Incentive-Robust Programme for Financial Reform." *Manchester School* 79 (s2): 39–72.

CGAP (Consultative Group to Assist the Poor). 2011. "Global Standard-Setting Bodies and Financial Inclusion for the Poor:

Towards Proportionate Standards and Guidance." CGAP and Global Partnership for Financial Inclusion, Washington, DC.

Chitu, Livia. 2012. "Was Official Dollarisation/Euroisation an Amplifier of the 'Great Recession' of 2007–2009 in Emerging Economies?" Working Paper 1473, European Central Bank, Frankfurt.

Cihak, Martin, Sonia Munoz, Shakira Teh Sharifuddin, and Kalin Tintchev. 2012. "Financial Stability Reports: What Are They Good For?" Working Paper WP/12/1, International Monetary Fund, Washington, DC.

Claessens, Stijn, Swati R. Ghosh, and Roxana Mihet. Forthcoming. "Macro-Prudential Policies to Mitigate Financial System Vulnerabilities." *Journal of International Money and Finance.*

Claessens, Stijn, M. Ayhan Kose, and Marco Terrones. 2012. "How Do Business and Financial Cycles Interact?" *Journal of International Economics* 87 (1): 178–90.

Clarke, Daniel J., Olivier Mahul, Kolli N. Rao, and Niraj Verma. 2012. "Weather Based Crop Insurance in India." Policy Research Working Paper 5985, World Bank, Washington, DC.

Cohen, Rebecca. 2007. "The Positive Impacts of Affordable Housing on Health: A Research Summary." Center for Housing Policy and Enterprise Commmunity Partners, Washington, DC.

Cole, Shawn, Martin Kanz, and Leora Klapper. 2012. "Incentivizing Calculated Risk-Taking: Evidence from an Experiment with Commercial Bank Loan Officers." Policy Research Working Paper 6146, World Bank, Washington, DC.

Collins, Daryl, Nicola Jentzsch, and Rafael Mazer. 2011. "Incorporating Consumer Research into Consumer Protection Policy Making." Focus Note 74, Consultative Group to Assist the Poor, Washington, DC.

Collins, Daryl, Jonathan Morduch, Stuart Rutherford, and Orlanda Ruthven. 2009. *Portfolios of the Poor: How the World's Poor Live on $2 a Day.* Princeton, NJ: Princeton University Press.

Cull, Robert, Asli Demirgüç-Kunt, and Timothy Lyman. 2012. "Financial Inclusion and Stability: What Does Research Show?" Brief 71305, Consultative Group to Assist the Poor, Washington, DC.

De Grauwe, Paul. 2010. "Crisis in the Eurozone and How to Deal with It." Policy Brief 204, Centre for European Policy Studies, Brussels.

Demirgüç-Kunt, Asli, and Leora Klapper. 2012. "Measuring Financial Inclusion: The Global Findex Database." Policy Research Working Paper 6025, World Bank, Washington, DC.

Demombynes, Gabriel, and Aaron Thegeya. 2012. "Kenya's Mobile Revolution and the Promise of Mobile Savings." Policy Research Working Paper 5988, World Bank, Washington, DC.

De Soto, Hernando. 2000. *The Mystery of Capital: Why Capitalism Triumphs in the West and Fails Everywhere Else.* New York: Basic Books.

Dowd, Kevin. 2009. "Moral Hazard and the Financial Crisis." *Cato Journal* 29 (1): 141–66.

Dziobek, Claudia, and Ceyla Pazarbasioglu. 1997. "Lessons from Systemic Bank Restructuring: A Survey of 24 Countries." Working Paper WP/97/161, International Monetary Fund, Washington, DC.

ECRI (European Credit Research Institute). Lending to Households in Europe (database). ECRI, Brussels. http://www.ecri.eu/new/node/165.

Ehrbeck, Tilman, Rajiv Lochan, Supriyo Sinha, Naveen Tahliyani, and Adil Zainulbhai. 2010. "Inclusive Growth and Financial Security: The Benefits of E-Payments to Indian Society." McKinsey & Company, New York.

European Commission. 2009. "Commission Recommendation of 30 April 2009 on Remuneration Policies in the Financial Services Sector." Commission Recommendation 2009/384/EC, European Commission, Brussels.

Faz, Xavier, and Paul Breloff. 2012. "A Structured Approach to Understanding the Financial Service Needs of the Poor in Mexico." Brief 71306, Consultative Group to Assist the Poor, Washington, DC.

FSB (Financial Stability Board). 2010. "Reducing the Moral Hazard Posed by Systemically Important Financial Institutions: FSB Recommendations and Time Lines." FSB, Basel.

———. 2013. "Thematic Review on Risk Governance: Peer Review Report." FSB, Basel.

Ghosh, Swati R., Ines Gonzalez del Mazo, and İnci Ötker-Robe. 2012. "Chasing the Shadow: How Significant Is Shadow Banking in Emerging Markets?" Economic Premise 88, World Bank, Washington, DC.

Green, Duncan. 2008. *From Poverty to Power: How Active Citizens and Effective States Can Change the World.* Oxford, U.K.: Oxfam International.

Gupta, Sunil. 2013. "The Mobile Banking and Payment Revolution." *European Financial Review* February: 3–6.

Han, Rui, and Martin Melecky. 2013. "Financial Inclusion for Stability: Access to Bank Deposits and the Deposit Growth during the Global Financial Crisis." Background paper for the *World Development Report 2014.*

Hardy, Daniel C. 2006. "Regulatory Capture in Banking." Working Paper WP/06/34, International Monetary Fund, Washington, DC.

Hashemi, Syed M., and Aude de Montesquiou. 2011. "Reaching the Poorest: Lessons from the Graduation Model." Focus Note 69, Consultative Group to Assist the Poor, Washington, DC.

Hoggarth, Glenn, Jack Reidhill, and Peter Sinclair. 2004. "On the Resolution of Banking Crises: Theory and Evidence." Working Paper 229, Bank of England, London.

Honohan, Patrick. 2008. "Cross-Country Variation in Household Access to Financial Services." *Journal of Banking & Finance* 32 (11): 2493–500.

———. 2010. "Partial Credit Guarantees: Principles and Practice." *Journal of Financial Stability* 6 (1): 1–9.

IMF (International Monetary Fund). 2012a. "The Interaction of Monetary and Macroprudential Policies—Background Paper." IMF, Washington, DC.

———. 2012b. "Macrofinancial Stress Testing: Principles and Practices—Background Material." IMF, Washington, DC.

Josefsson, Mats. 2006. "The Public Sector Recapitalization Program in Turkey." In *Bank Restructuring and Resolution,* edited by David S. Hoelscher, 369–84. New York: Palgrave Macmillan.

Klapper, Leora, Annamaria Lusardi, and Georgios Panos. 2012. "Financial Literacy and the Financial Crisis." Working Paper 17930, National Bureau of Economic Research, Cambridge, MA.

Laeven, Luc, and Fabian Valencia. 2012. "Systemic Banking Crises Database: An Update." Working Paper WP/12/163, International Monetary Fund, Washington, DC.

Lafley, Alan G., Roger L. Martin, Jan W. Rivkin, and Nicolaj Siggelkow. 2012. "Bringing Science to the Art of Strategy." *Harvard Business Review* 90 (9): 3–12.

Levine, Ross. 1997. "Financial Development and Economic Growth: Views and Agenda." *Journal of Economic Literature* 35 (2): 688–726.

Lim, Cheng Hoon, Francesco Columba, Alejo Costa, Piyabha Kongsamut, Akira Otani, Mustafa Saiyid, Torsten Wezel, and Xiaoyong Wu. 2011. "Macroprudential Policy: What Instruments and How to Use Them? Lessons from Country Experiences." Working Paper WP/11/238, International Monetary Fund, Washington, DC.

Maimbo, Samuel, and Martin Melecky. 2013. "Financial Policy Formulation: Addressing the Tradeoff between Development and Stability." Background paper for the *World Development Report 2014*.

Melecky, Martin, and Anca M. Podpiera. 2012. "Macroprudential Stress-Testing Practices of Central Banks in Central and Southeastern Europe: Comparison and Challenges Ahead." *Emerging Markets Finance and Trade* 48 (4): 118–43.

Mobarak, Ahmed Mushfiq, and Mark Rosenzweig. 2013. "Informal Risk Sharing, Index Insurance and Risk-Taking in Developing Countries." *American Economic Review* 103 (3): 375–80.

OECD (Organisation for Economic Co-operation and Development). 2011. "G20 High-Level Principles on Financial Consumer Protection." OECD, Paris.

Reinhart, Carmen M., and Kenneth S. Rogoff. 2009. *This Time Is Different: Eight Centuries of Financial Folly.* Princeton, NJ: Princeton University Press.

RTI International. 2005. "LAC Housing and Urban Upgrading Assistance Retrospective: Honduras and Ecuador, 1980–2005." Prepared for United States Agency for International Development, Washington, DC.

Senior Supervisors Group. 2009. "Risk Management Lessons from the Global Banking Crisis of 2008." Senior Supervisors Group.

Shin, Hyun Song. 2010. "Non-Core Liabilities Tax as a Tool for Prudential Regulation." Policy Memo, February 19, Seoul.

Willis, Lauren. 2009. "Evidence and Ideology in Assessing the Effectiveness of Financial Literacy Education." *San Diego Law Review* 46 (2): 415–58.

World Bank. 2012a. "Financial Inclusion Strategies Reference Framework." Prepared for the G-20 Mexico Presidency. Washington, DC: World Bank.

———. 2012b. *Global Financial Development Report 2013: Rethinking the Role of the State in Finance.* Washington, DC: World Bank.

———. 2013. *Global Financial Development Report 2014: Financial Inclusion.* Washington, DC: World Bank.

———. FinStats (internal database). World Bank, Washington, DC.

———. Global Financial Development Database. World Bank, Washington, DC, http://data.worldbank.org/data-catalog/global-financial-development.

———. Global Findex (database). World Bank, Washington, DC, http://data.worldbank.org/data-catalog/financial_inclusion.

Building resilience to global economic shocks in the Czech Republic, Peru, and Kenya

While the recent global economic downturn did not spare many developing countries, they were more resilient to the 2008 global crisis than to previous crises. The East Asian countries managed systemic risk especially well, but the performance of several countries in Central Europe, Latin America, and Sub-Saharan Africa has also been remarkable. The experiences of three of them—the Czech Republic, Peru, and Kenya—offer two main lessons. First, pursuing macroprudential policies in good times, while continuously strengthening the domestic financial system, is key to building resilience to severe economic downturns. Second, timely countercyclical macro policies not only help manage macroeconomic and financial cycles after crises hit but also boost preparation by building or preserving the necessary resources (fiscal space) to respond to a crisis.

A difficult period of reform

The Czech Republic started building stronger foundations for aggregate risk management following major lessons learned from the 1997–98 banking crisis. In 1997 the country abandoned its fixed exchange rate regime in favor of a monetary policy framework based on inflation targeting. In part thanks to its increased financial and political independence, the Czech National Bank managed to increase the credibility of monetary policy and achieve greater price stability. These achievements translated into low interest rates that, along with better fiscal discipline, helped the country maintain a sound external position, which benefited from a trade surplus and a modest current account deficit.

In addition to the strengthened policy framework, the Czech banking system was able to finance its lending activities mainly from local deposits and extended loans to households in domestic currency. Thus borrowers avoided unhedged exposures in foreign exchange, and the banks avoided the associated indirect credit risk.

Starting in 2006, all microprudential regulators were integrated under the Czech National Bank, which was already the monetary authority and macroprudential supervisor. Bringing microprudential and macroprudential supervision under one institution enabled the Czech Republic to conduct prudential supervision in a more comprehensive manner and to better monitor how the risks from individual financial institutions translate into systemic risk in the financial sector. Integrated financial sector supervision should also bring improvements to the coordination and timeliness of policy response in future crises.

Unlike the Czech Republic, until 2008, Peru had not been hit by a major economic turmoil for almost two decades. But until the late 1980s, the country experienced hyperinflation, severe macroeconomic imbalances, and massive capital outflows. In the 1990s, Peru put in place key reforms to stabilize the economy. It brought hyperinflation under control through explicit targets on the monetary base. Once inflation was reduced to single digits, the central bank adopted an inflation-targeting regime with a flexible exchange rate that kept inflation in check. The tax system and the financial sector were reformed. As a byproduct of these reforms and to safeguard against regional contagion from crisis episodes in emerging markets, banks built up adequate levels of capitalization and sufficient levels of liquidity.

Peru liberalized foreign trade in the early 1990s, drastically reducing tariff rates and eliminating nontariff barriers. A more favorable economic environment from 2002 to 2007 fueled economic growth. Increasing demand for the country's commodities (mineral ores and metals) from large dynamic emerging markets in East Asia produced a large positive income shock. Peru saved part of the revenues from natural resources. International reserves grew to the equivalent of more than 17 months of imports in 2007, and the fiscal primary surplus increased. Sustained annual gross domestic product (GDP) growth of nearly 7 percent from 2002 to 2008 helped reduce poverty. In light of these macroeconomic achievements, the international rating agencies upgraded Peru's sovereign rating, paving the way for major foreign investment.

Like Peru, Kenya successfully built resilience by strengthening both its financial and macrofiscal systems. Although it did not have to deal with a specific economic crisis before 2008, its economy was in trouble during the 1980s and early 1990s, after experiencing two decades of high growth. From 1991 to 1993, Kenya's GDP growth stagnated, agricultural production sharply contracted, and hyperinflation flared. The government decided to implement economic reforms to stabilize the financial sector and regain sustainable growth. The banking system was strengthened, notably through substantial capitalization of the banks, and access to finance for the population was improved. Kenya also managed to decrease its public debt and accumulate high international reserves (up to four months of import coverage) by adopting prudent fiscal policies and maintaining a healthy external position, with strong surpluses in the service balance (mainly tourism and information technology) and massive inflows of foreign capital that compensated for the trade deficit.

The benefits of good preparation

The relatively strong resilience of these three countries to the global crisis in 2008 was the result of an arduous process undertaken a decade or more before the shock. Although political leaders may have been tempted to adopt procyclical measures during good economic times, these three countries understood the necessity of strengthening their financial and macrofiscal systems to prepare for serious economic turmoil. This awareness proved its worth when the world economy crashed.

The Czech Republic demonstrated the utility of establishing an integrated supervisor at the national level within a strong and independent central bank. Overall, the Czech government did not have to undertake any major measures, and a simple relaxation of monetary policy proved sufficient to ensure adequate liquidity. The adequate loan-to-deposit ratio of the banking sector and low dollarization of loans through adequate pricing of foreign exchange risk by the banks were also key factors in weathering the global economic shock. Despite decreased lending during the crisis period, Czech banks continued to generate profits and further strengthen their capital buffers, which helped them cope with a notable increase in the share of nonperforming loans (figure S6.1). Other countries in the region, including Hungary and Ukraine, faced higher risk because of higher dollarization of loans.

Given the good conditions that Peru had created since the mid-1990s, the government was able to respond in an efficient and countercyclical manner to sustain the national economy during the global crisis. The central bank injected liquidity into the financial system, in both local currency (nuevos soles) and U.S. dollars, to prevent a liquidity squeeze and a credit crunch. The monetary policy rate was lowered to 1.25 percent, and the first package—equivalent to 3.4 percent of GDP—of a threefold stimulus plan was enacted in 2009, financed by fiscal savings. By investing in roads, housing, and hospitals; by giving incentives to nontraditional exporters; by supporting small and medium enterprises and farms; and by increasing expenditures in social programs, the government aimed to sustain domestic demand, boost business confidence, and extend guarantees to support firms, exporters, and smaller financial institutions. Peru also benefited from a key external factor: favorable terms of trade, with a rapid recovery of exports to Asia (particularly China).

Kenya's demonstration of risk management is arguably even more impressive, considering the quadruple shock it faced within a very short period: postelection violence in early 2008, oil and food price increases, catastrophic drought, and the global financial crisis. Although an increased perception of risk in the market was reflected in the commercial bank lending rates, with a particularly large impact on the agriculture sector, the central bank successfully implemented countercyclical monetary policies, reducing its rate, as well as the cash reserve ratio, to inject liquidity into the market. The banking sector was strong enough to maintain capital adequacy ratios (19.8 percent in 2009—well above the statutory requirement of 12 percent) and a low share of nonperforming loans. With public debt under control, and buoyed by large international reserves, the government was able to implement an ambitious fiscal stimulus program of $300 million, thereby protecting key expenditures. The stimulus boosted employment and economic activity, notably by increasing spending on infrastructure.

While many countries are still suffering from the crisis, the Czech Republic, Peru, and Kenya, have all demonstrated an impressive ability to manage macrofinancial risks—offering lessons that would benefit even developed countries.

FIGURE S6.1 *Bank nonperforming loans to total gross loans ratio, 2007–11*

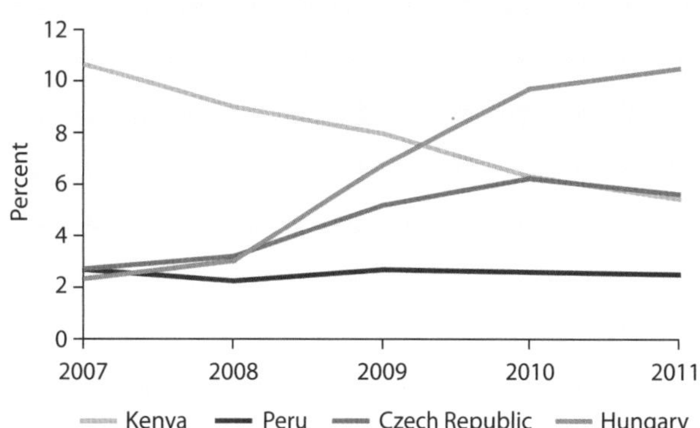

Source: WDR 2014 team based on data from World Bank Global Finance Development Database.

Note: While the share of nonperforming loans fell in Kenya during the crisis and remained relatively low and flat in Peru, it increased significantly in the Czech Republic; however, the country managed to stop the rise at the end of 2010. This can be considered a good performance in comparison with other Eastern European countries such as Hungary, where the share quadrupled over the same period and was still increasing at the end of 2011.

Sources

Castillo, Paul, and Daniel Barco. 2008. "Facing Up a Sudden Stop of Capital Flows: Policy Lessons from the 90's Peruvian Experience." Working Paper 2008-002, Central Reserve Bank of Peru, Lima.

De Gregorio, José. 2012. "Resilience in Latin America: Lessons from Macroeconomic Management and Financial Policies." Unpublished manuscript, University of Chile, Santiago.

De la Torre, Augusto, and Alain Ize. 2010. "Finance in Crisis: Causes, Lessons, Consequences, and Application to Latin America." In *The Day after Tomorrow*, edited by Otaviano Canuto and Marcelo Giugale, 143–59. Washington, DC: World Bank.

Ellingson, Amy. 2010. "Brazil and Peru: Economies Set to Flourish in Postrecession World." *EconSouth* 12 (1): 22–26.

IMF (International Monetary Fund). 2009. "The Implications of the Global Financial Crisis for Low-Income Countries." IMF, Washington, DC.

———. 2010. "Peru: Staff Report for the 2010 Article IV Consultation." IMF, Washington, DC.

———. 2012. "Resilience in Emerging Market and Developing Economies: Will It Last?" In *World Economic Outlook*, 129–71. Washington, DC: IMF.

Kirori, Gabriel, and Tabitha Kiriti Nganga. 2009. "Global Economic and Financial Crisis and Trade: Kenya's Experience." Paper prepared for the Rethinking African Economic Policy in Light of the Global Economic and Financial Crisis Conference organized by the African Economic Research Consortium.

Melecky, Martin. 2009. "Macroeconomic Management, Financial Sector Development and Crisis Resilience: Some Stylized Facts from Central and Eastern Europe." MPRA Paper 28214, University Library of Munich, Munich.

OECD (Organisation for Economic Co-operation and Development). 2009. *Latin American Economic Outlook 2010.* Paris: OECD.

Were, Maureen, and Samuel Tiriongo. 2012. "Central Bank's Response to Economic Crises from a Developing African Economy Perspective: Lessons from Kenya's Experience." Unpublished manuscript, Central Bank of Kenya, Nairobi.

World Bank. 2009. "Still Standing: Kenya's Slow Recovery from a Quadruple Shock, with a Special Focus on the Food Crisis." Kenya Economic Update, Edition 1, World Bank, Nairobi.

———. Global Financial Development Database. World Bank, Washington, DC, http://data.worldbank.org/data-catalog/global-financial-development.

A stable macroeconomy reduces uncertainty and enables economic agents to focus on productive decisions rather than on trying to mitigate high risks. A pensioner copes with the 1998 financial crisis in Russia.

CHAPTER 7

Managing macroeconomic risk

Building stronger institutions for better policy outcomes

Macroeconomy

Increasing resilience and promoting opportunity through sound macroeconomic policy

Peru has weathered a series of crises in the past 25 years. The first, driven by a money-financed fiscal expansion in the second half of the 1980s, led to high inflation and large macroeconomic imbalances. Declared ineligible for new loans from the International Monetary Fund (IMF) in 1986, Peru had no room for maneuver, and the new administration had to resort to severe monetary and fiscal tightening to bring inflation down, leading to a steep recession. The gross domestic product (GDP) plummeted more than 20 percent in 1990 from peak to trough. It took Peru 14 quarters to return to the real GDP level it had before the crisis.

By 1997, Peru's inflation reached single-digit levels. The government continued reconstituting reserves and reducing external debt. The country nonetheless remained vulnerable to reversals in capital flows, which became all too apparent when financial contagion, triggered by the East Asian crisis, led to a "sudden stop" in capital inflows. A recession again followed, but this one was milder (GDP fell around 4 percent from peak to trough), and the recovery was shorter (six quarters), if weak.

At the onset of the 2008–09 global crisis, Peru's economy was better equipped to withstand the unprecedented external shock. A credible inflation targeting regime kept inflation low and stable. Real GDP had grown strongly before the crisis (6.8 percent a year from 2002 to 2008). Sounder macroeconomic management and benign conditions internationally allowed Peru to build ample liquidity buffers and monetary and fiscal space, helping accommodate the global shock: unlike much of the rest of the world, the recession in Peru in 2008–09 was mild (minus 2.1 percent from peak to trough), and the recovery was swift (two quarters) and strong. Peru's GDP grew 10 percent the year after the economy hit its trough.

As Peru's experience illustrates, the national government can play a pivotal role helping individuals manage aggregate risks—domestic and international—that they are not equipped to manage on their own (cartoon 7.1). High inflation can worsen income distribution, increase poverty, and lower real wages. Unemployment rises in recessions—and even more in recessions associated with financial crises.[1] Aggregate risks like these can have a profound impact on people, households, communities, enterprises, and the financial system—and each of these agents' capacity to manage risk.

The government's conduct of macroeconomic policy plays a unique and pivotal role in managing risk at the national level. Macroeconomic policies that are adequately designed and implemented help overcome many obstacles in managing risk, including asymmetric information, coordination failures, externalities, and the provision of public goods (see chapter 2). Thus sound macroeconomic policy promotes development. A stable macroeconomic environment and ample revenues and resources—fiscal

CARTOON 7.1 Systemic risks. Individuals are unequipped to manage macroeconomic risks by themselves. © Jeff Parker/*Florida Today*

space—to finance government programs and policies reduce uncertainty and enable economic agents to concentrate on productive activities rather than on trying to mitigate high risks.

This chapter focuses on the conduct of macroeconomic risk management—more specifically, on monetary and fiscal policies aimed at achieving macroeconomic stability. To help people manage risks, monetary and fiscal policies should be credible, predictable, transparent, and sustainable. That requires building reputation and policy space in good times by keeping inflation low and stable, having exchange rate arrangements that absorb shocks from the international economy, and following fiscal practices that generate adequate surpluses and reduce the public debt burden. Consequently, macroeconomic policy makers should behave prudently during upswings. Accumulating resources in good times can help finance countercyclical policies—especially programs that protect the most vulnerable—and desired public investment programs. By reducing aggregate volatility—especially, that associated with crisis episodes—these policies will reduce uncertainty and help people plan, save, and invest for the longer term. Overall, to manage risk properly, policy makers must graduate from being crisis fighters to being cycle managers.[2]

That is the goal. In reality, policy makers may lack expertise and institutional capacity to manage the economy or may have difficulty in credibly committing to risk management policies. Government officials tend to provide resources to their constituents in the run-up to elections or fall prey to lobby groups competing for higher spending during upswings. Coordination failures among policy makers may also lead to less than optimal allocation of policy instruments to meet different macroeconomic targets. Problems like these can lead to uncertainty over the course of policy, which can in turn lead to greater instability and lower growth. Box 7.1 illustrates that uncertainty in global economic policy is growing. Reducing mismanagement of macroeconomic risk requires an adequate institutional framework that attains better information, improves the quality of analysis, and develops tools to help policy makers with the host of uncertainties they face. Greater public accountability for the likely costs of their policies will increase the quality of policy making. This chapter argues that credible, transparent, more flexible, and sustainable macroeconomic policy frameworks increase a country's resilience. It highlights examples of good monetary and fiscal management and offers policy recommendations suited to countries at different levels of institutional capacity facing different constraints and opportunities.

Gearing macroeconomic policies toward aggregate stability

Using macroeconomic policies to manage economic crises and cycles

Reducing instability and uncertainty. Macroeconomic volatility is a source of short-term concern and an impediment to achieving long-term development goals. Beyond regular business cycle fluctuations, volatility disrupts households' and firms' saving, investment, and production decisions. It reduces the ability of the financial system to transform liquid financial instruments into long-term capital investments, as agents in the economy become reluctant to enter long-term contracts. Greater output volatility—especially when accompanied by crisis episodes—lowers long-term growth. Increasing output volatility by one standard deviation leads to a 1.3 percentage point reduction in growth per capita; this decline is even more sizable (2.2 percentage points) during crises.[3] Macroeconomic volatility also worsens income inequality and poverty, as lower-income segments of the population are less protected from economic downturns. Doubling aggregate volatility reduces the income share of the poorest quintile of the population by 2.4 percent. Moreover, the average increase in income inequality during recessions (5 percent) tends to be larger than the

BOX 7.1 *The new normal in the world economy: Heightened macroeconomic policy uncertainty in developed countries*

Recent policy conflict and fiscal crisis in the world's biggest collective economies—the United States and the European Union—have generated considerable uncertainty, leading to concerns that firms and consumers may be postponing hiring and spending decisions, stalling the recovery. Uncertainty is a subjective concept, and measuring it is not easy. It can be approximated with an index of economic policy uncertainty that uses three groups of observable measures. The first component quantifies newspaper coverage of policy-related economic uncertainty. The second measures variability of forecasts of fiscal and monetary policies (as captured by the interquartile range of 1-year-ahead forecasts of inflation, government purchases, and state and local government purchases). The third reflects the number and size of tax code provisions set to expire in future years. The weight of each of these components varies according to the country or region.

Historically, policy uncertainty in the United States has surged around major wars, elections, and terrorist attacks. Recently, uncertainty spiked in 2008 and has remained high (panel a). A similar surge has occurred in Europe since 2008; together, the two have contributed to increased global policy uncertainty (panel b).

How big is the negative impact of policy uncertainty? In the United States, policy uncertainty of the size observed on average between 2006 and 2011 reduces industrial production by 2.5 percent and employment by 2.4 million workers. Moreover, policy uncertainty in the United States and the European Union spills over to the rest of the world through two channels. First, these two economic areas collectively account for more than half the world's trade and outbound foreign direct investment. Second, they are major financial centers, and the higher volatility of their stock markets due to increased uncertainty can have a global contagion effect.

The probability of disasters also affects people's perceptions of uncertainty; their decision making is disrupted by the greater likelihood of disasters. Economic disasters—as defined by a peak-to-trough cumulative drop in GDP or consumption larger than 10 percent—have a mean size of 21–22 percent, an average duration of 3.5 years, and an estimated probability of occurrence of 3.5 percent a year. Disasters have the potential to destroy part of the capital stock and impair productivity; thus they are characterized by declines in investment, corporate leverage, output, and employment, and account for part of increased risk premium in financial markets. Calibrated models for the United States estimate that doubling the probability of disaster reduces investment by 3.5 percent and unemployment by 0.8 percent.

Will policy uncertainty remain high? The prospects for a decline in U.S. policy uncertainty in the near term are not bright, largely because of the current U.S. political agenda and the polarization of its political system. In the European Union, policy uncertainty will remain high if concerted actions to address banking and fiscal problems at the national and supranational levels are delayed and pro-market reforms are not undertaken in southern European countries. In short, economic policy uncertainty is the new normal. With this in mind, firms and consumers should also actively manage risks—for instance, by attempting to reduce exposure to the most sensitive sectors. Such steps can help minimize the impact of international policy risk.

Economic policy uncertainty has increased in recent years in the United States and Europe

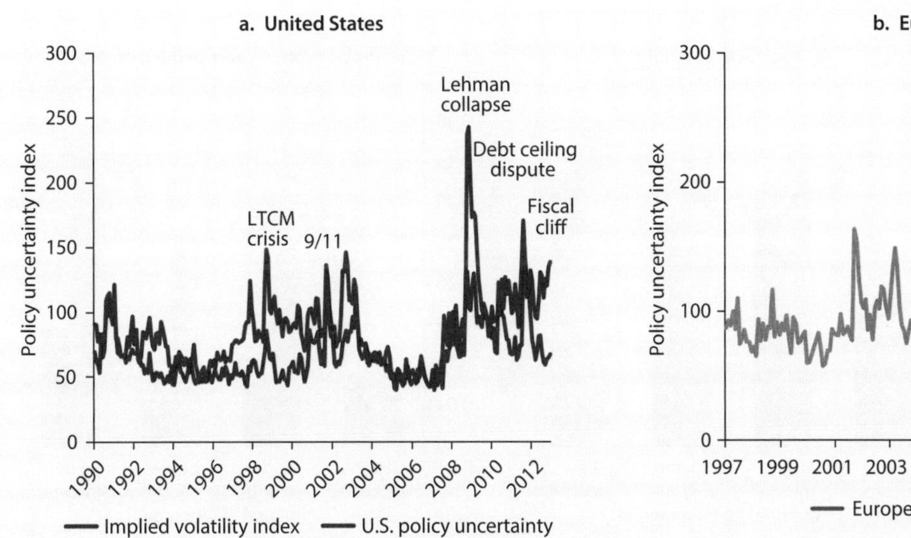

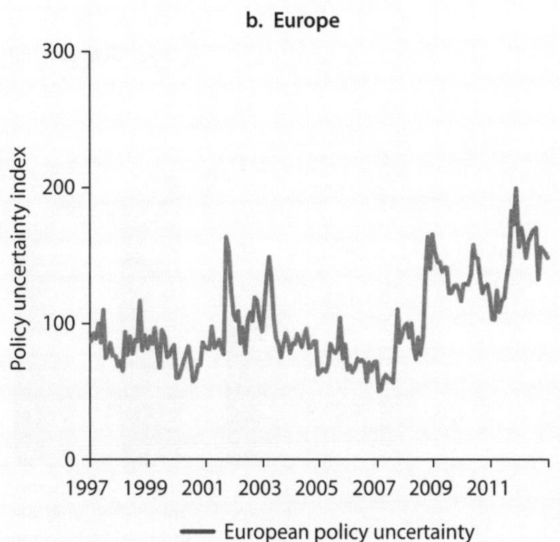

Sources: Bloom 2013 for the WDR 2014; Barro and Ursúa 2012; Gourio 2012.

Note: The index of policy uncertainty is normalized to 100 for January 2008. The data and description of these uncertainty indexes is available at http://www.policyuncertainty.com. This index may also capture macroeconomic and political uncertainty. The implied volatility index (VIX) is a measure of the implied volatility of S&P (Standard and Poor's) 500 index options. LCTM = Long-Term Capital Management L.P.

reduction during booms (0.9 percent).[4] A rising tide may lift all boats, as President Kennedy famously said, but a falling tide pushes them down deeper and longer. Macroeconomic policy will help manage aggregate risks—and avoid itself becoming a source of risk—and facilitate the development of risk-sharing mechanisms in the economy.

Managing the cycle in good times and coping in bad times. Macroeconomic policies help manage aggregate shocks—coming from abroad, from domestic policies themselves, or from systemically important domestic agents. In reality, developing countries' policies have been unable to contain boom-bust economic and financial cycles. These countries are exposed to larger and more frequent external shocks, have lower shock-absorbing capacity (including less diversified economic structures, underdeveloped financial markets, dollarized balance sheets, and poor institutional quality), and are more likely to experience macrofinancial crises. As a result, economic activity in developing countries is more volatile and prone to deep recessions (figure 7.1). Structural changes in advanced countries since the mid-1980s have led to a decrease in world output volatility. Better monetary frameworks that insulate the economy from shocks, financial innovations that reduce market frictions, labor market flexibility, and technological improvements in inventory management explain this reduction.[5] A stable external environment and improved macroeconomic frameworks not only explain the lower output volatility but also reduce the probability of recessions among developing countries (figure 7.1). Conversely, the unraveling of the Great Moderation period was also transmitted to emerging markets during the recent crisis. Most of these countries experienced a sharp slowdown. Aggressive monetary policy actions from advanced countries' central banks succeeded in restoring global financial conditions. As the world economy recovered (reflected in rising commodity prices and lower global risk aversion), the better-prepared emerging markets were able to resume rapid economic growth.

To manage risk properly, policy makers must graduate from being crisis fighters to being cycle managers.

FIGURE 7.1 ***Real economic activity is more volatile and more likely to decline sharply in developing countries***

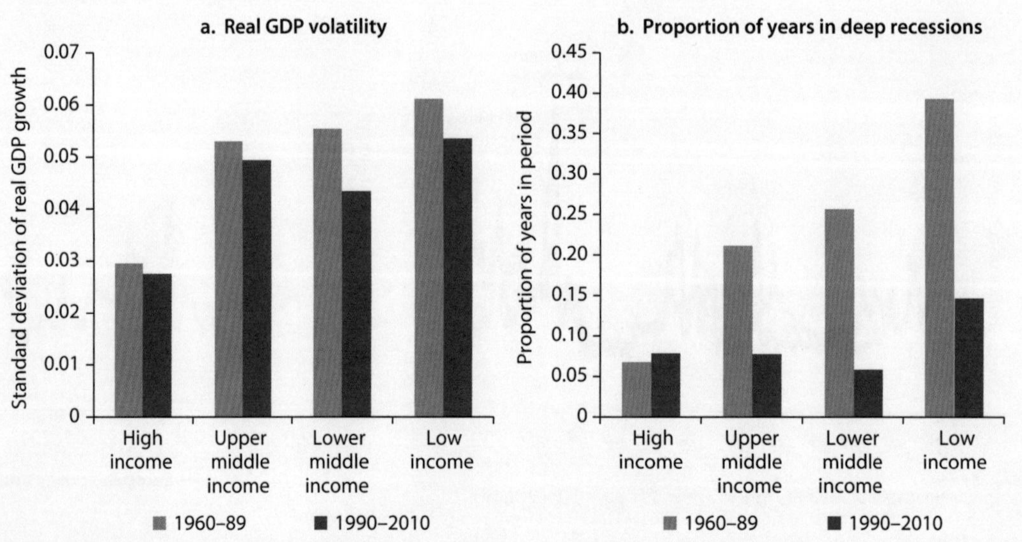

Source: WDR 2014 team based on data from World Bank World Development Indicators (database).

Note: Real GDP volatility is the standard deviation of GDP growth per capita. Proportion of years in deep recessions captures the share of years when per capita GDP declined more than 5 percent on a cumulative basis. Both measures have been computed for 1960–89 and 1990–2010.

Aiding longer-term planning and development. Macroeconomic stability broadens the set of tools for long-term planning available to households, firms, and governments. Increased price stability in countries that have wrestled with bouts of high and volatile inflation rates has led to the development of financial intermediaries, including local currency debt markets, the revival of mortgage markets, and the emergence of pension and mutual funds (see chapter 6). These developments have allowed economic agents to increase the average planning horizon of spending and investment decisions and raise the maturity of domestic government debt. For instance, if Brazil had the long-term inflation performance of Denmark, the depth of its local currency bond market would be almost triple its size.[6]

Delivering low inflation through sound monetary policy

High inflation distorts the saving and investment decisions of households and firms, thus leading to slower economic growth. Having a clearly defined (quantitative) nominal target helps central banks anchor expectations about the evolution of prices. To stop high inflation, countries have adopted either monetary aggregates or the exchange rate as their nominal anchors. Choosing an exchange rate anchor (hard peg) is sensible for countries with weak institutions, dollarized economies, underdeveloped financial markets, and low-credibility central banks. The exchange rate anchor is easy to implement and monitor and is verifiable by market participants. It has been successful in reducing inflation from historically high levels.[7] Small countries with greater international trade integration tend to have hard pegs, because greater exchange rate stability boosts their foreign trade and investment. Targeting monetary aggregates provides greater exchange rate flexibility and permits central banks to pursue independent monetary policy. However, these regimes proved to be inconsistent with long-term development. Exchange rate targeters were plagued by problems of fiscal indiscipline and monetary financing of deficits that led to a costly regime collapse.[8] Money growth targeters gradually lost the ability to anchor expectations as the relationship between monetary aggregates and inflation became unstable.[9]

Once high inflation was defeated, monetary frameworks targeted the inflation rate to coordinate expectations. Central banks set an inflation target to be achieved over a specific policy horizon. Monetary policy announcements shaped the expectations of the private sector concerning future interest rates and future inflation. Inflation targeting required having flexible exchange rates, so central banks could conduct independent monetary policy. Inflation targeting has been able to deliver low and stable inflation rates.[10] Its success rested on the better understanding of the monetary transmission mechanisms and on three strong institutional underpinnings.[11] First, central banks have a clear mandate (to maintain price stability) and are fully committed to achieving that goal. Second, central banks are independent from political interference in their decision making. They are instrument-independent: that is, they can choose and manage the instruments to achieve their primary goal. Third, greater central bank accountability creates incentives to fulfill the mandate. The effectiveness of monetary policy requires the absence of fiscal dominance, reduced currency mismatches, and sound domestic financial markets.[12]

The institutional push toward greater transparency has strengthened the reputation of central banks and enhanced efficiency in the implementation of monetary policy. Greater institutional capacity and flexibility to achieve the inflation target over time have permitted policy makers to use monetary policy instruments countercyclically. Historically, advanced countries have been able to implement expansionary monetary policies during recessions. They have lowered policy interest rates to withstand real shocks and stabilize output without jeopardizing their inflation target. In contrast, monetary authorities in many developing countries have acted procyclically, raising policy rates during contractions to avoid massive capital outflows and currency depreciation (fear of free falling) and cutting rates in good times to prevent surges in capital inflows and currency overvaluation (fear of capital inflows).[13] The adoption of sound macroeconomic policies (inflation targeting and flexible exchange rates), public debt management strategies, and market-friendly reforms (trade and financial liberalization) have helped many emerging markets sharply reduce the fear of free falling (figure 7.2). It thus comes as no surprise that in the midst of the recent global financial crisis, many emerging countries in Latin America and East Asia were able to reduce policy rates. For instance, the average monetary policy rate declined from 6.50 percent to 1.25 percent in Peru, and from 5.21 percent to 1.98 percent in the Republic of Korea, from September 2008 to September 2009.

The choice of exchange rate regime matters for its likely effects, both direct and indirect, on inflation and growth. Countries with higher per capita

FIGURE 7.2 *Monetary policy has become countercyclical in some developing countries*

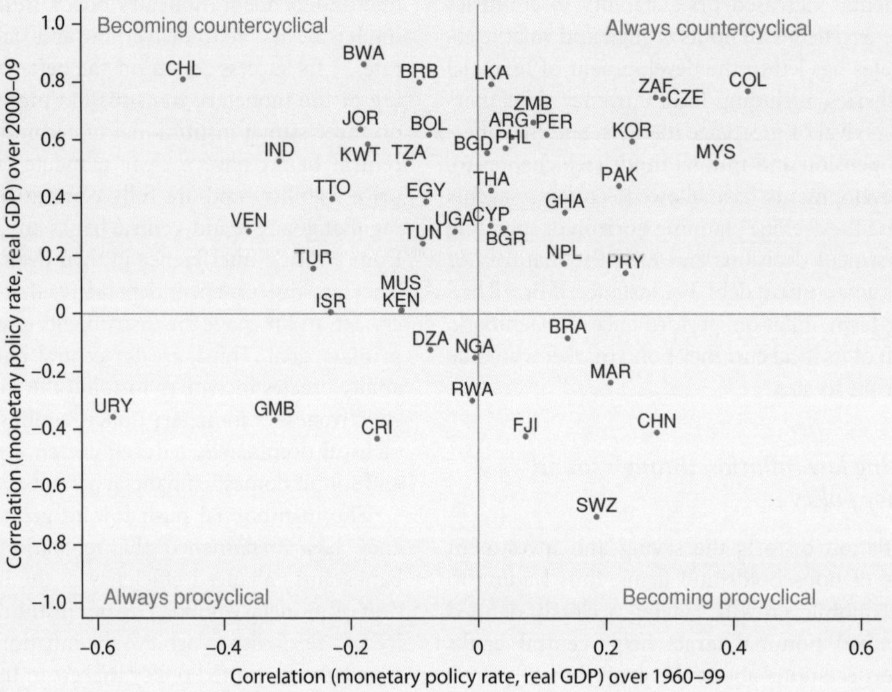

Source: WDR 2014 team based on data from Végh and Vuletin 2012.

Note: The figure compares the correlation between monetary policy rate and real GDP in 1960–99 with that in 2000–09. Both series are detrended using the Hodrick-Prescott filter. A positive (negative) correlation coefficient signals countercyclical (procyclical) monetary policy. The countries are classified as: (a) always countercyclical when the correlations are positive in both periods; (b) becoming countercyclical when the correlation is negative in 1960–99 and positive in 2000–10; (c) always procyclical when the correlations are negative in both periods; (d) becoming procyclical when the correlation is positive in 1960–99 and negative in 2000–10.

income and deeper financial markets have benefited from more flexible arrangements (floating regimes), which have delivered higher growth without higher inflation.[14] Floating regimes act as shock absorbers, helping countries accommodate adverse real shocks. In the presence of rigid prices, countries with floating rates will have smoother responses in real output to real shocks, thanks to the faster relative price adjustment that these regimes facilitate. Growth in per capita GDP declines 38 basis points, on average, for countries with flexible regimes facing a 10 percent deterioration in the terms of trade, whereas the decline is 83 basis points for countries with fixed regimes.[15] Countries with floating regimes also recover faster from natural hazards. Output growth averages 1.6 percentage points higher in countries with flexible regimes over a three-year period following a natural hazard, but only 0.24 percent in countries with fixed rates.[16] Finally, current account adjustment is faster in countries with flexible exchange rates. For instance, it takes 12 months to correct half the imbalance in the current account under floating exchange rates, compared with 21 months under fixed rates.[17] Overall, flexible exchange rate regimes are needed to guarantee the long-term viability of an independent and sound monetary policy framework. Box 7.2 illustrates the costs of not having an independent monetary policy (including a floating regime at the national level) within a currency union.

Before the global financial crisis, the prevailing monetary framework in advanced countries and some developing countries was characterized by a fragmented approach. Inflation targeting and flexible exchange rates were used to achieve low and stable inflation, stabilize fluctuations in output, and facilitate external adjustment. Meanwhile, microprudential regulation and bank supervision sought to prevent excessive risk taking in the financial sector. This arrangement did not account for the fact that macroeconomic and financial cycles are tightly linked—

BOX 7.2 *Relinquishing monetary policy flexibility: The ultimate sacrifice?*

Currency unions—either unilateral or multilateral arrangements—reduce cross-border transaction costs and foster trade among their members. In general, trade increases between 30 and 90 percent for countries that join a currency union, and between 4 and 16 percent for Euro Area countries. Joining a currency union poses a trade-off, however: a country must give up the power to have an independent (national) monetary policy to withstand idiosyncratic asymmetric shocks.

The recent Euro Area crisis underlines the costs of not having an independent monetary policy (including a floating regime at the national level) to accommodate negative real shocks and facilitate external adjustment. Costly coping with the crisis was exacerbated by poor preparation of the periphery countries: they had large external and fiscal imbalances. In the absence of monetary policy space, the burden of adjustment fell on the already stressed fiscal policy of these countries.

Lack of monetary flexibility at the national level sharply limits policy options for boosting growth and lifting the country out of recession. The alternative, an internal devaluation (a relative price decline in the absence of exchange rate devaluation), happens infrequently and entails a slow and painful adjustment. Only three episodes of internal devaluations have occurred among high-income countries since 1990, all during periods of severe recession and growing unemployment: Hong Kong SAR, China, in the early 2000s; Japan in the late 1990s and early 2000s; and Ireland in the recent crisis. Latvia, an upper-middle-income country, engineered an internal devaluation, but the recovery from the recent global crisis has been weak so far. There is compelling evidence of price and wage rigidity and lack of nominal wage declines (downward inflexibility). If trading partners' inflation does not outpace the country's inflation, internal devaluations will be slow and costly to achieve. For instance, competitiveness gains of 5 percent over three years would require a decade of internal devaluations in Greece. Finally, an internal devaluation would lead to a decline in nominal GDP—even if real economic activity increases—thus delaying the convergence to debt sustainability.

Some Euro Area policy makers are contemplating the option of fiscal devaluations—say, value added tax increases and payroll tax reductions—that have the potential to raise competitiveness faster than do internal devaluations. Whether that potential can be realized has not yet been shown.

Source: WDR 2014 team based on Rose and Stanley 2005; Micco, Stein, and Ordoñez 2003; Shambaugh 2012; Farhi, Gopinath, and Itskhoki 2011.

especially in advanced economies. For instance, real output and credit cycles of advanced countries are in the same cyclical phase (expansion or recession) 80 percent of the time, while the likelihood of a recession in economic activity in these countries conditional on a credit crunch is 40 percent.[18] The lack of a holistic approach led central bankers to tailor policy actions that addressed the trade-offs between inflation and output but did not address the buildup of financial imbalances. Yet mopping up the effects of burst bubbles by providing unlimited liquidity and sharply reducing interest rates—the preferred policy pursued in many advanced countries—can create moral hazard problems. In environments with low interest rates and excess liquidity, such as those currently experienced in advanced economies, financial institutions have incentives to take excessive risks and expand their balance sheets. Excessive leverage of financial institutions in advanced countries can be transmitted to emerging markets through surges in capital inflows and ensuing accumulation of financial imbalances.[19]

These developments have reignited the debate about including financial stability among central bank mandates and expanding the policy toolkit to include macroprudential instruments. Central banks need to assess whether monetary and financial conditions may lead to sharp credit and asset price reversals that disrupt economic activity. If so, they should deploy macroprudential tools to reduce the procyclicality of the financial system, avoid excessive bank risk taking, and increase the resilience of systemic institutions by imposing additional capital requirements.[20] Movements in monetary policy rates may prove ineffective in addressing financial bubbles, as higher interest rates may have adverse unintended consequences on output, unemployment, and volatility. Overall, macroprudential instruments—because they have more direct effect on leverage than the policy rate—can give central banks more instruments to achieve the goals of price and financial stability. For emerging markets, controls on capital inflows to limit the expansion of domestic credit and prevent the increase of currency and maturity mismatches may enhance financial stability.[21] So far, macroprudential policies have been effective in reducing systemic risk in the financial sector, but their impact on stabilizing output fluctuations is very much an open question. Box 7.3 examines the ability of one tool that is popular in the developing world to eliminate excessive fluctuations in real GDP: legal reserve requirements.

Promoting countercyclical fiscal policy

Countercyclical spending by the government is needed for two reasons: to transfer resources to less

BOX 7.3 ***Reserve requirement policy has substituted for monetary policy as a countercyclical tool in most developing countries***

Unlike industrial countries that tend to implement countercyclical monetary policies, many developing countries follow a procyclical stance. About half of developing countries use the legal reserve requirement both as a substitute for countercyclical monetary policy and as an instrument to stabilize output. In good times, policy makers in developing countries cut policy interest rates to reduce currency appreciation pressures and instead choose to increase reserve requirements to cool down the economy. In bad times, they increase policy interest rates to reduce depreciation pressures and decrease reserve requirements to help the economy get out of the recession. In other words, reserve requirement policy substitutes for monetary policy in its countercyclical role.

Increasing the legal reserve requirement by one standard deviation reduces output somewhat more than increasing the monetary policy rate (0.39 percent versus 0.21 percent) (see figure). In principle, both policy instruments could be used for stabilization purposes. In developing countries, however, monetary policy typically has been used to defend a nation's currency and contain inflationary pressures, but it has responded procyclically to fluctuations in output.

Reserve requirement policies can help stabilizing real GDP fluctuations

a. Reserve requirement policy

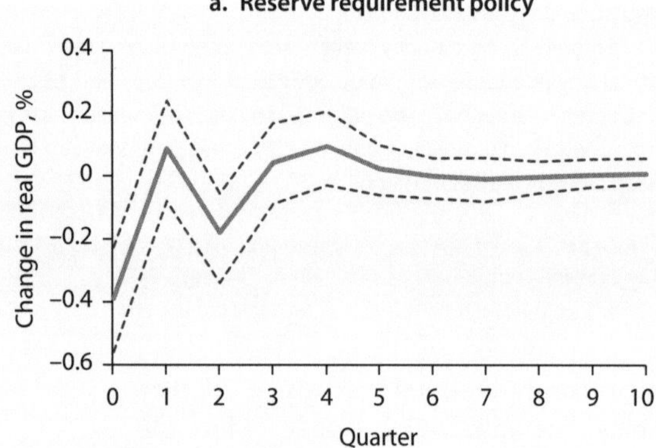

b. Monetary policy

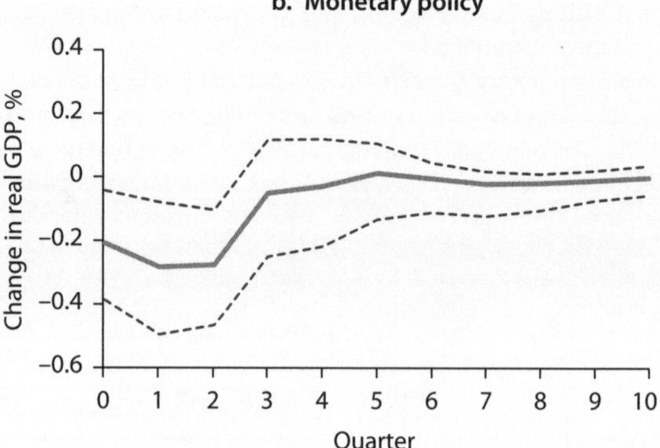

Source: Vuletin 2013 for the WDR 2014.
Note: The figure depicts the response of real GDP to a one standard deviation increase in the legal reserve requirement rate (panel a) and to an analogous increase in the monetary policy rate (panel b). These impulse-responses were estimated from a panel vector autoregression that evaluates the impact of exogenous changes in the reserve requirement, real GDP growth, and inflation in panel a; in panel b, the monetary policy rate was used instead of the reserve requirement. The dashed lines refer to 95 percent confidence intervals.

favored individuals, and to stimulate real economic activity in the event of shortfalls in aggregate demand. Contractions in economic activity and crisis episodes affect people and especially hurt those at lower income levels. The global financial crisis has added 53 million people to the number living below the $1.25-a-day poverty line, and that number is not expected to start declining until 2015.[22] Countercyclical social spending and timely stimulus packages are important to protect individuals during periods of hardship and stimulate employment. Historically, social security policies have been implemented or strengthened during financial crises. For instance, Mexico's social safety net for the poor, Programa de Educación, Salud y Alimentación (PROGRESA), was introduced after the 1994 "Tequila" crisis. The pension system in the Republic of Korea was broadened and universal health coverage was granted after the East Asian crisis. Unemployment insurance in the Republic of Korea was extended from 12.3 percent to about 50 percent of the unemployed from 1999 to 2004.[23]

Countercyclical fiscal policies in advanced countries are triggered by automatic increases in social security and welfare spending as the economy moves into recession—especially during crises. Historically, social security spending in advanced countries increases to 13.1 percent of GDP in the year of the financial crisis, from an average of 11.4 percent before the crisis.[24] A reduction of 1.0 percentage point in the growth rate of the economy is compensated by a 0.36 percentage point increase in social expenditures in these countries, on average. Social expenditures account for more than 80 percent of the overall contribution of fiscal policy to stabilizing output. Automatic movements in pensions and health spending, along with unemployment compensation, have been among the largest contributors.[25] Increasing transfers that are well-targeted and do not distort incentives to work (say, transfers to the unemployed and the poor) have been quite effective in the United States at stabilizing fluctuations in output. Cutting transfers (by 0.6 percent of GDP) in the United States increases output volatility by 4 percent, the variance of hours worked by 8 percent, and household consumption volatility by 35 percent.[26]

In contrast, most developing countries have been unwilling or unable to implement fiscal expansions during recessions.[27] Their behavior arises from the weakness of automatic stabilizers, their procyclical access to world capital markets, and political economy problems. Automatic stabilizers in developing countries are too small to have a significant smoothing effect on real economic activity: taxation is regressive, coverage and benefits of transfer programs are low, and unemployment insurance is almost nonexistent.[28] Spending on health, education, and infrastructure behaves procyclically in good times, and it expands faster than other types of spending. Social spending remains fairly constant during downturns, rather than declining. Deploying social spending in bad times may thus require only building up safety margins in good times—thereby breaking the cyclical pattern of boosting public spending in good times.[29] Procyclical discretionary fiscal interventions increase output volatility and hence undermine long-term growth. Heavy reliance on discretion may also create greater uncertainty and lead to greater instability. Governments may have less need for discretionary policy action if they have stronger built-in resilience or large automatic fiscal stabilizers.

Governments may have less need for discretionary policy action if they have flexible fiscal rules.

The procyclical bias of fiscal policy in developing countries stems partly from their generally procyclical access to capital markets. Governments' inability to borrow resources abroad or at home (or to borrow only at very high interest rates) during downturns leads them to cut spending or raise taxes. During upswings, they have access to markets and tend to borrow to increase public spending. Procyclical fiscal policies are also the outcome of political distortions and distributional conflicts. Governments tend to spend windfall revenues (stemming from rising commodity prices or higher-than-expected growth) during good times, when they are under pressure from powerful interest groups competing for public spending. In such situations, accumulating primary surpluses during upswings (saving for a rainy day) can be politically costly. Fiscal resources generated during upswings end up being captured by government agencies, state-owned enterprises, provinces or states, and rent-seekers.[30] Finally, voters may also seek to starve governments and reduce political rents—especially in corrupt democracies.[31]

Institutional development has helped some developing countries escape from the trap of fiscal procyclicality. An improvement in the quality of institutions, reflected in better fiscal institutions and sound fiscal rules, has helped some countries graduate from fiscal policy procyclicality. More than one-third of developing countries now follow a countercyclical fiscal policy stance (map 7.1).[32] Improved fiscal outcomes and frameworks in emerging markets have been rewarded in the markets by lower sovereign spreads. For instance, the sovereign spread of Brazil declined from 772 basis points to 145 basis points (over U.S. treasuries) from end-2000 to end-2012. Other factors that have contributed to developing countries' graduation from procyclicality are increases in the depth of domestic financial markets and greater credibility of fiscal policies.[33]

The effectiveness of discretionary fiscal stimulus is under intense debate in academic and policy circles. Discretionary actions to stimulate consumption and hence aggregate demand in the short run (the so-called Keynesian multiplier) through government spending should be distinguished from steps to increase productive capacity in the short and long run (such as public investment in infrastructure). Estimating these aggregate spending multipliers (that is, the increase in GDP for every dollar in additional government spending) is not a trivial issue. The estimation should consider changes in government spending that are independent from economic conditions; specifically, it needs to isolate the effects of government spending on output from reverse causality and from the influence of other forces in the economy such as natural hazards. The evidence consistent with this identification strategy suggests that the use of discretionary fiscal policy to stimulate demand in developing countries has not been overly successful—as witnessed over the past 30 years. The (short-term) aggregate government spending multiplier in developing countries is quite small: the one-year government spending multiplier

MAP 7.1 ***Government consumption became countercyclical in more than one-third of developing countries over the past decade***

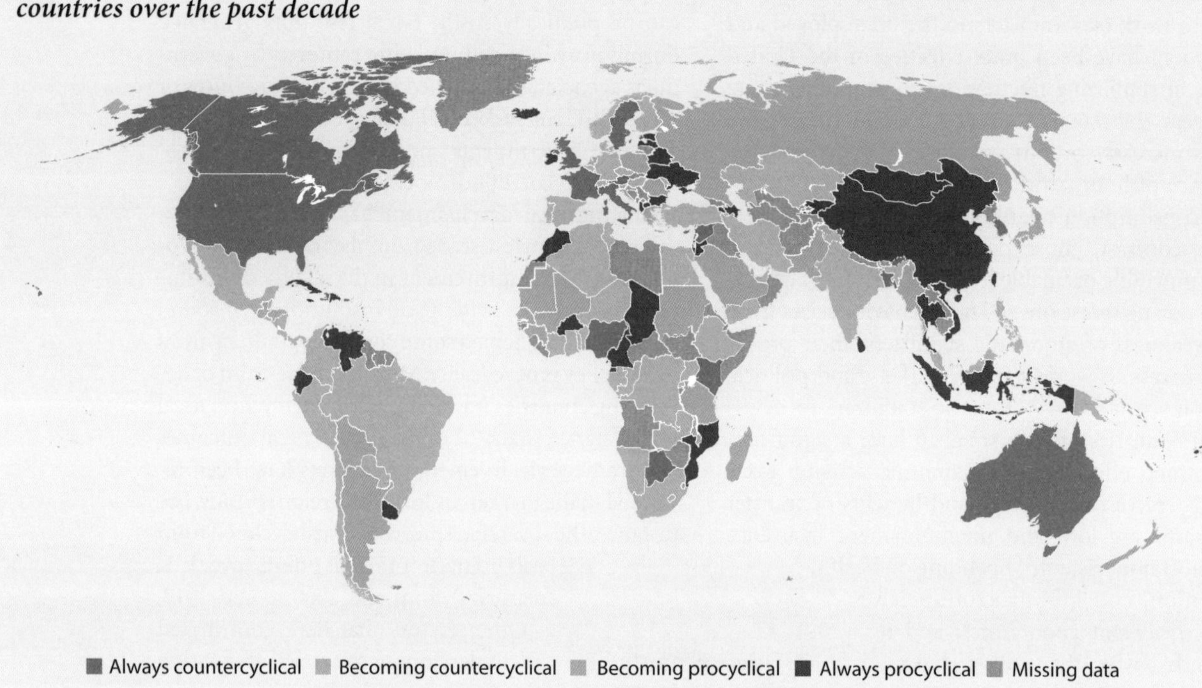

Source: WDR 2014 team estimations based on Frankel, Végh, and Vuletin 2013 methodology. Map number: IBRD 40099.

Note: The map shows the evolution of the cyclical stance of fiscal policy from 1960–99 to 2000–12. The cyclical stance is measured in a regression of the (Hodrick-Prescott) cyclical component of general government consumption expenditure on its own lagged value, and the cyclical component of real GDP. The sign of the coefficient on the cyclical component of real GDP indicates whether government consumption expenditure is procyclical (positive sign) or countercyclical (negative sign). The coefficient on the cyclical component of real GDP was estimated separately for the periods 1960–99 and 2000–12. Then, countries are classified as always countercyclical (in both periods); becoming countercyclical (only countercyclical in 2000–12); becoming procyclical (only procyclical in 2000–12); and always procyclical (in both periods). The likely endogeneity of the cyclical component of real GDP was controlled for by using as instruments the (current and lagged value of the) cyclical component of real GDP of the country's main trading partners and international oil prices, as well as the lagged value of the country's own cyclical component of real GDP.

fluctuates between 0.5 and 0.7, on average.[34] A recent survey for the United States suggests that one-year government spending multipliers are somewhere between 0.5 and 1.5, although, there is diversity in the methods used to identify exogenous fiscal policy changes.[35] Box 7.4 reviews a few contrasting experiences in industrial and developing countries.

The magnitude of the aggregate spending multiplier, however, depends on the country's initial conditions—and the evidence comes mostly from developed countries. Multipliers tend to be stronger in recessions than in booms. The one-year government spending multiplier is about 0.5 in recessions and booms; however, the response soon falls below zero in expansions, while it rises steadily to 2.5 after five years during recessions.[36] Aggregate multipliers are less than 1.0 when central banks can adjust interest rates in response to macroeconomic conditions. However, they are much larger if the nominal interest rate is unresponsive to increases in government spending—especially when interest rates are near zero. If government spending goes up for 12 quarters but the nominal interest rate does not vary, the impact multiplier is 1.6.[37]

The effectiveness of government expenditure in building productive capacity goes beyond the horizon of output impact multipliers. Public investment projects, especially infrastructure projects, can have lasting positive effects on GDP, investment, and productivity—especially when the economy's stock of infrastructure capital is relatively low.[38] The evidence shows that while the short-run impact of output to government investment is 0.6 in developing countries, its cumulative impact rises to a long-run value of 1.6.[39] Public infrastructure projects require coordination among different levels of government, and they undergo an extensive planning, bidding, contracting, construction, and evaluation process.

BOX 7.4 *Fiscal stimulus: The good, the bad, and the ugly*

China. China's response to the 1997–98 East Asian financial crisis is viewed as a successful countercyclical intervention by a developing country in the face of an external shock. The stimulus was timely, coincided with a growth slowdown, worked primarily through increases in infrastructure spending, and reversed at a good time. Several factors account for this success. First, China's public debt was very low before the crisis, giving China more scope to engage in deficit spending. Second, sustained growth and China's prohibition on subnational government borrowing ensured that credit-constrained local governments had strong need for financing for infrastructure projects. Third, the stimulus, although modest at 1 percent of GDP, was leveraged into larger investment spending. The central government participated in infrastructure projects only by cofinancing them; private banks provided the rest of the financing once the government provided loan guarantees. Finally, the fiscal expansion was implemented during a period when growth was still very rapid.

United States. The American Recovery and Reinvestment Act (enacted in February 2009) failed to stimulate the U.S. economy from 2009 to 2011. Temporary transfers to raise personal disposable incomes were not translated into higher consumption, as recipients used these resources to pay off debt and save. The amount of resources allotted to federal government purchases and services was quite small. Overall, purchases peaked at 0.2 percent of GDP and infrastructure spending at 0.05 percent of GDP in the third quarter of 2010. Finally, grants provided to state and local governments to start infrastructure projects and purchase goods and services were shifted toward reducing state and local net borrowing. In sum, the federal government stimulus compensated for collapsing state expenditures; the net increase in government spending was negligible.

Argentina. The risks of a mistimed expansionary change in fiscal policy are illustrated by Argentina in the mid-1990s. In the midst of the post-Tequila boom (1996–98), Argentina undertook an expansionary fiscal policy that further fueled the boom. This expansion was motivated by revenue shortfalls, partly linked to pension reform, whose adverse short-term draws on public revenue were not offset by increases in other taxes or reductions in spending. As a result, the ratio of public debt to GDP kept rising despite the economic bonanza. When the 1998 Russian financial crisis erupted, triggering sudden stops in capital inflows among emerging markets, Argentina's fiscal authorities had no room for maneuvering to mitigate the recession. Instead, they had to engage in a severe fiscal contraction that deepened the slump and eventually led to the collapse of the monetary policy regime.

Sources: Kraay and Servén 2013 for the WDR 2014; Taylor 2011.

Public infrastructure stimulus may not automatically translate into commensurate increases in the supply of infrastructure services because of limited or low-quality projects in the pipeline and inefficiencies in the selection and implementation of these projects. The disconnect between spending and asset accumulation is particularly acute when governance and fiscal institutions are weak, as is the case of many developing countries.

Elements of sound fiscal policy expansions

Fiscal expansions need to be credibly and sustainably financed. Only those developing countries with strong fiscal positions and large reserve stocks (such as Chile, China, Malaysia, and Turkey) can afford to finance fiscal expansions. This point underscores the importance of building up fiscal buffers in good times so that they are available in bad times.

Fiscal expansions should be timely but not rushed. Timely action is a challenge in developing countries, where data quality and fiscal institutions are often weak. Serious risk can arise from rushing to expand public spending without adequate oversight institutions and capacity to appraise new projects in place. Policy makers should first consider expanding well-functioning and already-tested projects and financing preappraised and "shovel-ready" new projects, before embarking on untried public spending projects that risk becoming "white elephants."

Fiscal expansions should focus on growth-enhancing spending programs or on areas where expenditures are reversible. Such expansions will not jeopardize long-run fiscal and debt sustainability. Policy makers should concentrate on projects that act as automatic stabilizers. Examples include means-tested social benefit programs that expand during downturns, as more people fall below eligibility thresholds, and then contract as the economy recovers. Similarly, workfare programs that clearly pay below-market wages will attract participants in downturns but will not be appealing once the economy recovers. The risks of unsustainable accumulation of public debt are also reduced to the extent that increases in spending occur in areas such as infrastructure, where costs may be recovered through future user fees. Overall, strengthening automatic stabilizers—or designing programs that resemble them for use during recessions—are sustainable ways to conduct countercyclical policies.

Historical experience in developing countries challenges the notion that expansionary fiscal policy is effective. That does not mean that expansionary policy cannot play a role in mitigating the effects of crises, however. It does mean that recommendations for countercyclical fiscal measures should incorporate the sobering lessons from past experience. Two priorities should be considered in the use of expansionary fiscal policy. First, social safety nets should be strengthened to help the most vulnerable and those most affected by the crisis to cope, especially in areas where short-term coping mechanisms can have severe long-term impact, such as cutbacks in children's food consumption or education (see chapter 3). Second, government spending should focus on areas that are likely to contribute to long-term growth, such as infrastructure.

Generating sustainable fiscal resources to finance stabilization policies and long-term social programs

Making fiscal room to maneuver to cope with shocks and unexpected obligations

Funding for stabilization policies and long-term social programs is limited by the ability of the government to save and borrow resources. In this context, creating space for policy actions requires assessing the sustainability of public debt, the nature and timing of desired expenditures, the responsiveness of public revenues to economic activity, the exposure to fiscal risks, and the government's capacity to repay its debt. In the latter case, debt defaults and the ensuing credit downgrades reduce the country's creditworthiness and deepen the downturn in economic activity.

Preparing to cope with macroeconomic disasters. Severe macroeconomic contractions are typically accompanied by declines in public revenue collection and the call for social expenditure increases. In the past 50 years, middle-income countries have been in recession 14 to 16 percent of the time, and low-income countries, a staggering 27 percent of the time. Meanwhile, industrial countries have spent 7 percent of the time in sharp recession, as defined by cumulative declines in real GDP per capita of more than 5 percent. The timely and appropriate response to a collapse in aggregate demand will be limited by the health of the government fiscal position.

Preparing to cope with budgetary surprises. Governments need to safeguard fiscal space to manage implicit obligations (such as social security programs) or obligations arising from explicit or implicit contingent liabilities. Explicit contingent liabilities stem from the government's need to meet the terms of contracts and regulations; examples include credit guarantees and public-private partnerships in infrastructure. Implicit contingent liabilities are taken by the government on the basis of political commitments (financial bailouts) or humanitarian grounds (disaster relief), or provision of public goods (environmental clean-up), for instance. Table 7.1 summarizes public policy actions to prevent or deal with recession and budgetary surprises (see also the discussion on contingent liabilities later in this chapter).

Creating space to cope with downturns and build resilience

Using fiscal rules appropriately. Fiscal rules have emerged in response to fiscal profligacy and to correct distorted incentives and contain pressures to overspend in good times. They typically impose year-by-year numerical limits on debt, expenditure, revenue, or budget balances. However, during the recent financial crisis, these annual numerical targets did not facilitate adjustment to adverse shocks, shifted expenditure composition away from social and investment spending, and created incentives in countries with large imbalances to erode transparency through the use of creative accounting.[40] Rules should recognize that fiscal sustainability is an intertemporal concept and allow for temporary deficits accompanied by subsequent offsetting surpluses. Fiscal rules targeting budget balances along the cycle provide flexibility to respond to shocks and meet the sustainability criteria. These rules are far from being a panacea, however. Their credibility and effectiveness rest on their design, adequate institutional capacity, clear operational procedures, and effective communication strategies (see the "Focus on policy reform" at the end of this Report).

Medium-term expenditure frameworks (MTEFs) constitute another option to implement forward-looking multiyear budget planning. Under these frameworks, spending may not exceed expected revenues and is allocated through medium-term sector strategies. MTEFs combine top-down approaches to allocate aggregate resources to spending agencies, bottom-up determination of the resource needs of spending agencies, and assessment of the links between funding and results. Currently, more than two-thirds of all countries have adopted MTEFs.[41]

Managing assets prudently. To weather adverse shocks, some countries have accumulated reserves

TABLE 7.1 *Policies to prevent or cope with fiscal risks*

Policies regarding asset management	Policies regarding liability management
Dealing with recessions/macroeconomic disasters	
Structural budget rules and sovereign wealth funds to safeguard savings in good times	Fiscal consolidation: debts and deficits reduction; sound debt management strategies (reduce interest rate, currency, and refinancing risks); hedge against currency and interest rates
Effective tax administration	Reprioritization of expenditures
Saving part of donor assistance (especially for low-income countries)	Integration of risk analysis and mitigation (especially for natural disasters) into a public investment frameworks; market insurance for future costs/damages of public investment
Commodity price hedging (for resource-rich countries)	Social security financing: encourage personal responsibility through setting up privately managed, fully funded contribution funds
Sound governance for state-owned enterprises to mitigate fluctuations of revenues	Increased transparency and disclosure of budget expenditures that are legally binding in the long term; reduce earmarking
Dealing with budgetary surprises	
Transparent tax frameworks to mitigate volatility of fiscal revenues due to tax competition	Establishment of a fiscal risk management unit in the ministry of finance to manage contingent liabilities
International diversification of assets to accommodate changes in global market sentiment	Guarantees: Build adequate incentives through risk sharing; valuing and provisioning
	Well-funded deposit insurance funds
	Increase transparency and build credibility to avoid legal claims against the government
	Adequate microprudential and macroprudential supervision to mitigate the need for financial bail-outs
	Adequate foreign exchange reserves for uncalled capital
	Rules on the subnational government borrowing operations to reduce the risk of bail-outs
	Preparation and implementation of sovereign disaster risk financing strategies, including retention instruments (such as reserves and contingency budgets) and risk transfer mechanisms (such as parametric insurance and catastrophe bonds)
	Adequate infrastructure and early warning systems for natural disasters
	Environmental norms to prevent residual damages associated with pollution

Source: WDR 2014 team.

while others have set up sovereign wealth funds in response to commodity price booms (such as oil-exporting countries) or large export-led booms in economic activity (as in China). Reserve accumulation can be used to limit exchange rate volatility and cushion aggregate domestic spending during current account reversals.[42] Holding reserves can be costly, however, because their return is lower than the interest rate offered on government debt. The cost of carrying reserves for the median emerging market was around 0.5 percent of GDP from 2001–09, on average.[43] International reserves as a share of GDP nearly tripled in upper-middle-income countries over the past decade (to 30.8 percent of GDP in 2010 from 10.9 percent in 2000). Safer assets (reserves and debt) have driven the accumulation of foreign assets in emerging market economies, as opposed to advanced countries, which accumulated riskier assets (equity and foreign direct investment). Compared relative to the rest of the world, emerging markets are now in a net creditor position in safe assets, while they are in a net debtor position in riskier assets.[44]

The net accumulation of foreign assets and persistent current account surpluses led to the emergence and growth of sovereign wealth funds (SWFs). According to their source of revenue, they can be classified as commodity SWFs, funded by revenues from commodity exports (such as the Government Pension Fund of Norway, and Saudi Arabian Monetary Authority Foreign Holdings); and noncommodity SWFs, funded by transferring assets from international reserves, government budget surpluses, and privatization revenues (such as China's SAFE Investment Company and Singapore's Temasek Holdings).

SWFs have multiple goals, including stabilizing government revenue, managing intergenerational savings and pension liabilities, and making long-term investments. SWFs need legitimacy and credibility to protect their capital from depletion by the government or the current generation.[45] Together, they manage more than $5 trillion in assets (with oil- and gas-related SWFs accounting for nearly 60 percent of the total), compared to world international reserves of $11 trillion and worldwide GDP of $71 trillion in 2012.[46] Countries have enacted laws and created institutions to set up management principles and investment policies for their funds. Procedures governing the funding, withdrawal, and spending of the capital should be tailored to the specific fund's goals. Stabilization and saving funds are typically made up of excess (commodity or government) revenues. Fund withdrawal is sometimes flexible; however, it requires an investment mandate to minimize unexpected resource demands from the government.[47] An SWF's spending plans should be part of a coherent policy framework, need to be flexible, and—if necessary—be able to be used to meet unexpected and large adverse shocks. For instance, Timor-Leste's Petroleum Fund has invested in the country's electricity grid and transportation networks. Chile has drawn upon its SWF to help rebuild areas damaged by the 2011 earthquake (box 7.5).[48] Greater accountability increases the credibility and effectiveness of these funds. All of them submit reports to the government on a regular basis. For instance, the Kuwait Investment Authority has an independent board that reports to the Council of Ministers.

Adopting sounder public debt management strategies. Along with sharp debt reduction, public debt managers in emerging markets have engineered a major shift in the risk and maturity profile of government debt portfolios. First, the development of local currency bond markets has allowed governments to issue debt in their own currency, thus reducing their dependence on external funding and exposure to exchange rate risk. Second, public bond issuances have gradually shifted from short-term and floating debt to fixed rate debt—thus reducing the exposure to interest rate fluctuations. Third, governments have raised the average life of their portfolio by issuing long-term, fixed-rate instruments. Established issuers such as Brazil, Colombia, Jamaica, Mexico, Peru, Turkey, and Uruguay have been issuing 30-year bonds since 2006. These longer maturities have allowed debt managers to reduce the risk of refinancing. Finally, the stable domestic macroeconomic environment and financial market reforms have allowed governments to diversify their funding sources. Domestic institutional investors are playing a larger role, with pension funds and insurance companies increasing their demand for government bonds. Foreign investors have increased their role as well, especially in countries that have (or have recently obtained) investment grade status.[49]

Enhancing the scope for public debt management with market insurance. Market instruments help governments secure the funds needed to deal with the aftermath of large negative shocks, such as fluctuations in interest rates, exchange rates, and commodity prices, and reversals of capital inflows. Some governments have issued explicit state-contingent debt to hedge against some of these risks—for instance, government debt indexed to GDP, exports, or export commodity prices (such as copper prices). The hedging potential of these instruments has not yet been fully realized, however. State-contingent securities, already traded in international markets, can provide additional insurance, helping governments build portfolios with countercyclical returns. For instance, the risk of reversals in capital flows (sudden stops)—driven by episodes of international flight to quality—is strongly correlated with jumps in the Chicago Board Options Exchange Market Volatility Index (VIX), which measures anticipated volatility in the Standard & Poor's 500 index. A strategy that "shorts" VIX-linked contracts may provide a good hedge against sudden-stop events. Similarly, market instruments are available to hedge against commodity price fluctuations, and the welfare gains from doing so are potentially large.[50] While these measures offer some potential insurance against shocks to external funding, their effectiveness relies on the presence of deep-pocketed and informed creditors who are willing to take on emerging market risks. That

BOX 7.5 *Managing commodity revenues in Chile: An example of sound institution building and management of public resources*

Chile is the world's largest producer of copper, accounting for 43 percent of world exports in 2010. Copper is an important source of government revenues: about half the income from copper is public, in the form of tax revenues and profits from Corporación Nacional del Cobre de Chile—a state-owned enterprise that controls about one-third of the country's copper production. How does Chile manage this natural wealth? The answer lies in the increasing institutionalization of prudent fiscal policies for better risk management.

In 2001, Chile became the only country besides Norway to correct for cyclical influences of the business cycle and the price of its main commodity export goods. A fiscal rule that commits the government to a target level for a cyclically adjusted balance (CAB) aims at saving during high-revenue periods and deploying resources in bad times, over and above the saving or dissaving target reflected by the CAB. The fiscal rule provides a predictable path for fiscal policy and has reduced uncertainty about fiscal revenues associated with copper prices. While the rule is a very sound measure, its workings are far from perfect. Chile has yet to establish an ex ante escape clause from the rule (that would apply under prespecified conditions) or ex post sanctions for violating the rule and ensuring corrections.

Chile also made fiscal policy a cornerstone for managing resource revenues. The Fiscal Responsibility Law enacted in 2006 (Law 20128) provided an institutional framework that strengthened the link between the fiscal rule and use of government savings. It also established two sovereign wealth funds (SWFs). The law contemplated greater disclosure and transparency in the conduct of fiscal policy. New government administrations are required to publish their fiscal policy framework for their four-year term and to issue an annual report on the financial state of the government, its fiscal sustainability, and its macrofinancial implications, along with an estimate of the CAB. In turn, the calculation of the CAB target requires an annual estimation of government contingent liabilities.

To finance the government's future pension liabilities, a Pension Reserve Fund was created. In good times, fiscal surpluses in excess of the structural target (and after contribution to the pension fund) are channeled to the new Economic and Social Stabilization Fund. In bad times, resources are withdrawn from the stabilization fund to finance budget deficits (including payments into the pension fund).

The international investment of the resources held in the two SWFs can be undertaken directly by the treasury or outsourced to the Central Bank of Chile—or to private fund managers hired by the central bank. The law also created a new independent committee, the Advisory Financial Committee for Fiscal Responsibility Funds, which provides nonbinding recommendations to the ministry of finance on fund investment policies and regulations, and publishes an annual report on the financial performance of the SWFs. Financial statements from the SWFs are audited by an independent international agency.

Source: Fuentes 2013 for the WDR 2014.

may be a problem, particularly when shocks to external funding often originate as shocks to the creditor's ability to lend.[51]

Implementing a management framework for sovereign assets and liabilities. Sound risk management by the government requires the effective implementation of a sovereign asset-liability management framework. This framework requires enhanced coordination by the various governmental institutions that control and manage specific sovereign financial assets and liabilities: for example, coordination between the treasury and the central bank, when the latter issues debt or holds windfall revenues (in the case of commodity-exporting countries). In practice, the management of assets and liabilities is rarely coordinated. Partial coordination efforts integrate the management of some (but not all) balance sheet items. For instance, Finland, Greece, and Turkey have integrated management of the net position on central government debt and cash reserves. In Hungary, the central bank prepares a consolidated balance sheet when an increase in the international reserves requires debt to be issued in foreign currency. In Canada, the country with the greatest degree of integration, the management of both assets and liabilities is assigned to one agency or ministry, which delegates responsibilities for day-to-day management (for example, to the central bank) and coordinates the borrowing and investing programs.[52]

Managing macroeconomic contingent liabilities

Managing public liabilities entails not only addressing current obligations but also focusing on contingent liabilities, thus reflecting the increased awareness of the ability of these liabilities to impair fiscal sustainability. For instance, calls on government guarantees will trigger budgetary obligations.

Controlling social security expenditures. In many countries, social security benefits (either publicly or privately provided) are implicit public guarantees.

To the extent that they are politically binding (and at times unavoidable), these benefits are ultimately a government obligation. Disclosure of long-term budgetary pressures associated with social security and demographic trends permits countries to manage the associated risks better. For instance, Australia, New Zealand, the United Kingdom, and the United States have published stand-alone, long-term fiscal sustainability reports. European Union countries, along with Brazil and Japan, report long-term fiscal outlooks on pension and social security spending.[53] The fiscal costs of social security can be mitigated by transforming these implicit open-ended guarantees into explicit but limited ones.[54] For example, the 1981 pension reform in Chile introduced privately managed individual retirement accounts. A similar reform was adopted by several countries in Latin America and Eastern Europe from 1981 to 2004. Nevertheless, the 2008 crisis brought up shortcomings in the effectiveness of the model, including high fees in private accounts, distributional effects, and political interference. In March 2008, Chile enacted a comprehensive pension reform law that addressed critical policy areas (related worker coverage, gender equity, pension adequacy, and administrative fees) and set up a basic universal pension as a supplement to the individual accounts system. Under the new law, the Sistema de Pensiones Solidarias has been added to the existing mandatory individual accounts to increase coverage. It also introduced a noncontributory basic solidarity pension (Pensión Básica Solidaria).[55]

Developing sound frameworks for explicit contingent liabilities. Optimal design of contingent contracts may reduce moral hazard by either the beneficiary or the guaranteed party. It is necessary to develop public-private risk-sharing mechanisms so that the guaranteed party or the beneficiary bears some risk. For instance, coverage ratios of credit guarantees should provide incentives for lenders to properly assess and monitor borrowers. Most practitioners argue that lenders should retain a significant part of the risk, from 30 to 40 percent. In practice, the median guarantee covers 80 percent of the loan, while some schemes offer guarantee to lenders up to 100 percent.[56] Governments should also consider other risk-sharing mechanisms, such as termination clauses that allow them to close arrangements when the instrument is no longer needed, requirements to post collateral or to have an ownership stake, and measures to share the upside potential along with the downside risks. Rather than implementing ad hoc mechanisms, governments need to develop fiscal frameworks to better assess and mitigate risks associated with contractual obligations. They should develop methods to project the costs, evaluate the merits of taking on these liabilities, and declare the conditions under which the government will meet these obligations. For instance, Australia and Canada have developed principles to regulate the participation of the government as a guarantor in loan operations—including the identification, pricing, coverage, and evaluation of the risk. In the case of public-private partnerships in infrastructure, the governments of Colombia and South Africa have established frameworks to ensure proper risk taking and the allocation of risks. The risk allocation under these schemes is reflected in national or international legislation.[57]

Enhancing fiscal policy decision making through transparency and disclosure. By enhancing the quality of information on fiscal risks, transparency builds support for prudent fiscal policies, promotes better policy actions, and leads to better risk mitigation. Disclosure strengthens confidence and credibility in public sector accounts and in the sustainability of fiscal policy. Credibility, in turn, reduces sovereign borrowing costs and improves the government's access to international capital markets. Greater fiscal transparency is positively associated with improvements in a country's credit rating: on average, credit spreads decline 11 percent when governments choose to become more transparent.[58] In best practice, some governments (Australia, Brazil, Chile, Colombia, Indonesia, New Zealand, and Pakistan) have published statements of fiscal risks to their balance sheets and hence to their policy stance. Sometimes, however, full disclosure of government obligations may lead to moral hazard. For instance, reporting some implicit contingent liabilities may lead some agents to take on excessive risk under the impression that the government may step in to cover any losses. Moreover, information that may endanger the government in the event of litigation should not be revealed. Box 7.6 highlights the experience of Colombia in disclosing fiscal risks.

Maintaining adequate regulatory and crisis resolution frameworks to protect against financial bailouts. Government bailout of the financial sector can both be costly and impair the sustainability of its financial accounts. The median fiscal cost of financial system bailouts in 87 crisis episodes from 1970 to 2011 was approximately 7 percent of GDP (4 percent of GDP

BOX 7.6 *Disclosing fiscal risks in Colombia: A path to greater transparency and credibility in risk management*

Colombia's resilience to the global economic turbulence is partly attributed to its sound fiscal institutions. The gradual consolidation of the fiscal framework over the past 15 years was strengthened with the enactment of the Responsibility and Transparency Law (Law 819) in 2003. This law established the Medium-Term Fiscal Framework (MTFF), a tool for macrofiscal programming that set high standards for fiscal policy transparency and risk management.

The MTFF must contain a 10-year fiscal programming framework and an assessment of the main fiscal risks and the fiscal impact of economic decisions adopted the previous year. This assessment is consolidated yearly in a public document submitted to Congress before the budget bill is discussed. The law requires the central government to analyze the country's macroeconomic and fiscal performance and its macroeconomic framework over a 10-year horizon, numerical targets for the nonfinancial public sector primary balance and its future financial plans, the fiscal cost of laws enacted the previous year, and the fiscal impact of quasi-fiscal operations (from the central bank and deposit insurance agency).

Evaluating nonexplicit debt and contingent liabilities. Law 448 of 1998 issued the first regulations for managing budgetary contingencies, giving the ministry of finance (MoF) responsibility to approve and monitor their assessment, and created a hedging mechanism, the Contingency Fund of State Entities. In 1999, for the first time, the National Planning Department estimated the present value of pension liabilities and built an "extended balance sheet" for the public sector, including an assessment of nonexplicit debt and contingent liabilities. In 2003, Law 819 required the MTFF to include an annual assessment of nonexplicit public debt associated with pension and severance liabilities, and a valuation of contingent liabilities related to state guarantees in public-private partnership (PPP) projects, loan guarantees, and lawsuits against the state. For instance, the MTFF estimated the net present value of pension liabilities at 114 percent of GDP in 2012.

Identifying contingent liabilities from guarantees for public-private partnerships in infrastructure. The MoF identifies, manages, and monitors risks affecting the expected financial results of infrastructure projects. It uses statistical models to estimate the probability of the occurrence and financial impact of risks. For instance, contingent liabilities arising from PPP contracts were estimated at 0.27 percent of GDP in 2012. The creation of the National Infrastructure Agency and new laws governing PPPs have also improved the technical and financial structuring of investment projects and reduced incentives to renegotiate contracts.

Assessing contingent liabilities related to lawsuits against the state. These liabilities are numerous and have growing fiscal impact: they represent an estimated 71.1 percent of GDP for 2011–21. To assess them, a probability tree is used to account for all stages of litigation. It is based on historical information of similar actions in similar jurisdictions and on qualitative analysis. The growing fiscal impact of these liabilities is partly explained by the low quality of public defense. The recent creation of the National Agency for the Legal Defense of the State is a step in the right direction to control these costs.

Determining contingent liabilities from guarantees in public credit operations. Assessing these contingencies is based on the estimation of solvency probability curves. Estimates suggest they amount to 0.22 percent of GDP for 2011–21.

Dealing with contingent liabilities related to disasters. Earthquakes and floods have had high fiscal impact in Colombia.[a] The government has strengthened its institutional and financial capacity to deal more efficiently with natural hazards by creating a national coordinating body in 1985, called the Prevention of and Attention to Disasters System; conducting impact evaluation studies of the potential costs and the financial capacity of the state; and creating a financial fund to recover and adapt infrastructure affected recently by floods. Currently, the MoF is designing a disaster risk financing strategy, which includes enhancing its management of the possible budgetary impacts of disasters through instruments such as contingent credit and parametric reinsurance, and improving insurance of public assets through risk pooling and standard insurance requirements for concession contracts.

Source: Salazar 2013 for the WDR 2014.

a. For example, damages from the 1999 earthquake in the coffee region totaled $1.6 billion. Floods from 2010 to 2012 caused around $4.5 billion in damage to transport infrastructure and the agricultural sector.

for industrial countries, and 10 percent for developing countries). Recent banking crises have been among the costliest in terms of government obligations: the fiscal costs of the bailout in Iceland and Ireland have exceeded 40 percent of GDP so far.[59] Protection against the risk associated with financial bailouts requires both an adequate institutional framework that regulates the behavior of financial intermediaries (through limits on risk taking) and sound entities to monitor their financial position. In addition, the government needs to formulate adequate frameworks for crisis resolution that provide clear expectations of ex post risk sharing.

Designing a comprehensive strategy to manage liabilities associated with natural hazards. Moving from postdisaster coping to proactive budget planning would help increase the financial and fiscal resilience of countries to natural hazards.[60] The Disaster Risk Finance Insurance (DRFI) program proposes a sovereign disaster risk financing framework built on a risk-layering, bottom-up approach to help countries formulate budget plans before natural hazards occur and reduce volatile and open-ended fiscal exposures to contingent liabilities associated with them. Government can effectively manage high probability, low-impact events (such as localized floods, storms, or landslides) through risk retention tools like annual budget allocation and domestic reserves. Mexico has an annual budget allocation of $800 million for its National Fund for Natural Disasters. Intermediate layers of risk can be addressed with contingent credit lines or budget reallocation, such as World Bank development policy loans with a catastrophe deferred drawdown option (CAT-DDO). Costa Rica, Guatemala, Colombia, and the Philippines drew down funds from their CAT-DDO after natural disasters. Financial market instruments—traditional and parametric insurance, and alternative risk transfer mechanisms, particularly catastrophe bonds—are better suited to manage liabilities associated with low frequency, high-impact events. For instance, Mexico issued the first CAT-bonds in 2006. Other risk-pooling mechanisms include regional disaster insurance facilities established in the Caribbean and in the Pacific Islands (see chapter 8). Governments can also acquire commercial insurance that will cover the costs of environmental cleanup of properties under their control that exceed their budgeted resources. The international community—multilateral agencies, more specifically—also provide contingent instruments and emergency loans to finance disaster risk (see chapter 8).

Putting it all together: What to avoid and what to do to improve risk management at the macroeconomic level

Do not generate uncertainty or greater risks

Maintain the predictability of economic policies and focus on sustainability. Governments should try to implement time-consistent, predictable, and sustainable policies. Otherwise, their policy actions may create a vicious cycle that leads to counterproductive procyclical responses later. Policy-induced volatility raises aggregate instability and reduces growth. An increase of one standard deviation in fiscal policy volatility, for example, reduces long-term economic growth by 0.74 percent a year.[61]

Provide the right incentives

To improve the predictability and credibility of policy responses, increase the autonomy and accountability of monetary policy makers. One of the major institutional achievements in monetary policy has been to shield the central bank's policy-making decisions from political interference and providing the monetary authority with independence to create policy instruments to achieve its goals. However, with greater autonomy comes greater responsibility. Advanced countries and some emerging market economies have made great strides in achieving greater transparency in monetary policy making. Currently, central banks must explain their policy frameworks, describe the ways they intend to reach their goals, and provide information about the models built to formulate economic policy analysis. The disclosure of this information improves the capacity of economic agents to anticipate monetary policy decisions and understand the central bank's decision-making process. Monetary policy decisions are more predictable when communication from the central bank is timely, clear, collegial, and tailored to its audience.

Promote flexibility

Create the right incentives for better fiscal policy making by shifting toward flexible rules within an adequate institutional framework. Political authorities in many countries have granted the monetary authority independence, a very precise mandate to guide monetary policy, and incentives to be more transparent and accountable. These changes would also benefit fiscal policy arrangements—although to different degrees. The goal of fiscal policy is to achieve long-term budgetary discipline while allowing for flexibility to pursue short-term countercyclical actions. Success requires rules that do not constrain short-term flexibility. These flexible rules, in turn, require the development of supporting institutions. In this context, independent fiscal agencies can help inform, evaluate, and implement rules-based fiscal policies.

Build the foundation for long-term risk management

Enhance fiscal policy credibility by creating independent fiscal agencies. Independent monetary policy committees have greatly improved monetary policy making. Similarly, independent fiscal councils could be created to monitor fiscal discipline and restrain policy makers from spending sprees in good times, thus helping overcome agency and common pool problems and fostering coordination (see chapter 2). Unlike monetary policy, there is less consensus on the goals of fiscal policy (such as the appropriate level of sustainable debt), and fiscal authorities have a wider set of instruments in their toolkit. Full delegation of policy-making decisions is implausible, given the redistributive nature of fiscal policy. However, government officials can empower councils to conduct and monitor some budget procedures.[62] For instance, fiscal councils can correct overly optimistic official forecasts of budget and GDP growth by providing independent (legally binding) ones (as in Chile and the United Kingdom) or by auditing them (as in Sweden). They can increase rule flexibility by defining ex ante contingencies that trigger escape clauses to the rule (Switzerland), provide positive analysis and normative assessments of policies (Belgium and the Netherlands), and identify rule deviations associated with bad policies. Greater accountability strengthens the reputation of these councils.[63] However, fiscal councils are not a panacea. They are subject to problems of time inconsistency, capture, and lack of legitimacy (see the "Focus on policy reform" at the end of this Report for more detail on their optimal design). In countries with weak institutions and capacity, a good foundation starts with more comprehensive fiscal frameworks—including top-down approaches to budget planning and cooperative bargaining that impose binding budget constraints and put a premium on fiscal policy transparency.[64]

The increasing complexity of macroeconomic management necessitates continuous strengthening of institutional capacity.

Ensure adequate institutional capacity to carry out macroeconomic policies and address implementation problems. The increasing complexity of macroeconomic management necessitates continuous strengthening of institutional capacity, which should be supported by qualified staff. For instance, the greater sophistication of monetary policy regimes and fiscal rules and the management of contingent liabilities demand rethinking and enhancing institutional arrangements. Effective policy implementation requires a high level of institutional coordination. Monitoring and managing fiscal risks associated with contingent liabilities may call for coordination among various risk management units, line ministries, and a supreme auditing institution. In addition, the design and application of a sovereign asset-liability management framework entail coordination among institutions controlling resources and generating obligations.[65]

Protect the vulnerable

Protect the vulnerable from the distributional consequences of shocks or of the policies themselves. Macroeconomic policies have distributional consequences. Lower-income groups tend to be more affected by external shocks and macroeconomic imbalances. Higher-income groups tend to be more strongly affected by financial crises. Macroeconomic mismanagement tends to disproportionately increase the unemployment rate among low-income households and the young. Wealth shocks associated with equity price busts tend to disproportionately affect those aged 26–35 years (the most leveraged age group). Deeper financial markets tend to amplify shocks, thus strengthening the case for tighter macroprudential regulation. More stringent regulations in product markets tend to have an adverse impact on young people and poorer segments of society. The negative consequences of macroeconomic shocks and policies on the less favored segments of society can be alleviated by institutions and policies that facilitate risk sharing. Positive measures include social protection (such as unemployment benefits) and policies that facilitate resource reallocation (such as more flexible entry and exit of firms, more flexible business regulation, trade openness, and prudent fiscal policies).[66]

Keep a long-run focus

Policy makers should be proactive and keep their sights on long-term development. Macroeconomic risk management should concentrate on managing the cycle prudently and on developing systematic, credible, and sustainable policy responses. Forward-looking policy makers should avoid making hasty decisions during crises and instead focus on building the resilience of individuals, households, communities, the enterprise sector, the financial system, and the economy as a whole. They need to build the proper economic institutions that can create incen-

TABLE 7.2 ***Policy priorities to improve risk management at the macroeconomic level***

	POLICIES TO SUPPORT RISK MANAGEMENT FOUNDATIONAL →	ADVANCED
Knowledge	Data collection and dissemination	
	Improve quality of data	Monetary policy transparency Disclosure of fiscal risks
Protection	Central bank independence	Inflation targeting Flexible exchange rate regime
	Build stronger fiscal frameworks/institutions	Debt/deficit reduction
Insurance	Countercyclical monetary policy; reserve accumulation	Hedging mechanisms; contingent bonds
	Design better automatic stabilizers	Strengthen automatic stabilizers and discretionary social spending
	Countercyclical social spending	
Coping	Support from international financial institutions	Contingent credit lines

Source: WDR 2014 team.

Note: The table presents a sequencing of policies based on the guidance of chapter 2 for establishing policy priorities: *be realistic* in designing policies tailored to the institutional capacity of the country, and *build a strong foundation* that addresses the most critical obstacles sustainably and that can be improved over time.

tives to invest and thus foster long-term development. Table 7.2 summarizes government policies for risk management, arrayed as priorities for countries at different levels of institutional development and capacity. Overall, safeguarding macroeconomic stability, building reserve funds to finance desirable public programs (notably, investments in human capital and infrastructure), and devising policies to take advantage of trade and financial integration in the global economy will create the right incentives to deliver sustained growth without undermining the management of aggregate volatility.

Notes

1. The increase in the unemployment rate relative to precrisis levels tends to be between 2 and 4.5 percentage points higher than in a regular recession. See Calvo, Coricelli, and Ottonello 2012.
2. Other macroeconomic policies, including trade and financial openness, also permit the national government to stabilize the economy by sharing risks internationally. Although important in the policy toolkit, their discussion goes beyond the scope of this chapter.
3. Hnatkovska and Loayza 2005.
4. Calderón and Levy Yeyati 2009.
5. Galí and Gambetti 2009.
6. Burger and Warnock 2006.
7. Levy Yeyati and Sturzenegger 2003.
8. Tornell and Velasco 2000.
9. Mishkin and Savastano 2001.
10. Mishkin and Schmidt-Hebbel 2007.
11. Mishkin 2004.
12. Fiscal dominance refers to the situation where monetary policy is used to alleviate problems of fiscal sustainability through the monetization of public debt—and with little regard for the inflationary consequences.
13. Végh and Vuletin 2012.
14. Husain, Mody, and Rogoff 2005.
15. Edwards and Levy Yeyati 2005.
16. Ramcharan 2007.
17. Ghosh, Qureshi, and Tsangarides 2013.
18. Claessens, Kose, and Terrones 2012.
19. Bruno and Shin 2013.
20. De Gregorio 2012; Canuto and Cavallari 2013.
21. Committee on International Economic Policy and Reform 2011.
22. Chen and Ravallion 2010.
23. Keum and others 2006.
24. Prasad and Gerecke 2010.
25. Darby and Melitz 2008.
26. McKay and Reis 2013.
27. Frankel, Végh, and Vuletin 2013.
28. Suescún 2007.
29. Arze del Granado, Gupta, and Hajdenberg 2010.
30. Tornell and Lane 1999.
31. Alesina, Campante, and Tabellini 2008.
32. Frankel, Végh, and Vuletin 2013.
33. Calderón and Schmidt-Hebbel 2008.
34. Kraay 2012; Barro and Redlick 2011.
35. Ramey 2011.
36. Auerbach and Gorodnichenko 2012.
37. Christiano, Eichenbaum, and Rebelo 2011.
38. Calderón, Moral-Benito, and Servén 2013.
39. Ilzetzki, Mendoza, and Végh 2013.
40. Fatás and Mihov 2010; Schaechter and others 2012.
41. World Bank 2013
42. Aizenman, Edwards, and Riera-Crichton 2011.
43. IMF 2011.
44. Didier, Hevia, and Schmukler 2012.
45. Aizenman and Glick 2009 document that countries with SWFs have superior governance to that of other developing countries, including better government effectiveness, regulatory quality, and control of corruption. The transparency and credibility of SWFs tend to reflect their national governance benchmark.
46. Sovereign Wealth Fund Institute, SWF Rankings http://www.swfinstitute.org/fund-rankings/.
47. Das and others 2009.
48. Ang 2012.
49. Anderson, Caputo Silva, and Velandia-Rubiano 2011.
50. Borensztein, Jeanne, and Sandri 2013.
51. Fostel and Geanakoplos 2008.
52. Das and others 2012.
53. Cebotari and others 2009.
54. Cebotari 2008.
55. Kritzer 2008.
56. Beck, Klapper, and Mendoza 2010.
57. Schick 2002.
58. Glennerster and Shin 2008.
59. Laeven and Valencia 2012 estimated the fiscal cost of bailouts as gross fiscal outlays related to the restructuring of the financial sector. The estimate includes fiscal costs related to bank recapitalizations and excludes asset purchases and direct liquidity assistance from the treasury.
60. This paragraph draws heavily from GFDRR 2012.
61. Fatás and Mihov 2013.
62. Calmfors and Wren-Lewis 2011.
63. Wyplosz 2013.
64. Dabla-Norris and others 2010.
65. Das and others 2012.
66. Ahrend, Arnold, and Moeser 2011.

References

Ahrend, Rudiger, Jens Arnold, and Charlotte Moeser. 2011. "The Sharing of Macroeconomic Risk: Who Loses (and Gains) from Macroeconomic Shocks." Economics Department Working Paper 877, OECD (Organisation for Economic Co-operation and Development), Paris.

Aizenman, Joshua, Sebastian Edwards, and Daniel Riera-Crichton. 2011. "Adjustment Patterns to Commodity Terms of Trade Shocks: The Role of Exchange Rate and International Reserves Policies." Working Paper 17692, National Bureau of Economic Research, Cambridge, MA.

Aizenman, Joshua, and Reuven Glick. 2009. "Sovereign Wealth Funds: Stylized Facts about Their Determinants and Governance." *International Finance* 12 (3): 351–86.

Alesina, Alberto, Filipe R. Campante, and Guido Tabellini. 2008. "Why Is Fiscal Policy Often Procyclical?" *Journal of the European Economic Association* 6 (5): 1006–36.

Anderson, Phillip R. D., Anderson Caputo Silva, and Antonio Velandia-Rubiano. 2011. "Public Debt Management in Emerging Market Economies: Has This Time Been Different?" Policy Research Working Paper 5399, World Bank, Washington, DC.

Ang, Andrew. 2012. "The Four Benchmarks of Sovereign Wealth Funds." In *Sovereign Wealth Funds and Long-Term Investing*, edited by Patrick Bolton, Frederic Samama, and Joseph E. Stiglitz, 94–105. New York: Columbia University Press.

Arze del Granado, Javier, Sanjeev Gupta, and Alejandro Hajdenberg. 2010. "Is Social Spending Procyclical?" Working Paper WP/10/234, International Monetary Fund, Washington, DC.

Auerbach, Alan J., and Yuriy Gorodnichenko. 2012. "Measuring the Output Responses to Fiscal Policy." *American Economic Journal: Economic Policy* 4 (2): 1–27.

Barro, Robert J., and Charles J. Redlick. 2011. "Macroeconomic Effects from Government Purchases and Taxes." *Quarterly Journal of Economics* 126 (1): 51–102.

Barro, Robert J., and José F. Ursúa. 2012. "Rare Macroeconomic Disasters." *Annual Review of Economics* 4 (1): 83–109.

Beck, Thorsten, Leora F. Klapper, and Juan Carlos Mendoza. 2010. "The Typology of Partial Credit Guarantee Funds around the World." *Journal of Financial Stability* 6 (1): 10–25.

Bloom, Nicholas. 2013. "Has Economic Policy Uncertainty Slowed Down the World Economy?" Background paper for the *World Development Report 2014*.

Borensztein, Eduardo, Olivier Jeanne, and Damiano Sandri. 2013. "Macro-Hedging for Commodity Exporters." *Journal of Development Economics* 101 (2): 105–16.

Bruno, Valentina, and Hyun Song Shin. 2013. "Capital Flows and the Risk-Taking Channel of Monetary Policy." Working Paper 18942, National Bureau of Economic Research, Cambridge, MA.

Burger, John D., and Francis E. Warnock. 2006. "Local Currency Bond Markets." *IMF Staff Papers* 53 (1): 133–46.

Calderón, César, and Eduardo Levy Yeyati. 2009. "Zooming in from Aggregate Volatility to Income Distribution." Policy Research Working Paper 4895, World Bank, Washington, DC.

Calderón, César, Enrique Moral-Benito, and Luis Servén. Forthcoming. "Is Infrastructure Capital Productive? A Dynamic Heterogeneous Approach." *Journal of Applied Econometrics*.

Calderón, César, and Klaus Schmidt-Hebbel. 2008. "Business Cycles and Fiscal Policies: The Role of Institutions and Financial Markets." Working Paper 481, Central Bank of Chile, Santiago, Chile.

Calmfors, Lars, and Simon Wren-Lewis. 2011. "What Should Fiscal Councils Do?" *Economic Policy* 26 (68): 649–95.

Calvo, Guillermo A., Fabrizio Coricelli, and Pablo Ottonello. 2012. "The Labor Market Consequences of Financial Crises with or without Inflation: Jobless and Wageless Recoveries." Working Paper 18480, National Bureau of Economic Research, Cambridge, MA.

Canuto, Otaviano, and Matheus Cavallari. 2013. "Monetary Policy and Macroprudential Regulation Whither Emerging Markets." Policy Research Working Paper 6310, World Bank, Washington, DC.

Cebotari, Aliona. 2008. "Contingent Liabilities: Issues and Practice." Working Paper WP/08/245, International Monetary Fund, Washington, DC.

Cebotari, Aliona, Jeffrey Davis, Lusine Lusinyan, Amine Mati, Paolo Mauro, Murray Petrie, and Ricardo Velloso. 2009. "Fiscal Risks: Sources, Disclosure, and Management." Departmental Paper 09/01, International Monetary Fund, Fiscal Affairs Department, Washington, DC.

Chen, Shaohua, and Martin Ravallion. 2010. "The Developing World Is Poorer Than We Thought, but No Less Successful in the Fight against Poverty." *Quarterly Journal of Economics* 125 (4): 1577–625.

Christiano, Lawrence J., Martin S. Eichenbaum, and Sergio Rebelo. 2011. "When Is the Government Spending Multiplier Large?" *Journal of Political Economy* 119 (1): 78–121.

Claessens, Stijn, M. Ayhan Kose, and Marco E. Terrones. 2012. "How Do Business and Financial Cycles Interact?" *Journal of International Economics* 87 (1): 178–90.

Committee on International Economic Policy and Reform. 2011. *Rethinking Central Banking*. Washington, DC: Brookings.

Dabla-Norris, Era, Richard Allen, Luis-Felipe Zanna, Tej Prakash, Eteri Kvintradze, Victor Duarte Lledo, and Irene Yackovlev. 2010. "Budget Institutions and Fiscal Performance in Low-Income Countries." Working Paper WP/10/80, International Monetary Fund, Washington, DC.

Darby, Julia, and Jacques Melitz. 2008. "Social Spending and Automatic Stabilizers in the OECD." *Economic Policy* 23 (56): 715–56.

Das, Udaibir S., Yinqiu Lu, Christian Mulder, and Amadou N. R. Sy. 2009. "Setting Up a Sovereign Wealth Fund: Some Policy and Operational Considerations." Working Paper WP/09/179, International Monetary Fund, Washington, DC.

Das, Udaibir S., Yinqiu Lu, Michael G. Papaioannou, and Iva Petrova. 2012. "Sovereign Risk and Asset and Liability Management Conceptual Issues." Working Paper WP/12/241, International Monetary Fund, Washington, DC.

De Gregorio, José. 2012. "Price and Financial Stability in Modern Central Banking." *Economía* 13 (1): 1–11.

Didier, Tatiana, Constantino Hevia, and Sergio L. Schmukler. 2012. "How Resilient and Countercyclical Were Emerging Economies during the Global Financial Crisis?" *Journal of International Money and Finance* 31 (8): 2052–77.

Edwards, Sebastian, and Eduardo Levy Yeyati. 2005. "Flexible Exchange Rates as Shock Absorbers." *European Economic Review* 49 (8): 2079–105.

Farhi, Emmanuel, Gita Gopinath, and Oleg Itskhoki. 2011. "Fiscal Devaluations." Working Paper 17662, National Bureau of Economic Research, Cambridge, MA.

Fatás, Antonio, and Ilian Mihov. 2010. "The Euro and Fiscal Policy." In *Europe and the Euro*, edited by Alberto Alesina and Francesco Giavazzi, 287–324. Chicago: University of Chicago Press.

———. 2013. "Policy Volatility, Institutions and Economic Growth." *Review of Economics and Statistics* 95 (2): 362–76.

Fostel, Ana, and John Geanakoplos. 2008. "Leverage Cycles and the Anxious Economy." *American Economic Review* 98 (4): 1211–44.

Frankel, Jeffrey A., Carlos A. Végh, and Guillermo Vuletin. 2013. "On Graduation from Fiscal Procyclicality." *Journal of Development Economics* 100 (1): 32–47.

Fuentes, Rodrigo. 2013. "Sovereign Wealth Funds: The Case of Chile." Background paper for the *World Development Report 2014.*

Galí, Jordi, and Luca Gambetti. 2009. "On the Sources of the Great Moderation." *American Economic Journal: Macroeconomics* 1 (1): 26–57.

GFDRR (Global Facility for Disaster Reduction and Recovery). 2012. "Disaster Risk Financing and Insurance Program." World Bank and GFDRR, Washington, DC.

Ghosh, Atish R., Mahvash S. Qureshi, and Charalambos G. Tsangarides. 2013. "Is the Exchange Rate Regime Really Irrelevant for External Adjustment?" *Economics Letters* 118 (1): 104–09.

Glennerster, Rachel, and Yongseok Shin. 2008. "Does Transparency Pay?" *IMF Staff Papers* 55 (1): 183–209.

Gourio, François. 2012. "Disaster Risk and Business Cycles." *American Economic Review* 102 (6): 2734–66.

Hnatkovska, Viktoria, and Norman Loayza. 2005. "Volatility and Growth." In *Managing Economic Volatility and Crises: A Practitioner's Guide*, edited by Joshua Aizenman and Brian Pinto, 65–100. Cambridge, UK: Cambridge University Press.

Husain, Aasim M., Ashoka Mody, and Kenneth S. Rogoff. 2005. "Exchange Rate Regime Durability and Performance in Developing Versus Advanced Economies." *Journal of Monetary Economics* 52 (1): 35–68.

Ilzetzki, Ethan, Enrique G. Mendoza, and Carlos A. Végh. 2013. "How Big (Small?) Are Fiscal Multipliers?" *Journal of Monetary Economics* 60 (2): 239–54.

IMF (International Monetary Fund). 2011. "Assessing Reserve Adequacy." IMF, Washington, DC.

Keum, Jaeho, Jiyeon Chang, Deok-Soon Hwang, Dong-Heon Kim, Jooseop Kim, Byung-Hee Lee, Kyu-Yong Lee, Seong-Jae Park, and Kil-sang Yoo. 2006. *Employment Insurance in Korea: The First Ten Years.* Seoul: Korea Labor Institute.

Kraay, Aart. 2012. "How Large Is the Government Spending Multiplier? Evidence from Lending by Official Creditors." *Quarterly Journal of Economics* 127 (2): 829–87.

Kraay, Aart, and Luis Servén. 2013. "Fiscal Policy as a Tool for Stabilization in Developing Countries." Background paper for the *World Development Report 2014.*

Kritzer, Barbara E. 2008. "Chile's Next Generation Pension Reform." *Social Security Bulletin* 68 (2): 69–84.

Laeven, Luc, and Fabian Valencia. 2012. "Systemic Banking Crises Database: An Update." Working Paper WP/12/163, International Monetary Fund, Washington, DC.

Levy Yeyati, Eduardo, and Federico Sturzenegger. 2003. "To Float or to Fix: Evidence on the Impact of Exchange Rate Regimes on Growth." *American Economic Review* 93 (4): 1173–93.

McKay, Alisdair, and Ricardo Reis. 2013. "The Role of Automatic Stabilizers in the U.S. Business Cycle." Working Paper 19000, National Bureau of Economic Research, Cambridge, MA.

Micco, Alejandro, Ernesto Stein, and Guillermo Ordoñez. 2003. "The Currency Union Effect on Trade: Early Evidence from EMU." *Economic Policy* 18 (37): 315–59.

Mishkin, Frederic S. 2004. "Can Inflation Targeting Work in Emerging Market Countries?" Working Paper 10646, National Bureau of Economic Research, Cambridge, MA.

Mishkin, Frederic S., and Miguel A. Savastano. 2001. "Monetary Policy Strategies for Latin America." *Journal of Development Economics* 66 (2): 415–44.

Mishkin, Frederic S., and Klaus Schmidt-Hebbel. 2007. "Does Inflation Targeting Make a Difference?" Working Paper 12876, National Bureau of Economic Research, Cambridge, MA.

Prasad, Naren, and Megan Gerecke. 2010. "Social Security Spending in Times of Crisis." *Global Social Policy* 10 (2): 1–30.

Ramcharan, Rodney. 2007. "Does the Exchange Rate Regime Matter for Real Shocks? Evidence from Windstorms and Earthquakes." *Journal of International Economics* 73 (1): 31–47.

Ramey, Valerie A. 2011. "Can Government Purchases Stimulate the Economy?" *Journal of Economic Literature* 49 (3): 673–85.

Rose, Andrew, and Tom D. Stanley. 2005. "A Meta-Analysis of the Effect of Common Currencies on International Trade." *Journal of Economic Surveys* 19 (3): 347–65.

Salazar, Natalia. 2013. "Fiscal Risk Management for Development: The Case of Colombia." Background paper for the *World Development Report 2014.*

Schaechter, Andrea, Tidiane Kinda, Nina Budina, and Anke Weber. 2012. "Fiscal Rules in Response to the Crisis toward the 'Next Generation' Rules: A New Dataset." Working Paper WP/12/187, International Monetary Fund, Washington, DC.

Schick, Allen. 2002. "Budgeting for Fiscal Risk." In *Government at Risk: Contingent Liabilities and Fiscal Risk*, edited by Hana Polackova Brixi and Allen Schick, 79–97. New York: Oxford University Press.

Shambaugh, Jay 2012. "The Euro's Three Crises." *Brookings Papers on Economic Activity* 1: 157–211.

Suescún, Rodrigo. 2007. "The Size and Effectiveness of Automatic Fiscal Stabilizers in Latin America." In *Fiscal Policy Stabilization and Growth: Prudence or Abstinence?*, edited by Guillermo E. Perry, Luis Servén, and Rodrigo Suescún, 75–120. Washington, DC: World Bank.

Taylor, John B. 2011. "An Empirical Analysis of the Revival of Fiscal Activism in the 2000s." *Journal of Economic Literature* 49 (3): 686–702.

Tornell, Aaron, and Philip R. Lane. 1999. "The Voracity Effect." *American Economic Review* 89 (1): 22–46.

Tornell, Aaron, and Andrés Velasco. 2000. "Fixed versus Flexible Exchange Rates: Which Provide More Fiscal Discipline?" *Journal of Monetary Economics* 45 (2): 399–436.

Végh, Carlos A., and Guillermo Vuletin. 2012. "Overcoming the Fear of Free Falling: Monetary Policy Graduation in Emerging Markets." Working Paper 18175, National Bureau of Economic Research, Cambridge, MA.

Vuletin, Guillermo. 2013. "Effects and Role of Macroprudential Policy." Background paper for the *World Development Report 2014.*

World Bank. 2013. *Beyond the Annual Budget: Global Experience with Medium-Term Expenditure Frameworks.* Washington, DC: World Bank.

———. World Development Indicators (database). World Bank, Washington, DC., http://data.worldbank.org/data-catalog/world-development-indicators.

Wyplosz, Charles. 2013. "Fiscal Rules: Theoretical Issues and Historical Experiences." In *Fiscal Policy after the Financial Crisis*, edited by Alberto Alesina and Francesco Giavazzi, 495–525. Chicago: University of Chicago Press for NBER.

Diseases without borders: Managing the risk of pandemics

Pandemics such as influenza (flu), AIDS, plague, and smallpox have caused episodes of overwhelming misery and economic and social disruptions throughout history. Today, a pathogen that originates in a chicken flock or a goat herd in a remote village in Asia or Africa and is then transmitted to humans can reach major cities on all continents within 36 hours. Because everyone is vulnerable, management of pandemic risk is the quintessential global public good that can yield benefits for all but can be supplied only through collective action. Any country's efforts to reduce the risk are of limited benefit unless all other countries take supportive measures.

Sources of pandemics and development implications

Pandemics do not start in a vacuum; their onset is shaped by human action. A staggering 2.3 billion infections by zoonotic (animal-borne) pathogens afflict people in developing countries every year. Some 75 percent of pathogens capable of causing human disease are now animal-borne. This is a major concern because health, nutrition, and food and income security all decline when livestock and people are diseased. The poorest, often living close to livestock or wild animals, are most vulnerable. This disease burden persists because of weak veterinary and human public health systems that fail to detect diseases and allow them to spread. Adding to the risks, livestock numbers are projected to grow very quickly in developing countries. Some pathogens spread not just across species but also through trade and travel across borders and continents. Even worse, some become capable of easy human-to-human spread and thus have great impact, like AIDS, flu, or severe acute respiratory syndrome (SARS). Any country's failure to stop contagion early at its animal source can cause a pandemic. A severe flu pandemic could more than double the total burden of disease. Moreover, economic activity would suffer from worker absenteeism, cascading service disruptions, and human reactions to fear and rumors, which can spread faster than the disease itself. Much of the economic costs would result from avoidance behaviors; these costs could account for as much as 60 percent of total economic costs. Poor countries, especially fragile and conflict-affected states, may be least able to cope.

Preventing a pandemic

To stop contagion, it is essential to act early, at the source, and quickly. Early warning requires cooperation from farmers and communities. If farmers who report disease are punished by having their livestock destroyed without compensation, they will hide disease from the authorities. The main cause of pandemic risk is low capacity of public veterinary and human health systems. Bringing them up to meet minimum international standards requires only modest resources: $3.4 billion a year for all developing countries, compared with the current level of barely $450 million. The expected annual benefits of robust systems are at least $37 billion, more than 10 times the costs. Because public health authorities failed to detect the disease early on—a failure of public health service delivery—AIDS spread unchecked for decades. The costs of this manmade delay are still rising. In contrast, prompt public health action to isolate infected people helped stop the SARS outbreak. Contagion is far less likely to take off in countries that detect disease early and implement effective control measures promptly. To date, no mechanism ensures the strengthening of veterinary and human public health systems in countries that are unable to detect and control diseases, although such "weak links" put all countries at risk.

Mitigating impacts of a pandemic

Contingency planning, and periodic simulation exercises by governments, firms, and communities, as part of disaster risk preparedness, can mitigate impacts. Health sector plans can help cope with surges of patients. Networked industries like power, transport, finance, and food distribution can avoid major disruptions when the main firms have business continuity plans. Likewise, security and other government services need operational continuity plans in the event of high worker absenteeism. Communications in-country and across borders are vital, as the differing degrees of SARS contagion within Canada clearly demonstrated. Advance planning for truthful, complete, coordinated, and timely communications about the disease and government responses can reduce uncertainty and rumors. Too few governments, communities, and firms make and test contingency plans for complex disasters (including pandemics), despite evidence that these activities are highly beneficial.

In short, pandemics are an undermanaged risk. Pandemic prevention and preparedness tend to be sidelined, especially in the health sector, where the responsibility often rests. Health authorities focus on immediate problems and do not readily work with veterinary authorities to prevent diseases of tomorrow or coordinate societywide preparedness. Why such neglect? The economic and social impacts of contagion are often ignored, so the total risk is underestimated. Recent experience shows how wide this gap can be. The 2003 SARS outbreak, which killed about 10 percent of the 8,000 people it infected, caused $54 billion in economic damage (mostly canceled travel, lost retail trade, and associated cross-border economic shocks). A severe flu pandemic could cost 4.8 percent of global gross domestic product (GDP), or more than $3 trillion, trigger-

BOX S7.1 *An emergency response to a top global catastrophic risk*

How H5N1 avian flu galvanized the international community

Why an emergency response? Two goals:

- Control H5N1 avian flu at its source in poultry to reduce pandemic risk to humans and the world economy.
- Prepare all countries to cope with a pandemic.

Results? Notable achievements, but risks remain:

- Largest global public health program to date reduced risk through prevention and preparedness; assistance was delivered quickly to over 100 developing countries.
- H5N1 avian flu was controlled in most of the 63 countries in Africa, Asia, and Europe where it appeared but still circulates in a dozen countries. Preventing renewed spread of this virus is technically possible and cost-effective, yet most of the required investments in veterinary and human public health systems are unfunded.
- Preparedness for pandemics was boosted, as evidenced by responses to the 2009 H1N1 flu pandemic.
- The onset of the financial crisis in 2008 and decline in media attention sidelined pandemic prevention, leaving weaknesses in veterinary and public health systems unaddressed and undermining the sustainability of investments made.

How did it work?

- Initiated by the United States and the European Commission, the International Partnership on Avian and Pandemic Influenzas *engaged all countries*.
- After launch at the United Nations (UN) General Assembly in 2005, *political support* was galvanized at five ministerial conferences in 2006–10.
- A UN System *coordinator* worked with the World Bank to support the World Health Organization (WHO), the World Organisation for Animal Health (OIE), the Food and Agriculture Organization of the United Nations (FAO), and others to develop a common strategy rapidly.
- *Financing* of $3.9 billion in 2005–10 helped over 100 developing countries. No new fund was created; instead, the World Bank monitored financing gaps in recipient countries and organizations.
- Partners agreed on *a strategy to reduce health risks* at the animal-human-environment interface (One Health), steered by the WHO-OIE-FAO tripartite.
- The United Nations and partners founded a *network for preparedness*, the Towards a Safer World Initiative, but sustainable funding and other support remain uncertain.

Source: WDR 2014 team.

ing a global recession. The international community has not yet expressed its demand for pandemic risk reduction by adopting explicit goals but instead resorts to emergency responses that contain the threat only temporarily (box S7.1). Because risk governance is not backed by resources and authority, numerous weak links persist in global defenses against contagion. Fearing trade and travel restrictions, countries may hide diseases, facilitating their spread; incentives for compliance with disease reporting are weak or absent. Governments with resources try to protect their own populations by spending large amounts on ex post measures (vaccines, masks, and antivirals), although prevention at the source of the threat has much higher benefit-cost ratios. In particular, the promising One Health approach to reducing disease risks through systematic collaboration between animal and human health services is underfunded.

Promising precedents

The international community has already eradicated two devastating scourges: smallpox in 1979, and rinderpest (cattle plague) in 2011. Smallpox killed as many as 500 million people in the 20th century alone. Rinderpest, with its high fatality rate, decimated herds and economies for centuries and catalyzed the founding of the World Organisation for Animal Health (OIE) in 1924. Intergovernmental cooperation, science-based disease control strategies, mass vaccination, and surveillance were among the elements behind these successful campaigns. The disease risk was reduced to zero. The benefits are lasting and already outweigh the control costs many times over. International coordination and strong public health agencies broke the chain of transmission of SARS. Faced with the H5N1 avian flu threat, the international community rapidly mobilized and deployed resources for zoonotic disease control and pandemic preparedness, but the effort dissipated soon after the threat left the headlines.

Current and future generations would benefit if the international community set a goal to reduce pandemic risk. The goal would empower international organizations to raise risk awareness and motivate prevention and preparedness; provide relevant knowledge, capacity building, and technical assistance to developing countries; assess the performance of national veterinary and human public health systems and their collaboration; and mobilize resources for strengthening these systems.

Sources

Barrett, Scott. 2007. *Why Cooperate? The Incentive to Supply Global Public Goods*. New York: Oxford University Press.

Burns, Andrew, Dominique van der Mensbrugghe, and Hans Timmer. 2008. "Evaluating the Economic Consequences of Avian Influenza." World Bank, Washington, DC.

Jonas, Olga. 2013. "Pandemic Risk." Background paper for the *World Development Report 2014*.

Mariner, Jeffrey C., James A. House, Charles A. Mebus, Albert E. Sollod, Dickens Chibeu, Bryony A. Jones, Peter L. Roeder, Berhanu Admassu, and Gijs G. M. van 't Klooster. 2012. "Rinderpest Eradication: Appropriate Technology and Social Innovations." *Science* 337 (6100): 1309–12.

The SARS Commission. 2006. "The Story of SARS." In *The SARS Commission Final Report: Spring of Fear*, vol. 2, 38–429. Ontario: Commission to Investigate the Introduction and Spread of SARS in Ontario.

UNSIC (United Nations System Influenza Coordination) and World Bank. 2010. *Animal and Pandemic Influenza: A Framework for Sustaining Momentum*. Fifth Global Progress Report. Bangkok: UNSIC.

World Bank. 2012. "People, Pathogens, and Our Planet: The Economics of One Health." World Bank, Washington, DC.

Warming Arctic waters: a risk with global impact. Scaling up risk management requires a cohesive international community that works collectively and has the capacity to mobilize resources and establish mechanisms to enforce agreements.

CHAPTER 8

The role of the international community

When risks exceed national capacity

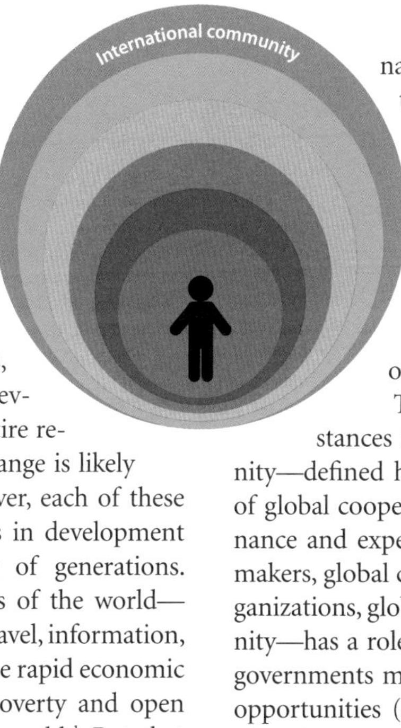

Global problems call for global players

Unmanaged risk does not respect boundaries. Once triggered, pandemics and financial crises can circle rapidly around an increasingly interconnected globe. Conflicts can quickly spill over into neighboring countries. Droughts, floods, and violent storms can devastate an area, a country, or an entire region. Left unmitigated, climate change is likely to intensify all these risks. Moreover, each of these risks is capable of reversing gains in development and jeopardizing the well-being of generations. The increasing interconnectedness of the world—through trade, communications, travel, information, and finance—has made possible the rapid economic growth that has helped reduce poverty and open opportunities for the developing world.[1] But that same interconnectedness also magnifies the potential impact of these global risks and complicates their management.

No one country or agent acting alone can deal effectively with a risk that crosses a national border. Clearly, risks that spread across and affect multiple countries or generations merit international attention. But international action is also justified when a country-specific shock is simply too large for a country to resolve on its own, even when its implications do not go beyond national boundaries. Managing these kinds of risks becomes a global public good, whose benefits also transcend boundaries, providing a central rationale for collective action by an international community that takes on the task of delivering it.[2] Global public goods benefit all countries and populations, but they are likely to yield the greatest benefit to those countries whose weak infrastructures and limited access to coping tools make them less equipped to deal with the adverse consequences of these kinds of risks.

This chapter looks at the circumstances in which the international community—defined here as a collection of organizations of global cooperation, providers of development finance and expertise, global standard setters, policy makers, global charities, other nongovernmental organizations, global media, and the scientific community—has a role to play in helping people and their governments manage risk and pursue development opportunities (diagram 8.1). The chapter explores what the international community can do that other economic and social systems cannot—and what it should (or should not) do to scale up collective efforts to manage risk. The chapter does not intend to address all possible risks at the global scale, but instead aims to illustrate the common factors that enhance or undermine the effectiveness of actions by the international community. It does so by focusing on five areas of risk: disasters, global financial crises, environmental risks, pandemics, and risks associated with fragile and conflict-affected states (FCSs).

In so doing, the chapter underscores a key message of this Report: risk management requires shared responsibility and actions by various economic and social systems, from households to the international

DIAGRAM 8.1 *The agents of the international community*

Source: WDR 2014 team.
Note: NGO = nongovernmental organization.

community. The international community is called on when managing risks requires efforts and public goods that go beyond the capacity of national economic and social systems. It can strengthen national efforts to manage risks that cross borders or generations or that produce outcomes exceeding the capacity of a country to manage alone. Its interventions aim to generate and disseminate global knowledge and expertise that improve risk awareness and the capacity to assess and manage risk, set rules and standards to make negative outcomes less likely or costly, and strengthen coping capacity through quick mobilization of global resources.

These are lofty goals. In practice, the international community has not been very effective in managing risks that transcend boundaries—but it can do better. Too often knowledge does not result in effective action. Less emphasis is put on preparing for risk than on responding to it after the fact. Sometimes, too much weight is placed on avoiding risk rather than on managing it to seize development opportunities. Diverging national interests and risk management capacities undermine cooperation and the effectiveness of global efforts. Scaling up risk management requires a cohesive international community that enables its actors to work collectively by facilitating information sharing, devoting more resources to capacity building, and protecting the most vulnerable. The international community must have the capacity to mobilize resources and establish mechanisms to enforce agreements, even when some countries are unwilling to cooperate, by using its various tools to realign incentives around basic, common goals.

What circumstances call for action by the international community and why?

Countries face many risks that may overwhelm national capacity—some country-specific, others shared; some simple, others more complex; some stemming from natural causes, and others generated by actions of other actors. Regardless of the type and cause, some risks are just too big for countries to handle alone. Beyond the national level, the international community provides assistance, expertise, and collaboration to better manage these risks.

Severe economic and humanitarian crises

Crises and disasters can put severe strains on people and the systems that support them. The international community can support people where national authorities, usually the first line of support, are overwhelmed by a negative shock that can expose economies to significant volatility, distress public resources, disrupt access to markets, and retard progress in development, as well as where states might be cut off from access to international resources.[3] The international community's risk-sharing tools can be particularly useful for lower-income countries that are disproportionately affected by economic risks and disasters (as measured in lives lost and damages relative to economic size), given their greater exposure to such shocks, weak institutional capacity, and limited access to insurance, credit markets, and other tools that can mitigate their effects (map 8.1; figure 8.1). Even in developed countries, prolonged periods of uncertainty and weak economic activity following crises can reverse years of economic and development advances and change people's lives dramatically.[4] The sovereign and financial crisis in the Euro Area and the subprime mortgage crisis in the United States appear to have undone 7 to 12 years of economic progress in several countries hardest hit by the crisis, resulting in unprecedented levels of unemployment and loss of economic and social well-being.[5]

People living in fragile and conflict-affected states face these risks on an ongoing basis. More than 1.5 billion people live in these states, in environments

MAP 8.1 ***Developing countries in general have suffered higher mortality associated with disasters***

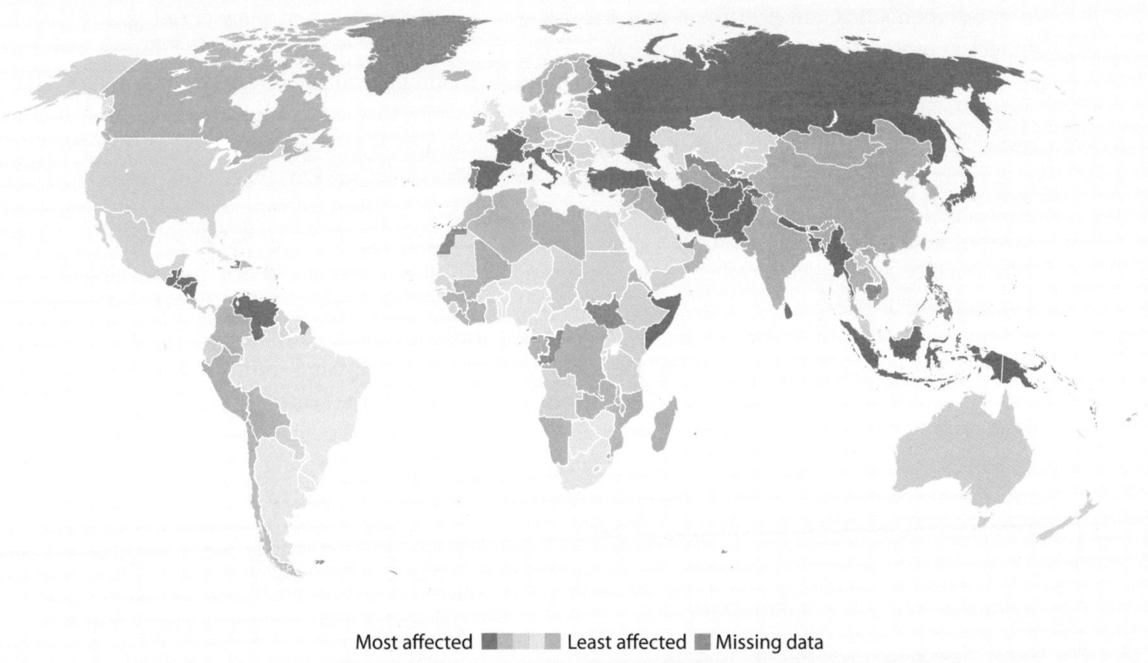

Source: WDR 2014 team based on data from EM-DAT OFDA/CRED International Disaster Database and World Bank World Development Indicators (database). Map number: IBRD 40100.

Note: The map depicts the extent to which countries experience deaths from disasters, with the number of deaths scaled by population, averaged over the period 1990–2011. Countries are divided into equally sized categories from the most affected to the least affected.

FIGURE 8.1 ***Damages from a disaster can exceed a country's annual GDP in developing countries***

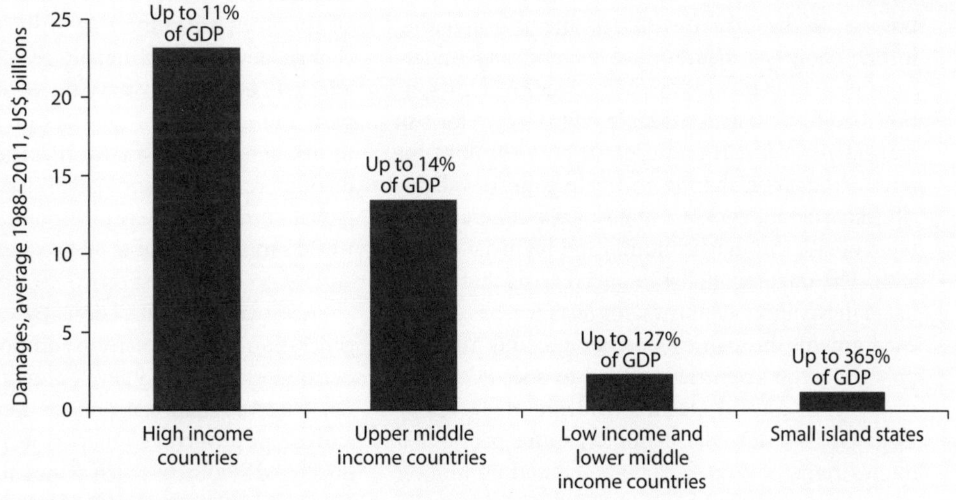

Source: WDR 2014 team based on data from EM-DAT OFDA/CRED International Disaster Database and World Bank World Development Indicators (database).

Note: GDP = gross domestic product.

typically characterized by corruption and weaknesses in governance and institutional capacity, with minimal access to functioning market mechanisms or governments that can help them manage risk—much less protect them from additional risks. These people make up 15 percent of the world population, but they represent nearly one-third of people in extreme poverty, one-third of the HIV-related deaths in poor countries, one-third of people lacking access to clean water, one-third of children who do not complete primary education, and half of all child deaths.[6] State fragility and violent conflict pose significant risks not only to citizens but to global and regional security in an interconnected world. By improving incomes, economic prospects, and the environment for health, security, and education, sustained and well-targeted engagement by the international community can help reduce social and economic tensions that inflame conflict, and instead create an environment that nurtures development opportunities.

Risks that recognize no boundaries

Some risks have implications that cross geographical borders—or even generations. The consequences of the risks taken today may not be visible for many years. Given their complexity, individual risk management actions may be insufficient, or even made ineffective by others' actions. The international community can facilitate risk sharing across countries and generations in cases where managing risks collectively encourages complementarities across individual actions and enhances their impact.

Global financial and economic crises are clear examples of cases where risks may transcend national borders. As the links intensify, problems originating in one country can introduce turmoil and undermine development elsewhere. International integration therefore presents a double-edged sword for risk management: it can create more opportunities for international risk sharing and help countries diversify idiosyncratic shocks, but it can also generate new types of risk through economic and financial contagion. The ongoing global financial crisis that originated in advanced countries, for instance, has dampened growth through close economic and financial linkages across countries and led to a slowdown in the progress toward meeting Millennium Development Goals (MDGs); 50 million more people fell into extreme poverty in 2009 alone and 64 million additional people had become poor by 2010.

Health risks can also cross national boundaries. Increased air travel and trade in goods and services can provide free passage to pathogens that cause infectious diseases, some of which can travel around the world in less than 36 hours.[7] Indeed, in recent years, greater mobility of people and goods has contributed to the spread of zoonotic diseases that originate in animals but then transfer to humans. The H5N1 (avian) flu killed 59 percent of the confirmed human cases in Asia and the Middle East during 2003–13. The H1N1 (swine) flu killed an estimated 151,700–575,400 people during the first year the virus circulated (2009).[8] AIDS, which also originated in animals, continues to destroy lives globally, although improved treatment has slowed fatalities since 2004; still, an estimated 1.7 million people died from AIDS in 2011 alone, and another 2.5 million contracted the disease. At the same time, globalization and scientific advances have improved understanding of many pathogens, including how they can be detected and diagnosed rapidly to enable disease control. Globalization also supports greater collaboration among scientists and public health officials and enables the media to inform people even in remote areas of risks (see spotlight 7 on managing pandemics).

Global efforts are also essential where risks may evolve slowly, with few immediately visible implications. HIV/AIDS was not detected until well after it had been established in populations around the world. Climate change risk is another example that has been building slowly and nearly invisibly for generations (box 8.1). Climate extremes such as heat waves and heavy precipitation have been increasing for the past 50 years and are expected to worsen as atmospheric concentrations of greenhouse gas emissions reach unprecedented levels, with potentially catastrophic and irreversible consequences.[9] While all countries are vulnerable to the effects of climate change, developing countries are disproportionately affected because they have the least capacity to prepare and cope; three-quarters of the people killed in disasters in the past two decades lived in lower-income countries and small island states.[10] The global community has a responsibility to help the world's most vulnerable people and provide broader and longer-term perspectives to tackle these risks.

Risk management actions by one country (or a generation) may also create additional risks and undermine stability and development efforts of others. For example, national policies to promote growth and escape poverty risk may create growing pressures on shared resources (such as oceans, waterways, fish stocks, and the atmosphere), resulting in degradation of resources that hurt other countries and future generations (the so-called tragedy of the commons).

BOX 8.1 *Climate change and implications for development*

Climate change is the rise in Earth's temperature associated with increased atmospheric concentrations of heat-trapping greenhouse gases such as carbon dioxide (CO_2). The steady rise, dating from the Industrial Revolution, has been attributed largely to human activities, including the burning of fossil fuels and deforestation. New research into climate change suggests that Earth is warmer today than at any time during the past 11,300 years as greenhouse gas concentrations have continued to rise: the concentration of the main greenhouse gas, CO_2, rose from its preindustrial level of 278 parts per million (ppm) to a daily average of 400 ppm in May 2013, approaching the 450 ppm threshold that corresponds to a likely increase in Earth's temperature of more than 2°C—the warming level that the international community committed itself to avoid because of its potentially catastrophic and irreversible consequences (see panel a).

The effects of climate change are already visible in widespread melting of Arctic glaciers, rising sea levels, and higher frequency and severity of extreme weather events and natural hazards (see panel b). If concentrations of greenhouse gases continue unabated, a warming of more than 4°C could occur as early as the 2060s, with large-scale impacts on human and ecological systems—including, heightened risk of inundation of coastal areas, spread of infectious diseases, declining water and food security, destruction of habitats for many species, and adverse social and economic consequences of large displaced populations. Climate change is hence a serious threat to development for both current and future generations; the estimated cumulative cost from damage to health, food security, and the physical environment ranges from $2 trillion to $4 trillion by 2030 depending on the climate scenario.

Mitigating climate change is a prime example of a global public good that requires collective action. Collective action is needed because while each country prefers that others supply the good (free-riding on others), each also recognizes that if everyone depended on others to supply the good, the result would be bad for everyone, suggesting that there is an advantage in collective provision. Climate change mitigation faces several important obstacles. First, despite improved confidence in climate models, significant scientific uncertainty remains on the critical warming thresholds (so-called tipping points) and on the magnitude of climate change effects. Second, climate change effects are not uniform across countries, creating diverging incentives for action. The absence of a global authority to enforce cooperation across nations undermines collective efforts, combined with the free-riding problems, as each country hopes that others will bear the cost of climate change mitigation. Third, short-termism and different valuations of ecosystems, biodiversity, and loss of life breed inaction and pass the risk to future generations. Despite general consensus that it is a serious threat, and decades of debate and negotiations notwithstanding, climate change risks are likely to grow until these challenges are effectively addressed.

a. Rising temperature and CO_2 concentrations

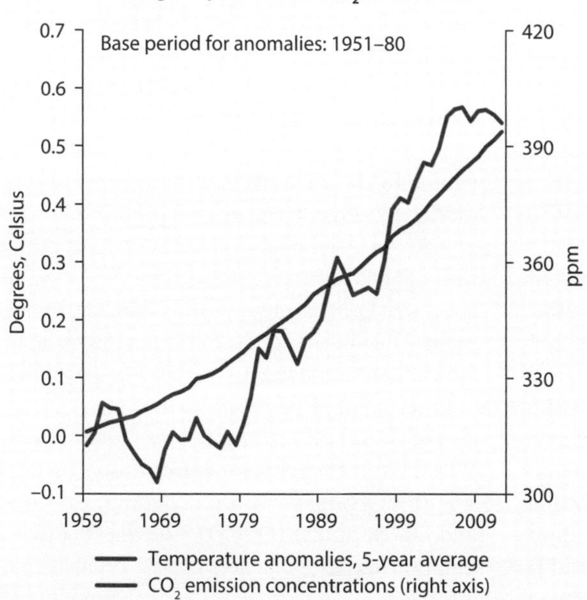

b. A changing pattern of natural disasters

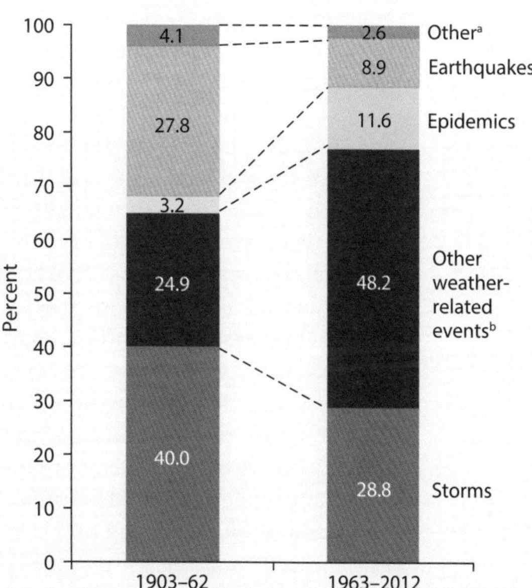

Source: WDR 2014 team based on Aldy, Orszag, and Stiglitz 2001; Barrett 2003, 2007, 2008; Cole 2007; DARA International 2012; IPCC 2007; Jacoby, Rabassa, and Skoufias 2011 (for loss estimates); Lenton and others 2008; Marcott and others 2013; Mercer 2011; Stern 2007; World Bank 2009, 2012c; and data from EM-DAT OFDA/CRED International Disaster Database; NASA Goddard Institute for Space Studies Surface Temperature Analysis (database); and Scripps Institution of Oceanography, Atmospheric CO_2 Concentration at Mauna Loa Observatory, Hawaii (database).

Note: CO_2 = carbon dioxide.

a. "Other" refers to volcanoes, insect infestations, and complex disasters.

b. "Other weather-related events" refers to floods, droughts, extreme temperatures, and wildfires.

Dams to control water levels and retain water can affect water security for millions of downstream users in neighboring countries. In each of these examples, countries acting in their own interest obtain immediate gain from their actions, while losses from the impact of adverse consequences are not felt immediately. If all countries try to safeguard their own interests, individual actions can collectively cause large damages to all involved, in some cases with irreversible consequences.

Similar beggar-thy-neighbor policies and collective action failures are observed in international finance and trade. National measures to protect the domestic financial system by ring-fencing affiliates of cross-border banks may reduce contagion risks and fiscal costs of a failing foreign bank, but they may also weaken the resilience of the home country financial system, raise the cost of capital and liquidity in both home and host countries, and limit the ability of banks to manage funding risks. Fear of ring-fencing may induce global banks to pull out of other host countries, hurting those with less developed financial markets. Similarly, history points to how international trade collapsed when many countries introduced beggar-thy-neighbor trade policies during the Great Depression.[11] More recently, increased export barriers by exporters and reduced import tariffs by importers during the food price crisis of 2008 caused the world price of grain to jump, forcing other countries to adopt similar measures. These uncoordinated actions turned out to be completely unsuccessful in protecting the poor against the food shock—close to half of the increase in the world price of rice is estimated to have come from countries' attempts to insulate themselves from higher rice prices.[12]

Not all risks that exceed national borders are truly global, however. Some risks, such as armed conflict between neighboring countries, may affect only a few countries, as may disputes over natural resources, such as those arising from management of waterways. Such risks may be more appropriately or efficiently managed by bilateral or regional institutions that provide appropriate forums, frameworks, and incentives for addressing the risks. The subsidiarity principle may suggest that the risk should be handled by the lowest level of authority capable of addressing the matter effectively, before it becomes a regional or global problem. Regional economic communities are important layers of support in Africa, Asia, and the Caribbean, dealing with risks and creating opportunities through cooperation and development actions in areas such as trade, energy, industry, security, and environment. The global community can step in when risks cannot be resolved effectively by individual countries or such regional bodies. Regional or international courts of justice, for instance, may deal with cross-border disputes that cannot be resolved because of mutually exclusive demands. Treatment of these issues deserves more extensive discussion and analyses than are possible within the scope of this Report.

How does the international community enhance risk management?

The international community supports national efforts to manage risks by addressing some of the key obstacles to effective management of risks that go beyond national capacity: information gaps, limited access to markets and resources, externalities imposed by actions of other actors, and cognitive and behavioral biases. Members of the international community contribute to strengthening the key pillars of risk management defined in chapter 1: knowledge, protection, insurance, and coping (diagram 8.2).

Generating and disseminating global knowledge and expertise

Lack of relevant knowledge is a key obstacle to effective risk management. Knowledge deficiencies become more formidable as risks grow in intensity and complexity and as the uncertainties about their sources, drivers, and potential impacts deepen. Lacking knowledge, countries or individuals may contribute to, or overlook, environmental risks; spread, or fail to protect against, communicable diseases; or take excessive risks in search of high returns. In this context, knowledge becomes a global public good that contributes, or limits damage, to development. The international community plays an important role in supplying it.

International financial institutions (IFIs)—such as the International Monetary Fund (IMF), the World Bank, the Bank for International Settlements, and the Organisation for Economic Co-operation and Development (OECD)—as well as other coordination agencies that accumulate extensive country information and experience, can provide a broad, impartial knowledge base for countries and individuals to draw upon to help bridge gaps between global objectives and national policies on a range of issues. Global knowledge and expertise can act as a guide and tool to raise awareness, especially where national agents fail to recognize far-reaching and longer-term implications of their actions, for them-

DIAGRAM 8.2 *Role of the international community*

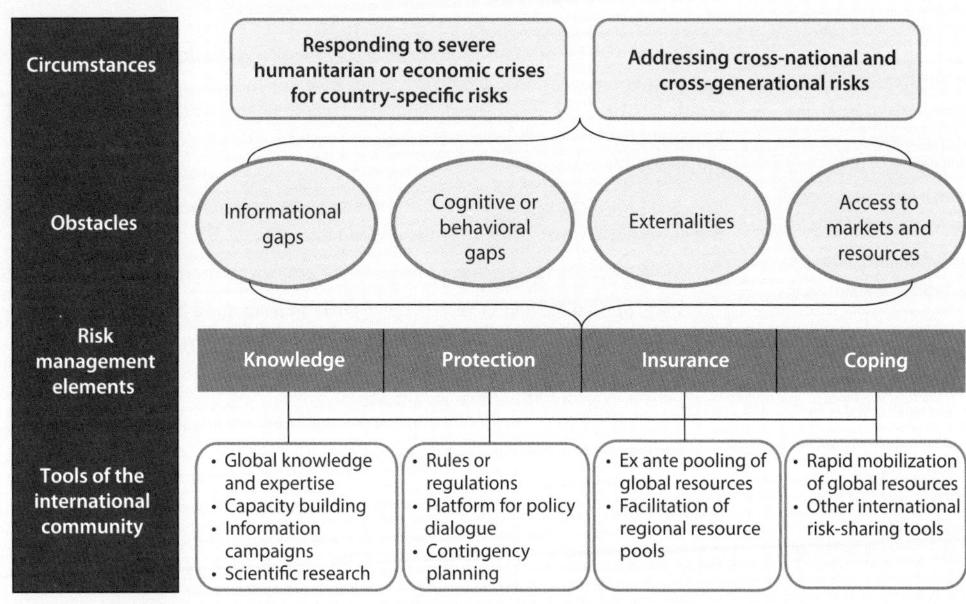

Source: WDR 2014 team.

selves or others. Clear and prompt communication of the knowledge is crucial, if it is to succeed in affecting behavior.

The international community offers a range of tools to fill knowledge gaps. From IFIs and coordination agencies to the scientific community, think tanks, media, and civil society, international organizations collect, review, analyze, synthesize, and disseminate information and research findings on economic, financial, health, environmental, safety, and other risks that have a bearing on development and stability, and publish cross-country information, research, and policy analyses that can help assess risks in an increasingly interconnected world. The international community can also provide platforms for knowledge exchange and publish periodic risk assessments or information at the global level on a variety of risks. These knowledge platforms can play an important role in bringing national interests closer to establish shared goals. With capacity-building technical assistance provided by IFIs, national authorities can design monitoring and early warning systems and contingency-planning frameworks for timely detection of problems and effective responses to them.[13] Global media can play a crucial role in disseminating alerts generated by these detection systems.

Improving protection through global rules, capacity building, and coordination

Accumulating knowledge about the drivers and potential effects of risks is necessary but not sufficient to encourage appropriate risk management action. Design and implementation of rules, regulations, standards, and frameworks for collective action can provide incentives and guidance to better manage a range of risks that affect multiple nations and generations. Some examples include the global financial sector reforms to strengthen the financial infrastructure and create a more resilient financial system following the 2008 financial crisis;[14] the Millennium Development Goals to reduce poverty and address a range of risk affecting development;[15] the United Nations effort to encourage preparedness for pandemics and incorporate pandemic response plans into disaster risk management (the Toward a Safer World Initiative);[16] and A New Deal for Engagement in Fragile States.[17] Several other examples, including those for managing environmental risks, are outlined more fully in table 8.1.

Technical capacity to implement rules, regulations, and standards is necessary for such efforts to succeed. Weak capacity in the veterinary and human public health systems in developing countries, for ex-

TABLE 8.1 *Examples of global actions and factors underlying their impact*

Goals and results	Underlying reasons for success or failure
Kyoto Protocol (1997)	
Goals: Reduce greenhouse gas emissions of 38 industrial countries as a confidence-building step to reach the goal of the United Nations (UN) Framework Convention on Climate Change (UNFCCC) to stabilize greenhouse gas concentrations at a level that would prevent dangerous interference with the climate. Required a 5.2% cut, on average, in the emissions of industrial countries below their 1990 levels between 2008 and 2012. **Results:** Took effect in February 2005 when the two conditions of ratification were met (ratification by 55 nations and ratification by nations that produce 55% of the emissions). By April 2006, 141 countries had ratified the protocol. Many countries did not meet their targets, however, and actually increased emissions, resulting in a global rise from 1990 levels.	Failed to attract broad-based support, ensure compliance (in the absence of an effective enforcement mechanism), and make parties take substantial actions; some of the largest emitters either did not participate (industrial countries such as the United States and Canada) or were not required to cut emissions (middle-income countries such as China and India). Bundled together targets for several greenhouse gases to achieve cost-effectiveness, but at the expense of lowering emission reduction targets. Diverging incentives and interests (no clear self-enforcing common goal): • Perception that an individual country is too small to make a change. • Climate change does not affect all countries the same way; some benefit from it in the short run, while some are hurt more than others. These differences create varying views about benefits and costs of action to mitigate climate change. • Competing domestic policy imperatives, including political factors, and short-term economic considerations; nonparticipation (particularly by developing countries) to avoid hurting growth. • Free-rider problems with costly steps to mitigate climate change.
Montreal Protocol (1987)	
Goals: Protect ozone layer by banning ozone-depleting chemicals (ODCs). **Results:** Emissions of most depleting substances have been brought under control; signs indicate that the ozone layer will recover within the next 100 years; developed countries have reduced their production, consumption, and emission of chemicals controlled by the protocol by 99%; developing countries by 72% and reductions are continuing. Some increase in some of the chemicals authorized for short-term substitution.	Broad participation: First treaty to reach universal ratification (197 UN nations). It started with 24 signatories and the European Economic Community in 1987, and was eventually signed by many, including developing countries. Addressed the problem by chemicals (source), not timetable (targets). Cost-effective substitutes for ODCs already existed. Negotiations included civil society and scientists to overcome informational barriers; high degree of scientific consensus and evidence provided credibility. Right incentives (and common interests): • Wide recognition that ozone depletion has serious, quickly visible consequences (health issues such as cancer). • Created strong incentives to participate and comply: the treaty set out reasonable plans for implementation with appropriate support coupled with trade restrictions—bans on trade between parties and nonparties in ozone-depleting substances and products containing the substances—to spur compliance. • Recognized importance of developing new technologies using nondepleting alternatives and providing access to developing countries. • Set up a multilateral fund to provide incremental funding to developing countries for transitioning to phase out harmful substances; provided institutional support (a key motivation for the participation of developing countries in the Protocol).
Smallpox eradication campaign (1967–79)	
Goals: Eradication of a pandemic disease that killed 300 million–500 million people.	Broad cooperation achieved. Strong leadership and commitment from the World Health Organization (WHO), backed by political commitment from governments. Financial and technical assistance from developed to developing countries that lacked resources and capacity to eradicate alone.

(continued)

TABLE 8.1 *Examples of global actions and factors underlying their impact* (continued)

Goals and results	Underlying reasons for success or failure
Results: WHO declared the world free of smallpox in May 1980. First disease eradicated by human effort. Seen as a unique achievement in the history of international cooperation.	Right incentives that were self-enforcing (no formal enforcement by WHO was needed): • Costs (about $300 million worldwide) were negligible, compared with benefits: the United States got back its entire contribution in 26 days (in health costs saved)—a benefit-cost ratio of over 400:1. • The disease affected every country (ease of spread with trade and movement of people) with direct consequences; eradication succeeded because smallpox was eliminated everywhere. Strong U.S. support (monetary and technical) and other support from U.S. Centers for Disease Control. Scientific research showing feasibility of eradication; technical breakthrough (with a new type of needle) lowered the cost of vaccination. Surveillance and containment strategy: strong focus on preventing the disease from spreading by seeking and monitoring new cases.
Controlling HIV/AIDS	
Goals: Eradication of the disease. **Results:** Progress in treatment research has decreased the number of people dying from HIV/AIDS. The number of new cases of HIV/AIDS has been decreasing since its peak in the late 1990s. But the number of people living with HIV is still rising.	Global cooperation has had some success: • In 2010, number of people on antiretroviral treatment in low- and middle-income countries reached 47% of the need, up from 39%. • Number of health facilities in these countries has risen significantly. • About 35% of pregnant women living with HIV in these countries receive care, up from 7% in 2005. Treatment 2.0 launched in 2010, aiming at higher efficiency: simplified, more affordable diagnosis and treatment; and integrated, decentralized HIV service delivery. Despite availability of prevention, there is a problem of incentives: • HIV takes 5–10 years to manifest; people with low life expectancy may not protect themselves and may spread the disease. • Promotion of treatment is a double-edge sword—treatment may create an externality and lower the incentive to protect. • Limited access to information and protection in low-income countries.
Hyogo Framework for Action (HFA) (2005–15)	
Goals: Reduce the impact of natural hazards by making prevention a priority at all levels under the coordination of UN International Strategy for Disaster Reduction. **Results:** Increasing number of reporting countries. Increase in disaster reduction and recovery activities at all levels. More progress needed in preparation.	Provide governments with a common set of terms, approach, and platform, facilitating cooperation at the international level. The structure of the HFA (organized by expected outcome, strategic goals, and priorities for actions) and guidance on its implementation supported development of comparable framework at regional and national levels. • Good communication and rising public awareness (various organizations have launched global campaigns). • Establishment of a scientific and technical committee. • Progress in implementation (creation of a special representative of the UN Secretary-General for implementation of the HFA). • Broad participation/acceptance of the framework. High and increasing damages caused by natural hazards provide strong incentives to reduce the risk. Consequences are concrete and immediate.

Source: WDR 2014 team based on United Nations Framework Convention on Climate Change 1998; Barrett 2006, 2008; UNEP 2007; Stern 2007; Rae 2012; Center for Global Development, "Case 1: Eradicating Smallpox," http://www.cgdev.org/doc/millions/MS_case_1.pdf; World Health Organization, http://www.who.int; UNISDR 2006, 2007; OECD and G20 2012.

ample, has undermined implementation of the International Health Regulations (2005) on surveillance, control, and reporting of contagious pathogens. The international community could help countries build implementation capacity. It could also make periodic assessments of whether national policies and practices have high potential for cross-border spillovers. These discussions could focus on areas where the lack of implementation capacity undermines a country's ability to conform to global agreements and manage risk effectively.

The international community can provide technical assistance to support initiatives designed to protect against various risks. It can support capacity building to strengthen governance; to build early warning and monitoring systems for infectious diseases, crises, and disasters; and to design proactive crisis and disaster management strategies that reduce the need for costly coping measures after the fact. The IFIs can support the development of markets for debt and reserve management and hedging instruments to manage financial risks, particularly where small or segmented markets can block efficient private sector solutions to risk and prevent the pooling of risk across markets. Specific risk management strategies include developing alternative risk-financing tools such as catastrophe bonds that transfer the risk of a disaster to markets by allowing the issuer to forgo repayment of the bond principal if a major disaster occurs.[18] Weather hedges are another example of an instrument that transfers the risk to financial markets; these hedges are based on an underlying weather index, with payments triggered by prespecified adverse weather events.

An important role for the international community lies in facilitating the collective action and cooperation necessary to supply global public goods. By providing a platform for policy dialogue and coordination among sovereign states (key building blocks of the international community), the international community can promote implementation of agreed rules and regulations that reduce global risks, as well as cooperation that improves development outcomes. Such cooperation could facilitate further liberalization of international trade and capital flows; support strong, sustainable, and inclusive growth, or engage with FCSs on a sustainable basis; and take a balanced approach to risks and opportunities. Cooperation can also limit potential externalities and inconsistencies in implementation that could jeopardize outcomes in a tightly integrated and interconnected world. Some of the challenges associated with securing effective cooperation among sovereign nations are discussed later in the chapter.

Mobilizing global resources for preparation, mitigation, coping, and recovery

Countries' efforts to prepare for risk notwithstanding, crises and disasters do happen, and when they do, significant resources are spent on coping with their consequences and recovery. The international community has a range of risk-sharing tools to help countries deal with extreme (tail-risk) scenarios such as disasters, both before and after the event (box 8.2).

Offering support for coping. In their most typical form, international risk-sharing solutions involve direct ex post support from bilateral or multilateral creditors or private organizations. A key driver of this support is the need for timely action to mitigate a sudden shortage of resources (monetary or human) following a severe crisis or a disaster. Direct international interventions can be justified when resources to protect vulnerable populations are unavailable from capital markets, self-insurance, or functioning communities and governments or when the risk that distress and contagion will escalate to other countries is high. Examples include the financial stabilization packages arranged for several Euro Area states, the liquidity provisions to unclog international financial markets during the global financial crisis, the support that 36 donors provided to more than 100 developing countries to control the H5N1 avian flu and prepare for a possible pandemic during 2005–10, and direct humanitarian help to people in FCSs.

Several international community actors play a role in coping. The IMF, the World Bank, and other IFIs, as part of their mandates, pool risk across countries and lend to countries experiencing actual or potential external funding pressure as countries work to restore stability or sustain development spending in the wake of a crisis and correct underlying problems. Remittances from immediate or extended family members abroad provide risk pooling at the family level, allowing for more direct and timely relief in the presence of adverse domestic shocks. Remittances and kinship support are among the traditional coping mechanisms for FCSs, especially when effective government support is not available. Civil societies, including global nongovernmental organizations, combine in-kind transfers with foreign onsite managerial services to deal with local bottlenecks. International investors also boost domestic capacity through portfolio and direct investment flows.

BOX 8.2 *International support for disaster risk management*

Disaster and climate risk management are increasingly recognized as key priorities for development, and many actors are working to shift the focus from ex post response toward preparation and prevention at all levels of government. At the international level, the UN Office for Disaster Risk Reduction coordinates efforts across the UN system and tracks progress toward the implementation of the Hyogo Framework for Action (HFA) to make prevention of natural disasters a priority. The scientific community, civil society, and international financial institutions, as well as regional intergovernmental organizations that foster regional disaster-risk-reduction cooperation, support the efforts for HFA implementation.

In 2006, the Global Facility for Disaster Reduction and Recovery (GFDRR) was created to forge a global partnership to intensify support for mainstreaming disaster risk management into national development planning. Housed within the World Bank, the GFDRR has helped the Bank move from a reactive approach to a more strategic, long-term approach focused on reducing risk. Bank disaster-related financing doubled from 1984–2006 to 2007–11. The share of funding by the International Development Association for climate adaptation rose from 9 percent to 16 percent, and for climate mitigation rose from 5 percent to 16 percent from fiscal 2011 to fiscal 2012.[a]

The Bank supports disaster resilience in developing countries through a five-pillar approach:

- *Risk identification.* By quantifying risks and anticipating the potential negative impacts of natural hazards on society and the economy, disaster and climate risk assessments can help governments, communities, and individuals make informed decisions about managing risk.
- *Risk reduction.* Anticipatory action can reduce existing risks and prevent the creation of new risks.
- *Preparedness.* Technical assistance and financing of climate services help establish early warning of extreme events. They also increase climate-modeling capacity to design effective adaptation policies.
- *Financial protection.* Advisory services on disaster risk financing and insurance help protect governments, businesses, and households from the economic burden of disasters; increase the state's financial capacity to respond to emergencies; promote deeper insurance markets at regional and sovereign levels; and support social protection strategies for the poorest.
- *Resilient recovery and reconstruction.* The Bank supports country-led Post-Disaster Needs Assessments, which estimate the impact on people, including development needs, and economic losses following a disaster. The estimates provide the basis for planning recovery and reconstruction efforts.

Source: Robert Reid for the WDR 2014.

a. IDA 2012.

Providing insurance mechanisms. Besides emergency assistance, international risk-sharing mechanisms include insurance that pools risk and transfers resources from good to bad times. IFIs such as the Multilateral Investment Guarantee Agency offer political risk insurance to reassure foreign investors and promote investment flows to countries as part of ex ante risk management. The IFIs also provide emergency disaster response tools by creating a range of products countries can access with great flexibility and speed, such as the World Bank's Immediate Response Mechanism and Catastrophe Deferred Drawdown Option (CAT DDO) instrument.[19] Moreover, the ongoing financial crisis facilitated the creation of insurance tools for countries experiencing volatility and instability despite relatively strong fundamentals, such as the IMF's Flexible Credit Line or the Bank's Development Policy Loan with DDO.[20]

These tools are also intended to reduce the demand for self-insurance through excessive reserve accumulation—a factor that contributed to global imbalances as external account deficits of systemically important economies widened because of higher demand for reserve currencies. Countries have been reluctant to use some of these tools, however, in part because of the stigma effect of seeking financial help. Finding an efficient design for global safety nets has also been a challenge, given the difficult trade-off between limiting moral hazard and preventing liquidity crises from turning into insolvency. Instead, stronger links among emerging economies triggered interest in regional reserve pooling and swap lines to serve as insurance; however, these schemes are of limited lending power and effectiveness in dealing with covariate liquidity shocks.[21]

Facilitating regional insurance. Besides its more direct engagement, the international community can also play a more indirect catalyzing and technical role by helping countries in a particular region pool resources that they can use in an emergency. Such mechanisms bode well for the principle of shared responsibility in managing risk and enhance countries' capacity to jointly access international markets at a lower premium than they could obtain individually. These facilities are particularly helpful for small states where private markets are nonexistent, small, segmented, poorly functioning, or unaffordable to the most vulnerable, and where access to credit, insurance, and reinsurance markets is limited. Three

BOX 8.3 *Regional risk-sharing solutions: Promoting financial resilience to disaster risks*

Innovative disaster risk financing and insurance (DRFI) solutions are being developed by international financial institutions, in partnership with donors and other members of the international community. These tools are particularly important for developing countries with high exposure to natural hazards, but limited resources, financial capacity, and access to cheap credit and insurance markets. The regional risk-pooling mechanisms discussed below illustrate four key roles the international community can play in advancing DRFI solutions: convening power; promotion of public goods that permit the development of risk market infrastructure; technical assistance and specialized expertise; and provision of initial seed capital, contingent loans, and credit enhancements.

Increasing access to catastrophe insurance in Southeast Europe

The Southeast Europe and the Caucasus Catastrophe Risk Insurance Facility (SEEC-CRIF) was launched in 2009 to support development of a catastrophe and weather risk insurance market for the region. The initiative simultaneously addresses three bottlenecks of market development: risk market infrastructure, regulatory framework, and government policy. It provides pivotal public goods, including country-specific catastrophe risk models and a web-based insurance underwriting platform to facilitate the sale of reliable, cost-efficient catastrophe insurance products. The CRIF also helps participating countries incorporate risk awareness, knowledge, and skills related to climate change and disasters into their development policies. The World Bank supports the CRIF with technical assistance and loans to the facility and member governments.

Providing technical assistance to launch state-of-the-art risk-pooling in the Caribbean

The Caribbean Catastrophe Risk Insurance Facility (CCRIF) is the first-ever multicountry risk pool to insure against disasters. Sixteen Caribbean countries are members of the facility, which provides them with immediate liquidity in case of a major hurricane or earthquake. Members pay an annual premium depending on their risk exposure. The CCRIF uses risk pooling (through joint reserves and lower reinsurance rates) and shared operating costs to provide coverage at a significantly lower cost than each country would pay acting separately. With technical assistance from the World Bank, the facility tackles the technical, actuarial, legal, fiduciary, and financial engineering aspects of designing and implementing an independent, sustainable facility. The CCRIF, which is funded by participating countries and donors, has provided immediate liquidity funding to governments on eight occasions since its launch in 2007.

Financing a proactive approach in the Pacific

Transitioning from relying on humanitarian aid and other ex post resources to more efficient ex ante DRFI requires investment in disaster risk assessment and financing tools—as well as funding to implement the solution (such as paying insurance premiums). The Pacific Catastrophe Risk Assessment and Financing Initiative has invested in the development of probabilistic catastrophe risk models acceptable to the international reinsurance market. The facility provides technical assistance on implementation and advises members on financial solutions to reduce their exposure and to improve financial and economic planning (insurance, donations, reserves, and contingencies). For the sovereign catastrophe-risk insurance pilot launched as part of the initiative in 2013, the Japanese government funded the first and part of the second year's premium for five participating countries.

Source: Laura Boudreau, Hannah Yi, and Olivier Mahul for the WDR 2014.

examples of regional facilities, designed with support from the international community, are outlined in box 8.3.

How effective is the international community in resolving global risks?

The international community has made significant progress in addressing risks through knowledge tools. It has put great effort into data collection and risk analysis to improve assessment of risks and has developed innovative tools and databases to analyze risk from adverse natural hazards (box 8.4). It has worked to reduce data and information gaps. In a recent joint effort, for example, the Bank for International Settlements, the Financial Stability Board, and the IMF developed a common data template for markets to use in monitoring excessive risk taking by global systemically important banks and for policy makers to use in assessing systemic risks.[22] The World Organisation for Animal Health has evaluated public veterinary systems in more than 100 countries for their ability to detect and control diseases and reduce contagion risks. The Intergovernmental Panel on Climate Change brings together scientists periodically to review research from around the world and update and fine-tune assessments on the drivers and consequences of climate change; the UN Framework Convention on Climate Change monitors trends in greenhouse gas emissions to inform policy analyses and discussions at national and international levels. IFIs monitor and analyze a wealth of economic, financial, environmental, and developmental data and trends that help inform national policies.

Significant efforts have also been made to apply this knowledge. The international community has put

BOX 8.4 *Global efforts to provide tools and databases for assessing disaster risk*

By anticipating and quantifying potential damages from natural hazards, disaster and climate risk assessments can help communities, companies, and governments make more informed decisions, such as where and how to build safer schools, how to insure farmers against drought, and how to protect coastal cities against rising sea levels.

Estimates of potential exposure of physical assets and populations to risk are necessary to develop any risk reduction strategy, as well as for effective emergency response and crisis management in general. Although the most detailed exposure data are available primarily in high-income countries, international actors are working with developing countries to build their own asset exposure inventories. For example, the Pacific Catastrophe Risk Assessment and Financing Initiative has created the largest-ever collection of geospatial information on disaster risks available for Pacific Island countries, with quantification of potential disaster losses from earthquakes, tsunamis, and tropical cyclones. Resulting exposure, hazard, and risk maps and data are shared with policy makers and the public.

The *Global Earthquake Model* is a global collaborative effort to pool knowledge and provide people with tools and resources to assess earthquake risk anywhere in the world. The goal is to provide a global exposure database by the end of 2013 that contains aggregate information on population and residential buildings. Building-by-building data will be available for a selected number of areas, and the number of areas will increase over time.

Probabilistic risk-modeling techniques are now increasingly used to evaluate uncertainty inherent in complex systems, including natural events. Probabilistic risk modeling is also being coupled with climate change models to assess the likelihood and severity of future hazards, over the time horizons needed for decision making in sectors such as urban planning.[a] A free platform, CAPRA (Central American Probabilistic Risk Assessment), has been developed to use a probabilistic methodology to visualize, quantify, and track sources of risk resulting from a range of hazards in Central America and is being rolled out in other regions.

Data sharing and open systems promote transparency and accountability and enlist a wide range of participants in the challenge of building resilience. For example, the *Open Data for Resilience Initiative* uses free and open-source software from eight leading international organizations and data providers to enable people and institutions to collaborate on building drought resilience in the Sahel. Similarly, *InaSAFE* is a free and open-source software that produces natural hazard impact scenarios, providing a simple yet rigorous way to combine data from scientists, local governments, and communities to assess likely effects of future disaster events. The tool was piloted by the city of Jakarta for emergency planning during the 2012 flood season.

Sources: Robert Reid for the WDR 2014.

a. Ranger and others 2011

in place rules and standards to encourage responsible risk management behavior. It has convened experts, national and global policy makers, and standard setters around the world to solve global problems. It has made progress in using risk assessments to generate and communicate predictions and warnings of natural hazards. Improved access to global media and the Internet has allowed rapid sharing of disease intelligence and scientific research on disease control, environmental risks, and financial risks, among others. Early warning systems have been developed for many types of hazards, helping to reduce the number of deaths from disasters. Enhanced monitoring of economic, financial, social, geopolitical, environmental, and technological risks is being used to assess low-probability, high-impact risks to the global system and to push for risk-mitigating policies, including those that would require international cooperation.[23] Global resources have been used when countries faced mounting difficulties that also risked spilling over to others.

But overall effectiveness has been limited. In particular, the international community as a whole could have been more forceful in addressing some of the key risks that cross boundaries. Five years after the onset of the global financial crisis, economies and financial systems of advanced and developing countries remain vulnerable to the risk of renewed tensions, as some underlying economic and structural weaknesses remain unresolved. Negative feedback loops across banking, sovereign, and real risks and competing macroeconomic priorities complicate policy responses. Progress remains limited in arresting climate change, despite substantial available knowledge and emphasis on the dangers of inaction. Progress in preventing and preparing for pandemic risk is limited, even as costly zoonotic disease outbreaks continue to occur (including the recent outbreaks of H7N9 and the coronavirus). The majority of the Millennium Development Goals are not expected to be met by fragile states by the 2015 target date (box 8.5); by that time, these countries also are expected to account for half of the world's poor.[24] The inability to move forward more aggressively to deal with these risks is costly, taking already scarce resources away from development efforts, in some cases slowing or reversing hard-won development gains and imposing huge costs on future generations.

Several common elements play a role in this poor performance. Insufficient access to available

BOX 8.5 *Well-managed risks can unleash development opportunities in fragile and conflict-affected states*

International engagement in fragile and conflict-affected states (FCSs) poses considerable risks for donors and implementing partners, who must contend with high levels of insecurity, political instability, weak institutions, and the failure of basic state functions that typically characterize such states. These characteristics undermine the social and economic support systems through which the international community provides support (including the state and local communities and institutions). In these complex and fast-changing environments, outcomes are hard to foresee and control, and the possibility of returning to violent conflict is always present. People's ability to manage risks is seriously constrained, and the consequences of a risk materializing are often a matter of life and death.

At the same time, international engagement in these high-risk environments can make particularly important contributions to development. Because of the low starting point, effective international assistance can achieve more in these transitional contexts than in most other situations.[a] Where state-society relations are renegotiated and state institutions redefined, international engagement, including aid, has the potential to provide critical catalytic and transformative support. Moreover, the risks of not engaging can be high—both for the countries themselves and for the international community, if the lack of international assistance allows conflict to continue or resume. In an interconnected world, such conflicts have significant economic and social costs that reach beyond national borders.

High degree of risk aversion

Yet within the donor community and its implementation partners, the emphasis tends to be on avoiding risk, both in where and how donors engage, and within the organizational cultures of donors. Aid flows to poor and fragile countries are volatile and unpredictable. High degrees of uncertainty and information gaps can also lead to overly pessimistic perception of risks and unrealistic expectations for what aid can achieve in short time frames. Concerns about corruption discourage donor and investor engagement. Tighter reporting and accountability requirements and less reliance on local initiative reduce the speed, flexibility, and innovation that are key to taking advantage of short-lived opportunities in these fast-changing situations. These shortfalls are manifested by a lack of progress in attaining the Millennium Development Goals (MDGs) in many FCSs (figure) and in a large number of countries returning to conflict. The absence of active engagement with and support of development over the long term prevents the building of national capacity.

Fragile and conflict-affected states have made slow progress toward the MDGs

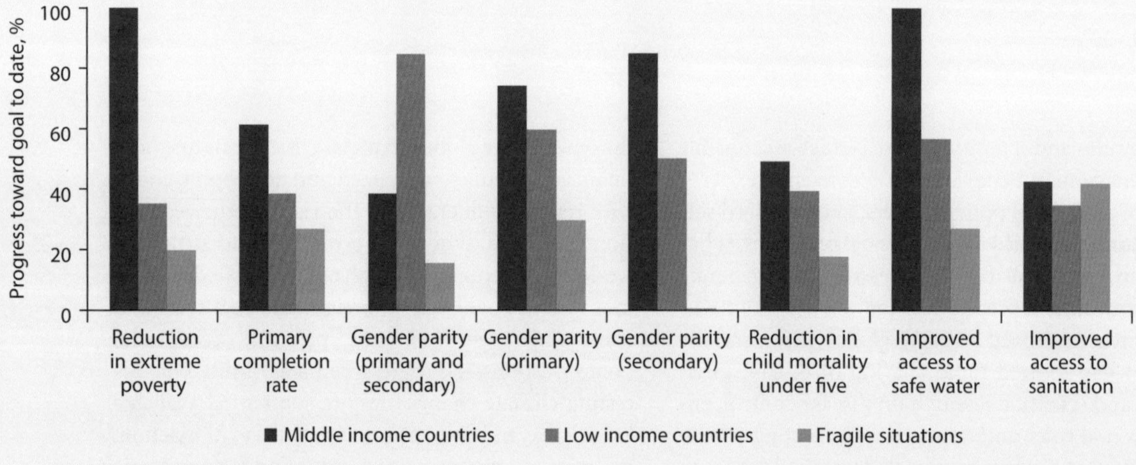

Progress toward goal to date, %

0 20 40 60 80 100

Reduction in extreme poverty | Primary completion rate | Gender parity (primary and secondary) | Gender parity (primary) | Gender parity (secondary) | Reduction in child mortality under five | Improved access to safe water | Improved access to sanitation

■ Middle income countries ■ Low income countries ■ Fragile situations

Source: WDR 2014 team based on World Bank and IMF 2010.

Some change in approach is under way

FCSs and development partners are now concluding that appropriate risk taking is essential for improved outcomes and that a better balance must be struck between risk and opportunity. The 2011 WDR on conflict suggested that poorly designed and rushed donor responses can exacerbate the significant risks in engaging in FCSs, and that risk-opportunity assessments should be used more frequently to see how aid itself might be a risk mitigation measure through its impact on local systems and capacities. The 2011 WDR recommended greater monitoring of government-executed programs, risk sharing through pooled funds, and proactive planning of risk contingencies based on risk-opportunity assessments. The New Deal for Engagement in Fragile States, agreed in 2011 in Busan, Republic of Korea, recognized that the risk of not engaging can outweigh most risks of engagement. It emphasized the need for joint assessments of the specific risks and context-specific, joint donor risk-mitigation strategies. The g7-plus group of states (those affected by conflict and now in transition to the next stage of development) and its development partners have committed to support developing countries' efforts to strengthen core institutions and policies by aiming to manage, rather than avoid, risk, and minimizing the risk of reverting to conflict through joint efforts of donors and fragile states.

Balancing risks and opportunities requires a parallel focus on contextual, programmatic, and institutional risks and collective

BOX 8.5 ***Well-managed risks can unleash development opportunities in fragile and conflict-affected states*** **(continued)**

approaches. Recent research by the OECD provided policy recommendations for donors to match aspiration with action and move from risk aversion to balancing risk and opportunity:

- *Establish institutional cultures that encourage appropriate risk taking in FCSs.* This would involve setting incentives for staff and implementing partners to consider risks in relation to opportunity and communicate openly about why some risks in FCSs are worth taking, along with devising specific risk-management frameworks.
- *Agree on realistic objectives and frameworks for measuring results.* Donors and partners should establish such frameworks for measuring results in complex environments, tailored to specific circumstances of FCSs.
- *Simplify procedures for the release and delivery of aid.* This step would facilitate rapid and flexible responses and transfer of funds to take advantage of the narrow windows of opportunity to influence the course of events.
- *Establish a common framework for understanding and assessing risk that ensures focus on people and contextual risks.* By conducting fragility assessments, several New Deal pilot countries have sought to develop a joint understanding with development partners and civil society of the causes, features, and drivers of fragility, and of sources of resilience that can form a basis for dialogue and joint risk mitigation strategies.
- *Identify options to share risks and maximize collective impact by pooling efforts and funding.* Joint efforts can reduce individual actors' exposures to political and reputational risks and dilute the risk of program failure. Options for sharing risks include pooled funds, joint guidelines, and mutual accountability frameworks.
- *Understand and facilitate the role of multilateral organizations as "risk-pooling mechanisms."* Donors need to give implementing partners the necessary scope and means to take risks and respond flexibly. Greater honesty and transparency about exposure to all risks is needed between donors and those they fund, with an explicit focus on building local capacities and a commitment to collectively manage associated risks.[b]

The broader international community could support donors' efforts to manage the risk of engagement in FCSs:

- It could help donors *identify, better understand, and monitor risks specific to the FCS,* notably by developing a set of indicators to monitor frequently. The New Deal Fragility Assessments will likely use a common set of indicators that can be applied flexibly to take country context and local needs into account. Better access to such knowledge could inform decision making and prioritization, alleviate risk aversion by the donor community, and identify the local capacities and institutions that need strengthening.
- *Contingency plans, early warning, and crisis and disaster management systems* could be developed to mitigate the extreme risks facing FCSs, in partnership with multilateral institutions. Targeted capacity-building assistance could strengthen implementation deficiencies, improve institutional capacity, and reduce corruption risks. Development agencies, civil society, and the media could partner in the effort, making wrongdoing costly. Coordinated donor involvement in reconstruction efforts proved useful after the 2004 tsunami in Aceh.
- *Both donors and FCSs could do risk pooling* with the international community's help (involving bilateral and multilateral partners). The positive experiences with regional risk-pooling facilities could provide useful guidance. The international community could help mobilize multilateral donor funding and design harmonized proactive risk-management frameworks and by providing political risk insurance in multilateral platforms.

Source: WDR 2014 team based on Laura Mazal, Diane Koester, and Sophie Walker for the WDR 2014; Asbjorn Wee for the WDR 2014; OECD 2011a, 2011c; OECD Development Assistance Committee 2012; Fengler and Kharas 2011; World Bank 2011; and World Bank and IMF 2010.

a. Transitional situations may include transitioning from conflict to peace or violence to security.

b. Ongoing case studies by the OECD and the U.K. Department for International Development highlight a number of interesting donor approaches and innovative practices on risk management already being used in FCSs. In Nepal, conflict-sensitive programming is used as a risk management practice that has been mainstreamed across donor operations. Specialized risk management units help pool resources in addressing security, fiduciary, and other risks encountered in operational work. In Somalia, a UN Risk Management Unit was set up to manage fiduciary risk and monitor implementing partners, where limited access and freedom of movement hamper the ability to undertake direct field monitoring.

knowledge, resources, and capacity hamper the accumulation and use of this knowledge to take appropriate risk management action. In some cases, more emphasis is put on avoiding risk than on taking well-informed risk and managing it (as with the international community's engagement with fragile states). Political economy constraints and lack of proper incentives, accountability, and effective enforcement mechanisms undermine international cooperation.

Problems in formulating and transforming knowledge to action

Continued gaps in information constrain knowledge and action in some areas. Information asymmetries continue to hamper global efforts to effectively manage risks in the financial sector. Despite the efforts of the global community, some key information needed to identify a buildup of systemic financial risks remains unavailable to markets and policy makers. In countries where financial systems are regionally or globally interconnected, the lack of exposure data across institutions hinders identification of emerging risks and undermines the usefulness of early warning systems to trigger appropriate action. Early warning systems for natural hazards are also of limited use when information is imprecise and is not communicated quickly or clearly, as experienced in some developing countries.[25] Similarly, infectious disease controls are often undermined by weak communication between public health authorities and within the public; delays in detection and diagnosis caused by information gaps lead to late and more costly control measures. Failure to translate scientific knowledge for use by local practitioners also limits the appreciation of, and response to, various risks. While extensive data are available on environmental risks, they remain scattered and lagged, with limited systematic dissemination of the key messages to summon national or global action.

Information asymmetries also affect the international community's ability to engage effectively in fragile and conflict-affected states, thus undermining their ability to support people's risk management. Corruption and political risks, which typically characterize these states, undermine the competitiveness and investment appeal of their economies.[26] Insufficient information about the extent of corruption, political risks, and local authorities' implementation will and capacity adds to donor risk aversion, reduces their willingness to engage, and may focus their attention on attaining results that, while safe, may not help these states strengthen national systems and address peace-building needs.[27] Missed opportunities for engagement (through market access or development aid), in turn, raise the risk that political transition will threaten prosperity and social cohesion and could create a vicious circle of fragility, poverty, despair, continued corruption, and conflict, with costs that can have broader cross-border implications, as observed in the Middle East and Africa. In such circumstances, risk of inaction can be very high.

Many tools designed by the international community to manage complex risks elude countries with limited resources and capacity to understand and implement them. Insufficient resources and capacity make it difficult for countries to access and apply available information and knowledge, afford insurance, reinsure, and take preventive actions. For instance, in the past five years, insurance covered less than 20 percent of total disaster losses in developing countries, on average, compared to about 60 percent in North America, according to SwissRe. Shortfalls in funding the cost of mitigation of, and adaptation to, climate change have been an obstacle to reducing greenhouse gas emissions in developing countries and to reaching agreements in global negotiations.[28] Although climate change risk and loss of biodiversity and resources are global problems, vulnerability as well as efforts to mitigate or adapt to these risks are local, and constrained by national and local authorities' capacity to implement necessary corrective actions.

Cognitive, behavioral, and political economy factors also get in the way of translating available information into actionable knowledge. Despite widespread availability of information on the evidence of drivers of climate change and other environmental risks, disasters, or the possibility of yet another pandemic, individuals, communities, and governments continue to overlook their potential exposure to what they view as rare or distant events, underestimate the potential cost, and fail to insure or otherwise protect themselves (and others). Similarly, small-probability, high-impact risks are often ignored in the face of short-term challenges, resulting in underinvestment in preventive steps. A recent global survey on climate change found, for instance, a clear indication of short-sighted attitudes to climate change risk and greater attention to what is seen as more pressing and urgent matters facing the world (figure 8.2). These responses suggest that a non-negligible part of the global population discount the future heavily and place a lower value on adverse consequences of climate change, such as loss of biodiversity and increased frequency and cost of disasters.

Deep uncertainty adds to the behavioral and cognitive biases. For example, the push to mitigate climate change risks is undermined by uncertainty about the benefits and costs of taking such action and by a lack of consensus on the critical thresholds (tipping points) for greenhouse gas concentrations beyond which small changes in Earth's temperature could have catastrophic consequences. The absence of scientific consensus on these thresholds undermines incentives for international cooperation. Recent experimental research suggests that if this threshold could be identified with certainty, and if the relative cost of avoiding it were low, the fear of crossing it could reduce the free-riding behavior of countries and induce them to join in the needed collective action to avoid catastrophe.[29] Deep uncertainty may also undermine the ability to assess complex macro-financial risks. The difficulty of anticipating the com-

FIGURE 8.2 ***A 2011 survey highlights divergent national interests and short-sighted views on climate change***

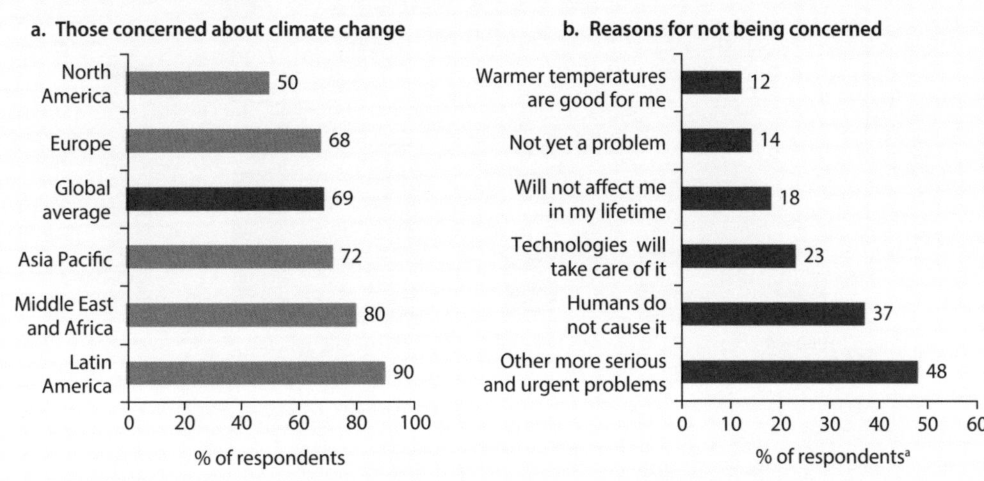

Source: WDR 2014 team based on data from survey responses of 51 countries in Nielsen Company 2011.
a. Percentages equal more than 100 percent because respondents could choose all choices that apply.

plex feedback loops between financial, sovereign, and real sector risks, for instance, has contributed both to the severity of the ongoing global financial crisis and to the challenges in resolving it.

Perverse incentives that discourage effective risk management

Emphasis on ex post risk management creates moral hazard. Ready availability of help to recover from a disaster or a crisis may encourage public and private agents to be less cautious in taking risk or in protecting or insuring against it. The ex post availability of disaster aid (given the reluctance to deny help to those who have not taken sufficient prevention measures—the Samaritan's dilemma) may, in some cases, weaken incentives of governments to invest in warning systems or enforce strict zoning and building regulations in disaster-prone areas, or for individuals to insure or avoid settling in such areas, when other options are available.[30] For governments (or donors), the political reward for well-funded and costly hazard prevention may be seen as small compared with the gain from an efficient ex post response.[31] Similarly, sustained investments in public health systems to prevent pandemics from developing may be crowded out by funding for mitigation programs, such as stockpiling of medications. In finance, the absence of effective cross-border resolution regimes to deal with failing systemic banks and national governments' tendency to rescue them create moral hazard, encouraging excessive risk taking by financial institutions perceived as too important to fail, and reducing their incentives to self-insure by holding capital and liquidity in line with the risks taken (see chapter 6).

Despite the high benefit-cost ratios of better preparation (see chapter 1), evidence suggests that more emphasis is placed on ex post risk management. This emphasis is evident in donor financing for disasters: of the total development assistance allocated for disaster-related activities between 1980 and 2009, only 3.6 percent ($3.3 billion) was devoted to prevention and preparedness (figure 8.3).[32] By contrast, the estimated economic losses from disasters over the past 30 years amount to $3.5 trillion—with a record $380 billion in 2012. Financial crises also divert resources from growth and development: the cost of direct support from national governments to financial institutions during the 1990 crisis ranged from less than 5 percent of gross domestic product (GDP) in Sweden to more than 55 percent in Indonesia. Since 2008, the cost of direct support and government guarantees to the financial system ranged from about 10 percent of GDP in the United States to more than 50 percent in Ireland.[33] Realization of these contingent liabilities reduces the fiscal room available for social spending (see chapter 7), and makes it more likely that national governments will call for international support when future problems hit. In the health area, the total cost of major zoonotic disease outbreaks reached an estimated $80 billion over 2007–09, compared with an annual estimated cost of $1.9 billion–$3.4 billion to

FIGURE 8.3 ***Disaster-related donor assistance has focused more on coping than preparedness and prevention***

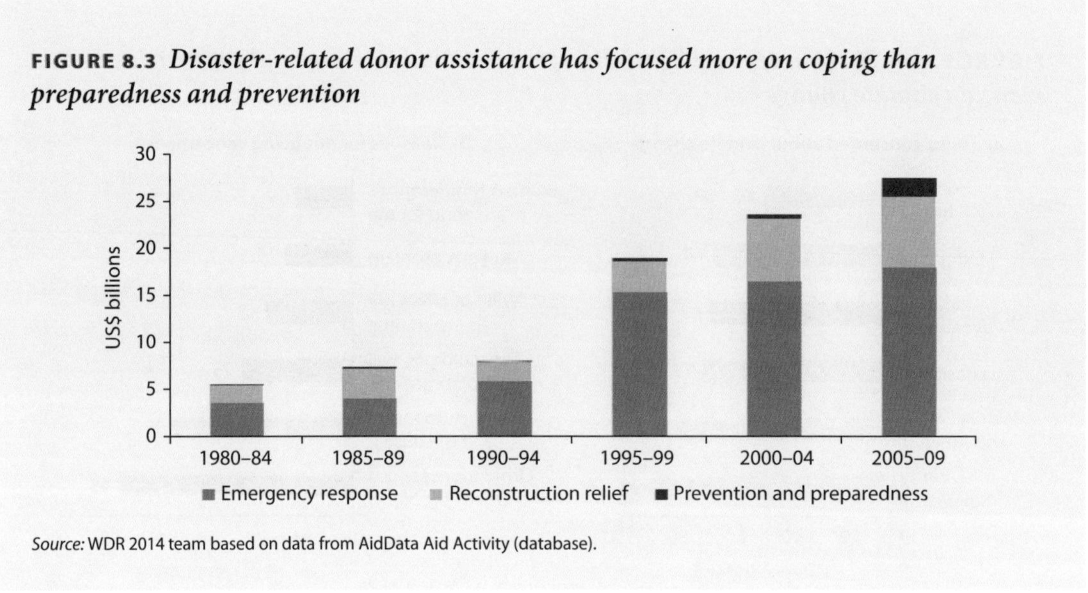

Source: WDR 2014 team based on data from AidData Aid Activity (database).

build and operate One Health approaches to prevent and control these diseases.[34]

Myopia about risks may also reduce the perceived urgency for action, while creating tendencies to pass the risk, and the associated cost of today's inaction, on to others. The costs of climate change mitigation not borne by today's generation will be passed to future generations when mitigation will likely be more costly and possibly too late to have the intended effect. A 2007 estimate by the Stern Review placed the cost of unmitigated climate change at a permanent annualized loss of 5–20 percent of global output by 2050, compared with a cost of 1 percent to stabilize carbon emissions.[35] Fears that other countries will impose trade and travel restrictions may also dampen a government's willingness to share information on the outbreak of a disease, increasing the eventual cost of stopping it.[36] Imprudent government spending raises the debt burden of future generations. And short-sighted domestic political considerations create incentives to delay tough policy measures to resolve a crisis, compounding the cost of an eventual resolution for all countries involved.

International cooperation works best when national interests are well aligned or when domestic policy imperatives are not overriding.

Finally, divergent national interests undermine international cooperation and create incentives for inaction in the absence of agreed common goals and standards that are enforceable. Global public goods (such as controlling climate change, arresting exploitation of natural resources, and curbing loss of biodiversity; restoring global financial stability; or containing pandemics) require global collective action by sovereign nations. Collective action depends, first, on recognition of shared interests. If there is no perceived commonality of interests, cooperation is unlikely. Cooperation also fails if there is no "global authority" that can assess global risks and exert coercive sanctions on sovereign countries that fail to take agreed-upon actions.[37] Without explicit enforcement mechanisms, international agreements to provide a global public good must rely on voluntary participation, which works only if the incentives are "right" or a "common goal" has been recognized.[38] That is, multilateral cooperation works best when national interests are well aligned, or when impediments arising from vested interests or other domestic policy priorities are not overriding.

Reducing greenhouse gas emissions to mitigate climate change and prevent its catastrophic consequences is a perfect illustration of the challenges facing collective action. Climate change affects countries and regions—and even populations within a given country—unevenly, benefiting some and hurting some more than others. Continued uncertainty about the level of climate change thresholds, the perceived unevenness of climate change effects across nations, and competing domestic policy imperatives create diverging incentives for taking mitigation action. As a result, countries have been unable to forge a lasting agreement ratified by all nations, let alone a mechanism to enforce it.[39] In contrast, in two successful examples of international cooperation—smallpox eradication and protection of the ozone layer—common interests helped remove barriers to collective action: everybody was vulnerable to the highly damaging and quickly visible health consequences (see table 8.1). The looming threat of a nuclear war, with devastating consequences for the world, also spurred 189 nations to sign the Nuclear Non-Proliferation Treaty in 1968, which helped contain the spread of nuclear weapons (to fewer than 10 countries), although long-term viability of the treaty remains vulnerable to the presence of several nations with the capacity to build nuclear weapons.[40]

Diverging incentives and collective action traps also play a role in the slow progress in resolving the ongoing global economic and financial crisis.[41] For example, the Basel III framework designed to strengthen the soundness of the global financial system following the ongoing financial crisis has faced challenges in its formulation and implementation. The desire of individual nations to protect their banking systems has led to divergent views among advanced countries and between advanced and developing countries on the stringency of the new standards and pace of their implementation; some countries have unilaterally introduced stricter national regulations as a result, in effect creating regulatory gaps. Similarly, the efforts of the Group of 20 worked well at the start of the financial crisis, when country leaders supported expansionary policies to restore financial stability and counter economic downturn. Continued cooperation has become more challenging as expansionary policies in advanced countries have stimulated large capital inflows to emerging market countries and complicated their macroeconomic management.

Diverging national interests also contribute to slow progress in resolving the problems facing fragile and conflict-affected states. Concerns about whether the resources devoted to FCSs are used effectively have made donors less inclined to engage, reducing the effectiveness of aid in many fragile states. On the one hand, expectations have risen that aid could help achieve peace-building and state-building objectives. On the other hand, applying the same reporting and accountability requirements as in more stable environments and requiring rapid and visible results often leave limited room for flexibility and innovation, undermining the effectiveness of engagement. While donors have been stressing since 2011 that they have a common interest in ensuring successful engagement with fragile states, they have struggled to adapt their systems for implementation and control to effectively meet these challenges.

The lack of international assistance leaves severe risks to people unaddressed and increases the eventual cost of engagement. Preventing states from falling into conflict can be more cost-effective than responding once they have failed: studies have estimated that each dollar spent on conflict prevention can generate, on average, savings of $4 to the international community.[42] Delayed response can also be very costly in terms of human lives, as demonstrated by recent events in Somalia, where a famine took many lives during 2010–11 despite 11 months of repeated early warnings, with opportunities for early intervention missed because of perceived political risk.[43] In an increasingly interconnected world, the cost of such inaction goes beyond national borders, resulting in increased refugee populations, spread of communicable diseases, crime, conflict, economic losses, and growing pressure on public goods (such as water, sanitation, education, housing, and health services) in neighboring countries that absorb affected populations.[44] One study estimated that sharing a border with a fragile state can reduce a country's economic growth by 0.4 percent annually.[45]

Policy implications and takeaways

The international community has made remarkable progress in providing a range of tools for effective risk management, but much more needs to be done to forge consensus on risks that transcend national and generational borders. In a world with a tight network of interconnections, "global problems require global solutions," but in the absence of an effective global risk governance mechanism with an international body that has appropriate accountability and enforcement powers over sovereign nations, the international architecture necessary to provide the global public goods and address global risks has not kept pace with the connectivity that glues the world together and the complexities such connectivity creates.[46]

The limited progress made in managing global risks has put into doubt the ability of the international community to foster collective action among a large number of nations with diverging interests, capacity constraints, and incentives to free ride on the actions of others. This collective inaction poses significant challenges to the goals the international community aims to safeguard, from eliminating poverty to restoring peace, building resilience and prosperity, and achieving a more equitable distribution of income around the world.

Does this mean the world should give up on the goal of attaining global solutions and turn its back

TABLE 8.2 ***Policy priorities to improve risk management at the international community level***

	POLICIES TO SUPPORT RISK MANAGEMENT FOUNDATIONAL →	ADVANCED
Knowledge	Improve data quality and availability	Eliminate information gaps on financial institutions and exposures
	Intensify scientific research, improve knowledge on global risks, and step up information/education campaigns to raise risk awareness on importance of preparation	
	Provide TA on basic RM tools, EWSs, contingency planning, market/institutional development, communication, governance	Advisory on EWSs, contingency planning, debt/reserve management, hedging instruments
Protection	Design targeted global rules, regulations, standards, and ensure collaboration through platforms for policy dialogue	
	Financing for disaster prevention and preparedness; mitigation and adaptation; contingency planning mechanisms/EWSs	Facilitate implementation of mitigation/adaptation, contingency planning mechanisms, EWSs
	Vaccination, basic nutrition, education programs, technology transfer, peacekeeping effort	Subsidies/financing of R&D
Insurance	Contingent credit lines with grant elements	Contingent credit lines including Global Safety Net
	Facilitate regional reserve pool and catastrophe insurance mechanisms	
Coping	Humanitarian, emergency response, and reconstruction relief (e.g., food, shelter, health)	Technical support for emergency response and reconstruction
	Stabilization and targeted development financing	Emergency liquidity/swap lines

Source: WDR 2014 team.

Note: The table presents a sequencing of policies based on the guidance of chapter 2 for establishing policy priorities: *be realistic* in designing policies tailored to the institutional capacity of the country, and *build a strong foundation* that addresses the most critical obstacles sustainably and that can be improved over time. EWSs = early warning systems. R&D = research and development. RM = risk management. TA = technical assistance.

on globalization, relying, instead, on individual, national actions to address the complex risks that have been collectively created? Individual and national actions are, of course, essential for any international action to be taken, but more ambitious and coordinated efforts are necessary to change the course and ensure that the whole is greater than the sum of its individual parts. Moving away from global cooperative solutions would be costly for development, especially for developing countries and the poor that have benefited the most from improved access to credit and foreign investment flows facilitated by globalization. The international community has much to lose by failing to cooperate. Taking advantage of the positive steps at the local, national, and individual levels, and building on the lessons learned from the successful examples of international cooperation, the international community should therefore strive to preserve the gains from globalization and continue its efforts to find the right tools, incentives, and institutions to achieve international cooperation.

Successful international cooperation requires a cohesive international community where national interests are well aligned. It requires an international community that has the capacity to mobilize resources and to establish mechanisms that can enforce agreements, even when not all countries are willing to cooperate. That capacity, in turn, rests on the international community's ability to realign incentives around shared goals and to attract participation of major players capable of achieving progress. The international community can scale up risk management to the extent it can devise innovative mechanisms that have a better chance of securing cooperation with appropriate combinations of knowledge, protection, insurance, and coping tools (table 8.2).

When incentives are well aligned: Pursue proactive and well-coordinated interventions

International cooperation works best when incentives are well aligned with a clear course of action. In this case, scaling up risk management requires proactive, well-coordinated interventions by the international community. For global risks such as financial crises or pandemics, the risk of rapid spillover in a tightly interconnected world helps align national interests that call for well-coordinated national actions to contain risks at the source. The effectiveness of these actions rests critically on prompt sharing of information and resources, effective coordination of actions, and appropriate capacity and infrastructure to monitor, identify, and prevent problems from arising and spreading beyond national borders.

Knowledge is fundamental to broadening perspectives and addressing the problems when they emerge. *Access to knowledge* is therefore the first step in boosting risk management capacity. Greater efforts are particularly needed to do the following:

- *Narrow existing information gaps and address cognitive and behavioral biases.* The international community could increase its own dissemination and communication of data and analysis and facilitate sharing of information and best practices, particularly for countries with limited access to information. More systematic, frequent, and targeted dissemination through knowledge platforms and information campaigns can help build longer-term perspectives on rare, high-impact, or distant risks, raising awareness of the dangers of inaction.
- *Reduce the degree of uncertainty about specific risks facing the global system.* More resources should be devoted to consolidating and disseminating scientific research that can expand knowledge and reduce uncertainty. Knowledge of the likelihood and nature of complex risks can heighten the ability to assess risks and the need for collective action. As the successful global campaigns to eradicate smallpox and protect the ozone layer demonstrate, partnership with the scientific community and civil society can prompt effective action.[47]

The international community should strive to preserve the gains from globalization and find the right tools, incentives, and institutions to achieve global cooperation.

International community efforts should focus on providing greater *resources for capacity building* and risk management actions:

- *Support capacity building for risk management.* The international community can further intensify efforts to assist countries where capacity constraints continue to undermine effective risk management. The efforts could focus on the capacity to design contingency plans and early-warning, monitoring, communication, and disease-control systems; and developing financial markets for catastrophe-risk financing to facilitate private sector risk solutions.
- *Ease resource constraints.* Financial support from the international community could augment national resources by facilitating and supporting regional risk-pooling solutions. Financing should focus on areas that matter the most and on people most vulnerable to shocks. The international assistance in cooperation with local and national authorities to rebuild infrastructure and establish early warning systems in Indonesia after the 2004 tsunami focused on reducing vulnerabilities to future disasters, whereas slow progress in restoring infrastructure and access to sanitation, treated water, and health care following the 2010 earthquake in Haiti added to vulnerabilities, including to deadly disease outbreaks like cholera (box 8.6).
- *Provide appropriate incentives for preparation and limit moral hazard.* Taking into account the degree of self-insurance and protection and making financing contingent on adequate risk management could help limit moral hazard. Donor aid to low-income countries and FCSs can be combined with targeted technical assistance to reduce vulnerability to future shocks and strengthen institutional and governance capacity and processes. National and international platforms can be strengthened to assure investors, unleashing capital necessary for growth and rebuilding.

When incentives are not well aligned: Use incremental approaches to global solutions

When major sovereigns are not fully engaged—that is, where progress on fostering collective action has been limited—new ways of thinking about international cooperation are necessary. Where the consequences of inaction are potentially catastrophic and irreversible, as with climate change, loss of biodiversity, or exhaustion of scarce natural resources, lack of full scientific certainty about the dangerous thresholds or tipping points should not be used as a reason for postponing action (cartoon 8.1). On the contrary, preventive action should be taken in the face of uncertainty.[48] For these risks, progress can still be made outside a multilateral treaty with full participation.[49]

The international community could embrace incremental deals and actions by an initially small group

BOX 8.6 *A tale of two disasters*

The international community typically provides valuable resources when countries are hit by a massive shock. How those resources are used to support national efforts has an important bearing on the results attained.

Aceh Province, a remote region of Indonesia then struggling with conflict, bore the brunt of a powerful earthquake and a massive tsunami that swept over the Indian Ocean in December 2004. More than 100,000 people in Aceh were killed and over 500,000 were left homeless. With the financial impact estimated at 97 percent of Aceh's gross domestic product, a special multidonor fund was created, pooling contributions from 15 countries and organizations to coordinate resources to support the national efforts and government reconstruction strategy. The funds helped communities to rebuild houses, local infrastructure, ports, and lost businesses; to offer scholarships to poor children; and to establish disaster warning and response systems in hazard-prone areas. Global efforts focused on helping local communities and the government to build earthquake-resistant homes and implement projects to reduce vulnerability to disasters.

Thousands of miles away from Aceh, a similar disaster hit Haiti, another very poor, fragile island country, where a powerful earthquake in 2010 left around 230,000 dead and 1.5 million homeless, after poorly constructed homes and infrastructure collapsed. The global community rushed to the scene, bringing supplies and vast sums of money. In the midst of this global mobilization, a second disaster hit Haiti, when deficient control measures and infrastructure led to a massive cholera outbreak, killing nearly 8,000—the cholera came from a faulty sanitation system at a base of peacekeeping troops from a cholera-infected region in South Asia. Only a small part of the massive foreign aid reached the government because of donor concerns about the funds' mismanagement by weak institutions and corruption. As of mid-2013, some 350,000 people remain in temporary housing, with little access to sanitation, piped or treated water, waste management, health care, or education.

Source: WDR 2014 team based on Larrimore and Sharkey 2013 and Global Facility for Disaster Reduction and Recovery, "Sendai dialogue: Resilience stories," https://www.gfdrr.org/node/1308.

of participants, while maintaining global collective action with full participation as the ultimate goal. If it can demonstrate benefits from action, the incremental approach can serve as a building block to global deals. Countries, international organizations, and specialized entities could form a "coalition of the willing" to coordinate, advocate, and take prompt action to address the risks, while creating incentives for others to join, converging over time on a global deal with full participation. The coalition should include the actors that contribute the most to the problem and those most affected by it, as well as engaging the scientific community, civil society, and media. After global climate change negotiations made only limited progress in 2009 and 2010, calls for such coalitions have increased, especially in Europe.[50]

The international community could continue to have a crucial role in this setting by developing approaches to tackle the problem collectively; providing platforms for policy discussion; monitoring, reporting, and aggregating actions; and anchoring them to existing global frameworks to demonstrate that incremental steps and global deals are connected and heading in the right direction. One way to achieve this is by establishing an international risk board that, as with the IPCC, would work with scientific and expert communities around the world, as well as relevant international financial and knowledge institutions, to pool all available knowledge to identify, assess, and manage the major risks that cross national and generational boundaries in the near and longer term.[51] The board could provide valuable inputs to the coalition of the willing on the specific issues that need urgent attention, and offer credibility and legitimacy to the coalition's efforts. Further details and background on the incremental approach are provided in the "Focus on policy reform" at the end of the Report.

The crucial step in this incremental approach is finding a common goal around which like-minded participants can work to realign national interests and incentives to examine complex issues and take concrete actions. A number of global or regional agreements have been reached through such incremental approaches that started from smaller-scale initiatives to address a pressing problem of common interest (including the Montreal Protocol, Nuclear Non-Proliferation Treaty, European Union, and World Trade Organization). Once that goal is found, the ways to achieve it are no different from the essential elements of reaching a global deal with full participation:

- *Improved access to knowledge and advocacy.* The international community could do more to facilitate information sharing and offer longer-term perspectives through focused information campaigns and open, transparent knowledge platforms where individual actions (or inactions) impose serious externalities on others. Such platforms and convincing evidence from the scientific community (including through an international risk board) can help bring diverging views closer, creating a greater sense of urgency for collective action. Such

CARTOON 8.1 Delayed action for climate change can have irreversible consequences.
© Kevin Kallaugher/*The Economist*

knowledge was crucial in the success of the Montreal Protocol and smallpox eradication.

- *Financial and technological incentives.* These incentives could help lower participation costs and encourage other countries to join the coalition—particularly developing countries that may be the most affected but have the least ability to cope. For climate change or loss of biodiversity, for example, technology transfers from developed countries could stimulate more environmentally friendly industries and induce the use of cleaner technologies and investments in research and development to devise methods to support climate change mitigation and adaptation and protection of scarce natural resources.[52] For example, developed countries made a collective commitment to provide new and additional resources for climate adaptation and mitigation in the 2009 and 2010 climate negotiations, but scaling up funding requires substantial efforts to mobilize existing and new sources of finance.[53] International cooperation benefited greatly from such transfers in the eradication of smallpox and the protection of the ozone layer.
- *Positive and negative financial incentives.* These incentives can also help internalize the cost of externalities created by individual actions (incentives include carbon taxes, cap-and-trade mechanisms, reduced fuel subsidies to encourage more environmentally friendly energy options,[54] or trade restrictions to encourage participation and compliance with agreements). Subsidies could reward companies that undertake research to develop green technologies. Carbon taxes and markets and other incentives to limit emissions are being introduced in many places in recent years, including in China and several U.S. states (see the "Focus on policy reform" at the end of the Report). Larger-scale and coordinated efforts would be needed, however, to make a material difference and avoid economic distortions.

The incremental approach discussed here is not without risks and is clearly a second best to a global solution with full cooperation, in effect formalizing free riding by those outside the coalition. There is also no guarantee that the incremental actions will succeed in scaling up efforts and participation to full global action. But the alternative of waiting until an acceptable deal is reached and all the uncertainties resolved is also not viable, if the irreversible consequences of inaction on key global risks are to be avoided. The international community therefore has a crucial responsibility to take and support the steps necessary to protect the world's vulnerable populations and its future generations from the costly and irreversible consequences of today's inaction.

Notes

1. Ghemawat and Altman 2012; IMF 2011.
2. Kaul 2003; Stiglitz 1999; World Bank 2007.
3. In the latter case, where the scope for risk management is potentially high, humanitarian instruments may be used to reach out to individuals and communities directly to deal with extreme human and financial costs of recurrent conflicts (OECD Development Assistance Committee 2012).
4. Crises can result in sharp output losses, increased debt, large fiscal costs, and average recovery time of two to three years; see Laeven and Valencia 2012.
5. *Economist* 2012; Calvo 2013 for the WDR 2014; Ötker-Robe and Podpiera 2013 for the WDR 2014.
6. OECD 2013; World Bank 2013.
7. Also see Jonas 2013 for the WDR 2014.
8. Centers for Disease Control and Prevention, "First Global Estimates of 2009 H1N1 Pandemic Mortality," http://www.cdc.gov/flu; World Health Organization Facts Sheet, http://www.who.int; U.S. Department of Health and Human Services, Pandemic Flu History, http://www.flu.gov. Pandemics can also have significant direct and indirect economic costs.
9. IPCC 2012. About three-fourths of the total number of disasters since 1903 have taken place in the past three decades, when the Earth's temperature started to rise rapidly.
10. Ghesquiere and others 2012.
11. Kindleberger 1973.
12. Anderson, Ivanic, and Martin 2013.
13. Early warning systems are an effective tool for preparation against risks. After the tsunami in 2004, for example, countries in the Indian Ocean region invested in tsunami warning systems. Similar systems have been set up for storms in Bangladesh and Cuba and are connected to a web of public shelters. Subbiah, Bildan, and Narasimhan (2008) calculate very high benefit-cost ratios for systems that warn of storm-related floods in Bangladesh. Also see World Bank and UN 2010.
14. BCBS 2009, 2011; FSB 2010; IMF and FSB 2011.
15. UN General Assembly 2000.
16. United Nations 2011, Towards a Safer World initiative.
17. OECD 2011a.
18. Examples from the World Bank include development of a platform for a multicountry, multiperil catastrophe bond (the MultiCat Program, in collaboration with Mexico) that transfers risk to private investors and allows pooling of multiple risks to take advantage of diversification benefits; intermediation services to help Malawi protect against the risk of severe drought; and advisory services to help Turkey establish national catastrophe insurance pool for earthquakes; see Mahul and Cummins 2009; Mahul and Ghesquiere 2010.
19. For example, since December 2011, the World Bank Immediate Response Mechanism has allowed low-income countries to rapidly access a portion of their undisbursed investment project balances to mitigate the impact of natural disasters or economic shocks on vulnerable groups and to protect critical development spending. Similarly, the Bank's Development Policy Loan (DPL) with CAT DDO has a contingent credit line that provides immediate liquidity to IBRD countries in the aftermath of a natural disaster; http://www.gfdrr.org/sites/gfdrr.org/files/documents/DRFI_CatDDO_ProductNote_Jan11.pdf.
20. Examples are the IMF's Flexible Credit Line, which allows qualified countries to draw on the credit line at any time within a specified window, and the World Bank's DPL with a DDO, a contingent credit line that allows the borrower country to rapidly meet its financing requirements following a shortfall in resources due to adverse economic events (see the experience of Indonesia, which used the DPL DDO in the midst of the 2008–09 financial crisis to support ongoing access to international capital markets at favorable terms thereby sending a strong positive signal to international and domestic markets about its economic strength). Detailed discussions on experiences with DDO instruments are provided in http://www.managingclimaterisk.org/document/CC_WB.pdf and http://treasury.worldbank.org/web/documents/DDO_MajorTermsConditions_July12013.pdf.
21. Kawai and Lombardi 2012.
22. Ötker-Robe and others 2011; IMF and FSB 2011.
23. International Monetary Fund and Financial Stability Board, IMF-FSB Early Warning Exercises 2012, http://www.imf.org; World Economic Forum, http://www3.weforum.org/docs/WEF_GlobalRisks_Report_2013.pdf; OECD 2011b.
24. Ötker-Robe 2013; OECD 2013; World Bank 2013.
25. UNISDR 2006.
26. See World Bank, World Governance Indicators database for corruption rankings, http://info.worldbank.org/governance/wgi/index.asp; and World Economic Forum Global Competitiveness Index, http://www.weforum.org/issues/global-competitiveness.
27. Evidence suggests that corruption can lower a countries' economic growth as much as 0.5–1.0 percent a year and decrease investments in health and education systems, leading to an increase in infant mortality, poverty, and inequality. Standard & Poor's estimates that in countries with corruption, investors, including donors, have a 50–100 percent chance of losing their investments within five years (up to $30 billion in aid to Africa has ended up in foreign bank accounts; see Transparency International, http://www.transparency.org/).
28. See, for example, World Bank 2009; Aldy, Orszag, and Stiglitz 2001; Barrett 2003.
29. Barrett and Dannenberg 2012.
30. For example, Nicaragua declined to pursue a weather-indexing program after it had been priced in the global reinsurance market, citing, among other things, international assistance following Hurricane Mitch in 1998 as an indication of dependable alternatives (World Bank and UN 2010).
31. Aizenman and Ötker-Robe 2013 for the WDR 2014; Noy 2012.
32. Ghesquiere and others 2012.
33. IMF 2012.
34. World Bank 2012a.
35. World Bank 2009.
36. Brahmbhatt and Dutta 2008 argue that efforts to avoid infection through reduced travel or trade account for 60 percent of the economic costs during a pandemic.
37. Aldy, Orszag, and Stiglitz 2001; Banerjee 2012; Barrett 2007, 2008; Dellink and Finus 2012; Kaul 2003; Stern 2007.
38. Stern 2007; Kaul 2003.
39. See Warner 2013, who discusses these challenges in detail.
40. Campbell, Einhorn, and Reiss 2004; Fitzpatrick 2009.
41. Sheng 2013.
42. Collier and Hoeffler 2004; Chalmers 2004.
43. Bailey 2013.
44. See Jim Yong Kim, "Spillover from Syria: Helping a Neighbor Cope," The Guardian Online—Global Development, July 29, 2013.
45. DFID 2005.

46. Goldin 2013; Hale 2011; Lagarde 2012.
47. See, among others, Barrett 2003, 2007, 2008; Barrett and Danneberg 2012; and Stern 2007.
48. See, for example, the United Nations Rio Declaration from the 1992 United Nations Earth Summit. http://www.unesco.org/education/nfsunesco/pdf/RIO_E.PDF.
49. See also Jim Yong Kim, "Make Climate Change a Priority," *Washington Post Opinions,* January 24, 2013, http://www.washingtonpost.com/opinions/make-climate-change-a-priority/2013/01/24/6c5c2b66-65b1-11e2-9e1b-07db1d2ccd5b_story.html.
50. Falkner, Stephan, and Vogler 2010; Goldin 2013; and Hale 2011. See also http://www.euractiv.com/climate-environment/europe-looks-coalition-willing-d-news-508909.
51. See a related proposal by the German Institute for Development 2009.
52. See, for example, Barrett 2003; The Royal Society 2009; World Bank 2009.
53. The agreements required provision of $30 billion in Fast Start Finance for 2010–12 and $100 billion a year by 2020. While the $30 billion goal is close to being realized, the second goal is falling short of the needs, in part because of the fiscal problems in advanced countries. World Bank 2009, 2012b, 2012c; Caravani and others 2012; Schalatek and others 2012a, 2012b.
54. Ending fuel subsidies globally could lead to a 5 percent fall in emissions by 2020. See Jim Yong Kim, "Make Climate Change a Priority," *Washington Post Opinions,* January 24, 2013, http://www.washingtonpost.com/opinions/make-climate-change-a-priority/2013/01/24/6c5c2b66-65b1-11e2-9e1b-07db1d2ccd5b_story.html.

References

AidData. AidData by Activity (database). AidData, Washington, DC, http://aiddata.org/content/index/data-search.

Aizenman, Joshua, and İnci Ötker-Robe. 2013. "Managing Risk for Development: International Risk Sharing Tools." Background paper for the *World Development Report 2014.*

Aldy, Joseph E., Peter R. Orszag, and Joseph E. Stiglitz. 2001. "Climate Change: An Agenda for Global Collective Action." Paper prepared for the Timing of Climate Change Policies Conference organized by Center for Climate and Energy Solutions, Washington, DC, October 10–12.

Anderson, Kym, Maros Ivanic, and Will Martin. 2013. "Food Price Spikes, Price Insulation, and Poverty." Policy Research Working Paper 6535, World Bank, Washington, DC.

Bailey, Rob. 2013. "Managing Famine Risk: Linking Early Warning to Early Action." Chatham House, London.

Banerjee, Subhabrata Bobby. 2012. "A Climate for Change? Critical Reflections on the Durban United Nations Climate Change Conference." *Organization Studies* 33 (12): 1761–86.

Barrett, Scott. 2003. "Creating Incentives for Cooperation: Strategic Choices." In *Providing Global Public Goods: Managing Globalization,* edited by Inge Kaul, Pedro Conceição, Katell Le Goulven, and Ronald U. Mendoza, 308–28. New York: Oxford University Press.

———. 2006. "The Smallpox Eradication Game." *Public Choice* 130 (1/2): 179–207.

———. 2007. *Why Cooperate? The Incentive to Supply Global Public Goods.* New York: Oxford University Press.

———. 2008. "Climate Treaties and the Imperative of Enforcement." *Oxford Review of Economic Policy* 24 (2): 239–58.

Barrett, Scott, and Astrid Dannenberg. 2012. "Climate Negotiations under Scientific Uncertainty." *PNAS* 109 (43): 17372–76.

BCBS (Basel Committee on Banking Supervision). 2009. "Strengthening the Resilience of the Banking Sector." Consultative Document, Bank for International Settlements, Basel.

———. 2011. "Basel III: A Global Regulatory Framework for More Resilient Banks and Banking Systems." Bank for International Settlements, Basel.

Brahmbhatt, Milan, and Arindam Dutta. 2008. "Economic Effects during Outbreaks of Infectious Disease." *World Bank Research Digest* 2 (2): 7.

Calvo, Sara. 2013. "Financial Crises, Social Impact, and Risk Management: Lessons and Challenges." Background paper for the *World Development Report 2014.*

Campbell, Kurt M., Robert J. Einhorn, and Mitchell B. Reiss. 2004. *The Nuclear Tipping Point: Why States Reconsider Their Nuclear Choices.* Washington, DC: Brookings Institution Press.

Caravani, Alice, Smita Nakhooda, Charlene Watson, and Liane Schalatek. 2012. "The Global Climate Finance Architecture." Climate Finance Fundamentals 2, http://www.climatefundsupdate.org.

Chalmers, Malcolm. 2004. "Spending to Save? An Analysis of the Cost Effectiveness of Conflict Prevention." Paper prepared for the Bottom Billion Conference organized by the Centre for the Study of African Economies, Oxford University, Oxford, U.K., June 27–29.

Cole, Daniel H. 2007. "Climate Change and Collective Action." Indiana University, Bloomington, IN.

Collier, Paul, and Anke Hoeffler. 2004. "Aid, Policy and Growth in Post-Conflict Societies." *European Economic Review* 48 (5): 1125–45.

DARA International. 2012. *Climate Vulnerability Monitor: A Guide to the Cold Calculus of a Hot Planet.* Madrid: DARA International.

Dellink, Rob, and Michael Finus. 2012. "Uncertainty and Climate Treaties: Does Ignorance Pay?" *Resources and Energy Economics* 34 (4): 565–84.

DFID (Department for International Development). 2005. "Why We Need to Work More Effectively in Fragile States." DFID, London.

Economist. 2012. "Lost Economic Time: The Proust Index." February 25.

Falkner, Robert, Hannes Stephan, and John Vogler. 2010. "International Climate Policy after Copenhagen: Towards a 'Building Blocks' Approach." *Global Policy* 1 (3): 252–62.

Fengler, Wolfgang, and Homi J. Kharas. 2011. "Delivering Aid Differently: Lessons from the Field." Economic Premise 49. World Bank, Washington, DC.

Fitzpatrick, Mark. 2009. "Successes and Failures of NPT or World without NPT?" Paper presented at a seminar on Nuclear Non-Proliferation: Challenges & Opportunities, Webster University, St. Louis, MO, October 29.

FSB (Financial Stability Board). 2010. "Progress since the Washington Summit in the Implementation of the G20 Recommendations for Strengthening Financial Stability." Report to G20 Leaders, FSB, Basel.

German Institute for Development. 2009. "Globalization at the Crossroad: An "International Panel on Systemic Risks in the Global Economy" is Needed." Briefing Paper 6/2009. German Institute for Development, Bonn.

Ghemawat, Pankaj, and Steven A. Altman. 2012. "DHL Global Connectedness Index 2012: Analyzing Global Flows and Their Power to Increase Prosperity." Deutsche Post DHL, Bonn.

Ghesquiere, Francis, Prashant, Robert Reid, Jan Kellett, Shyam KC, and Jack Campbell. 2012. "The Sendai Report: Managing Disaster Risks for a Resilient Future." Paper prepared for the Sendai Dialogue organized by World Bank, Sendai, Japan.

Goldin, Ian. 2013. *Divided Nations: Why Global Governance Is Failing and What We Can Do about It.* New York: Oxford University Press.

Hale, Thomas. 2011. "A Climate Coalition of the Willing." *Washington Quarterly* Winter 34 (1): 89–101.

IDA (International Development Association). 2012. "Implementation and Results Progress Report." IDA16 Mid-Term Review, World Bank, Washington, DC.

IMF (International Monetary Fund). 2011. "Mapping Cross-Border Financial Linkages: A Supporting Case for Global Financial Safety Nets." IMF, Washington, DC.

———. 2012. "Taking Stock: A Progress Report on Fiscal Adjustment." *Fiscal Monitor,* October, IMF, Washington, DC.

IMF and FSB. 2011. "The Financial Crisis and Information Gaps." Implementation Progress Report to the G20, IMF and FSB, Washington, DC.

IPCC (Intergovernmental Panel on Climate Change). 2007. "Climate Change 2007—Mitigation of Climate Change: Contribution of Working Group III to the Fourth Assessment Report of the Intergovernmental Panel on Climate Change." Cambridge University Press, Cambridge, U.K.

———. 2012. *Managing the Risks of Extreme Events and Disasters to Advance Climate Change Adaptation.* Special Report of the IPCC. Cambridge, U.K.: Cambridge University Press.

Jacoby, Hanan, Mariano Rabassa, and Emmanuel Skoufias. 2011. "Distributional Implications of Climate Change in India." Policy Research Working Paper 5623, World Bank, Washington, DC.

Jonas, Olga. 2013. "Pandemic Risk." Background paper for the *World Development Report 2014.*

Kaul, Inge. 2003. *Providing Global Public Goods: Managing Globalization.* New York: Oxford University Press.

Kawai, Masahiro, and Domenico Lombardi. 2012. "Financial Regionalism." *Finance and Development* 49 (3): 23–25.

Kindleberger, Charles P. 1973. *The World in Depression: 1929–1939.* Berkeley, CA: University of California Press.

Laeven, Luc, and Fabian Valencia. 2012. "Systemic Banking Crises Database: An Update." Working Paper WP/12/163, International Monetary Fund, Washington, DC.

Lagarde, Christine. 2012. "Fragmentation Risks." *Finance and Development* 49 (3): 26–27.

Larrimore, J. T., and Brielle Sharkey. 2013. "Haiti Continues to Struggle Three Years after the Earthquake." Council on Hemispheric Affairs, Washington, DC, January 18, http://www.coha.org/haiti-continues-to-struggle-three-years-after-the-earthquake/.

Lenton, Timothy M., Hermann Held, Elmar Kriegler, Jim W. Hall, Wolfgang Lucht, Stefan Rahmstorf, and Hans Joachim Schellnhuber. 2008. "Tipping Elements in the Earth's Climate System." *PNAS* 105 (6): 1786–93.

Mahul, Olivier, and J. David Cummins. 2009. *Catastrophe Risk Financing in Developing Countries: Principles for Public Intervention.* Washington, DC: World Bank.

Mahul, Olivier, and Francis Ghesquiere. 2010. "Financial Protection of the State against Natural Disasters: A Primer." Policy Research Working Paper 5429, World Bank, Washington, DC.

Marcott, Shaun A., Jeremy D. Shakun, Peter U. Clark, and Alan C. Mix. 2013. "A Reconstruction of Regional and Global Temperature for the Past 11,300 Years." *Science* 339 (6124): 1198–201.

Mercer. 2011. "Climate Change Scenarios: Implications for Strategic Asset Allocation." Mercer, New York.

NASA (National Aeronautics and Space Administration). Goddard Institute for Space Studies Surface Temperature Analysis (GISTEMP) (database), NASA, New York, http://data.giss.nasa.gov/gistemp/.

Nielsen Company. 2011. "Sustainable Efforts & Environmental Concerns around the World." A Nielsen Report. Nielsen, New York.

Noy, Ilan. 2012. "Investing in Early Warning Systems: A Global Fund for Disaster Preparedness." Paper prepared for the Copenhagen Consensus Project organized by Copenhagen Consensus Center, Copenhagen, March.

OECD (Organisation for Economic Co-operation and Development) 2011a. "A New Deal for Engagement in Fragile States." Paper prepared for the International Dialogue on Peacebuilding and Statebuilding organized by OECD, November 29–December 1.

———. 2011b. *Future Global Shocks: Improving Risk Governance.* OECD Reviews of Risk Management Policies. Paris: OECD.

———. 2011c. *Managing Risks in Fragile and Transitional Contexts. The Price of Success?* Paris: OECD.

———. 2012. *Fragile States 2013. Resource Flows and Trends in a Shifting World.* Paris: OECD.

———. 2013. *Fragile States: Resource Flows and Trends.* Conflict and Fragility Series. Paris: OECD.

OECD Development Assistance Committee (DAC). 2012. *International Support to Post-Conflict Transition: Rethinking Policy, Changing Practice.* DAC Guidelines and Reference Series. Paris: OECD.

OECD and G20 (Group of 20). 2012. *Disaster Risk Assessment and Risk Financing: A G20/OECD Methodological Framework.* Paris: OECD.

Ötker-Robe, İnci, 2013. "Seizing Opportunities under Extreme Risks: Fragile and Conflict-Affected States." *Let's Talk Development* (blog), May 17. http://blogs.worldbank.org/developmenttalk/seizing-opportunities-under-extreme-risks-fragile-and-conflict-affected-states.

Ötker-Robe, İnci, Aditya Narain, Anna Ilyina, and Jay Surti. 2011. "The Too-Important-to-Fail Conundrum: Impossible to Ignore and Difficult to Resolve." Staff Discussion Note SDN/11/12, International Monetary Fund, Washington, DC.

Ötker-Robe, İnci, and Anca Podpiera. 2013. "Social Impact of Financial Crises." Background paper for the *World Development Report 2014.*

Rae, Ian. 2012. "Saving the Ozone Layer: Why the Montreal Protocol Worked." *The Conversation,* September 10, http://theconversation.com/saving-the-ozone-layer-why-the-montreal-protocol-worked-9249.

Ranger, Nicola, Stephane Hallegatte, Sumana Bhattacharya, Murthy Bachu, Satya Priya, K. Dhore, Farhat Rafique, P. Mathur, Nicolas Naville, Fanny Henriet, Celine Herweijer, Sanjib Pohit, and Jan Corfee-Morlot. 2011. "An Assessment of the Potential Impact of Climate Change on Flood Risk in Mumbai." *Climate Change* 104 (1): 139–67.

The Royal Society. 2009. "Geoengineering the Climate: Science, Governance and Uncertainty." The Royal Society, London.

Schalatek, Liane, Smita Nakhooda, Sam Barnard, and Alice Caravani. 2012a. "Adaptation Finance." Climate Finance Fundamentals 3, http://www.climatefundsupdate.org.

———. 2012b. "Mitigation Finance." Climate Finance Fundamentals 4, http://www.climatefundsupdate.org.

Scripps Institution of Oceanography. Atmospheric CO_2 Concentration at Mauna Loa Observatory (Hawaii) (database), Scripps Institution of Oceanography, La Jolla, CA, http://scrippsco2.ucsd.edu/data/atmospheric_co2.html.

Sheng, Andrew. 2013. "The Contradictions of System Stability: One Asian View." Speech at Thirteenth IMF/World Bank/Federal Reserve Board Annual International Conference on Policy Challenges for the Financial Sector, Washington, DC, June.

Stern, Nicholas. 2007. *The Economics of Climate Change: The Stern Review.* Cambridge, UK: Cambridge University Press.

Stiglitz, Joseph E. 1999. "Knowledge as a Public Good." In *Global Public Goods: International Cooperation in the 21st Century,* edited by Isabelle Grunberg, Inge Kaul, and Marc A. Stern, 308–25. New York: Oxford University Press.

Subbiah, A., Lolita Bildan, and Ramraj Narasimhan. 2008. "Assessment of the Economics of Early Warning Systems for Disaster Risk Reduction." Background paper submitted to Global Facility for Disaster Reduction and Recovery, Washington, DC.

UNEP (United Nation Environment Programme). 2007. "Montreal Protocol: A Success in the Making." UNEP, Nairobi.

UNISDR (United Nations International Strategy for Disaster Reduction). 2006. "Global Survey of Early Warning Systems: An Assessment of Capacities, Gaps and Opportunities Towards Building a Comprehensive Global Early Warning System for All Natural Hazards." UNISDR, Geneva.

———. 2007. "Hyogo Framework for Action 2005–2015: Building the Resilience of Nations and Communities to Disasters." UNISDR, Geneva.

United Nations. 2011. "Beyond Pandemics: A Whole-of-Society Approach to Disaster Preparedness." Towards a Safer World initiative. September.

United Nations Framework Convention on Climate Change. 1998. "Kyoto Protocol." United Nations, New York.

UN General Assembly. 2000. "Resolution Adopted by the General Assembly: United Nations Millennium Declaration." A/RES/55/2, United Nations, New York, September 18.

Université Catholique de Louvain. EM-DAT: The OFDA/CRED International Disaster Database. Université Catholique de Louvain, Brussels, http://www.emdat.be.

Warner, Koko. 2013. "Climate Change and Global Warming: The Role of the International Community." Background paper for the *World Development Report 2014.*

World Bank. 2007. "Global Public Goods: A Framework for the Role of the World Bank." Paper prepared for the Development Commitee Meeting, Washington, DC, October 21.

———. 2009. *World Development Report 2010: Development and Climate Change.* Washington, DC: World Bank.

———. 2011. *World Development Report 2011: Conflict, Security, and Development.* Washington, DC: World Bank.

———. 2012a. "People, Pathogens and Our Planet: The Economics of One Health." World Bank, Washington, DC.

———. 2012b. "A Strategic Framework for the World Bank Group: Completion Report FY09–11." Development and Climate Change, World Bank, Washington, DC.

———. 2012c. "Turn Down the Heat: Why a 4°C Warmer World Must Be Avoided." World Bank, Washington, DC.

———. 2013. "Stop Conflict, Reduce Fragility and End Poverty: Doing Things Differently in Fragile and Conflict-Affected Situations." World Bank, Washington, DC.

———. World Development Indicators (database). World Bank, Washington, DC, http://data.worldbank.org/data-catalog/world-development-indicators.

World Bank and IMF. 2010. *Global Monitoring Report: The MDGs after the Crisis.* Washington, DC: World Bank.

World Bank and UN. 2010. *Natural Hazards, UnNatural Disasters: The Economics of Effective Prevention.* Washington, DC: World Bank.

Mainstreaming risk management into the development agenda: Selected institutional reforms

The discussion that follows expands on four selected areas where fundamental institutional reforms for better risk management are needed. The four areas cover integrated risk management, fiscal and financial risk management, social insurance and work status, and multinational approaches to address global risks. Why these four? They are by no means exhaustive, but they do represent a framework through which many specific recommendations provided in the Report could be implemented. They discuss innovative solutions to long-standing problems in developing countries. They cut across risks and social systems, using a holistic approach to risk management. Along with the other recommendations in the Report, they can contribute to mainstreaming risk management into the development agenda. The four reforms may require substantial changes in the way national governments develop and implement their general plans.

Reform 1. Establish a national risk board to assess and manage risks in an integrated way

What is the problem? Governments and public agencies often manage specific risks in an isolated manner, which can lead to ineffective formulation and implementation of risk management strategies. For example, while the ministry of finance can create and regulate a health care insurance system to better manage health risks, the usefulness of that system depends on the availability of competent health care providers, which is a responsibility of the health ministry. Shifting from one energy source to another (coal to gas or nuclear) may reduce one kind of pollution but increase other pollutants or security risks.

Such "risk-risk trade-offs" and coordination problems often arise from narrow decisions by risk managers with restricted perimeters of responsibility.[1] Ideally, broader analyses can help risk managers develop "risk-superior solutions" that reduce multiple risks at the same time.[2] Looking at risks in an integrated manner helps define policy priorities and avoids overspending on managing one risk while neglecting others, helping to achieve a good balance between preparation for low-probability but high-impact events (such as earthquakes) and less spectacular risks (such as truck accidents) that are more prevalent and are also costly to society.

Managing individual risks entails both trade-offs and synergies. A multistakeholder approach to national risk management helps identify and capture synergies across risks: for instance, developing the capacity to evacuate populations while taking into account the constraints of available crisis management infrastructure. National risk assessments undertaken in the Netherlands and the United Kingdom aim explicitly at identifying investments that increase the ability to anticipate and manage multiple risks—what the Dutch and U.K. authorities call risk management "capabilities."

Important trade-offs and synergies also exist across risks or across scales. For instance, providing a public retirement scheme reduces risks for individuals but may increase aggregate fiscal risks. And a watershed that covers multiple municipalities can be managed effectively only in a coordinated manner. An integrated and multistakeholder approach helps deal with these trade-offs and reduces the likelihood of simply transferring a risk of one type to a risk of another type (such as from idiosyncratic risk to systemic risk) or from one agent to another.

Involving more stakeholders (policy makers, industry experts, and academics) in the process of designing a national risk management strategy also makes the process more transparent and less prone to political capture and introduces natural accountability mechanisms. All too often, risks that evolve over long time horizons and the lack of clear indicators of success for risk management limit the accountability of decision makers for their risk management choices. This problem can be addressed, in part, by an independent and multistakeholder entity that analyzes and publishes assessments of risk management practices within a country and that makes expert and policy-relevant recommendations.

What is the solution? A national risk board should be created to provide integrated risk management at the national level. This recommendation builds on analogous proposals, including the national Council of Risk Analysts proposed by Graham and Wiener,[3] and the World Economic Forum's proposal to establish a country risk officer[4]—similar to the position of chief risk officer that has been created in many multinational companies, notably financial corporations. The board's expertise should cover the areas of military, security, and terrorism risk; economic risk; environmental, health, and technological risk; and social risk. It should also consider the actions undertaken by other countries, multinational firms, and the global community.

A national risk board can be set up as a standing (permanent) committee and should have powers to issue "act-or-explain" recommendations directed at the relevant authorities responsible for policy implementation. That is, government agencies and local authorities would have to act on the board's recommendations or explain why they have decided to discard them.

The board should analyze risks and risk management policies and practices, including synergies and trade-offs across risks or across entities; define priorities in risk management; and make recommendations for appropriate policies to pursue. Many countries already have regular national risk assessments conducted by multistakeholder teams involving various ministries and often including representatives of the private sector and civil society. The Netherlands, Singapore, the United Kingdom, and the United States have undertaken such assessments, and other countries, such as Morocco, are working to set up a national assessment process. But this process is usually carried out by a temporary, ad hoc group that exists only while the assessment is taking place. Moreover, the political relevance and accountability of such ad hoc groups generally have been weak.

Some countries go beyond risk assessments. Some have created multiministry bodies in charge of information exchange and coordination for risk management, but these bodies usually deal with a specific risk—most often natural disasters, as in Peru. Few countries actually have an integrated risk management agency that deals with multiple risks.

One country that does is Singapore, which has a framework, the Whole-of-Government Integrated Risk Management approach, dedicated to avoiding silo effects within the government and to managing risks in an integrated manner.[5] The institutional umbrella of the framework is the Strategy Committee, which is charged with steering and reviewing the implementation of the framework. The committee, which meets quarterly, comprises permanent secretaries from various ministries across government and is chaired by the Head of Civil Service. In addition, the Homefront Crisis Management system includes a ministerial committee chaired by the Minister of Domestic Affairs, which is responsible for crisis management. It is supported by the Homefront Crisis Executive Group, which comprises senior representatives from ministries and government agencies. This multirisk approach is complemented by more sectoral agencies, such as the National Security Coordination Secretariat, which focuses on national security issues. Singapore's institutional arrangement for integrated risk management involves a great deal of specialization and a complex coordination process that has evolved over time.

For developing countries, a simpler, consolidated arrangement that involves less specificity and specialization in the institutional design and more explicit and robust coordination mechanisms might be desirable. The proposed National Risk Board takes into account such considerations.

How can it be implemented? The board needs to have the required expertise, be credible and relevant, and have sufficient legitimacy. It could either be an advisory body or have powers to implement recommendations, or a combination of both. It could consist entirely of experts or policy makers or a combination of both. There are trade-offs among these design choices, which are illustrated in diagram F1.1. For instance, a board of experts with powers to implement policy could lack *legitimacy*, especially if it were to implement policies with significant redistribution effects (such as raising taxes to cover disaster insurance premiums).[6] In contrast, a board of experts issuing only nonbinding recommendations could lack *relevance* to policy making or be unable to influence actual decisions. If the board comprises only policy makers and issues nonbinding recommendations, it could lack *credibility*. Finally, if a board has implementation powers but consists only of policy makers, it could lack *expertise* and be vulnerable to political capture. To avoid becoming a powerless body, the board should have sufficient visibility: its chair should be a highly visible policy maker, and its annual meeting should be chaired by the head of government. The board should be held accountable by having to publish its recommendations, by issuing annual reports with policy priorities and their analytical substantiation, and by being subjected to annual hearings in front of a legislative committee.

The appropriate institutional design will depend on the country political and institutional context. For instance, rather than establishing an independent government agency, Jamaica, Mexico, and Morocco are considering placing the integrated risk management function within the government structure. Such an institutional design may be practical in countries with an effective and independent civil service, with the national risk board members appointed as expert technocrats with guaranteed positions for periods that extend beyond a political cycle. However, any institutional design should seek to balance legitimacy, relevance, credibility, and expertise (depicted as the balanced region in diagram F1.1).

DIAGRAM F1.1 ***Balancing the trade-offs in the institutional design of a national risk board***

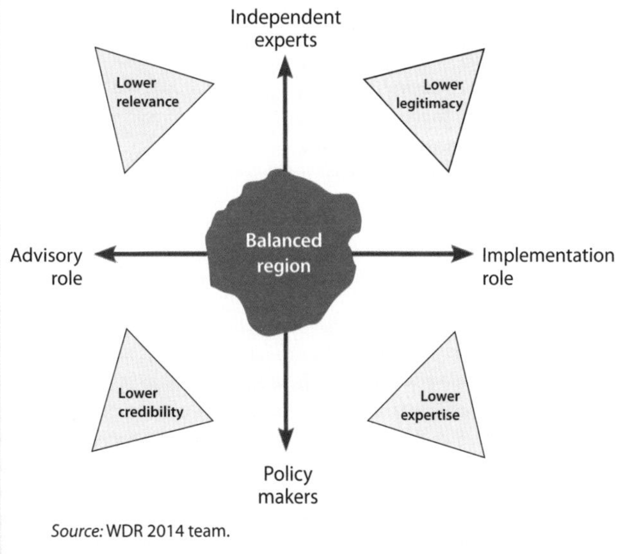

Source: WDR 2014 team.

Reform 2. Create independent fiscal and financial agencies to promote sustainable policies

Establish fiscal councils to promote fiscal sustainability

What is the problem? Very few developing countries have been able to conduct countercyclical fiscal policies.[7] Rather than saving during good times, policy makers typically increase government spending, run budget deficits, and accumulate debt. Over the past five decades, government spending has behaved procyclically in more than 90 percent of developing countries; in sharp contrast, it has been countercyclical in 80 percent of industrial countries.[8] Procyclical fiscal policies have increased output volatility and hindered long-term growth throughout the developing world.[9]

Two main factors explain this procyclical bias in developing countries. First, limited access to world capital markets during recessions forces governments to raise taxes and cut spending in bad times. Second, political economy considerations—including distributional conflicts and information asymmetries—prevent governments from acting prudently during upswings. Competition among multiple power blocs for greater revenue windfalls leads to overspending and overprovision of some public goods.[10] Voters' perception that their governments are rent-seeking leads to increasing popular pressure to lower taxes and increase spending in good times.[11]

By contrast, monetary authorities in several developing countries have succeeded in adopting a credible, predictable, and sustainable regime in the form of inflation targeting. Several developed and developing countries have maintained low and stable inflation, thanks to monetary frameworks that benefit from a clear mandate, independence from political interference, and accountability for policy makers' actions. A greater institutional push toward transparent monetary frameworks has provided central banks the flexibility to conduct countercyclical policies without jeopardizing inflationary goals. There is need for similar credible, predictable, and sustainable frameworks for fiscal policy.

What is the solution? The codification of flexible fiscal rules in legislation, along with the operation of autonomous fiscal councils, has the potential to restrain policy makers from spending sprees in normal times and to allow for additional (spending) stimulus in crisis times. Given the redistributive nature of fiscal policy, full delegation of policy making to these councils is unrealistic. Fiscal councils can nonetheless shape incentives more effectively than can a process that simply and mechanically follows numerical limits on budgetary aggregates. The councils should have a clear mandate, autonomy to operationalize budget procedures, and the power to monitor compliance with the fiscal rule. Fiscal councils should hold policy makers accountable for their actions and be accountable for their advice and recommendations. To put fiscal councils in place and uphold their powers, broad consensus needs to be built to implement these institutional reforms and encourage policy makers to deliver viable countercyclical actions. Severe crises may provide that opportunity—that has been the case in the European Union with the new Fiscal Compact Treaty and "Two-Pack" regulation proposal.[12] However, establishing these councils requires strong institutional underpinnings. In countries with weak governance and capacity, transparent and comprehensive fiscal frameworks (including top-down approaches to budgeting) would provide a good foundation for more institution building in the future.

How can it be implemented? Fiscal authorities have adopted quantitative limits on deficits, spending, debt, or some combination, to contain fiscal profligacy. However, these numerical limits have restricted countercyclical responses during downturns and have led politicians to circumvent them through the use of creative accounting, such as Stability and Growth Pact rules in the European Union.[13] Rather than imposing rigid numerical limits, fiscal authorities should focus on using flexible procedural rules that target the structural budget balance and provide a blueprint to achieve this target over time. Targeting structural budget balances—as is done in Chile and Norway—can deliver fiscal discipline and endow policy makers with flexibility to conduct countercyclical policies. Before the crisis, in 2007, strong economic performance and sharp increases in the prices of oil and copper allowed Chile and Norway—through their rules—to amass a significant amount of public savings. The general government primary surpluses that year were 11.8 of gross domestic product (GDP) in Chile and 15.7 percent in Norway, providing a comfortable cushion for countercyclical policies following the crisis.

Currently, more than 40 percent of advanced countries and about 20 percent of emerging market have a national fiscal rule targeting the structural budget balance.[14] However, the effectiveness of these rules rests upon their credibility and flexibility: they may lack credibility if not accompanied by budget transparency and clear operational guidance or if they are overly ambitious or unrealistic. Defining a structural budget balance rule can create monitoring and communication problems. Moreover, fiscal rules cannot anticipate every possible contingency. Their flexibility could be enhanced through the design and incorporation of escape clauses that would take into account extreme events (crises, disasters).[15] Fiscal councils can help identify the events that trigger escape clauses and decide on the treatment of cumulative deviations.[16]

Fiscal councils can shield some budget procedures from political pressure, thereby containing the government's incentives to overspend. Overspending and lack of budget discipline can be traced, in part, to overly optimistic government forecasts.[17] Fiscal councils can produce official forecasts for GDP growth and government budgetary items. The U.K. Treasury (ministry of finance), for instance, has delegated such forecasts to the Office for Budget Responsibility. Forecasting contains its own risks, however. Forecasting errors in uncertain environments can threaten the credibility of the council.[18] The accuracy of the council's real GDP growth and budget forecasts will be reduced by the greater volatility associated with higher economic uncertainty. Councils will have to be held accountable for incorrect predictions.

By providing independent analysis of fiscal plans and executed policies, councils raise voters' awareness of the consequences of policy actions. For instance, the Netherlands Bureau for Economic Policy Analysis (CPB) evaluates whether government policies threaten fiscal sustainability. Councils can also evaluate the cost of electoral platforms plans and coalition agreements after elections.[19] Finally, fiscal councils can hold policy makers accountable for choices made regarding the cyclical operation of the rule and define clear legal sanctions before the fact for noncompliance.[20]

Governments have incentives to dismiss the advice of fiscal councils. Councils can be dismantled if their critique of the government is too severe or if they are formed without adequate political consensus—as was the case in Hungary. Fiscal councils need legitimacy, as well as budgetary and political independence, to work effectively and to avoid political capture. So far, countries have not granted political autonomy to fiscal councils. Councils have had to rely on informal independence acquired through the buildup of reputation over time. Councils with the largest degree of informal independence are the oldest ones—Denmark's economic council, the Netherlands' CPB, and the U.S. Congressional Budget Office.[21] Limited resources and budget dependence on governmental offices can reduce the councils' quality of work—as has happened in Canada and Sweden.[22]

The council board members should be recruited competitively. Reputational costs of bad performance would act as a disciplining device. Nonetheless, members' idiosyncrasies or dismal performance can affect the work of the entire council. Regular evaluations are warranted to hold council members accountable, including testifying on a regular basis before the legislative body and continuous evaluation by international peer councils or expert groups.[23]

Put in place independent macroprudential supervisors for financial stability

What is the problem? The main difficulties for the financial system are managing systemic risk (stemming from negative externalities and herding behavior among individual financial firms) and avoiding regulatory capture by politicians and the financial industry (chapter 6).

What is the solution? The solution is to delegate the oversight of financial stability to an independent macroprudential committee, possibly under the central bank. In a number of emerging market countries, including the Czech Republic, South Africa, and Thailand, the responsibility for financial stability oversight already has been given to the central bank, while in many others, central banks have implicitly taken on this responsibility. Central banks seem to be best equipped to assume the statutory responsibility for macroprudential policy.[24]

The macroprudential committee should include selected policy stakeholders and independent experts, following the successful example of monetary policy committees. It should use selected indicators of systemic risk to detect excessive acceleration or concentration of indebtedness in the financial sector or the real economy. To manage any emerging excess, the committee would be directly equipped with macroprudential tools or with the ability to recommend actions to other regulators on an act-or-explain basis. The committee should be accountable to the legislative body.

How can it be implemented? A possible role model for other countries, including developing ones, is the United Kingdom's macroprudential committee—the Financial Policy Committee, or FPC. The FPC is chaired by the central bank governor and includes deputy governors for financial stability, monetary policy, and prudential regulation; the director of financial stability; the chief executive of the Financial Conduct Authority (business conduct regulator); four independent experts; and a representative of the U.K. Treasury, who has no voting rights.

The FPC has the statutory responsibility to identify, monitor, and take actions to remove or reduce systemic financial risk, with the view to protecting and enhancing the resilience of the U.K. financial system. It uses a set of systemic risk indicators to identify and monitor systemic risk.[25] Since mid-2011, it has been equipped with direct powers to adjust the capital requirements that banks must hold (the macroprudential buffer) to mitigate systemic risk. It can also issue act-or-explain recommendations to other policy makers in the financial sector, notably the microprudential regulator and the business conduct regulator, to implement measures to foster financial stability.[26] The FPC is likely to receive more direct tools to fulfill its statutory responsibility.[27]

Reform 3. For debate: Should access to social insurance be tied to work status?

Social insurance (including pensions and health insurance) protects people's income and consumption in the face of potentially devastating shocks such as illness or life-cycle transitions such as old age.[28] This is particularly true for the most vulnerable segments of the population, which lack the resources and access to financial markets to accumulate savings and purchase private insurance products. A good social insurance system is one that is *inclusive*, that protects people *equitably*, that is *fiscally sustainable* in the long term, and that *minimizes disincentives* to work, save, and participate in the formal economy.

What is the problem? Many countries have established so-called contributory social insurance systems, financed by mandatory payroll taxes levied on employers and contributions paid by employees. In economies with high levels of formality, this system has been successful in providing insurance to most people. By contrast, in countries with large shares of self-employed and agricultural workers, contributory systems cover only a minority of the population. The traditional approach thus ends up excluding many workers—mostly those who are low-income, are self-employed, or work in agriculture.

To narrow the coverage gap, a growing number of countries have introduced noncontributory insurance, where benefits are financed by general revenues (figure F1.1a). For example, 13 countries in Latin America and the Caribbean have both noncontributory and contributory systems. The introduction of noncontributory systems has helped increase coverage, reducing catastrophic health expenditures and curbing poverty among the elderly. In fact, aside from the former socialist countries in Eastern Europe and Central Asia, only in those developing countries with large noncontributory systems are more than half the households with elderly members in the poorest 40 percent of the population covered (figure F1.1b).[29]

However, combining contributory and noncontributory systems is particularly challenging. For workers and employers at the margin of the formal sector, participating in a mandatory contributory system is not worthwhile. Meanwhile, combined with other factors (such as minimum wages), the additional labor cost levied by the payroll tax for mandatory contributory systems discourages employers from hiring formally—or hiring at all—particularly for low-skill jobs. Thus if the benefits of contributing to social insurance are uncertain and the enforcement of mandated payments is weak, having these parallel systems may undermine both the incentives for employers to hire formally and for employees to seek formal employment. Evidence from Chile, Colombia, and Mexico shows that the interplay of contributory and noncontributory systems has led to declines in formal employment, and there is widespread evidence that smaller, informal firms tend to be less productive and pay lower wages.[30] For workers who move between formal and informal jobs or in and out of the labor force, replacement rates tend to be low, or in some cases they might not be eligible to receive benefits at all.[31] Moreover, workers in countries with rapidly aging populations make contributions toward increasingly uncertain benefits—all of which increases their perception

FIGURE F1.1 *Noncontributory pension programs have expanded coverage in developing countries, especially for the poorest*

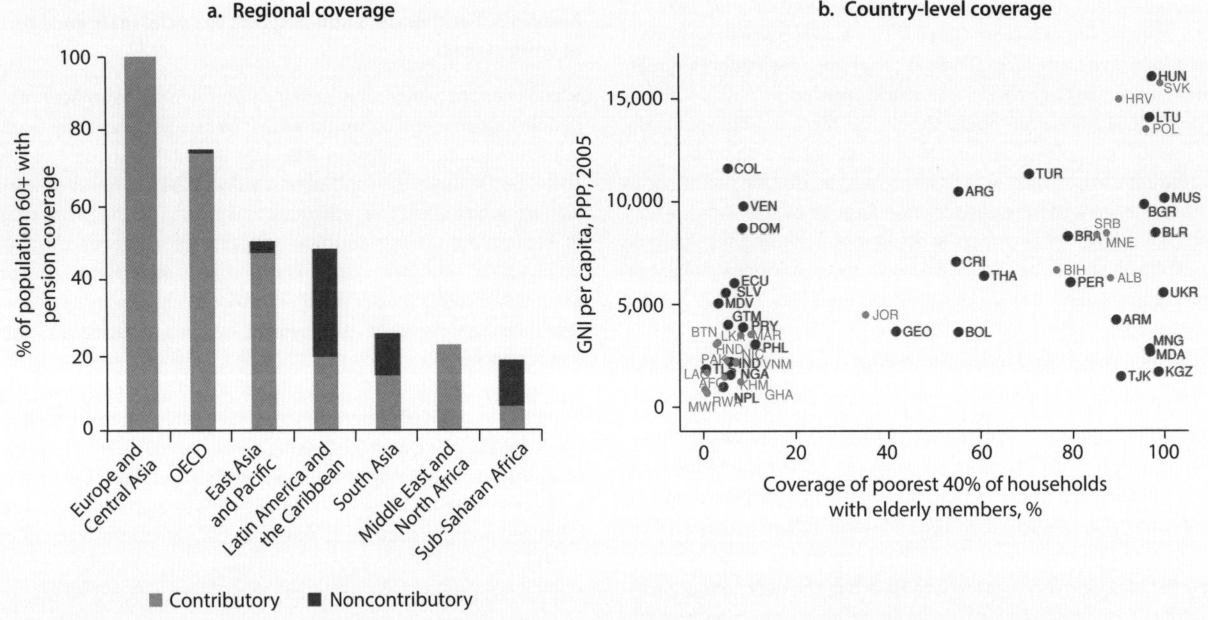

Sources: WDR 2014 team based on data from World Bank Pensions (database), United Nations 2009 (panel a); and Evans, forthcoming (panel b).

Note: For panel a, coverage rates are for total regional populations; years vary between 2001 and 2012. Organisation for Economic Co-operation and Development (OECD) countries in the figure are high-income countries that have been members of the OECD for at least 40 years. All other countries are grouped into geographic regions. For panel b, years vary between 2003 and 2010. Countries marked in blue have noncontributory programs. GNI = gross national income. PPP = purchasing power parity.

of contributions as a pure tax on labor, especially in the presence of parallel noncontributory systems. Finally, the rapid aging process taking place in many countries is threatening the fiscal sustainability of contributory systems, forcing governments to transfer additional resources.[32]

What could be done? One potential solution is to provide basic benefits using general revenues, instead of labor taxes. For health care, user fees could also be levied. The provision of basic benefits would make social insurance similar to other basic public services and recognize its level of priority in public spending. Funding basic social insurance through general revenues would make the insurance more inclusive by breaking the traditional eligibility condition linked to work status. Moreover, it could limit the distortions in the labor market, to the extent that general revenues are collected in a less distortionary way.[33]

Advanced countries such as Australia, New Zealand, and the United Kingdom rely mostly on universal basic pensions and provision of health care, whereas developing countries such as Mauritius and South Africa rely mostly on noncontributory systems for pensions.[34] Several low- and middle-income countries have also begun to offer universal access to health insurance, starting with the poor. China, India, Thailand, Turkey, and Vietnam are a few examples. In all these cases, benefits do not depend on labor taxes and therefore are accessible to people in the informal sector.

How would it work? While provision of universal benefits is desirable, not all countries are in a position to provide them at adequate levels in a fiscally sustainable manner. This is particularly true for countries where the old-age dependency ratio is growing rapidly (figure F1.2). In practice, many developing countries would be able to provide only a minimum level of benefits, possibly to only a targeted population. Thus countries would need to consider their long-term fiscal capacity in relation to their future commitments to decide what level of coverage and benefits would be appropriate. Countries might also choose different ways to raise the necessary revenue. Some countries would have to introduce new taxes or raise existing ones; in other cases, they may be able to reform spending items like energy subsidies or use resource-based revenues where available.

Noncontributory schemes provide crucial protection for the poor. However, if the benefits that can be sustainably offered by noncontributory systems are too basic, additional contributions to health and pension systems may be necessary. If contributory and noncontributory systems do coexist, policy makers should design both systems in a way that avoids creating distortions in the labor market. In some contexts, that implies reforming contributory systems to make contributions voluntary or reducing the mandatory contribution rates. In all cases, contributory systems should provide benefits that are clearly linked to contributions. Incentives to save can have a significant impact, as well, with examples including automatic enrollment, matching contributions, simplifying processes, and lowering information barriers through financial literacy. New Zealand's KiwiSaver scheme is an interesting example of an automatic enrollment program (with an "opt-out" option) that has increased retirement savings for about half the population.[35]

FIGURE F1.2 *Increasing coverage will require higher levels of spending in countries with aging populations*

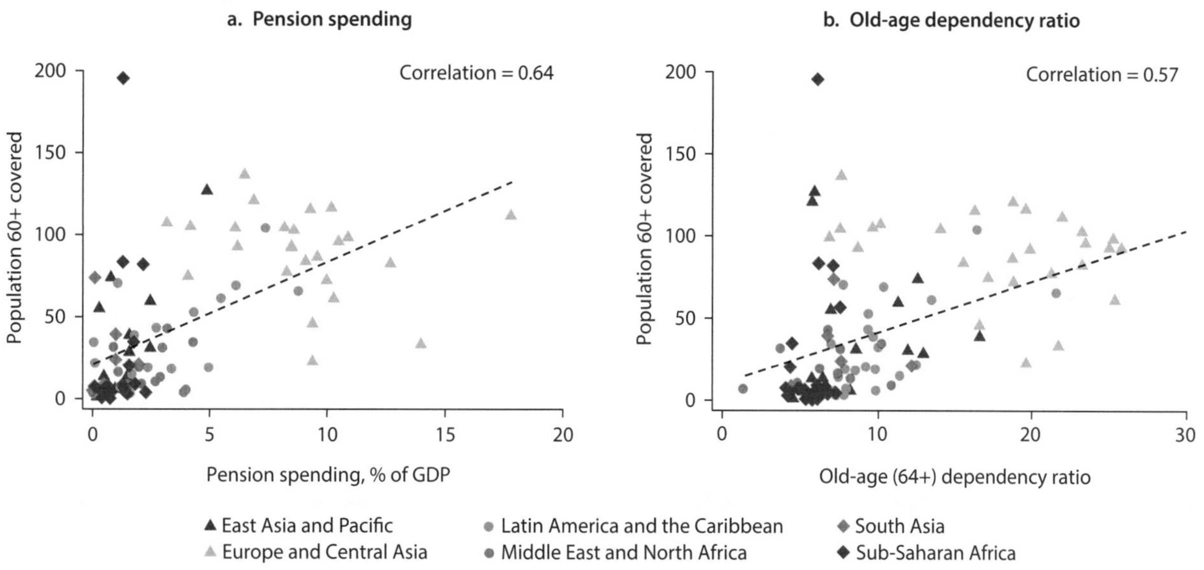

Sources: WDR 2014 team based on data from World Bank Pensions (database), United Nations 2009, and World Bank World Development Indicators (database).
Note: Years vary between 2001 and 2012. Coverage of the 60+ population might exceed 100 percent in some countries because people younger than 60 are eligible for pensions or because coverage includes disability or death benefits. In panel b, the old-age dependency ratio is calculated as the ratio of people 64+ to the working-age population. GDP = gross domestic product.

Reform 4. For the international community, embrace incremental approaches that can increase traction toward global solutions

What is the problem? Globalization has contributed to rapid economic growth and to reduced poverty around the world. But it has also made economic, social, and ecological systems more interdependent, generating gains from collaboration, while also increasing the prevalence of cross-border risks, such as climate change, loss of biodiversity, overuse of natural resources, global financial crises, and pandemics. Containing global risks requires timely, proactive, and concerted action because no country acting alone can manage them effectively and achieve the scale required to address them comprehensively. Unfortunately, in the absence of an effective global risk governance mechanism led by an international body that has appropriate accountability and enforcement powers over sovereign nations, the international architecture necessary to address global risks has not kept pace with the complexities arising from increased global connectivity.

The limited progress to reach a global deal in some areas, in turn, has cast into doubt the ability to foster collective action among a large number of nations with diverging interests, capacity constraints, and incentives to free ride. Global negotiations to secure agreements with full participation have stalled—most spectacularly for climate change, as atmospheric concentrations of greenhouse gases have continued to rise, with potentially catastrophic and irreversible consequences. The concentration of the main greenhouse gas, carbon dioxide (CO_2), rose from its preindustrial level of 278 parts per million (ppm) to more than 390 ppm as of May 2013 (hitting 399.91 ppm in Hawaii—a level not seen since 2 million to 4 million years ago). This approaches the 450 ppm threshold level that corresponds to a likely increase in temperature larger than 2°C degree—the warming level the international community has committed to avoid.[36]

In the absence of a global deal, many unilateral climate action plans to limit greenhouse gases have been put forward in recent years by private actors, civil society groups, and municipal and subnational governments (including in China and several U.S. states). Several countries have introduced measures, including incentives that can limit carbon emissions (table F1.1). These unilateral actions are welcome, but more ambitious and coordinated national and international efforts are needed to make a material difference and to ensure that the overall effort is greater than the sum of its individual parts. Yet some useful international actions, including cooperation to develop and share technologies and improvement in existing financial instruments, have been postponed in the expectation that they will be part of a soon-to-be-signed global agreement, reflecting differing views on who is responsible and incentives to free-ride on potential actions by others and to wait for new, equitable, financing instruments.

What is the solution? For certain global risks such as climate change or biodiversity loss, preserving collective action with full participation is the ultimate goal. In the interim, however, the international community is increasingly embracing incremental approaches that can increase traction toward global solutions. When incentives are misaligned, major sovereigns are not fully engaged, and the consequences of inaction are disastrous, progress can still be made outside a full-participation multilateral treaty. Incremental deals and actions by an initially small group of participants can serve as building blocks

TABLE F1.1 *National policy measures limiting carbon emissions*

	CO_2 emissions evolution and shares			Measures included in KPMG Green Tax Index							
Country	CO_2 emissions in metric tons per capita in 2009	Share of CO_2 emissions in 2009 (%)	Change in CO_2 emissions since 1990 (%)	Energy efficiency	Carbon and climate change	Green innovations	Renewable energy and fuels	Green vehicles and buildings	Water efficiency	Material resource efficiency and waste management	Pollution control and ecosystem protection
Australia	18.38	1.33	39.28	X	X	X	X	X	X	X	
United States	17.28	17.62	8.61	X	X	X	X	X	X	X	X
Canada	15.24	1.71	14.19		X	X	X	X	X		
Russian Federation	11.09	5.24	−26.23*	X					X		
Korea, Rep.	10.36	1.69	106.27		X	X	X	X	X	X	
Netherlands	10.26	0.56	3.36	X	X	X	X	X		X	
South Africa	10.12	1.66	49.62	X	X	X	X	X	X	X	X
Finland	10.03	0.18	3.52	X	X	X	X	X		X	
Belgium	9.60	0.34	−4.50	X	X	X		X	X	X	X
Ireland	9.34	0.14	32.59	X	X	X	X	X		X	
Germany***	8.97	2.44	−21.08**	X	X	X	X	X			
Japan	8.63	3.66	0.59	X	X	X	X	X		X	
United Kingdom	7.68	1.58	−16.77	X	X	X	X	X	X	X	X
Singapore	6.39	0.11	−32.05	X	X	X	X	X	X		X
Spain	6.28	0.96	31.69	X	X	X	X	X			X
China	5.77	25.56	212.39	X	X	X	X	X	X	X	
France	5.61	1.21	−8.94		X	X	X	X		X	X
Argentina***	4.36	0.58	55.15			X	X				
Mexico	3.98	1.48	41.93			X	X	X		X	X
Brazil	1.90	1.22	75.76			X		X		X	X
India	1.64	6.58	186.63	X	X	X	X	X			

Sources: WDR 2014 team based on data from KPMG Green Tax Index (database) (for national or subnational policy measures limiting carbon emissions), which analyzes the 21 largest economies of the world, and the World Bank World Development Indicators (database) (for CO_2 emissions data, as reported in the Carbon Dioxide Information Analysis Center, Environmental Science Division, Oak Ridge National Laboratory, Tennessee).

Note: X indicates the existence of a tax-related or non-tax-related measure in place at national or subnational levels. Energy efficiency refers to measures encouraging the purchase of energy efficient equipment (excluding measures specific to green vehicles or buildings). Carbon and climate change refers to penalties on high emissions (such as carbon taxes, emission trading systems or cap and trade mechanisms, and carbon sequestration incentives and penalties). Green innovation includes incentives for research and development for green technologies. Renewable energy and fuels refers to use of tax codes to encourage the production or use of renewable or alternative fuels and/or penalizing the use of fossil fuels. Green vehicle and buildings refers to tax incentives to reduce the energy consumption of buildings, increase their water efficiency and sustainability of building materials, and the purchase, lease and use of greener (fuel efficient, hybrid, electric) vehicles (excluding tax penalties and incentives related to fuels, which are included under renewable energy and fuels). Water efficiency includes use of taxes to encourage corporations to conserve and recycle water supplies. Material resource efficiency and waste management include use of taxes to promote conservation of material resources, reduction of waste, and recycling of waste materials. Pollution control and ecosystem protection include incentives to purchase equipment to reduce the pollution generated by the company or to encourage businesses to rehabilitate contaminated lands.

* 1991 value; ** 1992 value. *** Measures recorded by KPMG may not include some of the recent initiatives. For example, in Germany, recent information suggests additional measures in the areas of waste management, pollution control, and biodiversity protection (see German Federal Ministry for the Environment, Nature Conservation and Nuclear Safety (BMU), "The Energy Concept and its Accelerated Implementation," http://www.bmu.de/en/topics/climate-energy/transformation-of-the-energy-system/resolutions-and-measures/). In Argentina, recent information also suggests programs that limit carbon emissions, including energy efficiency, green buildings, waste management, pollution control, and ecosystem protection. CO_2 = carbon dioxide.

for global deals, by demonstrating benefits from action. The goal is to align incentives around a common goal in a group of like-minded participants that can examine complex issues and take concrete action. Over time, more public and private actors would be attracted to join the incremental approaches to build convergence toward a global deal.

The incremental approach has precedents. The Montreal Protocol to protect the ozone layer was signed by 24 countries in 1987, but received universal ratification during the 1990s through the combined efforts of governments, international organizations, nongovernmental organizations, and scientists, who presented and disseminated convincing evidence on the need for urgent action.[37] The 1968 Nuclear Non-Proliferation Treaty was helped by the earlier Limited Test Ban Treaty that expanded from 3 to 119 signatories from 1963 to 1992, setting a precedent for future arms negotiations. Several subnational governments (including the U.S. state of California) and countries (Australia, China, Japan, New Zealand) are using the lessons from Europe's Emissions Trading System introduced to meet emission commitments cost-effectively. Growing coalitions of more than 30 developed and developing countries include the Partnership of Market Readiness and the Climate, working on solutions to carbon pricing,[38] and the Clean Air Coalition of the United Nations Environment Programme, catalyzing rapid reductions in short-lived climate pollutants.[39]

How can it be implemented? Countries, international organizations, and private sector entities of the international community can form "coalitions of the willing" (or even better, "coalitions of the working") that could coordinate, advocate, and take action on some components of elusive global risks, such as climate change and the loss of biodiversity.[40] The coalitions should engage the scientific community, civil society, and media, and rely on information and peer pressure to demonstrate positive action and leadership, while inducing participants to comply and nonparticipants to join in a "race to the top." International organizations can continue to contribute by offering ways to develop approaches to tackle the problem collectively, by providing platforms for policy discussion and by monitoring, reporting, and aggregating the actions to ensure that incremental steps are heading in the right direction.

For legitimacy and fairness, these coalitions must include actors that contribute most to the problem, as well as those most affected by it. They should start with specific, concrete actions that can set the momentum for subsequent steps. The coalitions should create incentives for others to join over time to bring the coalition to a global scale. Steps could include, as appropriate, promoting technological change that lowers participation costs (such as supporting cheaper ways to cut emissions by providing subsidies or funding for green technologies, or backing technology transfers to developing countries).

Granted, there are risks with this approach—not least because it is a "second best" solution that in effect allows free-riding by those outside the coalition. Incremental deals may fail to scale up efforts sufficiently—or worse, reduce the urgency of global cooperation. Moreover, for certain risks, global collective action is still the only viable approach, given the rapid spillover risks in a tightly interconnected world. For example, once a pandemic is under way, no individual country or region can unilaterally protect itself without global cooperation that enables information to be shared and assists countries lacking the capacity to detect and contain the contagion.[41] Smallpox was declared eradicated in 1979 because it was eliminated in every country through global cooperation; if the disease had persisted in only one nation, all others would remain vulnerable.[42] Resolving global financial crises in a highly connected world also requires global cooperation, with well-coordinated policy responses and information sharing; uncoordinated actions are unable to prevent contagion and block movement of activities to less well-regulated and more-protected locations that retain systemic risk.

These limitations notwithstanding, the alternative—to wait until a universally acceptable deal is reached—is not viable for global risks such as climate change, biodiversity loss, or overuse of natural resources, if the irreversible consequences of inaction are to be avoided. That is especially the case for those who have done the least to cause the problem but will suffer some of the worst consequences. The international community therefore has the moral responsibility to take and support action on behalf of the vulnerable populations of today and the future. It should buttress the incremental approach with strategic thinking about which specific issues to tackle urgently first, while anchoring its actions to existing global frameworks to demonstrate that incremental and global deals are connected.[43]

One way to achieve this is to anchor the efforts of the coalition to the goals of the current global initiatives under the auspices of United Nations. Alternatively, an international risk board, similar to the national risk board proposed in Reform 1, could be established, in the form of an international panel on global systemic risks.[44] The panel could invite the scientific and expert community around the world to pool all available knowledge to identify, assess, and manage the major global risks that cross national and generational boundaries in the near and longer term. Through its long-term orientation, interdisciplinary nature, and the participation of global experts, the board could focus on providing credible, reliable, and impartial assessments of the causes, dynamics, and consequences of key systemic risks that pose threats to development. It could also analyze the interactions and prioritize across various risks and systematically bring its analysis to the attention of policy makers and the international community. In so doing, it could provide valuable inputs to the coalition of the willing on the specific issues that require urgent attention and offer credibility and legitimacy to the coalition's efforts.

Notes

1. Graham and Wiener 1995, chapter 1.
2. Graham and Wiener 1995, chapter 11.
3. Graham and Wiener 1995, chapter 11, 257–60.
4. WEF 2007.
5. OECD 2009.
6. However, in other cases when such a governmental body works with indirect policy tools, such as the monetary policy, an institutional design along these lines could be preferable.
7. Kaminsky, Reinhart, and Végh 2005.
8. Frankel, Végh, and Vuletin 2013.
9. Aghion and Marinescu 2008; Woo 2009.
10. Tornell and Lane 1999.
11. Alesina, Campante, and Tabellini 2008.
12. Barnes, Davidsson, and Rawdanowicz 2012.
13. Kumar and others 2009.
14. Schaechter and others 2012.
15. Wyplosz 2013.
16. Debrun, Hauner, and Kumar 2009.
17. Frankel 2011 shows that the authorities overestimate the persistence of booms and underestimate that of recessions.
18. Wren-Lewis 2010.
19. Bos and Teulings 2010.
20. Debrun 2011.
21. Debrun, Hauner, and Kumar 2009.
22. Calmfors and Wren-Lewis 2011; Page 2010.
23. Lane 2010.
24. BIS 2011; Bank of England 2013; IMF 2011; Nier and others 2011.
25. Bank of England 2013.
26. Financial Services Act 2012.
27. Bank of England 2013.
28. The term *social insurance* typically includes pensions, health, and unemployment insurance. Because most developing countries with social insurance offer only pensions and health benefits, the discussion in this section focuses on these two areas.
29. Evans, forthcoming; Levy and Schady 2013.
30. Levy and Schady 2013; Pagés-Serra 2010; ILO 2009; La Porta and Shleifer 2008.
31. Ribe, Robalino, and Walker 2012.
32. This is particularly true for "pay-as-you-go" systems, in which the current labor force finances the benefits provided to current beneficiaries.
33. Frölich and others, forthcoming.
34. Holzmann, Robalino, and Takayama 2009.
35. Hinz and others 2013.
36. World Bank 2012.
37. UNEP 2007.
38. See ongoing efforts to establish a carbon price at http://www.worldbank.org/en/news/opinion/2013/05/16/tackling-climate-change-robust-carbon-price.
39. For further details, see http://www.unep.org/ccac/.
40. See discussions in Falkner, Stephan, and Vogler 2010, Hale 2011, and Goldin 2013; and increased calls for such coalitions in Europe following the limited progress made in global negotiations in Copenhagen (2009) and Cancun (2010) at http://www.euractiv.com/climate-environment/europe-looks-coalition-willing-d-news-508909.
41. Goldin 2013; Jonas 2013.
42. Barrett 2006.
43. Falkner, Stephan, and Vogler 2010.
44. Bodies of this sort already exist for specific risks (such as the Intergovernmental Panel on Climate Change, or the Intergovernmental Platform on Biodiversity and Ecosystem Services) but none that consider multiple global risks in a systematic way. See a related proposal by the German Institute for Development 2009.

References

Aghion, Philippe, and Ioana Marinescu. 2008. "Cyclical Budgetary Policy and Economic Growth: What Do We Learn from OECD Panel Data?" In *NBER Macroeconomics Annual 2007,* vol. 22, edited by Daron Acemoglu, Kenneth Rogoff, and Michael Woodford, 251–78. Chicago: University of Chicago Press.

Alesina, Alberto, Filipe R. Campante, and Guido Tabellini. 2008. "Why Is Fiscal Policy Often Procyclical?" *Journal of the European Economic Association* 6 (5): 1006–36.

Bank of England. 2013. "The Financial Policy Committee's Powers to Supplement Capital Requirements: A Draft Policy Statement." Bank of England, London.

Barnes, Sebastian, David Davidsson, and Lukasz Rawdanowicz. 2012. "Europe's New Fiscal Rules." Economics Department Working Paper 972, Organisation for Economic Co-operation and Development, Paris.

Barrett, Scott. 2006. "The Smallpox Eradication Game." *Public Choice* 130 (1–2): 179–207.

BIS (Bank for International Settlements). 2011. "Central Bank Governance and Financial Stability: A Report by Study Group." BIS, Basel.

Bos, Frits, and Coen Teulings. 2010. "CPB and Dutch Fiscal Policy in View of the Financial Crisis and Ageing." Document 218, Bureau for Economic Policy Analysis (CPB), the Netherlands.

Calmfors, Lars, and Simon Wren-Lewis. 2011. "What Should Fiscal Councils Do?" *Economic Policy* 26 (68): 649–95.

Debrun, Xavier. 2011. "Democratic Accountability, Deficit Bias, and Independent Fiscal Agencies." Working Paper WP/11/173, International Montetary Fund, Washington, DC.

Debrun, Xavier, David Hauner, and Manmohan Kumar. 2009. "Independent Fiscal Agencies." *Journal of Economic Surveys* 23 (1): 44–81.

Evans, Brooks. Forthcoming. "An Examination of Pension Coverage of Elderly in the Developing World." Social Protection and Labor Policy Note, World Bank, Washington, DC.

Falkner, Robert, Hannes Stephan, and John Vogler. 2010. "International Climate Policy after Copenhagen: Towards a 'Building Blocks' Approach." *Global Policy* 1 (3): 252–62.

Financial Services Act. 2012. Chapter 21. London: TSO (The Stationery Office).

Frankel, Jeffrey A. 2011. "Over-Optimism in Forecasts by Official Budget Agencies and Its Implications." *Oxford Review of Economic Policy* 27 (4): 536–62.

Frankel, Jeffrey A., Carlos A. Végh, and Guillermo Vuletin. 2013. "On Graduation from Fiscal Procyclicality." *Journal of Development Economics* 100 (1): 32–47.

Frölich, Markus, David Kaplan, Carmen Pagés, Jamele Rigolini, and David Robalino. Forthcoming. *Social Insurance and Labor Markets: How to Protect Workers While Creating Good Jobs.* Washington, DC: World Bank, Inter-American Development Bank, and Institute for the Study of Labor.

German Institute for Development. 2009. "Globalization at the Crossroad: An "International Panel on Systemic Risks in the Global Economy" Is Needed." Briefing Paper 6/2009, Bonn. http://www.die-gdi.de/CMS-Homepage/openwebcms3.nsf/(ynDK_ contentByKey)/ANES-7T5J6U/$FILE/BP%206.2009.pdf.

Goldin, Ian. 2013. *Divided Nations: Why Global Governance Is Failing and What We Can Do about It.* Oxford: Oxford University Press.

Graham, John D., and Jonathan B. Wiener. 1995. *Risk Versus Risk: Tradeoffs in Protecting Health and the Environment.* Cambridge, MA: Harvard University Press.

Hale, Thomas. 2011. "A Climate Coalition of the Willing." *Washington Quarterly* 34 (1): 89–101.

Hinz, Richard, Robert Holzmann, David Tuesta, and Noriyuki Takayama. 2013. *Matching Contributions for Pensions: A Review of International Experience.* Washington, DC: World Bank.

Holzmann, Robert, David A. Robalino, and Noriyuki Takayama. 2009. *Closing the Coverage Gap: The Role of Social Pensions and Other Retirement Income Transfers.* Washington, DC: World Bank.

ILO (International Labour Organization). 2009. *The Informal Economy in Africa: Promoting Transition to Formality: Challenges and Strategies.* Geneva: ILO.

IMF (International Monetary Fund). 2011. "Macroprudential Policy: An Organizing Framework." IMF, Washington, DC.

Jonas, Olga. 2013. "Pandemic Risk." Background paper for the *World Development Report 2014.*

Kaminsky, Graciela L., Carmen M. Reinhart, and Carlos A. Végh. 2005. "When It Rains, It Pours: Procyclical Capital Flows and Macroeconomic Policies." In *NBER Macroeconomics Annual 2004,* vol. 19, edited by Mark Gertler and Kenneth Rogoff, 11–53. Cambridge, MA: MIT Press.

KPMG. Green Tax Index (database). KPMG, Amstelveen. http://www.kpmg.com/global/en/issuesandinsights/articlespublications/green-tax/pages/default.aspx.

Kumar, Manmohan, Emanuele Baldacci, Andrea Schaechter, Carlos Caceres, Daehaeng Kim, Xavier Debrun, Julio Escolano, Jiri Jonas, Philippe Karam, Irina Yakadina, and Robert Zymek. 2009. "Fiscal Rules—Anchoring Expectations for Sustainable Public Finances." International Monetary Fund, Washington, DC.

Lane, Philip. 2010. "Some Lessons for Fiscal Policy from the Financial Crisis." IIIS Discussion Paper 334, Trinity College, Dublin, Ireland.

La Porta, Rafael, and Andrei Shleifer. 2008. "The Unofficial Economy and Economic Development." *Brookings Papers on Economic Activity* 39 (2): 275–363.

Levy, Santiago, and Norbert Schady. 2013. "Latin America's Social Policy Challenge: Education, Social Insurance, Redistribution." *Journal of Economic Perspectives* 27 (2): 193–218.

Nier, Erlend W., Jacek Osinski, Luis I. Jacome, and Pamela Madrid. 2011. "Towards Effective Macroprudential Policy Frameworks: An Assessment of Stylized Institutional Models." Working Paper WP/11/250, International Monetary Fund, Washington, DC.

OECD (Organisation for Economic Co-operation and Development). 2009. "Innovation in Country Risk Mangement." OECD Studies in Risk Management, OECD, Paris.

Page, Kevin. 2010. "Lessons from Canada." Paper presented to the Conference on Independent Fiscal Institutions, Fiscal Council Republic of Hungary, Budapest.

Pagés-Serra, Carmen, ed. 2010. *The Age of Productivity: Transforming Economies from the Bottom Up.* Washington, DC: Inter-American Development Bank.

Ribe, Helena, David A. Robalino, and Ian Walker. 2012. *From Right to Reality: Incentives, Labor Markets, and the Challenge of Universal Social Protection in Latin America and the Caribbean.* Washington, DC: World Bank.

Schaechter, Andrea, Tidiane Kinda, Nina Budina, and Anke Weber. 2012. "Fiscal Rules in Response to the Crisis toward the 'Next Generation' Rules: A New Dataset." Working Paper WP/12/187, International Monetary Fund, Washington, DC.

Tornell, Aaron, and Philip R. Lane. 1999. "The Voracity Effect." *American Economic Review* 89 (1): 22–46.

UNEP (United Nations Environment Programme). 2007. "A Success in the Making: The Montreal Protocol on Substances that Deplete the Ozone Layer." UNEP, Nairobi.

United Nations. 2009. "World Population Prospects: The 2008 Revision." Department of Economic and Social Affairs Population Division, United Nations, New York.

WEF (World Economic Forum). 2007. "Global Risks 2007: A Global Risk Network Report." WEF, Geneva.

Woo, Jaejoon. 2009. "Why Do More Polarized Countries Run More Procyclical Fiscal Policy?" *Review of Economics and Statistics* 91 (4): 850–70.

World Bank. 2012. "Turn Down the Heat: Why a 4°C Warmer World Must Be Avoided." World Bank, Washington, DC.

———. Pensions (database). World Bank, Washington, DC. http://www.worldbank.org/pensions.

———. World Development Indicators (database). World Bank, Washington, DC. http://data.worldbank.org/data-catalog/world-development-indicators.

Wren-Lewis, Simon. 2010. "Macroeconomic Policy in Light of the Credit Crunch: The Return of Countercyclical Fiscal Policy?" *Oxford Review of Economic Policy* 26 (1): 71–86.

Wyplosz, Charles. 2013. "Fiscal Rules: Theoretical Issues and Historical Experiences." In *Fiscal Policy after the Financial Crisis,* edited by Alberto Alesina and Francesco Giavazzi. Chicago: University of Chicago Press.

Appendixes

Abbreviations and data notes

Abbreviations

AIDS	Acquired Immunodeficiency Syndrome
BIS	Bank for International Settlements
CAB	cyclically adjusted balance
CAT DDO	Catastrophe Deferred Drawdown Option
CCRIF	Caribbean Catastrophe Risk Insurance Facility
CCT	conditional cash transfer
CGAP	Consultative Group to Assist the Poor
CRIF	Catastrophe Risk Insurance Facility
DRFI	Disaster Risk Financing and Insurance
DRM	disaster risk management
EU	European Union
FAO	Food and Agriculture Organization of the United Nations
FCS	fragile and conflict-affected state
FDI	foreign direct investment
FONDEN	Fund for Natural Disasters
FX	foreign exchange/currency
G2P	government-to-person
GDP	gross domestic product
GEF	Global Environmental Facility
GFDRR	Global Facility for Disaster Reduction and Recovery
GFSN	Global Financial Safety Net
G-SIFI	global systemically important financial institution
GNI	gross national income
HFA	Hyogo Framework for Action
HIV	Human Immunodeficiency Virus
IBRD	International Bank for Reconstruction and Development
IFI	international financial institution
IMF	International Monetary Fund
IPP	independent power producer
ISO	International Organization for Standardization
MDG	Millennium Development Goal
MTEF	medium-term expenditure framework
MTFF	medium-term fiscal plan
NGO	nongovernmental organization
NRA	national risk assessment
ODC	ozone depleting chemical
OECD	Organisation for Economic Co-operation and Development
OIE	Office International des Epizooties, or World Organisation for Animal Health
ppm	parts per million

PPP	public-private partnership
SARS	severe acute respiratory syndrome
SEEC-CRIF	Southeast Europe and the Caucasus Catastrophe Risk Insurance Facility
SIFI	systemically important financial institution
S&P	Standard & Poor's
SWF	sovereign wealth fund
UN	United Nations
UNEP	United Nations Environment Programme
VIX	Volatility Index
WDI	World Development Indicators
WDR	World Development Report
WEF	World Economic Forum
WHO	World Health Organization

Data notes

The use of the term *countries* to refer to economies implies no judgment by the World Bank about the legal or other status of territory. The term *developing countries* includes low- and middle-income economies and thus may include economies in transition from central planning, as a matter of convenience. Dollar figures are current U.S. dollars, unless otherwise specified. *Billion* means 1,000 million; *trillion* means 1,000 billion.

For regional comparisons, figures in this Report use the following country groupings: Organisation for Economic Co-operation and Development (OECD), East Asia and Pacific (EAP), Europe and Central Asia (ECA), Latin America and Caribbean (LAC), Middle East and North Africa (MENA), South Asia (SAR), and Sub-Saharan Africa (SSA). The OECD group refers to high-income countries that have been members of the OECD for at least 40 years (Australia, Austria, Belgium, Canada, Denmark, Finland, France, Germany, Greece, Ireland, Italy, Japan, Luxembourg, Netherlands, New Zealand, Norway, Portugal, Spain, Sweden, Switzerland, United Kingdom, and United States). All other countries are grouped into geographic regions. Countries with less than 0.5 million population as of 2010 are not included in the sample for analytical purposes.

Income groupings are based on World Bank income classifications as of July 1, 2012, based on 2011 gross national income per capita—except for the tables in the selected indicators, which were prepared based on the income classifications as of July 1, 2013. See the selected indicators section for more details.

Maps

The maps numbered IBRD 40097, 40098, 40099, and 40100 were produced by the Map Design Unit of the World Bank.

The boundaries, colors, nominations, and any other information shown on those maps do not imply, on the part of the World Bank Group, any judgment on the legal status of any territory, or any endorsement or acceptance of such boundaries. Taiwan, China, receives the same ranking as China.

Background papers

Aizenman, Joshua, and İnci Ötker-Robe. 2013. "Managing Risk for Development: International Risk Sharing Tools."

Anderson, Phillip R. D. 2013. "Risk Market Transfer."

Ashwill, Maximillian, and Rasmus Heltberg. 2013. "Is There a Community-Level Adaptation Deficit?"

Ashwill, Maximillian, and Andrew Norton. 2013. "Rights and Social Action for Risk Management: Reflections on Global, National and Local Roles and Responses."

Auriol, Emmanuelle. 2013. "Taxation Base and Barriers to Entrepreneurship in Developing Countries."

Baliki, Ghassan. 2013. "Crime and Victimization."

Beck, Thorsten. 2013. "The Supply-Demand Mismatch in Provision of Financial Services."

Beck, Thorsten, and Olivier De Jonghe. 2013. "Lending Concentration, and its Implications for Bank Performance and Systemic Risk: Global Evidence."

Bloom, Nicholas. 2013. "Has Economic Policy Uncertainty Slowed Down the World Economy?"

Brown, Julia K., Ahmed Mushfiq Mobarak, and Tetyana V. Zelenska. 2013. "Barriers to Adoption of Products and Technologies That Aid Risk Management in Developing Countries."

Brown, Martin. 2013. "The Transmission of Banking Crises to Households: Lessons from the ECA Region 2008–2012."

Buncic, Daniel, and Martin Melecky. 2013. "Equilibrium Credit: The Reference Point for Macroprudential Supervisors."

Cáceres-Delpiano, Julio. 2013. "Literature Review: Family Formation and Fertility as Risk Coping Mechanisms."

Calvo, Sara Guerschanik. 2013. "Financial Crises, Social Impact, and Risk Management: Lessons and Challenges."

de la Fuente, Alejandro, Eduardo Ortiz-Juárez, and Carlos Rodriguez Castelan. 2013. "Living on the Edge: Vulnerability to Poverty and Public Transfers in Mexico."

Dutz, Mark A. 2013. "Resource Reallocation and Innovation: Converting Enterprise Risks into Opportunities."

Eden, Maya. 2013. "Managing Contingent Liabilities Using Market Risk Transfer Instruments: A Review of the Literature."

Fidas, Penelope D., and Najy Benhassine. 2013. "Transparency and Access to Information in Business Regulations."

Foa, Roberto. 2013. "Household Risk Preparation Indices: Construction and Diagnostics."

Fuentes, Rodrigo. 2013. "Sovereign Wealth Funds: The Case of Chile."

Genicot, Garance, and Ethan Ligon. 2013. "Risk and the Extent of Insurance."

Gereffi, Gary, and Xubei Luo. 2013. "Risks and Opportunities of Participation in Global Value Chains."

Ghani, Ejaz. 2013a. "Are Manufacturing Sectors Moving Out of Large Cities?"

———. 2013b. "Who Creates Jobs in India?"

———. 2013c. "Why Do Enterprises Get Attracted to Some Cities? Not to Others?"

Gooptu, Sudarshan, and Auguste T. Kouame. 2013. "The '4-3-2 Framework': A Framework for Dealing with the Debt-Related Risks of Highly Indebted Small States."

Grinbaum, Mikael, and Susan T. Jackson. 2013. "Managing Risk for Development: Expert Workshop on Local Violence in Developing Countries."

Gutierrez, Federico H. 2013. "Labor Contracts and Risk Sharing."

Hallegatte, Stéphane. 2013. "An Exploration of the Link between Development, Economic Growth, and Natural Risk."

Han, Rui, and Martin Melecky. 2013. "Financial Inclusion for Financial Stability: Access to Bank Deposits and the Deposits Growth in the Global Financial Crisis."

Heltberg, Rasmus, Ana María Oviedo, and Faiyaz Talukdar. 2013. "What Are the Sources of Risk and How Do People Cope? Insights from Household Surveys in 15 Countries."

Inglehart, Ronald. 2013. "Results from the Latest Wave of the World Values Survey."

Jonas, Olga B. 2013. "Pandemic Risk."

Kelman, Ilan. 2012. "Disaster Mitigation Is Cost Effective."

Khokhar, Tariq. 2013. "Leveraging New Technology for Data-Driven Risk Mitigation and Management: Selected Examples and Summaries."

Kraay, Aart, and Luis Servén. 2013. "Fiscal Policy as a Tool for Stabilization in Developing Countries."

Lakhani, Sadaf. 2013. "Forced Displacement: Moving from Managing Risk to Facilitating Opportunity."

Lambert, Sylvie, and Philippe de Vreyer. 2013. "Household Risk Management in Senegal."

Lasagabaster, Esperanza. 2013. "Policy Priorities for Innovative Entrepreneurship."

Maimbo, Samuel, and Martin Melecky. 2013. "Financial Policy Formulation: Addressing the Tradeoff between Development and Stability."

Maloney, William F. 2013. "Measuring Labor Market Risk."

Moscoso Boedo, Hernan J. 2013. "Enterprise Sector Risk."

Ötker-Robe, İnci, and Anca Podpiera. 2013. "Social Impact of Financial Crises: Evidence from the Recent Global Financial Crisis."

Oviedo, Ana María, and Harry Moroz. 2013. "The Impacts of Risk."

Petesch, Patti. 2013. "How Communities Manage Risks of Crime and Violence."

Premand, Patrick. 2013. "From Risk Coping to Risk Management: Productive Safety Nets in Africa."

Salazar, Natalia. 2013. "Fiscal Risk Management for Development: The Case of Colombia."

Teal, Francis J. 2013. "The Enterprise Sector: Providing Employment and Sharing Risk."

van Aalst, Maarten, Tom Mitchell, Jan Kellett, and Florence Pichon. 2013. "Incentives in Disaster Risk Management and Humanitarian Response."

Vuletin, Guillermo. 2013. "Effects and Role of Macroprudential Policy."

Warner, Koko. 2013. "Climate Change and Global Warming: The Role of the International Community."

Wethli, Kyla. 2013. "Benefit-Cost Analysis for Risk Management: Summary of Selected Examples."

Zhu, Nong, and Xubei Luo, 2013. "What Drives Productivity Volatility of Chinese Industrial Firms?"

Selected indicators

General notes

Tables 1 to 10 include 75 indicators relevant to the management of risk in the context of development. These indicators summarize the level and dimensions of risk facing each country, together with the capacity to manage risk along several different social, economic, financial, and environmental dimensions. Definitions of each indicator are provided in the technical notes that follow the tables.

Sources

The indicators in the tables come from a variety of authoritative sources, including the World Bank, other international organizations such as the United Nations and International Monetary Fund, government agencies, member country statistical publications, research institutes, and peer-reviewed academic papers. The source for each indicator is identified in the technical notes.

Many of the indicators in this section have been included in the World Bank's Open Data catalog and are available for download. The World Bank's Open Data terms of use allow users to use these data freely, subject to a limited set of conditions. We encourage readers to access the data at http://datacatalog.worldbank.org and to review the terms of use at http://data.worldbank.org/summary-terms-of-use. Several of the indicators available in the data catalog were obtained from research papers with the permission of the authors. These indicators in particular were developed for specific research studies and may not be suitable for other purposes. Neither the authors nor any institutions with which they are affiliated make any warranties with respect to the data and shall not be liable in connection with the data's use under any circumstances.

Country coverage

Tables 1 and 3 to 8 include data for 133 countries. Table 2 includes key development indicators for 81 economies with sparse data or with populations of less than 3 million. The term *country*, used interchangeably with economy, does not imply political independence but refers to any territory for which authorities report separate social or economic statistics. Data are shown for economies as they were constituted in 2012. Unless otherwise noted, data for China do not include data for Hong Kong SAR, China; Macao SAR, China; or Taiwan, China. Data for Indonesia include Timor-Leste through 1999. Data for Serbia include Montenegro through 2005 and exclude Kosovo from 1999 onward. Data for Sudan include South Sudan unless otherwise noted.

Classification of economies and summary measures

For operational and analytical purposes, the World Bank's main criterion for classifying economies is gross national income (GNI) per capita. Based on its GNI per capita, every economy is classified as low income, middle income (subdivided into lower-middle and upper-middle), or high income. Income classifications are set each year on July 1. These official analytical classifications are fixed during the World Bank's fiscal year (ending on June 30); thus countries remain in the categories in which they are classified irrespective of any revisions to their per capita income data. Low-income economies are those with a GNI per capita of $1,035 or less in 2012. Middle-income economies are those with a GNI per capita of more than $1,035 but less than $12,616. Lower-middle-income and upper-middle-income economies are separated at a GNI per capita of $4,086. High-income economies are those with a GNI per capita of $12,616 or more. When changes in classification are made, aggregates based on the new income classifications are recalculated for all past periods to ensure that a consistent time series is maintained.

Summary measures are either totals (indicated by a **t** if the aggregates include estimates for missing data and nonreporting countries, or by an **s** for simple sums of the data available), weighted averages (**w**), unweighted averages (**u**), or median values (**m**) calculated for groups of economies. Data for economies not appearing in the tables have been included in the summary measures, where data are available; otherwise it is assumed they follow the trend of reporting economies. Where missing data accounts for a third or more of the overall estimate, however, the group measure is reported as not available.

Symbols

.. means that data are not available or that aggregates cannot be calculated because of missing data in the years shown.

0 or 0.0 means zero or small enough that the number would round to zero at the displayed number of decimal places.

– in dates in column headings, as in 2003–12, refers to a time period that spans years. Unless otherwise noted in the column heading, these indicators are sums of annual values for the time period shown.

$ means current U.S. dollars unless otherwise noted.

Data in italics are for a year or period other than that specified in the column heading.

Classification of economies by region and income, FY2014

Low income
Afghanistan
Bangladesh
Benin
Burkina Faso
Burundi
Cambodia
Central African Republic
Chad
Congo, Dem. Rep.
Eritrea
Ethiopia
Guinea
Haiti
Kenya
Kyrgyz Republic
Liberia
Madagascar
Malawi
Mali
Mozambique
Myanmar
Nepal
Niger
Rwanda
Sierra Leone
Somalia
South Sudan
Tajikistan
Tanzania
Togo
Uganda
Zimbabwe

Lower middle income
Armenia
Bolivia
Cameroon
Congo, Rep.
Côte d'Ivoire
Egypt, Arab Rep.
El Salvador
Georgia
Ghana
Guatemala
Honduras
India
Indonesia
Lao PDR
Mauritania
Moldova
Morocco
Nicaragua
Nigeria
Pakistan
Papua New Guinea
Paraguay
Philippines
Senegal
Sri Lanka
Sudan
Syrian Arab Republic
Ukraine
Uzbekistan
Vietnam
West Bank and Gaza
Yemen, Rep.
Zambia

Upper middle income
Albania
Algeria
Angola
Argentina
Azerbaijan
Belarus
Bosnia and Herzegovina
Brazil
Bulgaria
China
Colombia
Costa Rica
Dominican Republic
Ecuador
Hungary
Iran, Islamic Rep.
Iraq
Jordan
Kazakhstan
Lebanon
Libya
Malaysia
Mexico
Panama
Peru
Romania
Serbia
South Africa
Thailand
Tunisia
Turkey
Turkmenistan
Venezuela, RB

High income
Australia
Austria
Belgium
Canada
Chile
Hong Kong SAR, China
Croatia
Czech Republic
Denmark
Finland
France
Germany
Greece
Ireland
Israel
Italy
Japan
Korea, Rep.
Lithuania
Netherlands
New Zealand
Norway
Poland
Portugal
Russian Federation
Saudi Arabia
Singapore
Slovak Republic
Spain
Sweden
Switzerland
United Arab Emirates
United Kingdom
United States
Uruguay

Selected island states (Tables 2 and 8 only)
Antigua and Barbuda
Bahamas
Barbados
Bermuda
Comoros
Dominica
Dominican Rep
Fiji
Grenada
Haiti
Jamaica
Maldives
Marshall Is
Micronesia Fed States
Philippines
Samoa
Seychelles
Solomon Is
St Kitts and Nevis
St Lucia
St Vincent and The Grenadines
Trinidad and Tobago

TABLE 1 *Key indicators of development*

	Population			Population age composition	Gross national income[a]		Gross national income, PPP[b]		Gross domestic product	Life expectancy at birth		Adult literacy rate
	Millions	Average annual growth, %	Density per sq. km	% ages 0–14	$ billions	$ per capita	$ billions	$ per capita	per capita growth, %	Years, male	Years, female	% ages 15 and older
	2012	2000–12	2012	2012	2012	2012	2012	2012	2012	2011	2011	2005–11[c]
Afghanistan	30	3.1	46	47	*16.6*	*570*	*40.7*[d]	*1,400*[d]	*4.4*	49	49	..
Albania	3	−0.4	115	21	12.9	4,090	29.7	9,390	0.5	74	80	96
Algeria	38	1.6	16	27	*155.1*	*4,110*	*285.0*[d]	*7,550*[d]	0.6	72	75	73
Angola	21	3.4	17	48	95.4	4,580	114.3	5,490	3.5	50	53	70
Argentina	41	0.9	15	24	..	..[e]	..	..	..	72	80	98
Armenia	3	−0.3	104	20	11.1	3,720	20.8	6,990	7.0	71	77	100
Australia	23	1.4	3	19	1,351.2	59,570	982.2	43,300	1.8	80	84	..
Austria	8	0.5	103	15	407.6	48,160	373.2	44,100	0.4	78	84	..
Azerbaijan	9	1.2	112	22	56.3	6,050	87.5	9,410	3.1	68	74	100
Bangladesh	155	1.3	1,188	31	129.2	840	319.9	2,070	5.1	68	70	57
Belarus	9	−0.5	47	15	61.8	6,530	143.9	15,210	1.6	65	77	100
Belgium	11	0.7	368	17	501.3	44,990	447.6	40,170	−1.1	78	83	..
Benin	10	3.1	89	43	7.5	750	15.8	1,570	2.6	54	58	42
Bolivia	10	1.8	10	35	23.3	2,220	52.1	4,960	3.5	64	69	91
Bosnia and Herzegovina	4	0.0	75	16	17.8	4,650	36.0	9,380	−0.6	73	78	98
Brazil	199	1.1	23	25	2,311.1	11,630	2,328.8	11,720	0.0	70	77	90
Bulgaria	7	−0.9	67	14	50.2	6,870	112.4	15,390	1.4	71	78	98
Burkina Faso	16	2.9	60	46	10.9	670	24.9	1,510	6.9	54	56	29
Burundi	10	3.2	384	44	2.4	240	5.5	560	0.7	49	52	67
Cambodia	15	1.6	84	31	13.0	880	35.1	2,360	5.4	62	64	74
Cameroon	22	2.6	46	43	25.4	1,170	50.3	2,320	2.1	51	53	71
Canada	35	1.0	4	16	1,777.9	50,970	1,483.6	42,530	0.6	79	83	..
Central African Republic	5	1.8	7	40	2.2	490	3.9	860	2.1	47	50	56
Chad	12	3.4	10	49	9.3	740	16.4	1,320	1.9	48	51	34
Chile	17	1.0	23	21	249.5	14,280	372.1	21,310	4.6	76	82	99
China	1,351	0.6	145	18	7,748.9	5,740	12,435.4	9,210	7.3	72	75	94
Hong Kong SAR, China	7	0.6	6,866	12	261.6	36,560	379.6	53,050	0.3	80	87	..
Colombia	48	1.5	43	28	333.6	6,990	482.2	10,110	2.6	70	77	93
Congo, Dem. Rep.	66	2.8	29	45	14.8	220	24.5	370	4.3	47	50	67
Congo, Rep.	4	2.7	13	42	11.1	2,550	15.2	3,510	1.1	56	59	..
Costa Rica	5	1.7	94	24	42.0	8,740	60.5[d]	12,590[d]	3.6	77	82	96
Côte d'Ivoire	20	1.7	62	41	24.2	1,220	38.8	1,960	7.0	54	57	56
Croatia	4	−0.3	76	15	56.7	13,290	84.3	19,760	−1.7	74	80	99
Czech Republic	11	0.2	136	15	190.6	18,130	259.8	24,710	−1.5	75	81	..
Denmark	6	0.4	132	18	334.1	59,770	242.3	43,340	−0.8	78	82	..
Dominican Republic	10	1.4	213	31	56.2	5,470	101.0[d]	9,820[d]	2.6	71	76	90
Ecuador	15	1.8	62	30	80.5	5,190	148.5	9,590	3.3	73	79	92
Egypt, Arab Rep.	81	1.7	81	31	241.8	3,000	536.3	6,640	0.5	71	75	72
El Salvador	6	0.5	304	31	22.5	3,580	42.8[d]	6,790[d]	1.0	67	77	84
Eritrea	6	3.7	61	43	2.8	450	3.4[d]	560[d]	3.6	59	64	68
Ethiopia	92	2.7	92	43	37.4	410	104.2	1,140	5.7	58	61	39
Finland	5	0.4	18	16	254.1	46,940	209.2	38,630	−0.7	77	84	..
France	66	0.6	120	18	2,742.9	41,750	2,412.6	36,720	−0.5	78	85	..
Georgia	5[f]	0.2[f]	65[f]	18	14.8[f]	3,280[f]	26.4[f]	5,860[f]	5.3[f]	70	77	100
Germany	82	0.0	235	13	3,603.9	44,010	3,430.1	41,890	0.6	78	83	..
Ghana	25	2.5	111	39	39.3	1,550	49.2	1,940	5.6	63	65	67
Greece	11	0.3	88	15	262.4	23,260	287.2	25,460	−6.2	79	83	97
Guatemala	15	2.5	141	41	47.0	3,120	74.8[d]	4,960[d]	0.4	68	75	75
Guinea	11	2.2	47	42	5.3	460	11.3	980	1.3	53	56	41
Haiti	10	1.4	369	35	7.7	760	12.6[d]	1,240[d]	1.4	61	63	49
Honduras	8	2.0	71	36	16.4	2,070	30.9[d]	3,890[d]	1.4	71	75	85
Hungary	10	−0.2	110	15	123.2	12,390	205.9	20,710	−1.4	71	79	99
India	1,237	1.4	416	29	1,890.4	1,530	4,749.2	3,840	1.9	64	67	63
Indonesia	247	1.4	136	29	844.0	3,420	1,188.0	4,810	4.9	68	71	93
Iran, Islamic Rep.	76	1.2	47	24	..	..[e]	..	..	..	71	75	85
Iraq	33	2.6	75	41	191.2	5,870	140.2	4,300	5.7	66	72	78
Ireland	5	1.6	67	22	178.8	38,970	164.6	35,870	0.7	78	83	..
Israel	8	1.9	365	28	*224.7*	*28,930*	*218.0*	*28,070*	*2.8*	80	84	..
Italy	61	0.6	207	14	2,061.3	33,840	2,002.3	32,870	−2.7	80	85	99
Japan	128	0.0	350	13	6,105.8	47,870	4,629.7	36,290	2.1	79	86	..
Jordan	6	2.3	71	34	29.9	4,720	38.8	6,130	0.6	72	75	93
Kazakhstan	17	1.0	6	25	163.5	9,730	200.7	11,950	3.5	64	74	100
Kenya	43	2.7	76	42	36.2	840	76.1	1,760	1.5	56	58	87
Korea, Rep.	50	0.5	515	15	1,133.8	22,670	1,548.7	30,970	1.6	78	84	..
Kyrgyz Republic	6	1.1	29	30	5.5	990	12.6	2,260	−2.1	66	74	99
Lao PDR	7	1.7	29	36	8.4	1,260	18.1	2,730	6.1	66	69	73
Lebanon	4	2.6	433	22	40.7	9,190	63.7	14,400	0.4	70	75	90
Liberia	4	3.1	44	43	1.6	370	2.5	600	7.9	56	58	61
Libya	6	1.4	3	29	..	..[e]	..	..	..	72	78	89
Lithuania	3	−1.3	48	15	41.3	13,850	67.9	22,760	5.3	68	79	100
Madagascar	22	2.9	38	43	9.7	430	21.2	950	0.3	65	68	64
Malawi	16	2.8	169	45	5.0	320	13.9	880	−1.0	54	54	75
Malaysia	29	1.8	89	27	286.4	9,800	483.2	16,530	3.9	72	77	93
Mali	15	3.1	12	47	9.8	660	17.2	1,160	−4.1	50	52	31
Mauritania	4	2.8	4	40	4.2	1,110	9.6	2,520	4.9	57	60	58
Mexico	121	1.3	62	29	1,176.9	9,740	2,015.8	16,680	2.6	75	79	93
Moldova	4[g]	−0.2[g]	108[g]	17	7.4[g]	2,070[g]	13.1[g]	3,690[g]	−0.8[g]	66	73	99
Morocco	33	1.0	73	28	97.1[h]	2,940[h]	166.6[h]	5,040[h]	1.2[h]	70	74	56

TABLE 1 *Key indicators of development* (continued)

	Population			Population age composition	Gross national income[a]		Gross national income, PPP[b]		Gross domestic product per capita growth, %	Life expectancy at birth		Adult literacy rate % ages 15 and older
	Millions	Average annual growth, %	Density per sq. km	% ages 0–14	$ billions	$ per capita	$ billions	$ per capita		Years, male	Years, female	
	2012	2000–12	2012	2012	2012	2012	2012	2012	2012	2011	2011	2005–11[c]
Mozambique	25	2.7	32	45	12.8	510	25.7	1,020	4.7	49	51	56
Myanmar	53	0.7	81	25	..	..[i]	..	..	..	63	67	92
Nepal	27	1.4	192	36	19.2	700	41.1	1,500	3.4	68	70	60
Netherlands	17	0.4	497	17	809.1	48,250	731.5	43,620	−1.4	79	83	..
New Zealand	4	1.2	17	20	*134.9*	*30,620*	*132.0*	*29,960*	2.3	79	83	..
Nicaragua	6	1.3	50	33	9.9	1,650	23.7[d]	3,960[d]	3.7	71	77	78
Niger	17	3.7	14	50	6.4	370	11.2	650	7.0	54	55	29
Nigeria	169	2.6	185	44	241.1	1,430	409.1	2,420	3.6	51	53	61
Norway	5	0.9	16	19	496.2	98,860	336.1	66,960	1.7	79	84	..
Pakistan	179	1.8	232	34	225.4	1,260	543.6	3,030	2.4	65	66	55
Panama	4	1.8	51	29	37.7	9,910	67.8[d]	17,830[d]	8.9	74	79	94
Papua New Guinea	7	2.4	16	38	12.8	1,790	19.9[d]	2,780[d]	5.7	61	65	61
Paraguay	7	1.9	17	33	22.0	3,290	37.5	5,610	−2.9	70	75	94
Peru	30	1.2	23	29	176.5	5,880	306.9	10,240	5.0	71	77	90
Philippines	97	1.8	324	35	238.7	2,470	425.2	4,400	4.8	66	72	95
Poland	39	0.0	127	15	488.3	12,670	816.0	21,170	1.9	73	81	100
Portugal	11	0.2	115	15	216.6	20,580	260.7	24,770	−3.0	78	84	95
Romania	21	−0.4	93	15	179.6	8,420	347.8	16,310	4.0	71	78	98
Russian Federation	144	−0.2	9	15	1,822.7	12,700	3,260.6	22,720	3.0	63	75	100
Rwanda	11	2.6	464	44	*6.2*	*560*	*13.9*	*1,250*	5.0	54	57	71
Saudi Arabia	28	2.8	13	30	*500.5*	*18,030*	*694.4*	*25,010*	4.8	73	75	87
Senegal	14	2.8	71	44	14.2	1,040	26.3	1,920	0.7	58	60	50
Serbia	7	−0.3	83	16	38.1	5,280	80.8	11,180	−1.2	72	77	98
Sierra Leone	6	3.1	83	42	3.5	580	8.1	1,360	13.0	47	48	42
Singapore	5	2.3	7,589	16	250.8	47,210	324.6	61,100	−1.1	80	84	96
Slovak Republic	5	0.0	113	15	92.9	17,170	134.0	24,770	1.8	72	80	..
Somalia	10	2.7	16	47	..	..[i]	..	..	..	50	53	..
South Africa	51	1.3	42	30	389.8	7,610	572.6	11,190	1.3	52	53	89
South Sudan	11	4.1	..	42	7.0	650	..	..	−57.7	..	..	..
Spain	46	1.1	93	15	1,391.4	30,110	1,493.8	32,320	−1.5	79	85	98
Sri Lanka	20	0.5	324	25	59.3	2,920	124.5	6,120	9.2	72	78	91
Sudan	37[j]	2.4[j]	16	41[j]	53.8[j]	1,450[j]	75.3[j]	2,030[j]	0.6[j]	60	63	71
Sweden	10	0.6	23	17	535.0	56,210	420.1	44,150	0.0	80	84	..
Switzerland	8	0.9	200	15	661.6	82,730	449.8	56,240	−0.1	81	85	..
Syrian Arab Republic	22	2.6	122	35	56.3	2,610	116.5	5,200	0.8	74	77	83
Tajikistan	8	2.2	57	36	6.9	860	17.8	2,220	5.4	64	71	100
Tanzania	48	2.8	54	45	26.7	570[k]	73.6[k]	1,590[k]	3.7[k]	57	59	73
Thailand	67	0.6	131	18	347.9	5,210	630.0	9,430	6.1	71	78	94
Togo	7	2.6	122	42	3.3	500	6.1	920	2.9	56	59	57
Tunisia	11	1.0	69	23	44.8	4,150	100.9	9,360	2.6	73	77	78
Turkey	74	1.3	96	26	801.1	10,830	1,345.7	18,190	0.9	72	76	91
Turkmenistan	5	1.2	11	29	28.7	5,550	49.9[d]	9,640[d]	9.7	61	69	100
Uganda	36	3.4	182	49	16.0	440	41.4	1,140	0.0	53	55	73
Ukraine	46	−0.6	79	14	159.6	3,500	332.5	7,290	0.4	66	76	100
United Arab Emirates	9	9.3	110	14	*321.7*	*36,040*	*378.3*	*42,380*	*−0.8*	76	78	90
United Kingdom	63	0.6	261	18	2,418.5	38,250	2,331.9	36,880	−0.5	79	83	..
United States	314	0.9	34	20	15,734.6	50,120	15,887.6	50,610	1.5	76	81	..
Uruguay	3	0.2	19	22	45.9	13,510	52.9	15,570	3.6	73	80	98
Uzbekistan	30	1.6	70	29	51.3	1,720	111.6[d]	3,750[d]	6.6	65	71	99
Venezuela, RB	30	1.7	34	29	373.5	12,470	393.0	13,120	3.9	71	77	96
Vietnam	89	1.1	286	23	124.1	1,400	305.6	3,440	3.9	73	77	93
West Bank and Gaza	4	2.7	672	41	..	..[l]	..	..	..	71	75	95
Yemen, Rep.	24	2.6	45	41	*26.0*	*1,110*	*53.7*	*2,310*	−2.2	64	67	64
Zambia	14	2.8	19	47	19.1	1,350	22.8	1,620	4.0	49	49	71
Zimbabwe	14	0.8	35	40	9.3	680	..	..	2.2	52	50	92
World	**7,046s**	**1.2w**	**54w**	**26w**	**70,571.6t**	**10,015w**	**85,463.2t**	**12,129w**	**1.0w**	**68w**	**72w**	**84w**
Low income	846	2.2	56	39	494.1	584	1,173.7	1,387	3.6	58	61	61
Middle income	4,898	1.2	77	27	21,396.9	4,369	35,469.4	7,242	3.8	67	71	83
Lower middle income	2,507	1.6	122	31	4,706.2	1,877	9,808.1	3,912	2.5	64	68	71
Upper middle income	2,391	0.8	56	22	16,704.9	6,987	25,679.4	10,741	4.5	71	75	94
Low & middle income	5,744	1.3	73	29	21,902.7	3,813	36,624.4	6,376	3.6	66	70	80
High income	1,302	0.6	25	17	48,952.3	37,595	49,167.5	37,760	0.7	76	82	..

a. Calculated using the World Bank Atlas method.
b. PPP = purchasing power parity; see the technical notes.
c. Data are for the most recent year available.
d. The estimate is based on regression; others are extrapolated from the 2005 International Comparison Program benchmark estimates.
e. Estimated to be upper middle income ($4,086–$12,615).
f. Excludes Abkhazia and South Ossetia.
g. Excludes Transnistria.
h. Includes Former Spanish Sahara.
i. Estimated to be low income ($1,035 or less).
j. Excludes South Sudan.
k. Covers mainland Tanzania only.
l. Estimated to be lower middle income ($1,036–$4,085).

TABLE 2 *Key indicators of development for other economies*

	Population			Population age composition	Gross national income[a]	
	Thousands	Average annual growth, %	Density per sq. km	% ages 0–14	$ millions	$ per capita
	2012	2000–12	2012	2012	2012	2012
American Samoa	55	−0.4	276	..	..	..[d]
Andorra	78	1.5	167	..	..	..[e]
Antigua and Barbuda	89	1.1	202	25	1,126	12,640
Aruba	102	1.0	569	20	..	..[e]
Bahamas, The	372	1.9	37	22	*7,795*	*21,280*
Bahrain	1,318	5.7	1,734	20	*20,084*	*16,050*
Barbados	283	0.5	659	19	..	..[e]
Belize	324	2.6	14	34	*1,322*	*4,180*
Bermuda	65	0.4	1,296	..	*6,903*	*106,920*
Bhutan	742	2.3	19	29	1,797	2,420
Botswana	2,004	1.1	4	34	15,477	7,720
Brunei Darussalam	412	1.8	78	26	..	..[e]
Cape Verde	494	0.9	123	30	1,882	3,810
Cayman Islands	58	2.7	240	..	..	..[e]
Channel Islands	161	0.7	849	15	..	..[e]
Comoros	718	2.6	386	42	605	840
Cuba	11,271	0.1	106	17	..	..[d]
Curacao	152	1.1	342	20	..	..[e]
Cyprus	1,129	1.5	122	17	22,708[g]	26,000[g]
Djibouti	860	1.4	37	34	..	..[h]
Dominica	72	0.2	96	..	463	6,460
Equatorial Guinea	736	2.9	26	39	9,983	13,560
Estonia	1,339	−0.2	32	16	21,200	15,830
Faeroe Islands	50	0.5	35	..	..	..[e]
Fiji	875	0.6	48	29	3,675	4,200
French Polynesia	274	1.2	75	23	..	..[e]
Gabon	1,633	2.4	6	38	16,438	10,070
Gambia, The	1,791	3.1	177	46	912	510
Greenland	57	0.1	0[i]	..	..	..[e]
Grenada	105	0.3	310	27	750	7,110
Guam	163	0.4	302	27	..	..[e]
Guinea-Bissau	1,664	2.2	59	42	916	550
Guyana	795	0.6	4	37	2,710	3,410
Iceland	320	1.1	3	21	12,393	38,710
Isle of Man	85	0.9	150	..	..	..[e]
Jamaica	2,712	0.4	250	28	13,929	5,140
Kiribati	101	1.6	124	32	228	2,260
Korea, Dem. Rep.	24,763	0.7	206	22	..	..[j]
Kosovo	1,806	0.5	166	*27*	6,576	3,640
Kuwait	3,250	4.4	182	25	*133,824*	*44,730*
Latvia	2,025	−1.3	33	15	28,725	14,180
Lesotho	2,052	0.8	68	37	2,823	1,380
Liechtenstein	37	0.9	229	..	..	..[e]
Luxembourg	531	1.6	205	17	40,898	76,960
Macao SAR, China	557	2.1	19,885	12	*30,440*	*55,720*
Macedonia, FYR	2,106	0.2	83	17	9,877	4,690
Maldives	338	1.8	1,128	29	1,947	5,750
Malta	418	0.8	1,307	15	8,268	19,760
Marshall Islands	53	0.1	292	..	217	4,140
Mauritius	1,291	0.7	636	20	11,063	8,570
Micronesia, Fed. Sts.	103	−0.3	148	36	342	3,310
Monaco	38	1.3	18,790	..	..	..[e]
Mongolia	2,796	1.3	2	27	8,844	3,160
Montenegro	621	0.1	46	19	4,309	6,940
Namibia	2,259	1.5	3	37	12,813	5,670
New Caledonia	258	1.6	14	23	..	..[e]
Northern Mariana Islands	53	−2.1	116	..	..	..[e]
Oman	3,314	3.4	11	24	*53,598*	*19,120*
Palau	21	0.7	45	..	205	9,860
Puerto Rico	3,667	−0.3	413	20	66,002	18,000
Qatar	2,051	10.3	177	13	*150,427*	*78,720*
Samoa	189	0.7	67	38	608	3,220
San Marino	31	1.2	521	..	..	..[e]
São Tomé and Príncipe	188	2.5	196	42	249	1,320
Seychelles	88	0.7	191	22	1,022	11,640
Sint Maarten (Dutch part)	39	2.1	1,150	..	..	..[e]
Slovenia	2,058	0.3	102	14	46,737	22,710
Solomon Islands	550	2.4	20	40	620	1,130
St. Kitts and Nevis	54	1.4	206	..	714	13,330
St. Lucia	181	1.2	297	24	1,181	6,530
St. Martin (French part)	31	0.7	569	..	..	..[e]
St. Vincent and the Grenadines	109	0.1	280	26	698	6,380
Suriname	535	1.1	3	28	4,534	8,480
Swaziland	1,231	1.2	72	38	3,518	2,860
Timor-Leste	1,210	2.9	81	46	4,447	3,670
Tonga	105	0.6	146	37	445	4,240
Trinidad and Tobago	1,337	0.4	261	21	19,258	14,400
Turks and Caicos Islands	32	4.5	34	..	..	..[e]
Tuvalu	10	0.4	329	..	60	6,070
Vanuatu	247	2.4	20	37	762	3,080
Virgin Islands (U.S.)	105	−0.3	301	21	..	..[e]

a. Calculated using the World Bank Atlas method.
b. PPP = purchasing power parity; see the technical notes.
c. Data are for the most recent year available.
d. Estimated to be upper middle income ($4,086–$12,615).
e. Estimated to be high income ($12,616 or more).
f. The estimate is based on regression; others are extrapolated from the 2005 International Comparison Program benchmark estimates.
g. Data are for the area controlled by the government of Cyprus.
h. Estimated to be lower middle income ($1,036–$4,085).
i. Less than 0.5.
j. Estimated to be low income ($1,035 or less).

	Gross national income, PPP[b]		Gross domestic product per capita	Life expectancy at birth		Adult literacy rate
	$ millions	$ per capita	% growth	Years, male	Years, female	% ages 15 and older
	2012	2012	2012	2011	2011	2005–11[c]
American Samoa	..	..	..	..	..	..
Andorra	..	..	..	..	..	..
Antigua and Barbuda	1,715[f]	19,260[f]	1.3	..	..	99
Aruba	..	..	..	73	78	97
Bahamas, The	*10,895*[f]	*29,740*[f]	0.3	72	79	..
Bahrain	*26,802*	*21,420*	*-0.5*	75	76	92
Barbados	..	..	..	74	80	..
Belize	*2,175*[f]	*6,880*[f]	*-0.5*	75	78	..
Bermuda	..	..	*-2.0*	77	82	..
Bhutan	4,678	6,310	7.6	65	69	53
Botswana	33,114	16,520	5.2	54	52	84
Brunei Darussalam	..	..	0.7	76	80	95
Cape Verde	2,144	4,340	3.5	70	78	84
Cayman Islands	..	..	..	..	..	99
Channel Islands	..	..	..	78	82	..
Comoros	882	1,230	0.5	60	62	75
Cuba	..	..	*2.1*	77	81	100
Curacao	..	..	..	*72*	*80*	..
Cyprus	25,671[g]	29,400[g]	-4.9[g]	77	82	98
Djibouti	..	..	3.2	56	59	..
Dominica	874[f]	12,190[f]	-1.8	..	..	..
Equatorial Guinea	13,901	18,880	-0.3	50	52	94
Estonia	29,511	22,030	3.3	71	81	100
Faeroe Islands	..	..	..	79	85	..
Fiji	4,265	4,880	1.4	67	72	..
French Polynesia	..	..	..	73	78	..
Gabon	23,328	14,290	3.6	62	64	88
Gambia, The	3,327	1,860	2.7	57	60	50
Greenland	..	..	..	*68*	*73*	..
Grenada	1,087[f]	10,300[f]	-1.2	74	77	..
Guam	..	..	..	74	79	..
Guinea-Bissau	1,981	1,190	-3.8	47	50	54
Guyana	2,703[f]	3,400[f]	4.2	67	73	..
Iceland	10,832	33,840	1.3	81	84	..
Isle of Man	..	..	..	..	..	..
Jamaica	..	..	-0.5	71	76	87
Kiribati	341[f]	3,380[f]	0.9	..	..	..
Korea, Dem. Rep.	..	..	..	66	72	100
Kosovo	..	..	2.9	68	72	..
Kuwait	*147,287*	*49,230*	*3.6*	74	76	94
Latvia	42,567	21,020	7.3	69	79	100
Lesotho	4,528	2,210	2.8	49	47	90
Liechtenstein	..	..	..	..	..	..
Luxembourg	34,646	65,190	-2.2	79	84	..
Macao SAR, China	*37,533*	*68,710*	7.9	79	83	93
Macedonia, FYR	24,354	11,570	-0.3	73	77	97
Maldives	2,602	7,690	1.4	76	78	98
Malta	11,291	26,990	0.6	80	84	92
Marshall Islands	..	..	1.8	..	..	..
Mauritius	20,425	15,820	2.7	70	77	89
Micronesia, Fed. Sts.	423[f]	4,090[f]	1.4	68	70	..
Monaco	..	..	..	..	..	..
Mongolia	14,265	5,100	10.6	65	73	97
Montenegro	8,654	13,930	0.4	72	77	98
Namibia	16,880	7,470	3.0	62	63	89
New Caledonia	..	..	..	73	80	96
Northern Mariana Islands	..	..	..	..	..	..
Oman	*71,696*	*25,580*	*-2.2*	71	76	87
Palau	356[f]	17,150[f]	4.5	..	..	..
Puerto Rico	..	..	1.3	75	83	90
Qatar	*161,789*	*84,670*	*8.8*	79	78	96
Samoa	807[f]	4,270[f]	0.4	70	76	99
San Marino	..	..	..	80	86	..
São Tomé and Príncipe	349	1,850	1.3	63	66	89
Seychelles	2,262[f]	25,760[f]	2.5	70	77	92
Sint Maarten (Dutch part)	..	..	..	*73*	*78*	..
Slovenia	56,072	27,240	-2.6	77	83	100
Solomon Islands	1,192[f]	2,170[f]	1.7	66	69	..
St. Kitts and Nevis	926[f]	17,280[f]	-2.2	..	..	..
St. Lucia	1,993[f]	11,020[f]	-3.9	72	77	..
St. Martin (French part)	..	..	..	..	..	..
St. Vincent and the Grenadines	1,182[f]	10,810[f]	1.5	70	74	..
Suriname	4,541[f]	8,500[f]	3.5	67	74	95
Swaziland	5,958	4,840	-3.0	49	48	87
Timor-Leste	7,761[f]	6,410[f]	5.5	62	63	58
Tonga	540[f]	5,140[f]	0.4	69	75	99
Trinidad and Tobago	29,957[f]	22,400[f]	0.9	67	74	99
Turks and Caicos Islands	..	..	..	..	..	..
Tuvalu	..	..	1.0	..	..	..
Vanuatu	1,112[f]	4,500[f]	0.0	69	73	83
Virgin Islands (U.S.)	..	..	..	76	82	..

TABLE 3 *Selected risk indicators*

	Large recessions		Incidence of natural hazards (droughts, earthquakes, floods, storms)		Incidence of epidemics		Adult mortality rate		Homicide rate
	Years in recession		Total events		Total epidemics		Per 1,000 male	Per 1,000 female	Per 100,000 people
	1991–2000	2001–10	1993–2002	2003–12	1993–2002	2003–12	2007–11[a]	2007–11[a]	2010
Afghanistan	0	0	26	62	18	3	407	374	*2.4*
Albania	3	0	6	6	2	0	93	45	4.0
Algeria	4	0	17	29	1	0	123	99	1.5
Angola	3	0	9	22	7	9	382	333	*19.0*
Argentina	2	2	25	20	0	1	158	72	*3.4*
Armenia	0	1	4	1	0	0	160	78	1.4
Australia	0	0	47	46	0	1	81	47	1.0
Austria	0	0	11	8	0	0	100	48	0.6
Azerbaijan	0	0	8	5	0	0	178	68	2.2
Bangladesh	0	0	80	55	10	4	161	134	2.7
Belarus	0	0	4	1	2	0	334	112	*4.9*
Belgium	0	0	13	9	0	0	107	61	1.7
Benin	0	0	6	8	11	8	327	271	*15.1*
Bolivia	0	0	12	15	4	4	221	164	8.9
Bosnia and Herzegovina	0	0	3	9	1	0	132	68	1.5
Brazil	2	0	30	47	7	3	214	112	21.0
Bulgaria	5	1	6	15	0	0	197	88	2.0
Burkina Faso	0	0	5	11	7	9	296	246	*18.0*
Burundi	6	0	5	27	10	2	410	373	*21.7*
Cambodia	0	0	11	11	4	3	258	217	..
Cameroon	4	0	6	7	10	6	404	372	*19.7*
Canada	2	0	16	33	2	1	92	55	1.6
Central African Republic	4	4	6	13	6	2	456	422	*29.3*
Chad	3	4	7	13	5	13	368	313	*15.8*
Chile	0	0	17	15	0	0	121	56	3.2
China	0	0	188	234	3	3	135	86	1.0
Hong Kong SAR, China	1	0	10	8	0	1	72	36	0.5
Colombia	2	0	31	39	1	1	191	88	33.4
Congo, Dem. Rep.	10	1	8	19	31	34	405	351	*21.7*
Congo, Rep.	5	0	4	7	5	11	330	295	*30.8*
Costa Rica	0	0	16	21	1	0	109	57	11.3
Côte d'Ivoire	6	3	1	4	6	6	366	337	*56.9*
Croatia	0	2	3	7	0	0	136	55	1.4
Czech Republic	0	1	7	11	0	0	138	63	*1.7*
Denmark	0	2	2	3	0	0	107	65	*0.9*
Dominican Republic	1	0	9	30	2	4	197	129	24.9
Ecuador	1	0	16	13	6	2	159	83	18.2
Egypt, Arab Rep.	0	0	9	4	0	2	138	83	*1.2*
El Salvador	0	0	15	17	4	2	278	118	64.7
Eritrea	3	7	3	4	0	0	338	255	*17.8*
Ethiopia	3	2	24	28	9	7	298	252	*25.5*
Finland	3	2	..	..	..	..	123	56	2.2
France	0	0	37	21	0	1	116	54	*1.1*
Georgia	4	0	7	8	0	0	175	66	4.3
Germany	0	1	20	22	1	1	101	54	0.8
Ghana	0	0	5	8	8	5	250	220	*15.7*
Greece	0	0	21	13	0	0	99	45	1.5
Guatemala	0	0	18	23	3	0	223	120	41.4
Guinea	4	0	4	7	5	7	347	298	*22.5*
Haiti	1	5	15	48	0	4	260	231	6.9
Honduras	0	0	20	24	4	2	162	113	82.1
Hungary	3	1	9	9	0	0	229	99	1.3
India	0	0	85	133	28	8	251	164	3.4
Indonesia	2	0	68	119	11	7	199	163	*8.1*
Iran, Islamic Rep.	0	0	59	41	1	0	162	75	*3.0*
Iraq	1	3	1	7	1	4	296	127	*2.0*
Ireland	0	0	7	4	1	1	97	57	1.2
Israel	0	3	4	1	1	0	79	45	2.1
Italy	0	2	24	19	1	1	78	41	0.9
Japan	0	2	47	55	1	0	85	42	*0.4*
Jordan	1	0	5	0	0	0	141	98	..
Kazakhstan	0	0	4	7	3	0	361	145	8.8
Kenya	4	0	11	34	18	12	370	348	*20.1*
Korea, Rep.	1	0	25	21	2	1	84	39	2.6
Kyrgyz Republic	5	0	2	9	2	1	305	130	20.1
Lao PDR	0	0	11	5	4	1	203	162	*4.6*
Lebanon	0	0	1	1	0	0	148	100	2.2
Liberia	5	2	2	5	7	3	340	305	*10.1*
Libya	0	2	1	0	0	0	135	83	*2.9*
Lithuania	0	1	2	4	0	0	271	93	6.6
Madagascar	6	1	14	29	3	2	213	166	*8.1*
Malawi	3	2	12	23	8	3	396	400	*36.0*
Malaysia	1	0	14	22	8	2	144	73	..

	Poverty headcount ratio				Volatility of GDP growth per capita		Volatility of household consumption growth per capita		Risk preparation index
	$2.50 a day, PPP (% population)		$10 a day, PPP (% population)		Standard deviation		Standard deviation		0–100 scale
	1990[b]	2010[c]	1990[b]	2010[c]	1990s	2000s	1990s	2000s	2013
Afghanistan	..	..	..	..	..	5.40	..	..	11
Albania	..	11.0	..	91.7	15.75	1.67	13.53	10.11	60
Algeria	36.6	..	95.7	..	2.73	1.50	3.89	8.83	59
Angola	..	77.1	..	98.9	11.65	6.90	..	..	..
Argentina	5.1[d]	2.6[d]	56.7[d]	29.2[d]	5.56	6.75	..	7.84	60
Armenia	..	36.1	..	97.5	19.68	8.07	12.85	4.31	59
Australia	..	..	..	..	1.79	1.06	1.27	1.47	94
Austria	..	..	..	..	1.19	2.02	1.26	0.63	80
Azerbaijan	54.0	7.3	98.4	86.4	14.85	8.32	..	15.36	49
Bangladesh	95.0	86.2	99.9	99.6	0.72	0.85	2.28	1.14	34
Belarus	0.3	0.2	57.1	19.8	8.89	2.94	10.39	5.21	78
Belgium	..	..	..	..	1.41	1.76	1.02	0.86	86
Benin	..	84.4	..	99.3	1.02	0.92	5.71	..	24
Bolivia	27.8	31.0	88.1	82.5	1.55	1.40	0.94	1.43	39
Bosnia and Herzegovina	..	0.5	..	36.7	..	2.66	..	..	60
Brazil	37.6	15.1	81.0	65.4	2.97	2.28	3.12	2.34	58
Bulgaria	0.1	2.5	14.1	68.3	5.36	3.63	10.57	4.94	76
Burkina Faso	90.3	82.2	99.3	99.1	3.69	2.05	11.82	..	38
Burundi	97.4	96.1	100.0	100.0	4.88	2.06	..	..	22
Cambodia	84.4	64.5	99.3	98.3	..	3.04	..	3.95	30
Cameroon	..	42.9	..	95.2	4.70	0.78	5.39	3.53	37
Canada	..	..	..	..	2.50	1.97	1.86	1.15	84
Central African Republic	93.5	86.2	99.6	99.3	4.57	3.13	..	3.18	9
Chad	..	89.5	..	99.8	7.99	9.06	11.74	..	13
Chile	21.2	4.3	78.4	52.9	3.40	1.98	3.78	3.28	70
China	91.7	36.5	99.9	91.1	2.99	1.62	3.46	1.42	69
Hong Kong SAR, China	..	..	..	..	3.64	3.23	4.56	3.26	73
Colombia	21.1	22.0	79.5	75.5	3.00	1.72	4.29	2.06	53
Congo, Dem. Rep.	..	97.0	..	100.0	5.26	4.26	..	4.70	8
Congo, Rep.	..	81.8	..	98.7	3.21	2.93	32.03	14.30	27
Costa Rica	20.7	8.1	80.1	59.4	2.64	2.81	2.69	1.98	58
Côte d'Ivoire	48.5	58.7	97.2	97.4	3.50	2.67	4.60	..	19
Croatia	..	0.1	..	8.1	..	3.78	..	4.05	72
Czech Republic	..	..	..	..	5.20	3.05	..	..	88
Denmark	..	..	..	..	1.39	2.52	1.92	2.37	87
Dominican Republic	36.0	16.1	88.8	75.9	4.57	3.22	5.98	4.80	45
Ecuador	29.8	15.9	85.4	75.5	3.16	2.35	3.27	1.47	61
Egypt, Arab Rep.	44.1	32.0	97.8	97.7	1.45	1.71	0.93	2.95	63
El Salvador	37.1	23.1	87.9	83.0	1.60	1.87	6.41	4.34	53
Eritrea	..	..	..	..	..	8.36	..	..	..
Ethiopia	90.9	79.9	99.9	99.4	7.28	4.39	9.36	5.28	30
Finland	..	..	..	..	4.08	3.80	3.71	1.94	94
France	..	..	..	..	1.20	1.67	1.33	0.92	82
Georgia	..	46.6	..	95.7	23.68	4.31	..	..	61
Germany	..	..	..	..	1.71	2.51	1.18	0.80	87
Ghana	86.5	63.9	99.7	97.8	0.68	2.73	..	..	30
Greece	..	..	..	..	1.81	4.29	1.27	4.40	78
Guatemala	63.5	33.9	94.7	85.2	0.69	1.41	0.95	0.91	43
Guinea	99.9	79.5	100.0	99.3	2.09	1.57	5.05	..	5
Haiti	..	83.0	..	97.8	..	3.04	..	..	16
Honduras	64.1	36.5	95.8	81.8	2.76	2.36	2.13	2.79	47
Hungary	..	0.6	..	42.4	5.03	3.29	4.82	4.25	81
India	90.8	81.1	99.7	99.2	2.11	2.25	1.83	2.00	31
Indonesia	91.4	60.4	99.9	98.4	6.85	0.91	5.94	1.10	42
Iran, Islamic Rep.	20.3	14.8	83.8	85.1	4.47	1.98	2.69	..	73
Iraq	..	36.4	..	97.4	..	20.52	..	..	38
Ireland	..	..	..	..	3.02	4.12	2.43	3.98	85
Israel	..	..	..	..	1.19	2.79	..	2.36	76
Italy	..	..	..	..	0.99	2.43	1.85	1.15	72
Japan	..	..	..	..	2.02	2.49	1.45	0.98	80
Jordan	24.6	5.4	89.3	81.9	5.25	2.10	11.89	5.08	64
Kazakhstan	..	4.2	..	87.4	6.41	3.78	11.39	4.34	78
Kenya	68.6	76.6	97.3	98.4	1.88	2.15	4.32	3.02	29
Korea, Rep.	..	..	..	..	4.77	2.09	7.16	3.25	78
Kyrgyz Republic	37.2	34.4	86.5	96.5	10.66	3.19	13.36	9.74	55
Lao PDR	..	78.1	..	99.1	1.34	1.09	..	5.05	38
Lebanon	..	..	..	..	10.77	3.16	..	3.84	40
Liberia	..	97.0	..	99.9	38.04	16.65	..	16.98	10
Libya	..	..	..	..	..	4.74	..	..	..
Lithuania	..	0.9	..	41.7	11.52	6.88	..	9.36	79
Madagascar	92.7	95.4	99.6	99.8	3.11	6.20	3.15	3.80	12
Malawi	..	88.5	..	99.4	7.62	3.82	..	..	39
Malaysia	18.3	6.2	80.8	55.1	5.18	2.71	6.28	3.21	67

TABLE 3 *Selected risk indicators* (continued)

	Large recessions		Incidence of natural hazards (droughts, earthquakes, floods, storms)		Incidence of epidemics		Adult mortality rate		Homicide rate
	Years in recession		Total events		Total epidemics		Per 1,000 male	Per 1,000 female	Per 100,000 people
	1991–2000	2001–10	1993–2002	2003–12	1993–2002	2003–12	2007–11[a]	2007–11[a]	2010
Mali	2	0	7	15	4	6	356	293	*8.0*
Mauritania	5	2	9	11	2	1	286	217	*14.7*
Mexico	1	2	68	55	1	1	130	72	22.7
Moldova	8	1	7	5	1	0	300	145	7.5
Morocco	3	0	11	12	0	0	141	89	1.4
Mozambique	1	0	17	28	9	11	477	443	..
Myanmar	0	0	7	14	0	1	231	181	*10.2*
Nepal	0	0	10	18	11	3	182	155	*2.8*
Netherlands	0	0	7	4	1	0	75	56	*1.1*
New Zealand	1	0	11	11	0	1	87	58	1.1
Nicaragua	3	0	21	17	6	2	194	109	13.6
Niger	5	0	9	13	15	14	309	267	*3.8*
Nigeria	0	0	18	24	23	16	387	359	*12.2*
Norway	0	0	4	3	0	0	82	50	0.6
Pakistan	0	0	31	46	6	3	188	157	7.6
Panama	0	0	8	21	2	0	131	69	21.6
Papua New Guinea	5	3	15	13	4	3	310	233	*13.0*
Paraguay	3	3	8	10	1	7	166	119	11.5
Peru	0	0	23	21	4	3	156	96	*10.3*
Philippines	3	0	100	163	5	7	257	142	*5.4*
Poland	0	0	7	13	0	0	198	76	1.1
Portugal	0	0	7	6	0	0	122	53	1.2
Romania	5	1	18	29	2	1	179	73	*2.0*
Russian Federation	1	1	49	37	9	1	367	137	10.2
Rwanda	2	0	6	8	7	2	345	312	*17.1*
Saudi Arabia	3	2	1	10	3	0	122	94	..
Senegal	4	0	8	11	4	3	287	235	*8.7*
Serbia	1	0	6	4	2	0	147	81	1.2
Sierra Leone	6	0	2	6	10	4	459	438	*14.9*
Singapore	1	2	0	0	2	1	75	44	0.4
Slovak Republic	3	1	5	7	0	0	184	74	*1.5*
Somalia	0	0	12	25	14	9	365	309	*1.5*
South Africa	3	0	28	20	4	3	572	574	31.8
South Sudan	0	0	..	..	..	..	..	..	..
Spain	0	3	16	12	2	1	94	43	0.8
Sri Lanka	0	0	17	24	3	3	182	78	3.6
Sudan	0	0	17	17	11	17	262	208	*24.2*
Sweden	3	2	2	1	1	1	71	44	1.0
Switzerland	0	0	9	10	0	1	76	42	0.7
Syrian Arab Republic	1	0	2	3	0	0	108	70	2.3
Tajikistan	6	1	16	18	3	2	221	125	2.1
Tanzania	4	0	17	21	12	8	351	331	*24.5*
Thailand	2	0	44	38	1	5	201	99	5.3
Togo	6	2	5	6	6	3	335	292	*10.9*
Tunisia	0	0	..	..	..	..	121	68	*1.1*
Turkey	1	3	29	32	0	2	133	74	*3.3*
Turkmenistan	7	0	2	0	0	0	302	158	..
Uganda	0	0	13	15	11	17	393	377	*36.3*
Ukraine	8	1	11	9	3	0	334	128	5.2
United Arab Emirates	5	0	..	..	..	..	89	67	..
United Kingdom	0	2	27	19	1	1	95	58	*1.2*
United States	0	2	211	184	3	1	135	79	4.8
Uruguay	2	2	10	5	0	0	130	58	6.1
Uzbekistan	6	0	1	2	1	0	242	138	*3.1*
Venezuela, RB	4	4	12	17	1	1	169	87	45.1
Vietnam	0	0	48	67	3	5	129	87	*1.6*
West Bank and Gaza	0	0	..	..	..	..	140	103	..
Yemen, Rep.	0	0	13	12	1	1	226	182	*4.2*
Zambia	6	0	4	12	7	7	486	489	*38.0*
Zimbabwe	4	7	6	10	10	10	517	571	*14.3*
World	**1u**	**1u**	**2,561s**	**3,132s**	**560s**	**425s**	**207w**	**147w**	**5.7w**
Low income	3	1	387	640	275	214	291	254	*14.5*
Middle income	1	0	1,431	1,809	251	191	199	134	6.2
Lower middle income	2	0	659	888	179	133	240	171	*4.8*
Upper middle income	1	0	772	921	72	58	160	100	7.2
Low & middle income	2	1	1,818	2,449	526	405	210	150	*5.8*
High income	0	1	743	683	34	20	147	72	4.0

a. Data are for the most recent year available between 2007 and 2011.
b. Country data are for the year closest to 1990 between 1985 and 1995.
c. Country data are for the most recent year available between 2001 and 2011.
d. Urban only.
e. Based on the 1990 income classification.

	Poverty headcount ratio				Volatility of GDP growth per capita		Volatility of household consumption growth per capita		Risk preparation index
	$2.50 a day, PPP (% population)		$10 a day, PPP (% population)		Standard deviation		Standard deviation		0–100 scale
	1990[b]	2010[c]	1990[b]	2010[c]	1990s	2000s	1990s	2000s	2013
Mali	95.9	87.2	99.7	100.0	3.52	2.45	4.31	..	18
Mauritania	74.9	60.9	99.0	97.8	4.57	4.97	..	8.88	19
Mexico	21.8	8.8	77.9	67.5	3.61	3.32	7.08	3.74	56
Moldova	..	10.7	..	87.8	14.13	3.92	..	8.19	57
Morocco	26.3	24.5	90.6	91.6	6.22	1.84	7.05	2.14	51
Mozambique	..	88.4	..	99.5	4.72	2.37	7.08	6.86	12
Myanmar	..	..	..	..	3.17	..	..	..	30
Nepal	..	71.8	..	99.3	1.44	1.58	..	..	23
Netherlands	..	..	..	..	1.15	2.12	1.67	1.44	93
New Zealand	..	..	..	..	3.31	1.90	3.07	1.77	89
Nicaragua	46.0	43.8	93.1	95.1	3.02	1.93	13.59	1.94	39
Niger	94.8	85.0	99.8	99.5	4.18	3.26	6.22	..	18
Nigeria	86.9	86.3	100.0	99.8	2.13	2.41	..	..	27
Norway	..	..	..	..	1.24	1.72	1.52	1.72	94
Pakistan	93.3	76.4	99.9	99.3	1.82	1.95	3.79	4.90	33
Panama	34.0	18.8	79.7	72.1	2.53	3.55	8.77	5.82	56
Papua New Guinea	..	..	..	..	7.62	3.60	12.39	..	22
Paraguay	7.7	18.4	68.5	73.2	1.91	5.36	3.82	6.12	50
Peru	..	18.3	..	73.2	5.04	3.08	5.22	2.24	52
Philippines	66.4	53.3	97.4	95.5	2.35	1.73	0.92	1.02	45
Poland	0.6	0.5	68.1	48.7	4.43	1.71	1.91	1.29	76
Portugal	..	..	..	..	2.20	1.77	2.06	2.10	77
Romania	..	4.3	..	85.3	6.42	4.97	8.12	7.56	65
Russian Federation	12.9	0.3	70.7	45.4	6.54	4.58	3.31	4.92	71
Rwanda	93.6	88.3	100.0	99.8	24.31	2.70	8.77	5.47	26
Saudi Arabia	..	..	..	..	2.89	2.50	..	..	83
Senegal	86.9	67.5	99.0	98.3	2.54	1.68	3.31	4.49	26
Serbia	..	1.3	..	61.3	17.42	2.98	..	4.75	61
Sierra Leone	80.8	87.6	99.1	99.6	9.09	5.54	..	..	14
Singapore	..	..	..	..	3.73	4.99	4.31	3.57	72
Slovak Republic	..	0.2	..	44.1	7.16	3.71	..	2.63	79
Somalia	..	..	..	..	..	..	..	..	..
South Africa	48.9	39.5	85.5	79.5	2.01	1.91	2.16	2.58	45
South Sudan	..	..	..	..	..	..	..	..	..
Spain	..	..	..	..	1.69	2.19	1.96	2.41	82
Sri Lanka	66.4	38.2	98.9	96.1	1.00	1.98	4.32	2.91	51
Sudan	..	58.5	..	98.8	4.19	1.90	1.76	5.71	22
Sweden	..	..	..	..	2.65	3.03	2.64	1.73	96
Switzerland	..	..	..	..	1.58	1.85	1.03	0.70	87
Syrian Arab Republic	..	29.0	..	94.2	4.07	1.90	6.97	..	46
Tajikistan	..	42.2	..	98.3	13.22	9.17	30.57	3.96	46
Tanzania	95.2	92.8	100.0	99.8	2.09	0.72	4.47	34.86	32
Thailand	50.1	9.6	93.9	81.2	6.62	2.79	6.88	2.02	62
Togo	..	64.9	..	98.6	8.93	2.47	12.54	6.51	28
Tunisia	28.5	8.3	92.0	78.8	2.03	2.28	2.03	2.41	59
Turkey	14.7	8.3	84.9	67.9	4.87	5.12	5.17	5.09	70
Turkmenistan	67.5	..	100.0	..	15.40	4.36	..	..	..
Uganda	90.9	76.0	99.7	98.7	2.27	1.80	3.35	3.91	25
Ukraine	14.2	0.2	84.3	56.3	7.73	7.07	9.87	9.00	71
United Arab Emirates	..	..	..	..	4.79	6.08	..	8.11	88
United Kingdom	..	..	..	..	1.77	2.41	2.11	2.61	82
United States	..	..	..	..	1.55	2.03	1.55	1.77	91
Uruguay	3.8	2.8	48.6	48.5	3.66	5.03	5.64	8.20	73
Uzbekistan	..	..	..	..	5.41	1.82	..	..	54
Venezuela, RB	20.2	18.8	83.2	80.2	4.66	7.67	4.42	8.17	52
Vietnam	91.3	58.2	99.8	98.2	1.72	0.91	..	2.39	56
West Bank and Gaza	..	1.3	..	65.1	..	..	..	..	46
Yemen, Rep.	..	61.7	..	98.4	1.19	4.64	..	..	30
Zambia	82.0	90.6	99.0	99.3	4.68	1.27	17.90	15.81	25
Zimbabwe	..	..	..	..	5.58	8.99	..	..	25
World	w	w	w	w	3.23 w	2.42 w	3.45 w	2.70 w	55 u
Low income	90.0	83.2	99.4	99.3	3.83	2.88	..	..	23
Middle income	73.6	48.1	95.1	89.8	3.32	2.32	3.61	2.47	52
Lower middle income	82.1	68.5	98.4	97.2	2.98	2.14	3.11	2.56	43
Upper middle income	65.8	26.8	92.0	82.0	3.64	2.50	4.03	2.38	61
Low & middle income	71.7[e]	50.0[e]	94.2[e]	88.8[e]	3.37	2.38	3.79	2.83	44
High income	..	..	..	..	2.72	2.58	2.22	2.21	81

TABLE 4 *Selected indicators related to risk management at the household level*

	Educational attainment			Education quality		Under-five mortality rate	Maternal mortality ratio	Access to social insurance		Savings
	% of adults 25+ with complete primary	% of adults 25+ with complete secondary	% of adults 25+ with complete tertiary	PISA mean score, math	PISA mean score, reading	Per 1,000 live births	Per 100,000 live births	Survey year	% coverage, adults 60+	% of people who saved in the past year
	2010	2010	2010	2009	2009	2011	2010			2011
Afghanistan	8.2	5.2	5.3	..	..	101	460	2006	8.5	14.6
Albania	9.6	30.6	5.0	377	385	14	27	2009	103.7	22.7
Algeria	1.4	34.5	5.6	..	..	30	97	2002	42.9	20.9
Angola	..	..	..	..	..	158	450	..	..	36.6
Argentina	32.0	30.8	3.3	388	398	14	77	2010	103.8	24.4
Armenia	4.8	64.6	12.7	..	..	18	30	2008	74.2	10.5
Australia	2.1	39.0	22.4	514	515	5	7	..	..	68.3
Austria	17.2	45.3	9.5	496	470	4	4	2006	85.1	78.3
Azerbaijan	..	..	..	431	362	45	43	2007	104.6	10.8
Bangladesh	21.5	18.4	3.0	..	..	46	240	2011	73.6	26.8
Belarus	..	..	..	..	..	6	4	2008	116.0	26.4
Belgium	11.1	33.3	20.4	515	506	4	8	2006	61.1	57.8
Benin	10.1	12.4	2.0	..	..	106	350	2004	2.9	32.4
Bolivia	11.8	35.5	9.5	..	..	51	190	2007	70.0	44.2
Bosnia and Herzegovina	..	..	..	..	..	8	8	2009	22.2	13.5
Brazil	26.2	25.1	5.2	386	412	16	56	2010	68.7	21.1
Bulgaria	24.4	27.1	12.1	428	429	12	11	2008	92.4	10.9
Burkina Faso	..	..	..	..	..	146	300	2005	2.6	38.0
Burundi	20.7	3.4	0.6	..	..	139	800	2004	6.3	25.2
Cambodia	33.3	5.3	0.5	..	..	43	250	2005	2.9	31.0
Cameroon	31.0	13.5	1.6	..	..	127	690	2002	4.4	51.9
Canada	2.6	37.5	28.0	527	524	6	12	2007	54.5	65.5
Central African Republic	16.5	8.5	1.2	..	..	164	890	2003	4.4	25.4
Chad	..	..	..	..	..	169	1,100	2001	0.6	28.7
Chile	13.6	29.7	11.7	421	449	9	25	2010	60.9	27.1
China	17.7	40.3	3.9	..	..	15	37	2010	59.2	38.4
Hong Kong SAR, China	14.3	35.4	7.3	555	533	..	..	2005	38.5	59.0
Colombia	28.9	31.8	8.5	381	413	18	92	2010	17.8	32.9
Congo, Dem. Rep.	8.4	7.9	1.1	..	..	168	540	..	..	24.1
Congo, Rep.	8.0	8.9	1.3	..	..	99	560	2001	5.6	30.4
Costa Rica	29.7	19.4	13.2	..	..	10	40	2009	42.9	41.0
Côte d'Ivoire	17.8	6.4	3.9	..	..	115	400	2004	6.6	..
Croatia	17.1	29.2	5.3	460	476	5	17	2010	60.6	21.9
Czech Republic	10.0	65.2	5.6	493	478	4	5	2007	91.6	49.0
Denmark	28.3	26.8	12.5	503	495	4	12	2006	82.7	72.6
Dominican Republic	7.8	8.1	4.5	..	..	25	150	2008	5.7	37.3
Ecuador	29.1	16.1	10.5	..	..	23	110	2009	38.4	30.2
Egypt, Arab Rep.	6.4	22.3	5.7	..	..	21	66	2004	31.1	8.1
El Salvador	15.9	16.9	8.5	..	..	15	81	2010	14.6	25.9
Eritrea	..	..	..	..	..	68	240	..	..	..
Ethiopia	..	..	..	..	..	77	350	..	..	..
Finland	22.1	26.4	13.1	541	536	3	5	2006	81.2	68.7
France	6.5	40.1	10.6	497	496	4	8	2006	103.1	61.8
Georgia	..	..	..	..	..	21	67	..	..	7.0
Germany	2.8	55.4	12.8	513	497	4	7	2006	86.1	67.3
Ghana	8.0	17.5	2.1	..	..	78	350	2010	8.1	36.6
Greece	28.2	32.3	22.4	466	483	4	3	2006	75.1	27.8
Guatemala	16.4	9.7	2.2	..	..	30	120	2008	6.9	24.8
Guinea	..	..	..	..	..	126	610	2001	2.9	27.1
Haiti	4.6	22.4	0.8	..	..	70	350	..	..	31.6
Honduras	35.3	13.3	4.0	..	..	21	100	2009	2.7	21.8
Hungary	3.9	52.2	12.6	490	494	6	21	2008	95.3	26.7
India	16.6	0.8	4.1	..	..	61	200	2010	23.7	22.4
Indonesia	32.0	11.1	1.7	371	402	32	220	2010	5.6	40.5
Iran, Islamic Rep.	12.5	24.4	12.9	..	..	25	21	2001	16.3	32.3
Iraq	20.4	11.8	6.5	..	..	38	63	2009	3.9	26.2
Ireland	10.9	32.4	20.2	487	496	4	6	2006	56.7	64.6
Israel	17.0	26.1	24.3	447	474	4	7	..	..	44.9
Italy	19.0	32.5	6.6	483	486	4	4	2006	84.6	26.4
Japan	14.0	30.3	24.0	529	520	3	5	2003	83.5	63.3
Jordan	8.0	38.0	6.4	387	405	21	63	2006	19.2	18.2
Kazakhstan	3.2	39.5	11.8	405	390	28	51	2009	106.8	21.9
Kenya	40.7	0.6	2.0	..	..	73	360	2006	6.9	40.1
Korea, Rep.	10.2	36.8	17.9	546	539	5	16	2005	28.1	64.5
Kyrgyz Republic	10.1	35.9	8.4	331	314	31	71	2008	103.9	36.4
Lao PDR	20.8	5.7	3.2	..	..	42	470	2005	5.7	54.5
Lebanon	..	..	..	..	..	9	25	2003	9.1	30.8
Liberia	6.2	5.8	5.3	..	..	78	770	..	..	34.9
Libya	21.4	19.4	10.3	..	..	16	58	..	..	..
Lithuania	4.0	55.5	16.4	477	468	6	8	2010	102.3	32.7

TABLE 4 *Selected indicators related to risk management at the household level* (continued)

	Educational attainment			Education quality		Under-five mortality rate	Maternal mortality ratio	Access to social insurance		Savings
	% of adults 25+ with complete primary	% of adults 25+ with complete secondary	% of adults 25+ with complete tertiary	PISA mean score, math	PISA mean score, reading	Per 1,000 live births	Per 100,000 live births	Survey year	% coverage, adults 60+	% of people who saved in the past year
	2010	2010	2010	2009	2009	2011	2010			2011
Madagascar	..	..	..	..	..	62	240	..	..	19.7
Malawi	12.6	8.1	0.3	..	..	83	460	..	..	33.0
Malaysia	12.9	33.8	5.0	..	..	7	29	2007	54.7	51.0
Mali	6.3	2.5	1.2	..	..	176	540	2010	20.0	37.4
Mauritania	23.7	6.3	1.5	..	..	112	510	2002	6.8	22.9
Mexico	18.9	17.7	13.9	419	425	16	50	2010	18.6	27.1
Moldova	4.5	39.2	9.0	..	..	16	41	2009	83.3	22.2
Morocco	17.5	9.9	5.9	..	..	33	100	2007	13.2	30.5
Mozambique	12.5	1.6	0.3	..	..	103	490	2004	8.8	42.6
Myanmar	24.3	9.0	4.0	..	..	62	200	..	..	..
Nepal	9.8	6.3	2.0	..	..	48	170	2006	39.2	18.4
Netherlands	7.6	40.5	16.5	526	508	4	6	2007	77.5	73.1
New Zealand	20.7	15.9	24.4	519	521	6	15	2007	68.5	72.6
Nicaragua	8.1	11.5	10.0	..	..	26	95	2008	13.8	26.1
Niger	9.8	2.1	0.7	..	..	125	590	2006	4.8	25.1
Nigeria	..	..	..	..	..	124	630	..	..	64.4
Norway	0.5	45.7	14.6	498	503	3	7	2006	70.3	..
Pakistan	14.3	19.0	5.2	..	..	72	260	2012	4.1	7.5
Panama	21.3	24.6	16.4	360	371	20	92	2009	32.0	34.9
Papua New Guinea	40.8	4.7	0.8	..	..	58	230	2005	0.8	..
Paraguay	25.4	30.4	3.1	..	..	22	99	2004	2.9	18.1
Peru	7.2	27.5	16.6	365	370	18	67	2008	20.0	29.1
Philippines	18.0	19.9	22.4	..	..	25	99	2007	13.0	45.5
Poland	15.9	11.4	9.1	495	500	6	5	2009	71.7	30.8
Portugal	42.4	13.6	3.8	487	489	3	8	2006	86.7	33.7
Romania	1.4	40.2	6.5	427	424	13	27	2009	76.7	18.2
Russian Federation	2.4	30.2	23.3	468	459	12	34	2007	120.5	22.7
Rwanda	27.0	3.4	0.7	..	..	54	340	2004	7.0	30.5
Saudi Arabia	15.3	24.0	8.7	..	..	9	24	..	..	33.4
Senegal	31.1	6.0	2.3	..	..	65	370	2010	34.5	15.4
Serbia	25.5	28.4	7.6	442	442	7	12	2007	32.7	14.9
Sierra Leone	8.7	1.2	0.9	..	..	185	890	..	..	32.6
Singapore	16.6	15.8	12.2	562	526	3	3	2009	30.1	60.9
Slovak Republic	10.6	36.7	6.5	497	477	8	6	2008	115.1	49.3
Somalia	..	..	..	..	..	180	1,000	..	..	21.8
South Africa	6.2	22.0	0.6	..	..	47	300	2010	81.7	31.5
South Sudan	..	..	..	..	..	121	..	..	..	..
Spain	18.9	21.9	16.6	483	481	4	6	2006	67.9	46.3
Sri Lanka	8.4	47.1	10.5	..	..	12	35	2010	20.9	36.3
Sudan	25.7	4.1	1.7	..	..	86[a]	730	2003	4.0	22.7
Sweden	8.2	52.3	16.7	494	497	3	4	2006	81.4	82.8
Switzerland	15.6	41.4	12.4	534	501	4	8	..	..	..
Syrian Arab Republic	14.5	5.2	2.3	..	..	15	70	..	..	48.3
Tajikistan	4.9	43.7	4.6	..	..	63	65	2004	98.5	13.8
Tanzania	49.0	1.2	0.6	..	..	68	460	2005	0.1	40.1
Thailand	27.4	10.1	8.8	419	421	12	48	2010	73.5	60.0
Togo	21.4	12.2	1.8	..	..	110	300	2003	3.7	19.6
Tunisia	18.0	15.1	6.2	371	404	16	56	2005	34.6	25.1
Turkey	45.8	17.7	5.9	445	464	15	20	2008	92.2	9.6
Turkmenistan	..	..	..	..	..	53	67	..	..	44.5
Uganda	24.5	3.1	2.6	..	..	90	310	2003	0.5	44.4
Ukraine	4.2	41.3	25.3	..	..	10	32	2010	111.3	25.0
United Arab Emirates	11.7	32.1	10.1	..	..	7	12	..	..	30.1
United Kingdom	24.2	1.3	13.6	492	494	5	12	..	..	56.7
United States	1.9	36.2	31.6	487	500	8	21	2008	58.1	66.8
Uruguay	35.3	18.6	6.4	427	426	10	29	2010	65.3	16.9
Uzbekistan	..	..	..	..	..	49	28	2005	136.1	31.4
Venezuela, RB	27.9	4.6	4.1	..	..	15	92	2006	18.6	28.4
Vietnam	38.5	11.4	3.0	..	..	22	59	2008	30.7	35.3
West Bank and Gaza	..	..	..	..	..	22	64	2009	5.5	16.2
Yemen, Rep.	8.6	6.1	1.9	..	..	77	200	2006	8.5	11.9
Zambia	29.8	10.0	1.0	..	..	83	440	2003	4.2	32.2
Zimbabwe	21.8	9.4	0.7	..	..	67	570	2005	3.7	39.9
World	16.7 w	24.1 w	8.7w			51w	210w		46.0w	35.9w
Low income	21.0	10.2	2.3			95	410		..	29.9
Middle income	18.9	22.4	5.3			46	190		40.0	31.0
Lower middle income	18.7	8.1	5.2			62	260		22.3	27.5
Upper middle income	19.1	33.8	5.4			20	64		56.8	34.5
Low & middle income	19.1	21.3	5.1			56	240		39.1	30.9
High income	9.3	32.9	20.0			6	16		77.0	53.9

a. Excludes South Sudan.

TABLE 5 *Selected indicators related to risk management at the enterprise sector level*

	Wage employment: Wage and salaried workers, % of total employed, annual average		Goods market efficiency: 1–7 scale		Labor market efficiency: 1–7 scale		Pension contributors		Formal production: % of economy, annual average	
	1991–2000	2001–10	2006–07	2012–13	2006–07	2012–13	Survey year	% of labor force	1999–2003	2004–07
Afghanistan	..	..	..	..	..	..	2006	3.7	..	..
Albania	..	..	3.46	4.33	4.05	4.40	2008	37.9	65.0	66.6
Algeria	..	46	3.66	2.99	3.52	2.79	2007	74.6	66.4	68.8
Angola	..	..	..	..	..	..	..	..	51.9	55.5
Argentina	71	75	3.66	3.18	3.44	3.29	2010	47.0	73.9	75.8
Armenia	55	52	3.74	4.22	4.59	4.72	2008	32.1	54.7	57.6
Australia	85	87	5.39	4.87	4.84	4.60	2005	90.7	85.8	86.4
Austria	86	87	5.33	4.91	4.47	4.69	2005	93.7	90.2	90.3
Azerbaijan	..	37	3.81	4.31	4.47	4.80	2007	35.4	39.8	44.7
Bangladesh	13	14	3.88	4.10	4.12	3.91	2004	2.5	64.3	65.2
Belarus	..	..	..	..	..	..	2008	93.5	52.2	55.3
Belgium	83	85	5.18	5.12	4.02	4.54	2005	91.4	77.8	78.4
Benin	..	10	3.60	3.66	3.76	4.40	2005	5.5	50.0	50.5
Bolivia	48	35	3.16	3.40	3.73	3.58	2009	12.2	32.6	35.6
Bosnia and Herzegovina	..	73	3.52	3.92	4.21	4.08	2009	24.5	66.0	66.9
Brazil	62	64	3.82	3.94	3.91	4.39	2010	59.3	60.0	62.2
Bulgaria	83	86	3.75	4.17	4.12	4.54	2008	78.7	63.5	66.2
Burkina Faso	4	6	3.70	3.80	4.18	4.42	2009	..	58.9	60.2
Burundi	6	5	2.94	3.28	4.21	3.97	2006	3.5	60.6	60.4
Cambodia	15	21	3.97	4.42	4.76	4.78	2010	0.5	50.1	52.7
Cameroon	14	19	3.55	4.15	3.82	4.48	2006	16.2	67.5	68.5
Canada	84	86	5.34	5.12	5.21	5.45	2009	87.4	84.1	84.6
Central African Republic	..	..	..	..	..	..	2003	1.5	56.1	53.7
Chad	5	..	2.67	3.08	3.73	4.12	2005	2.7	54.6	58.4
Chile	70	71	4.94	4.74	4.87	4.68	2010	57.7	80.3	81.2
China	..	..	4.17	4.31	4.27	4.60	2010	33.5	87.0	87.7
Hong Kong SAR, China	89	88	5.80	5.44	5.59	5.65	2009	78.9	83.4	84.7
Colombia	65	49	3.94	3.98	4.20	4.17	2010	27.8	61.2	64.6
Congo, Dem. Rep.	..	..	..	..	..	..	2009	..	52.3	53.2
Congo, Rep.	..	22	..	..	..	..	2008	9.7	52.3	55.3
Costa Rica	71	71	4.27	4.30	4.72	4.51	2010	58.6	73.8	74.9
Côte d'Ivoire	..	20	..	3.78	..	4.38	2004	12.8	55.9	53.5
Croatia	74	77	3.99	3.85	4.25	4.00	2010	76.0	67.0	69.0
Czech Republic	86	83	4.69	4.53	4.62	4.32	2007	95.4	81.0	82.4
Denmark	90	91	5.45	5.03	5.45	5.22	2007	92.9	81.9	82.7
Dominican Republic	56	52	3.67	3.97	3.99	4.00	2010	26.9	67.8	68.6
Ecuador	54	53	3.27	3.70	3.61	3.49	2007	26.4	66.3	69.2
Egypt, Arab Rep.	59	60	3.96	3.76	3.22	3.06	2009	55.1	64.6	65.8
El Salvador	55	55	4.39	4.21	4.53	3.86	2010	22.9	54.0	56.0
Eritrea	..	..	..	..	..	..	..	..	60.5	59.1
Ethiopia	7	8	3.44	3.79	4.13	4.18	..	..	60.0	63.1
Finland	85	87	5.40	5.05	4.70	5.00	2005	89.7	82.0	82.7
France	87	89	5.10	4.47	4.06	4.41	2005	87.3	84.8	85.2
Georgia	41	35	3.75	4.18	4.25	4.67	..	..	32.8	35.9
Germany	89	88	5.31	4.92	4.35	4.51	2005	86.9	83.9	84.3
Ghana	..	20	..	4.20	..	4.08	2012	8.7	58.3	60.7
Greece	55	63	4.28	3.92	3.63	3.56	2005	86.0	71.8	73.3
Guatemala	51	43	3.72	4.29	3.68	4.16	2008	20.3	48.7	50.6
Guinea	..	..	..	3.71	..	4.49	2005	12.1	60.8	61.3
Haiti	..	..	..	3.03	..	4.24	2010	8.1	44.2	42.9
Honduras	48	47	3.45	4.10	3.96	3.52	2009	17.3	50.4	53.3
Hungary	85	87	4.42	4.28	4.50	4.27	2008	92.0	75.2	76.1
India	15	17	4.60	4.21	3.90	4.24	2006	10.3	77.2	78.6
Indonesia	34	33	4.69	4.29	4.34	3.87	2010	11.0	80.6	81.6
Iran, Islamic Rep.	52	52	..	4.00	..	3.18	2010	40.5	81.2	82.3
Iraq	..	..	..	..	..	..	2009	43.1	..	..
Ireland	78	83	5.48	5.24	4.85	5.00	2005	88.9	84.0	84.4
Israel	85	87	5.08	4.51	4.93	4.61	2008	89.1	77.5	78.6
Italy	71	73	4.30	4.29	3.55	3.72	2005	90.1	72.9	73.1
Japan	81	85	5.21	4.98	5.20	4.89	2005	95.4	88.7	89.4
Jordan	..	83	4.42	4.50	4.04	4.02	2010	52.9	80.9	82.3
Kazakhstan	..	63	4.28	4.24	4.93	4.98	2009	62.5	57.5	60.6
Kenya	33	..	4.00	4.10	4.19	4.62	2009	..	65.7	68.3
Korea, Rep.	62	67	4.83	4.75	4.40	4.35	2011	79.9	72.6	73.9
Kyrgyz Republic	..	48	3.50	3.78	4.26	4.36	2008	40.4	58.9	60.4
Lao PDR	10	12	..	..	..	..	2008	1.4	69.7	71.3
Lebanon	..	62	..	4.57	..	4.00	2003	34.5	66.3	67.6
Liberia	..	17	..	4.54	..	4.45	..	..	56.3	55.3
Libya	..	..	..	3.45	..	3.46	2003	68.5	65.4	67.5
Lithuania	80	84	4.38	4.36	4.43	4.41	2009	82.9	66.9	69.3

TABLE 5 *Selected indicators related to risk management at the enterprise sector level* (continued)

	Wage employment: Wage and salaried workers, % of total employed, annual average		Goods market efficiency: 1–7 scale		Labor market efficiency: 1–7 scale		Pension contributors		Formal production: % of economy, annual average	
	1991–2000	2001–10	2006–07	2012–13	2006–07	2012–13	Survey year	% of labor force	1999–2003	2004–07
Madagascar	13	14	3.49	3.84	4.33	4.50	2009	5.3	58.7	59.8
Malawi	..	..	..	3.86	..	4.58	..	..	57.9	58.6
Malaysia	73	75	5.26	5.16	4.90	4.82	2010	53.5	68.5	69.8
Mali	..	11	3.58	3.87	4.00	3.89	2010	7.9	58.9	59.9
Mauritania	..	..	3.32	3.58	4.06	3.60	2000	13.1	64.2	66.3
Mexico	59	65	4.12	4.20	3.89	4.01	2010	27.8	69.6	70.5
Moldova	65	65	..	3.98	..	4.26	2011	71.0	55.2	56.1
Morocco	43	41	3.89	4.27	3.37	3.84	2011	29.1	64.2	66.2
Mozambique	..	9	3.31	3.77	3.98	3.72	2006	1.9	59.7	60.9
Myanmar	..	..	..	..	..	..	..	..	48.9	51.6
Nepal	..	25	3.75	3.78	3.64	3.75	2011	..	63.1	63.6
Netherlands	88	87	5.34	5.29	4.63	4.99	2005	90.7	86.8	86.9
New Zealand	79	82	5.56	5.35	5.19	5.19	..	..	87.4	88.0
Nicaragua	58	49	3.46	3.79	3.86	3.98	2008	21.7	54.7	56.4
Niger	..	5	..	..	..	..	2006	1.9	59.1	60.3
Nigeria	..	..	4.13	4.16	4.11	4.50	2010	..	42.5	46.0
Norway	91	92	5.04	4.79	4.97	4.98	2005	93.2	80.9	81.7
Pakistan	35	38	4.20	4.02	3.70	3.65	2009	..	63.2	65.6
Panama	66	66	4.22	4.59	4.01	4.17	..	..	35.4	38.3
Papua New Guinea	..	..	..	..	..	..	2009	4.4	63.5	63.1
Paraguay	58	47	3.33	4.19	3.47	3.92	2004	12.4	60.7	62.0
Peru	52	58	3.98	4.37	4.03	4.56	2009	21.7	40.4	43.9
Philippines	50	51	4.24	4.17	3.85	4.01	2011	26.3	57.1	60.1
Poland	71	75	4.26	4.39	4.44	4.48	2008	81.4	72.4	73.4
Portugal	72	75	4.49	4.31	4.12	3.80	2005	92.0	77.2	76.9
Romania	62	64	4.04	3.86	4.01	4.01	2008	67.9	66.3	68.9
Russian Federation	93	92	3.84	3.62	4.44	4.23	2011	65.1	54.7	58.1
Rwanda	6	..	..	4.54	..	5.10	2004	4.6	59.6	60.5
Saudi Arabia	..	..	..	5.12	..	4.47	2010	..	81.3	82.7
Senegal	11	22	..	4.20	..	4.27	2008	..	55.2	57.6
Serbia	..	70	..	3.57	..	4.04	2007	45.0	..	..
Sierra Leone	..	8	..	3.84	..	3.92	2004	5.5	53.0	56.2
Singapore	85	85	5.79	5.60	5.65	5.80	2009	62.1	86.8	87.5
Slovak Republic	93	88	4.59	4.37	4.73	4.20	2003	78.9	81.3	82.6
Somalia	..	..	..	..	..	..	..	..	..	..
South Africa	..	83	4.74	4.68	4.04	3.94	2010	6.7	71.8	73.8
South Sudan	..	..	..	..	..	..	..	..	..	..
Spain	76	82	4.67	4.37	4.01	3.98	2005	69.4	77.4	77.6
Sri Lanka	59	57	4.13	4.33	3.28	3.66	2006	24.1	55.5	56.9
Sudan	..	..	..	..	..	..	2005	5.2	65.9	..
Sweden	89	89	5.22	5.14	4.47	4.81	2005	88.8	80.9	81.7
Switzerland	83	84	5.24	5.26	5.58	5.90	2005	95.4	91.3	91.6
Syrian Arab Republic	..	58	..	..	..	..	2008	26.8	80.8	81.2
Tajikistan	..	53	3.50	4.04	4.12	4.55	..	..	57.1	58.7
Tanzania	9	9	3.92	3.89	4.33	4.55	2007	..	42.4	45.1
Thailand	36	43	4.72	4.56	5.02	4.32	2009	22.5	48.0	51.2
Togo	..	11	..	..	..	..	2009	..	65.1	65.1
Tunisia	69	67	..	..	..	..	2011	..	62.0	63.8
Turkey	43	55	4.47	4.55	3.53	3.79	2008	58.6	67.6	70.1
Turkmenistan	..	..	..	..	..	..	..	..	..	..
Uganda	..	18	3.67	3.95	4.72	4.83	2004	10.3	57.0	58.5
Ukraine	88	84	3.75	3.82	4.21	4.44	2010	62.1	48.6	52.3
United Arab Emirates	..	96	4.85	5.31	4.74	5.24	..	..	73.3	75.4
United Kingdom	87	87	5.48	5.09	5.41	5.42	2005	93.2	87.4	87.7
United States	92	93	5.55	4.88	5.80	5.37	2005	92.2	91.2	91.5
Uruguay	73	71	3.94	4.38	4.10	3.49	2009	78.5	47.8	51.3
Uzbekistan	..	..	..	..	..	..	2005	..	..	..
Venezuela, RB	61	62	3.42	2.78	3.52	2.88	2009	33.9	65.3	67.2
Vietnam	19	22	3.95	4.13	4.43	4.51	2010	20.7	84.5	85.3
West Bank and Gaza	63	61	..	..	..	..	2009	14.0	..	..
Yemen, Rep.	42	..	..	3.68	..	3.44	2006	10.4	72.7	73.2
Zambia	20	18	3.23	4.53	4.02	3.97	2010	..	51.6	54.5
Zimbabwe	38	38	3.29	3.63	3.50	3.40	2011	20.3	38.6	37.7
World	**..w**	**..w**	**4.24u**	**4.25u**	**4.28u**	**4.29u**		**37.9w**	**83.8w**	**83.1w**
Low income	..	..	3.54	3.84	4.11	4.29		..	58.3	59.9
Middle income	..	..	3.95	4.08	4.03	4.04		27.4	72.0	73.7
Lower middle income	26	26	3.84	4.06	3.92	4.03		15.3	69.6	71.1
Upper middle income	..	..	4.05	4.09	4.12	4.05		37.9	72.8	74.5
Low & middle income	..	..	3.84	4.00	4.05	4.12		25.5	71.7	73.4
High income	85	86	4.98	4.78	4.70	4.68		85.7	86.4	85.7

TABLE 6 *Selected indicators related to risk management at the financial sector level*

	Use of formal financial risk-management tools								Financial systems structure, % of GDP, 2005–10 average			
	Saved at a financial institution % age 15+ 2011	Loan from a financial institution % age 15+ 2011	Personally paid for health insurance % age 15+ 2011	Purchased agriculture insurance % of agriculture workers age 15+ 2011	Population using informal saving % age 15+ 2011	Population using informal credit % age 15+ 2011	Use of electronic payments Volume of transactions million 2009	Stock market capitalization	Bank assets	Mutual fund assets	Insurance assets	Pension assets
Afghanistan	2.8	7.4	0.1	10.8	11.7	36.8	..	..	7.5	..	..	..
Albania	8.6	7.5	11.2	73.3	14.2	12.9	7	..	50.8	0.0	1.4	0.0
Algeria	4.3	1.5	3.5	0.0	16.5	27.9	..	..	33.4	..	0.9	..
Angola	15.9	7.9	3.1	..	20.7	24.9	44	..	17.9	..	1.2	..
Argentina	3.8	6.6	9.1	0.0	20.6	9.0	47	24.2	23.4	2.0	2.4	12.7
Armenia	0.8	18.9	0.6	5.9	9.7	37.6	7	1.1	16.4	0.4	0.4	..
Australia	61.9	17.0	..	..	6.3	27.6	5,761	120.0	117.1	22.4	33.9	83.2
Austria	51.6	8.3	..	..	26.8	9.3	2,129	35.3	129.5	48.6	34.0	4.8
Azerbaijan	1.6	17.7	1.1	19.5	9.2	37.1	52	..	15.4	..	0.7	..
Bangladesh	16.6	23.3	2.1	0.0	10.2	14.0	..	7.5	53.3	..	2.1	..
Belarus	6.8	16.1	3.1	4.7	19.6	36.6	..	..	33.9	..	0.8	..
Belgium	42.6	10.5	..	..	15.2	7.4	2,211	68.1	109.7	30.2	65.4	3.5
Benin	7.0	4.2	0.7	1.4	25.3	32.4	..	..	21.4	..	1.9	..
Bolivia	17.1	16.6	3.7	4.3	27.2	9.1	4	17.6	36.0	3.0	4.0	23.1
Bosnia and Herzegovina	6.1	13.0	3.8	3.7	7.5	15.8	..	..	54.6	..	..	..
Brazil	10.3	6.3	7.6	11.2	10.8	17.5	16,509	61.4	75.8	40.8	7.5	14.9
Bulgaria	4.8	7.8	3.9	2.0	6.1	24.0	66	23.0	50.2	0.7	3.6	3.8
Burkina Faso	7.9	3.1	0.8	0.5	30.1	32.9	..	..	18.0	..	0.7	..
Burundi	3.3	1.7	3.5	7.6	21.9	50.6	..	..	23.1	..	..	..
Cambodia	0.8	19.5	2.6	14.3	30.2	40.1	..	..	17.1	..	0.5	..
Cameroon	9.9	4.5	1.2	3.4	42.0	45.6	..	..	11.9	..	1.7	..
Canada	53.2	20.3	..	..	12.3	21.6	8,441	120.9	138.3	45.3	34.6	60.3
Central African Republic	2.5	0.9	0.4	1.5	22.9	24.1	..	..	9.0	..	1.0	..
Chad	6.8	6.2	1.3	17.0	21.9	34.9	..	..	5.3	..	0.1	..
Chile	12.4	7.8	5.7	0.0	14.6	13.9	224	108.4	70.8	10.2	19.3	61.4
China	32.1	7.3	47.2	7.2	6.3	22.1	43,094	81.7	118.0	8.1	9.7	0.7
Hong Kong SAR, China	42.8	7.9	..	..	16.3	19.8	4,184	474.0	167.4	421.9	32.6	29.8
Colombia	9.2	11.9	5.6	8.3	23.7	22.0	287	40.9	36.4	2.6	4.9	15.1
Congo, Dem. Rep.	1.5	1.5	0.7	1.2	22.6	32.2	0	..	3.4	..	0.5	..
Congo, Rep.	5.5	2.8	0.1	2.8	25.0	29.2	..	..	3.1	..	..	..
Costa Rica	19.9	10.0	4.1	0.0	21.1	11.4	115	6.4	45.2	4.3	1.8	5.7
Côte d'Ivoire	..	..	..	..	..	..	..	26.1	18.8	..	3.3	..
Croatia	12.2	14.4	..	..	9.7	23.7	269	50.6	73.6	5.6	7.6	7.4
Czech Republic	35.5	9.5	..	..	13.5	19.9	175	28.9	59.5	3.6	10.0	5.1
Denmark	56.5	18.8	..	..	16.1	12.0	1,461	67.3	204.2	56.5	75.4	57.9
Dominican Republic	16.0	13.9	8.4	0.9	21.3	23.5	188	..	22.3	..	1.4	2.9
Ecuador	14.5	10.6	3.1	8.4	15.7	16.7	2	8.4	24.2	1.1	0.7	..
Egypt, Arab Rep.	0.7	3.7	0.5	6.6	7.4	26.9	1,292	66.7	71.3	4.1	3.6	2.5
El Salvador	12.9	3.9	1.0	5.4	13.0	7.4	7	23.8	44.0	..	2.3	20.8
Eritrea	..	..	..	..	..	..	0	..	..	..	..	..
Ethiopia	..	..	..	..	..	..	..	..	26.6	..	0.8	..
Finland	56.1	23.9	..	..	12.5	23.8	1,976	90.9	86.2	27.4	26.0	72.0
France	49.5	18.6	..	..	12.3	5.9	12,970	82.4	119.6	67.9	89.3	1.0
Georgia	1.0	11.0	3.2	0.4	5.9	18.0	32	6.8	24.4	..	1.6	..
Germany	55.9	12.5	..	..	11.4	12.7	..	45.7	131.4	43.6	59.5	12.0
Ghana	16.1	5.8	11.8	4.0	20.5	28.8	..	12.4	21.7	..	0.9	..
Greece	19.9	7.9	..	..	7.9	22.2	129	50.3	107.9	7.2	5.7	..
Guatemala	10.2	13.7	1.7	1.7	14.6	10.5	0	..	35.2	..	1.4	..
Guinea	2.0	2.4	0.3	49.5	25.1	42.1	..	..	7.7	..	..	..
Haiti	18.0	8.3	4.0	17.2	13.6	37.4	..	..	14.8	..	..	..
Honduras	8.5	7.1	1.3	2.8	13.3	12.9	..	..	47.3	..	3.0	..
Hungary	17.3	9.4	..	..	9.4	9.3	355	26.4	74.0	10.4	8.6	11.0
India	11.6	7.7	6.8	6.6	10.8	22.9	4,102	80.0	59.1	6.8	15.3	5.3
Indonesia	15.3	8.5	0.9	0.0	25.2	40.6	1,787	31.9	31.6	..	1.8	2.2
Iran, Islamic Rep.	19.7	30.7	19.3	24.3	12.6	40.4	1,658	16.9	33.1	..	1.0	..
Iraq	5.4	8.0	0.2	7.8	20.8	46.7	16	..	10.1	..	..	..
Ireland	51.3	15.7	..	..	13.3	13.6	..	42.0	200.6	363.4	83.4	45.5
Israel	24.8	16.7	..	..	20.1	23.3	940	97.0	99.3	..	..	38.7
Italy	15.5	4.6	..	..	10.9	6.6	3,252	36.0	121.6	15.9	33.8	2.2
Japan	51.3	6.1	..	..	12.0	11.6	1,428	87.7	164.1	13.2	74.4	19.9
Jordan	8.3	4.5	1.1	..	9.9	26.8	385	181.6	98.5	0.1	4.8	42.8
Kazakhstan	6.7	13.1	1.9	1.5	15.2	28.8	164	31.8	43.6	..	1.3	9.6
Kenya	23.3	9.7	5.4	3.3	16.9	57.7	..	38.4	38.6	..	7.6	12.9
Korea, Rep.	46.9	16.6	..	..	17.6	16.0	9,696	84.2	101.2	27.2	40.5	3.9
Kyrgyz Republic	0.9	11.3	0.0	2.7	35.5	24.2	6	2.0	10.1	..	0.4	..
Lao PDR	19.4	18.1	4.5	4.6	35.1	14.4	..	..	10.3	..	..	..
Lebanon	17.1	11.3	7.9	0.0	13.7	15.9	10	32.1	142.3	1.0	7.1	..
Liberia	13.9	6.5	5.9	18.8	20.9	44.7	..	..	11.2	..	..	..
Libya	..	..	..	..	..	..	0	..	10.7	..	..	..
Lithuania	20.5	5.6	14.6	31.1	12.2	30.2	217	21.1	58.0	0.7	3.2	2.3
Madagascar	1.4	2.3	0.3	1.2	18.3	61.4	3	..	12.2	..	1.8	..
Malawi	8.2	9.2	0.5	1.2	24.8	42.1	..	19.6	12.7	..	5.7	..
Malaysia	35.4	11.2	16.4	7.2	15.6	21.3	332	133.5	114.6	23.6	18.5	49.3
Mali	4.5	3.7	1.0	9.2	32.9	25.4	..	..	18.9	..	0.5	..
Mauritania	6.4	7.9	2.0	17.0	16.4	35.8	..	..	27.1	..	..	..

	Bank savings		Credit		Insurance premium (life + non-life)		Foreign currency mismatches on bank balance sheets				Loan-to-deposit ratio	
							Loan dollarization		Deposit dollarization			
	% of GDP		% of GDP		% of GDP		%		%		%	
	2000	2011	2000	2011	2000	2011	2000	2010	2000	2010	2000	2011
Afghanistan	..	..	..	..	..	..	..	..	..	..	..	..
Albania	43.8	66.7	4.7	39.0	0.4	0.6	53.2	72.6	29.1	43.1	10.7	58.4
Algeria	26.1	45.7	5.9	14.5	0.5	0.6	..	..	..	..	22.8	31.8
Angola	25.6	52.7	2.0	21.6	0.9	1.0	74.8	50.2	83.0	61.0	7.7	41.0
Argentina	27.4	20.6	23.2	16.0	2.4	2.4	66.1	12.5	44.1	..	84.5	77.9
Armenia	8.9	20.4	9.9	34.3	0.1	0.5	..	65.2	..	67.6	111.3	168.1
Australia	61.3	99.2	84.6	124.1	8.8	5.3	..	..	..	..	138.0	125.1
Austria	80.4	95.0	102.2	118.9	4.7	4.6	..	..	..	..	127.1	125.2
Azerbaijan	10.6	13.4	5.9	17.9	0.3	0.3	..	..	..	..	55.9	133.9
Bangladesh	29.8	54.2	24.3	48.6	0.5	1.1	..	..	..	..	81.7	89.6
Belarus	14.9	35.9	8.8	41.7	0.6	0.8	54.9	30.7	72.2	53.8	58.8	116.2
Belgium	82.3	106.1	77.8	92.6	7.4	7.6	..	..	..	..	94.6	87.2
Benin	15.6	29.7	11.6	25.3	0.6	0.8	..	..	..	..	74.3	85.3
Bolivia	46.1	44.7	58.7	36.8	0.8	1.0	96.3	69.2	92.6	52.0	127.2	82.3
Bosnia and Herzegovina	16.6	41.6	40.8	48.2	1.9	1.9	..	73.7	53.7	50.2	73.2	115.7
Brazil	44.3	66.5	31.7	58.0	1.4	2.4	18.0	..	6.1	..	71.5	87.2
Bulgaria	22.7	63.9	12.3	72.0	1.3	2.0	35.9	58.3	59.2	53.6	54.0	112.7
Burkina Faso	13.1	26.8	11.7	20.8	0.6	0.4	..	..	..	..	89.4	77.6
Burundi	14.5	19.0	20.8	19.2	0.4	0.2	..	..	..	..	143.9	100.7
Cambodia	18.7	32.3	6.4	28.8	..	0.1	97.0	98.1	93.2	96.6	34.2	89.2
Cameroon	11.1	18.2	8.2	12.7	0.7	0.9	..	..	..	..	73.8	70.1
Canada	70.1	..	76.1	..	5.4	1.8	..	..	..	..	108.5	..
Central African Republic	3.4	9.3	4.7	9.4	0.3	0.3	..	..	..	..	138.6	101.7
Chad	3.9	7.2	3.4	6.0	0.3	0.2	..	..	..	..	86.7	82.5
Chile	50.9	43.4	63.8	70.5	3.7	3.6	15.7	10.8	10.4	13.8	125.4	162.2
China	110.4	164.4	112.2	127.4	1.5	3.0	..	..	..	..	101.7	77.5
Hong Kong SAR, China	220.8	321.8	152.6	206.2	4.3	11.4	..	..	..	..	69.1	64.1
Colombia	22.4	20.9	20.8	35.1	1.6	2.1	..	4.2	..	..	92.7	168.0
Congo, Dem. Rep.	9.2	12.4	3.2	6.3	0.1	0.4	..	..	43.5	..	35.2	50.8
Congo, Rep.	8.6	21.5	4.8	7.3	0.1	0.4	..	..	..	..	55.8	33.8
Costa Rica	14.1	23.2	24.0	47.4	2.0	1.8	41.6	..	41.3	..	170.9	198.6
Côte d'Ivoire	13.3		14.9		1.2	1.4	..	..	..	..	..	68.0
Croatia	37.0	67.4	31.9	73.8	2.2	2.5	84.6	73.0	71.1	65.5	86.1	109.5
Czech Republic	58.1	64.1	47.0	55.8	3.0	3.7	21.6	13.4	15.3	8.9	80.9	87.0
Denmark	46.8	52.1	135.2	..	6.6	9.5	..	25.4	..	..	66.3	..
Dominican Republic	25.5	20.8	29.0	22.3	1.4	1.2	..	21.8	..	..	113.7	107.0
Ecuador	21.1	32.9	29.3	30.9	1.2	2.2	..	..	..	..	138.9	93.8
Egypt, Arab Rep.	64.7	63.1	52.0	31.3	0.6	0.7	23.1	31.2	..	..	80.3	49.5
El Salvador	42.5	38.6	45.1	39.0	1.4	1.8	..	..	..	..	106.2	101.0
Eritrea	131.0	89.7	29.9	13.6	1.2	0.4	..	..	..	..	22.8	15.2
Ethiopia	27.0	..	17.8	..	0.6	0.5	..	..	..	..	65.7	..
Finland	46.0	63.6	53.0	96.4	4.9	3.2	..	..	..	..	115.2	151.5
France	62.6	88.3	85.0	116.2	8.4	8.6	..	..	..	..	135.9	131.6
Georgia	5.2	23.4	7.4	32.8	0.2	0.5	81.4	74.3	77.9	71.0	143.1	140.5
Germany	91.5	117.2	119.4	105.5	5.1	5.3	..	..	..	..	130.5	90.0
Ghana	16.4	24.2	13.8	14.5	0.9	0.6	..	..	..	30.7	84.3	60.0
Greece	50.5	83.1	46.9	118.0	0.0	2.1	..	..	..	..	92.9	142.0
Guatemala	18.2	38.5	19.8	23.4	0.9	1.0	18.4	28.5	..	24.1	108.5	60.8
Guinea	4.8	23.7	3.4	9.1	0.1	0.0	..	..	..	..	70.3	38.5
Haiti	29.9	39.2	15.1	14.2	..	0.4	..	..	..	..	50.4	36.2
Honduras	35.2	46.4	34.1	48.0	1.5	1.6	23.2	26.1	29.0	30.1	96.8	103.6
Hungary	38.8	45.7	32.5	65.2	2.9	2.8	33.1	65.5	20.4	18.4	83.5	142.4
India	45.8	66.7	28.8	50.6	1.8	3.5	..	..	..	..	63.0	75.8
Indonesia	48.2	34.4	19.4	28.3	1.0	1.5	41.4	12.9	26.6	14.6	40.3	82.4
Iran, Islamic Rep.	31.6	14.5	19.5	13.7	0.6	1.1	2.6	14.9	1.1	8.3	61.7	94.9
Iraq	..	..	..	..	..	..	..	..	..	..	..	..
Ireland	77.6	103.1	104.6	204.3	9.7	8.0	..	..	..	..	134.8	198.2
Israel	79.0	94.9	77.2	94.8	4.5	4.3	34.9	14.8	31.6	27.2	97.7	99.9
Italy	49.9	86.2	74.8	122.1	5.3	6.6	..	..	..	..	149.9	141.7
Japan	228.4	222.1	190.8	105.0	6.9	1.6	..	..	..	..	83.5	47.3
Jordan	90.5	100.3	71.9	73.4	1.5	1.6	..	..	95.5	70.5	79.5	73.3
Kazakhstan	11.1	29.1	11.2	37.0	0.3	0.6	68.5	45.0	50.9	43.7	100.9	127.0
Kenya	29.8	45.9	25.8	38.0	2.0	2.6	..	..	..	..	86.5	82.6
Korea, Rep.	65.5	74.7	75.8	99.8	10.8	11.9	1.2	2.7	..	..	115.7	133.6
Kyrgyz Republic	5.0	..	4.1	..	0.1	0.2	68.6	55.8	57.9	52.2	81.3	..
Lao PDR	16.0	32.7	7.9	23.3	0.2	0.4	72.3	..	75.4	61.5	49.2	71.1
Lebanon	182.9	223.9	85.5	81.1	2.2	1.8	87.0	81.3	62.3	60.0	46.7	36.2
Liberia	1.6	11.1	0.8	5.7	..	..	..	..	..	..	51.4	51.7
Libya	36.9	83.1	22.7	17.6	0.5	0.3	..	..	..	..	61.4	21.2
Lithuania	16.9	38.0	13.1	53.7	0.8	1.5	67.7	72.4	45.3	32.4	77.3	141.2
Madagascar	14.0	17.4	8.8	10.9	0.6	0.6	..	..	..	..	62.8	62.7
Malawi	13.8	28.6	5.6	18.4	1.7	1.0	..	..	..	..	40.5	64.1
Malaysia	112.9	128.9	126.7	112.1	4.0	4.3	..	..	2.0	4.7	112.3	87.0
Mali	13.7	21.9	15.0	21.4	0.5	0.5	..	..	..	..	109.2	98.1
Mauritania	..	23.9	..	25.6	..	0.4	..	..	..	..	..	107.4

TABLE 6 *Selected indicators related to risk management at the financial sector level* (continued)

	Use of formal financial risk-management tools							Financial systems structure, % of GDP, 2005–10 average					
	Saved at a financial institution	Loan from a financial institution	Personally paid for health insurance	Purchased agriculture insurance	Population using informal saving	Population using informal credit	Use of electronic payments						
	% age 15+	% age 15+	% age 15+	% of agriculture workers age 15+	% age 15+	% age 15+	Volume of transactions million	Stock market capitalization	Bank assets	Mutual fund assets	Insurance assets	Pension assets
	2011	2011	2011	2011	2011	2011	2009					
Mexico	6.7	7.6	8.5	4.9	20.4	22.1	1,640	31.5	29.8	7.3	3.2	8.1
Moldova	3.5	6.4	1.6	2.6	18.7	41.5	27	..	33.4	..	2.2	..
Morocco	12.2	4.3	4.5	18.7	18.2	41.6	28	68.6	75.7	22.0	17.1	20.0
Mozambique	17.5	5.9	3.7	5.3	25.2	35.4	4	..	23.8	..	2.7	..
Myanmar	..	..	..	..	..	..	..	..	3.5	..	..	..
Nepal	9.9	10.8	1.8	2.2	8.5	43.4	0	29.2	45.6	..	0.6	..
Netherlands	57.8	12.6	..	..	15.2	7.2	4,807	87.4	194.7	12.9	61.5	119.9
New Zealand	60.4	26.6	..	..	12.2	23.7	..	36.8	138.2	10.9	..	11.6
Nicaragua	6.5	7.6	0.8	5.9	19.5	6.7	..	..	37.5	..	0.5	..
Niger	1.2	1.3	0.2	5.8	24.0	46.8	..	..	10.0	..	0.8	..
Nigeria	23.6	2.1	0.4	2.3	40.8	46.2	..	24.7	30.2	..	1.7	2.9
Norway	..	..	..	..	..	..	1,835	61.3	79.8	16.2	36.6	7.2
Pakistan	1.4	1.6	0.5	2.6	6.0	27.3	..	29.3	37.6	1.8	..	..
Panama	12.5	9.8	4.9	0.0	22.5	17.4	..	30.5	81.0	..	5.2	2.7
Papua New Guinea	..	..	..	..	..	..	..	117.6	32.3	..	..	..
Paraguay	9.7	12.9	5.9	1.7	8.4	16.6	..	3.5	23.2	..	1.2	..
Peru	8.6	12.7	3.5	11.1	20.6	16.4	103	56.5	22.1	3.2	3.5	15.5
Philippines	14.7	10.5	5.5	0.0	30.8	47.6	..	47.5	40.1	1.1	6.5	3.5
Poland	18.0	9.6	..	..	12.8	16.7	2,027	33.2	43.6	7.6	10.3	11.9
Portugal	25.6	8.3	..	..	8.2	6.9	1,457	41.2	169.1	13.9	33.0	12.4
Romania	8.7	8.4	5.9	6.5	9.5	18.3	278	18.8	33.9	0.4	2.8	0.4
Russian Federation	10.9	7.7	6.7	3.7	11.8	24.2	2,833	68.7	37.6	0.3	2.2	1.3
Rwanda	17.8	8.4	5.3	4.3	12.6	30.1	1	..	11.7	..	..	..
Saudi Arabia	17.2	2.1	..	..	16.1	34.8	159	104.6	52.5	6.9	1.7	..
Senegal	3.7	3.5	0.9	3.4	11.6	27.5	..	..	25.8	..	2.2	..
Serbia	3.2	12.3	3.7	2.2	11.7	31.4	398	30.6	37.4	..	3.2	0.2
Sierra Leone	14.5	6.1	0.5	17.3	18.1	43.0	0	..	11.4	..	..	..
Singapore	58.4	10.0	..	..	2.5	22.7	289	186.0	114.6	48.8	48.2	57.2
Slovak Republic	36.8	11.4	..	..	12.4	23.7	415	6.5	55.3	4.8	5.3	3.5
Somalia	13.6	1.6	0.5	20.1	8.2	34.7	..	..	..	..	..	..
South Africa	22.1	8.9	7.4	43.3	9.4	35.3	970	233.8	80.4	31.9	36.8	104.6
South Sudan	..	..	..	..	..	..	..	..	..	..	..	..
Spain	35.0	11.4	..	..	11.2	15.3	3,564	90.0	192.0	24.1	23.8	8.0
Sri Lanka	28.1	17.7	7.5	8.1	8.2	16.4	29	20.6	36.5	0.2	3.9	0.6
Sudan	3.4	1.8	9.5	20.7	19.3	63.3	10	..	13.3	..	0.5	..
Sweden	63.6	23.4	..	..	19.3	18.9	2,846	107.4	127.0	38.2	82.7	3.4
Switzerland	..	..	..	..	..	..	1,268	241.3	178.6	37.3	86.1	99.7
Syrian Arab Republic	5.1	13.1	9.5	2.6	43.2	49.3	..	..	36.1	..	..	..
Tajikistan	0.3	4.8	0.8	9.0	13.5	26.9	..	..	15.0	..	..	..
Tanzania	11.9	6.6	2.6	7.4	28.2	45.1	4	4.0	19.3	..	1.2	..
Thailand	42.8	19.4	24.1	7.4	17.2	7.8	558	62.8	106.1	17.9	11.4	5.3
Togo	3.6	3.8	0.7	2.2	16.0	20.4	..	..	23.4	..	1.9	..
Tunisia	5.0	3.2	6.1	0.0	20.1	23.2	..	14.0	59.7	7.0	0.8	..
Turkey	4.2	4.6	4.4	0.0	5.4	61.3	1,910	30.7	50.4	3.2	1.8	0.6
Turkmenistan	0.1	0.8	0.0	2.1	44.4	38.5	..	..	..	..	..	..
Uganda	16.3	8.9	0.7	9.1	28.1	43.9	29	9.6	16.4	..	1.1	..
Ukraine	5.4	8.1	1.7	0.0	19.6	36.3	..	29.8	55.0	..	2.8	0.1
United Arab Emirates	19.2	10.8	..	..	11.0	24.6	94	..	..	0.3	4.2	..
United Kingdom	43.8	11.8	..	..	12.9	17.0	13,486	123.9	183.3	36.3	95.9	76.2
United States	50.4	20.1	..	..	16.4	24.5	79,011	122.7	65.3	76.6	44.2	70.6
Uruguay	5.7	14.8	9.3	22.1	11.2	9.5	51	0.5	28.2	0.0	3.8	13.3
Uzbekistan	0.8	1.5	0.8	4.3	30.6	12.3	..	..	..	..	0.5	..
Venezuela, RB	13.6	1.7	6.0	41.2	14.8	11.7	27	2.9	19.5	..	..	..
Vietnam	7.7	16.2	17.5	3.1	27.5	27.8	..	13.2	90.1	0.2	4.2	..
West Bank and Gaza	5.5	4.1	5.1	9.8	10.7	49.6	2	68.4	9.5	..	..	..
Yemen, Rep.	1.1	0.9	0.0	0.0	10.8	56.2	8	..	13.1	..	..	..
Zambia	11.8	6.1	1.2	11.8	20.4	41.8	2	13.5	16.0	..	1.4	3.8
Zimbabwe	17.3	4.9	14.6	6.2	22.6	57.7	1	..	..	..	..	..
World	**22.4w**	**9.1w**	**17.1w**	**6.5w**	**13.5w**	**24.7w**	**249,527s**	**40.8m**	**42.1m**	**10.7m**	**4.3m**	**7.8m**
Low income	11.5	11.4	2.2	5.1	18.5	32.7	49	17.6	15.2	..	1.1	12.9
Middle income	18.1	7.6	19.1	6.7	12.9	25.9	77,239	28.6	35.5	3.6	3.1	5.2
Lower middle income	11.1	7.3	5.2	5.1	16.4	29.3	7,349	22.5	29.2	2.6	2.8	3.5
Upper middle income	24.9	7.9	32.6	8.3	9.6	22.7	69,890	32.5	47.6	3.9	3.4	6.4
Low & middle income	17.5	8.0	17.4	6.6	13.5	26.6	77,288	27.9	29.8	3.6	2.8	5.5
High income	40.4	13.0	..	..	13.5	18.1	172,239	69.9	99.1	17.9	25.7	11.6

	Bank savings		Credit		Insurance premium (life + non-life)		Foreign currency mismatches on bank balance sheets				Loan-to-deposit ratio	
	% of GDP		% of GDP		% of GDP		Loan dollarization %		Deposit dollarization %		%	
	2000	2011	2000	2011	2000	2011	2000	2010	2000	2010	2000	2011
Mexico	23.5	26.7	17.2	19.8	1.8	1.6	..	*9.7*	6.4	*8.6*	72.9	74.4
Moldova	13.1	36.6	12.6	33.6	0.5	1.1	40.8	*46.3*	42.4	*48.0*	96.4	91.7
Morocco	59.2	89.5	50.7	71.6	2.3	2.6	1.0	..	..	..	85.7	80.0
Mozambique	23.3	33.7	16.7	23.6	0.5	*1.1*	40.2	*32.4*	*46.7*	35.8	71.7	70.2
Myanmar	18.0	17.9	9.5	7.9	0.1	..	..	..	..	..	53.0	44.0
Nepal	38.8	63.9	30.3	52.4	0.5	1.5	..	..	..	..	78.1	82.0
Netherlands	92.3	131.9	134.1	197.9	7.2	4.9	..	..	..	..	145.3	150.1
New Zealand	78.7	*94.3*	110.0	*147.7*	3.8	2.7	..	..	..	..	139.8	*156.7*
Nicaragua	34.4	38.1	30.5	32.1	1.2	1.5	83.0	88.7	70.3	..	88.6	84.1
Niger	5.9	11.8	5.2	14.0	0.5	0.6	..	..	..	..	87.2	119.4
Nigeria	14.9	30.6	11.7	21.3	0.5	0.7	..	..	5.4	..	78.1	69.5
Norway	45.9	..	65.5	..	4.3	4.8	12.1	12.6	16.2	*25.4*	142.6	..
Pakistan	27.7	29.1	22.3	18.2	0.5	0.6	..	..	..	..	80.7	62.6
Panama	76.7	82.7	95.5	84.6	2.7	2.9	..	..	..	..	124.4	102.3
Papua New Guinea	29.0	41.8	17.1	22.4	1.5	*0.1*	..	..	..	..	59.1	53.5
Paraguay	22.2	27.3	27.1	41.0	1.1	1.1	49.0	42.0	59.7	39.6	122.4	150.4
Peru	25.8	29.5	25.7	26.3	0.9	1.3	81.4	52.3	77.2	52.6	99.4	89.1
Philippines	50.7	52.2	36.8	31.8	1.2	1.4	*27.1*	*18.4*	..	*22.6*	72.5	60.9
Poland	36.0	50.5	26.6	54.9	2.5	3.3	21.9	*30.2*	15.7	*8.8*	73.8	108.7
Portugal	89.3	133.5	126.1	192.1	4.7	5.9	..	..	..	..	141.2	143.9
Romania	19.7	31.4	7.1	38.0	0.8	1.3	59.5	*60.1*	47.0	*34.8*	36.2	121.1
Russian Federation	15.5	40.8	13.3	45.0	1.7	0.9	37.8	*24.1*	46.2	*29.8*	85.6	110.2
Rwanda	13.0	..	10.2	..	0.4	*0.5*	..	..	..	..	78.6	..
Saudi Arabia	37.4	51.7	24.4	39.7	0.2	*0.5*	25.4	*13.6*	18.6	*11.9*	65.2	76.8
Senegal	18.4	32.0	18.6	29.5	1.0	1.2	..	..	..	..	101.1	92.3
Serbia	14.1	43.2	49.1	51.0	2.1	1.5	..	*84.1*	76.7	*73.1*	..	118.1
Sierra Leone	9.1	18.9	2.0	8.9	..	*0.5*	..	..	..	..	22.3	47.0
Singapore	98.2	128.1	97.8	112.6	6.2	6.1	..	*42.9*	..	..	99.7	87.9
Slovak Republic	66.9	54.8	51.1	49.7	2.8	3.0	19.0	*18.1*	17.2	*17.1*	76.3	90.7
Somalia	..	..	..	..	..	..	..	..	..	..	..	..
South Africa	51.5	62.6	69.1	68.9	17.5	11.2	49.8	..	4.2	..	134.2	110.1
South Sudan	..	..	..	..	..	..	..	..	..	..	..	..
Spain	78.9	150.9	97.8	205.4	6.0	4.9	..	..	..	..	123.9	136.1
Sri Lanka	33.5	34.4	28.8	30.6	1.2	*1.2*	..	..	..	..	86.1	89.2
Sudan	5.7	15.9	2.1	11.2	0.3	*0.4*	..	..	..	..	37.5	70.6
Sweden	36.2	59.8	42.3	..	6.9	7.5	14.1	*23.0*	26.7	*26.1*	116.8	..
Switzerland	113.8	151.6	154.7	168.4	9.7	7.7	15.7	*15.1*	17.1	*33.4*	135.9	111.1
Syrian Arab Republic	38.3	*55.0*	8.5	*23.2*	0.4	*0.6*	..	..	..	..	22.1	*42.1*
Tajikistan	3.2	..	13.6	..	0.1	*0.4*	48.4	29.8	..	*72.2*	..	..
Tanzania	13.8	28.8	4.6	17.7	0.6	0.7	..	..	..	..	33.2	61.5
Thailand	106.6	103.8	108.3	108.6	2.5	4.2	*9.2*	..	..	*0.9*	101.6	104.5
Togo	16.0	38.3	16.0	31.1	1.0	*1.5*	..	..	..	..	99.9	81.0
Tunisia	46.8	55.1	60.5	72.2	1.4	1.6	..	..	..	..	129.3	131.1
Turkey	32.5	50.3	17.8	50.1	0.9	1.1	*62.3*	31.7	48.2	*33.5*	54.6	99.6
Turkmenistan	..	..	..	..	..	0.3	*90.3*	..	30.1	..	21.9	..
Uganda	12.1	18.1	5.6	15.2	0.4	0.6	..	..	..	..	46.3	83.8
Ukraine	11.0	37.1	11.1	55.8	1.1	*2.0*	46.0	60.3	38.4	..	100.4	150.7
United Arab Emirates	45.1	59.3	46.2	61.9	1.2	1.4	..	..	..	*18.9*	102.5	104.5
United Kingdom	103.9	162.6	128.6	186.7	17.0	*11.7*	36.5	*40.1*	55.9	*52.9*	123.7	114.9
United States	65.1	79.2	50.4	55.1	7.1	6.9	..	..	..	..	77.5	69.6
Uruguay	40.6	40.3	44.9	23.7	1.7	1.5	*86.3*	*75.8*	*90.7*	..	110.6	58.7
Uzbekistan	..	..	..	..	0.2	0.3	..	..	*8.1*	..	..	..
Venezuela, RB	15.2	32.1	10.5	20.4	1.2	*2.0*	..	..	0.2	..	69.0	63.6
Vietnam	32.8	94.8	35.3	111.6	0.6	1.3	20.7	17.8	..	..	107.6	117.8
West Bank and Gaza	..	..	..	..	..	..	..	..	..	..	..	..
Yemen, Rep.	13.9	15.3	4.3	4.1	0.2	0.2	41.9	45.0	52.7	*39.3*	30.9	27.0
Zambia	21.0	20.4	8.2	12.3	1.4	1.1	48.3	34.7	53.7	..	38.9	60.1
Zimbabwe	..	..	..	..	..	..	..	..	..	..	..	..
World	**34.5m**	**46.2m**	**28.8m**	**39.0m**	**1.3m**	**1.9m**					**80.7m**	**87.2m**
Low income	13.8	26.3	9.5	15.2	0.5	0.6					71.0	70.2
Middle income	31.6	41.2	22.7	34.7	1.0	1.3					77.4	85.6
Lower middle income	28.3	36.8	17.9	30.8	0.7	0.9					75.3	81.2
Upper middle income	32.5	51.5	25.7	47.8	1.5	1.6					78.7	89.4
Low & middle income	24.5	37.2	17.5	30.8	0.8	1.2					74.4	82.4
High income	62.6	79.2	63.8	90.0	4.3	3.9					97.7	106.6

TABLE 7 *Selected indicators related to risk management at the macroeconomy level*

	CPI inflation rate	Government primary surplus		Gross public debt		International reserves		Flexible exchange rate regimes			Worldwide Governance Indicators average
	Average annual growth, %	% of GDP, annual average		% of GDP, annual average		% of GDP, annual average		Coarse classification, 1–6 scale			(–2.5 to 2.5) (least to most)
	2010–12	2005–07	2010–12	2005–07	2010–12	2005–07	2010–12	1996–2000	2001–05	2006–10	2011
Afghanistan	6.2	–1.3	0.0	..	..	..	*33.8*	..	6	3	–1.75
Albania	2.7	–0.5	–0.4	56.0	59.0	19.1	19.9	4	3	3	–0.20
Algeria	6.7	11.1	–2.0	22.5	10.7	70.7	97.9	2	2	2	–0.93
Angola	11.9	..	..	29.3	32.8	16.8	27.0	..	1	2	–1.06
Argentina	9.8	3.7	0.1	77.0	46.3	16.0	11.0	1	3	2	–0.22
Armenia	5.1	–1.8	–2.2	17.0	36.3	16.2	19.1	2	2	3	–0.28
Australia	2.6	1.6	–3.6	10.2	23.9	5.6	3.4	4	4	4	1.63
Austria	2.9	0.7	–1.1	62.2	72.7	4.2	5.0	1	1	1	1.49
Azerbaijan	4.4	..	..	10.7	11.0	11.3	15.0	1	1	1	–0.84
Bangladesh	9.7	–1.2	–1.4	..	..	6.2	9.9	2	2	1	–0.87
Belarus	56.2	0.8	1.6	12.6	40.8	5.8	10.2	5	1	3	–1.01
Belgium	3.2	3.1	–0.6	88.0	97.6	3.4	5.1	1	1	1	1.37
Benin	4.7	0.0	–0.4	24.8	31.3	18.8	13.3	1	1	1	–0.29
Bolivia	7.2	..	..	58.7	35.4	29.1	47.6	2	2	1	–0.54
Bosnia and Herzegovina	2.9	..	..	21.8	41.3	28.6	24.9	1	1	1	–0.43
Brazil	6.0	3.5	2.6	67.0	66.2	9.1	14.7	3	3	3	0.13
Bulgaria	3.6	3.9	–1.8	23.8	16.3	35.7	34.8	1	1	1	0.18
Burkina Faso	3.3	1.9	–2.9	29.6	28.0	10.9	10.2	1	1	1	–0.38
Burundi	13.8	–0.2	–2.3	131.9	35.9	10.8	13.8	3	2	2	–1.19
Cambodia	4.2	–0.2	–3.1	33.1	28.7	20.9	32.0	..	2	2	–0.78
Cameroon	2.9	..	..	26.5	13.6	9.9	14.1	1	1	1	–0.89
Canada	2.2	2.4	–3.6	69.5	84.0	2.9	3.7	2	3	3	1.62
Central African Republic	*1.3*	3.0	–0.5	94.2	31.8	8.4	7.9	1	1	1	–1.30
Chad	2.4	2.3	–0.5	29.1	34.5	9.5	9.0	1	1	1	–1.30
Chile	3.2	6.8	0.7	5.3	10.3	12.0	15.0	3	3	3	1.21
China	4.0	..	..	17.8	27.3	40.3	44.7	1	1	1	–0.58
Hong Kong SAR, China	4.7	4.3	2.7	32.5	33.1	69.8	117.6	1	1	1	1.40
Colombia	3.3	1.8	0.0	36.0	35.0	9.9	9.7	3	3	3	–0.23
Congo, Dem. Rep.	..	1.4	2.7	141.0	35.8	1.8	9.1	4	4	..	–1.64
Congo, Rep.	2.6	17.5	13.2	101.7	22.5	20.7	38.9	1	1	1	–1.01
Costa Rica	4.7	2.8	–2.4	32.8	31.6	13.7	13.2	2	2	1	0.58
Côte d'Ivoire	3.1	0.4	–1.8	82.1	70.1	10.5	16.6	..	..	..	–1.16
Croatia	2.8	–0.7	–2.6	35.5	48.7	21.9	24.6	2	2	2	0.38
Czech Republic	2.6	–1.4	–3.1	28.2	40.6	21.1	20.9	1	3	3	0.95
Denmark	2.6	5.7	–2.5	32.5	46.4	11.9	25.8	1	1	1	1.86
Dominican Republic	6.1	0.8	–1.9	21.0	30.9	6.5	7.0	2	3	2	–0.36
Ecuador	4.8	..	..	30.3	19.8	5.5	3.0	1	1	1	–0.76
Egypt, Arab Rep.	8.6	–3.7	–4.6	91.3	76.7	24.4	9.8	1	2	2	–0.74
El Salvador	3.4	..	..	38.6	50.6	11.0	12.1	1	1	1	–0.07
Eritrea	..	..	..	154.8	134.2	*2.4*	*4.9*	..	1	1	–1.40
Ethiopia	28.2	..	..	50.6	25.0	6.9	..	2	2	..	–0.96
Finland	3.1	3.6	–2.0	38.8	50.3	4.3	3.8	1	1	1	1.85
France	2.0	–0.2	–3.2	65.0	86.2	4.1	4.9	1	1	1	1.21
Georgia	3.7	..	..	27.6	35.2	11.0	19.0	3	2	2	0.01
Germany	2.0	0.9	0.5	67.3	81.7	3.9	5.0	1	1	1	1.42
Ghana	8.9	..	..	35.1	48.7	12.6	14.8	5	2	2	0.14
Greece	2.4	–1.4	–2.8	105.3	159.0	1.1	1.7	1	1	1	0.36
Guatemala	5.0	–0.3	–1.3	21.7	24.6	13.3	13.3	2	2	2	–0.57
Guinea	18.2	1.5	–4.3	126.6	78.2	*1.4*	*2.5*	3	2	2	–1.19
Haiti	7.3	..	..	40.3	15.1	5.3	17.6	4	3	3	–1.16
Honduras	6.0	–2.2	–3.5	40.6	32.2	23.0	15.8	2	1	1	–0.55
Hungary	4.8	–3.6	3.0	64.9	80.7	17.9	35.2	2	3	3	0.74
India	9.1	–1.4	–4.2	78.4	67.2	19.2	16.1	2	2	2	–0.30
Indonesia	4.8	..	..	40.1	25.1	12.3	13.0	3	3	3	–0.46
Iran, Islamic Rep.	23.9	4.2	1.7	18.7	13.7	..	..	3	1	1	–1.16
Iraq	..	7.3	2.0	162.8	42.0	33.1	34.6	..	1	2	–1.34
Ireland	2.1	2.3	–14.5	25.6	105.3	0.4	0.8	1	1	1	1.45
Israel	2.6	2.9	–0.8	85.8	74.9	*19.4*	*31.7*	2	3	3	0.59
Italy	2.9	2.1	1.1	105.1	122.4	4.1	6.0	1	1	1	0.52
Japan	–0.2	–3.5	–9.0	185.1	228.1	20.5	20.8	4	4	4	1.17
Jordan	4.6	–1.9	–4.6	78.1	72.5	45.4	39.8	1	1	1	–0.12
Kazakhstan	6.7	5.6	3.9	6.9	11.2	17.6	15.2	2	2	2	–0.59
Kenya	11.7	–0.2	–3.0	47.9	48.9	10.9	13.8	2	2	3	–0.69
Korea, Rep.	3.1	1.5	1.0	30.1	33.8	25.0	28.3	3	3	3	0.76
Kyrgyz Republic	9.4	..	..	71.7	53.1	28.2	31.6	2	2	2	–0.83
Lao PDR	5.9	–2.3	–2.9	73.7	56.2	*13.8*	*14.9*	6	..	..	–0.91
Lebanon	*5.8*	..	..	176.6	139.6	81.3	108.6	1	1	1	–0.64
Liberia	7.7	2.9	–3.6	634.6	29.3	10.9	32.5	4	4	4	–0.74
Libya	10.7	29.5	4.9	0.4	0.0	107.1	..	6	6	6	–1.34
Lithuania	3.6	–0.1	–3.4	17.7	38.7	17.9	18.9	1	2	2	0.69

TABLE 7 *Selected indicators related to risk management at the macroeconomy level* (continued)

	CPI inflation rate	Government primary surplus		Gross public debt		International reserves		Flexible exchange rate regimes			Worldwide Governance Indicators average (−2.5 to 2.5) (least to most)
	Average annual growth, %	% of GDP, annual average		% of GDP, annual average		% of GDP, annual average		Coarse classification, 1–6 scale			
	2010–12	2005–07	2010–12	2005–07	2010–12	2005–07	2010–12	1996–2000	2001–05	2006–10	2011
Madagascar	7.9	..	..	50.9	37.3	10.6	12.7	3	3	3	−0.71
Malawi	14.2	..	..	71.0	44.8	5.6	5.0	3	2	2	−0.33
Malaysia	2.4	−1.7	−2.8	41.8	54.5	50.9	45.0	1	1	3	0.32
Mali	4.1	8.8	−1.9	31.5	31.2	15.7	13.4	1	1	1	−0.49
Mauritania	5.3	0.2	1.3	121.9	89.9	5.3	14.1	2	2	3	−0.88
Mexico	3.8	..	..	38.7	43.4	8.4	12.7	3	3	3	−0.13
Moldova	6.2	..	..	30.0	24.5	24.4	30.7	2	2	2	−0.30
Morocco	1.1	0.4	−3.9	59.5	55.1	30.8	21.2	2	1	1	−0.33
Mozambique	*10.4*	..	..	58.8	47.0	17.6	21.3	1	3	3	−0.30
Myanmar	*5.0*	−3.1	−4.4	84.3	51.0	..	..	6	6	6	−1.65
Nepal	9.5	0.6	0.0	48.1	34.0	*20.1*	*18.7*	2	1	1	−0.89
Netherlands	2.4	1.8	−3.3	48.2	66.8	3.4	5.0	1	1	1	1.71
New Zealand	2.6	3.8	−4.2	19.4	35.8	*11.2*	*12.0*	3	3	3	1.83
Nicaragua	7.6	1.5	0.9	85.9	57.0	13.3	19.5	2	2	2	−0.61
Niger	1.7	..	..	39.6	27.6	10.5	13.6	1	1	1	−0.58
Nigeria	11.5	9.5	−0.3	17.7	16.8	28.7	16.1	3	2	2	−1.15
Norway	1.0	14.5	10.6	54.3	39.2	15.9	11.0	3	3	3	1.70
Pakistan	10.8	−0.5	−2.9	59.4	61.4	10.4	7.5	2	2	2	−1.14
Panama	5.8	4.0	−0.1	54.2	39.4	8.5	8.1	1	1	1	0.08
Papua New Guinea	*8.4*	8.1	2.4	..	..	24.8	31.1	2	2	2	−0.69
Paraguay	5.9	..	..	25.3	12.3	16.2	19.3	3	3	1	−0.60
Peru	3.5	3.3	2.2	33.7	22.1	20.9	29.4	2	2	2	−0.18
Philippines	3.9	3.9	1.4	51.8	42.4	19.8	31.3	2	2	3	−0.49
Poland	4.0	−0.6	−2.7	46.6	55.5	14.6	20.0	3	3	3	0.83
Portugal	3.2	−2.0	−2.8	64.8	108.1	5.1	6.3	1	1	1	0.93
Romania	4.6	−1.0	−2.9	14.3	34.1	23.4	26.3	5	3	3	0.15
Russian Federation	6.7	8.2	−0.2	10.6	11.2	30.5	27.3	2	2	3	−0.74
Rwanda	6.0	−1.2	−0.7	41.4	25.0	*14.9*	*15.5*	..	2	2	−0.21
Saudi Arabia	4.7	20.9	10.4	26.8	5.8	*64.8*	*99.2*	1	1	1	−0.47
Senegal	2.4	−3.2	−4.4	30.3	40.2	14.2	14.7	1	1	1	−0.39
Serbia	9.2	..	..	44.4	53.4	33.4	36.1	..	3	3	−0.12
Sierra Leone	14.5	8.2	−2.4	93.4	49.2	10.1	14.5	..	4	2	−0.64
Singapore	4.9	7.6	5.2	88.5	105.2	97.9	100.1	3	3	3	1.47
Slovak Republic	3.8	−1.3	−4.5	31.3	45.5	22.4	2.0	2	2	1	0.79
Somalia	..	..	..	..	..	..	..		6	6	−2.30
South Africa	5.4	3.8	−1.8	31.9	39.2	9.9	11.9	4	4	4	0.25
South Sudan	*47.3*	..	..	..	..	..	..	..	..	..	−1.48
Spain	2.8	3.1	−7.9	39.7	71.5	1.5	2.7	1	1	1	0.94
Sri Lanka	6.8	−1.9	−1.5	..	..	10.7	12.2	2	2	2	−0.29
Sudan	..	..	..	80.2	80.6	4.9	0.7	2	2	2	−1.60
Sweden	1.9	2.2	−1.0	45.3	38.6	6.8	9.5	3	3	3	1.80
Switzerland	−0.2	1.5	0.8	62.7	49.0	15.9	58.1	3	3	3	1.71
Syrian Arab Republic	19.7	..	..	46.8	29.4	*52.1*	*34.9*	3	..	..	−1.10
Tajikistan	9.1	..	..	37.2	34.8	5.9	6.5	5	2	2	−1.10
Tanzania	14.3	..	..	42.4	39.7	15.8	15.7	2	2	2	−0.36
Thailand	3.4	2.4	−0.2	42.6	42.9	32.4	50.7	3	3	3	−0.29
Togo	3.1	−1.0	−2.9	93.8	47.5	14.5	18.4	1	1	1	−0.89
Tunisia	4.6	0.0	−1.3	49.1	43.0	18.3	19.0	2	2	2	−0.18
Turkey	7.7	4.5	1.7	46.4	39.3	11.5	11.9	3	4	3	−0.01
Turkmenistan		..	..	3.7	11.2	..	..	6	6	6	−1.41
Uganda	16.3	..	−3.3	57.8	31.2	18.2	15.7	3	2	2	−0.59
Ukraine	4.2	−1.2	−2.6	14.9	38.2	22.0	19.2	1	1	1	−0.58
United Arab Emirates	*0.9*	16.5	8.5	7.1	19.2	*18.0*	*10.7*	..	1	1	0.48
United Kingdom	3.7	−1.5	−6.2	42.8	85.1	2.0	3.7	3	3	3	1.34
United States	2.6	−0.7	−7.9	66.6	102.4	1.7	2.6	4	4	4	1.23
Uruguay	8.1	3.8	1.3	71.1	56.5	17.0	23.2	2	3	3	0.84
Uzbekistan	..	4.1	6.2	21.8	9.2	..	..	..	3	3	−1.29
Venezuela, RB	23.6	2.0	−17.2	36.4	40.8	18.4	6.3	2	1	1	−1.28
Vietnam	13.8	−0.2	−2.4	42.5	52.3	*24.1*	*11.3*	..	2	2	−0.54
West Bank and Gaza	..	..	..	..	..	..	..	1	1	1	−0.76
Yemen, Rep.	16.8	−0.4	−0.6	41.7	43.6	37.5	16.6	..	2	2	−1.33
Zambia	*6.4*	..	..	25.3	25.9	8.0	13.3	5	3	4	−0.30
Zimbabwe	..	..	..	58.0	67.8	2.4	7.3	1	5	1	−1.47
World		1.5m	−1.8m	42.6m	41.3m						
Low income		0.3	−1.9	58.0	35.9						
Middle income		0.8	−1.7	41.8	40.8						
Lower middle income		−0.3	−2.1	42.5	38.9						
Upper middle income		2.6	−0.9	38.7	41.3						
Low & middle income		0.8	−1.8	46.4	39.7						
High income		2.1	−1.6	34.8	48.6						

TABLE 8 *Natural disasters and climate change indicators*

	Consequences of natural hazards (droughts, earthquakes, floods, storms)								
	Total deaths		Average annual deaths per million population		Total damages $ millions		Average annual damages % of GDP		CO_2 emissions Per capita, metric tons
	1993–2002	2003–12	1993–2002	2003–12	1993–2002	2003–12	1993–2002	2003–12	2009
Afghanistan	8,787	1,908	45.1	7.1	20	167	..	0.16	0.2
Albania	11	5	0.3	0.2	18	0	0.06	0.00	1.0
Algeria	1,292	2,694	4.2	7.5	362	6,179	0.08	0.36	3.3
Angola	169	372	1.3	2.0	10	0	0.02	0.00	1.4
Argentina	86	109	0.2	0.3	3,307	1,198	0.11	0.04	4.4
Armenia	4	1	0.1	0.0	141	0	0.75	0.00	1.5
Australia	82	80	0.4	0.4	7,974	18,907	0.20	0.18	18.4
Austria	20	9	0.3	0.1	2,640	2,300	0.12	0.06	7.4
Azerbaijan	49	3	0.6	0.0	156	55	0.35	0.01	5.5
Bangladesh	5,891	7,772	4.6	5.3	6,342	5,384	1.44	0.68	0.3
Belarus	7	0	0.1	0.0	137	10	0.09	0.00	6.3
Belgium	16	11	0.2	0.1	183	947	0.01	0.02	9.6
Benin	34	85	0.5	0.9	3	0	0.01	0.00	0.5
Bolivia	323	305	4.0	3.1	291	746	0.34	0.45	1.4
Bosnia and Herzegovina	0	7	0.0	0.2	158	227	0.38	0.12	7.8
Brazil	401	2,142	0.2	1.1	262	7,619	0.00	0.05	1.9
Bulgaria	3	56	0.0	0.7	1	461	0.00	0.09	5.6
Burkina Faso	28	101	0.3	0.7	0	150	0.00	0.18	0.1
Burundi	6	180	0.1	2.1	0	0	0.00	0.00	0.0
Cambodia	1,029	311	8.8	2.2	315	592	1.01	0.57	0.3
Cameroon	63	57	0.4	0.3	0	0	0.00	0.00	0.3
Canada	77	26	0.3	0.1	2,549	3,186	0.04	0.02	15.2
Central African Republic	10	13	0.3	0.3	0	0	0.00	0.00	0.1
Chad	102	131	1.3	1.2	1	10	0.01	0.01	0.0
Chile	221	666	1.5	4.0	505	30,231	0.06	1.68	3.9
China	22,136	100,853	1.8	7.6	120,564	205,511	1.18	0.45	5.8
Hong Kong SAR, China	91	7	1.4	0.1	249	0	0.01	0.00	5.3
Colombia	1,935	1,635	5.0	3.6	1,863	3,442	0.19	0.14	1.6
Congo, Dem. Rep.	331	110	0.7	0.2	9	0	0.01	0.00	0.0
Congo, Rep.	2	32	0.1	0.8	0	0	0.00	0.00	0.5
Costa Rica	101	119	2.7	2.6	577	370	0.41	0.12	1.8
Côte d'Ivoire	28	24	0.2	0.1	0	0	0.00	0.00	0.4
Croatia	0	2	0.0	0.0	0	410	0.00	0.06	4.9
Czech Republic	56	39	0.5	0.4	4,438	698	0.69	0.03	10.3
Denmark	8	4	0.2	0.1	2,605	1,400	0.15	0.04	8.3
Dominican Republic	421	954	5.0	9.8	1,982	587	0.94	0.13	2.1
Ecuador	401	108	3.3	0.7	305	1,155	0.11	0.19	2.0
Egypt, Arab Rep.	669	71	1.0	0.1	142	0	0.02	0.00	2.8
El Salvador	1,669	479	28.3	7.8	2,432	2,342	2.02	1.09	1.0
Eritrea	3	0	0.1	0.0	5	0	0.07	0.00	0.1
Ethiopia	543	1,367	0.9	1.7	22	9	0.03	0.00	0.1
Finland	..	..	..	..	..	..	..	..	10.0
France	247	137	0.4	0.2	15,939	10,760	0.11	0.04	5.6
Georgia	14	13	0.3	0.3	582	96	1.61	0.08	1.3
Germany	112	70	0.1	0.1	19,619	10,202	0.09	0.03	9.0
Ghana	213	179	1.2	0.8	34	0	0.04	0.00	0.3
Greece	236	10	2.2	0.1	5,670	946	0.42	0.03	8.4
Guatemala	532	1,856	5.0	13.6	774	1,910	0.40	0.49	1.1
Guinea	25	10	0.3	0.1	0	0	0.00	0.00	0.1
Haiti	1,499	229,306	18.1	2,379.1	231	8,356	0.62	13.04	0.2
Honduras	15,270	333	255.3	4.5	4,061	340	7.81	0.24	1.0
Hungary	49	17	0.5	0.2	393	598	0.08	0.04	4.9
India	60,760	30,870	6.0	2.6	20,325	22,273	0.47	0.18	1.7
Indonesia	3,048	178,093	1.5	76.0	1,674	11,981	0.18	0.23	1.9
Iran, Islamic Rep.	4,786	28,093	7.5	38.7	5,726	1,183	0.56	0.03	8.2
Iraq	0	36	0.0	0.1	0	1	0.00	0.00	3.6
Ireland	16	2	0.4	0.0	239	325	0.03	0.01	9.3
Israel	18	2	0.3	0.0	118	0	0.01	0.00	9.0
Italy	214	395	0.4	0.7	25,552	22,586	0.21	0.10	6.7
Japan	5,885	20,781	4.7	16.3	123,726	280,055	0.32	0.58	8.6
Jordan	16	0	0.3	0.0	1	0	0.00	0.00	3.8
Kazakhstan	122	50	0.8	0.3	41	239	0.02	0.02	14.0
Kenya	300	874	1.0	2.3	12	201	0.01	0.07	0.3
Korea, Rep.	1,163	358	2.5	0.7	7,614	6,414	0.22	0.07	10.4
Kyrgyz Republic	1	81	0.0	1.5	4	3	0.03	0.01	1.2
Lao PDR	81	80	1.6	1.3	304	100	2.38	0.18	0.3
Lebanon	0	0	0.0	0.0	0	0	0.00	0.00	4.9
Liberia	10	4	0.4	0.1	0	0	0.00	0.00	0.1
Libya	0	0	0.0	0.0	42	0	0.02	0.00	10.5
Lithuania	8	4	0.2	0.1	5	256	0.00	0.05	3.8
Madagascar	571	1,101	3.9	5.5	69	805	0.19	0.86	0.1
Malawi	573	46	5.4	0.3	8	0	0.04	0.00	0.1
Malaysia	328	172	1.5	0.6	54	1,500	0.01	0.06	7.1
Mali	24	45	0.2	0.3	0	0	0.00	0.00	0.0
Mauritania	26	20	1.0	0.6	0	0	0.00	0.00	0.6

TABLE 8 *Natural disasters and climate change indicators* (continued)

	Consequences of natural hazards (droughts, earthquakes, floods, storms)								
	Total deaths		Average annual deaths per million population		Total damages \$ millions		Average annual damages % of GDP		CO_2 emissions Per capita, metric tons
	1993–2002	2003–12	1993–2002	2003–12	1993–2002	2003–12	1993–2002	2003–12	2009
Mexico	2,261	542	2.2	0.5	8,960	20,186	0.21	0.18	3.8
Moldova	62	4	1.7	0.1	386	414	2.36	0.68	1.3
Morocco	991	791	3.5	2.6	1,166	429	0.29	0.05	1.6
Mozambique	1,232	237	7.1	1.0	483	194	1.12	0.20	0.1
Myanmar	230	139,047	0.5	271.7	10	4,564	..	..	0.2
Nepal	2,620	1,254	11.8	4.8	237	63	0.49	0.05	0.1
Netherlands	8	7	0.1	0.0	2,065	578	0.05	0.01	10.3
New Zealand	4	191	0.1	4.5	177	24,842	0.03	1.91	7.4
Nicaragua	3,489	332	70.7	5.9	1,020	0	2.20	0.00	0.8
Niger	84	140	0.8	0.9	0	3	0.00	0.01	0.1
Nigeria	438	935	0.4	0.6	76	538	0.02	0.03	0.5
Norway	1	4	0.0	0.1	303	130	0.02	0.00	9.7
Pakistan	4,173	79,205	3.0	47.4	596	22,117	0.10	1.35	0.9
Panama	11	83	0.4	2.3	9	17	0.01	0.01	2.2
Papua New Guinea	2,359	180	46.2	2.7	162	27	0.43	0.03	0.5
Paraguay	100	9	1.9	0.1	7	7	0.01	0.00	0.7
Peru	1,055	958	4.2	3.3	362	600	0.06	0.05	1.6
Philippines	5,142	10,834	6.9	12.0	2,089	4,847	0.29	0.28	0.7
Poland	104	52	0.3	0.1	4,211	3,336	0.24	0.06	7.8
Portugal	50	48	0.5	0.5	48	2,958	0.00	0.12	5.4
Romania	143	212	0.6	1.0	1,062	1,313	0.25	0.06	3.7
Russian Federation	2,706	270	1.8	0.2	2,503	3,977	0.09	0.02	11.1
Rwanda	126	85	1.8	0.8	0	0	0.00	0.00	0.1
Saudi Arabia	19	295	0.1	1.1	0	1,200	0.00	0.03	16.2
Senegal	215	46	2.3	0.4	41	10	0.08	0.01	0.4
Serbia	12	2	0.2	0.0	0	0	0.00	0.00	6.3
Sierra Leone	25	154	0.6	2.8	0	0	0.00	0.00	0.3
Singapore	0	0	0.0	0.0	0	0	0.00	0.00	6.4
Slovak Republic	57	9	1.1	0.2	227	408	0.08	0.04	6.3
Somalia	2,485	482	36.0	5.3	0	100	..	..	0.1
South Africa	500	163	1.2	0.3	401	673	0.03	0.02	10.1
South Sudan	..	..	..	..	..	..	..	..	0.0
Spain	109	46	0.3	0.1	8,661	3,249	0.14	0.02	6.3
Sri Lanka	42	35,931	0.2	177.7	4	2,012	0.00	0.49	0.6
Sudan	369	330	1.4	1.0	42	484	0.04	0.09	0.3
Sweden	4	7	0.0	0.1	160	2,800	0.01	0.06	4.7
Switzerland	18	8	0.3	0.1	2,348	3,569	0.08	0.07	5.4
Syrian Arab Republic	27	11	0.2	0.1	0	0	0.00	0.00	3.1
Tajikistan	113	148	1.9	2.0	132	311	1.00	0.60	0.4
Tanzania	289	171	0.9	0.4	4	0	0.00	0.00	0.2
Thailand	1,244	10,008	2.0	15.1	2,929	42,573	0.26	1.56	4.1
Togo	3	69	0.1	1.2	0	0	0.00	0.00	0.2
Tunisia	..	..	..	..	..	..	..	..	2.4
Turkey	18,515	1,111	30.2	1.6	23,019	2,746	0.85	0.04	3.9
Turkmenistan	11	0	0.3	0.0	100	0	0.38	0.00	9.7
Uganda	319	160	1.4	0.5	73	0	0.11	0.00	0.1
Ukraine	57	46	0.1	0.1	426	2,816	0.10	0.16	5.9
United Arab Emirates	..	..	..	..	..	..	..	..	20.3
United Kingdom	108	58	0.2	0.1	11,439	13,938	0.08	0.05	7.7
United States	2,317	4,242	0.8	1.4	128,109	474,999	0.15	0.33	17.3
Uruguay	5	21	0.2	0.6	280	45	0.11	0.01	2.3
Uzbekistan	0	13	0.0	0.0	50	0	0.03	0.00	4.2
Venezuela, RB	30,233	212	128.7	0.8	3,249	330	0.36	0.01	6.5
Vietnam	7,852	2,692	10.4	3.2	3,250	5,605	1.19	0.62	1.7
West Bank and Gaza	..	..	..	..	..	..	..	..	0.6
Yemen, Rep.	562	278	3.4	1.3	1,212	0	1.92	0.00	1.1
Zambia	5	55	0.1	0.4	21	0	0.06	0.00	0.2
Zimbabwe	119	37	1.0	0.3	127	0	0.20	0.00	0.7
World	**240,551 s**	**911,500 s**	**4.1 w**	**13.7 w**	**656,227 s**	**1,340,427 s**	**0.21 w**	**0.22 w**	**4.7 w**[a]
Low income	27,921	386,806	4.6	50.5	31,429	21,249	0.56	0.51	0.3
Middle income	195,846	495,936	4.8	10.6	222,706	389,427	0.44	0.26	3.3
Lower middle income	109,266	344,583	5.5	14.6	41,440	80,026	0.39	0.24	1.6
Upper middle income	86,580	151,353	4.1	6.6	181,266	309,401	0.46	0.26	5.1
Low & middle income	223,767	882,742	4.7	16.3	254,135	410,675	0.45	0.26	2.9
High income	16,784	28,758	1.4	2.3	402,093	929,752	0.16	0.21	11.2
Selected island states	7,237	241,643	7.4	205.9	5,859	17,287	0.48	0.61	1.3

a. Includes emissions not allocated to specific countries.

TABLE 9 *Global temperature anomalies: Difference relative to 1951–80*

	Temperature means (degrees Celsius)					
	Dec–Feb	Mar–May	Jun–Aug	Sep–Nov	Jan–Dec	5 year average
1951	−0.32	−0.09	0.01	0.04	−0.06	−0.05
1952	0.12	−0.01	0.03	−0.04	0.02	−0.05
1953	0.10	0.14	0.05	0.03	0.09	−0.04
1954	−0.08	−0.16	−0.15	0.00	−0.12	−0.06
1955	−0.05	−0.23	−0.03	−0.13	−0.12	−0.06
1956	−0.23	−0.23	−0.17	−0.17	−0.18	−0.07
1957	−0.09	−0.01	0.12	0.06	0.04	−0.04
1958	0.25	0.05	−0.07	−0.01	0.04	−0.02
1959	0.04	0.11	0.02	−0.08	0.03	0.02
1960	0.03	−0.21	−0.03	−0.00	−0.04	0.02
1961	0.13	0.11	0.04	0.02	0.05	0.03
1962	0.02	0.04	0.01	0.02	0.04	−0.02
1963	0.06	−0.09	0.14	0.18	0.07	−0.03
1964	−0.06	−0.26	−0.12	−0.25	−0.20	−0.05
1965	−0.17	−0.13	−0.10	−0.09	−0.10	−0.06
1966	−0.07	−0.05	−0.00	−0.04	−0.04	−0.08
1967	−0.09	0.06	−0.02	−0.01	−0.01	−0.03
1968	−0.11	0.05	−0.07	−0.03	−0.05	0.00
1969	−0.13	0.10	0.02	0.12	0.06	−0.00
1970	0.22	0.05	−0.02	0.06	0.04	0.00
1971	−0.10	−0.09	−0.08	−0.01	−0.07	0.04
1972	−0.15	0.01	0.10	0.05	0.02	0.02
1973	0.26	0.26	0.11	0.09	0.16	0.01
1974	−0.15	−0.05	0.01	−0.08	−0.07	−0.00
1975	0.03	0.11	−0.06	−0.10	−0.01	0.02
1976	−0.10	−0.18	−0.14	−0.15	−0.12	−0.00
1977	0.10	0.24	0.21	0.05	0.15	0.04
1978	0.07	0.11	−0.05	0.07	0.05	0.09
1979	0.02	0.08	0.05	0.21	0.12	0.17
1980	0.35	0.28	0.20	0.18	0.23	0.16
1981	0.35	0.31	0.29	0.13	0.29	0.20
1982	0.18	0.03	0.06	0.09	0.09	0.20
1983	0.41	0.33	0.19	0.25	0.27	0.17
1984	0.17	0.21	0.09	0.09	0.12	0.14
1985	0.02	0.10	0.07	0.08	0.08	0.18
1986	0.23	0.23	0.09	0.04	0.15	0.20
1987	0.27	0.18	0.32	0.27	0.29	0.22
1988	0.44	0.41	0.36	0.26	0.36	0.29
1989	0.23	0.24	0.24	0.25	0.24	0.33
1990	0.34	0.54	0.33	0.34	0.40	0.31
1991	0.41	0.38	0.45	0.32	0.38	0.28
1992	0.37	0.31	0.13	0.01	0.19	0.29
1993	0.29	0.26	0.18	0.10	0.21	0.30
1994	0.14	0.30	0.28	0.38	0.29	0.29
1995	0.54	0.38	0.45	0.39	0.43	0.34
1996	0.33	0.31	0.36	0.28	0.33	0.43
1997	0.36	0.42	0.41	0.59	0.46	0.45
1998	0.68	0.64	0.70	0.45	0.61	0.44
1999	0.56	0.32	0.37	0.39	0.40	0.48
2000	0.41	0.51	0.42	0.34	0.41	0.51
2001	0.38	0.55	0.53	0.56	0.53	0.51
2002	0.66	0.70	0.56	0.59	0.62	0.54
2003	0.57	0.56	0.55	0.63	0.60	0.59
2004	0.65	0.54	0.36	0.60	0.52	0.60
2005	0.58	0.65	0.62	0.74	0.66	0.60
2006	0.62	0.49	0.59	0.65	0.59	0.58
2007	0.78	0.68	0.57	0.58	0.63	0.59
2008	0.34	0.55	0.46	0.61	0.49	0.59
2009	0.52	0.55	0.63	0.64	0.59	0.59
2010	0.66	0.80	0.59	0.65	0.67	0.57
2011	0.45	0.56	0.64	0.54	0.55	
2012	0.42	0.60	0.56	0.70	0.57	

	Dec–Feb	Mar–May	Jun–Aug	Sep–Nov	10 year average
1951–1960	−0.02	−0.06	−0.02	−0.03	−0.03
1961–1970	−0.02	−0.01	−0.01	−0.00	−0.01
1971–1980	0.03	0.08	0.03	0.03	0.05
1981–1990	0.26	0.26	0.20	0.18	0.23
1991–2000	0.41	0.38	0.37	0.33	0.37
2001–2010	0.58	0.61	0.55	0.63	0.59

TABLE 10 *Aid commitments*

	Emergency response		Reconstruction relief		Prevention and preparedness		Total
	$ millions	% of total	$ millions	% of total	$ millions	% of total	$ millions
1981	417.3	80.3	101.3	19.5	1.1	0.2	519.6
1982	698.4	71.3	242.0	24.7	39.1	4.0	979.5
1983	615.0	54.4	466.2	41.2	49.9	4.4	1,131.1
1984	1,226.2	65.3	596.6	31.8	53.6	2.9	1,876.4
1985	813.7	44.0	863.3	46.7	172.8	9.3	1,849.9
1986	838.1	62.7	497.5	37.3	0.0	0.0	1,335.6
1987	1,134.7	66.6	562.0	33.0	7.0	0.4	1,703.7
1988	535.2	52.4	461.2	45.1	25.9	2.5	1,022.3
1989	638.0	43.6	817.4	55.9	6.8	0.5	1,462.2
1990	930.0	58.1	579.5	36.2	91.6	5.7	1,601.1
1991	1,316.0	89.6	142.6	9.7	9.4	0.6	1,468.0
1992	1,252.4	76.5	377.1	23.0	8.3	0.5	1,637.7
1993	1,031.3	68.7	456.8	30.4	12.5	0.8	1,500.7
1994	1,253.9	71.0	511.3	29.0	0.5	0.0	1,765.7
1995	1,804.5	83.6	339.5	15.7	13.4	0.6	2,157.4
1996	2,818.5	93.7	186.5	6.2	3.5	0.1	3,008.6
1997	2,329.6	83.9	220.4	7.9	227.8	8.2	2,777.7
1998	3,107.5	72.4	1,143.5	26.7	38.1	0.9	4,289.2
1999	5,254.9	78.4	1,393.0	20.8	52.1	0.8	6,699.9
2000	2,403.7	70.0	975.4	28.4	56.5	1.6	3,435.6
2001	2,819.9	52.8	2,473.8	46.3	44.1	0.8	5,337.8
2002	3,871.9	69.6	1,609.1	28.9	84.5	1.5	5,565.5
2003	3,244.5	74.6	878.3	20.2	228.4	5.2	4,351.2
2004	4,097.1	83.1	789.7	16.0	43.0	0.9	4,929.8
2005	4,489.6	55.9	2,964.2	36.9	579.0	7.2	8,032.7
2006	3,039.4	65.5	1,374.0	29.6	227.8	4.9	4,641.3
2007	3,472.9	58.5	2,173.4	36.6	290.8	4.9	5,937.1
2008	3,227.9	74.9	573.7	13.3	509.5	11.8	4,311.1
2009	3,698.7	81.2	484.3	10.6	374.4	8.2	4,557.5
2010	225.9	37.2	276.4	45.5	105.6	17.4	607.9
Total	62,606.6	69.2	24,530.0	27.1	3,357.0	3.7	90,493.6
1981–1990	7,846.5	58.2	5,187.1	38.5	447.7	3.3	13,481.3
1991–2000	22,572.2	78.5	5,746.1	20.0	422.1	1.5	28,740.4
2001–2010	32,187.8	66.7	13,596.9	28.2	2,487.2	5.2	48,271.9

Technical notes

Data consistency and reliability

Considerable effort has been made to standardize the data, but full comparability cannot be assured, and care must be taken in interpreting the indicators. Many factors affect data availability, comparability, and reliability: statistical systems in many developing economies are still weak; statistical methods, coverage, practices, and definitions differ widely; and cross country and intertemporal comparisons involve complex technical and conceptual problems that cannot be resolved unequivocally. Data coverage may not be complete because of special circumstances affecting the collection and reporting of data, such as problems stemming from conflicts. For these reasons, although data are drawn from sources thought to be the most authoritative, they should be construed only as indicating trends and characterizing major differences among economies, rather than as offering precise quantitative measures of those differences.

Table 1: Key indicators of development

Population: Total population is based on the de facto definition of population, which counts all residents regardless of legal status or citizenship—except for refugees not permanently settled in the country of asylum, who are generally considered part of the population of their country of origin. The values shown are midyear estimates. **Data sources:** United Nations Population Division, World Population Prospects; United Nations Statistical Division, Population and Vital Statistics Report (various years); census reports and other statistical publications from national statistical offices; Eurostat: Demographic Statistics; Secretariat of the Pacific Community: Statistics and Demography Programme; U.S. Census Bureau: International Database.

Average annual population growth rate: Annual population growth rate for year *t* is the exponential growth rate of the total population (as defined above) from year *t - 1* to *t*, expressed as a percentage. **Data sources:** United Nations Population Division, World Population Prospects; United Nations Statistical Division, Population and Vital Statistics Report (various years); census reports and other statistical publications from national statistical offices; Eurostat: Demographic Statistics; Secretariat of the Pacific Community: Statistics and Demography Programme; U.S. Census Bureau: International Database.

Population density: Population density is the total population (as defined above) divided by land area, in square kilometers. Land area is a country's total area, excluding area under inland water bodies, national claims to continental shelves, and exclusive economic zones. In most cases the definition of inland water bodies includes major rivers and lakes. **Data sources:** Food and Agriculture Organization, at http://faostat.fao.org; population data from World Development Indicators, at http://data.worldbank.org/indicator/SP.POP.TOTL.

Population age composition, ages 0–14: Population age composition is the population between the ages 0 to 14 as a percentage of the total population (as defined above). **Data source:** United Nations Population Division, World Population Prospects, at http://esa.un.org/wpp.

Gross national income: Gross national income (GNI; formerly gross national product or GNP) is the sum of value added by all resident producers, plus any product taxes (less subsidies) not included in the valuation of output, plus net receipts of primary income (compensation of employees and property income) from abroad. **Data sources:** World Bank national accounts data, at http://data.worldbank.org; Organisation for Economic Co-operation and Development (OECD) National Accounts data, at http://stats.oecd.org/.

GNI per capita: GNI per capita is gross national income (as defined above) divided by the total population. **Data source:** World Bank, World Development Indicators, at http://data.worldbank.org/data-catalog/world-development-indicators.

Gross national income, PPP: PPP GNI (formerly PPP GNP) is gross national income (as defined above) converted to current international dollars using purchasing power parity (PPP) rates. An international dollar has the same purchasing power over gross national income as a U.S. dollar has in the United States. **Data sources:** World Bank national accounts data, at http://data.worldbank.org; OECD National Accounts data, at http://stats.oecd.org.

PPP GNI per capita: PPP GNI per capita is GNI per capita (as defined above), based on purchasing power parity (PPP). **Data source:** World Bank, International Comparison Program database, at http://www.worldbank.org/data/icp.

Gross domestic product per capita growth: Gross domestic product (GDP) per capita growth is the annual percentage growth rate of GDP per capita, based on constant local currency. (Aggregates are based on constant 2005 U.S. dollars.) GDP per capita is gross domestic product divided by the total population. GDP (at purchaser's prices) is the sum of gross value added by all resident producers in the economy, plus any product taxes and minus any subsidies not included in the value of the products. It is calculated without making deductions for depreciation of fabricated assets, or for depletion and degradation of natural resources. **Data sources:** World Bank national accounts data, at http://data.worldbank.org; OECD National Accounts data, at http://stats.oecd.org/.

Life expectancy at birth: Life expectancy at birth indicates the number of years a newborn infant would be expected to live if prevailing patterns of mortality at the time of its birth were to stay the same throughout its life. **Data sources:** United Nations Population Division, World Population Prospects; United Nations Statistical Division, Population and Vital Statistics Report (various years); census reports and other statistical publications from national statistical offices; Eurostat: Demographic Statistics; Secretariat of the Pacific Community: Statistics and Demography Programme; U.S. Census Bureau: International Database.

Adult literacy rate: The adult literacy rate is the percentage of people aged 15 and above who can—with understanding—read and write a short, simple statement on their everyday life. **Data source:** United Nations Educational, Scientific, and Cultural Organization Institute for Statistics, at http://www.uis.unesco.org.

Table 2: Key indicators of development for other economies

See indicator descriptions for table 1.

Table 3: Selected risk indicators

Large recessions, years in recession: Using real GDP per capita from the World Development Indicators, large recessions are identified by following Barro and Ursúa 2012 and using as a threshold a 5% decline in GDP per capita growth from peak to trough. The constructed variable is a dummy variable (1 if a country was in a large recession, and 0 otherwise). **Data sources:** Barro, Robert J., and José F. Ursúa, 2012, "Rare Macroeconomic Disasters," *Annual Review of Economics* 4 (1): 83–109), with data available at http://scholar.harvard.edu/barro/publications/barro-ursua-macroeconomic-data; World Bank national accounts data, at http://data.worldbank.org; OECD National Accounts data, at http://stats.oecd.org/.

Incidence of natural hazards (droughts, earthquakes, floods, storms): The incidence of natural hazards is the number of droughts, earthquakes, floods, and storms (as defined by the EM-DAT database) that occurred in the specified time period. Disasters that affect multiple countries are considered to be separate events for the purpose of calculating summary groups. **Data source:** EM-DAT: The OFDA/CRED International Disaster Database, at http://www.emdat.be.

Incidence of epidemics: The incidence of epidemics is the number of epidemics that were recorded in the specified time period. An epidemic is either an unusual increase in the number of cases of an infectious disease that already exists in a region or population, or the appearance of an infection previously absent from a region. Disasters that affect multiple countries are considered to be separate events for the purpose of calculating summary groups. **Data source:** EM-DAT: The OFDA/CRED International Disaster Database, at http://www.emdat.be.

Adult mortality rate (per 1,000 people): The adult mortality rate is the probability of dying between the ages 15 and 60, if subject to the age specific mortality rates of that year between those ages. **Data sources:** United Nations Population Division, World Population Prospects, at http://esa.un.org/wpp; University of California, Berkeley and Max Planck Institute for Demographic Research, Human Mortality Database, at http://www.mortality.org.

Homicide rate (per 100,000 people): Intentional homicides are estimates of unlawful homicides purposely inflicted as a result of domestic disputes, interpersonal violence, violent conflicts over land resources, intergang violence over turf or control, and predatory violence and killing by armed groups. Intentional homicide does not include all intentional killing; the difference is usually in the organization of the killing. Individuals or small groups usually commit homicide, whereas killing in armed conflict is usually committed by fairly cohesive groups of up to several hundred members and is thus usually excluded. **Data source:** United Nations Office on Drugs and Crime's International Homicide Statistics, at http://www.unodc.org/unodc/en/data-and-analysis/homicide.html.

Poverty headcount ratio ($2.50 a day and $10 a day, PPP; % population): The poverty headcount ratio is the percentage of the population living on less than $2.50 a day and $10 a day, respectively, at 2005 international prices. **Data source:** World Bank, PovcalNet (an online tool for poverty measurement), at http://iresearch.worldbank.org/PovcalNet/index.htm.

Volatility of household consumption growth per capita: Historical volatility is calculated by looking at past changes in household consumption per capita. Household consumption growth per capita is approximated using natural logarithm differences. The standard deviation of percentage changes in household consumption per capita (observed volatility) is calculated within decades with at least nine observations. **Data sources:** World Bank national accounts data, at http://data.worldbank.org; OECD National Accounts data, at http://stats.oecd.org.

Volatility of GDP growth per capita: Historical volatility is calculated by looking at past changes in GDP per capita. GDP per capita growth is approximated using natural logarithm differences. The standard deviation of percentage changes in GDP per capita (observed volatility) is calculated within decades with at least nine observations. **Data sources:** World Bank national accounts data, at http://data.worldbank.org; OECD National Accounts data, at http://stats.oecd.org.

Risk preparation index: The risk preparation index is a composite index that estimates preparation for risk across countries. The components of the index are average years of schooling; immunization rate (measles); proportion of households with less than $1,000 in net assets; access to finance index; contributors to a pension scheme (% of labor force); proportion of respondents stating that "in general, people can be trusted"; access to improved sanitation facilities (% of population); and gross public debt (% of revenues). The index follows the methodology suggested in Foa, R, 2013, "Household Risk Preparation Indices: Construction and Diagnostics," Background Paper for the *World Development Report 2014.* **Data source:** calculations by WDR staff.

Table 4: Selected indicators related to risk management at the household level

Educational attainment (primary, secondary, and tertiary): Educational attainment is the percentage of the population aged over 25 who have completed each level of education (primary, secondary, and tertiary). Observations are estimates based on population censuses. **Data source:** Robert J. Barro and Jong-Wha Lee, Barro-Lee Educational Attainment Dataset, at http://www.barrolee.com.

Education quality, PISA mean score (math and reading): The Programme for International Student Assessment (PISA) is an internationally comparable student assessment, coordinated by the OECD. The assessment has evaluated the knowledge and skills of 15 year olds by testing reading, mathematical, and scientific literacy every three years since 1997. Mean performance by subject refers to the average score of all students' scores in that country. **Data source:** OECD, at http://www.oecd.org/pisa.

Under-five mortality rate (per 1,000 live births): The under-five mortality rate is the probability that a newborn baby will die before reaching age five, if subject to the age specific mortality rates of that year. **Data source:** Level and Trends in Child Mortality, UN Inter-agency Group for Child Mortality Estimation (United Nations Children's Fund (UNICEF), World Health Organization (WHO), World Bank, and United Nations Population Division), at http://www.childmortality.org.

Maternal mortality ratio (per 100,000 live births): The maternal mortality ratio is number of women who die from pregnancy related causes while pregnant or within 42 days of pregnancy termination. **Data source:** Trends in Maternal Mortality: 1990–2010, WHO, UNICEF, United Nations Population Fund, and the World Bank, at http://www.who.int/reproductivehealth/publications/monitoring/9789241503631/en.

Access to social insurance: Access to social insurance is the percentage of the population aged 60 and over who are beneficiaries of social insurance. **Data sources:** World Bank, Pensions (database), at http://go.worldbank.org/8KO0DUVDS0; United Nations Population Division, World Population Prospects at http://esa.un.org/wpp.

Savings, % of people who saved in the past year: The percentage of people who saved in the past year denotes the percentage of respondents (aged 15+) who report saving or setting aside any money in the past 12 months. **Data source:** World Bank, Global Financial Inclusion Database, at http://data.worldbank.org/data-catalog/financial_inclusion.

Table 5: Selected indicators related to risk management at the enterprise sector level

Wage employment: Wage and salaried workers (employees) are those workers who hold the type of jobs defined as "paid employment jobs," where the incumbents hold explicit (written or oral) or implicit employment contracts that give them a basic remuneration that is not directly dependent upon the revenue of the unit for which they work. **Data source:**

International Labour Organization, Key Indicators of the Labour Market (database), at http://www.ilo.org/kilm.

Goods market efficiency: Goods market efficiency is a composite indicator of economies' capacities to produce the right mix of products and services given their particular supply and demand conditions, as well as to ensure that these goods can be most effectively traded. The indicator uses a 1–7 scale, where 1 indicates the lowest efficiency and 7 the highest efficiency. **Data source:** World Economic Forum, Global Competitiveness Report, 2006-07 and 2012-13 editions, at http://www.weforum.org/issues/competitiveness-0/gci2012-data-platform.

Labor market efficiency: Labor market efficiency is a composite indicator of economies' efficiency in allocating workers to their most effective uses and providing incentives for them to give their best efforts in their jobs. The indicator uses a 1–7 scale, where 1 indicates the lowest efficiency and 7 the highest efficiency. **Data source:** World Economic Forum, Global Competitiveness Report, 2006-07 and 2012-13 editions, at http://www.weforum.org/issues/competitiveness-0/gci2012-data-platform.

Pension contributors: Pension contributors are the total number of people who actively contribute to the pension system in a given year, as a percentage of the labor force. **Data sources:** World Bank, Pensions (database), at http://go.worldbank.org/8KO0DUVDS0; Pallares-Miralles, Montserrat, Carolina Romero, and Edward Whitehouse, 2012, "International Patterns of Pension Provision II: A Worldwide Overview of Facts and Figures," Social Protection and Labor Discussion Paper SP 1211, World Bank, Washington D.C.

Formal production: Formal production is production by the formal sector, as a share of the economy, computed as 100 minus the estimated size of the shadow economy. **Data source:** Schneider, Friedrich, Andreas Buehn, and Claudio E. Montenegro, 2010, "Shadow Economies All over the World: New Estimates for 162 Countries from 1999 to 2007," at http://documents.worldbank.org/curated/en/2010/06/12864844/shadow-economies-all-over-world-new-estimates-162-countries-1999-2007.

Table 6: Selected indicators related to risk management at the financial sector level

Saved at a financial institution: The percentage of people who have saved at a financial institution is the percentage of respondents (aged 15+) who report saving or setting aside any money by using an account at a formal financial institution such as a bank, credit union, microfinance institution, or cooperative in the past 12 months. **Data source:** World Bank, Global Financial Inclusion Database, at http://data.worldbank.org/data-catalog/financial_inclusion.

Loan from a financial institution: The percentage of people who have obtained a loan from a financial institution is the percentage of respondents (aged 15+) who report borrowing any money from a bank, credit union, microfinance institution, or other financial institution such as a cooperative in the past 12 months. **Data source:** World Bank, Global Financial Inclusion Database, at http://data.worldbank.org/data-catalog/financial_inclusion.

Personally paid for health insurance: The percentage of people who have personally paid for health insurance is the percentage of respondents (aged 15+) who have personally purchased health or medical insurance (in addition to any nationally provided health insurance). **Data source:** World Bank, Global Financial Inclusion Database, at http://data.worldbank.org/data-catalog/financial_inclusion.

Purchased agriculture insurance: The percentage of people who have purchased agriculture insurance is the percentage of respondents (aged 15+) who are farming, fishing, or forestry workers and have personally paid for crop, rainfall, or livestock insurance in the past 12 months. **Data source:** World Bank, Global Financial Inclusion Database, at http://data.worldbank.org/data-catalog/financial_inclusion.

Population using informal savings: The population using informal savings is calculated as the difference between the percentage of respondents (aged 15+) who have "saved any money in the past year" and those who "saved at a financial institution in the past year". **Data source:** World Bank, Global Financial Inclusion Database, at http://data.worldbank.org/data-catalog/financial_inclusion.

Population using informal credit: The population using informal credit is calculated as the difference between the percentage of respondents (aged 15+) who have obtained a "loan in the past year" and those who obtained a "loan from a financial institution in the past year". The percentage of people who have obtained a loan in the past year is the percentage of respondents who borrowed money in the past 12 months from a formal financial institution, a store (by using installment credit), family or friends, an employer, or another private lender. **Data source:** World Bank, Global Financial Inclusion Database, at http://data.worldbank.org/data-catalog/financial_inclusion.

Use of electronic payments: Use of electronic payments is the total transaction volume of direct credits and credit transfers, direct debits, payments by debit card, and payments by credit cards. **Data source:** World Bank, Global Payment Systems Survey, at http://go.worldbank.org/5MYOUCYBR0.

Stock market capitalization: Stock market capitalization is the total value of all listed shares in a stock market, as a percentage of GDP. **Data sources:** Standard & Poor's, *Global Stock Markets Factbook* and supplemental S&P data; World Bank, Global Financial Development Database, at http://data.worldbank.org/data-catalog/global-financial-development.

Bank assets (% of GDP): Banks assets to GDP is the ratio of total assets held by deposit money banks to GDP. Assets include claims on the domestic real nonfinancial sector (which includes central, state, and local governments); nonfinancial public enterprises; and the private sector. Deposit money banks comprise commercial banks and other financial institutions that accept transferable deposits, such as demand deposits. **Data source:** World Bank, Global Financial Development Database, at http://data.worldbank.org/data-catalog/global-financial-development.

Mutual fund assets (% of GDP): Mutual fund assets to GDP is the ratio of the total assets held by mutual funds to GDP. A mutual fund is a type of managed collective investment scheme that pools money from many investors to purchase securities. **Data source:** World Bank, Global Financial Development Database, at http://data.worldbank.org/data-catalog/global-financial-development.

Insurance assets (% of GDP): Insurance assets to GDP is the ratio of the total assets held by insurance companies to GDP. **Data source:** World Bank, Global Financial Development Database, at http://data.worldbank.org/data-catalog/global-financial-development.

Pension assets (% of GDP): Pension assets to GDP is the ratio of the total assets held by pension funds to GDP. A pension fund is any plan, fund, or scheme that provides retirement income. **Data source:** World Bank, Global Financial Development Database, at http://data.worldbank.org/data-catalog/global-financial-development.

Bank savings (% of GDP): Banks savings to GDP is the sum of domestic demand, time, and savings deposits in deposit money banks, expressed as a share of GDP. **Data source:** World Bank, Global Financial Development Database, at http://data.worldbank.org/data-catalog/global-financial-development.

Credit (% of GDP): Credit to GDP is the ratio of domestic private credit to the real sector by deposit money banks to GDP. **Data source:** World Bank, Global Financial Development Database, at http://data.worldbank.org/data-catalog/global-financial-development.

Insurance premiums (% of GDP): Insurance premiums to GDP is the ratio of insurance premiums (life and nonlife) to GDP. **Data source:** World Bank, Global Financial Development Database, at http://data.worldbank.org/data-catalog/global-financial-development.

Loan dollarization: Loan dollarizarion is the ratio of foreign currency denominated loans to total loans. **Data source:** Chitu, Livia, 2013, "Was Unofficial Dollarisation/Euroisation an Amplifier of the 'Great Recession' of 2007–09 in Emerging Economies," *Comparative Economic Studies* 55: 233–65, at http://www.palgrave-journals.com/ces/journal/v55/n2/full/ces20131a.html.

Deposit dollarization: Deposit dollarization is the ratio of foreign currency denominated deposits to total deposits. **Data source:** Chitu, Livia, 2013, "Was Unofficial Dollarisation/Euroisation an Amplifier of the 'Great Recession' of 2007–09 in Emerging Economies," *Comparative Economic Studies* 55: 233–65, at http://www.palgrave-journals.com/ces/journal/v55/n2/full/ces20131a.html.

Loan-to-deposit ratio: The loan-to-deposit ratio is the ratio of private credit by deposit money banks to the sum of domestic demand, time, and saving deposits in deposit money banks. **Data source:** World Bank, FinStats (internal database).

Table 7: Selected indicators related to risk management at the macroeconomy level

CPI inflation rate: The consumer price index (CPI) inflation rate is the annual percentage change in the cost to the average consumer of acquiring a basket of goods and services (which may be fixed or changed at specified intervals). The Laspeyres formula is generally used. **Data source:** International Monetary Fund (IMF) International Financial Statistics, at http://elibrary-data.imf.org/FindDataReports.aspx?d=33061&e=169393.

Government primary surplus: The government primary surplus is the gross fiscal balance plus net interest payments. **Data source:** IMF World Economic Outlook Database April 2013, at http://www.imf.org/external/ns/cs.aspx?id=28.

Gross public debt: Gross public debt is all liabilities that require payment or payments of interest and/or principal by the debtor to the creditor at a date or dates in the future. Gross public debt includes debt liabilities in the form of special drawing rights, currency and deposits, debt securities, loans, insurance, pensions and standardized guarantee schemes, and other accounts payable. **Data sources:** Abbas, S. Ali, Nazim Belhocine, Asmaa El Ganainy and Mark Horton, 2010, "A Historical Public Debt Database", IMF Working Paper WP/10/245, at http://www.imf.org/external/pubs/cat/longres.cfm?sk=24332.0; IMF World Economic Outlook Database April 2013, at http://www.imf.org/external/ns/cs.aspx?id=28.

International reserves: International reserves are holdings of monetary gold, special drawing rights, reserves of IMF members held by the IMF, and holdings of foreign exchange under the control of monetary authorities. The gold component of these reserves is valued at year end (December 31) London prices. Data are in current U.S. dollars. **Data source:** IMF International Financial Statistics, at http://elibrary-data.imf.org/FindDataReports.aspx?d=33061&e=169393.

Flexible exchange rate regimes: For each country, five year averages of observed exchange rate flexibility (1996–2000, 2001–05, 2006–10) are computed based on a taxonomy of de facto exchange rate arrangements. The coarse classification of exchange rate regimes takes values between 1 and 6, ranging from the least to most flexible exchange rate regimes. **Data source:** Calculations based on "Annual Coarse Classification 1946–2010" data in Ilzetzki, Ethan, Carmen M. Reinhart, and Kenneth S. Rogoff, 2010, "Exchange Rate Arrangements Entering the 21st Century: Which Anchor Will Hold?", at http://personal.lse.ac.uk/ilzetzki/IRRBack.htm.

Worldwide Governance Indicators average: Worldwide Governance Indicators average is the average of six indicators reflecting broad dimensions of governance (voice and accountability; political stability and absence of violence; government effectiveness; regulatory quality; rule of law; control of corruption) as defined by the Worldwide Governance Indicators project. **Data source:** World Bank, Worldwide Governance Indicators, at http://info.worldbank.org/governance/wgi/index.asp.

Table 8: Natural disasters and climate change indicators

Deaths from natural disasters (total, or per million): Deaths from natural disasters are the number of persons reported as dead or missing or presumed dead as a consequence of a drought, earthquake, flood, or storm (as defined by the EM-DAT database) during the specified time period. Deaths per million population is the number of deaths divided by the population for the same time period. **Data sources:** Guha-Sapir, D., and P. Heudtlass, forthcoming, "Standardized Indicators of Human and Economic Loss from Natural Disasters," CRED working paper, Université catholique de Louvain, Brussels; EM-DAT: The OFDA/CRED International Disaster Database, at http://www.emdat.be.

Damages from natural disasters (total, or % GDP): Damages from natural disasters are the reported economic impacts as a consequence of droughts, earthquakes, floods, and storms (as defined by the EM-DAT database) during the specified time period. The economic impact usually consists of direct (such as damage to infrastructure, crops, housing) and indirect (such as loss of revenues, unemployment, market destabilization) consequences to the local economy. Total damages are in current US dollars, according to when the events occurred. Damages as a percentage of GDP is the ratio of total reported damages to midyear GDP for the same time period. **Data sources:** Guha-Sapir, D., and P. Heudtlass, forthcoming, "Standardized Indicators of Human and Economic Loss from Natural Disasters," CRED working paper, Université catholique de Louvain, Brussels; EM-DAT: The OFDA/CRED International Disaster Database, at http://www.emdat.be.

CO_2 emissions per capita: CO_2 (carbon dioxide) emissions per capita are the emissions from the burning of fossil fuels and the manufacture of cement—including carbon dioxide produced during consumption of solid, liquid, and gas fuels and gas flaring—divided by the midyear population. **Data sources:** Carbon Dioxide Information Analysis Center, Oak Ridge National Laboratory, at http://cdiac.ornl.gov; population data from World Development Indicators, at http://data.worldbank.org/indicator/SP .POP.TOTL.

Table 9: Global temperature anomalies: Difference relative to 1951–80

Temperature anomalies are global average temperatures relative to the same time of year in the base period 1951–80. Temperature anomalies are shown in degrees Celsius. **Data source:** Combined Land-Surface Air and Sea-Surface Water Temperature Anomalies dataset (Land-Ocean Temperature Index, LOTI), NASA, at http://data.giss.nasa.gov/gistemp.

Table 10: Aid commitments

Aid commitments are commitments for emergency response, reconstruction relief, and prevention and preparedness. Commitment amounts are in constant 2009 US dollars and are five year running averages. These amounts are aggregated from AidData project level results and are collected from many sources including the OECD's Creditor Reporting System. **Data sources:** Disaster Aid Tracking Global Facility for Disaster Reduction and Recovery, at http://gfdrr.aiddata.org/dashboard; AidData Center for Development Policy, at http://www.aiddata.org/content/index/Research/research-datasets.

Index

The following letters denote special treatment in the material: "b" for boxes; "f" for cartoons, diagrams, figures, and illustrations; "m" for maps; "n" for notes; and "t" for tables and glossaries.

D

F

G

J

S

ECO-AUDIT

Environmental Benefits Statement

The World Bank is committed to preserving endangered forests and natural resources. The Publishing and Knowledge Division has chosen to print the ***World Development Report 2014: Risk and Opportunity—Managing Risk for Development*** on recycled paper with 50 percent postconsumer fiber in accordance with the recommended standards for paper usage set by the Green Press Initiative, a nonprofit program supporting publishers in using fiber that is not sourced from endangered forests. For more information, visit www.greenpressinitiative.org,

Saved:

- 136 trees
- 61 million Btu of total energy
- 11,704 pounds of net greenhouse gases
- 63,481 gallons of waste water
- 4,249 pounds of solid waste